Published 2007 by Prometheus Books

Inquiries should be addressed to
Prometheus Books
59 John Glenn Drive
Amherst, New York 14228–2197
VOICE: 716–691–0133, ext. 207
FAX: 716–564–2711
WWW.PROMETHEUSBOOKS.COM

11 10 09 08 07   5 4 3 2 1

Library of Congress Cataloging-in-Publication Data

United States. Constitutional Convention (1787)
    [Journal of the Federal Convention]
    The debates in the Federal convention of 1787 : which framed the Constitution of
the United States of America / reported by James Madison.
        p. cm.
    Includes bibliographical references and index.
    ISBN-13: 978–1–59102–471–2 (alk. paper)
    ISBN-10: 1–59102–471–4 (alk. paper)
    1. United States. Constitutional Convention (1787) 2. Constitutional history—
United States—Sources. I. Madison, James, 1751–1836. II. Hunt, Gaillard,
1862–1924. III. Scott, James Brown, 1866–1943. IV. Title.

KF4510.U583 2006
342.7302'9—dc22

                                                        2006051035

Printed in the United States of America on acid-free paper

THE DEBATES IN
THE FEDERAL CONVENTION OF 1787
WHICH FRAMED THE CONSTITUTION
OF THE UNITED STATES OF AMERICA

REPORTED BY

JAMES MADISON

A Delegate from the State of Virginia

VOLUME ONE

GAILLARD HUNT AND JAMES BROWN SCOTT
EDITORS

I send you enclos'd the propos'd new Federal Constitution for these States. I was engag'd 4 Months of the last Summer in the Convention that form'd it. It is now sent by Congress to the several States for their Confirmation. If it succeeds, I do not see why you might not in Europe carry the Project of good Henry the 4th into Execution, by forming a Federal Union and One Grand Republick of all its different States & Kingdoms; by means of a like Convention; for we had many Interests to reconcile. (Benjamin Franklin to Mr. Grand, October 22, 1787. *Documentary History of the Constitution*, Vol. IV, pp. 341-342.)

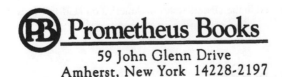
Prometheus Books
59 John Glenn Drive
Amherst, New York 14228-2197

THE DEBATES IN
THE FEDERAL CONVENTION OF 1787
WHICH FRAMED THE CONSTITUTION
OF THE UNITED STATES OF AMERICA

REPORTED BY

JAMES MADISON

A Delegate from the State of Virginia

JAMES MADISON MEMORIAL COMMITTEE

TABLE OF CONTENTS

---

[1] The Table of Contents to The Debates in the Federal Convention of 1787
is, with the exception of the first entry, the Session of Thursday, June 14, and
the various items in the Appendix, reproduced from *Documentary History of the
Constitution of the United States of America*, Vol. III (1900), pp. v-xix.

[Constitutional Convention Adjourns. End of volume one.]

PREFACE

The year 1987 marked the bicentennial of the Constitutional Convention in Philadelphia. While Madison's account is not the only source of information concerning the framing of the nation's future, it is the primary source for information about the debates in the Convention. It is absolutely indispensable for citizens who are concerned to comprehend the principles at issue and the process of construction. In his volume titled *1787: The Grand Convention*, the well-known scholar Clinton Rossiter noted: "As one learns in comparing his notes with those of other self-appointed but only part-time scribes (Yates, Lansing, King, McHenry, Paterson, Hamilton, Pierce), the record he (Madison) left us is remarkably full, impartial, and accurate." Coupled with *The Federalist*, the *Journal* is the ideal textbook for any study of the Constitution. The celebrations of 1987 would have been lamentably incomplete without the availability of Mr. Madison's labors. The man whom we have come to honor as the "Father of the Constitution" offers fellow citizens of every generation a "narrative so unique as to render it a major treasure of the Republic."

It has now been several decades since scholars directed their skills to the primary documents penned by Madison. In 1977 volume 10 of *The Papers of James Madison* published extensive excerpts from his writings but it noted that the "editors believe that it is beyond the scope of this present chronological series to reproduce the whole manuscript of JM's Federal Convention Debates" (p. 9). At some future time the editors may provide a newly edited and annotated edition of the *Journal*. Their interim decision to forego such an offering was clearly influenced by the already available publications on the Debates, of which they commented, "the most accurate are *Documentary History of the Constitution, III*; Farrand, *Records*; and *The Debates in the Federal Convention of 1787 which*

Framed the Constitution of the United States of America, Reported by James Madison, ed. Gaillard Hunt and James Brown Scott (New York, 1920)." Reproduced here is the Hunt/Scott version, the most recent and most readable. It has the additional advantage of having been "read against the text" of the *Documentary History* (1900) and Farrand (1911).

The present edition includes all the Madison notes and remarks, along with a selection of additional data deemed useful for interpreting the events of that summer.

A natural break in the *Journal* results from a Convention decision on July 2 to adjourn until July 5 that "time might be given to the Committee, and to such as chose to attend to the celebrations on the anniversary of Independence." That committee was to resolve the differences concerning representation in the two houses of Congress. On June 27 the Convention addressed the thorniest issue of the summer, "the rule of suffrage in the two branches." By July 2 the divisions were so acute that the Convention appointed the above-mentioned committee "to devise and report some compromise." July 5 marked the beginning of the process that ultimately led to what modern scholars term the "Great Compromise," without which there would have been no Constitution of 1787.

In that debate Mr. Madison was a key figure, one whose views were not accepted when, on July 16, the "Great Compromise" was adopted by a state vote of 8 to 3. Yet, even as Madison expressed skepticism concerning the resolution of the struggle between the large and small states, he was prepared to write to Thomas Jefferson two days later about the progress in Philadelphia.

> The Convention continue to sit. and have been closely employed since the Commencement of the Session. I am still under the mortification of being restrained from disclosing any part of their proceeding. . . . I have taken lengthy notes of every thing that has yet passed. and mean to go on with the drudgery, if no indisposition obliges me to discontinue it. It is not possible to form any judgment of the future duration of the Session. I am led by sundry circumstances to guess that the residue of the work will not be very quickly dispatched. The public mind is very impatient for the event, and various reports are circulating which tend to inflame curiosity. I do not learn however that any discontent is expressed at the concealment; and have little doubt that the people will be ready to receive as we shall be able to propose, a Government that will secure their liberties and happiness. (p. 105)

It is well known that Mr. Jefferson requested that his tombstone be inscribed with what he considered his chief accomplishments: writing the Virginia Statute on Religious Freedom, the founding of the University of Virginia, and the writing of the Declaration of Independence. In his later days Jefferson wrote to Madison, "Take care of me when I am dead." He was concerned for those testaments to his life that gave it substance and historic quality. Madison did not fail his most cherished friend. From 1826, the year of Jefferson's death, Rector Madison thrust his energies into establishing the Charlottesville University as a monument to free, open scholarship. This practical genius had already translated the Virginia Statute into law in 1786 and would do the same for the Declaration the following year. That friendship between two founders, one that Dumas Malone characterized as "one of the greatest in history," changed the face of world history. In keeping alive the Madison *Journal* a nation can care for him when he is dead.

One corrective to the notes by editor James Brown Scott does seem necessary. Writing in 1918, Scott employed Supreme Court decisions, particularly *State of Texas v. White* (1868) in order to alert readers to the "separate and independent existence" of the states and to the belief that there can "be no loss of separate and independent autonomy to the States, through their union under the Constitution."

Today constitutional scholars would view the future differently against the backdrop of the New Deal, massive social legislation, the Warren Court, and, most particularly, *Brown v. Board of Education* (1954). The resulting struggles in the nation throughout the 1950s and 1960s brought forth vigorous states rights challenges to the prevailing national mood. When the dust settled, interposition and militant state sovereignty arguments collapsed; at present they offer merely echoes of a lost cause. As the political pendulum swung toward the right in the 1980s, the center moved so dramatically that no serious attention was any longer paid to those who would insist upon the "independent autonomy" of the states. In the year 1987 citizens understood even more fully why Madison believed that the federal constitution would "secure their liberties and happiness."

Robert S. Alley
University of Richmond

INTRODUCTORY NOTE

I. Mr. Madison's Record

There have been three prints from Madison's manuscript notes of the debates in the Convention which framed the Constitution of the United States—that in Volume III of the *Documentary History of the Constitution*, published in 1900 by the State Department which is the custodian of the original manuscript; that in Volumes III and IV of *The Writings of James Madison*, edited by Mr. Hunt, published in 1902 and printed separately in two volumes in 1908 (G. P. Putnam's Sons); and that published by the Yale University Press in 1911, Max Farrand, editor, as the chief part of Volumes I and II of the three volume edition of *The Records of the Federal Convention of 1787*. All of these works are reasonably accurate prints of the Madison record, while none is nor can be perfectly accurate. In the *Documentary History* and Professor Farrand's work an attempt is made to indicate in the printed page the alterations which Madison made in his manuscript. In the *Documentary History* this is done by the use of the caret, interlineations and the words " stricken out " to show the words through which Madison had drawn his pen. Mr. Farrand has made use of " angular brackets " to indicate additions made by Madison to his original notes and has added numerous footnotes to show what words were struck out by Madison. The inevitable result is that we have texts which are confusing or disagreeable to read. Even the special student who cares more for the form than the substance, and the suspicious investigator, who thinks that Madison may have made alterations in his original record so as to suppress or distort the truth or give a coloring to the facts, will not be satisfied with these attempts to visualize manuscript by print. He must, in fact, see the manuscript itself or a good photograph of it. None other than the special student would however, tolerate a photograph in this case, for the penmanship is not easy to read, and is so microscopic at times as to be a severe strain upon the eye.

The chief source of Madison's corrections of his notes was the official *Journal* of the Convention which was printed in 1819 and Yates's *Secret Proceedings and Debates of the Federal Convention* which appeared in 1821. Whenever Madison thought either of these records more correct than his he changed or added to his; but he noted more frequently errors in the official *Journal* itself. Yates's record he

regarded as having little value. Nevertheless, he derived from it a
few lesser motions which had escaped him.

Madison began the revision of his Notes after he retired from the
Presidency in 1817 and had the manuscript copied under his own eye
by his amanuensis, John C. Payne, Mrs. Madison's brother. On December 27, 1821, he wrote to John G. Jackson that he had set about
arranging his papers " in earnest." On February 2, 1827, he wrote
to Samuel Harrison Smith, who urged him to publish his record, that
the world would not have long to wait for it. It was to be posthumous,
he said, and Rufus King, William Few and himself were the only
signers of the Constitution then surviving; " and of the lamps still
burning, none can now be far from the socket," he added. King died a
few months after this letter was written and Few in the following
year. It is probable that the transcript was completed when Madison
wrote, and the fact that it was being made caused a rumor to get
abroad that he was writing a history of some sort, for he was obliged to
deny to several correspondents that he had such a project.

At the end of the original manuscript of the debates in the Convention Madison wrote: " The few alterations and corrections made
in these debates which are not in my handwriting, were dictated by
me and made in my presence by John C. Payne." The entries made
in Payne's hand are indeed few, and a careful examination fails to
identify positively more than half-a-dozen, but when Payne wrote in
small characters his writing resembled Madison's, and there were
doubtless a few alterations made by him which can not be identified.

In Madison's will made in 1835 he says:

> In consideration of the particular and valuable aids received
> from my brother in law, John C. Payne and the affection which
> I bear him, I devise to him and his heirs two hundred and forty
> acres of land on which he lives.

The " particular and valuable aids," doubtless, were his services in
revising the record of the debates and transcribing it for publication.

Madison died on June 28, 1836. In replying to the letter of
condolence which the President, Andrew Jackson, sent to her, Mrs.
Madison wrote (August 20, 1836):

> The best return I can make for the sympathy of my coun-
> try is, to fulfil the sacred trust his confidence reposed in me—
> that of placing before it and the world what his pen prepared
> for their use—a legacy, the importance of which is deeply im-
> pressed on my mind.[1]

---

[1] *Executive Documents*, No. 8, 24th Congress, 2d Sess., Vol. I.

On November 15, 1836, she offered this legacy to the Government, and by act of March 3, 1837, the Government bought it for thirty thousand dollars. It was delivered to the Secretary of State, John Forsyth, by Mrs. Madison April 1, 1837, being described by her as: "the manuscript copy of the Debates in the Convention of 1787 and of the Debates &c in the Congress of the Confederation." In a letter of November 15, 1836, to President Jackson, she stated Mr. Madison's intention and gave a further description of the documents, saying:

> It was also intended to publish, with these debates, those taken by him in the Congress of the confederation in 1782, '3, and '7, of which he was then a member, and selections made by himself, and prepared under his eye, from his letters narrating the proceedings of that body during the periods of his service in it, prefixing the debates in 1776 on the declaration of independence by Thomas Jefferson, so as to embody all the memorials in that shape known to exist.[1]

These were "The Madison Papers." They comprised the original manuscripts and transcripts of them. Most of the transcripts, including the transcript of the debates in the Constitutional Convention, were made by Payne, but a few of the letters had been copied by Mrs. Madison herself. On July 9, 1838, a law was passed providing for the publication of "The Madison Papers." Henry D. Gilpin, Solicitor of the Treasury, was selected as the editor, and the joint committee of Senate and House on the Library ordered the withdrawal from the State Department of "one of the duplicate manuscript copies," which Mrs. Madison had deposited there. "The Madison Papers," being the debates and the other papers described by Mrs. Madison in her letter to the President, were published in three volumes in 1840 and from this edition several prints have since been made of the whole and of the debates separated from the other papers. The printer's copy for the publication of 1840 was returned to the joint Library Committee by the editor or printer, and the committee deposited it with the Librarian of Congress, instead of returning it to the Department of State whence it had come. It was not known until recently that this deposit was itself "one of the duplicate manuscript copies," which Mrs. Madison had deposited with the State Department. That part of it which concerns us, the debates in the Constitutional Convention, was Payne's transcript made under Madison's supervision; and Madison had himself gone over the transcript and had made a few additions and notes in his own hand. This printer's copy, therefore, has

---

[1] *Executive Documents*, No. 8, 24th Congress, 2d Sess., Vol. I.

more importance than commonly attaches to such material. It must, in fact, be considered when we are searching for an absolutely correct version of Madison's record. As, however, no transcript can be as correct as the original document which is transcribed, so the most correct version of the Madison record must be the original manuscript in Madison's own hand; but wherever Madison changed the transcript the change represents his final judgment and must be noticed in the interest of accuracy. Bringing the Payne transcript into comparison with the original record kept by Madison himself we have the last word in Madison's history of the Constitutional Convention.

In so far as any long text can be accurate the text which is printed here is believed to be accurate. Before it went to the printer it was collated with the original manuscript twice, each time by a different person. The galley proof was compared word for word with the original manuscript; the page proof was compared word for word by a different person with the original manuscript. The whole of the Payne transcript was read by the side of the Madison record to ascertain all variations and all corrections or additions which Madison made in the Payne transcript. With the exception of differences in spelling, abbreviation of words and punctuation, all variations between the two texts are stated in footnotes. The page proof was read against the text of the *Documentary History* and that of Professor Farrand in *The Records of the Federal Convention of 1787*, and the Madison manuscript was again consulted whenever a comparison showed any difference, however slight, in the three texts.

Finally, the foundry proof has, in the interest of accuracy, been read against Mr. Madison's original manuscript.

This is the first publication of the Madison record so compared.

GAILLARD HUNT.

WASHINGTON, D. C.,
November 11, 1918.

II. The Federal Convention of 1787 an International Conference

The notes which James Madison made of the proceedings of the Federal Convention which met in Philadelphia, May 25th and adjourned September 17, 1787, were in fact, though not in form, the notes of the proceedings of an international conference, to use the language of today, or of a continental conference, as its members might have phrased it had they not preferred the term federal, as we apparently prefer constitutional, convention. Each preference is, however, correct according to the point of view of the observer. It was indeed a constitutional convention or conference, in the sense that it drafted a constitution of a more perfect Union of and for the States ratifying it; it was a federal convention or conference, in the sense that it proposed a draft for a federation of the States which the framers of the Constitution called a more perfect Union than that created by the Articles of Confederation, which the Constitution was to replace; it was a continental convention or conference in that it was composed of twelve of the thirteen States of the American continent; it was an international convention or conference, in that it was composed of official representatives of twelve of the thirteen " sovereign, free and independent " States of America, acting under instructions and meeting " for the sole and express purpose of revising the Articles of Confederation " in order to " render the federal Constitution adequate to the exigencies of government and the preservation of the Union."

The Union to be preserved had been composed but a short time previously of the thirteen American colonies, whose official representatives in the Continental Congress, on July 4, 1776, declared,

> That these United Colonies are, and of Right ought to be Free and Independent States; that they are Absolved from all Allegiance to the British Crown, and that all political connection between them and the State of Great Britain, is and ought to be totally dissolved; and that as Free and Independent States, they have full Power to levy War, conclude Peace, contract Alliances, establish Commerce, and to do all other Acts and Things which Independent States may of right do.

The official representatives in the Congress of the States thus declared to be free and independent drafted, and on November 15, 1777, approved Articles of Confederation, which, ratified by each of the thirteen States at various times, became effective on March 1, 1781, by the ratification of the State of Maryland, the last so to do. The contracting parties were thus the thirteen States declared to be free and independent by the Declaration of Independence; and the origin, the form and nature of the Union, its name and the relation of the States to one another and to the Confederation and perpetual Union, are thus stated in the caption and in the first three of the Articles of Confederation:[1]

Articles of Confederation and perpetual Union between the states of Newhampshire, Massachusetts-bay, Rhodeisland and Providence Plantations, Connecticut, New-York, New-Jersey, Pennsylvania, Delaware, Maryland, Virginia, North-Carolina, South-Carolina and Georgia.

Article I. The Stile of this confederacy shall be " The United States of America."

Article II. Each state retains its sovereignty, freedom, and independence, and every Power, Jurisdiction and right, which is not by this confederation expressly delegated to the United States, in Congress assembled.

Article III. The said states hereby severally enter into a firm league of friendship with each other, for their common de- fence, the security of their Liberties, and their mutual and general welfare, binding themselves to assist each other, against all force offered to, or attacks made upon them, or any of them, on account of religion, sovereignty, trade, or any other pretence whatever.

The " Confederation and perpetual Union between the States " not proving to be " adequate to the exigencies of government & the preservation of the Union," the Congress, on February 21, 1787, deemed it " expedient that on the second Monday in May next a Convention of delegates who shall have been appointed by the several states be held at Philadelphia for the sole and express purpose of re- vising the Articles of Confederation and reporting to Congress and the several legislatures such alterations and provisions therein as shall when agreed to in Congress and confirmed by the states render the federal constitution adequate to the exigencies of Government & the preservation of the Union."

Pursuant to this resolution, twelve of the thirteen " sovereign, free and independent " States sent official delegates to the convention to be held in Philadelphia for the revision of the Articles of Confed-

[1] *Journals of the Continental Congress*, Library of Congress edition, Vol. XIX (1912), p. 214.

eration, and succeeded with much good will, concession, and compromise, in drafting, instead of revising the Articles, a constitution and a scheme of government of a more perfect Union, which, submitted to the Congress of the Confederation, referred by it to the States, ratified in the course of 1787-88 by conventions in eleven of the States, became effective in accordance with the 7th Article of the Constitution, providing that "The Ratification of the Conventions of nine States, shall be sufficient for the Establishment of this Constitution between the States so ratifying the Same."

The government of the more perfect Union was to go into operation on March 4, 1789, and, in the course of that and of the subsequent year, the people of the States of North Carolina and of Rhode Island ratified the Constitution, thus making it the union of all thirteen of the original States of America.

In the leading case of *Ware* v. *Hylton* (3 Dallas, 199, 224), decided in 1796, Mr. Justice Chase took occasion to consider the course of events leading to the Declaration of Independence of the colonies, the result of that Declaration upon the colonies, and the relation of the States to one another before the Articles of Confederation became binding by the ratification of the State of Maryland, on March 1, 1781. In the course of his opinion that learned Justice said, under a sense of judicial responsibility:

In *June* 1776, the Convention of *Virginia formally* declared, that *Virginia* was a free, sovereign, and independent state; and on the 4th of *July*, 1776, following, the *United States*, in Congress assembled, declared the *Thirteen United Colonies* free and independent states; and that as *such*, they had full power to levy war, conclude peace, &c. I consider this as a declaration, not that the United Colonies *jointly*, in a *collective* capacity, were independent states, &c. but that *each* of them was a sovereign and independent state, that is, that *each* of them had a right to govern itself by its own authority, and its own laws, without any controul from any other power upon earth.

Before these solemn acts of separation from the Crown of *Great Britain*, the war between *Great Britain* and the United Colonies, *jointly*, and *separately*, was a *civil* war; but instantly on that great and ever memorable event, the war changed its *nature*, and became a PUBLIC war between *independent governments;* and immediately thereupon ALL the *rights* of *public* war (and all the other rights of an independent nation) attached to the government of *Virginia;* and all the *former political* connexion between *Great Britain* and *Virginia,* and also between their respective subjects, were totally dissolved; and not only the *two nations,* but all the subjects of each, were in a state of war; precisely as

in the present war between *Great Britain* and *France*. *Vatt. lib.*
3. c. 18. § 292. to 295. *lib.* 3. c. 5. § 70. 72. and 73

From the 4th of *July*, 1776, the *American* States were *de facto*, as well as *de jure*, in the possession and actual exercise of *all* the *rights* of independent governments. . . .

The Supreme Court of the United States, of which Mr. Justice Chase was a member, apparently attaches great weight to this opinion in *Ware* v. *Hylton*, inasmuch as Mr. Justice Swayne, in delivering the unanimous opinion of this court in the case of *Hauenstein* v. *Lynham* (100 U. S., 483, 489), decided in 1879, said:

> We have quoted from the opinion of Mr. Justice Chase in that case, . . . because it shows the views of a powerful legal mind at that early period, when the debates in the convention which framed the Constitution must have been fresh in the memory of the leading jurists of the country.

It is proper to add, in this connection, that Mr. Justice Chase was a signer of the Declaration of Independence.

It is also interesting to note, in this connection, that John Marshall of Virginia, shortly to become and thereafter to remain, the great Chief Justice of the Supreme Court, appeared in 1796 as counsel for his State, in the case of *Ware* v. *Hylton*, and that in the course of his argument he said:

> 1st. It has been conceded, that independent nations have, in general, the right of confiscation; and that *Virginia*, at the time of passing her law [1777], was an independent nation.

Speaking of the nature of the Confederation, the relations of the States composing it both to themselves and to the Union, Mr. Chief Justice Marshall observed, speaking for the Supreme Court of the United States in *Sturges* v. *Crowninshield* (4 Wheaton, 122, 192), decided in 1819:

> It must be recollected, that previous to the formation of the new constitution, we were divided into independent States, united for some purposes, but, in most respects, sovereign.

And in the later case of *Gibbons* v. *Ogden*, (9 Wheaton, 1, 187), decided in 1824, the same great jurist, recurring to this matter, again remarked:

> As preliminary to the very able discussions of the constitution, which we have heard from the bar, and as having some influence on its construction, reference has been made to the political situation of these States, anterior to its formation. It has been said,

that they were sovereign, were completely independent, and were connected with each other only by a league. This is true.

As to the nature of the more perfect Union and the relation to it of the States whereof it is composed, Mr. Chief Justice Marshall solemnly declared, in the course of his opinion announcing and justifying the unanimous judgment of his brethren, in *McCulloch* v. *Maryland,* (4 Wheaton, 316, 410), decided in 1819, and which the late Professor Thayer considered the greatest of his cases:

> In America, the powers of sovereignty are divided between the government of the Union, and those of the States. They are each sovereign, with respect to the objects committed to it, and neither sovereign with respect to the objects committed to the other.

And in the great and leading case of the *State of Texas* v. *White,* (7 Wallace, 700, 725), decided in 1868, Mr. Chief Justice Chase thus restated and elaborated in classic terms the views of his vigorous namesake, Mr. Justice Chase, and of his illustrious predecessor, Mr. Chief Justice Marshall:

> Under the Articles of Confederation each State retained its sovereignty, freedom, and independence, and every power, jurisdiction, and right not expressly delegated to the United States. Under the Constitution, though the powers of the States were much restricted, still, all powers not delegated to the United States, nor prohibited to the States, are reserved to the States respectively, or to the people. And we have already had occasion to remark at this term, that "the people of each State compose a State, having its own government, and endowed with all the functions essential to separate and independent existence," and that "without the States in union, there could be no such political body as the United States." Not only, therefore, can there be no loss of separate and independent autonomy to the States, through their union under the Constitution, but it may be not unreasonably said that the preservation of the States, and the maintenance of their governments, are as much within the design and care of the Constitution as the preservation of the Union and the maintenance of the National government. The Constitution, in all its provisions, looks to an indestructible Union, composed of indestructible States.

The international import of the Constitution of a more perfect Union was not lost upon Benjamin Franklin, the keenest, shrewdest, most sagacious and far-sighted observer of his day, who, shortly after the adjournment of the Federal Convention, was pleased to say in a letter to a friend in Europe:

> I send you enclos'd the propos'd new Federal Constitution for these States. I was engag'd 4 Months of the last Summer

in the Convention that form'd it. It is now sent by Congress to the several States for their Confirmation.

And he was bold enough to suggest that:

> If it succeeds, I do not see why you might not in Europe carry the Project of good Henry the 4th into Execution, by forming a Federal Union and One Grand Republick of all its different States & Kingdoms; by means of a like Convention; for we had many Interests to reconcile.[1]

In view of the origin and nature of the Constitution drafted by official delegates of twelve of the thirteen " sovereign, free and independent " States of America, submitted to and ratified by the people of each of the several States in conventions assembled for that purpose, and binding only those States which had done so; and in view of the authoritative, conspicuous, and pertinent judgments of the Supreme Court of the United States regarding the nature and meaning of the Constitution thereof, it would appear that Madison's notes of the proceedings of that memorable and significant international conference from which there sprang " a more perfect Union . . . for the United States of America," are not only of interest to students of Federal Government, and to the good people of the United States, but also to students of International Law, and to the peoples of all the States forming the Society of Nations.

JAMES BROWN SCOTT.

WASHINGTON, D. C.,
November 11, 1918.

---

[1] Letter of October 22, 1787, to Mr. Grand. *Documentary History of the Constitution of the United States of America* (published by the Department of State of the United States), Vol. IV (1905), pp. 341-342.

PART I

ANTECEDENTS OF THE FEDERAL CONVENTION OF 1787

THE DECLARATION OF INDEPENDENCE—1776[1]

In Congress, July 4, 1776

The unanimous Declaration of the thirteen united States of America

When in the Course of human events, it becomes necessary for one people to dissolve the political bands which have connected them with another, and to assume among the powers of the earth, the separate and equal station to which the Laws of Nature and of Nature's God entitle them, a decent respect to the opinions of mankind requires that they should declare the causes which impel them to the separation.—We hold these truths to be self-evident, that all men are created equal, that they are endowed by their Creator with certain unalienable Rights, that among these are Life, Liberty and the pursuit of Happiness.—That to secure these rights, Governments are instituted among Men, deriving their just powers from the consent of the governed,—That whenever any Form of Government becomes destructive of these ends, it is the Right of the People to alter or to abolish it, and to institute new Government, laying its foundation on such principles and organizing its powers in such form, as to them shall seem most likely to effect their Safety and Happiness. Prudence, indeed, will dictate that Governments long established should not be changed for light and transient causes; and accordingly all experience hath shown, that mankind are more disposed to suffer, while evils are sufferable, than to right themselves by abolishing the forms to which they are accustomed. But when a long train of abuses and usurpations, pursuing invariably the same Object evinces a design to reduce them under absolute Despotism, it is their right, it is their duty, to throw off such Government, and to provide new Guards for their future security.—Such has been the patient sufferance of these Colonies; and such is now the necessity which constrains them to alter their former Systems of Government. The history of the present King of Great Britain is a history of repeated injuries and usurpations, all having in direct object the establishment of an absolute Tyranny over these States. To

---

[1] Printed from the facsimile of the engrossed copy of the original manuscript in the Library of the Department of State of the United States.

prove this, let Facts be submitted to a candid world.—He has refused his Assent to Laws, the most wholesome and necessary for the public good.—He has forbidden his Governors to pass Laws of immediate and pressing importance, unless suspended in their operation till his Assent should be obtained; and when so suspended, he has utterly neglected to attend to them.—He has refused to pass other Laws for the accommodation of large districts of people, unless those people would relinquish the right of Representation in the Legislature, a right inestimable to them and formidable to tyrants only.—He has called together legislative bodies at places unusual, uncomfortable, and distant from the depository of their public Records, for the sole purpose of fatiguing them into compliance with his measures.—He has dissolved Representative Houses repeatedly, for opposing with manly firmness his invasions on the rights of the people.—He has refused for a long time, after such dissolutions, to cause others to be elected; whereby the Legislative powers, incapable of Annihilation, have returned to the People at large for their exercise; the State remaining in the mean time exposed to all the dangers of invasion from without, and convulsions within.—He has endeavoured to prevent the population of these States; for that purpose obstructing the Laws for Naturalization of Foreigners; refusing to pass others to encourage their migration hither, and raising the conditions of new Appropriations of Lands.—He has obstructed the Administration of Justice, by refusing his Assent to Laws for establishing Judiciary powers.—He has made Judges dependent on his Will alone, for the tenure of their offices, and the amount and payment of their salaries. —He has erected a multitude of New Offices, and sent hither swarms of Officers to harrass our people, and eat out their substance.—He has kept among us, in times of peace, Standing Armies, without the Consent of our legislatures.—He has affected to render the Military independent of and superior to the Civil power.—He has combined with others to subject us to a jurisdiction foreign to our constitution, and unacknowledged by our laws; giving his Assent to their Acts of pretended Legislation:—For quartering large bodies of armed troops among us:—For protecting them, by a mock Trial, from punishment for any Murders which they should commit on the Inhabitants of these States:—For cutting off our Trade with all parts of the world:— For imposing Taxes on us without our Consent:—For depriving us in many cases, of the benefits of Trial by Jury:—For transporting us beyond Seas to be tried for pretended offences:—For abolishing the free System of English Laws in a neighbouring Province, establishing therein an Arbitrary government, and enlarging its Boundaries so as to render it at once an example and fit instrument for introducing the same absolute rule into these Colonies:—For taking away our Charters, abolishing our most valuable Laws, and altering fundamentally the Forms of our Governments:—For suspending our own Legislatures, and declaring themselves invested with power to legislate for us in all cases whatsoever.—He has abdicated Government here, by declaring us out of his Protection and waging War against us.—He has plundered our seas, ravaged our Coasts, burnt our towns, and destroyed the lives of our people.—He is at this time transporting large Armies of foreign Mercenaries to compleat the works of death, desolation and tyranny, already begun with circumstances of Cruelty & perfidy scarcely paralleled in the most barbarous ages, and totally unworthy the Head of a civilized nation.—He has constrained our fellow Citizens taken Captive on the high Seas to bear Arms against their Country, to become the executioners of their friends and Brethren, or to fall themselves by their Hands.—He has excited domestic insurrections amongst us, and has endeavoured to bring on the inhabitants of our frontiers, the merciless Indian Savages, whose known rule of warfare, is an undistinguished destruction of all ages, sexes and conditions. In every stage of these Oppressions We have Petitioned for Redress in the most humble terms: Our repeated Petitions have been answered only by repeated injury. A Prince, whose character is thus marked by every act which may define a Tyrant, is unfit to be the ruler of a free people. Nor have We been wanting in attentions to our Brittish brethren. We have warned them from time to time of attempts by their legislature to extend an unwarrantable jurisdiction over us. We have reminded them of the circumstances of our emigration and settlement here. We have appealed to their native justice and magnanimity, and we have conjured them by the ties of our common kindred to disavow these usurpations, which, would inevitably interrupt our connections and correspondence They too have been deaf to the voice of justice and of consanguinity. We must, therefore, acquiesce in the necessity, which denounces our Separation, and hold them, as we hold the rest of mankind, Enemies in War, in Peace Friends.—

WE, THEREFORE, the REPRESENTATIVES of the UNITED STATES OF AMERICA, in General Congress, Assembled, appealing to the Supreme Judge of the world for the rectitude of our intentions, do, in the Name, and by Authority of the good People of these Colonies, solemnly publish and declare, That these United Colonies are, and of Right ought to be FREE AND INDEPENDENT STATES; that they are Absolved from all Allegiance to the British Crown, and that all political connection between them and the State of Great Britain, is and ought to be totally dissolved; and that as Free and Independent States, they have full Power to levy War, conclude Peace, contract Alliances, establish Commerce, and to do all other Acts and Things which Independent States may of right do.—And for the support of this Declaration, with a firm reliance on the protection of Divine Providence, we mutually pledge to each other our Lives, our Fortunes and our sacred Honor.

JOHN HANCOCK.

New Hampshire
JOSIAH BARTLETT,
WM. WHIPPLE,
MATTHEW THORNTON

Massachusetts Bay
SAML. ADAMS,
JOHN ADAMS,
ROBT. TREAT PAINE,
ELBRIDGE GERRY.

Rhode Island
STEP. HOPKINS,
WILLIAM ELLERY.

Connecticut
ROGER SHERMAN,
SAM'EL HUNTINGTON,
WM. WILLIAMS,
OLIVER WOLCOTT.

New York
WM. FLOYD,
PHIL. LIVINGSTON,
FRANS. LEWIS,
LEWIS MORRIS.

New Jersey
RICHD. STOCKTON,
JNO. WITHERSPOON,
FRAS. HOPKINSON,
JOHN HART,
ABRA. CLARK.

Pennsylvania
ROBT. MORRIS,
BENJAMIN RUSH,
BENJA. FRANKLIN,
JOHN MORTON,
GEO. CLYMER,
JAS. SMITH,
GEO. TAYLOR,
JAMES WILSON,
GEO. ROSS.

Delaware
CAESAR RODNEY,
GEO. READ,
THO. M'KEAN.

Maryland
SAMUEL CHASE,
WM. PACA,
THOS. STONE,
CHARLES CARROLL of Carrollton.

Virginia
GEORGE WYTHE,
RICHARD HENRY LEE,
TH. JEFFERSON,
BENJA. HARRISON,
THS. NELSON, JR.,
FRANCIS LIGHTFOOT LEE,
CARTER BRAXTON.

North Carolina
WM. HOOPER,
JOSEPH HEWES,
JOHN PENN.

South Carolina
EDWARD RUTLEDGE,
THOS. HEYWARD, JUNR.,
THOMAS LYNCH, JUNR.,
ARTHUR MIDDLETON.

Georgia
BUTTON GWINNETT,
LYMAN HALL,
GEO. WALTON.

NOTE.—Mr. Ferdinand Jefferson, Keeper of the Rolls in the Department of State, at Washington, says: "The names of the signers are spelt above as in the facsimile of the original, but the punctuation of them is not always the same; neither do the names of the States appear in the facsimile of the original. The names of the signers of each State are grouped together in the facsimile of the original, except the name of Matthew Thornton, which follows that of Oliver Wolcott."—*Revised Statutes of the United States*, 2d Edition, 1878, page 6.

ARTICLES OF CONFEDERATION [1]

MARCH 1, 1781

To all to whom these Presents shall come, we the under signed Delegates of the States affixed to our Names, send greeting.

Whereas the Delegates of the United States of America, in Congress assembled, did, on the 15th day of November, in the Year of Our Lord One thousand Seven Hundred and Seventy seven, and in the Second Year of the Independence of America, agree to certain articles of Confederation and perpetual Union between the States of Newhampshire, Massachusetts-bay, Rhodeisland and Providence Plantations, Connecticut, New York, New Jersey, Pennsylvania, Delaware, Maryland, Virginia, North-Carolina, South-Carolina and Georgia in the words following, viz. " Articles of Confederation and perpetual Union between the states of Newhampshire, Massachusetts-bay, Rhodeisland and Providence Plantations, Connecticut, New-York, New-Jersey, Pennsylvania, Delaware, Maryland, Virginia, North-Carolina, South-Carolina and Georgia.

Article I. The Stile of this confederacy shall be " The United States of America."

Article II. Each state retains its sovereignty, freedom, and independence, and every Power, Jurisdiction and right, which is not by this confederation expressly delegated to the United States, in Congress assembled.

Article III. The said states hereby severally enter into a firm league of friendship with each other, for their common defence, the security of their Liberties, and their mutual and general welfare, binding themselves to assist each other, against all force offered to, or at-

---

[1] *Journals of the Continental Congress,* Library of Congress edition, Vol. XIX (1912), p. 214.

The Articles of Confederation were agreed to by the Congress, November 15, 1777. They were, as appears from the list of signatures affixed to these Articles, signed at different times by the delegates of the different American States. On March 1, 1781, the delegates from Maryland, the last of the States to take action, " did, in behalf of the said State of Maryland, sign and ratify the said articles, by which act the Confederation of the United States of America was completed, each and every of the Thirteen United States, from New Hampshire to Georgia, both included, having adopted and confirmed, and by their delegates in Congress, ratified the same." *Ibid.*, p. 214.

xxxii   DEBATES IN THE FEDERAL CONVENTION OF 1787

tacks made upon them, or any of them, on account of religion, sovereignty, trade, or any other pretence whatever.

Article IV. The better to secure and perpetuate mutual friendship and intercourse among the people of the different states in this union, the free inhabitants of each of these states, paupers, vagabonds and fugitives from justice excepted, shall be entitled to all privileges and immunities of free citizens in the several states; and the people of each state shall have free ingress and regress to and from any other state, and shall enjoy therein all the privileges of trade and commerce, subject to the same duties, impositions and restrictions as the inhabitants thereof respectively, provided that such restriction shall not extend so far as to prevent the removal of property imported into any state, to any other state, of which the Owner is an inhabitant; provided also that no imposition, duties or restriction shall be laid by any state, on the property of the united states, or either of them.

If any Person guilty of, or charged with treason, felony, or other high misdemeanor in any state, shall flee from Justice, and be found in any of the united states, he shall, upon demand of the Governor or executive power, of the state from which he fled, be delivered up and removed to the state having jurisdiction of his offence.

Full faith and credit shall be given in each of these states to the records, acts and judicial proceedings of the courts and magistrates of every other state.

Article V. For the more convenient management of the general interests of the united states, delegates shall be annually appointed in such manner as the legislature of each state shall direct, to meet in Congress on the first Monday in November, in every year, with a power reserved to each state, to recal its delegates, or any of them, at any time within the year, and to send others in their stead, for the remainder of the Year.

No state shall be represented in Congress by less than two, nor by more than seven Members; and no person shall be capable of being a delegate for more than three years in any term of six years; nor shall any person, being a delegate, be capable of holding any office under the united states, for which he, or another for his benefit receives any salary, fees or emolument of any kind.

Each state shall maintain its own delegates in a meeting of the states, and while they act as members of the committee of the states.

In determining questions in the united states in Congress assembled, each state shall have one vote.

Freedom of speech and debate in Congress shall not be impeached or questioned in any Court, or place out of Congress, and the members of congress shall be protected in their persons from arrests and imprisonments, during the time of their going to and from, and attendance on congress, except for treason, felony, or breach of the peace.

Article VI. No state, without the Consent of the united states in congress assembled, shall send any embassy to, or receive any embassy from, or enter into any conference, agreement, alliance or treaty with any King prince or state; nor shall any person holding any office of profit or trust under the united states, or any of them, accept of any present, emolument, office or title of any kind whatever from any king, prince or foreign state; nor shall the united states in congress assembled, or any of them, grant any title of nobility.

No two or more states shall enter into any treaty, confederation or alliance whatever between them, without the consent of the united states in congress assembled, specifying accurately the purposes for which the same is to be entered into, and how long it shall continue.

No state shall lay any imposts or duties, which may interfere with any stipulations in treaties, entered into by the united states in congress assembled, with any king, prince or state, in pursuance of any treaties already proposed by congress, to the courts of France and Spain.

No vessels of war shall be kept up in time of peace by any state, except such number only, as shall be deemed necessary by the united states in congress assembled, for the defence of such state, or its trade; nor shall any body of forces be kept up by any state, in time of peace, except such number only, as in the judgment of the united states, in congress assembled, shall be deemed requisite to garrison the forts necessary for the defence of such state; but every state shall always keep up a well regulated and disciplined militia, sufficiently armed and accoutred, and shall provide and constantly have ready for use, in public stores, a due number of field pieces and tents, and a proper quantity of arms, ammunition and camp equipage.

No state shall engage in any war without the consent of the united states in congress assembled, unless such state be actually invaded by enemies, or shall have received certain advice of a resolution being formed by some nation of Indians to invade such state, and the danger is so imminent as not to admit of a delay till the united states in congress assembled can be consulted: nor shall any state grant commissions to any ships or vessels of war, nor letters of marque or reprisal, except it be after a declaration of war by the united states in congress assembled, and then only against the kingdom or state and the subjects thereof, against which war has been so declared, and under such regulations as shall be established by the united states in congress assembled, unless such state be infested by pirates, in which case vessels of war may be fitted out for that occasion, and kept so long as the danger shall continue, or until the united states in congress assembled, shall determine otherwise.

Article VII. When land-forces are raised by any state for the common defence, all officers of or under the rank of colonel, shall be appointed by the legislature of each state respectively, by whom such forces shall be raised, or in such manner as such state shall direct, and all vacancies shall be filled up by the State which first made the appointment.

Article VIII. All charges of war, and all other expences that shall be incurred for the common defence or general welfare, and allowed by the united states in congress assembled, shall be defrayed out of a common treasury, which shall be supplied by the several states in proportion to the value of all land within each state, granted to or surveyed for any Person, as such land and the buildings and improvements thereon shall be estimated according to such mode as the united states in congress assembled, shall from time to time direct and appoint.

The taxes for paying that proportion shall be laid and levied by the authority and direction of the legislatures of the several states within the time agreed upon by the united states in congress assembled.

Article IX. The united states in congress assembled, shall have the sole and exclusive right and power of determining on peace and war, except in the cases mentioned in the sixth article—of sending and receiving ambassadors—entering into treaties and alliances, provided that no treaty of commerce shall be made whereby the legislative power of the respective states shall be restrained from imposing such imposts and duties on foreigners, as their own people are subjected to, or from prohibiting the exportation or importation of any species of goods or commodities whatsoever—of establishing rules for deciding in all cases, what captures on land or water shall be legal, and in what manner prizes taken by land or naval forces in the service of the united states shall be divided or appropriated—of granting letters of marque and reprisal in times of peace—appointing courts for the trial of piracies and felonies committed on the high seas and establishing courts for receiving and determining finally appeals in all cases of captures, provided that no member of congress shall be appointed a judge of any of the said courts.

The united states in congress assembled shall also be the last resort on appeal in all disputes and differences now subsisting or that hereafter may arise between two or more states concerning boundary, jurisdiction or any other cause whatever; which authority shall always be exercised in the manner following. Whenever the legislative or executive authority or lawful agent of any state in controversy with another shall present a petition to congress stating the matter in question and praying for a hearing, notice thereof shall be given by order of congress to the legislative or executive authority of the other state in controversy, and a day assigned for the appearance of the parties by their lawful agents, who shall then be directed to appoint by joint consent, commissioners or judges to constitute a court for hearing and determining the matter in question: but if they cannot agree, congress shall name three persons out of each of the united states, and from the list of such persons each party shall alternately strike out one, the petitioners beginning, until the number shall be reduced to thirteen; and from that number not less than seven, nor more than nine names as congress shall direct, shall in the presence of congress be drawn out by lot, and the persons whose names shall be so drawn or any five of them, shall be commissioners or judges, to hear and finally determine the controversy, so always as a major part of the judges who shall hear the cause shall agree in the determination: and if either party shall neglect to attend at the day appointed, without showing reasons, which congress shall judge sufficient, or being present shall refuse to strike, the congress shall proceed to nominate three persons out of each state, and the secretary of congress shall strike in behalf of such party absent or refusing; and the judgment and sentence of the court to be appointed, in the manner before prescribed, shall be final and conclusive; and if any of the parties shall refuse to submit to the authority of such court, or to appear or defend their claim or cause, the court shall nevertheless proceed to pronounce sentence, or judgment, which shall in like manner be final and decisive, the judgment or sentence and other proceedings being in either case transmitted to congress, and lodged among the acts of congress for the security of the parties concerned: provided that every commissioner, before he sits in judgment, shall take an oath to be administred by one of the judges of the supreme or superior court of the state, where the cause shall be tried, " well and truly to hear and determine the matter in question, according to the best of his judgment, without favour, affection or hope of reward: ''

provided also, that no state shall be deprived of territory for the benefit of the united states.

All controversies concerning the private right of soil claimed under different grants of two or more states, whose jurisdictions as they may respect such lands, and the states which passed such grants are adjusted, the said grants or either of them being at the same time claimed to have originated antecedent to such settlement of jurisdiction, shall on the petition of either party to the congress of the united states, be finally determined as near as may be in the same manner as is before prescribed for deciding disputes respecting territorial jurisdiction between different states.

The united states in congress assembled shall also have the sole and exclusive right and power of regulating the alloy and value of coin struck by their own authority, or by that of the respective states—fixing the standard of weights and measures throughout the united states—regulating the trade and managing all affairs with the Indians, not members of any of the states, provided that the legislative right of any state within its own limits be not infringed or violated—establishing or regulating post-offices from one state to another, throughout all the united states, and exacting such postage on the papers passing thro' the same as may be requisite to defray the expences of the said office—appointing all officers of the land forces, in the service of the united states, excepting regimental officers—appointing all the officers of the naval forces, and commissioning all officers whatever in the service of the united states—making rules for the government and regulation of the said land and naval forces, and directing their operations.

The united states in congress assembled shall have authority to appoint a committee, to sit in the recess of congress, to be denominated "A Committee of the States," and to consist of one delegate from each state; and to appoint such other committees and civil officers as may be necessary for managing the general affairs of the united states under their direction—to appoint one of their number to preside, provided that no person be allowed to serve in the office of president more than one year in any term of three years; to ascertain the necessary sums of Money to be raised for the service of the united states, and to appropriate and apply the same for defraying the public expences—to borrow money, or emit bills on the credit of the united states, transmitting every half year to the respective states an account of the sums of money so borrowed or emitted,—to build and equip a navy—to agree upon the number of land forces, and to make requisitions from each state for its quota, in proportion to the number of white inhabitants in such state; which requisition shall be binding, and thereupon the legislature of each state shall appoint the regimental officers, raise the men and cloath, arm and equip them in a soldier like manner, at the expence of the united states; and the officers and men so cloathed, armed and equipped shall march to the place appointed, and within the time agreed on by the united states in congress assembled: But if the united states in congress assembled shall, on consideration of circumstances judge proper that any state should not raise men, or should raise a smaller number than its quota, and that any other state should raise a greater number of men than the quota thereof, such extra number shall be raised, officered, cloathed, armed and equipped in the same manner as the quota of such state, unless the legislature of such state shall judge that such extra number cannot be safely spared out of the same, in which case they shall raise officer, cloath, arm and equip as many of such extra number as they judge can be safely spared. And the officers and men so cloathed, armed and equipped, shall march to the place appointed, and within the time agreed on by the united states in congress assembled.

The united states in congress assembled shall never engage in a war, nor grant letters of marque and reprisal in time of peace, nor enter into any treaties or alliances, nor coin money, nor regulate the value thereof, nor ascertain the sums and expences necessary for the defence and welfare of the united states, or any of them, nor emit bills, nor borrow money on the credit of the united states, nor appropriate money, nor agree upon the number of vessels of war, to be built or purchased, or the number of land or sea forces to be raised, nor appoint a commander in chief of the army or navy, unless nine states assent to the same: nor shall a question on any other point, except for adjourning from day to day be determined, unless by the votes of a majority of the united states in congress assembled.

The congress of the united states shall have power to adjourn to any time within the year, and to any place within the united states, so that no period of adjournment be for a longer duration than the space of six Months, and shall publish the Journal of their proceedings monthly, except such parts thereof relating to treaties, alliances or military operations, as in their judgment require secrecy; and the yeas and nays of the delegates of each state on any question shall be entered on the Journal, when it is desired by any delegate; and the delegates of a state, or any of them, at his or their request shall be furnished with a transcript of the said Journal, except such parts as are above excepted, to lay before the legislatures of the several states.

Article X. The committee of the states, or any nine of them, shall be authorized to execute, in the recess of congress, such of the powers of congress as the united states in congress assembled, by the consent of nine states, shall from time to time think expedient to vest them with; provided that no power be delegated to the said committee, for the exercise of which, by the articles of confederation, the voice of nine states in the congress of the united states assembled is requisite.

Article XI. Canada acceding to this confederation, and joining in the measures of the united states, shall be admitted into, and entitled to all the advantages of this union: but no other colony shall be admitted into the same, unless such admission be agreed to by nine states.

Article XII. All bills of credit emitted, monies borrowed and debts contracted by, or under the authority of congress, before the assembling of the united states, in pursuance of the present confederation, shall be deemed and considered as a charge against the united states, for payment and satisfaction whereof the said united states, and the public faith are hereby solemnly pledged.

Article XIII. Every state shall abide by the determinations of the united states in congress assembled, on all questions which by this confederation are submitted to them. And the Articles of this confederation shall be inviolably observed by every state, and the union shall be perpetual; nor shall any alteration at any time hereafter be made in any of them; unless such alteration be agreed to in a congress of the united states, and be afterwards confirmed by the legislatures of every state.

And Whereas it hath pleased the Great Governor of the World to incline the hearts of the legislatures we respectively represent in congress, to approve of, and to authorize us to ratify the said articles of confederation and perpetual union. Know Ye that we the undersigned delegates, by virtue of the power and authority to us given for that purpose, do by these presents, in the name and in behalf of our respective constituents, fully and entirely ratify and confirm each and every of the said articles of confederation and perpetual union, and all and singular the matters and things therein contained: And we do further solemnly plight and engage the faith of our respective constituents, that they shall abide by the determinations of the united states in congress assembled, on all questions, which by the said confederation are submitted to them. And that the articles thereof shall be inviolably observed by the states we respectively represent, and

that the union shall be perpetual. In Witness whereof we have hereunto set our hands in Congress. Done at Philadelphia in the state of
Pennsylvania the ninth day of July, in the Year of our Lord one
Thousand seven Hundred and Seventy-eight, and in the third year of
the independence of America.

Josiah Bartlett,
John Wentworth, jun^r
  August 8th, 1778,   } On the part & behalf of the State of New Hampshire.

John Hancock,
Samuel Adams,
Elbridge Gerry,
Francis Dana,   } On the part and behalf of the State of Massachusetts
James Lovell,   Bay.
Samuel Holten,

William Ellery,
Henry Marchant,   } On the part and behalf of the State of Rhode-Island
John Collins,   and Providence Plantations.

Roger Sherman,
Samuel Huntington,
Oliver Wolcott,   } On the part and behalf of the State of Connecticut.
Titus Hosmer,
Andrew Adams,

Ja^s Duane,
Fra: Lewis,
Wm Duer,   } On the part and behalf of the State of New York.
Gouv^r Morris,

Jno Witherspoon,
Nathl Scudder,   } On the Part and in Behalf of the State of New
                              Jersey, November 26th, 1778.

Robert Morris,
Daniel Roberdeau,
Jon. Bayard Smith,
William Clingar,   } On the part and behalf of the State of Pennsylvania.
Joseph Reed,
   22d July, 1778,

Thos McKean,
  Feby 22d, 1779,
John Dickinson,   } On the part & behalf of the State of Delaware.
  May 5th, 1779,
Nicholas Van Dyke,

John Hanson,
  March 1, 1781,   } On the part and behalf of the State of Maryland.
Daniel Carroll, do

Richard Henry Lee,
John Banister,
Thomas Adams,   } On the Part and Behalf of the State of Virginia.
Jno Harvie,
Francis Lightfoot Lee,

John Penn,
  July 21st, 1778,
Corn^s Harnett,
Jno Williams,

} On the part and behalf of the State of North Carolina.

Henry Laurens,
William Henry Drayton,
Jno Mathews,
Richd Hutson,
Thos Heyward, jun^r.

} On the part and on behalf of the State of South Carolina.

Jno Walton,
  24th July, 1778,
Edwd Telfair,
Edwd Langworthy,

} On the part and behalf of the State of Georgia.[1]

---

[1] The proceedings of this day with respect to the signing of the Articles of Confederation, the Articles themselves and the signers are entered in the *Papers of the Continental Congress*, No. 9 (History of the Confederation), but not in the Journal itself. The Articles are printed here from the original roll in the Bureau of Rolls and Library, Department of State.

LIST OF DELEGATES APPOINTED BY THE STATES REP-
RESENTED IN THE FEDERAL CONVENTION [1]

From		*Attended*
New Hampshire.	1. John Langdon,	July 23, 1787
	John Pickering,	
	2. Nicholas Gilman,	July 23,
	Benjamin West.	
Massachusetts.	*Francis Dana,*	
	Elbridge Gerry,	May 29,
	3. Nathaniel Gorham,	May 28,
	4. Rufus King,	May 25,
	Caleb Strong,	May 28,
Rhode Island.	[No appointment.]	
Connecticut.	5. Wm. Sam. Johnson,	June 2,
	6. Roger Sherman,	May 30,
	Oliver Elsworth,	May 29,
New York.	Robert Yates,	May 25,
	7. Alexander Hamilton,	do.
	John Lansing,	June 2,
New Jersey.	8. William Livingston,	June 5,
	9. David Brearley,	May 25,
	William C. Houston,	do.
	10. William Patterson,	do.
	John Neilson.	
	Abraham Clark.	
	11. Jonathan Dayton,	June 21,
Pennsylvania.	12. Benjamin Franklin,	May 28,
	13. Thomas Mifflin,	do.
	14. Robert Morris,	May 25,
	15. George Clymer,	May 28,
	16. Thomas Fitzsimons,	May 25,
	17. Jared Ingersoll,	May 28,

---

[1] Reprinted from *Journal, Acts and Proceedings of the Convention which formed the Constitution of the United States,* John Quincy Adams, Editor (1819), pp. 13-15.

For a more elaborate list including the names of delegates who were elected but declined, and fuller and revised details of attendance, see *The Records of the Federal Convention of 1787,* Max Farrand, Editor, Vol. III (1901), pp. 557-559, 586-590.

From		*Attended*
	18. James Wilson,	May 25,
	19. Gouverneur Morris,	do.
Delaware.	20. George Read,	do.
	21. Gunning Bedford, jr.	May 28,
	22. John Dickinson,	do.
	23. Richard Basset,	May 25,
	24. Jacob Broom,	do.
Maryland.	25. James M'Henry,	May 29,
	26. Daniel of St. Thomas Jenifer,	June 2,
	27. Daniel Carroll,	July 9,
	John Francis Mercer,	Aug. 6,
	Luther Martin,	June 9,
Virginia.	28. George Washington,	May 25,
	Patrick Henry,	(declined.)
	Edmund Randolph,	May 25,
	29. John Blair,	do.
	30. James Madison, jr	do.
	George Mason,	do.
	George Wythe,	do.
	James M'Clurg, (in the room of	
	P. Henry)	do.
North Carolina.	*Richard Caswell,*	(resigned.)
	Alexander Martin,	May 25,
	William R. Davie,	do.
	31. William Blount, (in the room of	
	R. Caswell)	June 20,
	Willie Jones,	(declined.)
	32. Richard D. Spaight,	May 25,
	33. Hugh Williamson, (in the room	
	of W. Jones)	May 25,
South Carolina.	34. John Rutledge,	do.
	35. Charles C. Pinckney,	do.
	36. Charles Pinckney,	do.
	37. Pierce Butler,	do.
Georgia.	38. William Few,	do.
	39. Abraham Baldwin,	June 11,
	William Pierce,	May 31,
	George Walton.	
	William Houstoun,	June 1,
	Nathaniel Pendleton.	

Those with numbers before their names, signed the Constitution..   39
Those in Italicks, never attended............................   10
Members who attended, but did not sign the Constitution.....   16
                                     —
                                     65

PART II
THE FEDERAL CONVENTION OF 1787

PREFACE TO DEBATES IN THE CONVENTION [1]

A Sketch Never Finished nor Applied. [2]

As the weakness and wants of man naturally lead to an association of individuals, under a common authority, whereby each may have the protection of the whole against danger from without, and enjoy in safety within, the advantages of social intercourse, and an exchange of the necessaries & comforts of life: in like manner feeble communities, independent of each other, have resorted to a Union, less intimate, but with common Councils, for the common safety agst powerful neighbors, and for the preservation of justice and peace among themselves. Ancient history furnishes examples of these confederal [3] associations, tho' with a very imperfect account, of their structure, and of the attributes and functions of the presiding Authority. There are examples of modern date also, some of them still existing, the modifications and transactions of which are sufficiently known.

It remained for the British Colonies, now United States, of North America, to add to those examples, one of a more interesting character than any of them: which led to a system without a [4] example ancient or modern, a system founded on popular rights, and so combing. a federal form with the forms of individual Republics, as may

---

[1] The proposed Preface has been printed from Madison's original manuscript in the Department of State. There is a transcript of the Preface in an unknown hand in the Library of Congress, which was sent to the printer and from which Henry D. Gilpin printed *The Papers of James Madison*, 3 volumes (1840). The text of the Preface as here printed has been read with the printer's copy thereof and important differences noted.

In the Preface, Madison referred in passing to documents which he evidently intended to embody in a finished draft which, unfortunately, he never completed. The matter referred to has been placed in footnotes or reference has been made to other pages of the present volume.

Footnotes bearing star or dagger instead of figures to indicate their order, are Madison's own notes and have been placed above the line. The editors' notes and indications of differences between the Madison manuscript and the transcript of the Preface have been numbered and placed below the line.

[2] These are the words which Madison wrote at the head of this document after he had scratched out the phrase "Preface to Debates in the Convention of 1787." It is a very rough and uneven draft, full of insertions and deletions. The last few pages are in Mrs. Madison's hand, having been written from her husband's dictation when his hands were crippled with rheumatism. A few words in the draft were written by John C. Payne (Mrs. Madison's brother) at Madison's direction. The date of the draft was between 1830 and 1836.

[3] The word "confederate" is substituted in the transcript for "confederal."

[4] The word "an" is substituted in the transcript for "a."

1

enable each to supply the defects of the other and obtain the advantages of both.[1]

Whilst the Colonies enjoyed the protection of the parent Country as it was called, against foreign danger; and were secured by its superintending controul, against conflicts among themselves, they continued independent of each other, under a common, tho' limited dependence, on the parental Authority. When however the growth of the offspring in strength and in wealth, awakened the jealousy and tempted the avidity of the parent, into schemes of usurpation & exaction, the obligation was felt by the former of uniting their counsels and efforts to avert the impending calamity.

As early as the year 1754, indications having been given of a design in the Brittish Government to levy contributions on the Colonies, without their consent; a meeting of Colonial deputies took place at Albany, which attempted to introduce a compromising substitute, that might at once satisfy the British requisitions, and save their own rights from violation. The attempt had no other effect, than by bringing these rights into a more conspicuous view, to invigorate the attachment to them, on [2] one side; and to nourish the haughty & encroaching spirit on the other.

In 1774. The progress made by G. B. in the open assertion of her pretensions, and in [3] the apprehended purpose of otherwise maintaining them than by Legislative enactments and declarations, had been such that the Colonies did not hesitate to assemble, by their deputies, in a formal Congress, authorized to oppose to the British innovations whatever measures might be found best adapted to the occasion; without however losing sight of an eventual reconciliation.

The dissuasive measures of that Congress, being without effect, another Congress was held in 1775, whose pacific efforts to bring about a change in the views of the other party, being equally unavailing, and the commencement of actual hostilities having at length put an end to all hope of reconciliation; the Congress finding moreover that the popular voice began to call for an entire & perpetual dissolution of the political ties which had connected them with G. B., proceeded on the memorable 4th of July, 1776 to declare the 13 Colonies, Independent States.[4]

During the discussions of this solemn Act, a Committee consisting of a member from each colony had been appointed to prepare &

---

[1] In place of "the advantages of both" the transcript reads "that advantage of both."

[2] The word "the" is here inserted in the transcript.

[3] The word "in" is omitted in the transcript.

[4] The words "Independent States" are italicized in the transcript.

digest a form of Confederation, for the future management of the common interests, which had hitherto been left to the discretion of Congress, guided by the exigences of the contest, and by the known intentions or occasional instructions of the Colonial Legislatures.

It appears that as early as the 21ˢᵗ of July 1775, A plan entitled " Articles of Confederation & *perpetual* Union of the Colonies " had been sketched by Docˢ Franklin, the plan being on that day submitted by him to Congress; and tho' not copied into their Journals remaining on their files in his handwriting. But notwithstanding the term " perpetual " observed in the title, the articles provided expressly for the event of a return of the Colonies to a connection with G. Britain.

This sketch became a basis for the plan reported by the Comᵉ on the 12 of July, now also remaining on the files of Congress, in the handwriting of Mʳ Dickinson. The plan, tho' dated after the Declaration of Independence, was probably drawn up before that event; since the name of *Colonies,* not *States* is used throughout the draught. The plan reported, was debated and amended from time to time, till the 17ᵗʰ of November 1777, when it was agreed to by Congress, and proposed to the Legislatures of the States, with an explanatory and recommendatory letter. The ratifications of these by their Delegates in Congᵉ duly authorized took place at successive dates; but were not compleated till March 1.[1] 1781. when Maryland who had made it a prerequisite that the vacant lands acquired from the British Crown should be a Common fund, yielded to the persuasion that a final & formal establishment of the federal Union & Govᵗ would make a favorable impression not only on other foreign Nations, but on G. B. herself.

The great difficulty experienced in so framing the fedˡ system as to obtain the unanimity required for its due sanction, may be inferred. from the long interval, and recurring discussions, between the commencement and completion of the work; from the changes made during its progress; from the language of Congˢ when proposing it to the States, wᶜʰ dwelt on the impracticability of devising a system acceptable to all of them; from the reluctant assent given by some; and the various alterations proposed by others; and by a tardiness in others again which produced a special address to them from Congˢ enforcing the duty of sacrificing local considerations and favorite opinions to to the public safety, and the necessary harmony: Nor was the assent of some of the States finally yielded without strong protests against par-

---

[1] The phrase " the first of March " is substituted in the transcript for " March 1."

ticular articles, and a reliance on future amendments removing their objections.

It is to be recollected, no doubt, that these delays might be occasioned in some degree, by an occupation of the public Councils both general & local, with the deliberations and measures, essential to a Revolutionary struggle; But there must have been a balance for these causes, in the obvious motives to hasten the establishment of a regular and efficient Gov^t; and in the tendency of the crisis to repress opinions and pretensions, which might be inflexible in another state of things.

The principal difficulties which embarrassed the progress, and retarded the completion of the plan of Confederation, may be traced to 1.[1] the natural repugnance of the parties to a relinquishment of power: 2[1] a natural jealousy of its abuse in other hands than their own: 3[1] the rule of suffrage among parties unequal in size, but equal in sovereignty. 4 the ratio of contributions in money and in troops, among parties,[2] whose inequality in size did not correspond with that of their wealth, or of their military or free population. 5.[3] the selection and definition of the powers, at once necessary to the federal head, and safe to the several members.

To these sources of difficulty, incident to the formation of all such Confederacies, were added two others one of a temporary, the other of a permanent nature. The first was the case of the Crown lands, so called because they had been held by the British Crown, and being ungranted to individuals when its authority ceased, were considered by the States within whose charters or asserted limits they lay, as devolving on them; whilst it was contended by the others, that being wrested from the dethroned authority, by the equal exertion of all, they resulted of right and in equity to the benefit of all. The lands being of vast extent and of growing value, were the occasion of much discussion & heart-burning; & proved the most obstinate of the impediments to an earlier consummation of the plan of federal Gov^t The State of Maryland the last that acceded to it held out as already noticed, till March 1,[4] 1781, and then yielded only to the hope that by giving a stable & authoritative character to the Confederation, a successful termination of the Contest might be accelerated. The dispute was happily compromised by successive surrenders of portions of the

---

[1] The figures 1, 2, and 3 are changed to " first," " secondly " and " thirdly " in the transcript.
[2] The phrase " unequal in size, but equal in sovereignty. 4 the ratio of contributions in money and in troops, among parties " is erroneously omitted in the transcript.
[3] The figure 5 is changed to " fourthly " in the transcript.
[4] In the transcript the date reads " the first of March, 1781."

territory by the States having exclusive claims to it, and acceptances of them by Congress.

The other source of dissatisfaction was the peculiar situation of some of the States, which having no convenient ports for foreign commerce, were subject to be taxed by their neighbors, thro whose ports, their commerce was carryed on. New Jersey, placed between Phil? & N. York, was likened to a cask tapped at both ends; and N. Carolina, between Virg? & S. Carolina to a patient bleeding at both arms. The Articles of Confederation provided no remedy for the complaint: which produced a strong protest on the part of N. Jersey; and never ceased to be a source of dissatisfaction & discord, until the new Constitution, superseded the old.

But the radical infirmity of the " art? of Confederation " was the dependance of Cong? on the voluntary and simultaneous compliance with its Requisitions, by so many independant Communities, each consulting more or less its particular interests & convenience and distrusting the compliance of the others. Whilst the paper emissions of Cong? continued to circulate they were employed as a sinew of war, like gold & silver. When that ceased to be the case, the fatal defect of the political System was felt in its alarming force. The war was merely kept alive and brought to a successful conclusion by such foreign aids and temporary expedients as could be applied; a hope prevailing with many, and a wish with all, that a state of peace, and the sources of prosperity opened by it, would give to the Confederacy in practice, the efficiency which had been inferred from its theory.

The close of the war however brought no cure for the public embarrasments. The States relieved from the pressure of foreign danger, and flushed with the enjoyment of independent and sovereign power; [instead of a diminished disposition to part with it,] persevered in omissions and in measures incompatible with their relations to the Federal Gov? and with those among themselves;

Having served as a member of Cong? through the period between Mar. 1780 & the arrival of peace in 1783, I had become intimately acquainted with the public distresses and the causes of them. I had observed the successful opposition to every attempt to procure a remedy by new grants of power to Cong? I had founnd moreover that despair of success hung over the compromising provision [1] of April 1783 for the public necessities which had been so elaborately planned, and so impressively recommended to the States.[*] Sympathizing, under this

* See address of Congress.[2]

---

[1] The word "principle" is substituted for "provision" in the transcript.
[2] This footnote is omitted in the transcript.

aspect of affairs, in the alarm of the friends of free Gov[t], at the threatened danger of an abortive result to the great & perhaps last experiment in its favour, I could not be insensible to the obligation to co-operate [1] as far as I could in averting the calamity. With this view I acceded to the desire of my fellow Citizens of the County that I should be one of its representatives in the Legislature, hoping that I might there best contribute to inculcate the critical posture to which the Revolutionary cause was reduced, and the merit of a leading agency of the State in bringing about a rescue of the Union and the blessings of liberty a [2] staked on it, from an impending catastrophe.

It required but little time after taking my seat in the House of Delegates in May 1784 to discover that, however favorable the general disposition of the State might be towards the Confederacy the Legislature retained the aversion of its predecessors to transfers of power from the State to the Gov[t] of the Union; notwithstanding the urgent demands of the Federal Treasury; the glaring inadequacy of the authorized mode of supplying it, the rapid growth of anarchy in the Fed[l] System, and the animosity kindled among the States by their conflicting regulations.

The temper of the Legislature & the wayward course of its proceedings may be gathered from the Journals of its Sessions in the years 1784 & 1785.

The failure however of the varied propositions in the Legislature, for enlarging the powers of Congress, the continued failure of the efforts of Cong[s] to obtain from them the means of providing for the debts of the Revolution; and of countervailing the commercial laws of G. B. a source of much irritation & ag[st] which the separate efforts of the States were found worse than abortive; these Considerations with the lights thrown on the whole subject, by the free & full discussion it had undergone led to an [3] general acquiescence in the Resol[n] passed, on the 21. of Jan[y] 1786. which proposed & invited a meeting of Deputies from all the States to " insert the Resol (See Journal.)1.[4]

The resolution had been brought forward some weeks before on the failure of a proposed grant of power to Congress to collect a revenue from commerce, which had been abandoned by its friends in consequence of material alterations made in the grant by a Committee of the whole. The Resolution tho introduced by M[r] Tyler an influ-

---

[1] The word "aid" is substituted in the transcript for "co-operate."
[2] The word "a" is omitted in the transcript.
[3] The word "a" is substituted in the transcript for "an."
[4] The phrase "to 'insert the Resol. (See Journal.) 1" is omitted in the transcript which substitutes the words "as follows: " and inserts the resolution which is printed in this volume at page xlvii.

encial member, who having never served in Congress, had more the ear of the House than those whose services there exposed them to an imputable bias, was so little acceptable that it was not then persisted in. Being now revived by him, on the last day of the Session, and being the alternative of adjourning without any effort for the crisis in the affairs of the Union, it obtained a general vote; less however with some of its friends from a confidence in the success of the experiment than from a hope that it might prove a step to a more comprehensive & adequate provision for the wants of the Confederacy

It happened also that Commissioners who had been [1] appointed by Virgᵃ & Maryᵈ to settle the jurisdiction on waters dividing the two States had, apart from their official reports, recommended a uniformity in the regulations of the 2 States on several subjects & particularly on those having relation to foreign trade. It apeared at the same time that Maryᵈ had deemed a concurrence of her neighbors Penᵃ & Delaware indispensable in such a case, who for like reasons would require that of their neighbors. So apt and forceable an illustration of the necessity of a uniformity throughout all the States could not but favour the passage of a Resolution which proposed a Convention having that for its object.

The commissioners appointed by the Legisl: & who attended the Convention were E. Randolph the Attorney of the State, Sᵗ Geo: Tucker & J. M.[2] The designation of the time & place for its meeting to be proposed and communicated to the States having been left to the Comʳˢ they named for the time early [3] September and for the place the City of Annapolis avoiding the residence of Congˢ and large Commercial Cities as liable to suspicions of an extraneous influence.

Altho the invited Meeting appeared to be generally favored, five States only assembled; some failing to make appointments, and some of the individuals appointed not hastening their attendance, the result in both cases being ascribed mainly, to a belief that the time had not arrived for such a political reform, as might be expected from a further experience of its necessity.

But in the interval between the proposal of the Convention and the time of its meeting, such had been the advance of public opinion in the desired direction, stimulated as it had been by the effect of the contemplated object, of the meeting, in turning the genal attention to the Critical State of things, and in calling forth the sentiments and exertions of the most enlightened & influencial patriots,

---

[1] The phrase "who had been" is omitted in the transcript.
[2] James Madison.
[3] In place of the word "early" the transcript reads "the first Monday in."

that the Convention thin as it was did not scruple to decline the limited task assigned to it and to recommend to the States a Convention with powers adequate to the occasion. Nor was it [1] unnoticed that the commission of the N. Jersey Deputation, had extended its object to a general provision for the exigencies of the Union. A recommendation for this enlarged purpose was accordingly reported by a Com.[e] to whom the subject had been referred. It was drafted by Col: H.[2] and finally agreed to unanimously [3] in the following form. Insert it.[4]

The recommendation was well rec.[d] by the Legislature of Virg.[a] which happened to be the *first* that *acted* on it, and the example of her compliance was made as conciliatory and impressive as possible. The Legislature were unanimous or very nearly so on the occasion, and [5] as a proof of the magnitude & solemnity attached to it, they placed Gen.[l] W. at the head of the Deputation from the State; and as a proof of the deep interest he felt in the case he overstepped the obstacles to his acceptance of the appointment.

The law complying with the recommendation from Annapolis was in the terms following: [6]

A resort to a General Convention to remodel the Confederacy, was not a new idea. It had entered at an early date into the conversations and speculations of the most reflecting & foreseeing observers of the inadequacy of the powers allowed to Congress. In a pamphlet published in May 81 at the seat of Cong.[s] Pelatiah Webster an able tho' not conspicuous Citizen, after discussing the fiscal system of the U. States, and suggesting among other remedial provisions [7] including a national Bank remarks that "the Authority of Cong.[s] at present is very inadequate to the performance of their duties; and this indicates the necessity of their calling a *Continental Convention* for the express purpose of ascertaining, defining, enlarging, and limiting, the duties & powers of their Constitution." [8]

---

[1] The words "had it been" are substituted in the transcript for the words "was it."

[2] Alexander Hamilton.

[3] The word "unanimously" is omitted in the transcript.

[4] Madison's direction "Insert it" is omitted in the transcript, and there is inserted the text of the proceedings and recommendation of the Annapolis Convention for which see, *ante*, pages xlviii-lii. The transcript text begins with the words "To the Honorable," and concludes with the paragraph beginning "Though your Commissioners," etc.

[5] The word "and" is omitted in the transcript.

[6] The text of this law of October 16, 1786 (printed *ante* pages lxviii-lxix) is inserted in the transcript beginning with the words "Whereas, the Commissioners," etc. and ending with the words ". . . States in the Union."

[7] The word "one" is here inserted in the transcript.

[8] Madison was in error. The pamphlet was written by William Barton.

On the 1. day of Ap! 1783, Col. Hamilton, in a debate in Cong:
observed that [1]

He alluded probably to [see Life of Schuyler in Longacre [2]

It does not appear however that his expectation had been fulfilled.]

In a letter to J. M. from R. H. Lee then President of Cong: dated
Nov: 26, 1784 He says [3]

The answer of J. M. remarks [4]

[5] In 1785, Noah Webster whose pol. & other valuable writings had
made him known to the public, in one of his publications of American
policy brought into view the same resort for supplying the defects
of the Fed! System [see his life in Longacre]

The proposed & expected Convention at Annapolis the first of a

---

See Gaillard Hunt, "Pelatiah Webster and the Constitution," in *The Nation*,
December 28, 1911.

[1] The following is supplied in the transcript: "he wished instead of them
[partial Conventions] to see a general Convention take place; and that he
should soon, in pursuance of instructions from his constituents, propose to Congress a plan for that purpose, the object [of which] would be to strengthen the
Federal Constitution."—See *The Writings of James Madison*, Hunt, Editor,
Vol. I (1900), pp. 438, 439.

[2] The phrase "[see Life of Schuyler in Longacre" is omitted in the transcript and the following quoted matter is substituted: "the resolutions introduced by General Schuyler in the Senate, and passed unanimously by the
Legislature of New York in the summer of 1782, declaring, that the Confederation was defective, in not giving Congress power to provide a revenue for itself,
or in not investing them with funds from established and productive sources;
and that it would be advisable for Congress to recommend to the States to call
a general Convention to revise and amend the Confederation."

The sketch is of Hamilton, not Schuyler, for which see *The National Portrait Gallery of Distinguished Americans*, conducted by Longacre and Herring,
Vol. II (1835), p. 7.

[3] The following sentence is supplied in the transcript: "It is by many here
suggested as a very necessary step for Congress to take, the calling on the
States to form a Convention for the sole purpose of revising the Confederation,
so far as to enable Congress to execute with more energy, effect and vigor the
powers assigned to it, than it appears by experience that they can do under the
present state of things." The letter referred to is among the Madison papers in
the Manuscript Division of the Library of Congress.

[4] The transcript here inserts the following: "I hold it for a maxim, that
the Union of the States is essential to their safety against foreign danger and
internal contention; and that the perpetuity and efficacy of the present system
cannot be confided in. The question, therefore, is, in what mode, and at what
moment, the experiment for supplying the defects ought to be made."—See,
also, *The Writings of James Madison*, Hunt, Editor, Vol. II (1901), pp. 99,
100.

[5] The paragraph beginning "In 1785" reads as follows in the transcript:
"In the winter of 1784-5, Noah Webster, whose political and other valuable
writings had made him known to the public, proposed, in one of his publications, 'a new system of government which should act, not on the States, but
directly on individuals, and vest in Congress full power to carry its laws into
effect.'"

See, also, *The National Portrait Gallery of Distinguished Americans*, conducted by Longacre and Herring, Vol. II (1835), p. 4.

general character that appears to have been realized, & the state of the public mind awakened by it had attracted the particular attention of Cong. and favored the idea there of a Convention with fuller powers for amending the Confederacy.[1]

It does not appear that in any of these cases, the reformed system was to be otherwise sanctioned than by the Legislative auth. of the States; nor whether or how far, a change was to be made in the structure of the Depository of Federal powers.

The act of Virg. providing for the Convention at Philad., was succeeded by appointments from [2] other States as their Legislatures were assembled, the appointments being selections from the most experienced & highest standing Citizens. Rh. I. was the only exception to a compliance with the recommendation from Annapolis, well known to have been swayed by an obdurate adherence to an advantage which her position gave her of taxing her neighbors thro' their consumption of imported supplies, an advantage which it was foreseen would be taken from her by a revisal of the " Articles of Confederation

As the pub. mind had been ripened for a salutary Reform of the pol. System, in the interval between the proposal & the meeting, of Com. at Annapolis, the interval between the last event, and the meeting of Dep. at Phil. had continued to develop more & more the necessity & the extent of a Systematic provision for the preservation and Gov. of the Union; among the ripening incidents was the Insurrection of Shays,[3] in Mass. against her Gov.; which was with difficulty suppressed, notwithstanding the influence on the insurgents of an apprehended interposition of the Fed. troops.

At the date of the Convention, the aspect & retrospect of the pol: condition of the U. S. could not but fill the pub. mind with a gloom which was relieved only by a hope that so select a Body would devise an adequate remedy for the existing and prospective evils so impressively demanding it

It was seen that the public debt rendered so sacred by the cause in which it had been incurred remained without any provision for its payment. The reiterated and elaborate efforts of Cong. to procure from the States a more adequate power to raise the means of payment had failed. The effect of the ordinary requisitions of Congress had

---

[1] In the transcript after the word "Confederacy" the following footnote is inserted: "The letters of Wm. Grayson, March 22d, 1786, and of James Monroe, of April 28th, 1786, both then members, to Mr. Madison, state that a proposition for such a Convention had been made."

[2] The word "the" is inserted in the transcript after "from."

[3] The final "s" is crossed off the word "Shays" in the transcript.

only displayed the inefficiency [1] of the auth? making them; none of the States having duly complied with them, some having failed altogether or nearly so; and [2] in one instance, that of N. Jersey [3] a compliance was expressly [4] refused; nor was more yielded to the expostulations of members of Cong? deputed to her Legislature, than a mere repeal of the law, without a compliance. [see letter of Grayson to J. M.[5]

The want of Auth? in Cong? to regulate Commerce had produced in Foreign nations particularly G. B. a monopolizing policy injurious to the trade of the U. S. and destructive to their navigation; the imbecilicity and anticipated dissolution of the Confederacy extinguish? all apprehensions of a Countervailing policy on the part of the U. States

The same want of a general power over Commerce, led to an exercise of the power separately, by the States, wch not only proved abortive, but engendered rival, conflicting and angry regulations. Besides the vain attempts to supply their respective treasuries by imposts, which turned their commerce into the neighbouring ports, and to co-erce a relaxation of the British monopoly of the W. Ind? navigation, which was attempted by Virg? [see the Journal of] [6] the States having ports for foreign commerce, taxed & irritated the adjoining States, trading thro' them, as N. Y. Pen? Virg? & S. Carolina. Some of the States, as Connecticut, taxed imports [7] as from Mass?

---

[1] The transcript substitutes the word "inefficacy" for the word "inefficiency" but the Gilpin edition prints the word as in the original notes.

[2] In the transcript the word "and" is crossed out and the word "which" [2] written above it.

[3] After the word "Jersey," reference is made in the transcript to the following footnote: "A letter of Mr. Grayson to Mr. Madison of March 22d, 1786, relating the conduct of New Jersey states this fact. Editor."

[4] The word "expressly" is italicized in the transcript.

[5] The phrase "[see letter of Grayson to J. M." is omitted in the transcript. An extract from the letter referred to reads as follows: "The Antients were surely men of more candor than we are; they contended openly for an abolition of debts in so many words, while we strive as hard for the same thing under the decent & specious pretense of a circulating medium. . . . There has been some serious thoughts in the minds of some of the members of Congress to recommend to the States the meeting of a general Convention, to consider, of an alteration of the Confederation, & there is a motion to this effect now under consideration: it is contended that the present Confederation is utterly inefficient, and that if it remains much longer in it's present state of imbecility we shall be one of the most contemptible nations on the face of the earth."— Letter from William Grayson to James Madison, March 22, 1786. The Madison Papers (manuscript), Library of Congress.

[6] In the transcript the footnote "See the Journal of her Legislature" is substituted for the phrase in brackets. The allusion is to the act of the Virginia Assembly passed January 21, 1786, imposing a tonnage tax of 5s. on vessels of foreigners.

[7] After the word "imports" down to the sentence beginning, "In sundry instances," the transcript reads "from others, as from Mass., which complained in a letter to the Executive of Virginia, and doubtless to those of other States."

higher than imports even from G. B. of wch Mass^ts complained to Virg^a and doubtless to other States. [See letter of J. M.[1] In sundry instances as of N. Y. N. J. P^a & Mary^d [see   ][2] the navigation laws treated the Citizens[3] other States as aliens.

In certain cases the auth^y of the Confederacy was disregarded, as in violations not only of the Treaty of peace; but of Treaties with France & Holland, which were complained of to Cong^s

In other cases the Fed^l Auth^y was violated by Treaties & wars with Indians, as by Geo: by troops raised & kept up with^t the consent of Cong^s as by Mass^ts by compacts with^t the consent of Cong^s as between Pen^a and N. Jersey, and between Virg^a & Mary^d From the Legisl: Journals of Virg^a it appears, that a vote refusing to apply for a sanction of Cong^s was followed by a vote ag^st the communication of the Compact to Cong^s

In the internal administration of the States a violation of Contracts had become familiar in the form of depreciated paper made a legal tender, of property substituted for money, of Instalment laws, and of the occlusions of the Courts of Justice; although evident that all such interferences affected the rights of other States, relatively creditor,[4] as well as Citizens Creditors within the State

Among the defects which had been severely felt was that of a uniformity in cases requiring it, as laws of naturalization,[5] bankruptcy, a Coercive authority operating on individuals and a guaranty of the internal tranquility of the States.

As natural consequences[6] of this distracted and disheartening condition of the union, the Fed^l Auth^y had ceased to be respected abroad, and dispositions[7] shewn there, particularly in G. B., to take advantage of its imbecility, and to speculate on its approaching downfall; at home it had lost all confidence & credit; the unstable and unjust career of the States had also forfeited the respect & confidence essential to order and good Gov^t, involving a general decay of confidence & credit between man & man. It was found moreover, that those least partial to popular Gov^t, or most distrustful of its efficacy were yielding to anticipations, that from an increase of the confusion a Gov^t might result more congenial with their taste or their opinions;

---

[1] The facts are given in Madison's letter to Jefferson, January 22, 1786. *The Writings of James Madison*, Hunt, Editor, Vol. II (1901), p. 218.
[2] Madison's direction " [see   ] " is omitted in the transcript.
[3] The word " of " is inserted in the transcript after " Citizens."
[4] The word " creditor " is plural in the transcript.
[5] The word " and " is inserted in the transcript after " naturalization."
[6] The words " a natural consequence " are substituted in the transcript for "natural consequences."
[7] The word " were " is inserted in the transcript after " dispositions."

whilst those most devoted to the principles and forms of Republics, were alarmed for the cause of liberty itself, at stake in the American Experiment, and anxious for a system that w^d avoid the inefficacy of a mere confederacy without passing into the opposite extreme of a consolidated gov^t it was known that there were individuals who had betrayed a bias towards Monarchy [see Knox to G. W. & him to Jay] (Marshall's life [1]) and there had always been some not unfavorable to a partition of the Union into several Confederacies; either from a better chance of figuring on a Sectional Theatre, or that the Sections would require stronger Gov^{ts}, or by their hostile conflicts lead to a monarchical consolidation. The idea of a [2] dismemberment had recently made its appearance in the Newspapers.

Such were the defects, the deformities, the diseases and the ominous prospects, for which the Convention were to provide a remedy, and which ought never to be overlooked in expounding & appreciating the Constitutional Charter the remedy that was provided.

As a sketch on paper, the earliest perhaps of a Constitutional Gov^t for the Union [organized into the regular Departments with physical means operating on individuals] to be sanctioned by *the people of the States,* acting in their original & sovereign character, was contained in [3] a letter of Apl. 8. 1787 from J. M. to Govr Randolph, a copy of the letter is here inserted.

The feature in the letter [4] which vested in the general Authy. a negative on the laws of the States, was suggested by the negative in the head of the British Empire, which prevented collisions between the parts & the whole, and between the parts themselves. It was supposed that the substitution, of an elective and responsible authority for an hereditary and irresponsible one, would avoid the appearance even of a departure from the principle of [5] Republicanism. But altho' the subject was so viewed in the Convention, and the votes on it were more than once equally divided, it was finally & justly abandoned see note

---

[1] This direction in Madison's notes is omitted in the transcript. His reference was to *The Life of George Washington*, by John Marshall, Vol. V (1807), pp. 91 *et seq.* For the text of the correspondence in question, see Appendix to Debates, I, Nos. 1, 2 and 3, pp. 585-588.

[2] The word " a " is omitted in the transcript.

[3] The phrase beginning with the words " a letter " down to the end of the paragraph is changed in the transcript to read as follows: " the letters of James Madison to Thomas Jefferson of the nineteenth of March; to Governor Randolph of the eighth of April; and to General Washington of the sixteenth of April, 1787, for which see these respective dates."

For the material portions of these letters see Appendix to Debates, II, Nos. 1, 2 and 3, pp. 589-595.

[4] The words " the letter " have been changed to " these letters " in the transcript.

[5] The words " the principle of " are omitted in the transcript.

for   for this erasure substitute the amend! marked * for this page [1] [as, apart from other objections, it was not practicable among so many states, increasing in number, and enacting, each of them, so many laws. Instead of the proposed negative, the objects of it were left as finally provided for in the Constitution.] [2]

On the arrival of the Virginia Deputies at Philad! it occurred to them that from the early and prominent part taken by that State in bringing about the Convention some initiative step might be expected from them. The Resolutions introduced by Governor Randolph were the result of a Consultation on the subject; with an understanding that they left all the Deputies entirely open to the lights of discussion, and free to concur in any alterations or modifications which their reflections and judgments might approve. The Resolutions as the Journals shew became the basis on which the proceedings of the Convention commenced, and to the developments, variations and modifications of which the plan of Gov! proposed by the Convention may be traced.

The curiosity I had felt during my researches into the History of the most distinguished Confederacies, particularly those of antiquity, and the deficiency I found in the means of satisfying it more especially in what related to the process, the principles, the reasons, & the anticipations, which prevailed in the formation of them, determined me to preserve as far as I could an exact account of what might pass in the Convention whilst executing its trust, with the magnitude of which I was duly impressed, as I was with [3] the gratification promised to future curiosity by an authentic exhibition of the objects, the opinions, & the reasonings from which the new System of Gov! was to receive its peculiar structure & organization. Nor was I unaware of the value of such a contribution to the fund of materials for the History of a Constitution on which would be staked the happiness of a people great even in its infancy, and possibly the cause of Liberty throught the world.

In pursuance of the task I had assumed I chose a seat in front of the presiding member, with the other members on my right & left hands. In this favorable position for hearing all that passed, I noted in terms legible & in abreviations & marks intelligible to myself what was read from the Chair or spoken by the members; and losing not a moment unnecessarily between the adjournment & reassembling of

---

[1] The words "see note for   for this erasure substitute the amend! marked * for this page" are omitted in the transcript.

[2] The passage enclosed in brackets is copied from the transcript. The original notes appear to have been lost since Gilpin's edition.

[3] The word "by" is substituted in the transcript for "with."

the Convention I was enabled to write out my daily notes [see page 18–[1] during the session or within a few finishing days after its close—see pa. 18 [2] in the extent and form preserved in my own hand on my files.

In the labour & correctness of doing [3] this, I was not a little aided by practice & by a familiarity with the style and the train of observation & reasoning which characterized the principal speakers. It happened, also that. I was not absent a single day, nor more than a cassual fraction of an hour in any day, so that I could not have lost a single speech, unless a very short one. Insert the Remark on the — slip of paper marked A [4]

[It may be proper to remark, that, with a very few exceptions, the speeches were neither furnished, nor revised, nor sanctioned, by the speakers, but written out from my notes, aided by the freshness of my recollections. A further remark may be proper, that views of the subject might occasionally be presented in the speeches and proceedings, with a latent reference to a compromise on some middle ground, by mutual concessions. The exceptions alluded to were,— first, the sketch furnished by Mr. Randolph of his speech on the introduction of his propositions, on the twenty-ninth day of May; secondly, the speech of Mr. Hamilton, who happened to call on me when putting the last hand to it, and who acknowledged its fidelity, without suggesting more than a very few verbal alterations which were made; thirdly, the speech of Gouverneur Morris on the second day of May, which was communicated to him on a like occasion, and who acquiesced in it without even a verbal change. The correctness of his language and the distinctness of his enunciation were particularly favorable to a reporter. The speeches of Doctor Franklin, excepting a few brief ones, were copied from the written ones read to the Convention by his colleague, Mr. Wilson, it being inconvenient to the Doctor to remain long on his feet.] [5]

Of the ability & intelligence of those who composed the Convention, the debates & proceedings may be a test; as the character of the work which was the offspring of their deliberations must be tested by the experience of the future, added to that of the nearly half century which has passed.[6]

---

[1] Madison's direction " [see page 18-" is omitted in the transcript.
[2] Madison's direction " see pa. 18 " is omitted in the transcript.
[3] The word "doing" is omitted in the transcript.
[4] Madison's direction "Insert the Remark," etc. is omitted in the transcript.
[5] The passage enclosed in brackets is copied from the transcript. The original notes appear to have been lost since Gilpin's edition.
[6] The phrase " of the nearly half century " is changed to " of nearly half a century " in the transcript.

But whatever may be the judgment pronounced on the competency of the architects of the Constitution, or whatever may be the destiny, of the edifice prepared by them, I feel it a duty to express my profound & solemn conviction, derived from my intimate opportunity of observing & appreciating the views of the Convention, collectively & individually, that there never was an assembly of men, charged with a great & arduous trust, who were more pure in their motives, or more exclusively or anxiously [devoted to the object committed to them, than were the members of the Federal Convention of 1787, to the object of devising and proposing a constitutional system which would best supply the defects of that which it was to replace, and best secure the permanent liberty and happiness of their country.] [1]

---

[1] The passage enclosed in brackets is copied from the transcript. The original notes appear to have been lost since Gilpin's edition.

[1] Monday May 14th 1787 was the day fixed for the meeting of the deputies in Convention for revising the federal system of Government. On that day a small number only had assembled. Seven States were not convened till,

Friday 25 of May, when the following members [2] appeared to wit: see Note A.[3]

viz,[3] From *Massachussetts* Rufus King. *N. York* Robert Yates,[4] Alex: Hamilton. *N. Jersey,* David Brearly, William Churchill Houston,[4] William Patterson. *Pennsylvania,* Robert Morris, Thomas Fitzsimmons, James Wilson,[4] Govurneur Morris. *Delaware,* George Read, Richard Basset,[4] Jacob Broome. *Virginia,* George Washington, Edmund Randolph, John Blair, James Madison, George Mason, George Wythe, [4] James M:Clurg. *N. Carolina,* Alexander Martin, William Richardson Davie, Richard Dobbs Spaight,[4] Hugh Williamson. *S. Carolina,* John Rutlidge, Charles Cotesworth Pinckney, Charles Pinckney,[4] Pierce Butler. *Georgia,* William Few.

M: Robert Morris informed the members assembled that by the instruction & in behalf, of the deputation of Pen: he proposed George Washington Esq: late Commander in chief for president of the Convention.[5] M: Jn? Rutlidge seconded the motion; expressing his confidence that the choice would be unanimous, and observing that the presence of Gen! Washington forbade any observations on the occasion which might otherwise be proper.

General Washington was accordingly unanimously elected by

---

[1] The text of the present edition of Madison's Debates has been read against the manuscript of the transcript in the Library of Congress, and every difference between Madison's original manuscript and the transcript has been noted except typographical differences such as capitalization, spelling (including abbreviation of words and figures), punctuation and paragraphing.
The word "Debates" is used as a heading in the transcript.

[2] Madison is not uniform in the spelling of proper names, but the correct form in each instance is to be found in the credentials of the delegates, pp. lvi-lxxxii.

[3] The words "to wit: see Note A. viz," are omitted in the transcript.

[4] The word "and" is here inserted in the transcript.

[5] The paragraph in brackets beginning with the words "The nomination" and ending with the word "house" (page 18) is printed as a footnote in the transcript with reference mark after the word "Convention."

ballot, and conducted to the Chair by M: R. Morris and M: Rutlidge; from which in a very emphatic manner he thanked the Convention for the honor they had conferred on him, reminded them of the novelty of the scene of business in which he was to act, lamented his want of better qualifications, and claimed the indulgence of the House towards the involuntary errors which his inexperience might occasion.

[1] [The nomination came with particular grace from Penna. as Doc: Franklin alone could have been thought of as a competitor. The Doc: was himself to have made the nomination of General Washington, but the state of the weather and of his health confined him to his house.]

M: WILSON moved that a Secretary be appointed, and nominated M: Temple Franklin.

Col HAMILTON nominated Major Jackson.

On the ballot Maj: Jackson had 5 votes & M: Franklin 2 votes.

On reading the credentials of the deputies it was noticed that those from Delaware were prohibited from changing the article in the Confederation establishing an equality of votes among the States.

The appointment of a Committee, consisting of Mess: Wythe, Hamilton & C. Pinckney, on the motion of M: C. PINCKNEY,[2] to prepare standing rules & orders was the only remaining step taken on this day.

MONDAY MAY 28.[3]—

[4] From Mass: Nat: Gorham & Caleb Strong. From Connecticut Oliver Elseworth. From Delaware, Gunning Bedford. From Maryland James M:Henry. From Penn: B. Franklin, George Clymer, Th: Mifflin & Jared Ingersol took their seats.

M: WYTHE from the Committee for preparing rules made a report which employed the deliberations of this day.

M: KING objected to one of the rules in the Report authorising any member to call for the yeas & nays and have them entered on the minutes. He urged that as the acts of the Convention were not to bind the Constituents, it was unnecessary to exhibit this evidence of the votes; and improper as changes of opinion would be frequent

---

[1] See footnote [5] on page 17.
[2] The phrase "on the motion of Mr. C. Pinckney" is transposed in the transcript so that it reads: "The appointment of a Committee, on the motion of Mr. C. Pinckney, consisting," etc.
[3] The year "1787" is here inserted in the transcript.
[4] The words "In Convention" are here inserted in the transcript.

in the course of the business & would fill the minutes with contradictions.

Col. MASON seconded the objection; adding that such a record of the opinions of members would be an obstacle to a change of them on conviction; and in case of its being hereafter promulged must furnish handles to the adversaries of the Result of the Meeting.

The proposed rule was rejected nem. contradicente. The standing rules * [1] agreed to were as follow: [see the Journal & copy here the printed rules] [2]

[viz. [3] A House to do business shall consist of the Deputies of not less than seven States; and all questions shall be decided by the greater number of these which shall be fully represented: but a less number than seven may adjourn from day to day.

Immediately after the President shall have taken the chair, and the members their seats, the minutes of the preceding day shall be read by the Secretary.

Every member, rising to speak, shall address the President; and whilst he shall be speaking, none shall pass between them, or hold discourse with another, or read a book, pamphlet or paper, printed or manuscript—and of two members rising [4] at the same time, the President shall name him who shall be first heard.

A member shall not speak oftener than twice, without special leave, upon the same question; and not the second time, before every other, who had been silent, shall have been heard, if he choose to speak upon the subject.

A motion made and seconded, shall be repeated, and if written, as it shall be when any member shall so require, read aloud by the

---

* Previous to the arrival of a majority of the States, the rule by which they ought to vote in the Convention had been made a subject of conversation among the members present. It was pressed by Governeur Morris and favored by Robert Morris and others from Pennsylvania, that the large States should unite in firmly refusing to the small states an equal vote, as unreasonable, and as enabling the small States to negative every good system of Government, which must in the nature of things, be founded on a violation of that equality. The members from Virginia, conceiving that such an attempt might beget fatal altercations between the large & small States, and that it would be easier to prevail on the latter, in the course of the deliberations, to give up their equality for the sake of an effective Government, than on taking the field of discussion to disarm themselves of the right & thereby throw themselves on the mercy of the large States, discountenanced & stifled the project.

---

[1] Madison's footnote reference mark after the word " rules " is placed in the transcript after the word " him " (page 20) thus placing the footnote at the end of the rules instead of at the beginning.

[2] Madison's direction is omitted from the transcript and the word " Rules " is inserted.

[3] The word " viz." is omitted in the transcript.

[4] The words " to speak " are inserted in the transcript after " rising."

Secretary, before it shall be debated; and may be withdrawn at any time, before the vote upon it shall have been declared.

Orders of the day shall be read next after the minutes, and either discussed or postponed, before any other business shall be introduced.

When a debate shall arise upon a question, no motion, other than to amend the question, to commit it, or to postpone the debate shall be received.]

[A question which is complicated, shall, at the request of any member, be divided, and put separately on [1] the propositions, of which it is compounded.

The determination of a question, altho' fully debated, shall be postponed, if the deputies of any State desire it until the next day.

A writing which contains any matter brought on to be considered, shall be read once throughout for information, then by paragraphs to be debated, and again, with the amendments, if any, made on the second reading; and afterwards, the question shall be put on [1] the whole, amended, or approved in its original form, as the case shall be.

[2] Committees shall be appointed by ballot; and [2] the members who have the greatest number of ballots, altho' not a majority of the votes present, shall [3] be the Committee— When two or more members have an equal number of votes, the member standing first on the list in the order of taking down the ballots, shall be preferred.

A member may be called to order by any other member, as well as by the President; and may be allowed to explain his conduct or expressions supposed to be reprehensible.— And all questions of order shall be decided by the President without appeal or debate.

Upon a question to adjourn for the day, which may be made at any time, if it be seconded, the question shall be put without a debate.

When the House shall adjourn, every member shall stand in his place, until the President pass him.][4]

A letter from sundry persons of the State of Rho. Island addressed to the Honorable [5] The Chairman of the General Convention was presented to the Chair by M: Gov: Morris, and being read, was ordered to lie on the table for further consideration. [For the letter see Note in the Appendix][6]

---

[1] The word "upon" is substituted for "on" in the transcript.
[2] The word "that" is here inserted in the transcript.
[3] The word "shall" is omitted in the transcript.
[4] See footnote [1] on page 19.
[5] The words "the Honorable" are omitted in the transcript.
[6] The footnote in the transcript reads as follows: "For the letter, see Appendix No. blank." The text referred to is printed in the Appendix to Debates, III, p. 595.

M̲ᵣ BUTLER moved that the House provide ag̲ˢ̲ᵗ interruption of business by absence of members, and against licentious publications of their proceedings—to which was added by—M̲ᵣ SPAIGHT—a motion to provide that on the one hand the House might not be precluded by a vote upon any question, from revising the subject matter of it, when they see cause, nor, on the other hand, be led too hastily to rescind a decision, which was the result of mature discussion.— Whereupon it was ordered that these motions be referred to [1] the consideration of the Committee appointed to draw up the standing rules and that the Committee make report thereon.

Adj̲ᵈ till tomorrow [2] 10. OClock.

TUESDAY MAY 29. [3]

John Dickenson, and Elbridge Gerry, the former from Delaware, the latter from Mass̲ᵗˢ took their seats. The following rules were added, on the report of M̲ᵣ Wythe from the Committee [see the Journal]—[4]

Additional rules. [see preceding page] [4]

That no member be absent from the House, so as to interrupt the representation of the State, without leave.

That Committees do not sit whilst the House shall be or ought to be, sitting.

That no copy be taken of any entry on the journal during the sitting of the House without leave of the House.

That members only be permitted to inspect the journal.

That nothing spoken in the House be printed, or otherwise published or communicated without leave.

That a motion to reconsider a matter which had [5] been determined by a majority, may be made, with leave unanimously given, on the same day on which the vote passed; but otherwise not without one day's previous notice: in which last case, if the House agree to the reconsideration, some future day shall be assigned for the [6] purpose.

M̲ᵣ C. PINKNEY moved that a Committee be appointed to superintend the Minutes.

---

[1] The word "for" is substituted in the transcript for the word "to."
[2] The word "at" is here inserted in the transcript.
[3] The words "In Convention" are here inserted in the transcript.
[4] Madison's directions "[see the Journal]—" and "[see preceding page]" are omitted in the transcript as are also the words "Additional rules."
[5] The word "has" is substituted in the transcript for "had."
[6] The word "that" is substituted in the transcript for "the."

M: Gov: Morris objected to it. The entry of the proceedings of the Convention belonged to the Secretary as their impartial officer. A committee might have an interest & bias in moulding the entry, according to their opinions and wishes.

The motion was negatived, 5 noes, 4 ays.

M: Randolph then opened the main business.

[Here insert his speech [1] including his resolutions.] [2]

(M: R. Speech A. to be inserted Tuesday May 29) [2]

He expressed his regret, that it should fall to him, rather than those, who were of longer standing in life and political experience, to open the great subject of their mission. But, as the convention had originated from Virginia, and his colleagues supposed that some proposition was expected from them, they had imposed this task on him.

He then commented on the difficulty of the crisis, and the necessity of preventing the fulfilment of the prophecies of the American downfal.

He observed that in revising the fœderal system we ought to inquire 1.[3] into the properties, which such a government ought to possess, 2.[3] the defects of the confederation, 3.[3] the danger of our situation & 4.[3] the remedy.

1. The Character of such a government ought to secure 1.[3] against foreign invasion: 2.[3] against dissentions between members of the Union, or seditions in particular states: 3.[3] to procure to the several States, various blessings, of which an isolated situation was incapable: 4.[3,4] to be able to defend itself against incroachment: & 5.[3] to be paramount to the state constitutions.

2. In speaking of the defects of the confederation he professed a high respect for its authors, and considered them, as having done all that patriots could do, in the then infancy of the science, of constitutions, & of confederacies,—when the inefficiency of requisitions was unknown—no commercial discord had arisen among any states—no rebellion had appeared as in Mass:—foreign debts had not become urgent—the havoc of paper money had not been foreseen—treaties.had not been violated—and perhaps nothing better could be obtained from the jealousy of the states with regard to their sovereignty.

---

[1] The speech is in Randolph's handwriting.
[2] Madison's direction is omitted in the transcript.
[3] The figures indicated by the reference mark [3] are changed in the transcript to "first," "secondly," "thirdly," etc.
[4] The words " it should " are here inserted in the transcript.

He then proceeded to enumerate the defects: 1.[1] that the confederation produced no security against foreign invasion; congress not being permitted to prevent a war nor to support it by their own authority—Of this he cited many examples; most of which tended to shew, that they could not cause infractions of treaties or of the law of nations, to be punished: that particular states might by their conduct provoke war without controul; and that neither militia nor draughts being fit for defence on such occasions, inlistments only could be successful, and these could not be executed without money.

2.[1] that the fœderal government could not check the quarrels between states, nor a rebellion in any, not having constitutional power nor means to interpose according to the exigency:

3.[1] that there were many advantages, which the U. S. might acquire, which were not attainable under the confederation—such as a productive impost—counteraction of the commercial regulations of other nations—pushing of commerce ad libitum—&c &c.

4.[1] that the fœderal government could not defend itself against the [2] incroachments from the states.

5.[1] that it was not even paramount to the state constitutions, ratified, as it was in may of the states.

3. He next reviewed the danger of our situation,[3] appealed to the sense of the best friends of the U. S.—the prospect of anarchy from the laxity of government every where; and to other considerations.

4. He then proceeded to the remedy; the basis of which he said must be the republican principle

He proposed as conformable to his ideas the following resolutions, which he explained one by one [Here insert ye Resolutions annexed].[4]

RESOLUTIONS PROPOSED BY Mr RANDOLPH IN CONVENTION MAY 29, 1787.[4]

1. Resolved that the Articles of Confederation ought to be so corrected & enlarged as to accomplish the objects proposed by their institution; namely, '' common defence, security of liberty and general welfare.''

2. Res^d therefore that the rights of suffrage in the National Legislature ought to be proportioned to the Quotas of contribution, or to

---

[1] The figures indicated by the reference mark [1] are changed in the transcript to '' First,'' '' Secondly,'' etc.
[2] The word '' the '' is crossed out in the transcript.
[3] The word '' and '' is here inserted in the transcript.
[4] This direction and the heading are omitted in the transcript.

the number of free inhabitants, as the one or the other rule may seem best in different cases.

3. Res^d that the National Legislature ought to consist of two branches.

4. Res^d that the members of the first branch of the National Legislature ought to be elected by the people of the several States every   for the term of   ; to be of the age of   years at least, to receive liberal stipends by which they may be compensated for the devotion of their time to[1] public service; to be ineligible to any office established by a particular State, or under the authority of the United States, except those beculiarly belonging to the functions of the first branch, during the term of service, and for the space of   after its expiration; to be incapable of re-election for the space of   after the expiration of their term of service, and to be subject to recall.

5. Resol^d that the members of the second branch of the National Legislature ought to be elected by those of the first, out of a proper number of persons nominated by the individual Legislatures, to be of the age of   years at least; to hold their offices for a term sufficient to ensure their independency;[2] to receive liberal stipends, by which they may be compensated for the devotion of their time to[3] public service; and to be ineligible to any office established by a particular State, or under the authority of the United States, except those peculiarly belonging to the functions of the second branch, during the term of service, and for the space of   after the expiration thereof.

6. Resolved that each branch ought to possess the right of originating Acts; that the National Legislature ought to be impowered to enjoy the Legislative Rights vested in Congress by the Confederation & moreover to legislate in all cases to which the separate States are incompetent, or in which the harmony of the United States may be interrupted by the exercise of individual Legislation; to negative all laws passed by the several States, contravening in the opinion of the National Legislature the articles of Union;[4] and to call forth the force of the Union agst any member of the Union failing to fulfill its duty under the articles thereof.

7. Res^d that a National Executive be instituted; to be chosen by

---

[1] The word " the " is here inserted in the transcript.
[2] The word " independency " is changed to " independence " in the transcript.
[3] The word " the " is here inserted in the transcript.
[4] The phrase " or any treaty subsisting under the authority of the Union " is here added in the transcript.

the National Legislature for the term of   years,[1] to receive punctually at stated times, a fixed compensation for the services rendered, in which no increase or [2] diminution shall be made so as to affect the Magistracy, existing at the time of increase or diminution, and to be ineligible a second time; and that besides a general authority to execute the National laws, it ought to enjoy the Executive rights vested in Congress by the Confederation.

8. Res? that the Executive and a convenient number of the National Judiciary, ought to compose a Council of revision with authority to examine every act of the National Legislature before it shall operate, & every act of a particular Legislature before a Negative thereon shall be final; and that the dissent of the said Council shall amount to a rejection, unless the Act of the National Legislature be again passed, or that of a particular Legislature be again negatived by   of the members of each branch.

9. Res? that a National Judiciary be established to consist of one or more supreme tribunals, and of inferior tribunals to be chosen by the National Legislature, to hold their offices during good behaviour; and to receive punctually at stated times fixed compensation for their services, in which no increase or diminution shall be made so as to affect the persons actually in office at the time of such increase or diminution. that the jurisdiction of the inferior tribunals shall be to hear & determine in the first instance, and of the supreme tribunal to hear and determine in the dernier resort, all piracies & felonies on the high seas, captures from an enemy; cases in which foreigners or citizens of other States applying to such jurisdictions may be interested, or which respect the collection of the National revenue; impeachments of any National officers, and questions which may involve the national peace and harmony.

10. Resolv? that provision ought to be made for the admission of States lawfully arising within the limits of the United States, whether from a voluntary junction of Government & Territory or otherwise, with the consent of a number of voices in the National legislature less than the whole.

11. Res? that a Republican Government & the territory of each State, except in the instance of a voluntary junction of Government & territory, ought to be guarantied by the United States to each State

12. Res? that provision ought to be made for the continuance of Congress and their authorities and privileges, until a given day after

---

[1] The word "years" is omitted in the transcript.
[2] The word "or" is changed to "nor" in the transcript.

the reform of the articles of Union shall be adopted, and for the completion of all their engagements.

13. Res.ᵈ that provision ought to be made for the amendment of the Articles of Union whensoever it shall seem necessary, and that the assent of the National Legislature ought not to be required thereto.

14. Res.ᵈ that the Legislative Executive & Judiciary powers within the several States ought to be bound by oath to support the articles of Union

15. Res.ᵈ that the amendments which shall be offered to the Confederation, by the Convention ought at a proper time, or times, after the approbation of Congress to be submitted to an assembly or assemblies of Representatives, recommended by the several Legislatures to be expressly chosen by the people, to consider & decide thereon.[1]

He concluded with an exhortation, not to suffer the present opportunity of establishing general peace, harmony, happiness and liberty in the U. S. to pass away unimproved.*

It was then Resolved—That the House will tomorrow resolve itself into a Committee of the Whole House to consider of the state of the American Union.—and that the propositions moved by M.ʳ Randolph be referred to the said Committee.

M.ʳ CHARLES PINKNEY laid before the house the draught of a federal Government which he had prepared, to be agreed upon between the free and independent States of America.[3]—M.ʳ P. plan[4] ordered

* This Abstract of the speech was furnished to J. M. by M.ʳ Randolph and is in his handwriting.   ² As a report of it from him had been relied on, it was omitted by J. M.

---

[1] The fifteen resolutions, constituting the "Virginia Plan," are in Madison's handwriting.

² This sentence is omitted in the transcript.

³ Robert Yates, a delegate from New York, gives the following account of Pinckney's motion: "Mr. C. Pinkney, a member from South-Carolina, then added, that he had reduced his ideas of a new government to a system, which he read, and confessed that it was grounded on the same principle as of the above resolutions." (*Secret Proceedings of the Federal Convention* (1821), p. 97.)

⁴ The words, "Mr. P. plan," are omitted in the transcript, and what purports to be the plan itself is here inserted.

Madison himself did not take a copy of the draft nor did Pinckney furnish him one, as he did a copy of his speech which he later delivered in the Convention and which is printed as a part of the debates (session of Monday, June 25), *infra*, pp. 155-161, and Madison's note, p. 161. Many years later, in 1818, when John Quincy Adams, then Secretary of State, was preparing the Journal of the Convention for publication, he wrote to Pinckney, requesting a copy of his plan, and, in compliance with this request, Pinckney sent him what purported to be the draft, but which appears to have been a copy of the report of the Committee of Detail of August 6, 1787, with certain alterations and additions. The alleged draft and Pinckney's letter transmitting it were written upon paper bearing the water-mark, "Russell & Co. 1797."

The Pinckney draft was not debated; it was neither used in the Committee of the Whole nor in the Convention. It was however referred to the Committee that the same be referred to the Committee of the Whole appointed to consider the state of the American Union.

adjourned.

WEDNESDAY MAY 30.

Roger Sherman (from Connecticut) took his seat.

The House went into Committee of the Whole on the State of the Union. M: Gorham was elected to the Chair by Ballot.

The propositions of M: RANDOLPH which had been referred to the Committee being taken up. He moved on the suggestion of M: G. Morris, that the first of his propositions to wit " Resolved that the articles of Confederation ought to be so corrected & enlarged, as to accomplish the objects proposed by their institution; namely, common defence, security of liberty & general welfare: [1]—should be postponed, in order to consider the 3 following:

1. that a Union of the States merely federal will not accomplish the objects proposed by the articles of Confederation, namely common defence, security of liberty, & gen! welfare.

2. that no treaty or treaties among the whole or part of the States, as individual Sovereignties, would be sufficient.

3. that a *national* Government ought to be established consisting of a *supreme* Legislative, Executive & Judiciary.

The motion for postponing was seconded by M: Gov: MORRIS and unanimously agreed to.

Some verbal criticisms were raised ag:t the first proposition, and it was agreed on motion of M: BUTLER seconded by M: RANDOLPH, to pass on to the third, which underwent a discussion, less however on its general merits than on the force and extent of the particular terms *national* & *supreme*.

M: CHARLES PINKNEY wished to know of M: Randolph whether he meant to abolish the State Govern:t altogether. M: R. replied that

---

of Detail, which appears to have made some use of it, as extracts from it have been identified by J. Franklin Jameson and an outline of it discovered by Andrew C. McLaughlin, among the papers and in the handwriting of James Wilson, a delegate from Pennsylvania, deposited with the Pennsylvania Historical Society.

For the main features of this plan as reconstructed by Professor McLaughlin according to Professor Jameson's and his own discoveries, see Appendix to Debates, IV, No. 1, 596-598.

For the text of the Pinckney plan submitted to John Quincy Adams and printed by him in the Journal of the Convention, for Madison's observations upon it and for further details concerning it, see Appendix to Debates, IV, Nos. 3 and 4, pp. 600-607.

[1] The resolution is italicized in the transcript.

he meant by these general propositions merely to introduce the particular ones which explained the outlines of the system he had in view.

M: BUTLER said he had not made up his mind on the subject, and was open to the light which discussion might throw on it. After some general observations he concluded with saying that he had opposed the grant of powers to Cong? heretofore, because the whole power was vested in one body. The proposed distribution of the powers into [1] different bodies changed the case, and would induce him to go great lengths.

Gen! PINKNEY expressed a doubt whether the act of Cong? recommending the Convention, or the Commissions of the Deputies to it, could [2] authorise a discussion of a System founded on different principles from the federal Constitution.

M: GERRY seemed to entertain the same doubt.

M: Gov: MORRIS explained the distinction between a *federal* and *national, supreme*, Gov:; the former being a mere compact resting on the good faith of the parties; the latter having a compleat and *compulsive* operation. He contended that in all Communities there must be one supreme power, and one only.

M: MASON observed that the present confederation was not only [3] deficient in not providing for coercion & punishment ag:t delinquent States; but argued very cogently that punishment could not in the nature of things be executed on the States collectively, and therefore that such a Gov: was necessary as could directly operate on individuals, and would punish those only whose guilt required it.

M: SHERMAN who took his seat today,[4] admitted that the Confederation had not given sufficient power to Cong? and that additional powers were necessary; particularly that of raising money which he said would involve many other powers. He admitted also that the General & particular jurisdictions ought in no case to be concurrent. He seemed however not [5] be disposed to make too great inroads on the existing system; intimating as one reason, that it would be wrong to lose every amendment, by inserting such as would not be agreed to by the States.

It was moved by M: READ [6] 2:d:d by M: Ch: COTESWORTH PINKNEY,

---

[1] The word "with" is substituted in the transcript for "into."
[2] The word "would" is substituted in the transcript for "could."
[3] The words "not only" are transposed in the transcript, which reads as follows: "Mr. Mason observed, not only that the present Confederation was deficient." . . .
[4] The phrase "who took his seat today" is omitted in the transcript.
[5] The word "to" is here inserted in the transcript.
[6] The word "and" is here inserted in the transcript.

to postpone the 3ᵈ proposition last offered by Mʳ Randolph viz that a national Government ought to be established consisting of a supreme Legislative Executive and Judiciary," in order to take up the following—viz. "Resolved that in order to carry into execution the Design of the States in forming this Convention, and to accomplish the objects proposed by the Confederation a more effective Government consisting of a Legislative, Executive and Judiciary ought to be established." The motion to postpone for this purpose was lost:

Yeas¹ Massachussetts, Connecticut, Delaware, S. Carolina—¹ 4

Nays.² N. Y. Pennsylvania, Virginia, North Carolina—² 4.

On the question as moved by Mʳ Butler, on the third proposition it was resolved in Committee of the whole that a national governᵗ ought to be established consisting of a supreme Legislative Executive & Judiciary." Mass.ᵗˢ being ay—Connect.—no. N. York divided [Col. Hamilton ay Mʳ Yates no] Penᵃ ay. Delaware ay. Virgᵃ ay. N. C. ay. S. C. ay.³

[Note E]⁴

Resol: 2. of Mʳ R's proposition towit—see May 29.⁴

The following Resolution, being the 2ᵈ of those proposed by Mʳ Randolph was taken up, viz—"that the rights of suffrage in the National Legislature ought to be proportioned to the quotas of contribution, or to the number of free inhabitants, as the one or the other rule may seem best in different cases."⁵

Mʳ MADISON observing that the words "*or to the number of free inhabitants,*" might occasion debates which would divert the Committee from the general question whether the principle of representation should be changed, moved that they might be struck out.

Mʳ KING observed that the quotas of contribution which would alone remain as the measure of representation, would not answer, because waving every other view of the matter, the revenue might hereafter be so collected by the general Govᵗ that the sums respectively drawn from the States would not appear; and would besides be continually varying.

Mʳ MADISON admitted the propriety of the observation, and that some better rule ought to be found.

---

¹ The word "Yeas" is omitted in the transcript and the word "aye" inserted before the figure "4."

² The word "Nays" is omitted in the transcript and the word "no" inserted before the figure "4."

³ In the transcript the vote reads: "Massachusetts, Pennsylvania, Delaware, Virginia, North Carolina, South Carolina, aye—6; Connecticut, no—1; New York, divided (Colonel Hamilton, aye, Mr. Yates, no)."

⁴ Madison's direction is omitted in the transcript.

⁵ The resolution is italicized in the transcript.

Col. HAMILTON moved to alter the resolution so as to read " that the rights of suffrage in the national Legislature ought to be proportioned to the number of free inhabitants. M: SPAIGHT 2^{ded} the motion.

It was then moved that the Resolution be postponed, which was agreed to.

M: RANDOLPH and M: MADISON then moved the following resolution—" that the rights of suffrage in the national Legislature ought to be proportioned."

It was moved and 2^{ded} to amend it by adding " and not according to the present system "—which was agreed to.

It was then moved and 2^{ded} to alter the resolution so as to read " that the rights of suffrage in the national Legislature ought not to be according to the present system."

It was then moved & 2^{ded} to postpone the Resolution moved by M: Randolph & M: Madison, which being agreed to:

M: MADISON, moved, in order to get over the difficulties, the following resolution—" that the equality of suffrage established by the articles of Confederation ought not to prevail in the national Legislature, and that an equitable ratio of representation ought to be substituted." This was 2^{ded} by M: Gov: MORRIS, and being generally relished, would have been agreed to; when,

M: REED moved that the whole clause relating to the point of Representation be postponed; reminding the Com: that the deputies from Delaware were restrained by their commission from assenting to any change of the rule of suffrage, and in case such a change should be fixed on, it might become their duty to retire from the Convention.

M: Gov: MORRIS observed that the valuable assistance of those members could not be lost without real concern, and that so early a proof of discord in the Convention as a secession of a State, would add much to the regret; that the change proposed was however so fundamental an article in a national Gov: that it could not be dispensed with.

M: MADISON observed that whatever reason might have existed for the equality of suffrage when the Union was a federal one among sovereign States, it must cease when a national Goverm: should be put into the place. In the former case, the acts of Cong: depended so much for their efficacy on the cooperation of the States, that these had a weight both within & without Congress, nearly in proportion to their extent and importance. In the latter case, as the acts of the Gen: Gov: would take effect without the intervention of the State legislatures, a vote from a small State w.ᵈ have the same efficacy & importance as a vote from a large one, and there was the same reason for different numbers of representatives from different States, as from Counties of different extents within particular States. He suggested as an expedient for at once taking the sense of the members on this point and saving the Delaware deputies from embarrassment, that the question should be taken in Committee, and the clause on report to the House be postponed without a question there. This however did not appear to satisfy M.ʳ Read.

By several it was observed that no just construction of the Act of Delaware, could require or justify a secession of her deputies, even if the resolution were to be carried thro' the House as well as the Committee. It was finally agreed however that the clause should be postponed: it being understood that in the event the proposed change of representation would certainly be agreed to, no objection or difficulty being started from any other quarter than from Delaware.

The motion of M.ʳ Read to postpone being agreed to,

The Committee then rose. The Chairman reported progress, and the House having resolved to resume the subject in Committee to-morrow,

Adjourned to 10 OClock.

THURSDAY MAY 31 [1]

William Pierce from Georgia took his seat.

In Committee of the whole on M.ʳ Randolph's propositions.

The 3.ᵈ Resolution "that the national Legislature ought to consist of two branches" was agreed to without debate or dissent, except that of Pennsylvania, given probably from complaisance to Doc.ʳ Franklin who was understood to be partial to a single House of Legislation.

Resol: 4.[2] first clause "that the members of the first branch of the National Legislature ought to be elected by the people of the several States" being taken up,

M.ʳ SHERMAN opposed the election by the people, insisting that it ought to be by the State Legislatures. The people he said, im-

---

[1] The year "1787" is here inserted in the transcript.
[2] The transcript changes "Resol: 4." to "The fourth Resolution."

mediately should have as little to do as may be about the Government. They want information and are constantly liable to be misled.

M� GERRY. The evils we experience flow from the excess of democracy. The people do not want virtue, but are the dupes of pretended patriots. In Mass⁺ˢ it had been fully confirmed by experience that they are daily misled into the most baneful measures and opinions by the false reports circulated by designing men, and which no one on the spot can refute. One principal evil arises from the want of due provision for those employed in the administration of Governm⁺ It would seem to be a maxim of democracy to starve the public servants. He mentioned the popular clamour in Mass⁺ᵗ for the reduction of salaries and the attack made on that of the Gov⁺ though secured by the spirit of the Constitution itself. He had he said been too republican heretofore: he was still however republican, but had been taught by experience the danger of the levilling spirit.

M⁺ MASON, argued strongly for an election of the larger branch by the people. It was to be the grand depository of the democratic principle of the Gov⁺ It was, so to speak, to be our House of Commons—It ought to know & sympathise with every part of the community; and ought therefore to be taken not only from different parts of the whole republic, but also from different districts of the larger members of it, which had in several instances particularly in Virg⁺, different interests and views arising from difference of produce, of habits &c &c. He admitted that we had been too democratic but was afraid we s⁴ incautiously run into the opposite extreme. We ought to attend to the rights of every class of the people. He had often wondered at the indifference of the superior classes of society to this dictate of humanity & policy; considering that however affluent their circumstances, or elevated their situations, might be, the course of a few years, not only might but certainly would, distribute their posterity throughout the lowest classes of Society. Every selfish motive therefore, every family attachment, ought to recommend such a system of policy as would provide no less carefully for the rights and happiness of the lowest than of the highest orders of Citizens.

M⁺ WILSON contended strenuously for drawing the most numerous branch of the Legislature immediately from the people. He was for raising the federal pyramid to a considerable altitude, and for that reason wished to give it as broad a basis as possible. No government could long subsist without the confidence of the people. In a republican Government this confidence was peculiarly essential.

He also thought it wrong to increase the weight of the State Legislatures by making them the electors of the national Legislature. All interference between the general and local Governm.ᵗˢ should be obviated as much as possible. On examination it would be found that the opposition of States to federal measures had proceded much more from the officers of the States, than from the people at large.

M.ʳ MADISON considered the popular election of one branch of the National Legislature as essential to every plan of free Government. He observed that in some of the States one branch of the Legislature was composed of men already removed from the people by an intervening body of electors. That if the first branch of the general legislature should be elected by the State Legislatures, the second branch elected by the first—the Executive by the second together with the first; and other appointments again made for subordinate purposes by the Executive, the people would be lost sight of altogether; and the necessary sympathy between them and their rulers and officers, too little felt. He was an advocate for the policy of refining the popular appointments by successive filtrations, but thought it might be pushed too far. He wished the expedient to be resorted to only in the appointment of the second branch of the Legislature, and in the Executive & judiciary branches of the Government. He thought too that the great fabric to be raised would be more stable and durable, if it should rest on the solid foundation of the people themselves, than if it should stand merely on the pillars of the Legislatures.

M.ʳ GERRY did not like the election by the people. The maxims taken from the British constitution were often fallacious when applied to our situation which was extremely different. Experience he said had shewn that the State legislatures drawn immediately from the people did not always possess their confidence. He had no objection however to an election by the people if it were so qualified that men of honor & character might not be unwilling to be joined in the appointments. He seemed to think the people might nominate a certain number out of which the State legislatures should be bound to choose.

M.ʳ BUTLER thought an election by the people an impracticable mode.

On the question for an election of the first branch of the national Legislature by the people,

Mass.ᵗˢ ay. Connect. div.ᵈ N. York ay. N. Jersey no. Pen. ay. Delaw. div.ᵈ V. ay. N. C. ay. S. C. no. Georg. ay.

The remaining Clauses of Resolution 4ᵗʰ ¹ relating to the qualifications of members of the National Legislature,¹ being posp.ᵈ nem. con., as entering too much into detail for general propositions;

The Committee proceeded to Resolution 5.² " that the second, [or senatorial] branch of the National Legislature ought to be chosen by the first branch out of persons nominated by the State Legislatures."

Mʳ. Spaight contended that the 2ᵈ branch ought to be chosen by the State Legislatures and moved an amendment to that effect.

Mʳ. Butler apprehended that the taking so many powers out of the hands of the States as was proposed, tended to destroy all that balance and security of interests among the States which it was necessary to preserve; and called on Mʳ. Randolph the mover of the propositions, to explain the extent of his ideas, and particularly the number of members he meant to assign to this second branch.

Mʳ. Rand. observed that he had at the time of offering his propositions stated his ideas as far as the nature of general propositions required; that details made no part of the plan, and could not perhaps with propriety have been introduced. If he was to give an opinion as to the number of the second branch, he should say that it ought to be much smaller than that of the first; so small as to be exempt from the passionate proceedings to which numerous assemblies are liable. He observed that the general object was to provide a cure for the evils under which the U. S. laboured; that in tracing these evils to their origin every man had found it in the turbulence and follies of democracy: that some check therefore was to be sought for ag.ˢᵗ this tendency of our Governments: and that a good Senate seemed most likely to answer the purpose.

Mʳ. King reminded the Committee that the choice of the second branch as proposed (by Mʳ. Spaight) viz. by the State Legislatures would be impracticable, unless it was to be very numerous, or *the idea of proportion* among the States was to be disregarded. According to this *idea*, there must be 80 or 100 members to entitle Delaware to the choice of one of them.—Mʳ. Spaight withdrew his motion.

Mʳ. Wilson opposed both a nomination by the State Legislatures, and an election by the first branch of the national Legislature, because the second branch of the latter, ought to be independent of both. He thought both branches of the National Legislature ought to

¹ In the transcript the words "Resolution 4ᵗʰ" are changed to "the fourth Resolution" and the phrase "the qualifications of members of the National Legislature" is italicized.
² In the transcript the words "Resolution 5," are changed to "the fifth Resolution" and the words of the resolution are italicized.

be chosen by the people, but was not prepared with a specific proposition. He suggested the mode of chusing the Senate of N. York to wit of uniting several election districts, for one branch, in chusing members for the other branch, as a good model.

M� MADISON observed that such a mode would destroy the influence of the smaller States associated with larger ones in the same district; as the latter would chuse from within themselves, altho' better men might be found in the former. The election of Senators in Virgˢ where large & small counties were often formed into one district for the purpose, had illustrated this consequence Local partiality, would often prefer a resident within the County or State, to a candidate of superior merit residing out of it. Less merit also in a resident would be more known throughout his own State.

Mʳ SHERMAN ̔favored an election of one member by each of the State Legislatures.

Mʳ PINKNEY moved to strike out the " nomination by the State Legislatures." On this question.

* Massᵗˢ. no. Conᵗ no. N. Y. no. N. J. no. Penᵃ no. Del divᵈ Vᵃ no. N. C. no. S. C. no. Georg no.[1]

On the whole question for electing by the first branch out of nominations by the State Legislatures, Mass. ay. Conᵗ no. N. Y. no. N. Jersey. no. Penᵃ no. Del. no. Virgᵃ ay. N. C. no. S. C. ay. Gᵃ no.[2]

So the clause was disagreed to & a chasm left in this part of the plan.

[3] The sixth Resolution stating the cases in which the national Legislature ought to legislate was next taken into discussion: On the question whether each branch shᵈ originate laws, there was an unanimous affirmative without debate. On the question for transferring all the Legislative powers of the existing Congˢ to this Assembly, there was also a silent affirmative nem. con.

* This question [1] omitted in the printed Journal, & the votes applied to the succeeding one, instead of the votes as here stated [this note to be in the bottom margin] [1]

---

[1] In the transcript the vote reads: " * Massachusetts, Connecticut, New York, New Jersey, Pennsylvania, Virginia, North Carolina, South Carolina, Georgia, no—9; Delaware divided"; and Madison's direction concerning the footnote is omitted. The word " is " is inserted after the word " question."·

[2] In the transcript the vote reads: " Massachusetts, Virginia, South Carolina, aye—3; Connecticut New York, New Jersey, Pennsylvania, Delaware, North Carolina, Georgia, no—7."

[3] In this paragraph the transcript italicizes the following phrases: " the cases in which the national Legislature ought to legislate," " whether each branch shᵈ originate laws," " for transferring all the Legislative powers of the existing Congˢ to this Assembly "; and the phrase " a silent affirmative nem. con." is changed to " an unanimous affirmative, without debate."

On the proposition for giving "Legislative power in all cases to which the State Legislatures were individually incompetent."

M. PINKNEY & M. RUTLEDGE objected to the vagueness of the term *incompetent*, and said they could not well decide how to vote until they should see an exact enumeration of the powers comprehended by this definition.

M. BUTLER repeated his fears that we were running into an extreme in taking away the powers of the States, and called on M. Randolp for the extent of his meaning.

M. RANDOLPH disclaimed any intention to give indefinite powers to the national Legislature, declaring that he was entirely opposed to such an inroad on the State jurisdictions, and that he did not think any considerations whatever could ever change his determination. His opinion was fixed on this point.

M. MADISON said that he had brought with him into the Convention a strong bias in favor of an enemeration and definition of the powers necessary to be exercised by the national Legislature; but had also brought doubts concerning its practicability. His wishes remained unaltered; but his doubts had become stronger. What his opinion might ultimately be he could not yet tell. But he should shrink from nothing which should be found essential to such a form of Gov as would provide for the safety, liberty and happiness of the community. This being the end of all our deliberations, all the necessary means for attaining it must, however reluctantly, be submitted to.

On the question for giving powers, in cases to which the States are not competent, Mass ay. Con div [Sharman no Elseworth ay] N. Y. ay. N. J. ay. P. ay. Del. ay. V. ay. N. C. ay. S. Carolina ay. Georg. ay.[1]

The other clauses [2] giving powers necessary to preserve harmony among the States to negative all State laws contravening in the opinion of the Nat. Leg. the articles of union, down to the last clause, (the words "or any treaties subsisting under the authority of the Union," being added after the words " contravening &c. the articles of the Union," on motion of D. FRANKLIN) were agreed to with debate or dissent.

---

[1] In the transcript the vote reads: "Massachusetts, New York, New Jersey, Pennsylvania, Delaware, Virginia, North Carolina, South Carolina, Georgia, aye—9; Connecticut divided (Sherman, no, Ellsworth, aye)."

[2] The phrase, "giving powers necessary to preserve harmony among the States to negative all State laws contravening in the opinion of the Nat. Leg. the articles of union" is italicized in the transcript.

The last clause of Resolution 6.[1] authorizing an exertion of the force of the whole ag.st a delinquent State came next into consideration.

M. MADISON, observed that the more he reflected on the use of force, the more he doubted the practicability, the justice and the efficacy of it when applied to people collectively and not individually.— A union of the States containing such an ingredient seemed to provide for its own destruction. The use of force ag.st a State, would look more like a declaration of war, than an infliction of punishment, and would probably be considered by the party attacked as a dissolution of all previous compacts by which it might be bound. He hoped that such a system would be framed as might render this recourse[2] unnecessary, and moved that the clause be postponed. This motion was agreed to nem. con.

The Committee then rose & the House
Adjourned

FRIDAY JUNE 1.st 1787.

William Houston from Georgia took his seat.

The Committee of the whole proceeded to Resolution 7.[3] " that a national Executive be instituted, to be chosen by the national Legislature—for the term of   years &c to be ineligible thereafter, to possess the executive powers of Congress &c."

M. PINKNEY was for a vigorous Executive but was afraid the Executive powers of the existing Congress might extend to peace & war &c., which would render the Executive a monarchy, of the worst kind, to wit an elective one.

M. WILSON moved that the Executive consist of a single person. M. C PINKNEY seconded the motion, so as to read " that a National Ex. to consist of a single person, be instituted.

A considerable pause ensuing and the Chairman asking if he should put the question, Doc. FRANKLIN observed that it was a point of great importance and wished that the gentlemen would deliver their sentiments on it before the question was put.

M. RUTLIDGE animadverted on the shyness of gentlemen on this and other subjects. He said it looked as if they supposed themselves

---

[1] The words " the sixth Resolution " are substituted in the transcript for " Resolution 6 " and the phrase " authorizing an exertion of the force of the whole ag.st a delinquent State " is italicized.

[2] The word " resource " is substituted in the transcript for " recourse."

[3] The words " the seventh Resolution " are substituted in the transcript for " Resolution 7 " and the words of the resolution are italicized.

precluded by having frankly disclosed their opinions from afterwards changing them, which he did not take to be at all the case. He said he was for vesting the Executive power in a single person, tho' he was not for giving him the power of war and peace. A single man would feel the greatest responsibility and administer the public affairs best.

Mʳ SHERMAN said he considered the Executive magistracy as nothing more than an institution for carrying the will of the Legislature into effect, that the person or persons ought to be appointed by and accountable to the Legislature only, which was the depositary of the supreme will of the Society. As they were the best judges of the business which ought to be done by the Executive department, and consequently of the number necessary from time to time for doing it, he wished the number might not be fixed, but that the legislature should be at liberty to appoint one or more as experience might dictate.

Mʳ WILSON preferred a single magistrate, as giving most energy dispatch and responsibility to the office. He did not consider the Prerogatives of the British Monarch as a proper guide in defining the Executive powers. Some of these prerogatives were of a Legislative nature. Among others that of war & peace &c. The only powers he conceived [1] strictly Executive were those of executing the laws, and appointing officers, not appertaining to and appointed by the Legislature.

Mʳ GERRY favored the policy of annexing a Council to the Executive in order to give weight & inspire confidence.

Mʳ RANDOLPH strenuously opposed a unity in the Executive magistracy. He regarded it as the fœtus of monarchy. We had he said no motive to be governed by the British Governmᵗ as our prototype. He did not mean however to throw censure on that Excellent fabric. If we were in a situation to copy it he did not know that he should be opposed to it; but the fixt genius of the people of America required a different form of Government. He could not see why the great requisites for the Executive department, vigor, despatch & responsibility could not be found in three men, as well as in one man. The Executive ought to be independent. It ought therefore in order to support its independence to consist of more than one.

Mʳ WILSON said that unity in the Executive instead of being the fetus of monarchy would be the best safeguard against tyranny. He repeated that he was not governed by the British Model which was

---

[1] The transcript here substitutes the word "considered" for "conceived."

inapplicable to the situation of this Country; the extent of which was so great, and the manners so republican, that nothing but a great confederated Republic would do for it.

M! Wilson's motion for a single magistrate was postponed by common consent, the Committee seeming unprepared for any decision on it; and the first part of the clause agreed to, viz—"that a National Executive be instituted."

M! MADISON thought it would be proper, before a choice sh⁴ be made between a unity and a plurality in the Executive, to fix the extent of the Executive authority; that as certain powers were in their nature Executive, and must be given to that departm⁴ whether administered by one or more persons, a definition of their extent would assist the judgment in determining how far they might be safely entrusted to a single officer. He accordingly moved that so much of the clause before the Committee as related to the powers of the Executive sh⁴ be struck out & that after the words "that a national Executive ought to be instituted" there be inserted the words following viz. "with power to carry into effect the national laws, to appoint to offices in cases not otherwise provided for, and to execute such other powers "not Legislative nor Judiciary in their nature," as may from time to time be delegated by the national Legislature." The words "not legislative nor judiciary in their nature" were added to the proposed amendment in consequence of a suggestion by Gen! Pinkney that improper powers might otherwise be delegated.

M! WILSON seconded this motion—

M! PINKNEY moved to amend the amendment by striking out the last member of it; viz: "and to execute such other powers not Legislative nor Judiciary in their nature as may from time to time be delegated." He said they were unnecessary, the object of them being included in the "power [1] to carry into effect the national laws."

M! RANDOLPH seconded the motion.

M! MADISON did not know that the words were absolutely necessary, or even the preceding words—"to appoint to offices &c. the whole being perhaps included in the first member of the proposition. He did not however see any inconveniency [2] in retaining them, and cases might happen in which they might serve to prevent doubts and misconstructions.

In consequence of the motion of M! Pinkney, the question on M! Madison's motion was divided; and the words objected to by

---

[1] The transcript uses the word "power" in the plural.
[2] The transcript changes the word "inconveniency" to "inconvenience."

M⁺ Pinkney struck out; by the votes of Connecticut, N. Y. N. J. Pen⁺ Del. N. C. & Geo.[1] ag⁺ Mass. Virg⁺ & S. Carolina [1] the preceding part of the motion being first agreed to; Connecticut divided, all the other States in the affirmative.

The next clause in Resolution 7,[2] relating to the mode of appointing, & the duration of, the Executive being under consideration,

M⁺ WILSON said he was almost unwilling to declare the mode which he wished to take place, being apprehensive that it might appear chimerical. He would say however at least that in theory he was for an election by the people. Experience, particularly in N. York & Mass⁺⁺, shewed that an election of the first magistrate by the people at large, was both a convenient & successful mode. The objects of choice in such cases must be persons whose merits have general notoriety.

M⁺ SHERMAN was for the appointment by the Legislature, and for making him absolutely dependent on that body, as it was the will of that which was to be executed. An independence of the Executive on the supreme Legislature, was in his opinion the very essence of tyranny if there was any such thing.

M⁺ WILSON moves that the blank for the term of duration should be filled with three years, observing at the same time that he preferred this short period, on the supposition that a re-eligibilty would be provided for.

M⁺ PINKNEY moves for seven years.

M⁺ SHERMAN was for three years, and ag⁺ the doctrine of rotation as throwing out of office the men best qualifyed to execute its duties.

M⁺ MASON was for seven years at least, and for prohibiting a re-eligibility as the best expedient both for preventing the effect of a false complaisance on the side of the Legislature towards unfit characters; and a temptation on the side of the Executive to intrigue with the Legislature for a re-appointment.

M⁺ BEDFORD was strongly opposed to so long a term as seven years. He begged the committee to consider what the situation of the Country would be, in case the first magistrate should be saddled on it for such a period and it should be found on trial that he did not possess the qualifications ascribed to him, or should lose them after his appointment. An impeachment he said would be no cure for this evil, as an impeachment would reach misfeasance only, not

---

[1] In the transcript the figures " 7 " and " 3 " are inserted after the States Georgia and South Carolina, respectively.
[2] The words " the seventh Resolution " are substituted in the transcript for " Resolution 7."

incapacity. He was for a triennial election, and for an ineligibility after a period of nine years.

On the question for seven years,[1]

Mass.^{ts} divid.^d Con.^t no. N. Y. ay. N. J. ay. Pen.^a ay. Del. ay. Virg.^a ay. N. C. no. S. C. no. Geor. no.[2] There being 5 ays, 4 noes, 1 div.^d, a question was asked whether a majority had voted in the affirmative? The President decided that it was an affirmative vote.

The *mode of appointing* the Executive was the next question.

Mr WILSON renewed his declarations in favor of an appointment by the people. He wished to derive not only both branches of the Legislature from the people, without the intervention of the State Legislatures but the Executive also; in order to make them as independent as possible of each other, as well as of the States;

Col. MASON favors the idea, but thinks it impracticable. He wishes however that Mr Wilson might have time to digest it into his own form.—the clause " to be chosen by the National Legislature "— was accordingly postponed.—

Mr RUTLIDGE suggests an election of the Executive by the second branch only of the national Legislature.

The Committee then rose and the House
Adjourned.

SATURDAY JUNE 2^D [3] IN COMMITTEE OF WHOLE.

* [Insert the words noted here] [4]   * William Saml Johnson from Connecticut, Daniel of St. Thomas Jennifer, from Mary.^d & John Lansing J.^r from N. York, took their seats.

It was mov.^d & 2^{ded} to postpone ye Resol: of Mr Randolph respecting the Executive, in order to take up the 2.^d branch of the Legislature; which being negatived by Mas: Con: Del: Virg: N. C. S. C. Geo:[5] ag.st N. Y. Pen.^a Mary.^d [5] The mode of appoint.^g ye Executive was resumed.

Mr WILSON made the following motion, to be substituted for the mode proposed by Mr Randolph's resolution, " that the Executive

---

[1] The transcript italicizes the phrase "for seven years."
[2] In the transcript the vote reads: "New York, New Jersey, Pennsylvania, Delaware, Virginia, aye—5; Connecticut, North Carolina, South Carolina, Georgia, no—4; Massachusetts, divided."
[3] The year " 1787 " is here inserted in the transcript.
[4] Madison's direction is omitted in the transcript.
[5] In the transcript the figures " 7 " and " 3 " are inserted after the States Georgia and Maryland, respectively.

Magistracy shall be elected in the following manner: That the States be divided into   districts: & that the persons qualified to vote in each district for members of the first branch of the national Legislature elect   members for their respective districts to be electors of the Executive magistracy, that the said Electors of the Executive magistracy meet at   and they or any of them so met shall proceed to elect by ballot, but not out of their own body   person   in whom the Executive authority of the national Government shall be vested.''

M! WILSON repeated his arguments in favor of an election without the intervention of the States. He supposed too that this mode would produce more confidence among the people in the first magistrate, than an election by the national Legislature.

M! GERRY, opposed the election by the national legislature. There would be a constant intrigue kept up for the appointment. The Legislature & the candidates w^d bargain & play into one another's hands, votes would be given by the former under promises or expectations from the latter, of recompensing them by services to members of the Legislature or to [1] their friends. He liked the principle of M! Wilson's motion, but fears it would alarm & give a handle to the State partisans, as tending to supersede altogether the State authorities. He thought the Community not yet ripe for stripping the States of their powers, even such as might not be requisite for local purposes. He was for waiting till people should feel more the necessity of it. He seemed to prefer the taking the suffrages of the States instead of Electors, or letting the Legislatures nominate, and the electors appoint. He was not clear that the people ought to act directly even in the choice of electors, being too little informed of personal characters in large districts, and liable to deceptions.

M! WILLIAMSON could see no advantage in the introduction of Electors chosen by the people who would stand in the same relation to them as the State Legislatures, whilst the expedient would be attended with great trouble and expence.

On the question for agreeing to M! Wilson's substitute, it was negatived: Mass^{ts} no. Con^t no. N. Y. no.* P^a ay. Del. no. Mar^d ay. Virg^a no. N. C. no. S. C. no. Geo^a no.[2]

* N. Y. in the printed Journal—'divided.'

---

[1] The word "to" is omitted in the transcript.

[2] In the transcript the vote reads: "Pennsylvania, Maryland, aye—2; Massachusetts, Connecticut, New York,* Delaware, Virginia, North Carolina, South Carolina, Georgia, no—8."

On the question for electing the Executive by the national Legislature for the term of seven years, it was agreed to Mass^t^ ay. Con^t^ ay. N. Y. ay. Pen^a^ no. Del. ay. Mary^d^ no. V^a^ ay. N. C. ay. S. C. ay. Geo. ay.[1]

Doc^r^ FRANKLIN moved that what related to the compensation for the services of the Executive be postponed, in order to substitute— " whose necessary expences shall be defrayed, but who shall receive no salary, stipend fee or reward whatsoever for their services "—He said that being very sensible of the effect of age on his memory, he had been unwilling to trust to that for the observations which seemed to support his motion, and had reduced them to writing, that he might with the permission of the Committee read instead of speaking them. Mr WILSON made an offer to read the paper, which was accepted—The following is a literal copy of the paper.

Sir.

It is with reluctance that I rise to express a disapprobation of any one article of the plan for which we are so much obliged to the honorable gentleman who laid it before us. From its first reading I have borne a good will to it, and in general wished it success. In this particular of salaries to the Executive branch I happen to differ; and as my opinion may appear new and chimerical, it is only from a persuasion that it is right, and from a sense of duty that I hazard it. The Committee will judge of my reasons when they have heard them, and their judgment may possibly change mine.—I think I see inconveniences in the appointment of salaries; I see none in refusing them, but on the contrary, great advantages.

Sir, there are two passions which have a powerful influence on the affairs of men. These are ambition and avarice; the love of power, and the love of money. Separately each of these has great force in prompting men to action; but when united in view of the same object, they have in many minds the most violent effects. Place before the eyes of such men, a post of *honour* that shall be at the same time a place of *profit*, and they will move heaven and earth to obtain it. The vast number of such places it is that renders the British Government so tempestuous. The struggles for them are the true sources of all those factions which are perpetually dividing the Nation, distracting its Councils, hurrying sometimes into fruitless &

---

[1] In the transcript the vote reads: "Massachusetts, Connecticut, New York, Delaware, Virginia, North Carolina, South Carolina, Georgia, aye—8; Pennsylvania, Maryland, no—2."

mischievous wars, and often compelling a submission to dishonorable terms of peace.

And of what kind are the men that will strive for this profitable pre-eminence, through all the bustle of cabal, the heat of contention, the infinite mutual abuse of parties, tearing to pieces the best of characters? It will not be the wise and moderate; the lovers of peace and good order, the men fittest for the trust. It will be the bold and the violent, the men of strong passions and indefatigable activity in their selfish pursuits. These will thrust themselves into your Government and be your rulers.—And these too will be mistaken in the expected happiness of their situation: For their vanquished competitors of the same spirit, and from the same motives will perpetually be endeavouring to distress their administration, thwart their measures, and render them odious to the people.

Besides these evils, Sir, tho' we may set out in the beginning with moderate salaries, we shall find that such will not be of long continuance. Reasons will never be wanting for proposed augmentations. And there will always be a party for giving more to the rulers, that the rulers may be able in return to give more to them.— Hence as all history informs us, there has been in every State & Kingdom a constant kind of warfare between the governing & governed: the one striving to obtain more for its support, and the other to pay less. And this has alone occasioned great convulsions, actual civil wars, ending either in dethroning of the Princes, or enslaving of the people. Generally indeed the ruling power carries its point, the revenues of princes constantly increasing, and we see that they are never satisfied, but always in want of more. The more the people are discontented with the oppression of taxes; the greater need the prince has of money to distribute among his partizans and pay the troops that are to suppress all resistance, and enable him to plunder at pleasure. There is scarce a king in a hundred who would not, if he could, follow the example of Pharoah, get first all the peoples money, then all their lands, and then make them and their children servants for ever. It will be said, that we don't propose to establish Kings. I know it. But there is a natural inclination in mankind to Kingly Government. It sometimes relieves them from Aristocratic domination. They had rather have one tyrant than five hundred. It gives more of the appearance of equality among Citizens, and that they like. I am apprehensive therefore, perhaps too apprehensive, that the Government of these States, may in future times, end in a Monarchy. But this Catastrophe I think may be long delayed, if in our proposed System we do not sow the seeds of contention, faction

& tumult, by making our posts of honor, places of profit. If we do, I fear that tho' we do employ at first a number, and not a single person, the number will in time be set aside, it will only nourish the fœtus of a King, as the honorable gentleman from Virginia very aptly expressed it, and a King will the sooner be set over us.

It may be imagined by some that this is an Utopian Idea, and that we can never find men to serve us in the Executive department, without paying them well for their services. I conceive this to be a mistake. Some existing facts present themselves to me, which incline me to a contrary opinion. The high Sheriff of a County in England is an honorable office, but it is not a profitable one. It is rather expensive and therefore not sought for. But yet, it is executed and well executed, and usually by some of the principal Gentlemen of the County. In France, the office of Counsellor or Member of their Judiciary Parliaments is more honorable. It is therefore purchased at a high price: There are indeed fees on the law proceedings, which are divided among them, but these fees do not amount to more than three per Cent on the sum paid for the place. Therefore as legal interest is there at five per C^t they in fact pay two per C^t for being allowed to do the Judiciary business of the Nation, which is at the same time entirely exempt from the burden of paying them any salaries for their services. I do not however mean to recommend this as an eligible mode for our Judiciary department. I only bring the instance to shew that the pleasure of doing good & serving their Country and the respect such conduct entitles them to, are sufficient motives with some minds to give up a great portion of their time to the public, without the mean inducement of pecuniary satisfaction.

Another instance is that of a respectable Society who have made the experiment, and practised it with success more than an [1] hundred years. I mean the Quakers. It is an established rule with them, that they are not to go to law; but in their controversies they must apply to their monthly, quarterly and yearly meetings. Committees of these sit with patience to hear the parties, and spend much time in composing their differences. In doing this, they are supported by a sense of duty, and the respect paid to usefulness. It is honorable to be so employed, but it was [2] never made profitable by salaries, fees, or perquisites. And indeed in all cases of public service the less the profit the greater the honor.

To bring the matter nearer home, have we not seen, the great and most important of our offices, that of General of our armies

---

[1] The word "one" is substituted in the transcript for "an."
[2] The word "is" is substituted in the transcript for "was."

executed for eight years together without the smallest salary, by a Patriot whom I will not now offend by any other praise; and this through fatigues and distresses in common with the other brave men his military friends & companions, and the constant anxieties peculiar to his station? And shall we doubt finding three or four men in all the U. States, with public spirit enough to bear sitting in peaceful Council for perhaps an equal term, merely to preside over our civil concerns, and see that our laws are duly executed. Sir, I have a better opinion of our Country. I think we shall never be without a sufficient number of wise and good men to undertake and execute well and faithfully the office in question.

Sir, The saving of the salaries that may at first be proposed is not an object with me. The subsequent mischiefs of proposing them are what I apprehend. And therefore it is, that I move the amendment. If it is not seconded or accepted I must be contented with the satisfaction of having delivered my opinion frankly and done my duty.

The motion was seconded by Col. HAMILTON with the view he said merely of bringing so respectable a proposition before the Committee, and which was besides enforced by arguments that had a certain degree of weight. No debate ensued, and the proposition was postponed for the consideration of the members. It was treated with great respect, but rather for the author of it, than from any apparent conviction of its expediency or practicability.

Mᵣ DICKENSON moved "that the Executive be made removeable by the National Legislature on the request of a majority of the Legislatures of individual States." It was necessary he said to place the power of removing somewhere. He did not like the plan of impeaching the Great officers of State. He did not know how provision could be made for removal of them in a better mode than that which he had proposed. He had no idea of abolishing the State Governments as some gentlemen seemed inclined to do. The happiness of this Country in his opinion required considerable powers to be left in the hands of the States.

Mᵣ BEDFORD seconded the motion.

Mᵣ SHERMAN contended that the National Legislature should have power to remove the Executive at pleasure.

Mᵣ MASON. Some mode of displacing an unfit magistrate is rendered indispensable by the fallibility of those who choose, as well as by the corruptibility of the man chosen. He opposed decidedly the making the Executive the mere creature of the Legislature as a violation of the fundamental principle of good Government.

M? MADISON & M? WILSON observed that it would leave an equality of agency in the small with the great States; that it would enable a minority of the people to prevent y? removal of an officer who had rendered himself justly criminal in the eyes of a majority; that it would open a door for intrigues ag?t him in States where his administration tho' just might be unpopular, and might tempt him to pay court to particular States whose leading partizans he might fear, or wish to engage as his partizans. They both thought it bad policy to introduce such a mixture of the State authorities, where their agency could be otherwise supplied.

M? DICKENSON considered the business as so important that no man ought to be silent or reserved. He went into a discourse of some length, the sum of which was, that the Legislative, Executive, & Judiciary departments ought to be made as independt as possible; but that such an Executive as some seemed to have in contemplation was not consistent with a republic: that a firm Executive could only exist in a limited monarchy. In the British Gov? itself the weight of the Executive arises from the attachments which the Crown draws to itself, & not merely from the force of its prerogatives. In place of these attachments we must look out for something else. One source of stability is the double branch of the Legislature. The division of the Country into distinct States formed the other principal source of stability. This division ought therefore to be maintained, and considerable powers to be left with the States. This was the ground of his consolation for the future fate of his Country. Without this, and in case of a consolidation of the States into one great Republic, we might read its fate in the history of smaller ones. A limited Monarchy he considered as *one* of the best Governments in the world. It was not *certain* that the same blessings were derivable from any other form. It was certain that equal blessings had never yet been derived from any of the republican form. A limited Monarchy however was out of the question. The spirit of the times—the state of our affairs, forbade the experiment, if it were desireable. Was it possible moreover in the nature of things to introduce it even if these obstacles were less insuperable. A House of Nobles was essential to such a Gov? could these be created by a breath, or by a stroke of the pen? No. They were the growth of ages, and could only arise under a complication of circumstances none of which existed in this Country. But though a form the most perfect *perhaps* in itself be unattainable, we must not despair. If antient republics have been found to flourish for a moment only & then vanish for ever, it only proves that they were badly constituted; and that we ought to seek for every remedy for their diseases. One of these remedies he conceived to be the accidental lucky division of this Country into distinct States; a division which some seemed desirous to abolish altogether. As to the point of representation in the national Legislature as it might affect States of different sizes, he said it must probably end in mutual concession. He hoped that each State would retain an equal voice at least in one branch of the National Legislature, and supposed the sums paid within each State would form a better ratio for the other branch than either the number of inhabitants or the quantum of property.

A motion being made to strike out "on request by a majority of the Legislatures of the individual States " and rejected, Connecticut, S. Carol: & Geo. being ay, the rest no: the question was taken—

On M: Dickenson's motion for making [1] Executive removeable by [1] Nat: Legislature at [1] request of [2] majority of State Legislatures [3] was also rejected—all the States being in the negative Except Delaware which gave an affirmative vote.

The Question for making y? Executive ineligible after seven years,[4] was next taken, and agreed to:

Mass: ay. Con: no. N. Y. ay. P: div: Del. ay. Mary: ay. V: ay. N. C. ay. S. C. ay. Geo. no:* [5]

M: Williamson 2ded by M: Davie moved to add to the last Clause, the words—" and to be removeable on impeachment & conviction of mal-practice or neglect of duty "—which was agreed to.

M: Rutlidge & M: C. Pinkney moved that the blank for the n? of persons in the Executive be filled with the words " one person." He supposed the reasons to be so obvious & conclusive in favor of one that no member would oppose the motion.

M: Randolph opposed it with great earnestness, declaring that he should not do justice to the Country which sent him if he were silently to suffer the establishm: of a Unity in the Executive department. He felt an opposition to it which he believed he should con-

* In [6] printed Journal Geo. ay.

---

[1] The word " the " is here inserted in the transcript.
[2] The word " a " is here inserted in the transcript.
[3] The word " which " is here inserted in the transcript.
[4] The phrase "ineligible after seven years" is italicized in the transcript.
[5] In the transcript the vote reads: " Massachusetts, New York, Delaware, Maryland, Virginia, North Carolina, South Carolina, aye—7; Connecticut, Georgia,* no—2; Pennsylvania, divided."
[6] The word " the " is here inserted in the transcript.

tinue to feel as long as he lived. He urged 1.[1] that the permanent temper of the people was adverse to the very semblance of Monarchy. 2.[1] that a unity was unnecessary a plurality being equally competent to all the objects of the department. 3.[1] that the necessary confidence would never be reposed in a single Magistrate. 4.[1] that the appointments would generally be in favor of some inhabitant near the center of the Community, and consequently the remote parts would not be on an equal footing. He was in favor of three members of the Executive to be drawn from different portions of the Country.

Mᵣ BUTLER contended strongly for a single magistrate as most likely to answer the purpose of the remote parts. If one man should be appointed he would be responsible to the whole, and would be impartial to its interests. If three or more should be taken from as many districts, there would be a constant struggle for local advantages. In Military matters this would be particularly mischievous. He said his opinion on this point had been formed under the opportunity he had had of seeing the manner in which a plurality of military heads [2] distracted Holland when threatened with invasion by the imperial troops. One man was for directing the force to the defence of this part, another to that part of the Country, just as he happened to be swayed by prejudice or interest.

The motion was then postpᵈ the Committee rose & the House Adjᵈ

MONDAY JUNE 4.[3] IN COMMITTEE OF THE WHOLE.

The Question was resumed on motion of Mᵣ PINKNEY 2ᵈᵉᵈ by [4] WILSON, " shall the blank for the number of the Executive be filled with a single person? "

Mᵣ WILSON was in favor of the motion. It had been opposed by the gentleman from Virgᵗ [Mᵣ Randolph] but the arguments used had not convinced him. He observed that the objections of Mᵣ R. were levelled not so much agˢᵗ the measure itself, as agˢᵗ its unpopularity. If he could suppose that it would occasion a rejection of the plan of which it should form a part, though the part was [5] an

---

[1] The figures " 1," " 2," " 3 " and " 4 " are changed to " first," " secondly," " thirdly " and " fourthly."
[2] The transcript italicizes the phrase " plurality of military heads."
[3] The year " 1787 " is here inserted in the transcript.
[4] The transcript inserts the word " Mr." before " Wilson."
[5] The word " was " is changed to " were " in the transcript.

important one, yet he would give it up rather than lose the whole. On examination he could see no evidence of the alledged antipathy of the people. On the contrary he was persuaded that it does not exist. All know that a single magistrate is not a King. One fact has great weight with him. All the 13 States tho agreeing in scarce any other instance, agree in placing a single magistrate at the head of the Govern! The idea of three heads has taken place in none. The degree of power is indeed different; but there are no co-ordinate heads. In addition to his former reasons for preferring a unity, he would mention another. The *tranquility* not less than the vigor of the Gov! he thought would be favored by it. Among three equal members, he foresaw nothing but uncontrouled, continued, & violent animosities; which would not only interrupt the public administration; but diffuse their poison thro' the other branches of Gov!, thro' the States, and at length thro' the people at large. If the members were to be unequal in power the principle of the [1] opposition to the unity was given up. If equal, the making them an odd number would not be a remedy. In Courts of Justice there are two sides only to a question. In the Legislative & Executive departm!! questions have commonly many sides. Each member therefore might espouse a separate one & no two agree.

M! SHERMAN. This matter is of great importance and ought to be well considered before it is determined. M! Wilson he said had observed that in each State a single magistrate was placed at the head of the Gov! It was so he admitted, and properly so, and he wished the same policy to prevail in the federal Gov! But then it should be also remarked that in all the States there was a Council of advice, without which the first magistrate could not act. A council he thought necessary to make the establishment acceptable to the people. Even in G. B. the King has a Council; and though he appoints it himself, its advice has its weight with him, and attracts the Confidence of the people.

M! WILLIAMSON asks M! WILSON whether he means to annex a Council.

M! WILSON means to have no Council, which oftener serves to cover, than prevent malpractices.

M! GERRY was at a loss to discover the policy of three members for the Executive. It w? be extremely inconvenient in many instances, particularly in military matters, whether relating to the militia, an army, or a navy. It would be a general with three heads.

---

[1] The word " the " is omitted in the transcript.

On the question for a single Executive it was agreed to Massᵗˢ ay. Conᵗ ay. N. Y. no. Penᵃ ay. Del. no. Maryᵈ no. Virg. ay. [Mʳ R. & Mʳ Blair no—Docʳ MᶜCᵍ Mʳ M. & Gen W. ay. Col. Mason being no, but not in house, Mʳ Wythe ay but gone home]. N. C. ay. S. C. ay. Georgᵃ ay.¹

First Clause of Proposition 8ᵗʰ ² relating *to a Council of Revision* taken into consideration.

Mʳ GERRY doubts whether the Judiciary ought to form a part of it, as they will have a sufficient check agˢᵗ encroachments on their own department by their exposition of the laws, which involved a power of deciding on their Constitutionality. In some States the Judges had actually set aside laws as being agˢᵗ the Constitution. This was done too with general approbation. It was quite foreign from the nature of yᵉ office to make them judges of the policy of public measures. He moves to postpone the clause in order to propose "that the National Executive shall have a right to negative any Legislative act which shall not be afterwards passed by   parts of each branch of the national Legislature."

Mʳ KING seconds the motion, observing that the Judges ought to be able to expound the law as it should come before them, free from the bias of having participated in its formation.

Mʳ WILSON thinks neither the original proposition nor the amendment go far enough. If the Legislative Exetv & Judiciary ought to be distinct & independent. The Executive ought to have an absolute negative. Without such a self-defence the Legislature can at any moment sink it into non-existence. He was for varying the proposition in such a manner as to give the Executive & Judiciary jointly an absolute negative.

On the question to postpone in order to take Mʳ Gerry's proposition into consideration it was agreed to, Massˢ ay. Conᵗ no. N. Y. ay. Pᵃ ay. Del. no. Maryᵈ no. Virgᵃ no. N. C. ay. S. C. ay. Gᵃ ay.³

Mʳ GERRY's proposition being now before ⁴ Committee, Mʳ WILSON & Mʳ HAMILTON move that the last part of it [viz. " wᶜʰ sˡ not be

---

¹ In the transcript the vote reads: "Massachusetts, Connecticut, Pennsylvania, Virginia, (Mr. Randolph and Mr. Blair, no; Doctor McClurg, Mr. Madison, and General Washington, aye; Colonel Mason being no, but not in the House, Mr. Wythe, aye, but gone home), North Carolina, South Carolina, Georgia, aye—7; New York, Delaware, Maryland, no—3."

² The phrase "the eighth Resolution" is substituted in the transcript for "Proposition 8ᵗʰ "

³ In the transcript the vote reads: "Massachusetts, New York, Pennsylvania, North Carolina, South Carolina, Georgia, aye—6; Connecticut, Delaware, Maryland, Virginia, no—4."

⁴ The word "the" is here inserted in the transcript.

afterw.^{ds} passed unless [1] by   parts of each branch of the National legislature] be struck out, so as to give the Executive an absolute negative on the laws. There was no danger they thought of such a power being too much exercised. It was mentioned by Col: Hamilton that the King of G. B. had not exerted his negative since the Revolution.

Mr Gerry sees no necessity for so great a controul over the legislature as the best men in the Community would be comprised in the two branches of it.

Doc.^r Franklin, said he was sorry to differ from his colleague for whom he had a very great respect, on any occasion, but he could not help it on this. He had had some experience of this check in the Executive on the Legislature, under the proprietary Government of Pen.^a The negative of the Governor was constantly made use of to extort money. No good law whatever could be passed without a private bargain with him. An increase of his salary, or some donation, was always made a condition; till at last it became the regular practice, to have orders in his favor on the Treasury, presented along with the bills to be signed, so that he might actually receive the former before he should sign the latter. When the Indians were scalping the western people, and notice of it arrived, the concurrence of the Governor in the means of self-defence could not be got, till it was agreed that his Estate should be exempted from taxation: so that the people were to fight for the security of his property, whilst he was to bear no share of the burden. This was a mischievous sort of check. If the Executive was to have a Council, such a power would be less objectionable. It was true, the King of G. B. had not, as was said, exerted his negative since the Revolution; but that matter was easily explained. The bribes and emoluments now given to the members of parliament rendered it unnecessary, every thing being done according to the will of the Ministers. He was afraid, if a negative should be given as proposed, that more power and money would be demanded, till at last eno' would be gotten [2] to influence & bribe the Legislature into a compleat subjection to the will of the Executive.

Mr Sherman was ag.st enabling any one man to stop the will of the whole. No one man could be found so far above all the rest in wisdom. He thought we ought to avail ourselves of his wisdom in revising the laws, but not permit him to overule the decided and cool opinions of the Legislature.

---

[1] The word " unless " is crossed out in the transcript.
[2] In the transcript the syllable "ten" is stricken from the word "gotten."

Mᵣ MADISON supposed that if a proper proportion of each branch should be required to overrule the objections of the Executive, it would answer the same purpose as an absolute negative. It would rarely if ever happen that the Executive constituted as ours is proposed to be would, have firmness eno' to resist the legislature, unless backed by a certain part of the body itself. The King of G. B. with all his splendid attributes would not be able to withstand yᵉ unanimous and eager wishes of both houses of Parliament. To give such a prerogative would certainly be obnoxious to the temper of this Country; its present temper at least.

Mᵣ WILSON believed as others did that this power would seldom be used. The Legislature would know that such a power existed, and would refrain from such laws, as it would be sure to defeat. Its silent operation would therefore preserve harmony and prevent mischief. The case of Penⁿ formerly was very different from its present case. The Executive was not then as now to be appointed by the people. It will not in this case as in the one cited be supported by the head of a Great Empire, actuated by a different & sometimes opposite interest. The salary too is now proposed to be fixed by the Constitution, or if Dᵣ F.'s idea should be adopted all salary whatever interdicted. The requiring a large proportion of each House to overrule the Executive check might do in peaceable times; but there might be tempestuous moments in which animosities may run high between the Executive and Legislative branches, and in which the former ought to be able to defend itself.

Mᵣ BUTLER had been in favor of a single Executive Magistrate; but could he have entertained an idea that a compleat negative on the laws was to be given him he certainly should have acted very differently. It had been observed that in all countries the Executive power is in a constant course of increase. This was certainly the case in G. B. Gentlemen seemed to think that we had nothing to apprehend from an abuse of the Executive power. But why might not a Cataline or a Cromwell arise in this Country as well as in others.

Mᵣ BEDFORD was opposed to every check on the Legislative,[1] even the Council of Revision first proposed. He thought it would be sufficient to mark out in the Constitution the boundaries to the Legislative Authority, which would give all the requisite security to the rights of the other departments. The Representatives of the people were the best Judges of what was for their interest, and ought to

---

[1] In the transcript the syllable "tive" is stricken from the word "Legislative" and "ture" is written above it.

be under no external controul whatever. The two branches would produce a sufficient controul within the Legislature itself.

Col. MASON observed that a vote had already passed he found
[he was out at the time] for vesting the executive powers in a single
person. Among these powers was that of appointing to offices in
certain cases. The probable abuses of a negative had been well explained by D: F. as proved by experience, the best of all tests.
Will not the same door be opened here. The Executive may refuse
its assent to necessary measures till new appointments shall be referred to him; and having by degrees engrossed all these into his
own hands, the American Executive, like the British, will by bribery
& influence, save himself the trouble & odium of exerting his negative afterwards. We are M: Chairman going very far in this business. We are not indeed constituting a British Government, but a
more dangerous monarchy, an elective one. We are introducing a
new principle into our system, and not necessary as in the British
Gov: where the Executive has greater rights to defend. Do gentlemen mean to pave the way to hereditary Monarchy? Do they flatter
themselves that the people will ever consent to such an innovation?
If they do I venture to tell them, they are mistaken. The people
never will consent. And do gentlemen consider the danger of delay,
and the still greater danger of a a rejection, not for a moment but
forever, of the plan which shall be proposed to them. Notwithstanding
the oppressions & injustice experienced among us from democracy;
the genius of the people is in favor of it, and the genius of the
people must be consulted. He could not but consider the federal
system as in effect dissolved by the appointment of this Convention
to devise a better one. And do gentlemen look forward to the dangerous interval between the extinction of an old, and the establishment
of a new Governm: and to the scenes of confusion which may ensue.
He hoped that nothing like a Monarchy would ever be attempted in
this Country. A hatred to its oppressions had carried the people
through the late Revolution. Will it not be eno' to enable the Executive to suspend offensive laws, till they shall be coolly revised, and
the objections to them overruled by a greater majority than was required in the first instance. He never could agree to give up all the
rights of the people to a single Magistrate. If more than one had
been fixed on, greater powers might have been entrusted to the
Executive. He hoped this attempt to give such powers would have
its weight hereafter as an argument for increasing the number of
the Executive.

Doc: FRANKLIN. A Gentleman from S. C. [M: Butler] a day or

two ago called our attention to the case of the U. Netherlands. He
wished the gentleman had been a little fuller, and had gone back to
the original of that Gov.^t The people being under great obligations to the Prince of Orange whose wisdom and bravery had
saved them, chose him for the Stadtholder. He did very well.
Inconveniences however were felt from his powers; which growing
more & more oppressive, they were at length set aside. Still however there was a party for the P. of Orange, which descended to
his son who excited insurrections, spilt a great deal of blood, mur-
dered the de Witts, and got the powers revested in the Stadtholder.
Afterwards another Prince had power to excite insurrections & to [1]
make the Stadtholdership hereditary. And the present Stadth.^{der} is
ready to wade thro a bloody civil war to the establishment of a monarchy. Col. Mason had mentioned the circumstance of appointing officers. He knew how that point would be managed. No new appointment would be suffered as heretofore in Pens.^a unless it be referred to
the Executive; so that all profitable offices will be at his disposal. The
first man put at the helm will be a good one. No body knows what
sort may come afterwards. The Executive will be always increasing
here, as elsewhere, till it ends in a Monarchy

On the question for striking out so as to give [2] Executive an abso-
lute negative—Mass.^{ts} no. Con.^t no. N. Y. no. P.^a no. Dl. no. M.^d no.
V.^a no. N. C. no. S. C. no. Georg.^a no.[3]

Mr BUTLER moved that the Resol.ⁿ be altered so as to read—" Resolved that the National Executive have a power to suspend any
Legislative act for the term of   ."

Doct.^r FRANKLIN seconds the motion.

Mr GERRY observed that a [4] power of suspending might do all the
mischief dreaded from the negative of useful laws; without answering the salutary purpose of checking unjust or unwise ones.

On [2] question " for giving this suspending power " all the States,
to wit Mass.^{ts} Con.^t N. Y. P.^a Del. Mary.^d Virg.^a N. C. S. C. Georgia,
were *No.*

On a question for enabling *two thirds* of each branch of the
Legislature to overrule the revisionary [5] check: it passed in the affirma-

---

[1] The word " to " is omitted in the transcript.
[2] The word " the " is here inserted in the transcript.
[3] In the transcript the vote reads " Massachusetts, Connecticut, New York,
Pennsylvania, Delaware, Maryland, Virginia, North Carolina, South Carolina,
Georgia, no—10."
[4] The word " the " is substituted in the transcript for " a."
[5] In the transcript the word " provisionary " was erroneously used in place
of " revisionary."

tive sub silentio; and was inserted in the blank of M: Gerry's motion.

On the question on M: Gerry's motion which gave the Executive alone without the Judiciary the revisionary controul on the laws unless overruled by ⅔ of each branch; Mass^{ts} ay. Con^t no. N. Y. ay. P^a ay. Del. ay. Mary^d no. V^a ay. N. C. ay. S. C. ay. Geo. ay.[1]

It was moved by M: WILSON 2^{ded} by M: MADISON—that the following amendment be made to the last resolution—after the words "National Ex." to add "& a convenient number of the National Judiciary."

An objection of order being taken by M: HAMILTON to the introduction of the last amendment at this time, notice was given by M: W. & M: M.—that the same w^d be moved tomorrow,—whereupon Wednesday (the day after)[2] was assigned to reconsider the amendment of M: Gerry.

It was then moved & 2^{ded} to proceed to the consideration of the 9th resolution submitted by M: Randolph—when on motion to agree to the first clause namely "Resolved that a National Judiciary be established"[3] It passed in the affirmative nem. con.

It was then moved & 2^{ded} to add these words to the first clause of the ninth resolution namely—"to consist of one supreme tribunal, and of one or more inferior tribunals," which passed in the affirmative—

The Comm^e then rose and the House
Adjourned.

TEUSDAY JUNE 5.   IN COMMITTEE OF THE WHOLE.

Governor Livingston from [4] New Jersey, took his seat.

The words, "one or more" were struck out before "inferior tribunals" as an amendment to the last clause of Resol^n 9th [5] The Clause—"that the National Judiciary be chosen by the National Legislature," being under consideration.

M: WILSON opposed the appointm^t of Judges by the National Legisl: Experience shewed the impropriety of such appointm^ts by numerous bodies. Intrigue, partiality, and concealment were the

---

[1] In the transcript this vote reads: "Massachusetts, New York, Pennsylvania, Delaware, Virginia, North Carolina, South Carolina, Georgia, aye—8; Connecticut, Maryland, no—2."

[2] The phrase " (the day after) " is crossed out in the transcript.

[3] The phrase "Resolved that a National Judiciary be established" is italicized in the transcript.

[4] The word "of" is substituted in the transcript for "from."

[5] The phrase "the ninth Resolution" is used in the transcript in place of "Resol^n 9th"

necessary consequences. A principal reason for unity in the Executive was that officers might be appointed by a single, responsible person.

M! RUTLIDGE was by no means disposed to grant so great a power to any single person. The people will think we are leaning too much towards Monarchy. He was against establishing any national tribunal except a single supreme one. The State tribunals are most proper to decide in all cases in the first instance.

Doc! FRANKLIN observed that two modes of chusing the Judges had been mentioned, to wit, by the Legislature and by the Executive. He wished such other modes to be suggested as might occur to other gentlemen; it being a point of great moment. He would mention one which he had understood was practiced in Scotland. He then in a brief and entertaining manner related a Scotch mode, in which the nomination proceeded from the Lawyers, who always selected the ablest of the profession in order to get rid of him, and share his practice among themselves. It was here he said the interest of the electors to make the best choice, which should always be made the case if possible.

Mr. MADISON disliked the election of the Judges by the Legislature or any numerous body. Besides, the danger of intrigue and partiality, many of the members were not judges of the requisite qualifications. The Legislative talents which were very different from those of a Judge, commonly recommended men to the favor of Legislative Assemblies. It was known too that the accidental circumstances of presence and absence, of being a member or not a member, had a very undue influence on the appointment. On the other hand he was not satisfied with referring the appointment to the Executive. He rather inclined to give it to the Senatorial branch, as numerous eno' to be confided in—as not so numerous as to be governed by the motives of the other branch; and as being sufficiently stable and independent to follow their deliberate judgments. He hinted this only and moved that the *appointment by the Legislature* might be struck out, & a blank left to be hereafter filled on maturer reflection. M! WILSON seconds it. On the question for striking out. Mass!! ay. Con! no. N. Y. ay. N. J. ay. Pen! ay. Del. ay. M! ay. V! ay. N. C. ay. S. C. no. Geo. ay.[1]

M! WILSON gave notice that he should at a future day move for a reconsideration of that clause which respects "inferior tribunals."

---

[1] In the transcript the vote reads: "Massachusetts, New York, New Jersey, Pennsylvania, Delaware, Maryland, Virginia, North Carolina, South Carolina, no, Georgia, aye—9; Connecticut, South Carolina,—2."

M! PINKNEY gave notice that when the clause respecting the appointment of the Judiciary should again come before the Committee he should move to restore the " appointment by the national Legislature."

The following clauses of Resol: 9.[1] were agreed to viz " to hold their offices during good behaviour, and to receive punctually at stated times, a fixed compensation for their services, in which no increase or diminution shall be made so as to affect the persons actually in office at the time of such increase or diminution."

The remaining clause of Resolution 9.[2] was posponed.

Resolution 10[3] was agreed to—viz—that provision ought to be made for the admission of States lawfully arising within the limits of the U. States, whether from a voluntary junction of Government & territory, or otherwise, with the consent of a number of voices in the National Legislature less than the whole.

The 11. propos:[4] " *for guarantying to States Republican* Gov! & territory &c., being read, M! PATTERSON wished the point of representation could be decided before this clause should be considered, and moved to postpone it: which was not opposed, and agreed to: Connecticut & S. Carolina only voting ag!ᵗ it.

Propos. 12[5] " *for continuing Cong! till a given day and for fulfilling their engagements,*" produced no debate.

On the question, Mass. ay. Con! no. N. Y. ay. N. J.* ay. P! ay. Del. no. M! ay. V! ay. N. C. ay. S. C. ay. G. ay.

Propos: 13.[6] " that *provision ought to be made for hereafter amending the system now to be established, without requiring the assent of the Nat! Legislature,*" being taken up,

M! PINKNEY doubted the propriety or necessity of it.

M! GERRY favored it. The novelty & difficulty of the experiment requires periodical revision. The prospect of such a revision would also give intermediate stability to the Gov! Nothing had yet happened in the States where this provision existed to prove its impropriety.—The proposition was postponed for further consideration:

---

* New Jersey omitted in the printed Journal.

---

[1] The transcript uses the phrase "the ninth Resolution" in place of "Resol: 9," and italicizes the resolution.

[2] The transcript here uses the phrase "the ninth Resolution."

[3] The phrase "The tenth Resolution" is here used in the transcript.

[4] In place of the words "The 11. propos:" the transcript reads: "The eleventh Resolution."

[5] The transcript changes "Propos. 12" to "The twelfth Resolution."

[6] The transcript changes "Propos: 13" to read as follows: "The thirteenth Resolution, to the effect."

the votes being, Mas: Con. N. Y. P? Del. Ma. N. C.—ay Virg? S. C.
Geo: no

Propos. 14.[1] *" requiring oath from the State officers to support
National Gov^t"* was postponed after a short uninteresting conversa-
tion: the votes, Con. N. Jersey. M^d Virg: S. C. Geo. ay N. Y. P?
Del. N. C. - - - no Massachusetts - - - divided.

Propos. 15[2] for *" recommending Conventions under appointment
of the people to ratify the new Constitution "* &c. being taken up.

Mr SHARMAN thought such a popular ratification unnecessary: the
articles of Confederation providing for changes and alterations with
the assent of Cong? and ratification of State Legislatures.

Mr MADISON thought this provision essential. The articles of
Confed^n themselves were defective in this respect, resting in many
of the States on the Legislative sanction only. Hence in conflicts
between acts of the States, and of Cong? especially where the former
are of posterior date, and the decision is to be made by State tribunals, an uncertainty must necessaily prevail, or rather perhaps
a certain decision in favor of the State authority. He suggested
also that as far as the articles of Union were to be considered as
a Treaty only of a particular sort, among the Governments of Independent States, the doctrine might be set up that a breach of any
one article, by any of the parties, absolved the other parties from
the whole obligation. For these reasons as well as others he thought
it indispensable that the new Constitution should be ratified in the
most unexceptionable form, and by the supreme authority of the
people themselves.

Mr GERRY observed that in the Eastern States the Confed^n had
been sanctioned by the people themselves. He seemed afraid of
referring the new system to them. The people in that quarter have
at this time the wildest ideas of Government in the world. They
were for abolishing the Senate in Mass^{ts} and giving all the other
powers of Gov? to the other branch of the Legislature.

Mr KING supposed that the last article of ye Confed^n rendered
the legislature competent to the ratification. The people of the
Southern States where the federal articles had been ratified by the
Legislatures only, had since *impliedly* given their sanction to it.
He thought notwithstanding that there might be policy in varying
the mode. A Convention being a single house, the adoption may
more easily be carried thro' it, than thro' the Legislatures where
there are several branches. The Legislatures also being to lose

---

[1] The transcript changes "Propos. 14" to "The fourteenth Resolution."
[2] The transcript changes "Propos. 15" to "The fifteenth Resolution."

power, will be most likely to raise objections. The people having already parted with the necessary powers it is immaterial to them, by which Government they are possessed, provided they be well employed.

M⸢ WILSON took this occasion to lead the Committee by a train of observations to the idea of not suffering a disposition in the plurality of States to confederate anew on better principles, to be defeated by the inconsiderate or selfish opposition of a few States. He hoped the provision for ratifying would be put on such a footing as to admit of such a partial union, with a door open for the accession of the rest.*

M⸢ PINKNEY hoped that in case the experiment should not unanimously take place, nine States might be authorized to unite under the same Govern⸢

The propos. 15.² was postponed nem. con⸢

M⸢ PINKNEY & M⸢ RUTLIDGE moved that tomorrow be assigned to reconsider that clause of Propos. 4:³ which respects the election of the first branch of the National Legislature—which passed in ⁴ affirmative: Con: N. Y. P⸢ Del: M⸢ V⸢—ay—6   Mas. N. J. N. C. S. C. Geo. no. 5.

M⸢ RUTLIDGE hav⸢ obtained a rule for reconsideration of the clause for establishing *inferior* tribunals under the national authority, now moved that that part of the clause in propos. 9.⁵ should be expunged: arguing that the State Tribunals might and ought to be left in all cases to decide in the first instance the right of appeal to the supreme national tribunal being sufficient to secure the national rights & uniformity of Judgm⸢: that it was making an unnecessary encroachment on the jurisdiction of the States and creating unnecessary obstacles to their adoption of the new system.—M⸢ SHERMAN 2ᵈᵉᵈ the motion.

M⸢ MADISON observed that unless inferior tribunals were dispersed throughout the Republic with *final* jurisdiction in *many* cases, appeals would be multiplied to a most oppressive degree; that besides, an appeal would not in many cases be a remedy. What was to be done after improper Verdicts in State tribunals obtained under

* The note in brackets to be transferred to bottom margin.¹
[This hint was probably meant in terrorem to the smaller States of N. Jersey & Delaware. Nothing was said in reply to it.]

---

¹ Madison's direction is omitted in the transcript.
² The transcript changes "The propos. 15" to "The fifteenth Resolution."
³ The transcript changes "Propos. 4" to "the fourth Resolution."
⁴ The word "the" is here inserted in the transcript.
⁵ The transcript changes "propos. 9" to "the ninth Resolution."

the biassed directions of a dependent Judge, or the local prejudices
of an undirected jury? To remand the cause for a new trial would
answer no purpose. To order a new trial at the Supreme bar would
oblige the parties to bring up their witnesses, tho' ever so distant
from the seat of the Court. An effective Judiciary establishment
commensurate to the legislative authority, was essential. A Government without a proper Executive & Judiciary would be the mere
trunk of a body, without arms or legs to act or move.

M⁹ WILSON opposed the motion on like grounds. he said the
admiralty jurisdiction ought to be given wholly to the national Government, as it related to cases not within the jurisdiction of particular states, & to a scene in which controversies with foreigners
would be most likely to happen.

M⁹ SHERMAN was in favor of the motion. He dwelt chiefly on the
supposed expensiveness of having a new set of Courts, when the
existing State Courts would answer the same purpose.

M⁹ DICKINSON contended strongly that if there was to be a National
Legislature, there ought to be a national Judiciary, and that the
former ought to have authority to institute the latter.

On the question for M⁹ Rutlidge's motion to strike out "inferior
tribunals" [1]

Mass⁹ᵗˢ divided. Con⁹ ay. N. Y. div⁹ N. J. ay. P⁹ no. Del. no.
M⁹ no. V⁹ no. N. C. ay. S. C. ay. Geo. ay.[2]

M⁹ WILSON & M⁹ MADISON then moved, in pursuance of the idea
expressed above by M⁹ Dickinson, to add to Resol: 9.[3] the words
following "that the National Legislature be empowered to institute
inferior tribunals." They observed that there was a distinction between establishing such tribunals absolutely, and giving a discretion
to the Legislature to establish or not establish them. They repeated
the necessity of some such provision.

M⁹ BUTLER. The people will not bear such innovations. The
States will revolt at such encroachments. Supposing such an establishment to be useful, we must not venture on it. We must follow
the example of Solon who gave the Athenians not the best Gov⁹ he
could devise; but the best they w⁹ receive.

M⁹ KING remarked as to the comparative expence that the estab-

---

[1] The phrase "it passed in the affirmative" is here inserted in the transcript.
[2] In the transcript the vote reads: "Connecticut, New York, New Jersey,
North Carolina, South Carolina, Georgia, aye—5; Pennsylvania, Delaware,
Maryland, Virginia, no—4; Massachusetts, divided." New York which was
"divided" was erroneously placed among the "ayes" in copying, although the
number was correctly given as "5."
[3] The transcript changes "Resol: 9" to "the ninth Resolution."

lishment of inferior tribunals w^d cost infinitely less than the appeals that would be prevented by them.

On this question as moved by Mr W. & M^r M.

Mass. ay. C^t no. N. Y. div^d N. J.* ay. P^a ay. Del. ay. M^d ay. V^a ay. N. C. ay. S. C. no. Geo. ay.

The Committee then rose & the House adjourned to 11 OC tom^w [1]

WEDNESDAY JUNE 6TH IN COMMITTEE OF THE WHOLE.

Mr PINKNEY according to previous notice & rule obtained, moved " that the first branch of the national Legislature be elected by the State Legislatures, and not by the people." contending that the people were less fit Judges in such a case, and that the Legislatures would be less likely to promote the adoption of the new Government, if they were to be excluded from all share in it.

Mr RUTLIDGE 2^{ded} the motion.

Mr GERRY. Much depends on the mode of election. In England, the people will probably lose their liberty from the smallness of the proportion having a right of suffrage. Our danger arises from the opposite extreme: hence in Mass^{ts} the worst men get into the Legislature. Several members of that Body had lately been convicted of infamous crimes. Men of indigence, ignorance & baseness, spare no pains, however dirty to carry their point agst men who are superior to the artifices practised. He was not disposed to run into extremes. He was as much principled as ever agst aristocracy and monarchy. It was necessary on the one hand that the people should appoint one branch of the Gov^t in order to inspire them with the necessary confidence. But he wished the election on the other to be so modified as to secure more effectually a just preference of merit. His idea was that the people should nominate certain persons in certain districts, out of whom the State Legislatures sh^d make the appointment.

Mr WILSON. He wished for vigor in the Gov^t, but he wished that vigorous authority to flow immediately from the legitimate source of all authority. The Gov^t ought to possess not only 1st the *force,* but 2dly the *mind or sense* of the people at large. The Legislature ought to be the most exact transcript of the whole Society. Representation is made necessary only because it is impossible for the people to act collectively. The opposition was to be expected he said from the

---

* In the printed Journal N. Jersey—no.

[1] The transcript omits the phrase " to 11 OC tom$_w$."

Governments, not from the Citizens of the States. The latter had parted as was observed [by M[r] King] with all the necessary powers;[1] and it was immaterial to them, by whom they were exercised, if well exercised. The State officers were to be the losers of power. The people he supposed would be rather more attached to the national Gov[t] than to the State Gov[ts] as being more important in itself, and more flattering to their pride. There is no danger of improper elections if made by *large* districts. Bad elections proceed from the smallness of the districts which give an opportunity to bad men to intrigue themselves into office.

M[r] SHERMAN. If it were in view to abolish the State Gov[ts] the elections ought to be by the people. If the State Gov[ts] are to be continued, it is necessary in order to preserve harmony between the National & State Gov[ts] that the elections to the former sh[d] be made by the latter. The right of participating in the National Gov[t] would be sufficiently secured to the people by their election of the State Legislatures. The objects of the Union, he thought were few. 1.[2] defence ag[st] foreign danger. 2[2] ag[st] internal disputes & a resort to force. 3.[2] Treaties with foreign nations. 4[2] regulating foreign commerce, & drawing revenue from it. These & perhaps a few lesser objects alone rendered a Confederation of the States necessary. All other matters civil & criminal would be much better in the hands of the States. The people are more happy in small than[3] large States. States may indeed be too small as Rhode Island, & thereby be too subject to faction. Some others were perhaps too large, the powers of Gov[t] not being able to pervade them. He was for giving the General Gov[t] power to legislate and execute within a defined province.

COL. MASON. Under the existing Confederacy, Cong[s] represent the *States*[4] not the *people* of the States: their acts operate on the *States,* not on the individuals.[5] The case will be changed in the new plan of Gov[t] The people will be represented; they ought therefore to choose the Representatives. The requisites in actual representation are that the Rep[s] should sympathize with their constituents; sh[d] think as they think, & feel as they feel; and that for these purposes sh[d] even be residents among them. Much he s[d] had been alledged ag[st] democratic elections. He admitted that much might be said; but

---

[1] The phrase "with all the necessary powers" is italicized in the transcript.
[2] The figures "1," "2," "3" and "4" are changed to "first," "secondly," etc. in the transcript.
[3] The word "in" is here inserted in the transcript.
[4] The word "and" is here inserted in the transcript.
[5] The transcript italicizes the word "individuals."

it was to be considered that no Gov.̈ was free from imperfections & evils; and that improper elections in many instances, were inseparable from Republican Gov.ᵗˢ But compare these with the advantage of this Form in favor of the rights of the people, in favor of human nature. He was persuaded there was a better chance for proper elections by the people, if divided into large districts, than by the State Legislatures. Paper money had been issued by the latter when the former were against it. Was it to be supposed that the State Legislatures then w.ᵈ not send to the Nat.ˡ legislature patrons of such projects, if the choice depended on them.

M.ͬ MADISON considered an election of one branch at least of the Legislature by the people immediately, as a clear principle of free Gov.ᵗ and that this mode under proper regulations had the additional advantage of securing better representatives, as well as of avoiding too great an agency of the State Governments in the General one.—He differed from the member from Connecticut [M.ͬ Sharman] in thinking the objects mentioned to be all the principal ones that required a National Gov.ᵗ Those were certainly important and necessary objects; but he combined with them the necessity of providing more effectually for the security of private rights, and the steady dispensation of Justice. Interferences with these were evils which had more perhaps than any thing else, produced this convention. Was it to be supposed that republican liberty could long exist under the abuses of it practised in some of the States. The gentleman [M.ͬ Sharman] had admitted that in a very small State, faction & oppression w.ᵈ prevail. It was to be inferred then that wherever these prevailed the State was too small. Had they not prevailed in the largest as well as the smallest tho' less than in the smallest; and were we not thence admonished to enlarge the sphere as far as the nature of the Gov.ᵗ would admit. This was the only defence ag.ˢᵗ the inconveniencies of democracy consistent with the democratic form of Gov.ᵗ All civilized Societies would be divided into different Sects, Factions, & interests, as they happened to consist of rich & poor, debtors & creditors, the landed, the manufacturing, the commercial interests, the inhabitants of this district or that district, the followers of this political leader or that political leader, the disciples of this religious Sect or that religious Sect. In all cases where a majority are united by a common interest or passion, the rights of the minority are in danger. What motives are to restrain them? A prudent regard to the maxim that honesty is the best policy is found by experience to be as little regarded by bodies of men as by individuals. Respect for character is always diminished in proportion to the number among whom the blame or praise is to be divided. Conscience, the only remaining tie, is known to be inadequate in individuals: In large numbers, little is to be expected from it. Besides, Religion itself may become a motive to persecution & oppression.—These observations are verified by the Histories of every Country antient & modern. In Greece & Rome the rich & poor, the creditors & debtors, as well as the patricians & plebeians alternately oppressed each other with equal unmercifulness. What a source of oppression was the relation between the parent cities of Rome, Athens & Carthage, & their respective provinces: the former possessing the power, & the latter being sufficiently distinguished to be separate objects of it? Why was America so justly apprehensive of Parliamentary injustice? Because G. Britain had a separate interest real or supposed, & if her authority had been admitted, could have pursued that interest at our expence. We have seen the mere distinction of colour made in the most enlightened period of time, a ground of the most oppressive dominion ever exercised by man over man. What has been the source of those unjust laws complained of among ourselves? Has it not been the real or supposed interest of the major number? Debtors have defrauded their creditors. The landed interest has borne hard on the mercantile interest. The Holders of one species of property have thrown a disproportion of taxes on the holders of another species. The lesson we are to draw from the whole is that where a majority are united by a common sentiment, and have an opportunity, the rights of the minor party become insecure. In a Republican Gov^t the Majority if united have always an opportunity. The only remedy is to enlarge the sphere, & thereby divide the community into so great a number of interests & parties, that in the 1st place a majority will not be likely at the same moment to have a common interest separate from that of the whole or of the minority; and in the 2^d place, that in case they sh^d have such an interest, they may not be [1] apt to unite in the pursuit of it. It was incumbent on us then to try this remedy, and with that view to frame a republican system on such a scale & in such a form as will controul all the evils wch have been experienced.

Mr DICKENSON considered it as [2] essential that one branch of the Legislature sh^d be drawn immediately from the people; and as expedient that the other sh^d be chosen by the Legislatures of the States. This combination of the State Gov^{ts} with the national Gov^t was as politic as it was unavoidable. In the formation of the

---

[1] The word " so " is here inserted in the transcript.
[2] The word " as " is omitted in the transcript.

Senate we ought to carry it through such a refining process as will assimilate it as near as may be to the House of Lords in England. He repeated his warm eulogiums on the British Constitution. He was for a strong National Gov^t but for leaving the States a considerable agency in the System. The objection agst making the former dependent on the latter might be obviated by giving to the Senate an authority permanent & irrevocable for three, five or seven years. Being thus independent they will speak [1] & decide with becoming freedom.

Mr Read. Too much attachment is betrayed to the State Govern^{ts}. We must look beyond their continuance. A national Gov^t must soon of necessity swallow all of them [2] up. They will soon be reduced to the mere office of electing the National Senate. He was agst patching up the old federal System: he hoped the idea w^d be dismissed. It would be like putting new cloth on an old garment. The confederation was founded on temporary principles. It cannot last: it cannot be amended. If we do not establish a good Gov^t on new principles, we must either go to ruin, or have the work to do over again. The people at large are wrongly suspected of being averse to a Genl Gov^t The aversion lies among interested men who possess their confidence.

Mr Pierce was for an election by the people as to the 1st branch & by the States as to the 2^d branch; by which means the Citizens of the States w^d be represented both *individually* & *collectively*.

General Pinkney wished to have a good National Gov^t & at the same time to leave a considerable share of power in the States. An election of either branch by the people scattered as they are in many States, particularly in S. Carolina was totally impracticable. He differed from gentlemen who thought that a choice by the people w^d be a better guard agst bad measures, than by the Legislatures. A majority of the people in S. Carolina were notoriously for paper money as a legal tender; the Legislature had refused to make it a legal tender. The reason was that the latter had some sense of character and were restrained by that consideration. The State Legislatures also he said would be more jealous, & more ready to thwart the National Gov^t, if excluded from a participation in it. The Idea of abolishing these Legislatures w^d never go down.

Mr Wilson, would not have spoken again, but for what had fallen from Mr Read; namely, that the idea of preserving the State Gov^{ts} ought to be abandoned. He saw no incompatibility between the

---

[1] The word " check " is substituted in the transcript for " speak."
[2] The words " them all " are substituted in the transcript for " all of them."

National & State Gov^{ts} provided the latter were restrained to certain local purposes; nor any probability of their being devoured by the former. In all confederated Systems antient & modern the reverse had happened; the Generality being destroyed gradually by the usurpations of the parts composing it.

On the question for electing the 1st branch by the State Legislatures as moved by Mr Pinkney: it was negatived:

Mass. no. C^{t} ay. N. Y. no. N. J. ay. P^{a} no. Del. no. M^{d} no. V^{a} no. N. C. no. S. C. ay. Geo. no.[1]

Mr Wilson moved to reconsider the vote excluding the Judiciary from a share in the revision of the laws, and to add after " National Executive " the words " with a convenient number of the national Judiciary "; remarking the expediency of reinforcing the Executive with the influence of that Department.

Mr Madison 2^{ded} the motion. He observed that the great difficulty in rendering the Executive competent to its own defence arose from the nature of Republican Gov^{t} which could not give to an individual citizen that settled pre-eminence in the eyes of the rest, that weight of property, that personal interest agst betraying the national interest, which appertain to an hereditary magistrate. In a Republic personal merit alone could be the ground of political exaltation, but it would rarely happen that this merit would be so pre-eminent as to produce universal acquiescence. The Executive Magistrate would be envied & assailed by disappointed competitors: His firmness therefore w^{d} need support. He would not possess those great emoluments from his station, nor that permanent stake in the public interest which w^{d} place him out of the reach of foreign corruption: He would stand in need therefore of being controuled as well as supported. An association of the Judges in his revisionary function w^{d} both double the advantage and diminish the danger. It w^{d} also enable the Judiciary Department the better to defend itself agst Legislative encroachments. Two objections had been made 1st that the Judges ought not to be subject to the bias which a participation in the making of laws might give in the exposition of them. 2dly that the Judiciary Departm^{t} ought to be separate & distinct from the other great Departments. The 1st objection had some weight; but it was much diminished by reflecting that a small proportion of the laws coming in question before a Judge w^{d} be such wherein he had been consulted; that a small part of this proportion w^{d} be so am-

---

[1] In the transcript the vote reads " Connecticut, New Jersey, South Carolina, aye—3; Massachusetts, New York, Pennsylvania Delaware, Maryland, Virginia, North Carolina, Georgia, no—8."

biguous as to leave room for his prepossessions; and that but a few cases w:d probably arise in the life of a Judge under such ambiguous passages. How much good on the other hand w:d proceed from the perspicuity, the conciseness, and the systematic character w:ch the Code of laws w:d receive from the Judiciary talents. As to the 2:d objection, it either had no weight, or it applied with equal weight to the Executive & to the Judiciary revision of the laws. The maxim on which the objection was founded required a separation of the Executive as well as of [1] the Judiciary from the Legislature & from each other. There w:d in truth however be no improper mixture of these distinct powers in the present case. In England, whence the maxim itself had been drawn, the Executive had an absolute negative on the laws; and the supreme tribunal of Justice [the House of Lords] formed one of the other branches of the Legislature. In short whether the object of the revisionary power was to restrain the Legislature from encroaching on the other co-ordinate Departments, or on the rights of the people at large; or from passing laws unwise in their principle, or incorrect in their form, the utility of annexing the wisdom and weight of the Judiciary to the Executive seemed incontestable.

M: GERRY thought the Executive, whilst standing alone w:d be more impartial than when he c:d be covered by the sanction & seduced by the sophistry of the Judges.

M: KING. If the Unity of the Executive was preferred for the sake of responsibility, the policy of it is as applicable to the revisionary as to the Executive power.

M: PINKNEY had been at first in favor of joining the heads of the principal departm:ts the Secretary at War, of foreign affairs &— in the council of revision. He had however relinquished the idea from a consideration that these could be called in [2] by the Executive Magistrate whenever he pleased to consult them. He was opposed to an [3] introduction of the Judges into the business.

Col. MASON was for giving all possible weight to the revisionary institution. The Executive power ought to be well secured ag:st Legislative usurpations on it. The purse & the sword ought never to get into the same hands whether Legislative or Executive.

M: DICKENSON. Secrecy, vigor & despatch are not the principal properties req:d in the Executive. Important as these are, that of responsibility is more so, which can only be preserved;

---

[1] The word "of" is omitted in the transcript.
[2] The word "on" is substituted in the transcript for "in."
[3] The word "the" is substituted in the transcript for "an."

by leaving it singly to discharge its functions. He thought too a junction of the Judiciary to it, involved an improper mixture of powers.

M: WILSON remarked, that the responsibility required belonged to his Executive duties. The revisionary duty was an extraneous one, calculated for collateral purposes.

M: WILLIAMSON, was for substituting a clause requiring ⅔ for every effective act of the Legislature, in place of the revisionary provision.

On the question for joining the Judges to the Executive in the revisionary business, Mass. no. Cont ay. N. Y. ay. N. J. no. P: no. Del. no. M⁴ no. V: ay. N. C. no. S. C. no. Geo. no.[1]

M: PINKNEY gave notice that tomorrow he should move for the reconsideration of that clause in the sixth Resolution adopted by the Comm: which vests a negative in the National Legislature on the laws of the several States.

The Com: rose & the House adj⁴ to 11 OC.[2]

THURSDAY JUNE 7ᵀᴴ 1787 [3]—IN COMMITTEE OF THE WHOLE.

M: PINKNEY according to notice moved to reconsider the clause respecting the negative on State laws, which was agreed to and tomorrow for fixed [4] the purpose.

The Clause providing for y: appointment of the 2ᵈ branch of the national Legislature, having lain blank since the last vote on the mode of electing it, to wit, by the 1ˢᵗ branch, M: DICKENSON now moved " that the members of the 2ᵈ branch ought to be chosen by the individual Legislatures."

M: SHARMAN seconded the motion; observing that the particular States would thus become interested in supporting the national Governm: and that a due harmony between the two Governments would be maintained. He admitted that the two ought to have separate and distinct jurisdictions, but that they ought to have a mutual interest in supporting each other.

M: PINKNEY. If the small States should be allowed one Senator only, the number will be too great, there will be 80 at least.

---

[1] In the transcript the vote reads: " Connecticut, New York, Virginia, aye—3; Massachusetts, New Jersey, Pennsylvania, Delaware, Maryland, North Carolina, South Carolina, Georgia, no—8."
[2] The expression " to 11 OC " is omitted in the transcript.
[3] The year " 1787 " is omitted in the transcript.
[4] The words " for fixed " are corrected in the transcript to " fixed for."

M: DICKENSON had two reasons for his motion. 1.[1] because the sense of the States would be better collected through their Governments; than immediately from the people at large; 2.[1] because he wished the Senate to consist of the most distinguished characters, distinguished for their rank in life and their weight of property, and bearing as strong a likeness to the British House of Lords as possible; and he thought such characters more likely to be selected by the State Legislatures, than in any other mode. The greatness of the number was no objection with him. He hoped there would be 80 and twice 80. of them. If their number should be small, the popular branch could not be balanced by them. The legislature of a numerous people ought to be a numerous body.

M: WILLIAMSON, preferred a small number of Senators, but wished that each State should have at least one. He suggested 25 as a convenient number. The different modes of representation in the different branches, will serve as a mutual check.

M: BUTLER was anxious to know the ratio of representation before he gave any opinion.

M: WILSON. If we are to establish a national Government, that Government ought to flow from the people at large. If one branch of it should be chosen by the Legislatures, and the other by the people, the two branches will rest on different foundations, and dissensions will naturally arise between them. He wished the Senate to be elected by the people as well as the other branch, and the people might be divided into proper districts for the purpose &[2] moved to postpone the motion of M: Dickenson, in order to take up one of that import.

M: MORRIS 2ᵈᵉᵈ him.

M: READ proposed " that the Senate should be appointed by the Executive Magistrate out of a proper number of persons to be nominated by the individual legislatures." He said he thought it his duty, to speak his mind frankly. Gentlemen he hoped would not be alarmed at the idea. Nothing short of this approach towards a proper model of Government would answer the purpose, and he thought it best to come directly to the point at once.—His proposition was not seconded nor supported.

M: MADISON, if the motion [of Mr. Dickenson] should be agreed to, we must either depart from the doctrine of proportional representation; or admit into the Senate a very large number of mem-

---

[1] The figures " 1 " and " 2 " are changed to " First " and " secondly " in the transcript.
[2] The word " he " is here inserted in the transcript.

bers. The first is inadmissible, being evidently unjust. The second is inexpedient. The use of the Senate is to consist in its proceeding with more coolness, with more system, & with more wisdom, than the popular branch. Enlarge their number and you communicate to them the vices which they are meant to correct. He differed from M: D. who thought that the additional number would give additional weight to the body. On the contrary it appeared to him that their weight would be in an inverse ratio to their number.[1] The example of the Roman Tribunes was applicable. They lost their influence and power, in proportion as their number was augmented. The reason seemed to be obvious: They were appointed to take care of the popular interests & pretensions at Rome, because the people by reason of their numbers could not act in concert;[2] were liable to fall into factions among themselves, and to become a prey to their aristocratic adversaries. The more the representatives of the people therefore were multiplied, the more they partook of the infirmities of their constituents, the more liable they became to be divided among themselves either from their own indiscretions or the artifices of the opposite faction, and of course the less capable of fulfilling their trust. When the weight of a set of men depends merely on their personal characters; the greater the number the greater the weight. When it depends on the degree of political authority lodged in them the smaller the number the greater the weight. These considerations might perhaps be combined in the intended Senate; but the latter was the material one.

M: GERRY. 4 modes of appointing the Senate have been mentioned. 1.[3] by the 1st branch of the National Legislature. This would create a dependence contrary to the end proposed. 2.[3] by the National Executive. This is a stride towards monarchy that few will think of. 3.[3] by the people. The people have two great interests, the landed interest, and the commercial including the stockholders. To draw both branches from the people will leave no security to the latter interest; the people being chiefly composed of the landed interest, and erroneously supposing, that the other interests are adverse to it. 4[3] by the Individual Legislatures. The elections being carried thro' this refinement, will be most likely to provide some check in favor of the commercial interest agst the landed; without which

---

[1] The transcript uses the word "number" in the plural.
[2] The word "and" is here inserted in the transcript.
[3] The figures "1," "2," "3" and "4" are changed to "First," "Secondly," etc., in the transcript.

oppression will take place, and no free Gov! can last long where that is the case. He was therefore in favor of this last.

M! DICKENSON.* The preservation of the States in a certain degree of agency is indispensable. It will produce that collision between the different authorities which should be wished for in order to check each other. To attempt to abolish the States altogether, would degrade the Councils of our Country, would be impracticable, would be ruinous. He compared the proposed National System to the Solar System, in which the States were the planets, and ought to be left to move freely in their proper orbits. The Gentleman from P? [M! Wilson] wished he said to extinguish these planets. If the State Governments were excluded from all agency in the national one, and all power drawn from the people at large, the consequence would be that the national Gov! would move in the same direction as the State Gov!! now do, and would run into all the same mischiefs. The reform would only unite the 13 small streams into one great current pursuing the same course without any opposition whatever. He adhered to the opinion that the Senate ought to be composed of a large number, and that their influence from family weight & other causes would be increased thereby. He did not admit that the Tribunes lost their weight in proportion as their n? was augmented and gave a historical sketch of this institution. If the reasoning of [M! Madison] was good it would prove that the number of the Senate ought to be reduced below ten, the highest n? of the Tribunitial corps.

M! WILSON. The subject it must be owned is surrounded with doubts and difficulties. But we must surmount them. The British Governm! cannot be our model. We have no materials for a similar one. Our manners, our laws, the abolition of entails and of primogeniture, the whole genius of the people, are opposed to it. He did not see the danger of the States being devoured by the Nation! Gov! On the contrary, he wished to keep them from devouring the national Gov! He was not however for extinguishing these planets as was supposed by M! D.—neither did he on the other hand, believe that they would warm or enlighten the Sun. Within their proper orbits they must still be suffered to act for subordinate purposes for which their existence is made essential by the great extent of our Country. He could not comprehend in what manner the landed interest w? be rendered less predominant in the Senate, by an election through the medium of the Legislatures than by the people themselves. If

* It will throw light on this discussion to remark that an election by the State Legislatures involved a surrender of the principle insisted on by the large States & dreaded by the small ones, namely that of a proportional representation in the Senate. Such a rule w? make the body too numerous, as the smallest State must elect one member at least.

the Legislatures, as was now complained, sacrificed the commercial to the landed interest, what reason was there to expect such a choice from them as would defeat their own views. He was for an election by the people in large districts which w.ᵈ be most likely to obtain men of intelligence & uprightness; subdividing the districts only for the accomodation of voters.

M.ʳ MADISON could as little comprehend in what manner family weight, as desired by M.ʳ D. would be more certainly conveyed into the Senate through elections by the State Legislatures, than in some other modes. The true question was in what mode the best choice w.ᵈ be made? If an election by the people, or thro' any other channel than the State Legislatures promised as uncorrupt & impartial a preference of merit, there could surely be no necessity for an appointment by those Legislatures. Nor was it apparent that a more useful check would be derived thro' that channel than from the people thro' some other. The great evils complained of were that the State Legislatures run into schemes of paper money &c. whenever solicited by the people, & sometimes without even the sanction of the people. Their influence then, instead of checking a like propensity in the National Legislature, may be expected to promote it. Nothing can be more contradictory than to say that the Nat.ˡ Legislature with.ᵗ a proper check, will follow the example of the State Legislatures, & in the same breath, that the State Legislatures are the only proper check.

M.ʳ SHARMAN opposed elections by the people in districts, as not likely to produce such fit men as elections by the State Legislatures.

M.ʳ GERRY insisted that the commercial & monied interest w.ᵈ be more secure in the hands of the State Legislatures, than of the people at large. The former have more sense of character, and will be restrained by that from injustice. The people are for paper money when the Legislatures are ag.ˢᵗ it. In Mass.ᵗˢ the County Conventions had declared a wish for a *depreciating* paper that w.ᵈ sink itself. Besides, in some States there are two Branches in the Legislature, one of which is somewhat aristocratic. There w.ᵈ therefore be so far a better chance of refinement in the choice. There seemed, he thought to be three powerful objections ag.ˢᵗ elections by districts. 1.[1] it is impracticable; the people cannot be brought to one place for the purpose; and whether brought to the same place or not, numberless frauds w.ᵈ be unavoidable. 2.[1] small States forming part of the same district with a large one, or [2] large part of a large one, w.ᵈ have no chance of gaining an appointment for its citizens of merit. 3 [1] a new

---

[1] The figures " 1," " 2 " and " 3 " are changed to " First," " Secondly " and " Thirdly " in the transcript.

[2] The word " a " is here inserted in the transcript.

source of discord w.ª be opened between different parts of the same district.

M.ʳ PINKNEY thought the 2.ª branch ought to be permanent & independent, & that the members of it w.ª be rendered more so by receiving their appointment [1] from the State Legislatures. This mode w.ª avoid the rivalships & discontents incident to the election by districts. He was for dividing the States into three classes according to their respective sizes, & for allowing to the 1.ˢᵗ class three members— to the 2.ª two, & to the 3.ª one.

On the question for postponing M.ʳ Dickinson's motion referring the appointment of the Senate to the State Legislatures, in order to consider M.ʳ Wilson's for referring it to the people

Mass. no. Con.ᵗ no. N. Y. no. N. J. no. P.ª ay Del. no. M.ª no. V.ª no. N. C. no. S. C. no. Geo. no.[2]

Col. MASON. whatever power may be necessary for the Nat.ˡ Gov.ᵗ a certain portion must necessarily be left in [3] the States. It is impossible for one power to pervade the extreme parts of the U. S. so as to carry equal justice to them. The State Legislatures also ought to have some means of defending themselves ag.ˢᵗ encroachments of the Nat.ˡ Gov.ᵗ In every other department we have studiously endeavored to provide for its self-defence. Shall we leave the States alone unprovided with the means for this purpose? And what better means can we provide than the giving them some share in, or rather to make them a constituent part of, the Nat.ˡ Establishment. There is danger on both sides no doubt; but we have only seen the evils arising on the side of the State Gov.ᵗˢ Those on the other side remain to be displayed. The example of Cong.ˢ does not apply. Cong.ˢ had no power to carry their acts into execution as the Nat.ˡ Gov.ᵗ will have.

On M.ʳ DICKINSON's motion for an appointment of the Senate by the State-Legislatures.

Mass. ay. C.ᵗ ay. N. Y. ay. P.ª ay Del. ay. M.ᵈ ay. V.ª ay N. C. ay. S. C. ay. Geo. ay.[4]

M.ʳ GERRY gave notice that he w.ª tomorrow move for a reconsidera-

---

[1] The word "appointment" is used in the plural in the transcript.

[2] In the transcript the vote reads: "Pennsylvania, aye—1; Massachusetts, Connecticut, New York, New Jersey, Delaware, Maryland, Virginia, North Carolina, South Carolina, Georgia, no—10."

[3] The word "with" is substituted in the transcript for "in."

[4] In the transcript the vote reads: "Massachusetts, Connecticut, New York, Pennsylvania, Delaware, Maryland, Virginia, North Carolina, South Carolina, Georgia, aye—10."

tion of the mode of appointing the Nat! Executive in order to substitute an appointm! by the State Executives

The Committee rose & The House adj?

FRIDAY JUNE 8?ᵀᴴ IN COMMITTEE OF THE WHOLE.

On a reconsideration of the clause giving the Nat! Legislature a
negative on such laws of the States as might be contrary to the
articles of Union, or Treaties with foreign nations,

M? PINKNEY moved "that the National Legislature sh? have
authority to negative all laws which they sh? judge to be improper."
He urged that such a universality of the power was indispensably
necessary to render it effectual; that the States must be kept in due
subordination to the nation; that if the States were left to act of
themselves in any case, it w? be impossible to defend the national
prerogatives, however extensive they might be on paper; that the
acts of Congress had been defeated by this means; nor had foreign
treaties escaped repeated violations; that this universal negative was
in fact the corner stone of an efficient national Gov!; that under
the British Gov! the negative of the Crown had been found beneficial,
and the *States* are more one nation now, than the *Colonies* were then.

M? MADISON seconded the motion. He could not but regard an
indefinite power to negative legislative acts of the States as abso
lutely necessary to a perfect system. Experience had evinced a con.
stant tendency in the States to encroach on the federal authority;
to violate national Treaties; to infringe the rights & interests of each
other; to oppress the weaker party within their respective jurisdictions. A negative was the mildest expedient that could be devised
for preventing these mischiefs. The existence of such a check would
prevent attempts to commit them. Should no such precaution be
engrafted, the only remedy w? lie [1] in an appeal to coercion. Was
such a remedy eligible? was it practicable? Could the national resources, if exerted to the utmost enforce a national decree ag?ᵗ Mass!ˢ
abetted perhaps by several of her neighbours? It w? not be possible. A small proportion of the Community, in a compact situation,
acting on the defensive, and at one of its extremities might at any
time bid defiance to the National authority. Any Gov! for the U.
States formed on the supposed practicability of using force ag?ᵗ the

---

[1] The word " be " is substituted in the transcript for " lie."

unconstitutional proceedings of the States, w.ᵈ prove as visionary & fallacious as the Gov.ᵗ of Cong.ˢ The negative w.ᵈ render the use of force unnecessary. The States c.ᵈ of themselves then[1] pass no operative act, any more than one branch of a Legislature where there are two branches, can proceed without the other. But in order to give the negative this efficacy, it must extend to all cases. A discrimination w.ᵈ only be a fresh source of contention between the two authorities. In a word, to recur to the illustrations borrowed from the planetary system. This prerogative of the General Gov.ᵗ is the great pervading principle that must controul the centrifugal tendency of the States; which, without it, will continually fly out of their proper orbits and destroy the order & harmony of the political System.

M.ʳ WILLIAMSON was ag.ˢᵗ giving a power that might restrain the States from regulating their internal police.

M.ʳ GERRY c.ᵈ not see the extent of such a power, and was ag.ˢᵗ every power that was not necessary. He thought a remonstrance ag.ˢᵗ unreasonable acts of the States w.ᵈ reclaim[2] them. If it sh.ᵈ not force might be resorted to. He had no objection to authorize a negative to paper money and similar measures. When the confederation was depending before Congress, Massachussetts was then for inserting the power of emitting paper money am.ᵍ the exclusive powers of Congress. He observed that the proposed negative w.ᵈ extend to the regulations of the Militia, a matter on which the existence of a[3] State might depend. The Nat.ˡ Legislature with such a power may enslave the States. Such an idea as this will never be acceded to. It has never been suggested or conceived among the people. No speculative projector, and there are eno' of that character among us, in politics as well as in other things, has in any pamphlet or newspaper thrown out the idea. The States too have different interests and are ignorant of each other's interests. The negative therefore will be abused. New States too having separate views from the old States will never come into the Union. They may even be under some foreign influence; are they in such case to participate in the negative on the will of the other States?

M.ʳ SHERMAN thought the cases in which the negative ought to be exercised, might be defined. He wished the point might not be decided till a trial at least sh.ᵈ be made for that purpose

M.ʳ WILSON would not say what modifications of the proposed power might be practicable or expedient. But however novel it

---

[1] The word "then" is omitted in the transcript.
[2] The word "restrain" is substituted in the transcript for "reclaim."
[3] The word "the" is substituted in the transcript for "a."

might appear the principle of it when viewed with a close & steady eye, is right. There is no instance in which the laws say that the individual sh.ᵈ be bound in one case, & at liberty to judge whether he will obey or disobey in another. The cases are parallel. Abuses of the power over the individual person may happen as well as over the individual States. Federal liberty is to [1] States, what civil liberty, is to private individuals. And States are not more unwilling to purchase it, by the necessary concession of their political sovereignty, that [2] the savage is to purchase civil liberty by the surrender of his [3] personal sovereignty, which he enjoys in a State of nature. A definition of the cases in which the Negative should be exercised, is impracticable. A discretion must be left on one side or the other? will it not be most safely lodged on the side of the Nat.ˡ Gov.ᵗ? Among the first sentiments expressed in the first Cong.ˢ one was that Virg.ᵃ is no more, that Mas.ᵗˢ is no [4], that P.ᵃ is no more &c. We are now one nation of brethren. We must bury all local interests & distinctions. This language continued for some time. The tables at length began to turn. No sooner were the State Gov.ᵗˢ formed than their jealousy & ambition began to display themselves. Each endeavoured to cut a slice from the common loaf, to add to its own morsel, till at length the confederation became frittered down to the impotent condition in which it now stands. Review the progress of the articles of Confederation thro' Congress & compare the first & last draught of it. To correct its vices is the business of this convention. One of its vices is the want of an effectual controul in the whole over its parts. What danger is there that the whole will unnecessarily sacrifice a part? But reverse the case, and leave the whole at the mercy of each part, and will not the general interest be continually sacrificed to local interests?

M.ʳ DICKENSON deemed it impossible to draw a line between the cases proper & improper for the exercise of the negative. We must take our choice of two things. We must either subject the States to the danger of being injured by the power of the Nat.ˡ Gov.ᵗ or the latter to the danger of being injured by that of the States. He thought the danger greater from the States. To leave the power doubtful, would be opening another spring of discord, and he was for shutting as many of them as possible.

M.ʳ BEDFORD. In answer to his colleague's question where w.ᵈ be

---

[1] The word " the " is here inserted in the transcript.
[2] The word " that " is changed to " than " in the transcript.
[3] The word " the " is substituted in the transcript for " his."
[4] The word " more " is here inserted in the transcript.

the danger to the States from this power, would refer him to the smallness of his own State which may be injured at pleasure without redress. It was meant he found to strip the small States of their equal right of suffrage. In this case Delaware would have about ⅟₉₀ for its share in the General Councils, whilst Pᵃ & Vᵃ would possess ⅓ of the whole. Is there no difference of interests, no rivalship of commerce, of manufactures? Will not these large States crush the small ones whenever they stand in the way of their ambitious or interested views. This shews the impossibility of adopting such a system as that on the table, or any other founded on a change in the principle of representation. And after all, if a State does not obey the law of the new System, must not force be resorted to as the only ultimate remedy, in this as in any other system. It seems as if Pᵃ & Vᵃ by the conduct of their deputies wished to provide a system in which they would have an enormous & monstrous influence. Besides, How can it be thought that the proposed negative can be exercised? are the laws of the States to be suspended in the most urgent cases until they can be sent seven or eight hundred miles, and undergo the deliberations [1] of a body who may be incapable of Judging of them? Is the National Legislature too to sit continually in order to revise the laws of the States?

Mʳ MADISON observed that the difficulties which had been started were worthy of attention and ought to be answered before the question was put. The case of laws of urgent necessity must be provided for by some emanation of the power from the Natˡ Govᵗ into each State so far as to give a temporary assent at least. This was the practice in Royal Colonies before the Revolution and would not have been inconvenient, if the supreme power of negativing had been faithful to the American interest, and had possessed the necessary information. He supposed that the negative might be very properly lodged in the senate alone, and that the more numerous & expensive branch therefore might not be obliged to sit constantly.—He asked Mʳ B. what would be the consequence to the small States of a dissolution of the Union wᶜʰ seemed likely to happen if no effectual substitute was made for the defective System existing, and he did not conceive any effectual system could be substituted on any other basis than that of a proportional suffrage? If the large States possessed the avarice & ambition with which they were charged, would the small ones in their neighbourhood, be more secure when all controul of a Genˡ Govᵗ was withdrawn.

---

[1] The transcript uses the word " deliberations " in the singular.

M: BUTLER was vehement ag:t the Negative in the proposed extent, as cutting off all hope of equal justice to the distant States. The people there would not he was sure give it a hearing.

On the question for extending the negative power to all cases as propos:d by [M: P. & M: M—] Mass. ay. Con: no. N. Y. no. N. J. no. P: ay. Del. div:d M: Read & M: Dickenson ay. M: Bedford & M: Basset no. Mary:d no. V: ay. M: R. M: Mason no. M: Blair, Doc: M:C: M: M. ay. Gen:l W. not consulted. N. C. no. S. C. no. Geo. no.[1]

On motion of M: GERRY and M: KING tomorrow was assigned for reconsidering the mode of appointing the National Executive: the reconsideration being voted for by all the States except Connecticut & N. Carolina.

M: PINKNEY and M: RUTLIDGE moved to add to Resol:n 4.[2] agreed to by the Com:e the following, viz. " that the States be divided into three classes, the 1:st class to have 3 members, the 2:d two. & the 3:d one member each; that an estimate be taken of the comparative importance of each State at fixed periods, so as to ascertain the number of members they may from time to time be entitled to" The Committee then rose and the House adjourned.

SATURDAY JUNE 9:TH M:R LUTHER MARTIN FROM MARYLAND TOOK HIS
SEAT IN COMMITTEE OF THE WHOLE.

M: GERRY, according to previous notice given by him, moved " that the National Executive should be elected by the Executives of the States whose proportion of votes should be the same with that allowed to the States in the election of the Senate." If the appointm:t should be made by the Nat:l Legislature, it would lessen that independence of the Executive which ought to prevail, would give birth to intrigue and corruption between the Executive & Legislature previous to the election, and to partiality in the Executive afterwards to the friends who promoted him. Some other mode therefore appeared to him necessary. He proposed that of appointing by the State Executives as most analogous to the principle observed in elect-

---

[1] In the transcript the vote reads: " Massachusetts, Pennsylvania, Virginia, [Mr. Randolph and Mr. Mason, no; Mr. Blair, Doctor McClurg and Mr. Madison, aye; General Washington not consulted,] aye—3; Connecticut, New York, New Jersey, Maryland, North Carolina, South Carolina, Georgia, no—7; Delaware, divided, [Mr. Read and Mr. Dickinson, aye; Mr. Bedford and Mr. Basset, no)."

[2] The words " the fourth Resolution " are substituted in the transcript for " Resol:n 4."

ing the other branches of the Nat! Gov!; the first branch being chosen by the *people* of the States, & the 2ᵈ by the Legislatures of the States; he did not see any objection agˢᵗ letting the Executive be appointed by the Executives of the States. He supposed the Executives would be most likely to select the fittest men, and that it would be their interest to support the man of their own choice.

Mʳ RANDOLPH, urged strongly the inexpediency of Mʳ Gerry's mode of appointing the Nat! Executive. The confidence of the people would not be secured by it to the Nat! magistrate. The small States would lose all chance of an appointmᵗ from within themselves. Bad appointments would be made; the Executives of the States being little conversant with characters not within their own small spheres. The State Executives too notwithstanding their constitutional independence, being in fact dependent on the State Legislatures will generally be guided by the views of the latter, and prefer either favorites within the States, or such as it may be expected will be most partial to the interests of the State. A Nat! Executive thus chosen will not be likely to defend with becoming vigilance & firmness the National rights agˢᵗ State encroachments. Vacancies also must happen. How can these be filled? He could not suppose either that the Executives would feel the interest in supporting the Nat! Executive which had been imagined. They will not cherish the great Oak which is to reduce them to paltry shrubs.

On the question for referring the appointment of the Nat! Executive to the State Executives as propᵈ by Mʳ Gerry Massᵗˢ no. Conᵗ no. N. Y. no. N. J. no. Pᵃ no. Del. divᵈ Mᵈ no. Vᵃ no. S. C. no. Geo. no.[1]

Mʳ PATTERSON moves that the Committee resume the clause relating to the rule of suffrage in the Nat! Legislature.

Mʳ BREARLY seconds him. He was sorry he said that any question on this point was brought into view. It had been much agitated in Congˢ at the time of forming the Confederation, and was then rightly settled by allowing to each sovereign State an equal vote. Otherwise the smaller States must have been destroyed instead of being saved. The substitution of a ratio, he admitted carried fairness on the face of it; but on a deeper examination was unfair and unjust. Judging of the disparity of the States by the quota of Congˢ Virgᵃ would have 16 votes, and Georgia but one. A like proportion to the others will make the whole number ninity. There

---

[1] In the transcript the vote reads: "Massachusetts, Connecticut, New York, New Jersey, Pennsylvania, Maryland, Virginia, South Carolina, Georgia, no; Delaware divided."

will be 3. large states, and 10 small ones. The large States by which he meant Mass^{ts}. Pen^a. & Virg^a. will carry every thing before them. It had been admitted, and was known to him from facts within N. Jersey that where large & small counties were united into a district for electing representatives for the district, the large counties always carried their point, and Consequently that[1] the large States would do so. Virg^a. with her sixteen votes will be a solid column indeed, a formidable phalanx. While Georgie with her Solitary vote, and the other little States will be obliged to throw themselves constantly into the scale of some large one, in order to have any weight at all. He had come to the convention with a view of being as useful as he could in giving energy and stability to the federal Government. When the proposition for destroying the equality of votes came forward, he was astonished, he was alarmed. Is it fair then it will be asked that Georgia should have an equal vote with Virg^a? He would not say it was. What remedy then? One only, that a map of the U. S. be spread out, that all the existing boundaries be erased, and that a new partition of the whole be made into 13 equal parts.

M^r. PATTERSON considered the proposition for a proportional representation as striking at the existence of the lesser States. He w^d. premise however to an investigation of this question some remarks on the nature structure and powers of the Convention. The Convention he said was formed in pursuance of an Act of Cong^s. that this act was recited in several of the Commissions, particularly that of Mass^ts. which he required to be read: that the amendment of the confederacy was the object of all the laws and commissions on the subject; that the articles of the Confederation were therefore the proper basis of all the proceedings of the Convention.[2] We ought to keep within its limits, or we should be charged by our Constituents with usurpation, that the people of America were sharpsighted and not to be deceived. But the Commissions under which we acted were not only the measure of our power, they denoted also the sentiments of the States on the subject of our deliberation. The idea of a national Gov^t. as contradistinguished from a federal one, never entered into the mind of any of them, and to the public mind we must accomodate ourselves. We have no power to go beyond the federal scheme, and if we had the people are not ripe for any other. We must follow the people; the people will not follow us.—The *proposition* could not be maintained whether considered in reference to us as a nation, or as a confederacy. A confederacy supposes sov-

---

[1] The word "that" is omitted in the transcript.
[2] The word "that" is here inserted in the transcript.

ereignty in the members composing it & sovereignty supposes equality. If we are to be considered as a nation, all State distinctions must be abolished, the whole must be thrown into hotchpot, and when an equal division is made, then there may be fairly an equality of representation. He held up Virg? Mass?ᵗˢ & P? as the three large States, and the other ten as small ones; repeating the calculations of M? Brearly as to the disparity of votes which w? take place, and affirming that the small States would never agree to it. He said there was no more reason that a great individual State contributing much, should have more votes than a small one contributing little, than that a rich individual citizen should have more votes than an indigent one. If the rateable property of A was to that of B as 40 to 1, ought A for that reason to have 40 times as many votes as B. Such a principle would never be admitted, and if it were admitted would put B entirely at the mercy of A. As A. has more to be protected than B so he ought to contribute more for the common protection. The same may be said of a large State w? has more to be protected than a small one. Give the large States an influence in proportion to their magnitude, and what will be the consequence? Their ambition will be proportionally increased, and the small States will have every thing to fear. It was once proposed by Galloway & some others that America should be represented in the British Parl? and then be bound by its laws. America could not have been entitled to more than ⅓ of the n? of [1] Representatives which would fall to the share of G. B. Would American rights & interests have been safe under an authority thus constituted? It has been said that if a Nat? Gov? is to be formed so as to operate on the people and not on the States, the representatives ought to be drawn from the people. But why so? May not a Legislature filled by the State Legislatures operate on the people who chuse the State Legislatures? or may not a practicable coercion be found. He admitted that there was none such in the existing System.—He was attached strongly to the plan of the existing confederacy, in which the people chuse their Legislative representatives; and the Legislatures their federal representatives. No other amendments were wanting than to mark the orbits of the States with due precision, and provide for the use of coercion, which was the great point. He alluded to the hint thrown out heretofore by M? Wilson of the necessity to which the large States might be reduced of confederating among themselves, by a refusal of the others to concur. Let them unite if they please, but let them re-

---

[1] The words " n? of " are omitted in the transcript.

member that they have no authority to compel the others to unite. N. Jersey will never confederate on the plan before the Committee. She would be swallowed up. He had rather submit to a monarch, to a despot, than to such a fate. He would not only oppose the plan here but on his return home do every thing in his power to defeat it there.

Mͬ Wilson. hoped if the Confederacy should be dissolved, that a *majority*, that a *minority* of the States would unite for their safety. He entered elaborately into the defence of a proportional representation, stating for his first position that as all authority was derived from the people, equal numbers of people ought to have an equal nͦ of representatives, and different numbers of people different numbers of representatives. This principle had been improperly violated in the Confederation, owing to the urgent circumstances of the time. As to the case of A. & B, stated by Mͬ Patterson, he observed that in districts as large as the States, the number of people was the best measure of their comparative wealth. Whether therefore wealth or numbers were [1] to form the ratio it would be the same. Mͬ P. admitted persons, not property to be the measure of suffrage. Are not the Citizens of Penᵃ equal to those of N. Jersey? does it require 150 of the former to balance 50 of the latter? Representatives of different districts ought clearly to hold the same proportion to each other, as their respective Constituents hold to each other. If the small States will not confederate on this plan, Penᵃ & he presumed some other States, would not confederate on any other. We have been told that each State being sovereign, all are equal. So each man is naturally a sovereign over himself, and all men are therefore naturally equal. Can he retain this equality when he becomes a member of Civil Government? He can not. As little can a Sovereign State, when it becomes a member of a federal Governͭ If N. J. will not part with her Sovereignty it is in vain to talk of Govͭ A new partition of the States is desireable, but evidently & totally impracticable.

Mͬ Williamson, illustrated the eases by a comparison of the different States, to Counties of different sizes within the same State; observing that proportional representation was admitted to be just in the latter case, and could not therefore be fairly contested in the former.

The Question being about to be put Mͬ Patterson hoped that as

---

[1] The word "was" is substituted in the transcript for "were."

so much depended on it, it might be thought best to postpone the decision till tomorrow, which was done nem. con.

The Com? rose & the House adjourned.

MONDAY. JUNE 11ᵀᴴ Mᴿ ABRAHAM BALDWIN FROM GEORGIA TOOK HIS SEAT. IN COMMITTEE OF THE WHOLE.

The clause concerning the rule of suffrage in the nat! Legislature postponed on Saturday was resumed.

Mᴿ SHARMAN proposed that the proportion of suffrage in the 1ˢᵗ branch should be according to the respective numbers of free inhabitants; and that in the second branch or Senate, each State should have one vote and no more. He said as the States would remain possessed of certain individual rights, each State ought to be able to protect itself: otherwise a few large States will rule the rest. The House of Lords in England he observed had certain particular rights under the Constitution, and hence they have an equal vote with the House of Commons that they may be able to defend their rights.

Mᴿ RUTLIDGE proposed that the proportion of suffrage in the 1ˢᵗ branch should be according to the quotas of contribution. The justice of this rule he said could not be contested. Mᴿ BUTLER urged the same idea: adding that money was power; and that the States ought to have weight in the Gov! in proportion to their wealth.

Mᴿ KING & Mᴿ WILSON,* in order to bring the question to a point moved " that the right of suffrage in the first branch of the national Legislature ought not to be according [1] the rule established in the articles of Confederation, but according to some equitable ratio of representation." The clause so far as it related to suffrage in the first branch was postponed in order to consider this motion.

Mᴿ DICKENSON contended for the *actual* contributions of the States as the rule of their representation & suffrage in the first branch. By thus connecting the interest [2] of the States with their duty, the latter would be sure to be performed.

Mᴿ KING remarked that it was uncertain what mode might be used in levying a national revenue; but that it was probable, imposts would be one source of it. If the *actual* contributions were to be the rule the non-importing States, as Con! & N. Jersey, wᵈ be in a

---

* In the printed Journal Mr. Rutlidge is named as the seconder of the motion.

[1] The word " to " is here inserted in the transcript.
[2] The transcript uses the word " interest " in the plural.

bad situation indeed. It might so happen that they w.^d have no representation. This situation of particular States had been always one powerful argument in favor of the 5 Per C.^t impost.

The question being ab.^t to be put Doc.^r FRANKLIN s.^d he had thrown his ideas of the matter on a paper wch Mr Wilson read to the Committee in the words following—

Mr CHAIRMAN

It has given me great pleasure to observe that till this point, the proportion of representation, came before us, our debates were carried on with great coolness & temper. If any thing of a contrary kind, has on this occasion appeared, I hope it will not be repeated; for we are sent here to *consult*, not to *contend*, with each other; and declarations of a fixed opinion, and of determined resolution, never to change it, neither enlighten nor convince us. Positiveness and warmth on one side, naturally beget their like on the other; and tend to create and augment discord & division in a great concern, wherein harmony & Union are extremely necessary to give weight to our Councils, and render them effectual in promoting & securing the common good.

I must own that I was originally of opinion it would be better if every member of Congress, or our national Council, were to consider himself rather as a representative of the whole, than as an Agent for the interests of a particular State; in which case the proportion of members for each State would be of less consequence, & it would not be very material whether they voted by States or individually. But as I find this is not to be expected, I now think the[+] number of Representatives should bear some proportion to the number of the Represented; and that the decisions sh.^d be by the majority of members, not by the majority of [1] States. This is objected to from an apprehension that the greater States would then swallow up the smaller. I do not at present clearly see what advantage the greater States could propose to themselves by swallowing [2] the smaller, and therefore do not apprehend they would attempt it. I recollect that in the beginning of this Century, when the Union was proposed of the two Kingdoms, England & Scotland, the Scotch Patriots were full of fears, that unless they had an equal number of Representatives in Parliament, they should be ruined by the superiority of the English. They finally agreed however that the different proportions of importance in the Union, of the two Nations should

---

[1] The word " the " is here inserted in the transcript.
[2] The word " up " is here inserted in the transcript.

be attended to, whereby they were to have only forty members in the House of Commons, and only sixteen in the House of Lords; A very great inferiority of numbers! And yet to this day I do not recollect that any thing has been done in the Parliament of Great Britain to the prejudice of Scotland; and whoever looks over the lists of public officers, Civil & military of that nation will find I believe that the North Britons enjoy at least their full proportion of emolument.

But, Sir, in the present mode of voting by States, it is equally in the power of the lesser States to swallow up the greater; and this is mathematically demonstrable. Suppose for example, that 7 smaller States had each 3 members in the House, and the 6 larger to have one with another 6 members; and that upon a question, two members of each smaller State should be in the affirmative and one in the Negative; they will [1] make

Affirmatives .... 14 ...... Negatives   7
And that all the larger States
    should be unanimously in
    the Negative, they would
    make ....Negatives 36
                                              ——
    In all   43

It is then apparent that the 14 carry the question against the 43. and the minority overpowers the majority, contrary to the common practice of Assemblies in all Countries and Ages.

The greater States Sir are naturally as unwilling to have their property left in the disposition of the smaller, as the smaller are to have theirs in the disposition of the greater. An honorable gentleman has, to avoid this difficulty, hinted a proposition of equalizing the States. It appears to me an equitable one, and I should, for my own part, not be against such a measure, if it might be found practicable. Formerly, indeed, when almost every province had a different Constitution, some with greater others with fewer privileges, it was of importance to the borderers when their boundaries were contested, whether by running the division lines, they were placed on one side or the other. At present when such differences are done away, it is less material. The Interest of a State is made up of the interests of its individual members. If they are not injured, the State is not injured. Small States are more easily well & hap-

---

[1] The word "will" is changed to "would" in the transcript.

pily governed than large ones. If therefore in such an equal division, it should be found necessary to diminish Pennsylvania, I should not be averse to the giving a part of it to N. Jersey, and another to Delaware. But as there would probably be considerable difficulties in adjusting such a division; and however equally made at first, it would be continually varying by the augmentation of inhabitants in some States, and their [1] fixed proportion in others; and thence frequent occasion for new divisions, I beg leave to propose for the consideration of the Committee another mode, which appears to me, to be as equitable, more easily carried into practice, and more permanent in its nature.

Let the weakest State say what proportion of money or force it is able and willing to furnish for the general purposes of the Union.

Let all the others oblige themselves to furnish each an equal proportion.

The whole of these joint supplies to be absolutely in the disposition of Congress.

The Congress in this case to be composed of an equal number of Delegates from each State.

And their decisions to be by the Majority of individual members voting.

If these joint and equal supplies should on particular occasions not be sufficient, Let Congress make requisitions on the richer and more powerful States for farther aids, to be voluntarily afforded, leaving to each State the right of considering the necessity and utility of the aid desired, and of giving more or less as it should be found proper.

This mode is not new, it was formerly practised with success by the British Government with respect to Ireland and the Colonies. We sometimes gave even more than they expected, or thought just to accept; and in the last war carried on while we were united, they gave us back in 5 years a million Sterling. We should probably have continued such voluntary contributions, whenever the occasions appeared to require them for the common good of the Empire. It was not till they chose to force us, and to deprive us of the merit and pleasure of voluntary contributions that we refused & resisted. Those [2] contributions however were to be disposed of at the pleasure of a Government in which we had no representative. I am therefore

---

[1] The word " more " is in the Franklin manuscript.
[2] The word " These " is substituted in the transcript for " Those."

persuaded, that they will not be refused to one in which the Representation shall be equal

My learned Colleague [M: Wilson] has already mentioned that the present method of voting by States, was submitted to originally by Congress, under a conviction of its impropriety, inequality, and injustice. This appears in the words of their Resolution. It is of Sep: 6. 1774. The words are

"Resolved that in determining questions in this Cong? each Colony or province shall have one vote: The Cong? not being possessed of or at present able to procure materials for ascertaining the importance of each Colony."

On the question for agreeing to M: Kings and M: Wilsons motion it passed in the affirmative

Mass'? ay. C? ay. N. Y. no. N. J. no. P? ay. Del. no. M? div?. V? ay. N. C. ay. S. C. ay. Geo. ay.[1]

It was then moved by M: RUTLIDGE 2?ed by M: BUTLER to add to the words " equitable ratio of representation " at the end of the motion just agreed to, the words " according to the quotas of contribution." On motion of M: WILSON seconded by M: C. PINCKNEY, this was postponed; in order to add, after, after the words "equitable ratio of representation " the words following " in proportion to the whole number of white & other free Citizens & inhabitants of every age sex & condition including those bound to servitude for a term of years and three fifths of all other persons not comprehended in the foregoing description, except Indians not paying taxes, in each State," this being the rule in the Act of Congress agreed to by eleven States, for apportioning quotas of revenue on the States, and requiring a Census only every 5-7, or 10 years.

M: GERRY thought property not the rule of representation. Why then sh? the blacks, who were property in the South, be in the rule of representation more than the Cattle & horses of the North.

On the question,—Mass: Con: N. Y. Pen: Mary? Virg? N. C. S. C. & Geo: were in the affirmative:[2] N. J. & Del: in the negative.[2]

M: SHARMAN moved that a question be taken whether each State shall have one vote in the 2? branch. Every thing he said depended on this. The smaller States would never agree to the plan on any

---

[1] In the transcript the vote reads: " Massachusetts, Connecticut, Pennsylvania, Virginia, North Carolina, South Carolina, Georgia, aye—7; New York, New Jersey, Delaware, no—3; Maryland divided."
[2] In place of the phrase " were in the affirmative " the transcript substitutes " aye—9; " and instead of " in the negative " the expression " no—2 " is used.

other principle than an equality of suffrage in this branch. M.ʳ ELSWORTH seconded the motion. On the question for allowing each State one vote in the 2ᵈ branch.

Mass.ᵗˢ no. Con.ᵗ ay. N. Y. ay. N. J. ay. P.ᵃ no. Del. ay. M.ᵈ ay. V.ᵃ no. N. C. no. S. C. no. Geo. no.[1]

M.ʳ WILSON & M.ʳ HAMILTON moved that the right of suffrage in the 2ᵈ branch ought to be according to the same rule as in the 1.ˢᵗ branch. On this question for making the ratio of representation the same in the 2ᵈ as in the 1.ˢᵗ branch it passed in the affirmative: Mass.ᵗˢ ay. Con.ᵗ no. N. Y. no. N. J. no. P.ᵃ ay. Del. no. M.ᵈ no. V.ᵃ ay. N. C. ay. S. C. ay. Geo. ay.[2]

Resol: 11,[3] for guarantying Republican Gov.ᵗ & territory to each State being considered: the words " or partition " were, on motion of M.ʳ MADISON, added, after the words " voluntary junction: "

Mas. N. Y. P. V.ᵃ \N. C. S. C. G. ay[4] Con: N. J. Del. M.ᵈ no.[4]

M.ʳ READ disliked the idea of guarantying territory. It abetted the idea of distinct States w.ᶜʰ would be a perpetual source of discord. There can be no cure for this evil but in doing away States altogether and uniting them all into one great Society.

Alterations having been made in the Resolution, making it read "that a republican Constitution & its existing laws ought to be guaranteed to each State by the U. States " the whole was agreed to nem. con.

Resolution 13,[5] for amending the national Constitution hereafter without consent of [6] Nat.ˡ Legislature being considered, several members did not see the necessity of the Resolution at all, nor the propriety of making the consent of the Nat.ˡ Legisl. unnecessary.

Col. MASON urged the necessity of such a provision. The plan now to be formed will certainly be defective, as the Confederation has been found on trial to be. Amendments therefore will be necessary, and it will be better to provide for them, in an easy, regular and Constitutional way than to trust to chance and violence. It

---

[1] In the transcript the vote reads: " Connecticut, New York, New Jersey, Delaware, Maryland, aye—5; Massachusetts, Pennsylvania, Virginia, North Carolina, South Carolina, Georgia, no—6."

[2] In the transcript the vote reads: " Massachusetts, Pennsylvania, Virginia, North Carolina, South Carolina, Georgia, aye; Connecticut, New York, New Jersey, Delaware, Maryland, no."

[3] The words " The eleventh Resolution " are substituted in the transcript for " Resol: 11."

[4] The figures " 7 " and " 4 " are inserted in the transcript after " ay" and " no," respectively.

[5] The words " The thirteenth Resolution " are substituted in the transcript for " Resolution 13."

[6] The word " the " is here inserted in the transcript.

would be improper to require the consent of the Nat! Legislature, because they may abuse their power, and refuse their consent [1] on that very account. The opportunity for such an abuse, may be the fault of the Constitution calling for amendm!

M� RANDOLPH enforced these arguments.

The words, "without requiring the consent of the Nat! Legislature" were postponed. The other provision in the clause passed nem. con.

Resolution 14,[2] requiring oaths from the members of the State Gov!ts to observe the Nat! Constitution & laws, being considered.

M� SHARMAN opposed it as unnecessarily intruding into the State jurisdictions.

M� RANDOLPH considered it as [3] necessary to prevent that competition between the National Constitution & laws & those of the particular States, which had already been felt. The officers of the States are already under oath to the States. To preserve a due impartiality they ought to be equally bound to the Nat! Gov! The Nat! authority needs every support we can give it. The Executive & Judiciary of the States, notwithstanding their nominal independence on the State Legislatures are in fact, so dependent on them, that unless they be brought under some tie to the Nat! System, they will always lean too much to the State systems, whenever a contest arises between the two.

M⁰speaker GERRY did not like the clause. He thought there was as much reason for requiring an oath of fidelity to the States, from Nat! officers, as vice. versa.

M⁰speaker LUTHER MARTIN moved to strike out the words requiring such an oath from the State officers, viz "within the several States" observing that if the new oath should be contrary to that already taken by them it would be improper; if coincident the oaths already taken will be sufficient.

On the question for striking out as proposed by M⁰ L. Martin

Mass!ts no. Con! ay. N. Y. no. N. J. ay. P⁰ no. Del. ay. M⁰ ay. V⁰ no. N. C. no. S. C. no. Geo. no.[4]

Question on [5] whole Resolution as proposed by M⁰ Randolph;

---

[1] The word "assent" is substituted in the transcript for "consent."

[2] The words "The fourteenth Resolution" are substituted in the transcript for "Resolution 14."

[3] The word "as" is crossed out in the transcript.

[4] In the transcript the vote reads: "Connecticut, New Jersey, Delaware, Maryland, aye—4; Massachusetts, New York, Pennsylvania, Virginia, North Carolina, South Carolina, Georgia, no—7."

[5] The word "the" is here inserted in the transcript.

Mass^{ts} ay. Con^t no. N. Y. no. N. J. no. P^a ay. Del. no. M^d
no. V^a ay. N. C. ay. S. C. ay. Geo. ay.[1]
  [2] Com^e rose & [2] House adj^d

Teusday June 12TH in Committee of [2] whole

The Question [3] taken on Resolution 15,[4] to wit, referring the new
system to the people of the [5] States for ratification it passed in the
affirmative: Mass^{ts} ay. Con^t no. N. Y. no. N. J. no. P^a * ay. Del.
div^d M^d div^d V^a ay. N. C. ay. S. C. ay. Geo. ay.[6]

Mr Sharman & Mr Elseworth moved to fill the blank left in the
4th Resolution for the periods of electing the members of the first
branch with the words, "every year." Mr Sharman observing that
he did it in order to bring on some question.

Mr Rutlidge proposed "every two years."

Mr Jennifer prop^d "every three years," observing that the too
great frequency of elections rendered the people indifferent to them,
and made the best men unwilling to engage in so precarious a service.

Mr Madison seconded the motion for three years. Instability is
one of the great vices of our republics, to be remedied. Three years
will be necessary, in a Government so extensive, for members to form
any knowledge of the various interests of the States to which they
do not belong, and of which they can know but little from the situation and affairs of their own. One year will be almost consumed in
preparing for and travelling to & from the seat of national business.

Mr Gerry. The people of New England will never give up the
point of annual elections, they know of the transition made in England from triennial to septennial elections, and will consider such an
innovation here as the prelude to a like usurpation. He considered
annual elections as the only defence of the people agst tyranny. He
was as much agst a triennial House as agst a hereditary Executive.

---

* Pennsylvania omitted in the printed Journal. The vote is there entered
as of June 11th.

---

[1] In the transcript the vote reads: "Massachusetts, Pennsylvania, Virginia,
North Carolina, South Carolina, Georgia, aye—6; Connecticut, New York, New
Jersey, Delaware, Maryland, no—5."
[2] The word "the" is here inserted in the transcript.
[3] The word "was" is here inserted in the transcript.
[4] The words "the fifteenth Resolution" are substituted in the transcript
for "Resolution 15."
[5] The word "United" is here inserted in the transcript.
[6] In the transcript the vote reads: "Massachusetts, Pennsylvania,* Virginia,
North Carolina, South Carolina, Georgia, aye—6; Connecticut, New York, New
Jersey, no—3; Delaware, Maryland, divided."

M� MADISON, observed that if the opinions of the people were to be our guide, it w⁴ be difficult to say what course we ought to take. No member of the Convention could say what the opinions of his Constituents were at this time; much less could he say what they would think if possessed of the information & lights possessed by the members here; & still less what would be their way of thinking 6 or 12 months hence. We ought to consider what was right & necessary in itself for the attainment of a proper Governm⁶ A plan adjusted to this idea will recommend itself—The respectability of this convention will give weight to their recommendation of it. Experience will be constantly urging the adoption of it, and all the most enlightened & respectable citizens will be its advocates. Should we fall short of the necessary & proper point, this influential class of Citizens will be turned against the plan, and little support in opposition to them can be gained to it from the unreflecting multitude.

M⁶ GERRY repeated his opinion that it was necessary to consider what the people would approve. This had been the policy of all Legislators. If the reasoning of M⁶ Madison were just, and we supposed a limited Monarchy the best form in itself, we ought to recommend it, tho' the genius of the people was decidedly adverse to it, and having no hereditary distinctions among us, we were destitute of the essential materials for such an innovation.

On the question for [1] triennial election of the 1ˢᵗ branch

Mass. no. [M⁶ King ay.] M⁶ Ghorum wavering. Con⁴ no. N. Y. ay. N. J. ay. P⁶ ay. Del. ay. M⁴ ay. V⁶ ay. N. C. no. S. C. no. Geo. ay.[2]

The words requiring members of yᵉ 1ˢᵗ branch to be of the age of   years were struck out Maryland alone, no. The words "*liberal compensation for members*" being consid⁴ M⁶ MADISON moves to insert the words, "*& fixt.*" He observed that it would be improper to leave the members of the Nat¹ legislature to be provided for by the State Legisl⁶ because it would create an improper dependence; and to leave them to regulate their own wages, was an indecent thing, and might in time prove a dangerous one. He thought wheat or some other article of which the average price throughout a reasonable period preceding might be settled in some convenient mode, would form a proper standard.

Col. MASON seconded the motion; adding that it would be im-

---

[1] The word "the" is here inserted in the transcript.
[2] In the transcript the vote reads: "New York, New Jersey, Pennsylvania, Delaware, Maryland, Virginia, Georgia, aye—7; Massachusetts [Mr. King, aye, Mr. Gorham, wavering] Connecticut, North Carolina, South Carolina, no—4."

proper for other reasons to leave the wages to be regulated by the States. 1.[1] the different States would make different provision for their representatives, and an inequality would be felt among them, whereas he thought they ought to be in all respects equal. 2.[1] the parsimony of the States might reduce the provision so low that as had already happened in choosing delegates to Congress, the question would be not who were most fit to be chosen, but who were most willing to serve.

On the question for inserting the words "and fixt."

Mass[ts] no. Con[t] no. N. Y. ay. N. J. ay. P[a] ay. Del. ay. M[d] ay. V[a] ay. N. C. ay. S. C. no. Geo. ay.[2]

Doct[r] FRANKLYN said he approved of the amendment just made for rendering the salaries as fixed as possible; but disliked the word "*liberal.*" he would prefer the word moderate if it was necessary to substitute any other. He remarked the tendency of abuses in every case, to grow of themselves when once begun, and related very pleasantly the progression in ecclesiastical benefices, from the first departure from the gratuitous provision for the Apostles, to the establishment of the papal system. The word "liberal" was struck out nem. con.

On the motion of M[r] PIERCE, that the wages should be paid out of the National Treasury, Mass[ts] ay. C[t] no. N. Y. no. N. J. ay. P[a] ay. Del. ay. M[d] ay. V[a] ay. N. C. ay. S. C. no. G. ay.[3]

Question on the clause relating to term of service & compensation of [4] 1st branch

Mass[ts] ay. C[t] no. N. Y no. N. J. ay. P[a] ay. Del. ay. M[d] ay. V[a] ay. N. C. ay. S. C. no. Geo. ay.[5]

On a question for striking out the "*ineligibility* of members of [4]Nat[l] Legis: to *State offices.*"

Mass[ts] div[d] Con[t] ay. N. Y. ay. N. J. no. P[a] no. Del. no. M[d] div[d] V[a] no. N. C. ay. S. C. ay. Geo. no[6]

---

[1] The figures "1" and "2" are changed to "First" and "Secondly" in the transcript.

[2] In the transcript the vote reads: New York, New Jersey, Pennsylvania, Delaware, Maryland, Virginia, North Carolina, Georgia, aye—8; Massachusetts, Connecticut, South Carolina, no—3."

[3] In the transcript the vote reads: "Massachusetts, New Jersey, Pennsylvania, Delaware, Maryland, Virginia, North Carolina, Georgia, aye—8; Connecticut, New York, South Carolina, no—3."

[4] The word "the" is here inserted in the transcript.

[5] In the transcript the vote reads: "Massachusetts, New Jersey, Pennsylvania, Delaware, Maryland, Virginia, North Carolina, Georgia, aye—8; Connecticut, New York, South Carolina, no—3."

[6] In the transcript the vote reads: "Connecticut, New York, North Carolina, South Carolina, aye—4; New Jersey, Pennsylvania, Delaware, Virginia, Georgia, no—5; Massachusetts, Maryland, divided."

On the question for agreeing to the clause as amended.

Mass⁺ ay. Con⁺ no. N. Y. ay. N. J. ay. P⁺ ay. Del. ay M⁴ ay. V⁺ ay. N. C. ay. S. C. ay. Geo. ay.[1]

On a question for making Members of [2] Nat! legislature *ineligible* to any office under the Nat! Gov⁺ for the term of 3 years after ceasing to be members.

Mass⁺ no. Con⁺ no. N. Y. no. N. J. no. P⁺ no. Del. no. M⁴ ay V⁺ no. N C. no. S. C. no. Geo. no.[3]

On the question for such ineligibility for one year

Mass⁺ ay. C⁺ ay. N. Y. no. N. J. ay. P⁺ ay. Del. ay. M⁴ div⁴ V⁺ ay. N. C. ay. S. C. ay. Geo. no.[4]

On [2] question moved by M⁺ PINCKNEY for striking out "incapable of re-election into [2] 1⁺ᵗ branch of [2] Nat! Legisl. for   years, and subject to recall" ag⁴ to nem. con.

On [2] question for striking out from Resol: 5 [5] the words requiring members of the senatorial branch to be of the age of   years at least

Mass⁺ no. Con⁺ ay. N. Y. no. N. J. ay. P⁺ ay. Del. no. M⁴ no. V⁺ no. N. C. div⁴ S. C. no. Geo. div⁴ [6]

On the question for filling the blank with 30 years as the qualification; it was agreed to.

Mass⁺ ay. Con⁺ no. N. Y. ay N. J. no. P⁺ ay Del. no M⁴ ay V⁺ ay N. C. ay S. C. ay Geo. no [7]

M⁺ SPAIGHT moved to fill the blank for the duration of the appointm⁺ to the 2⁴ branch of the National Legislature with the words "7 years.

M⁺ SHERMAN, thought 7 years too long. He grounded his opposition he said on the principle that if they did their duty well, they would be reelected. And if they acted amiss, an earlier opportunity

---

[1] In the transcript the vote reads: "Massachusetts, New York, New Jersey, Pennsylvania, Delaware, Maryland, Virginia, North Carolina, South Carolina, Georgia, aye—10; Connecticut, no—1."

[2] The word "the" is here inserted in the transcript.

[3] In the transcript the vote reads: "Maryland, aye—1; Massachusetts, Connecticut, New York, New Jersey, Pennsylvania, Delaware, Virginia, North Carolina, South Carolina, Georgia, no—10."

[4] In the transcript the vote reads: "Massachusetts, Connecticut, New Jersey, Pennsylvania, Delaware, Virginia, North Carolina, South Carolina, aye—8; New York, Georgia, no—2; Maryland, divided."

[5] The words "the fifth Resolution" are substituted in the transcript for "Resol: 5."

[6] In the transcript the vote reads: "Connecticut, New Jersey, Pennsylvania, aye—3; Massachusetts, New York, Delaware, Maryland, Virginia, South Carolina, no—6; North Carolina, Georgia, divided."

[7] In the transcript the vote reads: "Massachusetts, New York, Pennsylvania, Maryland, Virginia, North Carolina, South Carolina, aye—7; Connecticut, New Jersey, Delaware, Georgia, no—4."

should be allowed for getting rid of them.   He preferred 5 years which w.^{d} be between the terms of [1] 1.st branch & of the executive

Mr PIERCE proposed 3 years.   7 years would raise an alarm. Great mischiefs had [2] arisen in England from their septennial act which was reprobated by most of their patriotic Statesmen.

Mr RANDOLPH was for the term of 7 years.   The democratic licentiousness of the State Legislatures proved the necessity of a firm Senate.   The object of this 2.^{d} branch is to controul the democratic branch of the Nat^l Legislature.   If it be not a firm body, the other branch being more numerous, and coming immediately from the people, will overwhelm it.   The Senate of Maryland constituted on like principles had been scarcely able to stem the popular torrent. No mischief can be apprehended, as the concurrence of the other branch, and in some measure, of the Executive, will in all cases be necessary.   A firmness & independence may be the more necessary also in this branch, as it ought to guard the Constitution agst encroachments of the Executive who will be apt to form combinations with the demagogues of the popular branch.

Mr MADISON, considered 7 years as a term by no means too long. What we wished was to give to the Gov^t that stability which was every where called for, and which the Enemies of the Republican form alledged to be inconsistent with its nature.   He was not afraid of giving too much stability by the term of Seven years.   His fear was that the popular branch would still be too great an overmatch for it. It was to be much lamented that we had so little direct experience to guide us.   The Constitution of Maryland was the only one that bore any analogy to this part of the plan.   In no instance had the Senate of Mary^d created just suspicions of danger from it.   In some instances perhaps it may have erred by yielding to the H. of Delegates. In every instance of their opposition to the measures of the H. of D. they had had with them the suffrages of the most enlightened and impartial people of the other States as well as of their own.   In the States where the Senates were chosen in the same manner as the other branches, of the Legislature, and held their seats for 4 years, the institution was found to be no check whatever agst the instabilities of the other branches.   He conceived it to be of great importance that a stable & firm Gov^t organized in the republican form should be held out to the people.   If this be not done, and the people be left to judge of this species of Gov^t by ye operations of the defective systems under which they now live, it is much to be feared

---

[1] The word " the " is here inserted in the transcript.
[2] The word " have " is substituted in the transcript for " had."

the time is not distant when, in universal disgust, they will renounce the blessing which they have purchased at so dear a rate, and be ready for any change that may be proposed to them.

On the question for " seven years " as the term for the 2ᵈ branch Massᵗˢ divided (Mʳ King, Mʳ Ghorum ay—Mʳ Gerry, Mʳ Strong, no) Conⁿ no. N. Y. divᵈ N. J. ay. Pᵃ ay Del. ay. Mᵈ ay. Vᵃ ay. N. C. ay. S. C. ay. Geo. ay.¹

Mʳ BUTLER & Mʳ RUTLIDGE proposed that the members of the 2ᵈ branch should be entitled to no salary or compensation for their services On the question,*

Massᵗˢ divᵈ Conⁿ ay. N. Y. no. N. J. no. P. no. Del. ay. Mᵈ no. Vᵃ no. N. C. no. S. C. ay. Geo. no.³

It was then moved & agreed that the clauses respecting the stipends & ineligibility of the 2ᵈ branch be the same as, of the 1ˢᵗ branch: Con: disagreeing to the ineligibility.

It was moved & 2ᵈᵉᵈ to alter Resol: 9.⁴ so as to read " that the jurisdiction of the supreme tribunal shall be to hear & determine in the dernier resort, all piracies, felonies &c."

It was moved & 2ᵈᵉᵈ to strike out " all piracies & felonies on the high seas," which was agreed to.

It was moved & agreed to strike out " all captures from an enemy."

It was moved & agreed to strike out " other States " and insert " two distinct States of the Union "

It was moved & agreed to postpone the consideration of Resolution 9,⁴ relating to the Judiciary:

The Comᵉ then rose & the House adjourned

WEDNESDAY JUNE 13. IN COMMITTEE OF THE WHOLE

Resol: 9 ⁴ being resumed

The latter parts of the clause relating to the jurisdiction of the

---

* [It is probable yᵉ votes here turned chiefly on the idea that if the salaries were not here provided for, the members would be paid by their respective States]
This note for the bottom margin.³

---

¹ In the transcript the vote reads: " New Jersey, Pennsylvania, Delaware, Maryland, Virginia, North Carolina, South Carolina, Georgia, aye—8; Connecticut, no—1; Massachusetts [Mr. Gorham and Mr. King, aye; Mr. Gerry and Mr. Strong, no] New York, divided."
² Madison's direction is omitted in the transcript.
³ In the transcript the vote reads: " Connecticut, Delaware, South Carolina, aye—3; New York, New Jersey, Pennsylvania, Maryland, Virginia, North Carolina, Georgia, no—7; Massachusetts, divided."
⁴ The words " the ninth Resolution " are substituted in the transcript for " Resol: 9."

Nati! tribunals, was struck out nem. con in order to leave full room for their organization.

M! RANDOLPH & M! MADISON, then moved the following resolution respecting a National Judiciary, viz "that the jurisdiction of the National Judiciary shall extend to cases, which respect the collection of the national revenue, impeachments of any national officers, and questions which involve the national peace and harmony " which was agreed to.

M! PINKNEY & M! SHERMAN moved to insert after the words " one supreme tribunal " the words " the Judges of which to be appointed by the national Legislature."

M! MADISON, objected to an app! by the whole Legislature. Many of them were[1] incompetent Judges of the requisite qualifications. They were too much influenced by their partialities. The candidate who was present, who had displayed a talent for business in the legislative field, who had perhaps assisted ignorant members in business of their own, or of their Constituents, or used other winning means, would without any of the essential qualifications for an expositor of the laws prevail over a competitor not having these recommendations, but possessed of every necessary accomplishment. He proposed that the appointment should be made by the Senate, which as a less numerous & more select body, would be more competent judges, and which was sufficiently numerous to justify such a confidence in them.

M! SHARMAN & M! PINKNEY withdrew their motion, and the app! by the Senate was ag! to nem. con.

M! GERRY. moved to restrain the Senatorial branch from originating money bills. The other branch was more immediately the representatives of the people, and it was a maxim that the people ought to hold the purse-strings. If the Senate should be allowed to originate such bills, they w! repeat the experiment, till chance should furnish a sett of representatives in the other branch who will fall into their snares.

M! BUTLER saw no reason for such a discrimination. We were always following the British Constitution when the reason of it did not apply. There was no analogy between the H. of Lords and the body proposed to be established. If the Senate should be degraded by any such discriminations, the best men would be apt to decline serving in it in favor of the other branch. And it will lead the latter into the practice of tacking other clauses to money bills.

M! MADISON observed that the Commentators on the Brit: Const:

---

[1] The word " are " is substituted in the transcript for " were."

had not yet agreed on the reason of the restriction on the H. of L. in money bills. Certain it was there could be no similar reason in the case before us. The Senate would be the representatives of the people as well as the 1ˢᵗ branch. If they sᵈ have any dangerous influence over it, they would easily prevail on some member of the latter to originate the bill they wished to be passed. As the Senate would be generally a more capable sett of men, it wᵈ be wrong to disable them from any preparation of the business, especially of that which was most important, and in our republics, worse prepared than any other. The Gentleman in pursuance of his principle ought to carry the restraint to the *amendment*, as well as the originating of money bills, since, an addition of a given sum wᵈ be equivalent to a distinct proposition of it.

Mͬ KING differed from Mͬ GERRY, and concurred in the objections to the proposition.

Mͬ READ favored the proposition, but would not extend the restraint to the case of amendments.

Mͬ PINKNEY thinks the question premature. If the Senate shᵈ be formed on the *same* proportional representation as it stands at present, they sᵈ have equal power, otherwise if a different principle sᵈ be introduced.

Mͬ SHERMAN. As both branches must concur, there can be no danger whichever way the Senate [1] be formed. We establish two branches in order to get more wisdom, which is particularly needed in the finance business—The Senate bear their share of the taxes, and are also the representatives of the people. What a man does by another, he does by himself is a maxim. In Conͭ both branches can originate in all cases, and it has been found safe & convenient. Whatever might have been the reason of the rule as to The H. of Lords, it is clear that no good arises from it now even there.

Genͤ PINKNEY. This distinction prevails in S. C. & has been a source of pernicious disputes between yͤ 2 branches. The Constitution is now evaded, by informal schedules of amendments handed from yͤ Senate to the other House.

Mͬ WILLIAMSON wishes for a question chiefly to prevent re-discussion. The restriction will have one advantage, it will oblige some member in [2] lower branch to move, & people can then mark him.

On the question for excepting money bills as propᵈ by Mͬ Gerry,

---

[1] The word "may" is here inserted in the transcript.
[2] The word "the" is here inserted in the transcript.

Mass. no. Con� no. N. Y. ay. N. J. no. Del. ay. M͎ no. V͎ ay. N. C. no. S. C. no. Geo. no.[1]

[2] Committee rose & M͎ GHORUM made report, which was postponed till tomorrow, to give an opportunity for other plans to be proposed. The report was in the words following:

REPORT OF THE COMMITTEE OF WHOLE ON M͎ RANDOLPH'S PROPOSITIONS [3]

1. Res͎ that it is the opinion of this Committee that a National Governm͎ ought to be established, consisting of a supreme Legislative, Executive & Judiciary.

2. Resol͎ that the National Legislature ought to consist of two branches.

3. Res͎ that the members of the first branch of the National Legislature ought to be elected by the people of the several States for the term of three years, to receive fixed Stipends by which they may be compensated for the devotion of their time to [2] public service, to be paid out of the National Treasury: to be ineligible to any office established by a particular State, or under the authority of the U. States, (except those peculiarly belonging to the functions of the first branch), during the term of service, and under the national Government for the space of one year after its expiration.

4. Res͎ that the members of the second branch of the Nat͎ Legislature ought to be chosen by the individual Legislatures, to be of the age of 30 years at least, to hold their offices for a term sufficient to ensure their independency,[4] namely, seven years, to receive fixed stipends by which they may be compensated for the devotion of their time to [2] public service to be paid out of the National Treasury; to be ineligible to any office established by a particular State, or under the authority of the U. States, (except those peculiarly belonging to the functions of the second branch) during the term of service, and under the Nat͎ Gov͎ for the space of one year after its expiration.

5. Res͎ that each branch ought to possess the right of originating Acts

6. Res͎ that the Nat͎ Legislature ought to be empowered to enjoy the Legislative rights vested in Cong͎ by the Confederation, and moreover to legislate in all cases to which the separate States are incompetent; or in which the harmony of the U. S. may be interrupted by the exercise of individual legislation; to negative all laws passed by the several States contravening in the opinion of the National Legislature the articles of Union, or any treaties subsisting under the authority of the Union.

---

[1] In the transcript the vote reads: "New York, Delaware, Virginia, aye—3; Massachusetts, Connecticut, New Jersey, Maryland, North Carolina, South Carolina, Georgia no—7."

[2] The word "the" is here inserted in the transcript.

[3] This heading is omitted in the transcript.

[4] The word "independency" is changed to "independence" in the transcript.

7. Res^d that the rights of suffrage in the 1.st branch of the National Legislature, ought not to be according to the rule established in the articles of confederation but according to some equitable ratio of representation, namely, in proportion to the whole number of white & other free citizens & inhabitants, of every age sex and condition, including those bound to servitude for a term of years, & three fifths of all other persons, not comprehended in the foregoing description, except Indians not paying taxes in each State:

8. Resolved that the right of suffrage in the 2^d branch of the National Legislature ought to be according to the rule established for the first.

9. Resolved that a National Executive be instituted to consist of a single person, to be chosen by the Nati^l Legislature for the term of seven years, with power to carry into execution the national laws, to appoint to offices in cases not otherwise provided for—to be ineligible a second time, & to be removeable on impeachment and conviction of malpractices or neglect of duty—to receive a fixed stipend by which he may be compensated for the devotion of his time to [1] public service to be paid out of the national Treasury.

10. Resol^d that the Nat^l Executive shall have a right to negative any Legislative Act, which shall not be afterwards passed unless [2] by two thirds of each branch of the National Legislature.

11. Resol^d that a Nat^l Judiciary be established, to consist of one supreme tribunal, the Judges of which to [3] be appointed by the 2^d branch of the Nat^l Legislature, to hold their offices during good behaviour, & to receive punctually at stated times a fixed compensation for their services, in which no increase or diminution shall be made, so as to affect the persons actually in office at the time of such increase or diminution.

12. Resol^d that the Nat^l Legislature be empowered to appoint inferior Tribunals.

13. Res^d that the jurisdiction of the Nat^l Judiciary shall extend to all cases which respect the collection of the Nat^l revenue, impeachments of any Nat^l Officers, and questions which involve the national peace & harmony.

14. Res^d that provision ought to be made for the admission of States lawfully arising within the limits of the U. States, whether from a voluntary junction of Government & territory or otherwise, with the consent of a number of voices in the Nat^l Legislature less than the whole.

15. Res^d that provision ought to be made for the continuance of Congress and their authorities and privileges untill a given day after the reform of the articles of Union shall be adopted and for the completion of all their engagements.

16. Res^d that a Republican Constitution & its existing laws ought to be guaranteed to each State by the U. States.

---

[1] The word "the" is here inserted in the transcript.
[2] The word "unless" is omitted in the transcript.
[3] The word "shall" is substituted in the transcript for "to."

17. Res.^d that provision ought to be made for the amendment of the Articles of Union whensoever it shall seem necessary.

18. Res.^d that the Legislative, Executive & Judiciary powers within the several States ought to be bound by oath to support the articles of Union.

19. Res.^d that the amendments which shall be offered to the confederation by the Convention ought at a proper time or times after the approbation of Cong.^s to be submitted to an Assembly or Assemblies recommended by the several Legislatures to be expressly chosen by the people to consider and decide thereon.

THURSDAY JUNE 14. IN CONVENTION [1]

Mr PATTERSON, observed to the Convention that it was the wish of several deputations, particularly that of N. Jersey, that further time might be allowed them to contemplate the plan reported from the Committee of the Whole, and to digest one purely federal, and contradistinguished from the reported plan. He said they hoped to have such an one ready by tomorrow to be laid before the Convention: And the Convention adjourned that leisure might be given for the purpose.

FRIDAY JUNE 15.TH 1787.[2]

[3] Mr PATTERSON, laid before the Convention the plan which he said several of the deputations wished to be substituted in place of that proposed by Mr Randolph. After some little discussion of the most proper mode of giving it a fair deliberation it was agreed that it should be referred to a Committee of the whole, and that in order to place the two plans in due comparison, the other should be recommitted. At the earnest desire [4] of Mr Lansing & some other gentlemen, it was also agreed that the Convention should not go into Committee of the whole on the subject till tomorrow, by which delay the friends of the plan proposed by Mr Patterson w.^d be better prepared to explain & support it, and all would have an opportu.^y of taking copies.*

[* this plan had been concerted among the deputations or members thereof, from Con.^t N. Y. N. J. Del. and perhaps Mr Martin from Mary.^d who made with

---

[1] The words " In Convention " are crossed out in the transcript.
[2] The year " 1787 " is omitted in the transcript.
[3] The words " In Convention " are here inserted in the transcript.
[4] The word " request " is substituted in the transcript for " desire."

The propositions from N. Jersey moved by M: Patterson were in the words following.

1. Res? that the articles of Confederation ought to be so revised, corrected & enlarged, as to render the federal Constitution adequate to the exigencies of Government, & the preservation of the Union.

2. Res? that in addition to the powers vested in the U. States in Congress, by the present existing articles of Confederation, they be authorized to pass acts for raising a revenue, by levying a duty or duties on all goods or merchandizes of foreign growth or manufacture, imported into any part of the U. States, by Stamps on paper, vellum or parchment, and by a postage on all letters or packages passing through the general post-office, to be applied to such federal purposes as they shall deem proper & expedient; to make rules & regulations for the collection thereof; and the same from time to time, to alter & amend in such manner as they shall think proper: to pass Acts for the regulation of trade & commerce as well with foreign nations as with each other: provided that all punishments, fines, forfeitures & penalties to be incurred for contravening such acts rules and regulations shall be adjudged by the Common law Judiciaries of the State in which any offence contrary to the true intent & meaning of such Acts rules & regulations shall have been committed or perpetrated, with liberty of commencing in the first instance all suits & prosecutions for that purpose in the superior common law Judiciary in such State, subject nevertheless, for the correction of all errors, both in law & fact in rendering Judgment, to an appeal to the Judiciary of the U. States.

3. Res? that whenever requisitions shall be necessary, instead of the rule for making requisitions mentioned in the articles of Confederation, the United States in Cong: be authorized to make such requisitions in proportion to the whole number of white & other free citizens & inhabitants of every age sex and condition including those bound to servitude for a term of years & three fifths of all other

them a common cause [1] on different principles. Cont: & N. Y. were ag:t a departure from the principle of the Confederation, wishing rather to add a few new powers to Cong: than to substitute, a National Gov: The States of N. J. & Del. were opposed to a National Gov: because its patrons considered a proportional representation of the States as the basis of it. The eagourness displayed by the members opposed to a Nat: Gov: from these different motives began now to produce serious anxiety for the result of the Convention. M: Dickenson said to M: Madison—You see the consequence of pushing things too far. Some of the members from the small States wish for two branches in the General Legislature, and are friends to a good National Government; but we would sooner submit to a foreign power, than submit to be deprived of an equality of suffrage,[2] in both branches of the legislature, and thereby be thrown under the domination of the large States.]
   * The note in brackets for the margin.[3]

---

[1] The word "though" is here inserted in the transcript.
[2] The phrase "of an equality of suffrage" is transposed so that the transcript reads "deprived, in both branches of the legislature of an equality of suffrage, and thereby" . . .
[3] Madison's direction is omitted in the transcript.

persons not comprehended in the foregoing description, except Indians not paying taxes; that if such requisitions be not complied with, in the time specified therein, to direct the collection thereof in the non complying States & for that purpose to devise and pass acts directing & authorizing the same; provided that none of the powers hereby vested in the U. States in Cong: shall be exercised without the consent of at least   States, and in that proportion if the number of Confederated States should hereafter be increased or diminished.

4. Res⁴ that the U. States in Cong⁵ be authorized to elect a federal Executive to consist of   persons, to continue in office for the term of   years, to receive punctually at stated times a fixed compensation for their services, in which no increase or diminution shall be made so as to affect the persons composing the Executive at the time of such increase or diminution, to be paid out of the federal treasury; to be incapable of holding any other office or appointment during their time of service and for   years thereafter; to be ineligible a second time, & removeable by Cong⁵ on application by a majority of the Executives of the several States; that the Executives [1] besides their general authority to execute the federal acts ought to appoint all federal officers not otherwise provided for, & to direct all military operations; provided that none of the persons composing the federal Executive shall on any occasion take command of any troops, so as personally to conduct any [2] enterprise as General or in other capacity.

5. Res⁴ that a federal Judiciary be established to consist of a supreme Tribunal the Judges of which to be appointed by the Executive, & to hold their offices during good behaviour, to receive punctually at stated times a fixed compensation for their services in which no increase or diminution shall be made, so as to affect the persons actually in office at the time of such increase or diminution; that the Judiciary so established shall have authority to hear & determine in the first instance on all impeachments of federal officers, & by way of appeal in the dernier resort in all cases touching the rights of Ambassadors, in all cases of captures from an enemy, in all cases of piracies & felonies on the high Seas, in all cases in which foreigners may be interested, in the construction of any treaty or treaties, or which may arise on any of the Acts for [3] regulation of trade, or the collection of the federal Revenue: that none of the Judiciary shall during the time they remain in office be capable of receiving or holding any other office or appointment during their time [4] of service, or for   thereafter.

6. Res⁴ that all Acts of the U. States in Cong⁵ made by virtue & in pursuance of the powers hereby & by the articles of Confederation vested in them, and all Treaties made & ratified under the authority of the U. States shall be the supreme law of the respective

---

[1] The transcript uses the word "Executives" in the singular.
[2] The word "military" is here inserted in the transcript.
[3] The word "the" is here inserted in the transcript.
[4] The word "term" is substituted in the transcript for "time."

States so far forth as those Acts or Treaties shall relate to the said States or their Citizens, and that the Judiciary of the several States shall be bound thereby in their decisions, any thing in the respective laws of the Individual States to the contrary notwithstanding; and that if any State, or any body of men in any State shall oppose or prevent y⁰ carrying into execution such acts or treaties, the federal Executive shall be authorized to call forth y⁰ power of the Confederated States, or so much thereof as may be necessary to enforce and compel an obedience to such Acts, or an observance of such Treaties.

7. Res⁰ that provision be made for the admission of new States into the Union.

8. Res⁰ ¹ the rule for naturalization ought to be the same in every State.

9. Res⁰ that a Citizen of one State committing an offence in another State of the Union, shall be deemed guilty of the same offence as if it had been committed by a Citizen of the State in which the offence was committed.*

Adjourned.

Saturday June 16. In Committee of the whole on ² Resolutions proposᴰ by Mᴿ P. & Mᴿ R

Mᴿ Lansing called for the reading of the 1ˢᵗ resolution of each plan, which he considered as involving principles directly in contrast; that of Mᴿ Patterson says he sustains the sovereignty of the respective States, that of Mᴿ Randolph distroys it: the latter requires a negative on all the laws of the particular States; the former, only certain general powers for the general good. The plan of Mᴿ R. in short absorbs all power except what may be exercised in the little local matters of the States which are not objects worthy of the supreme cognizance. He grounded his preference of Mᴿ P.'s plan, chiefly on two objections agᵗ ³ that of Mᴿ R. 1.⁴ want of power in the Convention to discuss & propose it. 2⁴ the improbability of its being

---

* This copy of Mᴿ Patterson's propositions varies in a few clauses from that in the printed Journal furnished from the papers of Mᴿ Brearley a Colleague of Mᴿ Patterson. A confidence is felt, notwithstanding, in its accuracy. That the copy in the Journal is not entirely correct is shewn by the ensuing speech of Mᴿ Wilson [June 16] in which he refers to the mode of removing the Executive by impeachment & conviction as a feature in the Virgᵃ plan forming one of its contrasts to that of Mᴿ Patterson, which proposed a removal on the application of a majority of the Executives of the States. In the copy printed in the Journal, the two modes are combined in the same clause; whether through inadvertence, or as a contemplated amendment does not appear.

¹ The word "that" is here inserted in the transcript.
² The word "the" is here inserted in the transcript.
³ The word "to" is substituted in the transcript for "agᵗ"
⁴ The figures "1" and "2" are changed to "first" and "secondly" in the transcript.

adopted. 1. He was decidedly of opinion that the power of the Convention was restrained to amendments of a federal nature, and having for their basis the Confederacy in being. The Act of Congress The tenor of the Acts of the States, the Commissions produced by the several deputations all proved this. And this limitation of the power to an amendment of the Confederacy, marked the opinion of the States, that it was unnecessary & improper to go farther. He was sure that this was the case with his State. N. York would never have concurred in sending deputies to the convention, if she had supposed the deliberations were to turn on a consolidation of the States, and a National Government.

2. was it probable that the States would adopt & ratify a scheme, which they had never authorized us to propose? and which so far exceeded what they regarded as sufficient? We see by their several Acts particularly in relation to the plan of revenue proposed by Cong. in 1783, not authorized by the Articles of Confederation, what were the ideas they then entertained. Can so great a change be supposed to have already taken place. To rely on any change which is hereafter to take place in the sentiments of the people would be trusting to too great an uncertainty. We know only what their present sentiments are. And it is in vain to propose what will not accord with these. The States will never feel a sufficient confidence in a general Government to give it a negative on their laws. The Scheme is itself totally novel. There is no parallel to it to be found. The authority of Congress is familiar to the people, and an augmentation of the powers of Congress will be readily approved by them.

M⠂ PATTERSON, said as he had on a former occasion given his sentiments on the plan proposed by M⠂ R. he would now avoiding repetition as much as possible give his reasons in favor of that proposed by himself. He preferred it because it accorded 1.[1] with the powers of the Convention, 2 [1] with the sentiments of the people. If the confederacy was radically wrong, let us return to our States, and obtain larger powers, not assume them of ourselves. I came here not to speak my own sentiments, but the sentiments of those who sent me. Our object is not such a Governm⠄ as may be best in itself, but such a one as our Constituents have authorized us to prepare, and as they will approve. If we argue the matter on the supposition that no Confederacy at present exists, it can not be denied that all the

---

[1] The figures " 1 " and " 2 " are changed to " first " and " secondly " in the transcript.

States stand on the footing of equal sovereignty. All therefore must concur before any can be bound. If a proportional representation be right, why do we not vote so here? If we argue on the fact that a federal compact actually exists, and consult the articles of it we still find an equal Sovereignty to be the basis of it. He reads the 5th art: of [1] Confederation giving each State a vote—& the 13th declaring that no alteration shall be made without unanimous consent. This is the nature of all treaties. What is unanimously done, must be unanimously undone. It was observed [by Mr Wilson] that the larger States gave up the point, not because it was right, but because the circumstances of the moment urged the concession. Be it so. Are they for that reason at liberty to take it back. Can the donor resume his gift without the consent of the donee. This doctrine may be convenient, but it is a doctrine that will sacrifice the lesser States. The large States acceded readily to the confederacy. It was the small ones that came in reluctantly and slowly. N. Jersey & Maryland were the two last, the former objecting to the want of power in Congress over trade: both of them to the want of power to appropriate the vacant territory to the benefit of the whole.—If the sovereignty of the States is to be maintained, the Representatives must be drawn immediately from the States, not from the people: and we have no power to vary the idea of equal sovereignty. The only expedient that will cure the difficulty, is that of throwing the States into Hotchpot. To say that this is impracticable, will not make it so. Let it be tried, and we shall see whether the Citizens of Mass^{ts} Pen^a & V^a accede to it. It will be objected that Coercion will be impracticable. But will it be more so in one plan than the other? Its efficacy will depend on the quantum of power collected, not on its being drawn from the States, or from the individuals; and according to his plan it may be exerted on individuals as well as according [2] that of Mr R. A distinct executive & Judiciary also were equally provided by his plan. It is urged that two branches in the Legislature are necessary. Why? for the purpose of a check. But the reason of [3] the precaution is not applicable to this case. Within a particular State, where party heats prevail, such a check may be necessary. In such a body as Congress it is less necessary, and besides, the delegations of the different States are checks on each other. Do the people at large complain of Cong^s? No, what they wish is that Cong^s may have more power. If the power now proposed be not eno',

---

[1] The word "the" is here inserted in the transcript.
[2] The word "to" is here inserted in the transcript.
[3] The word "for" is substituted in the transcript for "of."

the people hereafter will make additions to it.   With proper powers Cong. will act with more energy & wisdom than the proposed Nat! Legislature; being fewer in number, and more secreted & refined by the mode of election.   The plan of M. R. will also be enormously expensive.   Allowing Georgia & Del. two representatives each in the popular branch the aggregate number of that branch will be 180. Add to it half as many for the other branch and you have 270. members coming once at least a year from the most distant as well as the most central parts of the republic.   In the present deranged state of our finances can so expensive a system be seriously thought of?   By enlarging the powers of Cong. the greatest part of this expence will be saved, and all purposes will be answered.   At least a trial ought to be made.

M. WILSON entered into a contrast of the principal points of the two plans so far he said as there had been time to examine the one last proposed.   These points were 1. in the Virg. plan there are 2 & in some degree 3 branches in the Legislature: in the plan from N. J. there is to be a *single* legislature only—2. Representation of the people at large is the basis of the [1] one:—the State Legislatures, the pillars of the other—3. proportional representation prevails in one; —equality of suffrage in the other—4. A single Executive Magistrate is at the head of the one:—a plurality is held out in the other.—5. in the one the [2] majority of the people of the U. S. must prevail:—in the other a minority may prevail.   6. the Nat! Legislature is to make laws in all cases to which the separate States are incompetent &-:— in place of this Cong. are to have additional power in a few cases only—7. A negative on the laws of the States:—in place of this coertion to be substituted—8. The Executive to be removeable on impeachment & conviction;—in one plan: in the other to be remove-able at the instance of [3] majority of the Executives of the States— 9. Revision of the laws provided for in one:—no such check in the other—10. inferior national tribunals in one:—none such in the other. 11.   In y. one jurisdiction of Nat! tribunals to extend &c—; an appellate jurisdiction only allowed in the other.   12. Here the juris-diction is to extend to all cases affecting the Nation! peace & har-mony: there, a few cases only are marked out.   13. finally y. ratifica-tion is in this to be by the people themselves:—in that by the legis-lative authorities according to the 13 art: of [4] Confederation.

---

[1] The word "the" is omitted in the transcript.
[2] The word "a" is substituted in the transcript for "the."
[3] The word "a" is here inserted in the transcript.
[4] The word "the" is here inserted in the transcript.

With regard to the *power of the Convention,* he conceived himself authorized to *conclude nothing,* but to be at liberty to *propose any thing.* In this particular he felt himself perfectly indifferent to the two plans.

With *regard to the sentiments of the people,* he conceived it difficult to know precisely what they are. Those of the particular circle in which one moved, were commonly mistaken for the general voice. He could not persuade himself that the State Gov^{ts.} & Sovereignties were so much the idols of the people, nor a Nat! Gov! so obnoxious to them, as some supposed. Why s^d a Nat! Gov! be unpopular? Has it less dignity? will each Citizen enjoy under it less liberty or protection? Will a Citizen of *Delaware* be degraded by becoming a Citizen of the *United States?* [1] Where do the people look at present for relief from the evils of which they complain? Is it from an internal reform of their Gov^{ts.}? no, Sir. It is from the Nat! Councils that relief is expected. For these reasons he did not fear, that the people would not follow us into a national Gov! and it will be a further recommendation of Mr R.'s plan that it is to be submitted to *them,* and not to the *Legislatures,* for ratification.

proceeding now to the 1st point on which he had contrasted the two plans, he observed that anxious as he was for some augmentation of the federal powers, it would be with extreme reluctance indeed that he could ever consent to give powers to Cong^s he had two reasons either of wch was sufficient. 1.[2] Cong^s as a Legislative body does not stand on the people. 2.[2] it is a *single* body. 1. He would not repeat the remarks he had formerly made on the principles of Representation. he would only say that an inequality in it, has ever been a poison contaminating every branch of Gov! In G. Britain where this poison has had a full operation, the security of private rights is owing entirely to the purity of Her tribunals of Justice, the Judges of which are neither appointed nor paid, by a venal Parliament. The political liberty of that Nation, owing to the inequality of representation is at the mercy of its rulers. He means not to insinuate that there is any parallel between the situation of that Country & ours at present. But it is a lesson we ought not to disregard, that the smallest bodies in G. B. are notoriously the most corrupt. Every other source of influence must also be stronger in small than [3] large bodies of men. When Lord Chesterfield had told us that one of the Dutch provinces

---

[1] The transcript does not italicize the word "States."
[2] The figures "1" and "2" are changed to "first" and "secondly" in the transcript.
[3] The word "in" is here inserted in the transcript.

had been seduced into the views of France, he need not have added, that it was not Holland, but one of the *smallest* of them.   There are facts among ourselves which are known to all.   Passing over others, he [1] will only remark that the *Impost*, so anxiously wished for by the public was defeated not by any of the *larger* States in the Union.   2. *Congress is a single Legislature.*   Despotism comes on Mankind in different Shapes, sometimes in an Executive, sometimes in a Military, one.   Is there no danger of a Legislative despotism? Theory & practice both proclaim it.   If the Legislative authority be not restrained, there can be neither liberty nor stability; and it can only be restrained by dividing it within itself, into distinct and independent branches.   In a single House there is no check, but the inadequate one, of the virtue & good sense of those who compose it.

On another great point, the contrast was equally favorable to the plan reported by the Committee of the whole.   It vested the Executive powers in a single Magistrate.   The plan of N. Jersey, vested them in a plurality.   In order to controul the Legislative authority, you must divide it.   In order to controul the Executive you must unite it.   One man will be more responsible than three. Three will contend among themselves till one becomes the master of his colleagues.   In the triumvirates of Rome first Cæsar, then Augustus, are witnesses of this truth.   The Kings of Sparta, & the Consuls of Rome prove also the factious consequences of dividing the Executive Magistracy.   Having already taken up so much time he w⁴ not he s⁴ proceed to any of the otłfer points.   Those on which he had dwelt, are sufficient of themselves: and on a decision of them, the fate of the others will depend.

M⁛ Pinkney, the whole comes to this, as he conceived.   Give N. Jersey an equal vote, and she will dismiss her scruples, and concur in the Nati! system.   He thought the Convention authorized to go any length in recommending, which they found necessary to remedy the evils which produced this Convention.

M⁛ Elseworth proposed as a more distinctive form of collecting the mind of the Committee on the subject, "that the Legislative power of the U. S. should remain in Cong⁵" This was not seconded, though it seemed better calculated for the purpose than the 1ˢᵗ proposition of M⁛ Patterson in place of which M⁛ E. wished to substitute it.

M⁛ Randolph, was not scrupulous on the point of power.   When the salvation of the Republic was at stake, it would be treason to

---

[1] The word " we " is substituted in the transcript for " he."

our trust, not to propose what we found necessary. He painted in strong colours, the imbecility of the existing Confederacy, & the danger of delaying a substantial reform. In answer to the objection drawn from the sense of our Constituents as denoted by their acts relating to the Convention and the objects of their deliberation, he observed that as each State acted separately in the case, it would have been indecent for it to have charged the existing Constitution with all the vices which it might have perceived in it. The first State that set on foot this experiment would not have been justified in going so far, ignorant as it was of the opinion of others, and sensible as it must have been of the uncertainty of a successful issue to the experiment. There are certainly seasons [1] of a peculiar nature where the ordinary cautions must be dispensed with; and this is certainly one of them. He w^d not as far as depended on him leave any thing that seemed necessary, undone. The present moment is favorable, and is probably the last that will offer.

The true question is whether we shall adhere to the federal plan, or introduce the national plan. The insufficiency of the former has been fully displayed by the trial already made. There are but two modes, by which the end of a Genl Gov^t can be attained: the 1st is [2] by coercion as proposed by Mr P.s plan 2.[3] by real legislation as prop^d by the other plan. Coercion he pronounced to be *impracticable, expensive, cruel to individuals*. It tended also to habituate the instruments of it to shed the blood & riot in the spoils of their fellow Citizens, and consequently trained them up for the service of ambition. We must resort therefore to a National [4] *Legislation over individuals*, for which Cong^s are unfit. To vest such power in them, would be blending the Legislative with the Executive, contrary to the rec^d maxim on this subject: If the Union of these powers heretofore in Cong^s has been safe, it has been owing to the general impotency of that body. Cong^s are moreover not elected by the people, but by the Legislatures who retain even a power of recall. They have therefore no will of their own, they are a mere diplomatic body, and are always obsequious to the views of the States, who are always encroaching on the authority of the U. States. A provision for harmony among the States, as in trade, naturalization &c.—for crushing rebellion whenever it may rear its crest—and for certain other general

---

[1] The words "certainly seasons" are transposed to read "seasons certainly" in the transcript; but the word "seasons" was erroneously printed "reasons," which error has been followed in other editions of Madison's notes.
[2] The word "is" is omitted in the transcript.
[3] The figure "2" is changed to "the second" in the transcript.
[4] The transcript italicizes the word "National."

benefits, must be made. The powers for these purposes, can never be given to a body, inadequate as Congress are in point of representation, elected in the mode in which they are, and possessing no more confidence than they do: for notwithstanding what has been said to the contrary, his own experience satisfied him that a rooted distrust of Congress pretty generally prevailed. A Nat! Gov⸴ alone, properly constituted, will answer the purpose; and he begged it to be considered that the present is the last moment for establishing one. After this select experiment, the people will yield to despair.

The Committee rose & the House adjourned.

MONDAY JUNE 18. IN COMMITTEE OF THE WHOLE ON THE PROPOSITIONS OF M⸴ PATTERSON & M⸴ RANDOLPH

On motion of M⸴ DICKINSON to postpone the 1ˢᵗ Resolution in M⸴ Patterson's plan, in order to take up the following viz—" that the Articles of Confederation ought to be revised and amended, so as to render the Government of the U. S. adequate to the exigences, the preservation and the prosperity of the Union " the postponement was agreed to by 10 States, Pen: divided.

M⸴ HAMILTON, had been hitherto silent on the business before the Convention, partly from respect to others whose superior abilities age & experience rendered him unwilling to bring forward ideas dissimilar to theirs, and partly from his delicate situation with respect to his own State, to whose sentiments as expressed by his Colleagues, he could by no means accede. The crisis however which now marked our affairs, was too serious to permit any scruples whatever to prevail over the duty imposed on every man to contribute his efforts for the public safety & happiness. He was obliged therefore to declare himself unfriendly to both plans. He was particularly opposed to that from N. Jersey, being fully convinced, that no amendment of the Confederation, leaving the States in possession of their Sovereignty could possibly answer the purpose. On the other hand he confessed he was much discouraged by the amazing extent of Country in expecting the desired blessings from any general sovereignty that could be substituted.—As to the powers of the Convention, he thought the doubts started on that subject had arisen from distinctions & reasonings too subtle. A *federal* Gov⸴ he conceived to mean an association of independent Communities into one. Different Confederacies have different powers, and exercise them in different ways. In some instances the powers are exercised over collective bodies; in others over individuals, as in the German Diet—& among ourselves in cases of piracy. Great latitude therefore must be given to the signification of the term. The plan last proposed departs itself from the *federal* idea, as understood by some, since it is to operate eventually on individuals. He agreed moreover with the Honble gentleman from V? [M: R.] that we owed it to our Country, to do on this emergency whatever we should deem essential to its happiness. The States sent us here to provide for the exigences of the Union. To rely on & propose any plan not adequate to these exigences, merely because it was not [1] clearly within our powers, would be to sacrifice the means to the end. It may be said that the *States* can not *ratify* a plan not within the purview of the article of [2] Confederation providing for alterations & amendments. But may not the States themselves in which no constitutional authority equal to this purpose exists in the Legislatures, have had ·in view a reference to the people at large. In the Senate of N. York, a proviso was moved, that no act of the Convention should be binding untill it should be referred to the people & ratified; and the motion was lost by a single voice only, the reason assigned agst it being, that it might possibly be found an inconvenient shackle.

The great question is what provision shall we make for the happiness of our Country? He would first make a comparative examination of the two plans—prove that there were essential defects in both—and point out such changes as might render a *national one,* efficacious.—The great & essential principles necessary for the support of Government are 1. an active & constant interest in supporting it. This principle does not exist in the States in favor of the federal Gov? They have evidently in a high degree, the esprit de corps. They constantly pursue internal interests adverse to those of the whole. They have their particular debts—their particular plans of finance &c. All these when opposed to, invariably prevail over the requisitions & plans of Congress. 2. The love of power. Men love power. The same remarks are applicable to this principle. The States have constantly shewn a disposition rather to regain the powers delegated by them than to part with more, or to give effect to what they had parted with. The ambition of their demagogues is known to hate the controul of the Gen? Government. It may be remarked too

---

[1] The word "not" is blotted in the notes but is retained because it is in the transcript.
[2] The word "the" is here inserted in the transcript.

that the Citizens have not that anxiety to prevent a dissolution of the Gen! Gov! as of the particular Gov!? A dissolution of the latter would be fatal; of the former would still leave the purposes of Gov! attainable to a considerable degree. Consider what such a State as Virg? will be in a few years, a few compared with the life of nations. How strongly will it feel its importance & self-sufficiency? 3. An habitual attachment of the people. The whole force of this tie is on the side of the State Gov! Its sovereignty is immediately before the eyes of the people: its protection is immediately enjoyed by them. From its hand distributive justice, and all those acts which familiarize & endear [1] Gov! to a people, are dispensed to them. 4. *Force* by which may be understood a *coertion of laws* or *coertion of arms.* Cong? have not the former except in few cases. In particular States, this coercion is nearly sufficient; tho' he held it in most cases, not entirely so. A certain portion of military force is absolutely necessary in large communities. Mass! is now feeling this necessity & making provision for it. But how can this force be exerted on the States collectively. It is impossible. It amounts to a war between the parties. Foreign powers also will not be idle spectators. They will interpose, the confusion will increase, and a dissolution of the Union ensue. 5. *influence.* he did not mean corruption, but a dispensation of those regular honors & emoluments, which produce an attachment to the Gov! Almost all the weight of these is on the side of the States; and must continue so as long as the States continue to exist. All the passions then we see, of avarice, ambition, interest, which govern most individuals, and all public bodies, fall into the current of the States, and do not flow in the stream of the Gen! Gov! The former therefore will generally be an overmatch for the Gen! Gov! and render any confederacy, in its very nature precarious. Theory is in this case fully confirmed by experience. The Amphyctionic Council had it would seem ample powers for general purposes. It had in particular the power of fining and using force ag:t delinquent members. What was the consequence. Their decrees were mere signals of war. The Phocian war is a striking example of it. Philip at length taking advantage of their disunion, and insinuating himself into their Councils, made himself master of their fortunes. The German Confederacy affords another lesson. The authority of Charlemagne seemed to be as great as could be necessary. The great feudal chiefs however, exercising their local sovereignties, soon felt the spirit & found the means of, encroachments, which reduced

---

[1] The word " a " is here inserted in the transcript.

the imperial authority to a nominal sovereignty. The Diet has succeeded, which tho' aided by a Prince at its head, of great authority independently of his imperial attributes, is a striking illustration of the weakness of Confederated Governments. Other examples instruct us in the same truth. The Swiss cantons have scarce any Union at all, and have been more than once at war with one another—How then are all these evils to be avoided? only by such a compleat sovereignty in the general Governm.t as will turn all the strong principles & passions above mentioned on its side. Does the scheme of N. Jersey produce this effect? does it afford any substantial remedy whatever? On the contrary it labors under great defects, and the defect of some of its provisions will destroy the efficacy of others. It gives a direct revenue to Cong.s but this will not be sufficient. The balance can only be supplied by requisitions: which experience proves can not be relied on. If States are to deliberate on the mode, they will also deliberate on the object of the supplies, and will grant or not grant as they approve or disapprove of it. The delinquency of one will invite and countenance it in others. Quotas too must in the nature of things be so unequal as to produce the same evil. To what standard will you resort? Land is a fallacious one. Compare Holland with Russia: France or Eng.d with other countries of Europe. Pen.a with N. Carol.a will the relative pecuniary abilities in those instances, correspond with the relative value of land. Take numbers of inhabitants for the rule and make like comparison of different countries, and you will find it to be equally unjust. The different degrees of industry and improvement in different Countries render the first object a precarious measure of wealth. Much depends too on *situation.* Con.t N. Jersey & N. Carolina, not being commercial States & contributing to the wealth of the commercial ones, can never bear quotas assessed by the ordinary rules of proportion. They will & must fail in their duty, their example will be followed, and the Union itself be dissolved. Whence then is the national revenue to be drawn? from Commerce? even from exports which notwithstanding the common opinion are fit objects of moderate taxation, from excise, &c &c. These tho' not equal, are less unequal than quotas. Another destructive ingredient in the plan, is that equality of suffrage which is so much desired by the small States. It is not in human nature that V.a & the large States should consent to it, or if they did that they sh.d long abide by it. It shocks too much the [1] ideas of Justice, and every human feeling. Bad principles in a Gov.t tho slow are sure in their

---

[1] The word " all " is substituted in the transcript for " the."

operation, and will gradually destroy it. A doubt has been raised whether Cong? at present have a right to keep Ships or troops in time of peace. He leans to the negative. M.^r P? plan provides no remedy.—If the powers proposed were adequate, the organization of Cong? is such that they could never be properly & effectually exercised. The members of Cong? being chosen by the States & subject to recall, represent all the local prejudices. Should the powers be found effectual, they will from time to time be heaped on them, till a tyrannic sway shall be established. The general power whatever be its form if it preserves itself, must swallow up the State powers. Otherwise it will be swallowed up by them. It is ag.st all the principles of a good Government to vest the requisite powers in such a body as Cong? Two Sovereignties can not co-exist within the same limits. Giving powers to Cong? must eventuate in a bad Gov! or in no Gov! The plan of N. Jersey therefore will not do. What then is to be done? Here he was embarrassed. The extent of the Country to be governed, discouraged him. The expence of a general Gov.^t was also formidable; unless there were such a diminution of expence on the side of the State Gov.^{ts} as the case would admit. If they were extinguished, he was persuaded that great œconomy might be obtained by substituting a general Gov! He did not mean however to shock the public opinion by proposing such a measure. On the other hand he saw no *other* necessity for declining it. They are not necessary for any of the great purposes of commerce, revenue, or agriculture. Subordinate authorities he was aware would be necessary. There must be district tribunals: corporations for local purposes. But cui bono, the vast & expensive apparatus now appertaining to the States. The only difficulty of a serious nature which occurred to him, was that of drawing representatives from the extremes to the center of the Community. What inducements can be offered that will suffice? The moderate wages for the 1.st branch would [1] only be a bait to little demagogues. Three dollars or thereabouts he supposed would be the utmost. The Senate he feared from a similar cause, would be filled by certain undertakers who wish for particular offices under the Gov! This view of the subject almost led him to despair that a Republican Gov! could be established over so great an extent. He was sensible at the same time that it would be unwise to propose one of any other form. In his private opinion he had no scruple in declaring, supported as he was by the opinions of so many of the wise & good, that the British Gov! was the best in the world: and that he

---

[1] The word "could" is substituted in the transcript for "would."

doubted much whether any thing short of it would do in America. He hoped Gentlemen of different opinions would bear with him in this, and begged them to recollect the change of opinion on this subject which had taken place and was still going on. It was once thought that the power of Cong! was amply sufficient to secure the end of their institution. The error was now seen by every one. The members most tenacious of republicanism, he observed, were as loud as any in declaiming agst the vices of democracy. This progress of the public mind led him to anticipate the time, when others as well as himself would join in the praise bestowed by Mr Neckar on the British Constitution, namely, that it is the only Govt in the world "which unites public strength with individual security."—In every community where industry is encouraged, there will be a division of it into the few & the many. Hence separate interests will arise. There will be debtors & creditors &c. Give all power to the many, they will oppress the few. Give all power to the few, they will oppress the many. Both therefore ought to have [1] power, that each may defend itself agst the other. To the want of this check we owe our paper money, instalment laws &c. To the proper adjustment of it the British owe the excellence of their Constitution. Their house of Lords is a most noble institution. Having nothing to hope for by a change, and a sufficient interest by means of their property, in being faithful to the national interest, they form a permanent barrier agst every pernicious innovation, whether attempted on the part of the Crown or of the Commons. No temporary Senate will have firmness eno' to answer the purpose. The Senate [of Maryland] which seems to be so much appealed to, has not yet been sufficiently tried. Had the people been unanimous & eager, in the late appeal to them on the subject of a paper emission they would would have yielded to the torrent. Their acquiescing in such an appeal is a proof of it.—Gentlemen differ in their opinions concerning the necessary checks, from the different estimates they form of the human passions. They suppose seven years a sufficient period to give the senate an adequate firmness, from not duly considering the amazing violence & turbulence of the democratic spirit. When a great object of Govt is pursued, which seizes the popular passions, they spread like wild fire, and become irresistable. He appealed to the gentlemen from the N. England States whether experience had not there verified the remark.—As to the Executive, it seemed to be admitted that no good one could be established on Republican principles. Was not this giving up the merits of the ques-

---

[1] The word "the" is here inserted in the transcript.

tion: for can there be a good Gov.? without a good Executive. The English model was the only good one on this subject. The Hereditary interest of the King was so interwoven with that of the Nation, and his personal emoluments so great, that he was placed above the danger of being corrupted from abroad—and at the same time was both sufficiently independent and sufficiently controuled, to answer the purpose of the institution at home. one of the weak sides of Republics was their being liable to foreign influence & corruption. Men of little character, acquiring great power become easily the tools of intermedling Neibours. Sweeden was a striking instance. The French & English had each their parties during the late Revolution which was effected by the predominant influence of the former.—What is the inference from all these observations? That we ought to go as far in order to attain stability and permanency, as republican principles will admit. Let one branch of the Legislature hold their places for life or at least during good behaviour. Let the Executive also be for life. He appealed to the feelings of the members present whether a term of seven years, would induce the sacrifices of private affairs which an acceptance of public trust would require, so so as to ensure the services of the best Citizens. On this plan we should have in the Senate a permanent will, a weighty interest, which would answer essential purposes. But is this a Republican Gov.?, it will be asked? Yes if all the Magistrates are appointed, and vacancies are filled, by the people, or a process of election originating with the people. He was sensible that an Executive constituted as he proposed would have in fact but little of the power and independence that might be necessary. On the other plan of appointing him for 7 years, he thought the Executive ought to have but little power. He would be ambitious, with the means of making creatures; and as the object of his ambition w.? be to *prolong* his power, it is probable that in case of a [1] war, he would avail himself of the emergence,[2] to evade or refuse a degradation from his place. An Executive for life has not this motive for forgetting his fidelity, and will therefore be a safer depository of power. It will be objected probably, that such an Executive will be an *elective Monarch,* and will give birth to the tumults which characterize that form of Gov.? He w.? reply that *Monarch* is an indefinite term. It marks not either the degree or duration of power. If this Executive Magistrate w.? be a monarch for life —the other prop.? by the Report from the Comtte of the whole, w.?

---

[1] The word " a " is omitted in the transcript.
[2] The word " emergence " is changed to " emergency " in the transcript.

be a monarch for seven years. The circumstance of being elective was also applicable to both. It had been observed by judicious writers that elective monarchies w^d be the best if they could be guarded agst the *tumults* excited by the ambition and intrigues of competitors. He was not sure that tumults were an inseparable evil. He rather thought this character of Elective Monarchies had been taken rather from particular cases than from general principles. The election of Roman Emperors was made by the *Army*. In *Poland* the election is made by great rival *princes* with independent power, and ample means, of raising commotions. In the German Empire, the appointment is made by the Electors & Princes, who have equal motives & means, for exciting cabals & parties. Might not such a mode of election be devised among ourselves as will defend the community agst these effects in any dangerous degree? Having made these observations he would read to the Committee a sketch of a plan which he sh^d prefer to either of those under consideration. He was aware that it went beyond the ideas of most members. But will such a plan be adopted out of doors? In return he would ask will the people adopt the other plan? At present they will adopt neither. But he sees the Union dissolving or already dissolved—he sees evils operating in the States which must soon cure the people of their fondness for democracies—he sees that a great progress has been already made & is still going on in the public mind. He thinks therefore that the people will in time be unshackled from their prejudices; and whenever that happens, they will themselves not be satisfied at stopping where the plan of M^r. R. w^d place them, but be ready to go as far at least as he proposes. He did not mean to offer the paper he had sketched as a proposition to the Committee. It was meant only to give a more correct view of his ideas, and to suggest the amendments which he should probably propose to the plan of M^r. R. in the proper stages of its future discussion. He read [1] his sketch in the words following: towit

I. " The Supreme Legislative power of the United States of America to be vested in two different bodies of men; the one to be called the Assembly, the other the Senate who together shall form the Legislature of the United States with power to pass all laws whatsoever subject to the Negative hereafter mentioned.

II. The Assembly to consist of persons elected by the people to serve for three years.

III. The Senate to consist of persons elected to serve during good behaviour; their election to be made by electors chosen for that pur-

---

[1] The word "reads" is substituted in the transcript for "read."

pose by the people: in order to this the States to be divided into election districts. On the death, removal or resignation of any Senator his place to be filled out of the district from which he came.

IV. The supreme Executive authority of the United States to be vested in a Governour to be elected to serve during good behaviour— the election to be made by Electors chosen by the people in the Election Districts aforesaid—The authorities & functions of the Executive to be as follows: to have a negative on all laws about to be passed, and the execution of all laws passed; to have the direction of war when authorized or begun; to have with the advice and approbation of the Senate the power of making all treaties; to have the sole appointment of the heads or chief officers of the departments of Finance, War and Foreign Affairs; to have the nomination of all other officers (Ambassadors to foreign Nations included) subject to the approbation or rejection of the Senate; to have the power of pardoning all offences except Treason; which he shall not pardon without the approbation of the Senate.

V. On the death resignation or removal of the Governour his authorities to be exercised by the President of the Senate till a Successor be appointed.

VI. The Senate to have the sole power of declaring war, the power of advising and approving all Treaties, the power of approving or rejecting all appointments of officers except the heads or chiefs of the departments of Finance War and foreign affairs.

VII. The supreme Judicial authority to be vested in   Judges to hold their offices during good behaviour with adequate and permanent salaries.   This Court to have original jurisdiction in all causes of capture, and an appellative jurisdiction in all causes in which the revenues of the general Government or the Citizens of foreign Nations are concerned.

VIII. The Legislature of the United States to have power to institute Courts in each State for the determination of all matters of general concern.

IX. The Governour Senators and all officers of the United States to be liable to impeachment for mal- and corrupt conduct; and upon conviction to be removed from office, & disqualified for holding any place of trust or profit—All impeachments to be tried by a Court to consist of the Chief   or Judge of the superior Court of Law of each State, provided such Judge shall hold his place during good behavior, and have a permanent salary.

X. All laws of the particular States contrary to the Constitution or laws of the United States to be utterly void; and the better to prevent such laws being passed, the Governour or president of each State shall be appointed by the General Government and shall have a negative upon the laws about to be passed in the State of which he is [1] Governour or President.

XI. No State to have any forces land or Naval; and the Militia of all the States to be under the sole and exclusive direction of the

---

[1] The word "the" is here inserted in the transcript.

United States, the officers of which to be appointed and commissioned by them.

On these several articles he entered into explanatory observations[1] corresponding with the principles of his introductory reasoning.[2]

[3] Committee rose & the House Adjourned.

TEUSDAY JUNE 19TH IN COMMITTEE OF [3] WHOLE ON THE PROPOSITIONS OF MR. PATTERSON

The substitute offered yesterday by Mr Dickenson being rejected by a vote now taken on it; Con. N. Y. N. J. Del. ay.[4] Mas. Pa V. N. C. S. C. Geo. no:[5] Mayd divided. Mr Patterson's plan was again at large before the Committee.

Mr MADISON. Much stress had [6] been laid by some gentlemen on the want of power in the Convention to propose any other than a *federal* plan. To what had been answered by others, he would only add, that neither of the characteristics attached to a *federal* plan would support this objection. One characteristic, was that in a *federal* Government, the power was exercised not on the people individually;[7] but on the people *collectively*, on the *States*. Yet in some instances as in piracies, captures &c. the existing Confederacy, and in many instances, the amendments to it proposed by Mr Patterson, must operate immediately on individuals. The other characteristic was, that a *federal* Govt derived its appointments not immediately from the people, but from the States which they respectively composed. Here too were facts on the other side. In two of the States, Connect and Rh. Island, the delegates to Congs were chosen, not by the Legisla-

---

[1] In the transcript the following footnote was inserted with reference mark after " observations ":

"The speech introducing the plan, as above taken down & written out was seen by Mr. Hamilton, who approved its correctness, with one or two verbal changes, which were made as he suggested. The explanatory observations which did not immediately follow, were to have been furnished by Mr. H. who did not find leisure at the time to write them out, and they were not obtained.

" Judge Yates, in his notes, appears to have consolidated the explanatory with the introductory observations of Mr. Hamilton (under date of June 19th, a typographical error). It was in the former, Mr. Madison observed, that Mr. Hamilton, in speaking of popular governments, however modified, made the remark attributed to him by Judge Yates, that they were ' *but pork still with a little change of sauce.*' "

[2] For the text of Hamilton's Plan handed to Madison about the close of the Convention, but not actually submitted to that body, see Appendix to Debates, V, pp. 608-618.

[3] The word " The " is here inserted in the transcript.

[4] The figure " 4 " is here inserted in the transcript.

[5] The figure " 6 " is here inserted in the transcript.

[6] The word " has " is substituted in the transcript for " had."

[7] The transcript italicizes the word " individually."

tures, but by the people at large; and the plan of M: P. intended no
change in this particular.

It had been alledged [by M: Patterson], that the Confederation
having been formed by unanimous consent, could be dissolved by
unanimous Consent only. Does this doctrine result from the nature
of compacts? does it arise from any particular stipulation in the
articles of Confederation? If we consider the federal union as
analogous to the fundamental compact by which individuals compose
one Society, and which must in its theoretic origin at least, have been
the unanimous act of the component members, it can not be said that
no dissolution of the compact can be effected without unanimous consent. A breach of the fundamental principles of the compact by a
part of the Society would certainly absolve the other part from their
obligations to it. If the breach of *any* article by *any* of the parties,
does not set the others at liberty, it is because, the contrary is *implied*
in the compact itself, and particularly by that law of it, which gives
an indifinite authority to the majority to bind the whole in all cases.
This latter circumstance shews that we are not to consider the federal
Union as analogous to the social compact of individuals: for if it
were so, a Majority would have a right to bind the rest, and even
to form a new Constitution for the whole, which the Gent: from N.
Jersey would be among the last to admit. If we consider the federal
Union as analogous not to the social compacts among individual
men: but to the conventions among individual States. What is the
doctrine resulting from these conventions? Clearly, according to
the Expositors of the law of Nations, that a breach of any one article,
by any one party, leaves all the other parties at liberty, to consider
the whole convention as dissolved, unless they choose rather to compel the delinquent party to repair the breach. In some treaties indeed it is expressly stipulated that a violation of particular articles
shall not have this consequence, and even that particular articles
shall remain in force during war, which in general is [1] understood to
dissolve all subsisting Treaties. But are there any exceptions of
this sort to the Articles of confederation? So far from it that there
is not even an express stipulation that force shall be used to compell
an offending member of the Union to discharge its duty. He observed
that the violations of the federal articles had been numerous & notorious. Among the most notorious was an act of N. Jersey herself;
by which she *expressly refused* to comply with a constitutional
requisition of Cong: and yielded no farther to the expostulations of

---

[1] The words " in general is " are transposed to read " is in general " in the
transcript.

their deputies, than barely to rescind her vote of refusal without passing any positive act of compliance. He did not wish to draw any rigid inferences from these observations. He thought it proper however that the true nature of the existing confederacy should be investigated, and he was not anxious to strengthen the foundations on which it now stands.

Proceeding to the consideration of M.ʳ Patterson's plan, he stated the object of a proper plan to be twofold. 1.¹ to preserve the Union. 2.¹ to provide a Governm.ᵗ that will remedy the evils felt by the States both in their united and individual capacities. Examine M.ʳ P.s plan, & say whether it promises satisfaction in these respects.

1. Will it prevent those violations of the law of nations & of Treaties which if not prevented must involve us in the calamities of foreign wars? The tendency of the States to these violations has been manifested in sundry instances. The files of Cong.ˢ contain complaints already, from almost every nation with which treaties have been formed. Hitherto indulgence has been shewn to us. This can not be the permanent disposition of foreign nations. A rupture with other powers is among the greatest of national calamities. It ought therefore to be effectually provided that no part of a nation shall have it in its power to bring them on the whole. The existing Confederacy does not sufficiently provide against this evil. The proposed amendment to it does not supply the omission. It leaves the will of the States as uncontrouled as ever.

2. Will it prevent encroachments on the federal authority? A tendency to such encroachments has been sufficiently exemplified, among ourselves, as well² in every other confederated republic antient and Modern. By the federal articles, transactions with the Indians appertain to Cong.ˢ Yet in several instances, the States have entered into treaties & wars with them. In like manner no two or more States can form among themselves any treaties &c. without the consent of Cong.ˢ Yet Virg.ᵃ & Mary.ᵈ in one instance—Pen.ᵃ & N. Jersey in another, have entered into compacts, without previous application or subsequent apology. No State again can of right raise troops in time of peace without the like consent. Of all cases of the league, this seems to require the most scrupulous observance. Has not Mass.ᵗˢ, notwithstanding, the most powerful member of the Union, already raised a body of troops? Is she not now augmenting them, without having even deigned to apprise Cong.ˢ of Her intention? In

---

¹ The figures " 1 " and " 2 " are changed to " first " and " secondly " in the transcript.
² The word " as " is here inserted in the transcript.

fine—Have we not seen the public land dealt out to Con! to bribe her
acquiescence in the decree constitutionally awarded ag.ˢᵗ her claim on
the territory of Pen.ᵃ? for no other possible motive can account for the
policy of Cong.ˢ in that measure?—If we recur to the examples of
other confederacies, we shall find in all of them the same tendency of
the parts to encroach on the authority of the whole. He then reviewed
the Amphyctionic & Achæan confederacies among the antients, and
the Helvetic, Germanic & Belgic among the moderns, tracing their
analogy to the U. States—in the constitution and extent of their
federal authorities—in the tendency of the particular members to
usurp on these authorities; and to bring confusion & ruin on the
whole.—He observed that the plan of Mr. Pat–son besides omitting
a controul over the States as a general defence of the federal prerogatives was particularly defective in two of its provisions. 1.[1] Its
ratification was not to be by the people at large, but by the *legislatures*.
It could not therefore render the Acts of Cong.ˢ in pursuance of their
powers, even legally *paramount* to the Acts of the States. 2.[2] It gave
to the federal Tribunal an appellate jurisdiction only—even in the
criminal cases enumerated, The necessity of any such provision supposed a danger of undue acquittals[3] in the State tribunals. Of what
avail c.ᵈ[4] an appellate tribunal be, after an acquittal? Besides in most
if not all of the States, the Executives have by their respective *Constitutions* the right of pard? How could this be taken from them by
a *legislative*[5] ratification only?

3. Will it prevent trespasses of the States on each other? Of these
enough has been already seen. He instanced Acts of Virg.ᵃ & Maryland which give[6] a preference to their own Citizens in cases where the
Citizens of other States are entitled to equality of privileges by the
Articles of Confederation. He considered the emissions of paper
money & other kindred measures as also aggressions. The States
relatively to one an other being each of them either Debtor or
Creditor; The creditor States must suffer unjustly from every emission by the debtor States. We have seen retaliating acts on this
subject which threatened danger not to the harmony only, but the
tranquility of the Union. The plan of M.ʳ Paterson, not giving even
a negative on the acts of the States, left .them as much at liberty
as ever to execute their unrighteous projects ag.ˢᵗ each other.

---

[1] The figure " 1 " is changed to " In the first place " in the transcript.
[2] The figure " 2 " is changed to " and in the second place " in the transcript.
[3] The transcript uses the word " acquittals " in the singular.
[4] The word " would " is substituted in the transcript for " c.ᵈ "
[5] The word " *legislative* " is not italicized in the transcript.
[6] The word " gave " is substituted in the transcript for " give."

4. Will it secure the internal tranquility of the States themselves? The insurrections in Mass.ᵗˢ admonished all the States of the danger to which they were exposed. Yet the plan of M.ʳ P. contained no provisions for supplying the defect of the Confederation on this point. According to the Republican theory indeed, Right & power being both vested in the majority, are held to be synonimous. According to fact & experience, a minority may in an appeal to force be an overmatch for the majority. 1.[1] If the minority happen to include all such as possess the skill & habits of military life, with such as possess the great pecuniary resources, one third may conquer the remaining two thirds. 2.[2] one third of those who participate in the choice of rulers may be rendered a majority by the accession of those whose poverty disqualifies them from a suffrage, & who for obvious reasons may [3] be more ready to join the standard of sedition than that of the [4] established Government. 3.[5] where slavery exists, the Republican Theory becomes still more fallacious.

5. Will it secure a good internal legislation & administration to the particular States? In developing the evils which vitiate the political system of the U. S. it is proper to take into view those which prevail within the States individually as well as those which affect them collectively: Since the former indirectly affect the whole; and there is great reason to believe that the pressure of them had a full share in the motives which produced the present Convention. Under this head he enumerated and animadverted on 1.[6] the multiplicity of the laws passed by the several States. 2.[6] the mutability of their laws. 3.[6] the injustice of them. 4.[7] the impotence of them: observing that M.ʳ Patterson's plan contained no remedy for this dreadful class of evils, and could not therefore be received as an adequate provision for the exigences of the Community.

6. Will it secure the Union ag.ˢᵗ the influence of foreign powers over its members. He pretended not to say that any such influence had yet been tried: but it was naturally to be expected that occasions would produce it. As lessons which claimed particular attention, he cited the intrigues practised among the Amphyctionic Confederates first by the Kings of Persia, and afterwards fatally by Philip of Macedon: among the Achæans, first by Macedon & afterwards no less

---

[1] The figure "1" is changed to "in the first place" in the transcript.

[2] The figure "2" is changed to "in the second place" in the transcript.

[3] The word "must" is substituted in the transcript for "may."

[4] The word "the" is omitted in the transcript.

[5] The figure "3" is changed to "and in the third place."

[6] The figures "1," "2" and "3" are changed to "first," "secondly" and "thirdly" in the transcript.

[7] The figure "4" is changed to "and fourthly" in the transcript.

fatally by Rome: among the Swiss by Austria, France & the lesser neighbouring powers: among the members of the Germanic Body by France, England, Spain & Russia—: and in the Belgic Republic, by all the great neighbouring powers. The plan of M: Patterson, not giving to the general Councils any negative on the will of the particular States, left the door open for the like pernicious machinations among ourselves.

7. He begged the smaller States which were most attached to M: Pattersons plan to consider the situation in which it would leave them. In the first place they would continue to bear the whole expence of maintaining their Delegates in Congress. It ought not to be said that if they were willing to bear this burden, no others had a right to complain. As far as it led the small States to forbear keeping up a representation, by which the public business was delayed, it was evidently a matter of common concern. An examination of the minutes of Congress would satisfy every one that the public business had been frequently delayed by this cause; and that the States most frequently unrepresented in Cong: were not the larger States. He reminded the convention of another consequence of :aving on a small State the burden of maintaining a Representation in Cong: During a considerable period of the War, one of the Representatives of Delaware, in whom alone before the signing of the Confederation the entire vote of that State and after that event one half of its vote, frequently resided, was a Citizen & Resident of Pen: and held an office in his own State incompatible with an appointment from it to Cong: During another period, the same State was represented by three delegates two of whom were citizens of Penn: and the third a Citizen of New Jersey. These expedients must have been intended to avoid the burden of supporting delegates from their own State. But whatever might have been y: cause, was not in effect the vote of one State doubled, and the influence of another increased by it? In the 2d place The coercion, on which the efficacy of the plan depends, can never be exerted but on themselves. The larger States will be impregnable, the smaller only can feel the vengeance of it. He illustrated the position by the history of the Amphyctionic Confederates: and the ban of the German Empire. It was the cobweb wch could entangle the weak, but would be the sport of the strong.

8. He begged them to consider the situation in which they would remain in case their pertinacious adherence to an inadmissible plan, should prevent the adoption of any plan. The contemplation of such an event was painful; but it would be prudent to submit to the task of examining it at a distance, that the means of escaping it might be

the more readily embraced. Let the Union of the States be dissolved, and one of two consequences must happen. Either the States must remain individually independent & sovereign; or two or more Confederacies must be formed among them. In the first event would the small States be more secure agst the ambition & power of their larger neighbours, than they would be under a general Government pervading with equal energy every part of the Empire, and having an equal interest in protecting every part agst every other part? In the second, can the smaller expect that their larger neighbours would confederate with them on the principle of the present confederacy, which gives to each member, an equal suffrage; or that they would exact less severe concessions from the smaller States, than are proposed in the scheme of Mr Randolph?

The great difficulty lies in the affair of Representation; and if this could be adjusted, all others would be surmountable. It was admitted by both the gentlemen from N. Jersey, [Mr Brearly and Mr Patterson] that it would not be *just to allow Virg^a* which was 16 times as large as Delaware an equal vote only. Their language was that it would not be *safe for Delaware* to allow Virg^a 16 times as many votes. The expedient proposed by them was that all the States should be thrown into one mass and a new partition be made into 13 equal parts. Would such a scheme be practicable? The dissimilarities existing in the rules of property, as well as in the manners, habits and prejudices of the [1] different States, amounted to a prohibition of the attempt. It had been found impossible for the power of one of the most absolute princes in Europe [K. of France] directed by the wisdom of one of the most enlightened and patriotic Ministers [Mr Neckar] that any age has produced to equalize in some points only the different usages & regulations of the different provinces. But admitting a general amalgamation and repartition of the States to be practicable, and the danger apprehended by the smaller States from a proportional representation to be real; would not a particular and voluntary coalition of these with their neighbours, be less inconvenient to the whole community, and equally effectual for their own safety. If N. Jersey or Delaware conceived that an advantage would accrue to them from an equalization of the States, in which case they would necessaryly form a junction with their neighbours, why might not this end be attained by leaving them at liberty by the Constitution to form such a junction whenever they pleased? And why should they wish to obtrude a like arrangement

---

[1] The word "the" is crossed out in the transcript.

on all the States, when it was, to say the least, extremely difficult, would be obnoxious to many of the States, and when neither the inconveniency,[1] nor the benefit of the expedient to themselves, would be lessened, by confining it to themselves.—The prospect of many new States to the Westward was another consideration of importance. If they should come into the Union at all, they would come when they contained but few inhabitants. If they sh^d be entitled to vote according to their proportions of inhabitants, all would be right & safe. Let them have an equal vote, and a more objectionable minority than ever might give law to the whole.

On a question for postponing generally the 1st proposition of Mr Patterson's plan, it was agreed to: N. Y. & N J. only being no—

On the question moved by Mr King whether the Committee should rise & Mr Randolphs propositions be re-reported without alteration, which was in fact a question whether Mr R.'s should be adhered to as preferable to those of Mr Patterson:

Mass^ts ay. Con^t ay. N. Y. no. N. J. no. P^a ay. Del. no. M^d div^d V^a ay. N. C. ay. S. C. ay. Geo. ay.[2]

Insert here from Printed Journal p. 13[3] copy of the Resol^ns of Mr R. as altered in the Com^e and reported to the House[4]

[State of the resolutions submitted to the consideration of the House by the honorable Mr. Randolph, as altered, amended, and agreed to, in a Committee of the whole House.

1. Resolved that it is the opinion of this Committee that a national government ought to be established consisting of a Supreme Legislative, Judiciary, and Executive.
2. Resolved. that the national Legislature ought to consist of Two Branches.
3 Resolved that the members of the first branch of the national Legislature ought to be elected by the People of the several States for the term of Three years. to receive fixed stipends, by which they may be compensated for the devotion of their time to public service to be paid out of the National-Treasury. to be ineligible to any Office established by a particular State or under the authority of the United-States (except those peculiarly belonging to the functions of the first branch) during the term of service, and under the national government for the space of one year after it's expiration.

---

[1] The word "inconveniency" is changed to "inconvenience" in the transcript.

[2] In the transcript the vote reads: "Massachusetts, Connecticut, Pennsylvania, Virginia, North Carolina, South Carolina, Georgia, aye—7; New York, New Jersey, Delaware, no—3; Maryland divided."

[3] Found at page 134 instead of page 13, and here printed from the original manuscript deposited in the Department of State by President Washington.

[4] Madison's direction concerning Mr. Randolph's Resolutions and the Resolutions themselves are omitted in the transcript.

4 Resolved. that the members of the second Branch of the national Legislature ought to be chosen by the individual Legislatures. to be of the age of thirty years at least. to hold their offices for a term sufficient to ensure their independency, namely seven years. to receive fixed stipends, by which they may be compensated for the devotion of their time to public service—to be paid out of the National Treasury to be ineligible to any office established by a particular State, or under the authority of the United States (except those peculiarly belonging to the functions of the second branch) during the term of service, and under the national government, for the space of one year after it's expiration.

5. Resolved that each branch ought to possess the right of originating acts.

6. Resolved. that the national Legislature ought to be empowered to enjoy the legislative rights vested in Congress by the confederation—and moreover to legislate in all cases to which the separate States are incompetent: or in which the harmony of the United States may be interrupted by the exercise of individual legislation. to negative all laws passed by the several States contravening, in the opinion of the national Legislature, the articles of union, or any treaties subsisting under the authority of the union.

7. Resolved. that the right of suffrage in the first branch of the national Legislature ought not to be according to the rule established in the articles of confederation: but according to some equitable ratio of representation—namely, in proportion to the whole number of white and other free citizens and inhabitants of every age, sex, and condition including those bound to servitude for a term of years, and three fifths of all other persons not comprehended in the foregoing description, except Indians, not paying taxes in each State.

8 Resolved. that the right of suffrage in the second branch of the national Legislature ought to be according to the rule established for the first.

9 Resolved. that a national Executive be instituted to consist of a single person. to be chosen by the National Legislature. for the term of seven years. with power to carry into execution the national Laws, to appoint to Offices in cases not otherwise provided for to be ineligible a second time, and to be removable on impeachment and conviction of mal practice or neglect of duty. to receive a fixed stipend, by which he may be compensated for the devotion of his time to public service to be paid out of the national Treasury.

10 Resolved. that the national executive shall have a right to negative any legislative act: which shall not be afterwards passed unless by two third parts of each branch of the national Legislature.

11 Resolved. that a national Judiciary be established to consist of One Supreme Tribunal. The Judges of which to be appointed by the second Branch of the National Legislature. to hold their offices during good behaviour to receive, punctually, at stated times, a fixed compensation for their services: in which no encrease or diminution shall be made so as to affect the persons actually in office at the time of such encrease or diminution

12 Resolved. That the national Legislature be empowered to appoint inferior Tribunals.

13 Resolved. that the jurisdiction of the national Judiciary shall extend to cases which respect the collection of the national revenue: impeachments of any national officers: and questions which involve the national peace and harmony.

14. Resolved. that provision ought to be made for the admission of States, lawfully arising within the limits of the United States,

whether from a voluntary junction of government and terri‚
tory, or otherwise, with the consent of a number of voices in
the national Legislature less than the whole.

15. Resolved. that provision ought to be made for the continuance of Congress
and their authorities until a given day after the reform of the
articles of Union shall be adopted; and for the completion of
all their engagements.

16. Resolved that a republican constitution, and its existing laws, ought to
be guaranteed to each State by the United States.

17. Resolved. that provision ought to be made for the amendment of the
articles of Union, whensoever it shall seem necessary.

18 Resolved. that the Legislative, Executive, and Judiciary powers within
the several States ought to be bound by oath to support the
articles of Union.

19 Resolved. that the amendments which shall be offered to the confederation
by the Convention, ought at a proper time or times, after the
approbation of Congress to be submitted to an assembly or
assemblies of representatives, recommended by the several
Legislatures, to be expressly chosen by the People to consider
and decide thereon.

(Of [1] M: Randolph's plan as reported from the Committee) [2]. the
1. propos: "that a Nat! Gov! ought to be established consisting &c."
being taken up in the House.[3]

M: WILSON observed that by a Nat! Gov! he did not mean one
that would swallow up the State Gov.ᵗˢ as seemed to be wished by
some gentlemen. He was tenacious of the idea of preserving the
latter. He thought, contrary to the opinion of [Col. Hamilton] that
they might not only subsist but subsist on friendly terms with the
former. They were absolutely necessary for certain purposes which
the former could not reach. All large Governments must be subdivided into lesser jurisdictions. As Examples he mentioned Persia,
Rome, and particularly the divisions & subdivisions of England by
Alfred.

Col. HAMILTON coincided with the proposition as it stood in the
Report. He had not been understood yesterday. By an abolition of
the States, he meant that no boundary could be drawn between the
National & State Legislatures; that the former must therefore have
indefinite authority. If it were limited at all, the rivalship of the
States would gradually subvert it. Even as Corporations the extent
of some of them as V: Mass'ᵗˢ &c. would be formidable. As *States*, he
thought they ought to be abolished. But he admitted the necessity of
leaving in them, subordinate jurisdictions. The examples of Persia
& the Roman Empire, cited by [M: Wilson] were he thought in favor
of his doctrine: the great powers delegated to the Satraps & pro-

---

[1] The word "of" is omitted in the transcript.
[2] The words "June 13 being before the house" are here inserted in the
transcript.
[3] The words "in the House" are omitted in the transcript.

consuls, having frequently produced revolts, and schemes of independence.

M: KING, wished as every thing depended on this proposition, that no objections might be improperly indulged ag:ᵗ the phraseology of it. He conceived that the import of the terms " States " " Sovereignty " " *national* " " federal," had been often used & applied in the discussions inaccurately & delusively. The States were not " Sovereigns " in the sense contended for by some. They did not possess the peculiar features of sovereignty, they could not make war, nor peace, nor alliances nor treaties. Considering them as political Beings, they were dumb, for they could not speak to any foreign Sovereign whatever. They were deaf, for they could not hear any propositions from such Sovereign. They had not even the organs or faculties of defence or offence, for they could not of themselves raise troops, or equip vessels, for war. On the other side, if the Union of the States comprizes the idea of a confederation, it comprizes that also of consolidation. A Union of the States is a Union of the men composing them, from whence a *national* character results to the whole. Cong: can act alone without the States—they can act & their acts will be binding ag:ᵗ the Instructions of the States. If they declare war: war is de jure declared—captures made in pursuance of it are lawful—No acts of the States can vary the situation, or prevent the judicial consequences. If the States therefore retained some portion of their sovereignty, they had certainly divested themselves of essential portions of it. If they formed a confederacy in some respects—they formed a Nation in others—The Convention could clearly deliberate on & propose any alterations that Cong: could have done under y: federal articles, and could not Cong: propose by virtue of the last article, a change in any article whatever: and as well that relating to the equality of suffrage, as any other. He made these remarks to obviate some scruples which had been expressed. He doubted much the practicability of annihilating the States; but thought that much of their power ought to be taken from them.

M: MARTIN, said he considered that the separation from G. B. placed the 13 States in a state of Nature towards each other; that they would have remained in that state till this time, but for the confederation; that they entered into the confederation on the footing of equality; that they met now to to amend it on the same footing; and that he could never accede to a plan that would introduce an inequality and lay 10 States at the mercy of V: Mass:ᵗˢ and Penn:

M: WILSON, could not admit the doctrine that when the Colonies became independent of G. Britain, they became independent also of each other. He read the declaration of Independence, observing thereon that the *United Colonies* were declared to be free & independent States; and inferring that they were independent, not *individually* but *Unitedly* and that they were confederated as they were independent, States.

Col. HAMILTON, assented to the doctrine of M: Wilson. He denied the doctrine that the States were thrown into a State of Nature He was not yet prepared to admit the doctrine that the Confederacy, could be dissolved by partial infractions of it. He admitted that the States met now on an equal footing but could see no inference from that against concerting a change of the system in this particular. He took this occasion of observing for the purpose of appeasing the fears of the small States, that two circumstances would render them secure under a National Gov: in which they might lose the equality of rank they now held: one was the local situation of the 3 largest States Virg: Mas:, & P: They were separated from each other by distance of place, and equally so, by all the peculiarities which distinguish the interests of one State from those of another. No combination therefore could be dreaded. In the second place, as there was a gradation in the States from V: the largest down to Delaware the smallest, it would always happen that ambitious combinations among a few States might & w: be counteracted by defensive combinations of greater extent among the rest. No combination has been seen among [1] large Counties merely as such, ag:t lesser Counties. The more close the Union of the States, and the more compleat the authority of the whole: the less opportunity will be allowed [2] the stronger States to injure the weaker.

Adj:

WEDNESDAY JUNE 20. 1787.[3]   IN CONVENTION

M: William Blount from N. Carolina took his seat.

1:t propos: [4] of the Report of Com: of the whole [5] before the House.

M: ELSEWORTH 2:ded by M: GORHAM, moves to alter it so as to run " that the Government of the United States ought to consist of a supreme legislative, Executive and Judiciary." This alteration he

---

[1] The word "the" is here inserted in the transcript.
[2] The word "to" is here inserted in the transcript.
[3] The year "1787" is omitted in the transcript.
[4] The words "The first Resolution" are substituted in the transcript for "1st propos."
[5] The word "being" is here inserted in the transcript.

said would drop the word *national,* and retain the proper title "the United States." He could not admit the doctrine that a breach of any of the federal articles could dissolve the whole. It would be highly dangerous not to consider the Confederation as still subsisting. He wished also the plan of the Convention to go forth as an amendment to [1] the articles of [2] Confederation, since under this idea the authority of the Legislatures could ratify it. If they are unwilling, the people will be so too. If the plan goes forth to the people for ratification several succeeding Conventions within the States would be unavoidable. He did not like these conventions. They were better fitted to pull down than to build up Constitutions.

M! RANDOLPH, did not object to the change of expression, but apprised the gentlemen [3] who wished for it that he did not admit it for the reasons assigned; particularly that of getting rid of a reference to the people for ratification. The motion of M! Ellsew!ᵗʰ was acquiesced in nem: con:

The 2ᵈ Resol: "that the national Legislature ought to consist of two branches"[4] taken up, the word "national" struck out as of course.

M! LANSING, observed that thé true question here was, whether the Convention would adhere to or depart from the foundation of the present Confederacy; and moved instead of the 2ᵈ Resolution, "that the powers of Legislation be vested in the U. States in Congress." He had already assigned two reasons ag!ᵗ such an innovation as was proposed: 1.[5] the want of competent powers in the Convention.—2.[5] the state of the public mind. It had been observed by [M! Madison] in discussing the first point, that in two States the Delegates to Cong! were chosen by the people. Notwithstanding the first appearance of this remark, it had in fact no weight, as the Delegates however chosen, did not represent the people merely as so many individuals; but as forming a Sovereign State. [M! Randolph] put it, he said, on its true footing namely that the public safety superseded the scruple arising from the review of our powers. But in order to feel the force of this consideration, the same impression must be had of the public danger. He had not himself the same impression, and could not therefore dismiss his scruple. [M! Wilson] contended that as the Convention were only to recommend, they might recommend

---

[1] The word "of" is substituted in the transcript for "to."
[2] The word "the" is here inserted in the transcript.
[3] The word "gentlemen" is used in the singular in the transcript.
[4] The word "being" is here inserted in the transcript.
[5] The figures "1" and "2" are changed to "first" and "secondly" in the transcript.

what they pleased. He differed much from him. Any act whatever of so respectable a body must have a great effect, and if it does not succeed, will be a source of great dissentions. He admitted that there was no certain criterion of the public mind on the subject. He therefore recurred to the evidence of it given by the opposition in the States to the scheme of an Impost. It could not be expected that those possessing Sovereignty could ever voluntarily part with it. It was not to be expected from any one State, much less from thirteen. He proceeded to make some observations on the plan itself and the argum^{ts} urged in support of it. The point of Representation could receive no elucidation from the case of England. The corruption of the boroughs did not proceed from their comparative smallness: but from the actual fewness of the inhabitants, some of them not having more than one or two. A great inequality existed in the Counties of England. Yet the like complaint of peculiar corruption in the small ones had not been made. It had been said that Congress represent the State prejudices: will not any other body whether chosen by the Legislatures or people of the States, also represent their prejudices? It had been asserted by his colleague [Col. Hamilton] that there was no coincidence of interests among the large States that ought to excite fears of oppression in the smaller. If it were true that such a uniformity of interests existed among the States, there was equal safety for all of them, whether the representation remained as heretofore, or were proportioned as now proposed. It is proposed that the Genl Legislature shall have a negative on the laws of the States. Is it conceivable that there will be leisure for such a task? there will on the most moderate calculation, be as many Acts sent up from the States as there are days in the year. Will the members of the general Legislature be competent Judges? Will a gentleman from Georgia be a Judge of the expediency of a law which is to operate in N. Hamshire. Such a Negative would be more injurious than that of Great Britain heretofore was. It is said that the National Gov^t must have the influence arising from the grant of offices and honors. In order to render such a Government effectual he believed such an influence to be necessary. But if the States will not agree to it, it is in vain, worse than in vain to make the proposition. If this influence is to be attained, the States must be entirely abolished. Will any one say this would ever be agreed to? He doubted whether any Genl Government equally beneficial to all can be attained. That now under consideration he is sure, must be utterly unattainable. He had another objection. The system was too novel & complex. No man could foresee what its operation will be either with respect to the Gen! Gov! or the State Gov!? One or other it has been surmised must absorb the whole.

Col. MASON, did not expect this point would have been reagitated. The essential differences between the two plans, had been clearly stated. The principal objections ag?! that of M? R. were the *want of power* & the *want of practicability*. There can be no weight in the first as the fiat is not to be *here*, but in the people. He thought with his colleague M? R. that there were besides certain crisises, in which all the ordinary cautions yielded to public necessity. He gave as an example, the eventual Treaty with G. B. in forming which the Comrs. of the U. S. had boldly disregarded the improvident shackles of Cong? had given to their Country an honorable & happy peace, and instead of being censured for the transgression of their powers, had raised to themselves a monument more durable than brass. The *impracticability* of gaining the public concurrence he thought was still more groundless. [M? Lansing] had cited the attempts of Congress to gain an enlargement of their powers, and had inferred from the miscarriage of these attempts, the hopelessness of the plan which he [M? L] opposed. He thought a very different inference ought to have been drawn; viz that the plan which [M? L] espoused, and which proposed to augment the powers of Congress, never could be expected to succeed. He meant not to throw any reflections on Cong? as a body, much less on any particular members of it. He meant however to speak his sentiments without reserve on this subject; it was a privilege of Age, and perhaps the only compensation which nature had given for the privation of so many other enjoyments: and he should not scruple to exercise it freely. Is it to be thought that the people of America, so watchful over their interests; so jealous of their liberties, will give up their all, will surrender both the sword and the purse, to the same body, and that too not chosen immediately by themselves? They never will. They never ought. Will they trust such a body, with the regulation of their trade, with the regulation of their taxes; with all the other great powers, which are in contemplation? Will they give unbounded confidence to a secret Journal—to the intrigues—to the factions which in the nature of things appertain to such an Assembly? If any man doubts the existence of these characters of Congress, let him consult their Journals for the years 78, 79, & 80.—It will be said, that if the people are averse to parting with power, why is it hoped that they will part with it to a National Legislature. The proper answer is that in this case they do not part with power: they only transfer it from one sett of immediate Representatives to another sett.—Much has been said of the unsettled state of the mind of the people, he believed the mind of the people of America, as elsewhere, was unsettled as to some points; but settled as to others. In two points he was sure it was well settled. 1.[1] in an attachment to Republican Government. 2.[1] in an attachment to more than one branch in the Legislature. Their constitutions accord so generally in both these circumstances, that they seem almost to have been pre-concerted. This must either have been a miracle, or have resulted from the genius of the people. The only exceptions to the establishm[t] of two branches in the Legislatures are the State of P[a]. & Cong[s]. and the latter the only single one not chosen by the people themselves. What has been the consequence? The people have been constantly averse to giving that Body further powers—It was acknowledged by [M[r] Patterson] that his plan could not be enforced without military coertion. Does he consider the force of this concession. The most jarring elements of Nature; fire & water themselves are not more incompatible that[2] such a mixture of civil liberty and military execution. Will the militia march from one State to[3] another, in order to collect the arrears of taxes from the delinquent members of the Republic? Will they maintain an army for this purpose? Will not the Citizens of the invaded State assist one another till they rise as one Man, and shake off the Union altogether. Rebellion is the only case, in which the military force of the State can be properly exerted ag[st] its Citizens. In one point of view he was struck with horror at the prospect of recurring to this expedient. To punish the non-payment of taxes with death, was a severity not yet adopted by despotism itself: yet this unexampled cruelty would be mercy compared to a military collection of revenue, in which the bayonet could make no discrimination between the innocent and the guilty. He took this occasion to repeat, that notwithstanding his solicitude to establish a national Government, he never would agree to abolish the State Gov[ts] or render them absolutely insignificant. They were as necessary as the Gen[l] Gov[t] and he would be equally careful to preserve them. He was aware of the difficulty of drawing the line between them, but hoped it was not insurmountable. The Convention, tho' comprising so many distinguished characters, could not be expected to make a faultless Gov[t] And he would prefer trusting to posterity the amendment of its defects, rather than to push the experiment too far.

---

[1] The figures " 1 " and " 2 " are changed to " first " and " secondly " in the transcript.
[2] The word " than " is substituted in the transcript for " that."
[3] The word " into " is substituted in the transcript for " in."

M.ʳ LUTHER MARTIN agreed with [Col Mason] as to the importance of the State Gov.ᵗˢ he would support them at the expence of the Gen.ˡ Gov.ᵗ which was instituted for the purpose of that support. He saw no necessity for two branches, and if it existed Congress might be organized into two. He considered Cong.ˢ as representing the people, being chosen by the Legislatures who were chosen by the people. At any rate, Congress represented the Legislatures; and it was the Legislatures not the people who refused to enlarge their powers. Nor could the rule of voting have been the ground of objection, otherwise ten of the States must always have been ready, to place further confidence in Cong.ˢ The causes of repugnance must therefore be looked for elsewhere.—At the separation from the British Empire, the people of America preferred the establishment of themselves into thirteen separate sovereignties instead of incorporating themselves into one: to these they look up for the security of their lives, liberties & properties: to these they must look up. The federal Gov.ᵗ they formed, to defend the whole ag.ˢᵗ foreign nations, in case of war, and to defend the lesser States ag.ˢᵗ the ambition of the larger: they are afraid of granting powers [1] unnecessarily, lest they should defeat the original end of the Union; lest the powers should prove dangerous to the sovereignties of the particular States which the Union was meant to support; and expose the lesser to being swallowed up by the larger. He conceived also that the people of the States having already vested their powers in their respective Legislatures, could not resume them without a dissolution of their Governments. He was ag.ˢᵗ Conventions in the States: was not ag.ˢᵗ assisting States ag.ˢᵗ rebellious subjects; thought the *federal* plan of M.ʳ Patterson did not require coercion more than the *National one,* as the latter must depend for the deficiency of its revenues on requisitions & quotas, and that a national Judiciary extended into the States would be ineffectual, and would be viewed with a jealousy inconsistent with its usefulness.

M.ʳ SHERMAN 2.ᵈᵉᵈ & supported M.ʳ Lansings motion. He admitted two branches to be necessary in the State Legislatures, but saw no necessity for them in a Confederacy of States. The examples were all, of a single Council. Cong.ˢ carried us thro' the war, and perhaps as well as any Gov.ᵗ could have done. The complaints at present are not that the views of Cong.ˢ are unwise or unfaithful; but that their powers are insufficient for the execution of their views. The national debt & the want of power somewhere to draw forth

---

[1] The transcript uses the word "powers" in the singular.

the National resources, are the great matters that press. All the States were sensible of the defect of power in Cong⁹ He thought much might be said in apology for the failure of the State Legislatures to comply with the confederation. They were afraid of bearing too hard on the people, by accumulating taxes; no *constitutional* rule had been or could be observed in the quotas—the accounts also were unsettled & every State supposed itself in advance, rather than in arrears. For want of a general system, taxes to a due amount had not been drawn from trade which was the most convenient resource. As almost all the States had agreed to the recommendation of Cong⁹ on the subject of an impost, it appeared clearly that they were willing to trust Cong⁹ with power to draw a revenue from Trade. There is no weight therefore in the argument drawn from a distrust of Cong⁹ for money matters being the most important of all, if the people will trust them with power as to them, they will trust them with any other necessary powers. Cong⁹ indeed by the confederation have in fact the right of saying how much the people shall pay, and to what purpose it shall be applied: and this right was granted to them in the expectation that it would in all cases have its effect. If another branch were to be added to Cong⁹ to be chosen by the people, it would serve to embarrass. The people would not much interest themselves in the elections, a few designing men in the large districts would carry their points, and the people would have no more confidence in their new representatives than in Cong⁹ He saw no reason why the State Legislatures should be unfriendly as had been suggested, to Cong⁹ If they appoint Cong⁹ and approve of their measures, they would be rather favorable and partial to them. The disparity of the States in point of size he perceived was the main difficulty. But the large States had not yet suffered from the equality of votes enjoyed by the small ones. In all great and general points, the interests of all the States were the same. The State of Virg⁹ notwithstanding the equality of votes, ratified the Confederation without, or ¹ even proposing, any alteration. Mass⁹ also ratified without any material difficulty &c. In none of the ratifications is the want of two branches noticed or complained of. To consolidate the States as some had proposed would dissolve our Treaties with foreign Nations, which had been formed with us, as *confederated* States. He did not however suppose that the creation of two branches in the Legislature would have such an effect. If the difficulty on the subject of representation can not be otherwise got over, he would agree

---

¹ The word " or " is stricken out in the transcript.

to have two branches, and a proportional representation in one of them; provided each State had an equal voice in the other. This was necessary to secure the rights of the lesser States; otherwise three or four of the large States would rule the others as they please. Each State like each individual had its peculiar habits usages and manners, which constituted its happiness. It would not therefore give to others a power over this happiness, any more than an individual would do, when he could avoid it.

M⸢r⸣ WILSON, urged the necessity of two branches; observed that if a proper model were [1] not to be found in other Confederacies it was not to be wondered at. The number of them was small & the duration of some at least short. The Amphyctionic & Achæan were formed in the infancy of political Science; and appear by their History & fate, to have contained radical defects. The Swiss & Belgic Confederacies were held together not by any vital principle of energy but by the incumbent pressure of formidable neighbouring nations: The German owed its continuance to the influence of the H. of Austria. He appealed to our own experience for the defects of our Confederacy. He had been 6 years in [2] the 12 since the commencement of the Revolution, a member of Congress, and had felt all its weaknesses. He appealed to the recollection of others whether on many important occasions, the public interest had not been obstructed by the small members of the Union. The success of the Revolution was owing to other causes, than the Constitution of Congress. In many instances it went on even ag⸢st⸣ the difficulties arising from Cong⸢s⸣ themselves. He admitted that the large States did accede as had been stated, to the Confederation in its present form. But it was the effect of necessity not of choice. There are other instances of their yielding from the same motive to the unreasonable measures of the small States. The situation of things is now a little altered. He insisted that a jealousy would exist between the State Legislatures & the General Legislature: observing that the members of the former would have views & feelings very distinct in this respect from their constituents. A private Citizen of a State is indifferent whether power be exercised by the Gen⸢l⸣ or State Legislatures, provided it be exercised most for his happiness. His representative has an interest in its being exercised by the body to which he belongs. He will therefore view the National Legisl: with the eye of a jealous rival. He observed that the addresses of Cong⸢s⸣ to the people at

---

[1] The word " was " is substituted in the transcript for " were."
[2] The word " of " is substituted in the transcript for " in."

large, had always been better received & produced greater effect, than those made to the Legislatures.

On the question for postponing in order to take up M: Lansings proposition " to vest the powers of Legislation in Cong: "

Mass: no. Con: ay. N. Y. ay. N. J. ay. P: no. Del. ay M: div: V: no. N. C. no. S. C. no. Geo. no [1]

On motion of the Deputies from Delaware, the question on the 2: Resolution in the Report from the Committee of the whole was postponed till tomorrow.

Adj:

THURSDAY JUNE 21. IN CONVENTION

M: Jonathan Dayton from N. Jersey took his seat.[*]

[3] Doc: JOHNSON. On a comparison of the two plans which had been proposed from Virginia & N. Jersey, it appeared that the peculiarity which characterized the latter was its being calculated to preserve the individuality of the States.' The plan from V: did not profess to destroy this individuality altogether, but was charged with such a tendency. One Gentleman alone (Col. Hamilton) in his animadversions on the plan of N. Jersey, boldly and decisively contended for an abolition of the State Gov'? M: Wilson & the gentlemen from Virg: who also were adversaries of the plan of N. Jersey held a different language. They wished to leave the States in possession of a considerable, tho' a subordinate jurisdiction. They had not yet however shewn how this c: consist with, or be secured ag?t the general sovereignty & jurisdiction, which they proposed to give to the national Government. If this could be shewn in such a manner as to satisfy the patrons of the N. Jersey propositions, that the individuality of the States would not be endangered, many of their objections would no doubt be removed. If this could not be shewn their objections would have their full force. He wished it therefore to be well considered whether in case the States, as was

[*] From June 21 to July 18 inclusive not copied by M: Eppes.[2]

---

[1] In the transcript the vote reads: " Connecticut, New York, New Jersey, Delaware, aye—4; Massachusetts, Pennsylvania, Virginia, North Carolina, South Carolina, Georgia, no—6; Maryland divided."

[2] This footnote is omitted in the transcript. It refers to a copy of Madison's journal made by John W. Eppes, Jefferson's son-in-law, for Jefferson's use some time between 1799 and 1810. " The Writings of James Madison, Hunt, Editor, Vol. VI (1906), 329, n; Documentary History of the Constitution, Vol. V (1905), 294-296.

[3] The transcript here inserts the following: " The second Resolution in the Report from the Committee of the Whole, being under consideration."

proposed, sh.^d retain some portion of sovereignty at least, this portion could be preserved, without allowing them to participate effectually in the Genl Gov.^t, without giving them each a distinct and equal vote for the purpose of defending themselves in the general Councils.

Mr WILSON's respect for Doc.^r Johnson, added to the importance of the subject led him to attempt, unprepared as he was, to solve the difficulty which had been started. It was asked how the Genl Gov.^t and individuality of the particular States could be reconciled to each other; and how the latter could be secured ag.st the former? Might it not, on the other side be asked how the former was to be secured ag.st the latter? It was generally admitted that a jealousy & rivalship would be felt between the Genl & particular Gov.^{ts} As the plan now stood, tho' indeed contrary to his opinion, one branch of the Genl Gov.^t (the Senate or second branch) was to be appointed by the State Legislatures. The State Legislatures, therefore, by this participation in the Genl Gov.^t would have an opportunity of defending their rights. Ought not a reciprocal opportunity to be given to the Genl Gov.^t of defending itself by having an appointment of some one constituent branch of the State Gov.^{ts}? If a security be necessary on one side, it w.^d seem reasonable to demand it on the other. But taking the matter in a more general view, he saw no danger to the States from the Genl Gov.^t In case a combination should be made by the large ones it w.^d produce a general alarm among the rest; and the project w.^d be frustrated. But there was no temptation to such a project. The States having in general a similar interest, in case of any proposition [1] in the National Legislature to encroach on the State Legislatures, he conceived a general alarm w.^d take place in the National Legislature itself, that it would communicate itself to the State Legislatures, and w.^d finally spread among the people at large. The Genl Gov.^t will be as ready to preserve the rights of the States as the latter are to preserve the rights of individuals; all the members of the former, having a common interest, as representatives of all the people of the latter, to leave the State Gov.^{ts} in possession of what the people wish them to retain. He could not discover, therefore any danger whatever on the side from which it had been [2] apprehended. On the contrary, he conceived that in spite of every precaution the general Gov.^t would be in perpetual danger of encroachments from the State Gov.^{ts}

---

[1] The transcript uses the word "proposition" in the plural.
[2] The word "was" is substituted in the transcript for "had been."

M: MADISON was of opinion [1] that there was 1. less danger of encroachment from the Genl Gov.^t than from the State Gov.^{ts} 2.[2] that the mischief from encroachments would be less fatal if made by the former, than if made by the latter. 1. All the examples of other confederacies prove the greater tendency in such systems to anarchy than to tyranny; to a disobedience of the members than to [3] usurpations of the federal head. Our own experience had fully illustrated this tendency.—But it will be said that the proposed change in the principles & form of the Union will vary the tendency; that the Genl Gov.^t will have real & greater powers, and will be derived in one branch at least from the people, not from the Gov.^{ts} of the States. To give full force to this objection, let it be supposed for a moment that indefinite power should be given to the Genl Legislature, and the States reduced to corporations dependent on the Genl Legislature; Why sh.^d it follow that the Genl Gov.^t w.^d take from the States any branch of their power as far as its operation was beneficial, and its continuance desireable to the people? In some of the States, particularly in Connecticut, all the Townships are incorporated, and have a certain limited jurisdiction. Have the Representatives of the people of the Townships in the Legislature of the State ever endeavored to despoil the Townships of any part of their local authority? As far as this local authority is convenient to the people they are attached to it; and their representatives chosen by & amenable to them naturally respect their attachment to this, as much as their attachment to any other right or interest. The relation of a General Gov.^t to State Gov.^{ts} is parallel. 2. Guards were more necessary ag.st encroachments of the State Gov.^{ts} on the Genl Gov.^t than of the latter on the former. The great objection made ag.st an abolition of the State Gov.^{ts} was that the Genl Gov.^t could not extend its care to all the minute objects which fall under the cognizance of the local jurisdictions. The objection as stated lay not ag.st the probable abuse of the general power, but ag.st the imperfect use that could be made of it throughout so great an extent of country, and over so great a variety of objects. As far as as its operation would be practicable it could not in this view be improper; as far as it would be impracticable, the conveniency [4] of the Genl Gov.^t itself would concur with that of the people in the maintenance of subordinate Governments. Were it practicable for the Genl Gov.^t to extend its care to every

---

[1] The phrase " in the first place " is here inserted in the transcript and the figure " 1 " is omitted.

[2] The figure " 2 " is changed to " and in the second place " in the transcript.

[3] The word " to " is omitted in the transcript.

[4] The word " conveniency " is changed to " convenience " in the transcript.

requisite object without the cooperation of the State Govᵗˢ the people would not be less free as members of one great Republic than as members of thirteen small ones. A Citizen of Delaware was not more free than a Citizen of Virginia: nor would either be more free than a Citizen of America. Supposing therefore a tendency in the Genˡ Government to absorb the State Govᵗˢ no fatal [1] consequence could result. Taking the reverse of [2] the supposition, that a tendency should be left in the State Govᵗˢ towards an independence on the General Govᵗ and the gloomy consequences need not be pointed out. The imagination of them, must have suggested to the States the experiment we are now making to prevent the calamity, and must have formed the chief motive with those present to undertake the arduous task.

On the question for resolving "that the Legislature ought to consist of two Branches"

Mass. ay. Conᵗ ay. N. Y. no. N. Jersey no Pᵃ ay. Del. no. Mᵈ divᵈ Vᵃ ay. N. C. ay. S. C. ay. Geo. ay.[3]

The *third* resolution of the Report [4] taken into consideration.

Genˡ PINKNEY moved "that the 1ˢᵗ branch, instead of being elected by the people, shᵈ be elected in such manner as the Legislature of each State should direct." He urged 1.[5] that this liberty would give more satisfaction, as the Legislatures could then accomodate the mode to the conveniency [6] & opinions of the people. 2.[5] that it would avoid the undue influence of large Counties which would prevail if the elections were to be made in districts as must be the mode intended by the Report of the Committee. 3.[5] that otherwise disputed elections must be referred to the General Legislature which would be attended with intolerable expence and trouble to the distant parts of the republic.

Mʳ L. MARTIN seconded the Motion.

Col. HAMILTON considered the motion as intended manifestly to transfer the election from the people to the State Legislatures, which would essentially vitiate the plan. It would increase that State influence which could not be too watchfully guarded agˢᵗ All too must admit the possibility, in case the Genˡ Govᵗ shᵈ maintain itself,

---

[1] The transcript italicizes the word "fatal."

[2] The word "as" is substituted in the transcript for "of."

[3] In the transcript the vote reads: "Massachusetts, Connecticut, Pennsylvania, Virginia, North Carolina, South Carolina, Georgia, aye—7; New York, New Jersey, Delaware, no—3; Maryland, divided."

[4] The word "being" is here inserted in the transcript.

[5] The figures "1," "2" and "3" are changed to "first," "secondly" and "thirdly" in the transcript.

[6] The word "conveniency" is changed to "convenience" in the transcript.

that the State Gov^{ts} might gradually dwindle into nothing. The system therefore sh^d not be engrafted on what might possibly fail.

Mr MASON urged the necessity of retaining the election by the people. Whatever inconveniency [1] may attend the democratic principle, it must actuate one part of the Gov^t It is the only security for the rights of the people.

Mr SHERMAN, would like an election by the Legislatures best, but is content with [2] plan as it stands.

Mr RUTLIDGE could not admit the solidity of the distinction between a mediate & immediate election by the people. It was the same thing to act by oneself, and to act by another. An election by the Legislature would be more refined than an election immediately by the people: and would be more likely to correspond with the sense of the whole community. If this Convention had been chosen by the people in districts it is not to be supposed that such proper characters would have been preferred. The Delegates to Cong^s he thought had also been fitter men than would have been appointed by the people at large.

Mr WILSON considered the election of the 1st branch by the people not only as the corner Stone, but as the foundation of the fabric: and that the difference between a mediate & immediate election was immense. The difference was particularly worthy of notice in this respect: that the Legislatures are actuated not merely by the sentiment of the people; but have an official sentiment opposed to that of the Genl Gov^t and perhaps to that of the people themselves.

Mr KING enlarged on the same distinction. He supposed the Legislatures w^d constantly choose men subservient to their own views as contrasted to the general interest; and that they might even devise modes of election that w^d be subversive of the end in view. He remarked several instances in which the views of a State might be at variance with those of the Genl Gov^t: and mentioned particularly a competition between the National & State debts, for the most certain & productive funds.

Genl PINKNEY was for making the State Gov^{ts} a part of the General System. If they were to be abolished, or lose their agency, S. Carolina & other States would have but a small share of the benefits of Gov^t

On the question for Genl Pinkney motion to substitute election

---

[1] The word " inconveniency " is changed to " inconvenience " in the transcript.

[2] The word " the " is here inserted in the transcript.

of [1] 1ˢᵗ branch in such mode as the Legislatures should appoint, in stead of its being elected by the people."

Massᵗˢ no. Conᵗ ay. N. Y. no. N. J. ay. Pᵃ no. Del. ay. Mᵈ divᵈ Vᵃ no. N. C. no. S. C. ay Geo. no.[2]

General PINKNEY then moved that the 1ˢᵗ branch be elected *by the people* in such mode as the Legislatures should direct; but waved it on its being hinted that such a provision might be more properly tried in the detail of the plan.

On the question for yᵉ election of the 1ˢᵗ branch by the *people*."

Massᵗˢ ay. Conᵗ ay. N. Y. ay. N. J. no. Pᵃ ay. Del. ay. Mᵈ divᵈ Vᵃ ay. N. C. ay. S. C. ay Geo. ay.[3]

[1] Election of the 1ˢᵗ branch " for the term of three years,"[4] considered

Mʳ RANDOLPH moved to strike out, " three years " and insert " two years "—he was sensible that annual elections were a source of great mischiefs in the States, yet it was the want of such checks agˢᵗ the popular intemperence as were now proposed, that rendered them so mischievous. He would have preferred annual to biennial, but for the extent of the U. S. and the inconveniency [5] which would result from them to the representatives of the extreme parts of the Empire. The people were attached to frequency of elections. All the Constitutions of the States except that of S. Carolina, had established annual elections.

Mʳ DICKENSON. The idea of annual elections was borrowed from the antient usage of England, a country much less extensive than ours. He supposed biennial would be inconvenient. He preferred triennial: and in order to prevent the inconveniency [5] of an entire change of the whole number at the same moment, suggested a rotation, by an annual election of one third.

Mʳ ELSEWORTH was opposed to three years, supposing that even one year was preferable to two years. The people were fond of frequent elections and might be safely indulged in one branch of the Legislature. He moved for 1 year.

Mʳ STRONG seconded & supported the motion.

---

[1] The word " the " is here inserted in the transcript.
[2] In the transcript the vote reads: " Connecticut, New Jersey, Delaware, South Carolina, aye—4; Massachusetts, New York, Pennsylvania, Virginia, North Carolina, Georgia, no—6; Maryland, divided."
[3] In the transcript the vote reads: " Massachusetts, Connecticut, New York, Pennsylvania, Delaware, Virginia, North Carolina, South Carolina, Georgia, aye—9; New Jersey, no—1; Maryland, divided."
[4] The word " being " is here inserted in the transcript.
[5] The word " inconveniency " is changed to " inconvenience " in the transcript.

M⸢ WILSON being for making the 1ˢᵗ branch an effectual representation of the people at large, preferred an annual election of it. This
frequency was most familiar & pleasing to the people. It would
be not [1] more inconvenient to them, than triennial elections, as the
people in all the States have annual meetings with which the election
of the National representatives might be made to co-incide. He
did not conceive that it would be necessary for the Nat⸾ Legisl:
to sit constantly; perhaps not half—perhaps not one fourth of the
year.

M⸢ MADISON was persuaded that annual elections would be extremely inconvenient and apprehensive that biennial would be too
much so: he did not mean inconvenient to the electors; but to the
representatives. They would have to travel seven or eight hundred
miles from the distant parts of the Union; and would probably not
be allowed even a reimbursement of their expences. Besides, none of
those who wished to be re-elected would remain at the seat of Gov-
ernm⸾; confiding that their absence would not affect them. The
members of Cong⸾ had done this with few instances of disappoint-
ment. But as the choice was here to be made by the people themselves who would be much less complaisant to individuals, and much
more susceptible of impressions from the presence of a Rival candidate, it must be supposed that the members from the most distant
States would travel backwards & forwards at least as often as the
elections should be repeated. Much was to be said also on the time
requisite for new members who would always form a large proportion, to acquire that knowledge of the affairs of the States in general
without which their trust could not be usefully discharged.

M⸢ SHERMAN preferred annual elections, but would be content
with biennial. He thought the Representatives ought to return home
and mix with the people. By remaining at the seat of Gov⸾ they
would acquire the habits of the place which might differ from those
of their Constituents.

Col. MASON observed that the States being differently situated
such a rule ought to be formed as would put them as nearly as possible on a level. If elections were annual the middle States would
have a great advantage over the extreme ones. He wished them to
be biennial; and the rather as in that case they would coincide with
the periodical elections of S. Carolina as well of the other States.

Col. HAMILTON urged the necessity of 3 years. There ought to
be neither too much nor too little dependence, on the popular senti-

---

[1] The words " be not " are transposed to read " not be " in the transcript.

ments. The checks in the other branches of Govern.^t would be but feeble, and would need every auxiliary principle that could be interwoven. The British House of Commons were elected septennially, yet the democratic spirit of ye Constitution had not ceased. Frequency of elections tended to make the people listless to them; and to facilitate the success of little cabals. This evil was complained of in all the States. In Virg.^a it had been lately found necessary to force the attendance & voting of the people by severe regulations.

On the question for striking out " three years "

Mass.^{ts} ay. Con.^t ay. N. Y. no. N. J. div.^d P.^a ay. Del. no. M.^d no. V.^a ay. N. C. ay. S. C. ay. Geo. ay.[1]

The motion for " two years " was then inserted nem. con.

Adj.^d

FRIDAY JUNE 22. IN CONVENTION

The clause in Resol. 3.[2] " to receive fixed stipends to be paid out of the Nation.^l Treasury "[3] considered.

Mr ELSEWORTH, moved to substitute payment by the States out of their own Treasurys: observing that the manners of different States were very different in the Stile of living and in the profits accruing from the exercise of like talents. What would be deemed therefore a reasonable compensation in some States, in others would be very unpopular, and might impede the system of which it made a part.

Mr WILLIAMSON favored the idea. He reminded the House of the prospect of new States to the Westward. They would be[4] poor—would pay little into the common Treasury—and would have a different interest from the old States. He did not think therefore that the latter ought to pay the expences of men who would be employed in thwarting their measures & interests.

Mr GHORUM, wished not to refer the matter to the State Legislatures who were always paring down salaries in such a manner as to keep out of offices men most capable of executing the functions of them. He thought also it would be wrong to fix the compensations[5] by the constitutions,[5] because we could not venture to make it as liberal

---

[1] In the transcript the vote reads: "Massachusetts, Connecticut, Pennsylvania, Virginia, North Carolina, South Carolina, Georgia, aye—7; New York, Delaware, Maryland, no—3; New Jersey, divided."

[2] The words "the third Resolution" are substituted in the transcript for "Resol. 3."

[3] The word "being" is here inserted in the transcript.

[4] The word "too" is here inserted in the transcript.

[5] The transcript uses the words "conpensations" and "constitutions" in the singular.

as it ought to be without exciting an enmity ag.ᵗ the whole plan. Let the Nat.ˡ Legisl.: provide for their own wages from time to time; as the State Legislatures do. He had not seen this part of their power abused, nor did he apprehend an abuse of it.

M.ʳ RANDOLPH [1] feared we were going too far, in consulting popular prejudices. Whatever respect might be due to them, in lesser matters, or in cases where they formed the permanent character of the people, he thought it neither incumbent on nor honorable for the Convention, to sacrifice right & justice to that consideration. If the States were to pay the members of the Nat.ˡ Legislature, a dependence would be created that would vitiate the whole System. The whole nation has an interest in the attendance & services of the members. The Nation.ˡ Treasury therefore is the proper fund for supporting them.

M.ʳ KING, urged the danger of creating a dependence on the States by leav.ᵍ to them the payment of the members of the Nat.ˡ Legislature. He supposed it w.ᵈ be best to be explicit as to the compensation to be allowed. A reserve on that point, or a reference to the Nat.ˡ Legislature of the quantum, would excite greater opposition than any sum that would be actually necessary or proper.

M.ʳ SHERMAN contended for referring both the quantum and the payment of it to the State Legislatures.

M.ʳ WILSON was ag.ᵗ *fixing* the compensation as circumstances would change and call for a change of the amount. He thought it of great moment that the members of the Nat.ˡ Gov.ᵗ should be left as independent as possible of the State Gov.ᵗˢ in all respects.

M.ʳ MADISON concurred in the necessity of preserving the compensations for the Nat.ˡ Gov.ᵗ independent on the State Gov.ᵗˢ but at the same time approved of *fixing* them by the Constitution, which might be done by taking a standard which w.ᵈ not vary with circumstances. He disliked particularly the policy suggested by M.ʳ Wiliamson of leaving the members from the poor States beyond the Mountains, to the precarious & parsimonious support of their constituents. If the Western States hereafter arising should be admitted into the Union, they ought to be considered as equals & as brethren. If their representatives were to be associated in the Common Councils, it was of common concern that such provisions should be made as would invite the most capable and respectable characters into the service.

M.ʳ HAMILTON apprehended inconveniency [2] from *fixing* the wages.

---

[1] The words " said he " are here inserted in the transcript.
[2] The word " inconveniency " is changed to " inconvenience " in the transcript.

He was strenuous agst making the National Council dependent on the Legislative rewards of the States. Those who pay are the masters of those who are paid. Payment by the States would be unequal as the distant States would have to pay for the same term of attendance and more days in travelling to & from the seat of the [1] Gov^t He expatiated emphatically on the difference between the feelings & views of the *people*—& the *Governments* of the States arising from the personal interest & official inducements which must render the latter unfriendly to the Genl Gov^t

Mr WILSON moved that the Salaries of the 1st branch " *be ascertained by the National Legislature,* " [2] and be paid out of the Nat^l Treasury.

Mr MADISON, thought the members of the Legis^l too much interested to ascertain their own compensation. It w^d be indecent to put their hands into the public purse for the sake of their own pockets.

On this question [3] Mas. no. Con^t no. N. Y. div^d N. J. ay. P^a ay. Del. no. M^d no. V^a no. N. C. no. S. C. no. Geo. div^d [4]

On the question for striking out " Nat^l Treasury " as moved by Mr Elseworth

Mr HAMILTON renewed his opposition to it. He pressed the distinction between [5] State Gov^{ts} & the people. The former w^d be the rivals of the Genl Gov^t The State legislatures ought not therefore to be the paymasters of the latter.

Mr ELSEWORTH. If we are jealous of the State Gov^{ts} they will be so of us. If on going home I tell them we gave the Gen: Gov^t such powers because we c^d not trust you, will they adopt it, and with^t y^r approbation it is a nullity.

[6] Mass^{ts} ay. Con^t ay. N. Y. div^d N. J. no Pen^a no. Del. no. M^d no. V^a no. N. C. ay. S. C. ay. Geo. div^d * [7]

* Note. [It appeared that Mass^{ts} concurred, not because they thought the State Treasy ought to be substituted; but because they thought nothing should be said on the subject, in which case it w^d silently devolve on the Nat^l Treasury to support the National Legislature.]

---

[1] The word " the " is omitted in the transcript.
[2] The transcript does not italicize the phrase " *be ascertained by the National Legislature.* "
[3] The transcript here inserts the following: " shall the salaries of the first branch be ascertained by the National Legislature? "
[4] In the transcript the vote reads: " New Jersey, Pennsylvania, aye—2; Massachusetts, Connecticut, Delaware, Maryland, Virginia, North Carolina, South Carolina, no—7; New York, Georgia, divided."
[5] The word " the " is here inserted in the transcript.
[6] The words " On the question " are here inserted in the transcript.
[7] In the transcript the vote reads: " Massachusetts,* Connecticut, North Carolina, South Carolina, aye—4; New Jersey, Pennsylvania, Delaware, Maryland, Virginia, no—5; New York, Georgia, divided; so it passed in the negative."

On a question for substituting " adequate compensation " in place of " fixt stipends " it was agreed to nem. con. the friends of the latter being willing that the practicability of *fixing* the compensation should be considered hereafter in forming the details.

It was then moved by M: BUTLER that a question be taken on both points jointly; to wit " adequate compensation to be paid out of the Nat! Treasury." It was objected to as out of order, the parts having been separately decided on. The Presid! refer⁴ the question of order to the House, and it was determined to be in order. Con. N. J. Del. M⁴ N. C. S. C.—ay—¹ N. Y. P! V! Geo. no—¹ Mass: divided. The question on the sentence was then postponed by S. Carolina in right of the State.

Col. MASON moved to insert " twenty-five years of age as a qualification for the members of the 1ˢᵗ branch." He thought it absurd that a man to day should not be permitted by the law to make a bargain for himself, and tomorrow should be authorized to manage the affairs of a great nation. It was the more extraordinary as every man carried with him in his own experience a scale for measuring the deficiency of young politicians; since he would if interrogated be obliged to declare that his political opinions at the age of 21. were too crude & erroneous to merit an influence on public measures. It had been said that Cong! had proved a good school for our young men. It might be so for any thing he knew but if it were, he chose that they should bear the expence of their own education.

M: WILSON was ag! abridging the rights of election in any shape. It was the same thing whether this were done by disqualifying the objects of choice, or the persons chusing. The motion tended to damp the efforts of genius, and of laudable ambition. There was no more reason for incapacitating *youth* than *age*, where the requisite qualifications were found. Many instances might be mentioned of signal services rendered in high stations to the public before the age of 25: The present M: Pitt and Lord Bolingbroke were striking instances.

On the question for inserting " 25 years of age "

Mass!ˢ no. Con! ay. N. Y. div⁴ N. J. ay. P! no. Del. ay. M⁴ ay. V! ay. N. C. ay. S. C. ay. Geo. no.²

---

¹ In the transcript the figures " 6 " and " 4 " are inserted after " ay " and " no " respectively.

² In the transcript the vote reads: " Connecticut, New Jersey, Delaware, Maryland, Virginia, North Carolina, South Carolina, aye—7; Massachusetts, Pennsylvania, Georgia, no—3; New York, divided."

M̠ GHORUM moved to strike out the last member of 3 Resol:[1] concerning ineligibility of members of the 1ˢᵗ branch to offices[2] during the term of their membership & for one year after. He considered it as[3] unnecessary & injurious. It was true abuses had been displayed in G. B. but no one c̠ᵈ say how far they might have contributed to preserve the due influence of the Gov̠ᵗ nor what might have ensued in case the contrary theory had been tried.

M̠ BUTLER opposed it. This precaution ag̠ˢᵗ intrigue was necessary. He appealed to the example of G. B. where men got[4] into Parl̠ᵗ that they might get offices for themselves or their friends. This was the source of the corruption that ruined their Gov̠ᵗ

M̠ KING, thought we were refining too much. Such a restriction on the members would discourage merit. It would also give a pretext to the Executive for bad appointments, as he might always plead this as a bar to the choice he wished to have made.

M̠ WILSON was ag̠ˢᵗ fettering elections, and discouraging merit. He suggested also the fatal consequence in time of war, of rendering perhaps the best Commanders ineligible: appealing[5] to our situation during the late war, and indirectly leading to a recollection of the appointment of the Commander in Chief out of Congress.

Col. MASON was for shutting the door at all events ag̠ˢᵗ corruption. He enlarged on the venality and abuses in this particular in G. Britain: and alluded to the multiplicity of foreign Embassies by Cong̠ˢ The disqualification he regarded as a corner stone in the fabric.

Col. HAMILTON. There are inconveniences on both sides. We must take man as we find him, and if we expect him to serve the public must interest his passions in doing so. A reliance on pure patriotism had been the source of many of our errors. He thought the remark of M̠ Ghorum a just one. It was impossible to say what w̠ᵈ be[6] effect in G. B. of such a reform as had been urged. It was known that one of the ablest politicians [M̠ Hume,] had pronounced all that influence on the side of the crown, which went under the name of corruption,[7] an essential part of the weight which maintained the equilibrium of the Constitution.

---

[1] The words "the third Resolution" are substituted in the transcript for "3 Resol: "

[2] The letter "s" is stricken out of the word "offices" in the transcript.

[3] The word "as" is stricken out in the transcript.

[4] The word "get" is substituted in the transcript for "got."

[5] The word "appealed" is substituted in the transcript for "appealing."

[6] The word "the" is here inserted in the transcript.

[7] The transcript italicizes the word "corruption."

On M: Ghorum's Motion for striking out " ineligibility,"[1]
Mas. ay. Con. no. N. Y. div. N. J. ay. P. div. Del. div.
Mar. no. V. no. N. C. ay. S. C. no. Geo. ay.[2]

Adj.

SATURDAY JUNE 23.   IN CONVENTION

The 3. Resol: resumed.[3]

On[4] Question yesterday postponed by S. Carol: for agreeing to
the whole sentence " for allowing an adequate compensation to be
paid out of the *Treasury of the U. States* "
Mast. ay. Con. no. N. Y. no. N. J. ay. Pen. ay Del. no.
M. ay. V. ay. N. C. no. S. C. no. Geo divided.[5] So the question
was lost, & the sentence not inserted:

Gen. PINKNEY moves to strike out the ineligibility of members of
the 1st branch to offices established " by a particular State." He
argued from the inconveniency[6] to which such a restriction would
expose both the members of the 1st branch, and the States wishing
for their services;[7] from the smallness of the object to be attained
by the restriction.

It w. seem from the ideas of some that we are erecting a Kingdom to be divided ag.t itself, he disapproved such a fetter on the
Legislature.

M. SHERMAN seconds the motion. It w. seem that we are erecting a Kingdom at war with itself. The Legislature ought not to[8]
fettered in such a case. on the question

Mast. no. Con. ay. N. Y. ay. N. J. ay. P. no. Del. no.
M. ay. V. ay. N. C. ay. S. C. ay. Geo. ay.[9]

---

[1] The transcript here inserts the following: " it was lost by an equal
division of the votes."

[2] In the transcript the vote reads: " Massachusetts, New Jersey, North
Carolina, Georgia, aye—4; Connecticut, Maryland, Virginia, South Carolina,
no—4; New York, Pennsylvania, Delaware, divided."

[3] In the transcript this sentence reads: " The third Resolution being resumed."

[4] The word " the " is here inserted in the transcript.

[5] In the transcript the vote reads: " Massachusetts, New Jersey, Pennsylvania, Maryland, Virginia, aye—5; Connecticut, New York, Delaware, North
Carolina, South Carolina, no—5; Georgia, divided."

[6] The word " inconveniency " is changed to " inconvenience " in the transcript.

[7] The word " and " is here inserted in the transcript.

[8] The word " be " is here inserted in the transcript.

[9] In the transcript the vote reads: " Connecticut, New York, New Jersey,
Maryland, Virginia, North Carolina, South Carolina, Georgia, aye—8; Massachusetts, Pennsylvania, Delaware, no—3."

M: MADISON renewed his motion yesterday made & waved to render the members of the 1ˢᵗ branch "ineligible during their term of service, & for one year after—to such offices only as should be established, or the emoluments thereof, augmented by the Legislature of the U. States during the time of their being members." He supposed that the unnecessary creation of offices, and increase of salaries, were the evils most experienced, & that if the door was shut agˢᵗ them: it might properly be left open for the appointᵗ of members to other offices as an encouragemᵗ to the Legislative service.

M: Alex: MARTIN seconded the motion.

M: BUTLER. The amendᵗ does not go far eno' & wᵈ be easily evaded

M: RUTLIDGE, was for preserving the Legislature as pure as possible, by shutting the door against appointments of its own members to offices,[1] which was one source of its corruption.

M: MASON. The motion of my colleague is but a partial remedy for the evil. He appealed to him as a witness of the shameful partiality of the Legislature of Virginia to its own members. He enlarged on the abuses & corruption in the British Parliament, connected with the appointment of its members. He cᵈ not suppose that a sufficient number of Citizens could not be found who would be ready, without the inducement of eligibility to offices, to undertake the Legislative service. Genius & virtue it may be said, ought to be encouraged. Genius, for aught he knew, might, but that virtue should be encouraged by such a species of venality, was an idea, that at least had the merit of being new.

M: KING remarked that we were refining too much in this business; and that the idea of preventing intrigue and solicitation of offices was chimerical. You say that no member shall himself be eligible to any office. Will this restrain him from from availing himself of the same means which would gain appointments for himself, to gain them for his son, his brother, or any other object of his partiality. We were losing therefore the advantages on one side, without avoiding the evils on the other.

M: WILSON supported the motion. The proper cure he said for corruption in the Legislature was to take from it the power of appointing to offices. One branch of corruption would indeed remain, that of creating unnecessary offices, or granting unnecessary salaries, and for that the amendment would be a proper remedy. He animadverted on the impropriety of stigmatizing with the name

---

[1] The transcript uses the word "offices" in the singular.

of venality the laudable ambition of rising into the honorable offices of the Government; an ambition most likely to be felt in the early & most incorrupt period of life, & which all wise & free Gov^{ts} had deemed it sound policy, to cherish, not to check. The members of the Legislature have perhaps the hardest & least profitable task of any who engage in the service of the state. Ought this merit to. be made a disqualification?

Mr SHERMAN, observed that the motion did not go far enough. It might be evaded by the creation of a new office, the translation to it of a person from another office, and the appointment of a member of the Legislature to the latter. A new Embassy might be established to a new Court, & an ambassador taken from another, in order to *create* a vacancy for a favorite member. He admitted that inconveniencies lay on both sides. He hoped there w^d be sufficient inducements to the public service without resorting to the prospect of desireable offices, and on the whole was rather agst the motion of Mr Madison.

Mr GERRY thought there was great weight in the objection of Mr Sherman. He added as another objection agst admitting the eligibility of members in any case that it would produce intrigues of ambitious men for displacing proper officers, in order to create vacancies for themselves. In answer to Mr King he observed that although members, if disqualified themselves might still intrigue & cabal for their sons, brothers &c, yet as their own interest would be dearer to them, than those of their nearest connections, it might be expected they would go greater lengths to promote it.

Mr MADISON had been led to this motion as a middle ground between an eligibility in all cases, and an absolute disqualification. He admitted the probable abuses of an eligibility of the members, to offices, particularly within the gift of the Legislature He had witnessed the partiality of such bodies to their own members, as had been remarked of the Virginia assembly by his colleague [Col. Mason]. He appealed however to him, in turn to vouch another fact not less notorious in Virginia, that the backwardness of the best citizens to engage in the Legislative service gave but too great success to unfit characters. The question was not to be viewed on one side only. The advantages & disadvantages on both ought to be fairly compared. The objects to be aimed at were to fill all offices with the fittest characters, & to draw the wisest & most worthy citizens into the Legislative service. If on one hand, public bodies were partial to their own members; on the other they were as apt to be misled by taking characters on report, or the authority of patrons and dependents. All who had been concerned in the appointment of strangers on those recommedations must be sensible of this truth. Nor w^d the partialities of such Bodies be obviated by disqualifying their own members. Candidates for office would hover round the seat of Gov^t or be found among the residents there, and practise all the means of courting the favor of the members. A great proportion of the appointments made by the States were evidently brought about in this way. In the general Gov^t the evil must be still greater, the characters of distant states, being much less known throughout the U. States than those of the distant parts of the same State. The elections by Congress had generally turned on men living at the seat of the fed^l Gov^t or in its neighbourhood.—As to the next object, the impulse to the Legislative service, was evinced by experience to be in general too feeble with those best qualified for it. This inconveniency [1] w^d also be more felt in the Nat^l Gov^t than in the State Gov^{ts} as the sacrifices req^d from the distant members, w^d be much greater, and the pecuniary provisions, probably, more disproportiate. It w^d therefore be impolitic to add fresh objections to the Legislative service by an absolute disqualification of its members. The point in question was whether this would be an objection with the most capable citizens. Arguing from experience he concluded that it would. The Legislature of Virg^a would probably have been without many of its best members, if in that situation, they had been ineligible to Cong^s to the Gov^t & other honorable offices of the State.

Mr BUTLER thought Characters fit for office w^d never be unknown.

Col. MASON. If the members of the Legislature are disqualified, still the honors of the State will induce those who aspire to them to enter that service, as the field in which they can best display & improve their talents, & lay the train for their subsequent advancement.

Mr JENIFER remarked that in Maryland, the Senators chosen for five years, c^d hold no other office & that this circumstance gained them the greatest confidence of the people.

On the question for agreeing to the motion of Mr Madison.

Mass^{ts} div^d C^t ay. N. Y. no. N. J. ay. P^a no. Del. no. M^d no. V^a no. N. C. no. S. C. no. Geo. no.[2]

Mr SHERMAN mov^d to insert the words " and incapable of hold-

---

[1] The word " inconveniency " is changed to " inconvenience " in the transcript.

[2] In the transcript the vote reads: " Connecticut, New Jersey, aye—2; New York, Pennsylvania, Delaware, Maryland, Virginia, North Carolina, South Carolina, Georgia, no—8; Massachusetts, divided."

ing " after the words " eligible to offices " [1] wch was agreed to without opposition.

The word " established " & the words " [2] Nat^l Gov^t " were struck out of Resolution 3^d : [3]

Mr SPAIGHT called for a division of the question, in consequence of which it was so put, as that it turned in [4] the first member of it, " on the ineligibility of the [5] members *during the term for which they were elected* "—whereon the States were,

Mass^{ts} div^d C^t ay. N. Y. ay. N. J. ay. P^a no. Del. ay. M^d ay. V^a ay. N. C. ay. S. C. ay. Geo. no.[6]

On the 2^d member of the sentence extending ineligibility of members to one year after the term for which they were elected Col MASON thought this essential to guard agst evasions by resignations, and stipulations for office to be fulfilled at the expiration of the legislative term. Mr GERRY, had known such a case. Mr HAMILTON. Evasions c^d not be prevented—as by proxies—by friends holding for a year, & them [7] opening the way &c. Mr RUTLIDGE admitted the possibility of evasions but was for controuling them as possible.[8]

[9] Mass. no. C^t no. N. Y. ay. N. J. no. P^a div^d Del. ay. Mar^d ay V^a no. N. C. no. S. C. ay. Geo. no [10]

Adj^d

MONDAY. JUNE 25. IN CONVENTION.

Resolution 4.[11] being taken up.

Mr PINKNEY [12] spoke as follows— The efficacy of the System will

---

[1] The words " ineligible to any office " are substituted in the transcript for " eligible to offices."

[2] The words " under the " are here inserted in the transcript.

[3] The words " the third Resolution " are substituted in the transcript for " Resolution 3d "

[4] The word " on " is substituted in the transcript for " in."

[5] The word " the " is omitted in the transcript.

[6] In the transcript the vote reads: " Connecticut, New York, New Jersey, Delaware, Maryland, Virginia, North Carolina, South Carolina, aye—8; Pennsylvania, Georgia, no—2; Massachusetts, divided."

[7] The word " then " is substituted in the transcript for " them."

[8] The phrase " contracting them as far as possible " is substituted in the transcript for " controuling them as possible."

[9] The words " On the question " are here inserted in the transcript.

[10] In the transcript the vote reads: " New York, Delaware, Maryland, South Carolina, aye—4; Massachusetts, Connecticut, New Jersey, Virginia, North Carolina, Georgia, no—6; Pennsylvania, divided."

[11] The words " The fourth Resolution " are substituted in the transcript for " Resolution 4."

[12] Pinckney furnished Madison with a copy of this speech which he transcribed, but apparently not with the whole of it, as Madison's note at the end

depend on this article. In order to form a right judgmᵗ in the case, it will be proper to examine the situation of this Country more accurately than it has yet been done. The people of the U. States are perhaps the most singular of any we are acquainted with. Among them there are fewer distinctions of fortune & less of rank, than among the inhabitants of any other nation. Every freeman has a right to the same protection & security; and a very moderate share of property entitles them to the possession of all the honors and privileges the public can bestow: hence arises a greater equality, than is to be found among the people of any other country, and an equality which is more likely to continue—I say this equality is likely to continue, because in a new Country, possessing immense tracts of uncultivated lands, where every temptation is offered to emigration & where industry must be rewarded with competency, there will be few poor, and few dependent—Every member of the Society almost, will enjoy an equal power of arriving at the supreme offices & consequently of directing the strength & sentiments of the whole Community. None will be excluded by birth, & few by fortune, from voting for proper persons to fill the offices of Government— the whole community will enjoy in the fullest sense that kind of political liberty which consists in the power the members of the State reserve to themselves, of arriving at the public offices, or at least, of having votes in the nomination of those who fill them.

If this State of things is true & the prospect of its continuing[1] probable, it is perhaps not politic to endeavour too close an imitation of a Government calculated for a people whose situation is, & whose views ought to be extremely different

Much has been said of the Constitution of G. Britain. I will confess that I believe it to be the best Constitution in existence; but at the same time I am confident it is one that will not or can not be introduced into this Country, for many centuries.—If it were proper to go here into a historical dissertation on the British Constitution, it might easily be shewn that the peculiar excellence, the distinguishing feature of that Governmᵗ can not possibly be introduced into our System—that its balance between the Crown & the people can not be made a part of our Constitution.—that we neither have or can have the members to compose it, nor the rights, privileges & properties of so distinct a class of Citizens to guard.—that the materials for form-

---

indicates. The original Pinckney draft is among the Madison papers, and shows Madison's copying to have been accurate.

    [1] The word "continuance" is substituted in the transcript for "continuing."

ing this balance or check do not exist, nor is there a necessity for having so permanent a part of our Legislative, until the Executive power is so constituted as to have something fixed & dangerous in its principle—By this I mean a sole, hereditary, though limited Executive.

That we cannot have a proper body for forming a Legislative balance between the inordinate power of the Executive and the people, is evident from a review of the accidents & circumstances which gave rise to the peerage of Great Britain—I believe it is well ascertained that the parts which compose the British Constitution arose immediately from the forests of Germany; but the antiquity of the establishment of nobility is by no means clearly defined. Some authors are of opinion that the dignity denoted by the titles of dux et [1] comes, was derived from the old Roman to the German Empire; while others are of opinion that they existed among the Germans long before the Romans were acquainted with them. The institution however of nobility is immemorial among the nations who may probably be termed the ancestors of [2] Britain.—At the time they were summoned in England to become a part of the National Council, and [3] the circumstances which have [3] contributed to make them a constituent part of that constitution, must be well known to all gentlemen who have had industry & curiosity enough to investigate the subject— The nobles with their possessions & and dependents composed a body permanent in their nature and formidable in point of power. They had a distinct interest both from the King and the people; an interest which could only be represented by themselves, and the guardianship [4] could not be safely intrusted to others.—At the time they were originally called to form a part of the National Council, necessity perhaps as much as other cause, induced the Monarch to look up to them. It was necessary to demand the aid of his subjects in personal & pecuniary services. The power and possessions of the Nobility would not permit taxation from any assembly of which they were not a part: & the blending [5] the deputies of the Commons with them, & thus forming what they called their parler-ment [6] was perhaps as much the effect of chance as of any thing else. The Commons were at that time compleatly subordinate to the nobles, whose

---

[1] The word "and" is substituted in the transcript for "et."
[2] The word "Great" is here inserted in the transcript.
[3] The words "and" and "have" are crossed out in the transcript.
[4] The words "of which" are here inserted in the transcript.
[5] The word "of" is here inserted in the transcript.
[6] The transcript italicizes the word "parler-ment."

consequence & influence seem to have been the only reasons for their superiority; a superiority so degrading to the Commons that in the first Summons we find the peers are called upon to consult,[1] the commons to consent.[1] From this time the peers have composed a part of the British Legislature, and notwithstanding their power and influence have diminished & those of the Commons have increased, yet still they have always formed an excellent balance agst either the encroachments of the Crown or the people.

I have said that such a body cannot exist in this Country for ages, and that untill the situation of our people is exceedingly changed no necessity will exist for so permanent a part of the Legislature. To illustrate this I have remarked that the people of the United States are more equal in their circumstances than the people of any other Country—that they have very few rich men among them,—by rich men I mean those whose riches may have a dangerous influence, or such as are esteemed rich in Europe—perhaps there are not one hundred such on the Continent; that it is not probable this number will be greatly increased: that the genius of the people, their mediocrity of situation & the prospects which are afforded their industry in a Country which must be a new one for centuries are unfavorable to the rapid distinction of ranks. The destruction of the right of primogeniture & the equal division of the property of Intestates will also have an effect to preserve this mediocrity; for laws invariably affect the manners of a people. On the other hand that vast extent of unpeopled territory which opens to the frugal & industrious a sure road to competency & independence will effectually prevent for a considerable time the increase of the poor or discontented, and be the means of preserving that equality of condition which so eminently distinguishes us.

If equality is as I contend the leading feature of the U. States, where then are the riches & wealth whose representation & protection is the peculiar province of this permanent body. Are they in the hands of the few who may be called rich; in the possession of less than a hundred citizens? certainly not. They are in the great body of the people, among whom there are no men of wealth, and very few of real poverty.—Is it probable that a change will be created, and that a new order of men will arise? If under the British Government, for a century no such change was probable,[2] I think it

---

[1] The transcript italicizes the words "consult" and "consent."
[2] The word "produced" is substituted for the word "probable" in the transcript.

may be fairly concluded it will not take place while even the semblance of Republicanism remains.—How is this change to be effected? Where are the sources from whence it is to flow? From the landed interest? No. That is too unproductive & too much divided in most of the States. From the Monied interest? If such exists at present, little is to be apprehended from that source. Is it to spring from commerce? I believe it would be the first instance in which a nobility sprang from merchants. Besides, Sir, I apprehend that on this point the policy of the U. States has been much mistaken. We have unwisely considered ourselves as the inhabitants of an old instead of a new country. We have adopted the maxims of a State full of people & manufactures & established in credit. We have deserted our true interest, and instead of applying closely to those improvements in domestic policy which would have ensured the future importance of our commerce, we have rashly & prematurely engaged in schemes as extensive as they are imprudent. This however is an error which daily corrects itself & I have no doubt that a few more severe trials will convince us, that very different commercial principles ought to govern the conduct of these States.

The people of this country are not only very different from the inhabitants of any State we are acquainted with in the modern world; but I assert that their situation is distinct from either the people of Greece or Rome, or of any State we are acquainted with among the antients.—Can the orders introduced by the institution of Solon, can they be found in the United States? Can the military habits & manners of Sparta be resembled to our habits & manners? Are the distinctions of Patrician & Plebeian known among us? Can the Helvetic or Belgic confederacies, or can the unwieldy, unmeaning body called the Germanic Empire, can they be said to possess either the same or a situation like ours? I apprehend not.—They are perfectly different, in their distinctions of rank, their Constitutions, their manners & their policy.

Our true situation appears to me to be this.—a new extensive Country containing within itself the materials for forming a Government capable of extending to its citizens all the blessings of civil & religious liberty—capable of making them happy at home. This is the great end of Republican Establishments. We mistake the object of our Government, if we hope or wish that it is to make us respectable abroad. Conquest or superiority among other powers is not or ought not ever to be the object of republican systems. If they are sufficiently active & energetic to rescue us from contempt & preserve our domestic happiness & security, it is all we can expect from them,—it is more than almost any other Government ensures to its citizens.

I believe this observation will be found generally true:—that no two people are so exactly alike in their situation or circumstances as to admit the exercise of the same Government with equal benefit: that a system must be suited to the habits & genius of the people it is to govern, and must grow out of them.

The people of the U. S. may be divided into three classes— *Professional men* who must from their particular pursuits always have a considerable weight in the Government while it remains popular—*Commercial men*, who may or may not have weight as a wise or injudicious commercial policy is pursued.—If that commercial policy is pursued which I conceive to be the true one, the merchants of this Country will not or ought not for a considerable time to have much weight in the political scale.—The third is the *landed interest*, the owners and cultivators of the soil, who are and ought ever to be the governing spring in the system.—These three classes, however distinct in their pursuits are individually equal in the political scale, and may be easily proved to have but one interest. The dependence of each on the other is mutual. The merchant depends on the planter. Both must in private as well as public affairs be connected with the professional men; who in their turn must in some measure depend upon [1] them. Hence it is clear from this manifest connection, & the equality which I before stated exists, & must for the reasons then assigned, continue, that after all there is one, but one great & equal body of citizens composing the inhabitants of this Country among whom there are no distinctions of rank, and very few or none of fortune.

For a people thus circumstanced are we then to form a government & the question is what kind [2] of Government is best suited to them.

Will it be the British Gov? No. Why? Because G. Britain contains three orders of people distinct in their situation, their possessions & their principles.—These orders combined form the great body of the Nation, and as in national expences the wealth of the whole community must contribute, so ought each component part to be properly & duly [3] represented—No other combination of power could form this due representation, but the one that exists.—Neither

---

[1] The word "on" is substituted in the transcript for "upon."
[2] The word "sort" is substituted in the transcript for "kind."
[3] The words "properly & duly" are transposed in the transcript to read "duly and properly."

the peers or the people could represent the royalty, nor could the Royalty & the people form a proper representation for the Peers.— Each therefore must of necessity be represented by itself, or the sign of itself; and this accidental mixture has certainly formed a Government admirably well balanced.

But the U. States contain but one order that can be assimilated to the British Nation,—this is the order of Commons. They will not surely then attempt to form a Government consisting of three branches, two of which shall have nothing to represent. They will not have an Executive & Senate [hereditary] because the King & Lords of England are so. The same reasons do not exist and therefore the same provisions are not necessary.

We must as has been observed suit our Governm⸢t⸣ to the people it is to direct. These are I believe as active, intelligent & susceptible of good Governm⸢t⸣ as any people in the world. The Confusion which has produced the present relaxed State is not owing to them. It is owing to the weakness & [defects] of a Gov⸢t⸣ incapable of combining the various interests it is intended to unite, and destitute of energy.— All that we have to do then is to distribute the powers of Gov⸢t⸣ in such a manner, and for such limited periods, as while it gives a proper degree of permanency to the Magistrate, will reserve to the people, the right of election they will not or ought not frequently to part with.— I am of opinion that this may be easily [1] done; and that with some amendments the propositions before the Committee will fully answer this end.

No position appears to me more true than this; that the General Gov⸢t⸣ can not effectually exist without reserving to the States the possession of their local rights. They are the instruments upon which the Union must frequently depend for the support & execution of their powers, however immediately operating upon the people, and not upon the States.

Much has been said about the propriety of abolishing the distinction of State Governments, & having but one general System. Suffer me for a moment to examine this question.*

* The residue of this speech was not furnished like the above by M⸢r⸣ Pinckney.[2]

---

[1] The words "be easily" are transposed in the transcript to "easily be."
[2] "The residue" of Pinckney's speech, according to Robert Yates was as follows:
"The United States include a territory of about 1500 miles in length, and in breadth about 400; the whole of which is divided into states and districts. While we were dependent on the crown of Great Britain, it was in contemplation to have formed the whole into one—but it was found impracticable. No legislature could make good laws for the whole, nor can it now be done. It would

The mode of constituting the 2.ᵈ branch being under consideration.
The word " national " was struck out and " United States "
inserted.

M.ʳ GHORUM, inclined to a compromise as to the rule of proportion. He thought there was some weight in the objections of the small
States. If V.ᵃ should have 16. votes & Del.ʳᵉ with several other States
together 16. those from Virg.ᵃ would be more likely to unite than the
others, and would therefore have an undue influence. This remark
was applicable not only to States, but to Counties or other districts of
the same State. Accordingly the Constitution of Mass.ᵗˢ had provided that the representatives of the larger districts should not be in
an exact ratio to their numbers. And experience he thought had shewn
the provision to be expedient.

M.ʳ READ. The States have heretofore been in a sort of partner-
ship. They ought to adjust their old affairs before they open [1] a
new account. He brought into view the appropriation of the common
interest in the Western lands, to the use of particular States. Let
justice be done on this head; let the fund be applied fairly & equally
to the discharge of the general debt, and the smaller States who
had been injured; would listen then perhaps to those ideas of just
representation which had been held out.

M.ʳ GHORUM. did [2] not see how the Convention could interpose in
the case. Errors he allowed had been committed on the subject.
But Cong.ˢ were now using their endeavors to rectify them. The
best remedy would be such a Government as would have vigor enough
to do justice throughout. This was certainly the best chance that
could be afforded to the smaller States.

M.ʳ WILSON. the question is shall the members of the 2.ᵈ branch
be chosen by the Legislatures of the States? When he considered the
amazing extent of Country—the immense population which is to fill
it, the influence which [3] the Gov.ᵗ we are to form will have, not only on
the present generation of our people & their multiplied posterity,

---

necessarily place the power in the hands of the few, nearest the seat of government.   State governments must therefore remain, if you mean to prevent confusion.   The general negative powers will support the general government.
Upon these considerations I am led to form the second branch differently from
the report.   Their powers are important and the number not too large, upon
the principle of proportion.   I have considered the subject with great attention;
and I propose this plan (reads it) and if no better plan is proposed, I will
then move its adoption."   *Secret Proceedings and Debates of the Convention
Assembled at Philadelphia, in the year 1787, for the purpose of forming the
Constitution of the United States of America*, by Robert Yates (1821), p. 163.
    [1] The word " opened " is substituted in the transcript for " open."
    [2] The word " could " is substituted in the transcript for " did."
    [3] The word " of " is substituted in the transcript for " which."

but on the whole Globe, he was lost in the magnitude of the object. The project of Henry the 4ᵗʰ & his Statesmen was but the picture in miniature of the great portrait to be exhibited. He was opposed to an election by the State Legislatures. In explaining his reasons it was necessary to observe the twofold relation in which the people would stand. 1.[1] as Citizens of the Genˡ Govᵗ 2.[1] as Citizens of their particular State. The Genˡ Govᵗ was meant for them in the first capacity: the State Govᵗˢ in the second. Both Govᵗˢ were derived from the people—both meant for the people—both therefore ought to be regulated on the same principles. The same train of ideas which belonged to the relation of the Citizens to their State Govᵗˢ were applicable to their relation to the Genˡ Govᵗ and in forming the latter, we ought to proceed, by abstracting as much as possible from the idea of[2] State Govᵗˢ With respect to the province & objects[3] of the Genˡ Govᵗ they should be considered as having no existence. The election of the 2ᵈ branch by the Legislatures, will introduce & cherish local interests & local prejudices. The Genˡ Govᵗ is not an assemblage of States, but of individuals for certain political purposes— it is not meant for the States, but for the individuals composing them; the *individuals* therefore not the *States,* ought to be represented in it: A proportion in this representation can be preserved in the 2ᵈ as well as in the 1ˢᵗ branch; and the election can be made by electors chosen by the people for that purpose. He moved an amendment to that effect which was not seconded.

Mʳ ELSEWORTH saw no reason for departing from the mode contained in the Report. Whoever chooses the member, he will be a Citizen of the State he is to represent & will feel the same spirit & act the same part whether he be appointed by the people or the Legislature. Every State has its particular views & prejudices, which will find their way into the general councils, through whatever channel they may flow. Wisdom was one of the characteristics which it was in contemplation to give the second branch. Would not more of it issue from the Legislatures; than from an immediate election by the people. He urged the necessity of maintaining the existence & agency of the States. Without their co-operation it would be impossible to support a Republican Govᵗ over so great an extent of Country. An army could scarcely render it practicable. The largest States are the worst Governed. Virgᵃ is obliged to

---

[1] The figure " 1 " is changed in the transcript to " first," and the figure " 2 " to " and secondly."

[2] The word " the " is here inserted in the transcript.

[3] The word " objects " is used in the singular in the transcript.

acknowledge her incapacity to extend her Gov: to Kentucky. Mas:
can not keep the peace one hundred miles from her capitol and is
now forming an army for its support. How long Pen: may be free
from a like situation can not be foreseen. If the principles & materials of our Gov: are not adequate to the extent of these single
States; how can it be imagined that they can support a single Gov:
throughout the U. States. The only chance of supporting a Gen!
Gov: lies in engrafting [1] it on that [2] of the individual States.

Doc: JOHNSON urged the necessity of preserving the State Gov'*
which would be at the mercy of the Gen! Gov: on M: Wilson's plan.

M: MADISON thought it w⁴ obviate difficulty if the present resol:
were postponed. & the 8ᵗʰ taken up, which is to fix the right of suffrage in the 2ᵈ branch.

Doc: [3] WILLIAMSON professed himself a friend to such a system as
would secure the existence of the State Gov'*. The happiness of the
people depended on it. He was at a loss to give his vote as to the
Senate untill he knew the number of its members. In order to
ascertain this, he moved to insert these words [4] after " 2ᵈ branch of
the Nat! Legislature "—[5] " who shall bear such proportion to the n:
of the 1ˢᵗ branch as 1 to   ." He was not seconded.

M: MASON. It has been agreed on all hands that an efficient
Gov: is necessary that to render it such it ought to have the faculty
of self-defence, that to render its different branches effectual each of
them ought to have the same power of self defence. He did not
wonder that such an agreement should have prevailed in [6] these points.
He only wondered that there should be any disagreement about the
necessity of allowing the State Gov'* the same self-defence. If they
are to be preserved as he conceived to be essential, they certainly
ought to have this power, and the only mode left of giving it to
them, was by allowing them to appoint the 2ᵈ branch of the Nat!
Legislature.

M: BUTLER observing that we were put to difficulties at every
step by the uncertainty whether an equality or a ratio of representation w⁴ prevail finally in the 2ᵈ branch, moved to postpone the 4ᵗʰ
Resol: & to proceed to the [7] Resol: on that point. M: MADISON seconded him.

---

[1] The word " grafting " is substituted in the transcript for " engrafting."
[2] The word " those " is substituted in the transcript for " that."
[3] The word " Mr." is substituted in the transcript for " Doc: "
[4] The words " these words " are omitted in the transcript.
[5] The words " the words " are here inserted in the transcript.
[6] The word " on " is substituted in the transcript for " in."
[7] The word " eighth " is here inserted in the transcript.

On the question

Mass⁺⁆ no. Con⁺ no. N. Y. ay. N. J. no. P⁺ no. Del. no. M⁴ no. V⁺ ay. N. C. no. S. C. ay. Geo. ay.[1]

On a question to postpone the 4 and take up the 7. Resol: ays [2] — Mar⁴ V⁺ N. C. S. C. Geo:—Noes [3] Mas. C⁺ N. Y. N. J. P⁺ Del: [3]

On the question to agree " that the members of the 2⁴ branch be chosen by the indiv⁆ Legislatures " Mas⁺⁆ ay. Con⁺ ay. N. Y. ay. N. J. ay. P⁺ no. Del. ay. M⁴ ay. V⁺ no. N. C. ay. S. C. ay. Geo. ay.* [4]

On a question on the clause requiring the age of 30 years at least—" it was agreed to unanimously: [5]

On a question to strike out—the words " sufficient to ensure their independency [6] " after the word " term " it was agreed to.

[7] That the 2⁴ branch hold their offices for [8] term of seven years,[9] considered

M⁺ GHORUM suggests a term of " 4 years," ¼ to be elected every year.

M⁺ RANDOLPH. supported the idea of rotation, as favorable to the wisdom & stability of the Corps, which might possibly be always sitting, and aiding the Executive. And moves after " 7 years " to add, " to go out in fixt proportion " which was agreed to.

M⁺ WILLIAMSON. suggests " 6 years," as more convenient for Rotation than 7 years.

M⁺ SHERMAN seconds him.

M⁺ REED proposed that they s⁴ hold their offices " during good " behaviour. M⁺ R. MORRIS seconds him.

* It must be kept in view that the largest States particularly Pennsylvania & Virginia always considered the choice of the 2⁴ Branch by the State Legislatures as opposed to a proportional Representation to which they were attached as a fundamental principle of just Government. The smaller States who had opposite views, were reinforced by the members from the large States most anxious to secure the importance of the State Governments.

---

[1] In the transcript the vote reads: " New York, Virginia, South Carolina, Georgia, aye—4; Massachusetts, Connecticut, New Jersey, Pennsylvania, Delaware, Maryland, North Carolina, no—7."

[2] The word " ays " is omitted in the transcript.

[3] The word " noes " is omitted in the transcript; " aye—5 " being inserted after " Georgia " and " no—6 " after " Delaware."

[4] In the transcript this vote reads: " Massachusetts, Connecticut, New York, New Jersey, Delaware, Maryland, North Carolina, South Carolina, Georgia, aye—9; Pennsylvania, Virginia, no—2."

[5] The words " agreed to unanimously " are transposed in the transcript to read " unanimously agreed to."

[6] The word " independency " is changed to " independence " in the transcript.

[7] The words " The clause " are here inserted in the transcript.

[8] The word " a " is here inserted in the transcript.

[9] The word " being " is here inserted in the transcript.

Gen! PINKNEY proposed " 4 years." A longer term [1] w⁴ fix them at the seat of Gov! They w⁴ acquire an interest there, perhaps transfer their property & lose sight of the States they represent. Under these circumstances the distant States w⁴ labour under great disadvantages.

M! SHERMAN moved to strike out " 7 years " in order to take questions on the several propositions.

On the question to strike out " seven "

Mas!ˢ ay. Con! ay. N. Y. ay. N. J. ay. P! no. Del. no. M⁴ div⁴ V! no. N. C. ay. S. C. ay. Geo. ay.[2]

On the question to insert " 6 years, which failed 5 St! being ay. 5 no. & 1 divided

Mas!ˢ no. Con! ay. N. Y. no. N. J. no. P! ay. Del ay. M⁴ div⁴ V! ay. N. C. ay. S. C. no. Geo. no.[3]

On a motion to adjourn, the votes were 5 for 5 ag!ᵗ it & 1 divided, —Con. N. J. P! Del. V! —ay.[4] Mass!ˢ N. Y. N. C. S. C. Geo: no.[4] Mary⁴ divided.

On the question for " 5 years " it was lost.

Mas!ˢ no. Con! ay. N. Y. no. N. J. no. P! ay. Del. ay. M⁴ div⁴ V! ay. N. C. ay. S. C. no. Geo no.[5]

Adj⁴

TUESDAY. JUNE 26. IN CONVENTION

The duration of the 2⁴ branch [6] under consideration.

M! GHORUM moved to fill the blank with " six years," one third of the members to go out every second year.

M! WILSON 2ᵈᵉᵈ the motion.

Gen! PINKNEY opposed six years in favor of four years. The States he said had different interests. Those of the Southern, and of S. Carolina in particular were different from the Northern. If the

---

[1] The word " time " is substituted in the transcript for " term."

[2] In the transcript the vote reads: " Massachusetts, Connecticut, New York, New Jersey, North Carolina, South Carolina, Georgia, aye—7; Pennsylvania, Delaware, Virginia, no—3; Maryland, divided."

[3] In the transcript the vote reads: " Connecticut, Pennsylvania, Delaware, Virginia, North Carolina, aye—5; Massachusetts, New York, New Jersey, South Carolina, Georgia, no—5; Maryland, divided."

[4] The figure " 5 " is here inserted in the transcript.

[5] In the transcript the vote reads: " Connecticut, Pennsylvania, Delaware, Virginia, North Carolina, aye—5; Massachusetts, New York, New Jersey, South Carolina, Georgia, no—5; Maryland, divided."

[6] The word " being " is here inserted in the transcript.

Senators should be appointed for a long term, they w⁴ settle in the State where they exercised their functions; and would in a little time be rather the representatives of that than of the State appoint⁵ them.

M⁺ Read mov⁴ that the term be nine years. This w⁴ admit of a very convenient rotation, one third going out triennially. He w⁴ still prefer "during good behaviour," but being little supported in that idea, he was willing to take the longest term that could be obtained.

M⁺ Broome 2ᵈᵉᵈ the motion.

M⁺ Madison. In order to judge of the form to be given to this institution, it will be proper to take a view of the ends to be served by it. These were first to protect the people agˢᵗ their rulers: secondly to protect the people agˢᵗ the transient impressions into which they themselves might be led. A people deliberating in a temperate moment, and with the experience of other nations before them, on the plan of Gov⁺ most likely to secure their happiness, would first be aware, that those charg⁴ with the public happiness, might betray their trust. An obvious precaution agˢᵗ this danger w⁴ be to divide the trust between different bodies of men, who might watch & check each other. In this they w⁴ be governed by the same prudence which has prevailed in organizing the subordinate departments of Gov⁺, where all business liable to abuses is made to pass thro' separate hands, the one being a check on the other. It w⁴ next occur to such a people, that they themselves were liable to temporary errors, thro' want of information as to their true interest, and that men chosen for a short term, & employed but a small portion of that in public affairs, might err from the same cause. This reflection w⁴ naturally suggest that the Gov⁺ be so constituted, as that one of its branches might have an opp⁷ of acquiring a competent knowledge of the public interests. Another reflection equally becoming a people on such an occasion, w⁴ be that they themselves, as well as a numerous body of Representatives, were liable to err also, from fickleness and passion. A necessary fence agˢᵗ this danger would be to select a portion of enlightened citizens, whose limited number, and firmness might seasonably interpose agˢᵗ impetuous councils. It ought finally to occur to a people deliberating on a Gov⁺ for themselves, that as different interests necessarily result from the liberty meant to be secured, the major interest might under sudden impulses be tempted to commit injustice on the minority. In all civilized Countries the people fall into different classes hav⁵ a real or supposed difference of interests. There will be creditors & debtors, farmers, merch⁺ˢ & manufacturers.

There will be particularly the distinction of rich & poor. It was true as had been observ^d [by Mr Pinkney] we had not among us those hereditary distinctions, of rank which were a great source of the contests in the ancient Gov^{ts} as well as the modern States of Europe, nor those extremes of wealth or poverty which characterize the latter. We cannot however be regarded even at this time, as one homogeneous mass, in which every thing that affects a part will affect in the same manner the whole. In framing a system which we wish to last for ages, we sh^d not lose sight of the changes which ages will produce. An increase of population will of necessity increase the proportion of those who will labour under all the hardships of life, & secretly sigh for a more equal distribution of its blessings. These may in time outnumber those who are placed above the feelings of indigence. According to the equal laws of suffrage, the power will slide into the hands of the former. No agrarian attempts have yet been made in in this Country, but symtoms, of a leveling spirit, as we have understood, have sufficiently appeared in a certain quarters to give notice of the future danger. How is this danger to be guarded agst on republican principles? How is the danger in all cases of interested coalitions to oppress the minority to be guarded agst? Among other means by the establishment of a body in the Gov^t sufficiently respectable for its wisdom & virtue, to aid on such emergences, the preponderance of justice by throwing its weight into that scale. Such being the objects of the second branch in the proposed Gov^t he thought a considerable duration ought to be given to it. He did not conceive that the term of nine years could threaten any real danger; but in pursuing his particular ideas on the subject, he should require that the long term allowed to the 2^d branch should not commence till such a period of life, as would render a perpetual disqualification to be re-elected little inconvenient either in a public or private view. He observed that as it was more than probable we were now digesting a plan which in its operation w^d decide for ever the fate of Republican Gov^t we ought not only to provide every guard to liberty that its preservation c^d require, but be equally careful to supply the defects which our own experience had particularly pointed out.

Mr Sherman. Gov^t is instituted for those who live under it. It ought therefore to be so constituted as not to be dangerous to their liberties. The more permanency it has the worse if it be a bad Gov^t Frequent elections are necessary to preserve the good behavior of rulers. They also tend to give permanency to the Government, by preserving that good behavior, because it ensures their re-election.

In Connecticut elections have been very frequent, yet great stability & uniformity both as to persons & measures have been experienced from its original establishm![to] the present time; a period of more than 130 years. He wished to have provision made for steadiness & wisdom in the system to be adopted; but he thought six or four years would be sufficient. He sh![d] be content with either.

M![r] READ wished it to be considered by the small States that it was their interest that we should become one people as much as possible; that State attachments sh![d] be extinguished as much as possible; that the Senate sh![d] be so constituted as to have the feelings of Citizens of the whole.

M![r] HAMILTON. He did not mean to enter particularly into the subject. He concurred with M![r] Madison in thinking we were now to decide for ever the fate of Republican Government; and that if we did not give to that form due stability and wisdom, it would be disgraced & lost among ourselves, disgraced & lost to mankind for ever. He acknowledged himself not to think favorably of Republican Government; but addressed his remarks to those who did think favorably of it, in order to prevail on them to tone their Government as high as possible. He professed himself to be as zealous an advocate for liberty as any man whatever, and trusted he should be as willing a martyr to it though he differed as to the form in which it was most eligible.—He concurred also in the general observations of [M![r] Madison] on the subject, which might be supported by others if it were necessary. It was certainly true: that nothing like an equality of property existed: that an inequality would exist as long as liberty existed, and that it would unavoidably result from that very liberty itself. This inequality of property constituted the great & fundamental distinction in Society. When the Tribunitial power had levelled the boundary between the *patricians* & *plebeians*, what followed? The distinction between rich & poor was substituted. He meant not however to enlarge on the subject. He rose principally to remark that [M![r] Sherman] seemed not to recollect that one branch of the proposed Gov![t] was so formed, as to render it particularly the guardians of the poorer orders of Citizens; nor to have adverted to the true causes of the stability which had been exemplified in Con![t] Under the British system as well as the federal, many of the great powers appertaining to Gov![t] particularly all those relating to foreign Nations were not in the hands of the Gov![t] there. Their internal affairs also were extremely simple, owing to sundry causes many of which were peculiar to that Country. Of late the Goverm![t] had entirely given way to the people, and had in fact suspended many of its ordinary functions in order to prevent those turbulent scenes which had appeared elsewhere. He asks M.ʳ S. whether the State at this time, dare impose & collect a tax on y.ᵉ people? To these causes & not to the frequency of elections, the effect, as far as it existed ought to be chiefly ascribed.

M.ʳ GERRY. wished we could be united in our ideas concerning a permanent Gov.ᵗ All aim at the same end, but there are great differences as to the means. One circumstance He thought should be carefully attended to. There were not 1/1000 part of our fellow citizens who were not ag.ˢᵗ every approach towards Monarchy. Will they ever agree to a plan which seems to make such an approach. The Convention ought to be extremely cautious in what they hold out to the people. Whatever plan may be proposed will be espoused with warmth by many out of respect to the quarter it proceeds from as well as from an approbation of the plan itself. And if the plan should be of such a nature as to rouse a violent opposition, it is easy to foresee that discord & confusion will ensue, and it is even possible that we may become a prey to foreign powers. He did not deny the position of M.ʳ Madison, that the majority will generally violate justice when they have an interest in so doing; But did not think there was any such temptation in this Country. Our situation was different from that of G. Britain: and the great body of lands yet to be parcelled out & settled would very much prolong the difference. Notwithstanding the symtoms of injustice which had marked many of our public Councils, they had not proceeded so far as not to leave hopes, that there would be a sufficient sense of justice & virtue for the purpose of Gov.ᵗ He admitted the evils arising from a frequency of elections: and would agree to give the Senate a duration of four or five years. A longer term would defeat itself. It never would be adopted by the people.

M.ʳ WILSON did not mean to repeat what had fallen from others, but w.ᵈ add an observation or two which he believed had not yet been suggested. Every nation may be regarded in two relations 1.[1] to its own citizens. 2[1] to foreign nations. It is therefore not only liable to anarchy & tyranny within, but has wars to avoid & treaties to obtain from abroad. The Senate will probably be the depositary of the powers concerning the latter objects. It ought therefore to be made respectable in the eyes of foreign Nations. The true reason why G. Britain has not yet listened to a commercial treaty with us has been, because she had no confidence in the stability or

---

[1] The figures "1" and "2" are changed to "first" and "secondly" in the transcript.

efficacy of our Government. 9 years with a rotation, will provide these desirable qualities; and give our Gov: an advantage in this respect over Monarchy itself. In a monarchy much must always depend on the temper of the man. In such a body, the personal character will be lost in the political. He w^d add another observation. The popular objection agst appointing any public body for a long term was that it might by gradual encroachments prolong itself first into a body for life, and finally become a hereditary one. It would be a satisfactory answer to this objection that as ⅓ would go out triennially, there would be always three divisions holding their places for unequal terms,[1] and consequently acting under the influence of different views, and different impulses—On the question for 9 years, ⅓ to go out triennially

Mass^{ts} no. Con^t no. N. Y. no. N. J. no. P^a ay. Del. ay. M^d no. V^a ay. N. C. no. S. C. no. Geo. no.[2]

On the question for 6 years ⅓ to go out biennially

Mass^{ts} ay. Con^t ay. N. Y. no. N. J. no. P^a ay. Del. ay. M^d ay. V^a ay. N. C. ay. S. C. no. Geo. no.[3]

[4] " To receive fixt stipends by which they may be compensated for their services." [5] considered

General PINKNEY proposed " that no Salary should be allowed." As this [the Senatorial] branch was meant to represent the wealth of the Country, it ought to be composed of persons of wealth; and if no allowance was to be made the wealthy alone would undertake the service. He moved to strike out the clause.

Doct^r FRANKLIN seconded the motion. He wished the Convention to stand fair with the people. There were in it a number of young men who would probably be of the Senate. If lucrative appointments should be recommended we might be chargeable with having carved out places for ourselves. On the question, Mas^{ts} Connecticut * P^a M^d S. Carolina ay.[7] N. Y. N. J. Del. Virg^a N. C. Geo. no.[8]

* Quer. whether Connecticut should not be—no, & Delaware, ay.[6]

---

[1] The word " times " is substituted in the transcript for " terms."

[2] In the transcript the vote reads: " Pennsylvania, Delaware, Virginia, aye—3; Massachusetts, Connecticut, New York, New Jersey, Maryland, North Carolina, South Carolina, Georgia, no—8."

[3] In the transcript the vote reads: " Massachusetts, Connecticut, Pennsylvania, Delaware, Maryland, Virginia, North Carolina, aye—7; New York, New Jersey, South Carolina, Georgia, no—4."

[4] The words " The clause of the fourth Resolution " are here inserted in the transcript.

[5] The word " being " is here inserted in the transcript.

[6] An interrogation mark and the initials " J.M." are here inserted in the transcript. According to the Journal, Connecticut was " ay " and Delaware " no."

[7] The figure " 5 " is here inserted in the transcript.

[8] The figure " 6 " is here inserted in the transcript.

M! WILLIAMSON moved to change the expression into these words towit " to receive a compensation for the devotion of their time to the public Service." The motion was seconded by M! Elseworth. And was [1] agreed to by all the States except S. Carol? It seemed to be meant only to get rid of the word " fixt " and leave greater room for modifying the provision on this point.

M! ELSEWORTH moved to strike out " to be paid out of the nati! Treasury " and insert " to be paid by their respective States." If the Senate was meant to strengthen the Gov! it ought to have the confidence of the States. The States will have an interest in keeping up a representation, and will make such provision for supporting the members as will ensure their attendance.

M! MADISON considered this [2] a departure from a fundamental principle, and subverting the end intended by allowing the Senate a duration of 6 years. They would if this motion should be agreed to, hold their places during pleasure; during the pleasure of the State Legislatures. One great end of the institution was, that being a firm, wise and impartial body, it might not only give stability to the Gen! Gov! in its operations on individuals, but hold an even balance among different States. The motion would make the Senate like Congress, the mere Agents & Advocates of State interests & views, instead of being the impartial umpires & Guardians of justice and [3] general Good. Cong! had lately by the establishment of a board with full powers to decide on the mutual claims be- between the U. States & the individual States, fairly acknowledged themselves to be unfit for discharging this part of the business referred to them by the Confederation.

M! DAYTON considered the payment of the Senate by the States as fatal to their independence. he was decided for paying them out of the Nat! Treasury.

On the question for payment of the Senate to be left to the States as moved by M! Elseworth.[4]

Mass!. no.   Con! ay.   N. Y. ay.   N. J. ay.   P? no.   Del. no. M? no.   V? no.   N. C. no.   S. C. ay.   Geo. ay.[5]

Col. MASON. He did not rise to make any motion, but to hint an idea which seemed to be proper for consideration. One impor-

---

[1] The word " was " is omitted in the transcript.
[2] The word " as " is here inserted in the transcript.
[3] The word " the " is here inserted in the transcript.
[4] The phrase " it passed in the negative " is here inserted in the transcript.
[5] In the transcript the vote reads: " Connecticut, New York, New Jersey, South Carolina, Georgia, aye—5; Massachusetts, Pennsylvania, Delaware, Maryland, Virginia, North Carolina, no—6."

tant object in constituting the Senate was to secure the rights of property. To give them weight & firmness for this purpose, a considerable duration in office was thought necessary. But a longer term than 6 years, would be of no avail in this respect, if needy persons should be appointed. He suggested therefore the propriety of annexing to the office a qualification of property. He thought this would be very practicable; as the rules of taxation would supply a scale for measuring the degree of wealth possessed by every man.

A question was then taken whether the words " to be paid out of the public [1] treasury," should stand."

Mass[ts] ay. Con[t] no. N. Y. no. N. J. no. P[a] ay. Del. ay. M[d] ay. V[a] ay. N. C. no. S. C. no. Geo. no.[2]

M[r] BUTLER moved to strike out the ineligibility of Senators to *State offices.*

M[r] WILLIAMSON seconded the motion.

M[r] WILSON remarked the additional dependence this w[d] create in the Senators on the States. The longer the time he observed allotted to the officer, the more compleat will be the dependance, if it exists at all.

Gen[l] PINKNEY was for making the States as much as could be conveniently done, a part of the Gen[l] Gov[t]: If the Senate was to be appointed by the States, it ought in pursuance of the same idea to be paid by the States: and the States ought not to be barred from the opportunity of calling members of it into offices at home. Such a restriction would also discourage the ablest men from going into the Senate.

M[r] WILLIAMSON moved a resolution so penned as to admit of the two following questions. 1.[s] whether the members of the Senate should be ineligible to & incapable of holding offices *under the U. States*

2.[s] Whether &c. under the *particular States.*

On the Question to postpone in order to consider [4] Williamson's Resol[n] Mass[ts] no. Con[t] ay. N. Y. no. N. J. no. P[a] ay. Del. ay. M[d] ay. V[a] ay. N. C. ay. S. C. ay. Geo. ay.[5]

M[r] GERRY & M[r] MADISON—move to add to M[r] Williamsons 1,[s] Quest: " and for 1 year thereafter." On this amend[t]

---

[1] The word "public" is changed to "national" in the transcript.
[2] In the transcript the vote reads: "Massachusetts, Pennsylvania, Delaware, Maryland, Virginia, aye—5; Connecticut, New York, New Jersey, North Carolina, South Carolina, Georgia, no—6."
[3] The figures "1" and "2" are changed to "first" and "secondly" in the transcript.
[4] The word "Mr." is here inserted in the transcript.
[5] In the transcript the vote reads: "Connecticut, Pennsylvania, Delaware, Maryland, Virginia, North Carolina, South Carolina, Georgia, aye—8; Massachusetts, New York, New Jersey, no—3."

Mas.[ts] no. Con[t] ay. N. Y. ay. N. J. no. P. no. Del. ay. M.[d] ay. V.[a] ay. N. C. ay. S. C. ay. Geo. no.[1]

On M.[r] Will–son's 1 Question as amend.[ed] vz. inelig: & incapable &c. &c for 1 year &c. ag.[d] [2] unanimously.

On the 2.[3] question as to ineligibility &c. to State offices.[4]

Mas. ay. C.[t] no. N. Y. no. N. J. no. P. ay. Del. no. M.[d] no. V.[a] ay. N. C. no. S. C. no. Geo. no.[5]

The 5.[6] Resol: " that each branch have the right of originating acts " was agreed to nem: con:

Adj.[d]

WEDNESDAY JUNE 27.   IN CONVENTION

M.[r] RUTLIDGE moved to postpone the 6th Resolution, defining the powers of Cong.[s] in order to take up the 7 & 8 which involved the most fundamental points; the rules of suffrage in the 2 branches which was agreed to nem. con.

A question being proposed on Resol: 7 [7]: declaring that the suffrage in the first branch s.[d] be according to an equitable ratio.

M.[r] L. MARTIN contended at great length and with great eagerness that the General Gov.[t] was meant merely to preserve the State Govern.[ts]: not to govern individuals: that its powers ought to be kept within narrow limits; that if too little power was given to it, more might be added; but that if too much, it could never be resumed: that individuals as such have little to do but with their own States; that the Gen.[l] Gov.[t] has no more to apprehend from the States composing the Union, while it pursues proper measures, that [8] a Gov.[t] over individuals has to apprehend from its subjects: that to resort to the Citizens at large for their sanction to a new Govern.[t] will be throwing them back into a State of Nature: that the dissolution of the State Gov.[ts] is involved in the nature of the process: that the

---

[1] In the transcript the vote reads: " Connecticut, New York, Delaware, Maryland, Virginia, North Carolina, South Carolina, aye—7; Massachusetts, New Jersey, Pennsylvania, Georgia, no—4."

[2] The word " to " is here inserted in the transcript.

[3] The figure " 2 " is changed to " second " in the transcript.

[4] The transcript italicizes the words " State offices."

[5] In the transcript the vote reads: " Massachusetts, Pennsylvania, Virginia, aye—3; Connecticut, New York, New Jersey, Delaware, Maryland, North Carolina, South Carolina, Georgia, no—8."

[6] The figure " 5 " is changed to " fifth " in the transcript.

[7] The words " the seventh Resolution " are substituted in the transcript for " Resol: 7."

[8] The word " than " is substituted in the transcript for " that."

people have no right to do this without the consent of those to whom
they have delegated their power for State purposes: through their
tongue only they can. speak, through their ears, only, can hear: that
the States have shewn a good disposition to comply with the Acts, of
Cong⁸. weak, contemptibly weak as that body has been; and have
failed through inability alone to comply: that the heaviness of the
private debts, and the waste of property during the war, were the
chief causes of this inability: that he did not conceive the instances
mentioned by M⁰ʳ Madison of compacts between V⁰ᵃ & M⁰ᵈ between
P⁰ᵃ & N. J. or of troops raised by Mass⁰ᵗˢ for defence against the Rebels,
to be violations of the articles of confederation—that an equal vote in
each State was essential to the federal idea, and was founded in justice
& freedom, not merely in policy: that tho' the States may give up this
right of sovereignty, yet they had not, and ought not: that the States
like individuals were in a State of nature equally sovereign & free. In
order to prove that individuals in a State of nature are equally free
& independent he read passages from Locke, Vattel, Lord Summers—
Priestly. To prove that the case is the same with States till they surrender their equal sovereignty, he read other passages in Locke &
Vattel, and also Rutherford: that the States being equal cannot treat
or confederate so as to give up an equality of votes without giving
up their liberty: that the propositions on the table were a system
of slavery for 10 States: that as V⁰ᵃ Mas⁰ᵗˢ & P⁰ᵃ have ⁴²⁄₉₀ of the votes
they can do as they please without a miraculous Union of the other
ten: that they will have nothing to do, but to gain over one of the
ten to make them compleat masters of the rest: that they can then
appoint an Execut⁰ᵉ & Judiciary & legislate [1] for them as they please:
that there was & would continue a natural predilection & partiality
in men for their own States; that the States, particularly the smaller,
would never allow a negative to be exercised over their laws: that
no State in ratifying the Confederation had objected to the equality
of votes; that the complaints at present run not ag⁰ᵗ this equality
but the want of power; that 16 members from V⁰ᵃ would be more
likely to act in concert than a like number formed of members from
different States; that instead of a junction of the small States as a
remedy, he thought a division of the large States would be more
eligible.—This was the substance of a speech which was continued
more than three hours. He was too much exhausted he said to
finish his remarks, and reminded the House that he should tomorrow,
resume them.

Adj⁰ᵈ

---

[1] The word "legislature" is substituted in the transcript for "legislate."

THURSDAY JUNE 28TH IN CONVENTION

M: L. MARTIN resumed his discourse, contending that the Genl Govt ought to be formed for the States, not for individuals: that if the States were to have votes in proportion to their numbers of people, it would be the same thing whether their representatives were chosen by the Legislatures or the people; the smaller States would be equally enslaved; that if the large States have the same interest with the smaller as was urged, there could be no danger in giving them an equal vote; they would not injure themselves, and they could not injure the large ones on that supposition without injuring themselves and if the interests, were not the same, the inequality of suffrage wd be dangerous to the smaller States: that it will be in vain to propose any plan offensive to the rulers of the States, whose influence over the people will certainly prevent their adopting it: that the large States were weak at present in proportion to their extent: & could only be made formidable to the small ones, by the weight of their votes; that in case a dissolution of the Union should take place, the small States would have nothing to fear from their power; that if in such a case the three great States should league themselves together, the other ten could do so too: & that he had rather see partial confederacies take place, than the plan on the table.

This was the substance of the residue of his discourse which was delivered with much diffuseness & considerable vehemence.

M: LANSING & M: DAYTON moved to strike out "not." so that the 7 art: might read that the rights [1] of suffrage in the 1st branch ought to be according to the rule established by the Confederation."

M: DAYTON expressed great anxiety that the question might not be put till tomorrow; Governr Livingston being kept away by indisposition, and the representation of N. Jersey thereby suspended.

M: WILLIAMSON. thought that if any political truth could be grounded on mathematical demonstration, it was that if the States were equally sovereign now, and parted with equal proportions of sovereignty, that they would remain equally sovereign. He could not comprehend how the smaller States would be injured in the case, and wished some Gentleman would vouchsafe a solution of it. He observed that the small States, if they had a plurality of votes would have an interest in throwing the burdens off their own shoul-

---

[1] The transcript uses the word "rights" in the singular.

ders on those of the large ones. He begged that the expected addition of new States from the Westward might be kept in [1] view. They would be small States, they would be poor States, they would be unable to pay in proportion to their numbers; their distance from market rendering the produce of their labour less valuable; they would consequently be tempted to combine for the purpose of laying burdens on commerce & consumption which would fall with greatest [2] weight on the old States.

M⁫ MADISON, s⁙ he was much disposed to concur in any expedient not inconsistent with fundamental principles, that could remove the difficulty concerning the rule of representation. But he could neither be convinced that the rule contended for was just, nor [3] necessary for the safety of the small States ag⁙ the large States. That it was not just, had been conceded by M⁫ Breerly & M⁫ Patterson themselves. The expedient proposed by them was a new partition of the territory of the U. States. The fallacy of the reasoning drawn from the equality of Sovereign States in the formation of compacts, lay in confounding mere Treaties, in which were specified certain duties to which the parties were to be bound, and certain rules by which their subjects were to be reciprocally governed in their intercourse, with a compact by which an authority was created paramount to the parties, & making laws for the government of them. If France, England & Spain were to enter into a Treaty for the regulation of commerce &c with the Prince of Monacho & 4 or 5 other of the smallest sovereigns of Europe, they would not hesitate to treat as equals, and to make the regulations perfectly reciprocal. W⁙ the case be the same, if a Council were to be formed of deputies from each with authority and discretion, to raise money, levy troops, determine the value of coin &c? Would 30 or 40. million [4] of people submit their fortunes into the hands, of a few thousands? If they did it would only prove that they expected more from the terror of their superior force, than they feared from the selfishness of their feeble associates. Why are Counties of the same states represented in proportion to their numbers? Is it because the representatives are chosen by the people themselves? So will be the representatives in the Nation! Legislature. Is it because, the larger have more at stake than the smaller? The case will be the same with the larger & smaller States. Is it because the laws are to operate immediately

---

[1] The words " taken into " are substituted in the transcript for " kept in."
[2] The word " greater " is substituted in the transcript for " greatest."
[3] The words " that it was " are here inserted in the transcript.
[4] The transcript uses the word " million " in the plural.

on their persons & properties? The same is the case in some degree
as the articles of confederation stand; the same will be the case in
a far greater degree under the plan proposed to be substituted. In
the cases of captures, of piracies, and of offences in a federal army;
the property & persons of individuals depend on the laws of Cong!
By the plan proposed a compleat power of taxation, the highest
prerogative of supremacy is proposed to be vested in the National
Gov! Many other powers are added which assimilate it to the Gov!
of individual States. The negative proposed on the State laws, will
make it an essential branch of the State Legislatures & of course will
require that it should be exercised by a body established on like principles with the other [1] branches of those Legislatures.—That it is not
necessary to secure the small States ag.st the large ones he conceived
to be equally obvious: Was a combination of the large ones dreaded?
this must arise either from some interest common to V.^{a} Mas.^{ts} & P.^{a}
& distinguishing them from the other States or from the mere circumstance of similarity of size. Did any such common interest exist?
In point of situation they could not have been more effectually
separated from each other by the most jealous citizen of the most
jealous State. In point of manners, Religion, and the other circumstances which sometimes beget affection between different communities, they were not more assimilated than the other States.—In
point of the staple productions they were as dissimilar as any three
other States in the Union. The Staple of Mas.^{ts} was *fish*, of P.^{a}
flower, of V.^{a} *Tob*? Was a combination to be apprehended from the
mere circumstance of equality of size? Experience suggested no
such danger. The journals of Cong.^{s} did not present any peculiar
association of these States in the votes recorded. It had never been
seen that different Counties in the same State, conformable in extent, but disagreeing in other circumstances, betrayed a propensity
to such combinations. Experience rather taught a contrary lesson.
Among individuals of superior eminence & weight in Society, rivalships were much more frequent than coalitions. Among independent
nations, pre-eminent over their neighbours, the same remark was
verified. Carthage & Rome tore one another to pieces instead of uniting their forces to devour the weaker nations of the Earth. The
Houses of Austria & France were hostile as long as they remained
the greatest powers of Europe. England & France have succeeded
to the pre-eminence & to the enmity. To this principle we owe
perhaps our liberty. A coalition between those powers would have

---

[1] The word " other " is omitted in the transcript.

been fatal to us. Among the principal members of antient & Modern confederacies, we find the same effect from the same cause. The contintions, not the Coalitions of Sparta, Athens & Thebes, proved fatal to the smaller members of the Amphyctionic Confederacy. The contentions, not the combinations of Prussia & Austria, have distracted & oppressed the Germanic [1] empire. Were the large States formidable *singly* to their smaller neighbours? On this supposition the latter ought to wish for such a general Gov! as will operate with equal energy on the former as on themselves. The more lax the band, the more liberty the larger will have to avail themselves of their superior force. Here again Experience was an instructive monitor. What is ye situation of the weak compared with the strong in those stages of civilization in which the violence of individuals is least controuled by an efficient Government? The Heroic period of Antient Greece the feudal licentiousness of the middle ages of Europe, the existing condition of the American Savages, answer this question. What is the situation of the minor sovereigns in the great society of independent nations, in which the more powerful are under no controul but the nominal authority of the law of Nations? Is not the danger to the former exactly in proportion to their weakness. But there are cases still more in point. What was the condition of the weaker members of the Amphyctionic Confederacy. Plutarch [2 life of Themistocles] will inform us that it happened but too often that the strongest cities corrupted & awed the weaker, and that Judgment went in favor of the more powerful party. What is the condition of the lesser states in the German Confederacy? We all know that they are exceedingly trampled upon; and that they owe their safety as far as they enjoy it, partly to their enlisting themselves, under the rival banners of the pre-eminent members, partly to alliances with neighbouring Princes which the Constitution of the Empire does not prohibit. What is the state of things in the lax system of the Dutch Confederacy? Holland contains about ½ the people, supplies about ½ of [3] the money, and by her influence, silently & indirectly governs the whole republic. In a word; the two extremes before us are a perfect separation & a perfect incorporation, of the 13 States. In the first case they would be independent nations subject to no law, but the law of nations. In the last, they would be mere counties of one entire republic, subject to one common law. In the first case the smaller States would have every thing to fear

---

[1] The word " German " is substituted in the transcript for " Germanic."
[2] The word " see " is here inserted in the transcript.
[3] The word " of " is omitted in the transcript.

from the larger. In the last they would have nothing to fear. The true policy of the small States therefore lies in promoting those principles & that form of Gov! which will most approximate the States to the condition of counties. Another consideration may be added. If the Gen! Gov! be feeble, the large States distrusting its continuance, and foreseeing that their importance & security may depend on their own size & strength, will never submit to a partition. Give to the Gen! Gov! sufficient energy & permanency, & you remove the objection. Gradual partitions of the large, & junctions of the small States will be facilitated, and time may effect that equalization, which is wished for by the small States now, but can never be accomplished at once.

Mᴿ WILSON. The leading argument of those who contend for equality of votes among the States is that the States as such being equal, and being represented not as districts of individuals, but in their political & corporate capacities, are entitled to an equality of suffrage. According to this mode of reasoning the representation of the boroughs in Engᴵᵈ which has been allowed on all hands to be the rotten part of the Constitution, is perfectly right & proper. They are like the States represented in their corporate capacity like the States therefore they are entitled to equal voices, old Sarum to as many as London. And instead of the injury supposed hitherto to be done to London, the true ground of complaint lies with old Sarum: for London instead of two which is her proper share, sends four representatives to Parliament.

Mᴿ SHERMAN. The question is not what rights naturally belong to men [1]; but how they may be most equally & effectually guarded in Society. And if some give up more than others in order to attain [2] this end, there can be no room for complaint. To do otherwise, to require an equal concession from all, if it would create danger to the rights of some, would be sacrificing the end to the means. The rich man who enters into Society along with the poor man, gives up more than the poor man, yet with an equal vote he is equally safe. Were he to have more votes than the poor man in proportion to his superior stake, the rights of the poor man would immediately cease to be secure. This consideration prevailed when the articles of Confederation were formed.

The determination of the question from [3] striking out the word " not " was put off till tomorrow at the request of the Deputies of

---

[1] The word "men" is used in the singular in the transcript.
[2] The word "obtain" is substituted in the transcript for "attain."
[3] The word "from" is changed to "for" in the transcript.

N. York.   See opposite page & insert the Speech of Doct? F in this place.[1]

M? President

The small progress we have made after 4 or five weeks close attendance & continual reasonings with each other—our different sentiments on almost every question, several of the last producing as many noes as ays, is methinks a melancholy proof of the imperfection of the Human Understanding. We indeed seem to feel our own want of political wisdom, since we have been running about in search of it. We have gone back to ancient history for models of Government, and examined the different forms of those Republics which having been formed with the seeds of their own dissolution now no longer exist. And we have viewed Modern States all round Europe, but find none of their Constitutions suitable to our circumstances.

In this situation of this Assembly, groping as it were in the dark to find political truth, and scarce able to distinguish it when presented to us, how has it happened, Sir, that we have not hitherto once thought of humbly applying to the Father of lights to illuminate our understandings? In the beginning of the Contest with G. Britain, when we were sensible of danger we had daily prayer in this room for the divine protection.—Our prayers, Sir, were heard, & they were graciously answered. All of us who were engaged in the struggle must have observed frequent instances of a superintending providence in our favor. To that kind providence we owe this happy opportunity of consulting in peace on the means of establishing our future national felicity. And have we now forgotten that powerful friend? or do we imagine that we no longer need his assistance? I have lived, Sir, a long time, and the longer I live, the more convincing proofs I see of this truth—*that God Governs in the affairs of men.* And if a sparrow cannot fall to the ground without his notice, is it probable that an empire can rise without his aid? We have been assured, Sir, in the sacred writings, that " except the Lord build the House they labour in vain that build it." I firmly believe this; and I also believe that without his concurring aid we shall succeed in this political building no better, than the Builders of Babel: We shall be divided by our little partial local interests; our projects will be confounded, and we ourselves shall become a reproach and bye word down to future ages. And what is worse, mankind may hereafter from this unfortunate instance, despair of establishing

---

[1] Madison's direction is omitted in the transcript and the words " Doctor Franklin " are inserted.

Governments by Human wisdom and leave it to chance, war and conquest.

I therefore beg leave to move—that henceforth prayers imploring the assistance of Heaven, and its blessings on our deliberations, be held in this Assembly every morning before we proceed to business, and that one or more of the Clergy of this City be requested to officiate in that Service—

M�速 SHARMAN seconded the motion.

M⁸ HAMILTON & several others expressed their apprehensions that however proper such a resolution might have been at the beginning of the convention, it might at this late day, 1.[1] bring on it some disagreeable animadversions. & 2.[2] lead the public to believe that the embarrassments and dissensions within the Convention, had suggested this measure. It was answered by Doc⁸ F. M⁸ SHERMAN & others, that the past omission of a duty could not justify a further omission—that the rejection of such a proposition would expose the Convention to more unpleasant animadversions than the adoption of it: and that the alarm out of doors that might be excited for the state of things within, would at least be as likely to do good as ill.

M⁸ WILLIAMSON, observed that the true cause of the omission could not be mistaken. The Convention had no funds.

M⁸ RANDOLPH proposed in order to give a favorable aspect to y⁸ measure, that a sermon be preached at the request of the convention on [3] 4ᵗʰ of July, the anniversary of Independence; & thenceforward prayers be used [4] in y⁸ Convention every morning. D⁸ FRANK⁸ 2ᵈᵉᵈ this motion After several unsuccessful attempts for silently postponing the [5] matter by adjourn⁸ the adjournment was at length carried, without any vote on the motion.

FRIDAY JUNE 29ᵀᴴ IN CONVENTION

Doct⁸ JOHNSON. The controversy must be endless whilst Gentlemen differ in the grounds of their arguments; Those on one side considering the States as districts of people composing one political Society; those on the other considering them as so many political

---

[1] The figure " 1 " is changed to " in the first place " in the transcript.
[2] The figure " 2 " is changed to " in the second place " in the transcript.
[3] The word " the " is here inserted in the transcript.
[4] The words " &c to be read " are substituted in the transcript for " be used."
[5] The word " this " is substituted in the transcript for " the."

societies. The fact is that the States do exist as political Societies, and a Gov! is to be formed for them in their political capacity, as well as for the individuals composing them. Does it not seem to follow, that if the States as such are to exist they must be armed with some power of self-defence. This is the idea of [Col. Mason] who appears to have looked to the bottom of this matter. Besides the Aristocratic and other interests, which ought to have the means of defending themselves, the States have their interests as such, and are equally entitled to likes means. On the whole he thought that as in some respects the States are to be considered in their political capacity, and in others as districts of individual citizens, the two ideas embraced on different sides, instead of being opposed to each other, ought to be combined; that in *one* branch the *people*, ought to be represented; in the *other* the *States*.

M! GHORUM. The States as now confederated have no doubt a right to refuse to be consolidated, or to be formed into any new system. But he wished the small States which seemed most ready to object, to consider which are to give up most, they or the larger ones. He conceived that a rupture of the Union w⁴ be an event unhappy for all, but surely the large States would be least unable to take care of themselves, and to make connections with one another. The weak therefore were most interested in establishing some general system for maintaining order. If among individuals, composed partly of weak, and partly of strong, the former most need the protection of law & Government, the case is exactly the same with weak & powerful States. What would be the situation of Delaware (for these things he found must be spoken out, & it might as well be done [1] first as last) what w⁴ be the situation of Delaware in case of a separation of the States? Would she not lie [2] at the mercy of Pennsylvania? would not her true interest lie in being consolidated with her, and ought she not now to wish for such a union with P? under one Gov! as will put it out of the power of Pen! to oppress her? Nothing can be more ideal than the danger apprehended by the States, from their being formed into one nation. Mass!! was originally three colonies, viz old Mass!! Plymouth—& the province of Mayne. These apprehensions existed then. An incorporation took place; all parties were safe & satisfied; and every distinction is now forgotᵗen. The case was similar with Connecticut & Newhaven. The dread of union was reciprocal; the consequence of it equally salutary and satisfactory. In like manner N. Jersey has been made

[1] The word " at " is here inserted in the transcript.
[2] The word " be " is substituted in the transcript for " lie."

one society out of two parts. Should a separation of the States take place, the fate of N. Jersey w.ᵈ be worst of all. She has no foreign commerce & can have but little. P.ᵃ & N. York will continue to levy taxes on her consumption. If she consults her interest she w.ᵈ beg of all things to be annihilated. The apprehensions of the small States ought to be appeased by another reflection. Mass.ᵗˢ will be divided. The province of Maine is already considered as approaching the term of its annexation to it; and P.ᵃ will probably not increase, considering the present state of her population, & other events that may happen. On the whole he considered a Union of the States as necessary to their happiness, & a firm Gen.ˡ Gov.ᵗ as necessary to their Union. He sh.ᵈ consider it as [1] his duty if his colleagues viewed the matter in the same light he did to stay here as long as any other State would remain with them, in order to agree on some plan that could with propriety be recommended to the people.

M.ʳ Elsworth, did not despair. He still trusted that some good plan of Gov.ᵗ w.ᵈ be divised & adopted.

M.ʳ Read. He sh.ᵈ have no objection to the system if it were truly national, but it has too much of a federal mixture in it. The little States he thought had not much to fear. He suspected that the large States felt their want of energy, & wished for a Gen.ˡ Gov.ᵗ to supply the defect. Mass.ᵗˢ was evidently labouring under her weakness and he believed Delaware w.ᵈ not be in much danger if in her neighbourhood. Delaware had enjoyed tranquility & he flattered himself w.ᵈ continue to do so. He was not however so selfish as not to wish for a good Gen.ˡ Gov.ᵗ In order to obtain one the whole States must be incorporated. If the States remain, the representatives of the large ones will stick together, and carry every thing before them. The Executive also will be chosen under the influence of this partiality, and will betray it in his administration. These jealousies are inseparable from the scheme of leaving the States in existence. They must be done away. The ungranted lands also which have been assumed by particular States must also [2] be given up. He repeated his approbation of the plan of M.ʳ Hamilton, & wished it to be substituted in place of [3] that on the table.

M.ʳ Madison agreed with Doc.ʳ Johnson, that the mixed nature of the Gov.ᵗ ought to be kept in view; but thought too much stress was laid on the rank of the States as political societies. There was a gradation, he observed from the smallest corporation, with the most

---

[1] The word " as " is omitted in the transcript.
[2] The word " also " is stricken out in the transcript.
[3] The word " for " is substituted in the transcript for " in place of."

limited powers, to the largest empire with the most perfect sovereignty. He pointed out the limitations on the sovereignty of the States, as now confederated their laws in relation to the paramount law of the Confederacy were analogous to that of bye laws to the supreme law within a State. Under the proposed Gov.[t] the powers of the States will be much farther reduced. According to the views of every member, the Gen.[l] Gov.[t] will have powers far beyond those exercised by the British Parliament, when the States were part of the British Empire. It will in particular have the power, without the consent of the State Legislatures, to levy money directly on [1] the people themselves; and therefore not to divest such *unequal* portions of the people as composed the several States, of an *equal* voice, would subject the system to the reproaches & evils which have resulted from the vicious representation in G. B.

He entreated the gentlemen representing the small States to renounce a principle w.[ch] was confessedly unjust, which c.[d] never be admitted, & [2] if admitted must infuse mortality into a Constitution which we wished to last forever. He prayed them to ponder well the consequences of suffering the Confederacy to go to pieces. It had been s.[d] that the want of energy in the large states w.[d] be a security to the small. It was forgotten that this want of energy proceeded from the supposed security of the States ag.[st] all external danger. Let each state depend on itself for its security, & let apprehensions arise arise of danger, from distant powers or from neighbouring States, & the languishing condition of all the States, large as well as small, w.[d] soon be transformed into vigorous & high toned Gov.[ts] His great fear was that their Gov.[ts] w.[d] then have too much energy, that these [3] might not only be formidable in the large to the small States, but fatal to the internal liberty of all. The same causes which have rendered the old world the Theatre of incessant wars, & have banished liberty from the face of it, w.[d] soon produce the same effects here. The weakness & jealousy of the small States w.[d] quickly introduce some regular military force ag.[st] sudden danger from their powerful neighbours. The example w.[d] be followed by others, and w.[d] soon become universal. In time of actual war, great discretionary powers are constantly given to the Executive Magistrate. Constant apprehension of war, has the same tendency to render the head too large for the body. A standing military force, with an overgrown

---

[1] The word " from " is substituted in the transcript for " on."
[2] The word " which " is here inserted in the transcript.
[3] The word " these " is stricken out in the transcript and " this " is written above it.

Executive will not long be safe companions to liberty. The means of defence ag.ᵗ foreign danger, have been always the instruments of tyranny at home. Among the Romans it was a standing maxim to excite a war, whenever a revolt was apprehended. Throughout all Europe, the armies kept up under the pretext of defending, have enslaved the people. It is perhaps questionable, whether the best concerted system of absolute power in Europe c.ᵈ maintain itself, in a situation, where no alarms of external danger c.ᵈ tame the people to the domestic yoke. The insular situation of G. Britain was the principal cause of her being an exception to the general fate of Europe. It has rendered less defence necessary, and admitted a kind of defence w.ᶜʰ c.ᵈ not be used for the purpose of oppression.— These consequences he conceived ought to be apprehended whether the States should run into a total separation from each other, or sh.ᵈ enter into partial confederacies. Either event w.ᵈ be truly deplorable; & those who might be accessary to either, could never be forgiven by their Country, nor by themselves.

* M.ʳ HAMILTON observed that individuals forming political Societies modify their rights differently, with regard to suffrage. Examples of it are found in all the States. In all of them some individuals are deprived of the right altogether, not having the requisite qualification of property. In some of the States the right of suffrage is allowed in some cases and refused in others. To vote for a member in one branch, a certain quantum of property, to vote for a member in another branch of the Legislature, a higher quantum of property is required. In like manner States may modify their right of suffrage differently, the larger exercising a larger, the smaller a smaller share of it. But as States are a collection of individual men which ought we to respect most, the rights of the people composing them, or of the artificial beings resulting from the composition. Nothing could be more preposterous or absurd than to sacrifice the former to the latter. It has been s.ᵈ that if the smaller States renounce their *equality,* they renounce at the same time their *liberty.* The truth is it is a contest for power, not for liberty. Will the men composing the small States be less free than those composing the larger. The State of Delaware having 40,000 souls will *lose* [2] *power,* if she has ⅒ only of the votes allowed to P.ᵃ having 400,000: but will the people of Del: *be less free,* if each citizen

* From this date he was absent till the   of [1]

---

[1] The date, " 13th of August," is supplied in the transcript.
[2] The transcript does not italicize the word " *lose.*"

has an equal vote with each citizen of P? He admitted that common residence within the same State would produce a certain degree of attachment; and that this principle might have a certain influence in[1] public affairs. He thought however that this might by some precautions be in a great measure excluded: and that no material inconvenience could result from it, as there could not be any ground for combination among the States whose influence was most dreaded. The only considerable distinction of interests, lay between the carrying & non-carrying States, which divide[2] instead of uniting the largest States. No considerable inconvenience had been found from the division of the State of N. York into different districts of different sizes.

Some of the consequences of a dissolution of the Union, and the establishment of partial confederacies, had been been pointed out. He would add another of a most serious nature. Alliances will immediately be formed with different rival & hostile nations of Europes, who will foment disturbances among ourselves, and make us parties to all their own quarrels. Foreign Nations having American dominions[3] are & must be jealous of us. Their representatives betray the utmost anxiety for our fate, & for the result of this meeting, which must have an essential influence on it.—It had been said that respectability in the eyes of foreign Nations was not the object at which we aimed; that the proper object of republican Government was domestic tranquility & happiness. This was an ideal distinction. No Governm.t could give us tranquility & happiness at home, which did not possess sufficient stability and strength to make us respectable abroad. This was the critical moment for forming such a Government. We should run every risk in trusting to future amendments. As yet we retain the habits of union. We are weak & sensible of our weakness. Henceforward the motives will become feebler, and the difficulties greater. It is a miracle that we were[4] now here exercising our tranquil & free deliberations on the subject. It would be madness to trust to future miracles. A thousand causes must obstruct a reproduction of them.

M.r PIERCE considered the equality of votes under the Confederation as the great source of the public difficulties. The members of Cong.s were advocates for local advantages. State distinctions must be sacrificed as far as the general good required, but without destroy-

---

[1] The word " on " is substituted in the transcript for " in."
[2] The word " divides " is substituted in the transcript for " divide."
[3] The transcript uses the word " dominions " in the singular.
[4] The word " are " is substituted in the transcript for " were."

ing the States. Tho' from a small State he felt himself a Citizen of the U. S.

Mr GERRY, urged that we never were independent States, were not such now, & never could be even on the principles of the Confederation. The States & the advocates for them were intoxicated with the idea of their *sovereignty*. He was a member of Congress at the time the federal articles were formed. The injustice of allowing each State an equal vote was long insisted on. He voted for it, but it was ag.st his Judgment, and under the pressure of public danger, and the obstinacy of the lesser States. The present confederation he considered as dissolving. The fate of the Union will be decided by the Convention. If they do not agree on something, few delegates will probably be appointed to Cong.s If they do Cong.s will probably be kept up till the new System should be adopted. He lamented that instead of coming here like a band of brothers, belonging to the same family, we seemed to have brought with us the spirit of political negociators.

Mr L. MARTIN. remarked that the language of the States being *sovereign & independent*, was once familiar & understood; though it seemed now so strange & obscure. He read those passages in the articles of Confederation, which describe them in that language.

On the question as moved by Mr Lansing. Shall the word " not " be struck out.

Mass.ts no. Con.t ay. N. Y. ay. N. J. ay. P.a no. Del. ay. M.d div.d V.a no. N. C. no. S. C. no. Geo. no.[1]

On the motion to agree to the clause as reported, " that the rule of suffrage in the 1.st branch ought not to be according to that established by the articles of [2] Confederation.

Mass. ay. Con.t no. N. Y. no. N. J. no. P.a ay. Del. no. M.d div.d V.a ay. N. C. ay. S. C. ay. Geo. ay.[3]

Doc.r JOHNSON & Mr ELSEWORTH moved to postpone the residue of the clause, & take up—y.e 8—Resol:

On [2] question.

Mas. no. Con.t ay. N. Y. ay. N. J. ay. P.a ay. Del. no. M.d ay. V.a ay. N. C. ay. S. C. ay. Geo. ay.[4]

---

[1] In the transcript the vote reads: " Connecticut, New York, New Jersey, Delaware, aye—4; Massachusetts, Pennsylvania, Virginia, North Carolina, South Carolina, Georgia, no—6; Maryland, divided."

[2] The word " the " is here inserted in the transcript.

[3] In the transcript the vote reads: " Massachusetts, Pennsylvania, Virginia, North Carolina, South Carolina, Georgia, aye—6; Connecticut, New York, New Jersey, Delaware, no—4; Maryland, divided."

[4] In the transcript the vote reads: " Connecticut, New York, New Jersey, Pennsylvania, Maryland, Virginia, North Carolina, South Carolina, Georgia, aye—9; Massachusetts, Delaware, no—2."

Mᵣ Elseworth moved that the rule of suffrage in the 2ᵈ branch be the same with that established by the articles of confederation.'' He was not sorry on the whole he said that the vote just passed, had determined against this rule in the first branch. He hoped it would become a ground of compromise with regard to the 2ᵈ branch. We were partly national; partly federal. The proportional representation in the first branch was conformable to the national principle & would secure the large States agˢᵗ the small. An equality of voices was conformable to the federal principle and was necessary to secure the Small States agˢᵗ the large. He trusted that on this middle ground a compromise would take place. He did not see that it could on any other. And if no compromise should take place, our meeting would not only be in vain but worse than in vain. To the Eastward he was sure Massᵗˢ was the only State that would listen to a proposition for excluding the States as equal political Societies, from an equal voice in both branches. The others would risk every consequence rather than part with so dear a right. An attempt to deprive them of it, was at once cutting the body of America in two, and as he supposed would be the case, somewhere about this part of it. The large States he conceived would notwithstanding the equality of votes, have an influence that would maintain their superiority. Holland, as had been admitted [by Mᵣ Madison] had, notwithstanding a like equality in the Dutch Confederacy, a prevailing influence in the public measures. The power of self-defence was essential to the small States. Nature had given it to the smallest insect of the creation. He could never admit that there was no danger of combinations among the large States. They will like individuals find out and avail themselves of the advantage to be gained by it. It was true the danger would be greater, if they were contiguous and had a more immediate ¹ common interest. A defensive combination of the small States was rendered more difficult by their greater number. He would mention another consideration of great weight. The existing confederation was founded on the equality of the States in the article of suffrage: was it meant to pay no regard to this antecedent plighted faith. Let a strong Executive, a Judiciary & Legislative power be created; but Let not too much be attempted; by which all may be lost. He was not in general a half-way man, yet he preferred doing half the good we could, rather than do nothing at all. The other half may be added, when the necessity shall be more fully experienced.

---

¹ The word " and " is here inserted in the transcript.

M: BALDWIN could have wished that the powers of the General Legislature had been defined, before the mode of constituting it had been agitated. He should vote against the motion of M: Elseworth, tho' he did not like the Resolution as it stood in the Report of the Committee of the whole. He thought the second branch ought to be the representation of property, and that in forming it therefore some reference ought to be had to the relative wealth of their Constituents, and to the principles on which the Senate of Mass:ᵗˢ was constituted. He concurred with those who thought it wᵈ be impossible for the Genᴸ Legislature to extend its cares to the local matters of the States.

Adjᵈ

SATURDAY JUNE 30. 1787.[1]   IN CONVENTION

M: BREARLY moved that the Presidᵗ write to the Executive of N. Hamshire, informing it that the business depending before the Convention was of such a nature as to require the immediate attendance of the deputies of that State. In support of his motion he observed that the difficulties of the subject and the diversity of opinions called for all the assistance we could possibly obtain. [it was well understood that the object was to add N. Hamshire to the nᵒ of States opposed to the doctrine of proportional representation, which it was presumed from her relative size she must be adverse to].

M: PATTERSON seconded the motion

M: RUTLIDGE could see neither the necessity nor propriety of such a measure. They are not unapprized of the meeting, and can attend if they choose. Rho. Island might as well be urged to appoint & send deputies. Are we to suspend the business until the deputies arrive? if we proceed he hoped all the great points would be adjusted before the letter could produce its effect.

M: KING. said he had written more than once as a private correspondent, & the answers[2] gave him every reason to expect that State would be represented very shortly, if it shᵈ be so at all. Circumstances of a personal nature had hitherto prevented it. A letter cᵈ have no effect.

M: WILSON wished to know whether it would be consistent with the rule or reason of secresy, to communicate to N. Hamshire that

---

[1] The year " 1787 " is omitted in the transcript.
[2] The transcript uses the word " answers " in the singular.

the business was of such a nature as the motion described. It w<u>d</u> spread a great alarm. Besides he doubted the propriety of soliciting any State on the subject; the meeting being merely voluntary—on the [1] motion of M<u>r</u> Brearly Mas<u>ts</u> no. Con<u>t</u> no. N. Y. ay. N. J. ay. P<u>a</u> not on y<u>e</u> floor. Del. not on floor. M<u>d</u> div<u>d</u> V<u>a</u> no. N. C. no. S. C. no. Geo. not on floor.[2]

The motion of M<u>r</u> Elseworth[3] resumed for allowing each State an equal vote in y<u>e</u> 2<u>d</u> branch.

M<u>r</u> WILSON did not expect such a motion after the establishment of y<u>e</u> contrary principle in the 1<u>st</u> branch; and considering the reasons which would oppose it, even if an equal vote had been allowed in the 1<u>st</u> branch. The Gentleman from Connecticut [M<u>r</u> Elseworth] had pronounced that if the motion should not be acceded to, of all the States North of Pen<u>a</u> one only would agree to any Gen<u>l</u> Government. He entertained more favorable hopes of Conn<u>t</u> and of the other Northern States. He hoped the alarms exceeded their cause, and that they would not abandon a Country to which they were bound by so many strong and endearing ties. But should the deplored event happen, it would neither stagger his sentiments nor his duty. If the minority of the people of America refuse to coalesce with the majority on just and proper principles, if a separation must take place, it could never happen on better grounds. The votes of yesterday ag<u>st</u> the just principle of representation, were as 22 to 90 of the people of America. Taking the opinions to be the same on this point, and he was sure if there was any room for change, it could not be on the side of the majority, the question will be shall less than ¼ of the U. States withdraw themselves from the Union; or shall more than ¾. renounce the inherent, indisputable, and unalienable rights of men, in favor of the artificial systems of States. If issue must be joined, it was on this point he would chuse to join it. The gentleman from Connecticut in supposing that the prepondenancy[4] secured to the majority in the 1<u>st</u> branch had removed the objections to an equality of votes in the 2<u>d</u> branch for the security of the minority, narrowed the case extremely. Such an equality will enable the minority to controul in all cases whatsoever, the sentiments and interests of the majority. Seven States will controul six: Seven

---

[1] The word "the" is omitted in the transcript.

[2] In the transcript the vote reads: "New York, New Jersey, aye—2; Massachusetts, Connecticut, Virginia, North Carolina, South Carolina, no—5; Maryland, divided; Pennsylvania, Delaware, Georgia, not on the floor."

[3] The word "being" is here inserted in the transcript.

[4] The word "prepondenancy" is changed to "preponderance" in the transcript.

States, according to the estimates that had been used, composed $^{2}\%_{0}$. of the whole people. It would be in the power then of less than ⅛ to overrule ⅔ whenever a question should happen to divide the States in that manner. Can we forget for whom we are forming a Government? Is it for *men*, or for the imaginary beings called *States?* Will our honest Constituents be satisfied with metaphysical distinctions? Will they, ought they to be satisfied with being told that the one third compose the greater number of States? The rule of suffrage ought on every principle to be the same in the 2^{d} as in the 1st branch. If the Government be not laid on this foundation, it can be neither solid nor lasting. Any other principle will be local, confined & temporary. This will expand with the expansion, and grow with the growth of the U. States.—Much has been said of an imaginary combination of three States. Sometimes a danger of monarchy, sometimes of aristocracy, has been charged on it. No explanation however of the danger has been vouchsafed. It would be easy to prove both from reason & history that rivalships would be more probable than coalitions; and that there are no coinciding interests that could produce the latter. No answer has yet been given to the observations of [Mr Madison] on this subject. Should the Executive Magistrate be taken from one of the large States would not the other two be thereby thrown into the scale with the other States? Whence then the danger of monarchy? Are the people of the three large States more aristocratic than those of the small ones? Whence then the danger of aristocracy from their influence? It is all a mere illusion of names. We talk of States, till we forget what they are composed of. Is a real & fair majority, the natural hot-bed of aristocracy? It is a part of the definition of this species of Gov^{t} or rather of tyranny, that the smaller number governs the greater. It is true that a majority of States in the 2^{d} branch can not carry a law agst a majority of the people in the 1st But this removes half only of the objection. Bad Govern^{ts} are of two sorts. 1.[1] that which does too little. 2.[1] that which does too much: that which fails thro' weakness; and that which destroys thro' oppression. Under which of these evils do the U. States at present groan? under the weakness and inefficiency of its Govern^{t} To remedy this weakness we have been sent to this Convention. If the motion should be agreed to, we shall leave the U. S. fettered precisely as heretofore; with the additional mortification of seeing the good purposes of ye fair

---

[1] The figures " 1 " and " 2 " are changed to " first " and " secondly " in the transcript.

representention of the people in the 1ˢᵗ branch, defeated in¹ 2ᵈ Twenty four will still controul sixty six. He lamented that such a disagreement should prevail on the point of representation, as he did not foresee that it would happen on the other point most contested, the boundary between the Genˡ & the local authorities. He thought the States necessary & valuable parts of a good system.

Mʳ ELSEWORTH. The capital objection of Mʳ Wilson " that the minority will rule the majority " is not true. The power is given to the few to save them from being destroyed by the many. If an equality of votes had been given to them in both branches, the objection might have had weight. Is it a novel thing that the few should have a check on the many? Is it not the case in the British Constitution the wisdom of which so many gentlemen have united in applauding? Have not the House of Lords, who form so small a proportion of the nation a negative on the laws, as a necessary defence of their peculiar rights agˢᵗ the encroachmˢ of the Commons. No instance of a Confederacy has existed in which an equality of voices has not been exercised by the members of it. We are running from one extreme to another. We are razing the foundations of the building, when we need only repair the roof. No salutary measure has been lost for want of *a majority of the States*, to favor it. If security be all that the great States wish for the 1ˢᵗ branch secures them. The danger of combinations among them is not imaginary. Altho' no particular abuses could be foreseen by him, the possibility of them would be sufficient to alarm him. But he could easily conceive cases in which they might result from such combinations. Suppose that in pursuance of some commercial treaty or arrangement, three or four free ports & no more were to be established would not combinations be formed in favor of Boston—Philadᵃ & & some port in² Chesapeak? A like concert might be formed in the appointment of the great officers. He appealed again to the obligations of the federal pact which was still in force, and which had been entered into with so much solemnity; persuading himself that some regard would still be paid to the plighed faith under which each State small as well as great, held an equal right of suffrage in the general Councils. His remarks were not the result of partial or local views. The State he represented [Connecticut] held a middle rank.

Mʳ MADISON did justice to the able & close reasoning of Mʳ E. but must observe that it did not always accord with itself. On

---

¹ The word "the" is here inserted in the transcript.
² The words "of the" are substituted in the transcript for "in."

another occasion, the large States were described by him as the Aristocratic States, ready to oppress the small. Now the small are the House of Lords requiring a negative to defend them ag:t the more numerous commons. Mr. E. had also erred in saying that no instance had existed in which confederated States had not retained to themselves a perfect equality of suffrage. Passing over the German system in which the K. of Prussia has nine voices, he reminded Mr. E. of the Lycian confederacy, in which the component members had votes proportioned to their importance, and which Montesquieu recommends as the fittest model for that form of Government. Had the fact been as stated by Mr. E. it would have been of little avail to him, or rather would have strengthened the arguments ag:t him; the History & fate of the several confederacies modern as well as Antient, demonstrating some radical vice in their structure. In reply to the appeal of Mr. E. to the faith plighted in the existing federal compact, he remarked that the party claiming from others an adherence to a common engagement ought at least to be guiltless itself of a violation. Of all the States however Connecticut was perhaps least able to urge this plea. Besides the various omissions to perform the stipulated acts from which no State was free, the Legislature of that State had by a pretty recent vote, *positively, refused* to pass a law for complying with the Requisitions of Cong: and had transmitted a copy of the vote to Cong. It was urged, he said, continually that an equality of votes in the 2d branch was not only necessary to secure the small, but would be perfectly safe to the large ones whose majority in the 1st branch was an effectual bulwark. But notwithstanding this apparent defence, the majority of States might still injure the majority of [1] people. 1.[2] they could *obstruct* the wishes and interests of the majority. 2.[2] they could *extort* measures repugnant to the wishes & interest of the Majority. 3.[2] they could *impose* measures adverse thereto; as the 2d branch will probly exercise some great powers, in which the 1st will not participate. He admitted that every peculiar interest whether in any class of citizens, or any description of States, ought to be secured as far as possible. Wherever there is danger of attack there ought[3] be given a constitutional power of defence. But he contended that the States were divided into different interests not by their difference of size, but by other circumstances; the most material of which resulted partly

---

[1] The word "the" is here inserted in the transcript.
[2] The figures "1," "2" and "3" are changed to "In the first place," "Secondly" and "Thirdly."
[3] The word "to" is here inserted in the transcript.

from climate, but principally from the effects of their having or not having slaves. These two causes concurred in forming the great division of interests in the U. States. It did not lie between the large & small States: It lay between the Northern & Southern, and if any defensive power were necessary, it ought to be mutually given to these two interests. He was so strongly impressed with this important truth that he had been casting about in his mind for some expedient that would answer the purpose. The one which had occurred was that instead of proportioning the votes of the States in both branches, to their respective numbers of inhabitants computing the slaves in the ratio of 5 to 3, they should be represented in one branch according to the number of free inhabitants only; and in the other according to the whole n? counting the slaves as if [1] free. By this arrangement the Southern Scale would have the advantage in one House, and the Northern in the other. He had been restrained from proposing this expedient by two considerations: one was his unwillingness to urge any diversity of interests on an occasion where it is but too apt to arise of itself—the other was, the inequality of powers that must be vested in the two branches, and which w?. destroy the equilibrium of interests.

M? ELSEWORTH assured the House that whatever might be thought of the Representatives of Connecticut the State was entirely federal in her disposition. He appealed to her great exertions during the war, in supplying both men & money. The muster rolls would show she had more troops in the field than Virg? If she had been Delinquent, it had been from inability, and not more so than other States.

M? SHERMAN. M? Madison has [2] animadverted on the delinquency of the States, when his object required him to prove that the Constitution of Cong? was faulty. Cong? is not to blame for the faults of the States. Their measures have been right, and the only thing wanting has been, a further power in Cong? to render them effectual.

M? DAVY was much embarrassed and wished for explanations. The Report of the Committee allowing the Legislatures to choose the Senate, and establishing a proportional representation in it, seemed to be impracticable. There will according to this rule be ninety members in the outset, and the number will increase as new States are added. It was impossible that so numerous a body could possess the activity and other qualities required in it. Were he to vote on the comparative merits of the report as it stood, and the amendment, he

---

[1] The word " if " is omitted in the transcript.
[2] The word " has " is omitted in the transcript.

should be constrained to prefer the latter. The appointment of the Senate by electors chosen by the people for that purpose was he conceived liable to an insuperable difficulty. The larger Counties or districts thrown into a general district, would certainly prevail over the smaller Counties or districts, and merit in the latter would be excluded altogether. The report therefore seemed to be right in referring the appointment to the Legislatures, whose agency in the general System did not appear to him objectionable as it did to some others. The fact was that the local prejudices & interests which could not be denied to exist, would find their way into the national councils whether the Representatives should be chosen by the Legislatures or by the people themselves. On the other hand, if a proportional representation was attended with insuperable difficulties, the making the Senate the Representative of the States, looked like bringing us back to Cong⁵ again, and shutting out all the advantages expected from it. Under this view of the subject he could not vote for any plan for the Senate yet proposed. He thought that in general there were extremes on both sides. We were partly federal, partly national in our Union, and he did not see why the Gov⁵ might not in some respects operate on the States, in others on the people.

M⁵ WILSON admitted the question concerning the number of Senators, to be embarrassing. If the smallest States be allowed one, and the others in proportion, the Senate will certainly be too numerous. He looked forward to the time when the smallest States will contain 100,000 souls at least. Let there be then one Senator in each for every 100,000 souls and let the States not having that n⁰ of inhabitants be allowed one. He was willing himself to submit to this temporary concession to the small States; and threw out the idea as a ground of compromise.

Doc⁵ FRANKLIN The diversity of opinions turns on two points. If a proportional representation takes place, the small States contend that their liberties will be in danger. If an equality of votes is to be put in its place, the large States say their money will be in danger. When a broad table is to be made, and the edges of planks do not fit, the artist takes a little from both, and makes a good joint. In like manner here both sides must part with some of their demands, in order that they may join in some accomodating proposition. He had prepared one which he would read, that it might lie on the table for consideration. The proposition was in the words following "

"That the Legislatures of the several States shall choose & send an equal number of Delegates, namely   who are to compose the 2ᵈ branch of the General Legislature—

That in all cases or questions wherein the Sovereignty of individual States may be affected, or whereby their authority over their own Citizens may be diminished, or the authority of the General Government within the several States augmented, each State shall have equal suffrage.

That in the appointment of all Civil officers of y⁀ Gen⁀ Gov⁀ in the election of whom the 2⁀ branch may by the Constitution have part, each State shall have equal suffrage.

That in fixing the Salaries of such officers, and in all allowances for public services, and generally in all appropriations & dispositions of money to be drawn out of the General Treasury; and in all laws for supplying that Treasury, the Delegates of the several States shall have suffrage in proportion to the Sums which their respective States do actually contribute to the Treasury." Where a Ship had many owners this was the rule of deciding on her expedition. He had been one of the Ministers from this Country to France during the joint war and w⁀ have been very glad if allowed a vote in distributing the money to carry it on.

M⁀ KING observed that the simple question was whether each State should have an equal vote in the 2⁀ branch; that it must be apparent to those gentlemen who liked neither the motion for this equality, nor the report as it stood, that the report was as susceptible of melioration as the motion; that a reform would be nugatory & nominal only if we should make another Congress of the proposed Senate: that if the adherence to an equality of votes was fixed & unalterable, there could not be less obstinacy on the other side, & that we were in fact cut insunder [1] already, and it was in vain to shut our eyes against it: that he was however filled with astonishment that if we were convinced that every *man* in America was secured in all his rights, we should be ready to sacrifice this substantial good to the phantom of *State* sovereignty: that his feelings were more harrowed & his fears more agitated for his Country than he could express, that he conceived this to be the last opportunity of providing for its liberty & happiness: that he could not therefore but repeat his amazement that when a just Govern⁀ founded on a fair representation of the *people* of America was within our reach, we should renounce the blessing, from an attachment to the ideal freedom & importance of *States:* that should this wonderful illusion continue to prevail, his mind was prepared for every event, rather than to [2] sit down under a Gov⁀ founded in [3] a vicious principle of representation, and which must be as short lived as it would be unjust. He

---

[1] The word " asunder " is substituted in the transcript for " insunder."
[2] The word " to " is omitted in the transcript.
[3] The word " on " is substituted in the transcript for " in."

might prevail on himself to accede to some such expedient as had been hinted by M: Wilson: but he never could listen to an equality of votes as proposed in the motion.

M: DAYTON. When assertion is given for proof, and terror substituted for argument, he presumed they would have no effect however eloquently spoken. It should have been shewn that the evils we have experienced have proceeded from the equality now objected to: and that the seeds of dissolution for the State Governments are not sown in the Gen! Government. He considered the system on the table as a novelty, an amphibious monster; and was persuaded that it never would be rec^d by the people.

M: MARTIN, w^d never confederate if it could not be done on just principles

M: MADISON would acquiesce in the concession hinted by M: Wilson, on condition that a due independence should be given to the Senate. The plan in its present shape makes the Senate absolutely dependent on the States. The Senate therefore is only another edition of Cong^s He knew the faults of that Body & had used a bold language agst it. Still he w^d preserve the State rights, as carefully as the trials by jury.

M: BEDFORD, contended that there was no middle way between a perfect consolidation and a mere confederacy of the States. The first is out of the question, and in the latter they must continue if not perfectly, yet equally sovereign. If political Societies possess ambition avarice, and all the other passions which render them formidable to each other, ought we not to view them in this light here? Will not the same motives operate in America as elsewhere? If any gentleman doubts it let him look at the votes. Have they not been dictated by interest, by ambition? Are not the large States evidently seeking to aggrandize themselves at the expense of the small? They think no doubt that they have right on their side, but interest had blinded their eyes. Look at Georgia. Though a small State at present, she is actuated by the prospect of soon being a great one. S. Carolina is actuated both by present interest & future prospects. She hopes too to see the other States cut down to her own dimensions. N. Carolina has the same motives of present & future interest. Virg^a follows. Mary^d is not on that side of the Question. Pen^a has a direct and future interest. Mass^{ts} has a decided and palpable interest in the part she takes. Can it be expected that the small States will act from pure disinterestedness. Look at G. Britain. Is the Representation there less unequal? But we shall be told again that that is the rotten part of the Constitution. Have not

the boroughs however held fast their constitutional rights? and are
we to act with greater purity than the rest of mankind. An exact
proportion in the Representation is not preserved in any one of the
States. Will it be said that an inequality of power will not result
from an inequality of votes. Give the opportunity, and ambition will
not fail to abuse it. The whole History of mankind proves it. The
three large States have a common interest to bind them together in
commerce. But whether a combination as we suppose, or a competition as others suppose, shall take place among them, in either
case, the smaller [1] States must be ruined. We must like Solon make
such a Govern! as the people will approve. Will the smaller States
ever agree to the proposed degradation of them. It is not true that
the people will not agree to enlarge the powers of the present Cong!
The Language of the people has been that Cong! ought to have the
power of collecting an impost, and of coercing the States when [2] it
may be necessary. On The first point they have been explicit &, in
a manner, unanimous in their declarations. And must they not agree
to this & similar measures if they ever mean to discharge their
engagements. The little States are willing to observe their engagements, but will meet the large ones on no ground but that of
the Confederation. We have been told with a dictatorial air that
this is the last moment for a fair trial in favor of a good Governm!
It will be the last indeed if the propositions reported from the Committee go forth to the people. He was under no apprehensions. The
Large States dare not dissolve the Confederation. If they do the
small ones will find some foreign ally of more honor and good faith,
who will take them by the hand and do them justice. He did not
mean by this to intimidate or alarm. It was a natural consequence;
which ought to be avoided by enlarging the federal powers not
annihilating the federal system. This is what the people expect. All
agree in the necessity of a more efficient Gov! and why not make
such an one; as they desire.

M! ELSEWORTH,. Under a National Gov! he should participate in
the National Security, as remarked by [M! King] but that was all.
What he wanted was domestic happiness. The Nat! Gov! could not
descend to the local objects on which this depended. It could only
embrace objects of a general nature. He turned his eyes therefore
for the preservation of his rights to the State Gov!! From these alone
he could derive the greatest happiness he expects in this life. His

---

[1] The word "small" is substituted in the transcript for "smaller."
[2] The word "where" is substituted in the transcript for "when."

happiness depends on their existence, as much as a new born infant on its mother for nourishment. If this reasoning was not satisfactory, he had nothing to add that could be so.

M.ʳ KING was for preserving the States in a subordinate degree, and as far as they could be necessary for the purposes stated by M.ʳ Elsewth. He did not think a full answer had been given to those who apprehended a dangerous encroachment on their jurisdictions. Expedients might be devised as he conceived that would give them all the security the nature of things would admit of. In the establishm.ᵗ of Societies the Constitution was to the Legislature what the laws were to individuals. As the fundamental rights of individuals are secured by express provisions in the State Constitutions; why may not a like security be provided for the Rights of States in the National Constitution. The articles of Union between Engl.ᵈ & Scotland furnish an example of such a provision in favor of sundry rights of Scotland. When that Union was in agitation, the same language of apprehension which has been heard from the smaller States, was in the mouths of the Scotch patriots. The articles however have not been violated and the Scotch have found an increase of prosperity & happiness. He was aware that this will be called a mere *paper security*. He thought it a sufficient answer to say that if fundamental articles of compact, are no sufficient defence against physical power, neither will there be any safety ag.ˢᵗ it if there be no compact. He could not sit down, without taking some notice of the language of the honorable gentleman from Delaware [M.ʳ Bedford]. It was not he that had uttered a dictatorial language. This intemperance had marked the honorabl gentleman himself. It was not he who with a vehemence unprecedented in that House, had declared himself ready to turn his hopes from our common Country, and court the protection of some foreign hand. This too was the language of the Honbl member himself. He was grieved that such a thought had entered into [1] his heart. He was more grieved that such an expression had dropped from his lips. The gentleman c.ᵈ only excuse it to himself on the score of passion. For himself whatever might be his distress, he w.ᵈ never court relief from a foreign power.

Adjourned

---

[1] The word "into" is omitted in the transcript.

MONDAY JULY 2�12 IN CONVENTION

On the question for allowing each State one vote in the second branch as moved by Mʳ Elseworth,[1] Massᵗˢ no. Conᵗ ay. N. Y. ay. N. J. ay. Pᵃ no. Del. ay. Mᵈ ay. Mʳ Jenifer being not present Mʳ Martin alone voted Vᵃ no. N. C. no. S. C. no. Geo. divᵈ Mʳ Houston no. Mʳ Baldwin ay.

Mʳ PINKNEY thought an equality of votes in the 2ᵈ branch inadmissible. At the same time candor obliged him to admit that the large States would feel a partiality for their own Citizens & give them a preference, in appointments: that they might also find some common points in their commercial interests, and promote treaties favorable to them. There is a real distinction [2] the Northern & Southⁿ interests. N. Carolᵗ S. Carol: & Geo. in their Rice & Indigo had a peculiar interest which might be sacrificed. How then shall the larger States be prevented from administering the Genˡ Govᵗ as they please, without being themselves unduly subjected to the will of the smaller? By allowing them some but not a full proportion. He was extremely anxious that something should be done, considering this as the last appeal to a regular experiment. Congˢ have failed in almost every effort for an amendment of the federal System. Nothing has prevented a dissolution of it, but the appointmᵗ of this Convention; & he could not express his alarms for the consequences of such an event He read his motion, to form the States into classes, with an apportionment of Senators among them, [see art. 4, of his plan].[3]

General PINKNEY. was willing the motion might be considered. He did not entirely approve it. He liked better the motion of Docʳ Franklin [which see Saturday June 30]. Some compromise seemed to be necessary: the States being exactly divided on the question for an equality of votes in the 2ᵈ branch. He proposed that a Committee consisting of a member from each State should be appointed to devise & report some compromise.

Mʳ L. MARTIN had no objection to a commitment, but no modifications whatever could reconcile the Smaller States to the least diminution of their equal Sovereignty.

---

[1] The phrase "it was lost by an equal division of votes," is here inserted in the transcript and the vote reads: "Connecticut, New York, New Jersey, Delaware, Maryland,* aye—5; Massachusetts, Pennsylvania, Virginia, North Carolina, South Carolina, no—5; Georgia, divided [Mr. Baldwin, aye, Mr. Houston, no]." The footnote referring to Maryland reads: "Mr. Jenifer not being present, Mr. Martin alone voted."

[2] The word "between" is here inserted in the transcript.

[3] See Appendix to Debates, IV, No. 3, p. 600.

Mr SHARMAN. We are now at a full stop, and nobody he supposed meant that we sh^d break up without doing something. A committee he thought most likely to hit on some expedient.

* Mr Govr MORRIS. thought a Com^e adviseable as the Convention had been equally divided. He had a stronger reason also. The mode of appointing the 2^d branch tended he was sure to defeat the object of it. What is this object? to check the precipitation, changeableness, and excesses of the first branch. Every man of observation had seen in the democratic branches of the State Legislatures, precipitation— in Congress changeableness, in every department excesses agst personal liberty private property & personal safety. What qualities are necessary to constitute a check in this case? *Abilities* and *virtue*, are equally necessary in both branches. Something more then is now wanted. 1.[2] the checking branch must have a personal interest in checking the other branch, one interest must be opposed to another interest. Vices as they exist, must be turned agst each other. 2.[3] It must have great personal property, it must have the aristocratic spirit; it must love to lord it thro' pride, pride is indeed the great principle that actuates both the poor & the rich. It is this principle which in the former resists, in the latter abuses authority. 3.[4] It should be independent. In Religion the Creature is apt to forget its Creator. That it is otherwise in political affairs, the late debates here are an unhappy proof. The aristocratic body, should be as independent & as firm as the democratic. If the members of it are to revert to a dependence on the democratic choice, the democratic scale will preponderate. All the guards contrived by America have not restrained the Senatorial branches of the Legislatures from a servile complaisance to the democratic. If the 2^d branch is to be dependent we are better without it. To make it independent, it should be for life. It will then do wrong, it will be said. He believed so: He hoped so. The Rich will strive to establish their dominion & enslave the rest. They always did. They always will. The proper security agst them is to form them into a separate interest. The two forces will then controul each other. Let the rich mix with the poor and in a Commercial Country, they will establish an oligarchy. Take away commerce, and the democracy will triumph. Thus it has been

* Transfer hither the marginal note.[1]
* He had just returned from N. Y. hav^g left ye Convention a few days after it commenced business.

---

[1] Madison's direction concerning the footnote is omitted in the transcript.
[2] The figure " 1 " is changed to " In the first place " in the transcript.
[3] The figure " 2 " is changed to " In the second place " in the transcript.
[4] The figure " 3 " is changed to " In the third place " in the transcript.

all the world over. So it will be among us. Reason tells us we are
but men: and we are not to expect any particular interference of
Heaven in our favor. By thus combining & setting apart, the aristocratic interest, the popular interest will be combined ag:t it. There
will be a mutual check and mutual security. 4.[1] An independence
for life, involves the necessary permanency. If we change our
measures no body will trust us: and how avoid a change of measures,
but by avoiding a change of men. Ask any man if he confides in
Cong: if he confides in the State of Pen: if he will lend his money
or enter into contract? He will tell you no. He sees no stability.
He can repose no confidence. If G. B. were to explain her refusal to
treat with us, the same reasoning would be employed.—He disliked
the exclusion of the 2ᵈ branch from holding offices. It is dangerous.
It is like the imprudent exclusion of the military officers during
the war, from civil appointments. It deprives the Executive of the
principal source of influence. If danger be apprehended from the
Executive what a lift-handed way is this of obviating it? If the
son, the brother or the friend can be appointed, the danger may be
even increased, as the disqualified father &c. can then boast of a
disinterestedness which he does not possess. Besides shall the best,
the most able, the most virtuous citizens not be permitted to hold
offices? Who then are to hold them? He was also ag:t paying the
Senators. They will pay themselves if they can. If they can not
they will be rich and can do without it. Of such the 2ᵈ branch
ought to consist; and none but such can compose it if they are not
to be paid—He contended that the Executive should appoint the
Senate & fill up vacancies. This gets rid of the difficulty in the
present question. You may begin with any ratio you please; it will
come to the same thing. The members being independ: & for life,
may be taken as well from one place as from another.—It should be
considered too how the scheme could be carried through the States.
He hoped there was strength of mind eno' in this House to look
truth in the face. He did not hesitate therefore to s..y that loaves
& fishes must bribe the Demagogues. They must be made to expect
higher offices under the general than the State Gov:t. A Senate for
life will be a noble bait. Without such captivating prospects, the
popular leaders will oppose & defeat the plan. He perceived that
the 1:t branch was to be chosen by the people of the States: the 2ᵈ
by those chosen by the people. Is not here a Gov:t by the States. A
Govern:t by Compact between Virg: in the 1:t & 2ᵈ branch; Mas:ts in

---

[1] The figure " 4 " is changed to " In the fourth place " in the transcript.

the 1st & 2d branch &c. This is going back to mere treaty. It is no Govt at all. It is altogether dependent on the States, and will act over again the part which Congs has acted. A firm Governt alone can protect our liberties. He fears the influence of the rich. They will have the same effect here as elsewhere if we do not by such a Govt keep them within their proper sphere.[1] We should remember that the people never act from reason alone. The Rich will take [2] advantage of their passions & make these the instruments for oppressing them. The Result of the Contest will be a violent aristocracy, or a more violent despotism. The schemes of the Rich will be favored by the extent of the Country. The people in such distant parts can not communicate & act in concert. They will be the dupes of those who have more knowledge & intercourse. The only security agst encroachments will be a select & sagacious body of men, instituted to watch agst them on all sides. He meant only to hint these observations, without grounding any motion on them

Mr RANDOLPH favored the commitment though he did not expect much benefit from the expedient. He animadverted on the warm & rash language of Mr Bedford on Saturday; reminded the small States that if the large States should combine some danger of which he did not deny there would be a check in the revisionary power of the Executive, and intimated that in order to render this still more effectual, he would agree that in the choice of the [3] Executive each State should have an equal vote. He was persuaded that two such opposite bodies as Mr Morris had planned, could never long co-exist. Dissentions would arise as has been seen even between the Senate and H. of Delegates in Maryland, appeals would be made to the people; and in a little time, commotions would be the result—He was far from thinking the large States could subsist of themselves any more than the small; an avulsion would involve the whole in ruin, and he was determined to pursue such a scheme of Government as would secure us agst such a calamity.

Mr STRONG was for the Commitment; and hoped the mode of constituting both branches would be referred. If they should be established on different principles, contentions would prevail, and there would never be a concurrence in necessary measures.

Docr WILLIAMSON. If we do not concede on both sides, our business must soon be at an end. He approved of the Commitment,

---

[1] The transcript uses the word "sphere" in the plural.
[2] The word "the" is here inserted in the transcript.
[3] The word "an" is substituted in the transcript for "the."

supposing that as the Com! w⁴ be a smaller body, a compromise would be pursued with more coolness

M! Wilson objected to the Committee, because it would decide according to that very rule of voting which was opposed on one side. Experience in Cong! had also proved the inutility of Committees consisting of members from each State

M! Lansing w⁴ not oppose the commitment, though expecting little advantage from it.

M! Madison opposed the Commitment. He had rarely seen any other effect than delay from *such* Committees in Cong! Any scheme of compromise that could be proposed in the Committee might as easily be proposed in the House; and the report of the Committee when [1] it contained merely the *opinion* of the Com! would neither shorten the discussion, nor influence the decision of the House.

M! Gerry was for the Commitm! Something must be done, or we shall disappoint not only America, but the whole world. He suggested a consideration of the State we should be thrown into by the failure of the Union. We should be without an Umpire to decide controversies and must be at the mercy of events. What too is to become of our treaties—what of our foreign debts, what of our domestic? We must make concessions on both sides. Without these the Constitutions of the several States would never have been formed.

On the question " for committing," generally:

Mast! ay. Con! ay. N. Y. ay. N. J. no. P. ay. Del. no. M⁴ ay. V! ay. N. C. ay. S. C. ay. Geo. ay.[2]

On the question for committing [3] " to a member from each State."

Mass!! ay. Con! ay. N. Y. ay. N. J. ay. P! no. Del. ay. M⁴ ay. V! ay. N. C. ay. S. C. ay. Geo. ay.[4]

The Committee elected by ballot, were M! Gerry, M! Elseworth, M! Yates, M! Patterson, D! Franklin, M! Bedford, M! Martin, M! Mason, M! Davy, M! Rutlidge, Mr. Baldwin.

That time might be given to the Committee, and to such as chose to attend to the celebrations on the anniversary of Independence, the Convention adjourned till Thursday.

---

[1] The word "where" is substituted in the transcript for "when."

[2] In the transcript the vote reads: "Massachusetts, Connecticut, New York, Pennsylvania, Maryland, Virginia, North Carolina, South Carolina, Georgia, aye—9; New Jersey, Delaware, no—2."

[3] The word "it" is here inserted in the transcript.

[4] In the transcript the vote reads: "Massachusetts, Connecticut, New York, New Jersey, Delaware, Maryland, Virginia, North Carolina, South Carolina, Georgia, aye—10; Pennsylvania, no—1."

THURSDAY JULY 5TH IN CONVENTION

M? GERRY delivered in from the Committee appointed on Monday last the following Report.

" The Committee to whom was referred the 8th. Resol. of the Report from the Committee of the whole House, and so much of the 7th as has not been decided on, submit the following Report: That the subsequent propositions be recommended to the Convention on condition that both shall be generally adopted. 1. that in the I?t branch of the Legislature each of the States now in the Union shall be allowed 1 member for every 40,000 inhabitants of the description reported in the 7th Resolution of the Com? of the whole House: that each State not containing that number shall be allowed 1 member: that all bills for raising or appropriating money, and for fixing the Salaries of the officers of the Govern? of the U. States shall originate in the 1?t branch of of the Legislature, and shall not be altered or amended by the 2d branch: and that no money shall be drawn from the public Treasury. but in pursuance of appropriations to be originated in the 1?t branch " II. That in the 2d branch each State shall have an equal vote." *

M? GHORUM observed that as the report consisted of propositions mutually conditional he wished to hear some explanations touching the grounds on which the conditions were estimated.

M? GERRY. The Committee were of different opinions as well as the Deputations from which the Com? were taken, and agreed to the Report merely in order that some ground of accomodation might be proposed. Those opposed to the equality of votes have only assented conditionally; and if the other side do not generally agree will not be under any obligation to support the Report.

M? WILSON thought the Committee had exceeded their powers.

M? MARTIN was for taking the question on the whole report.

---

* This report was founded on a motion in the Committe made by D? Franklin. It was barely acquiesced in by the members from the States opposed to an equality of votes in the 2d branch and was evidently considered by the members on the other side, as a gaining of their point. A motion was made by M? Sherman [he [1] acted in place of M? Elseworth who was kept away by indisposition.] In the Committee to the following effect " that each State should have an equal vote in the 2d branch; provided that no decision therein should prevail unless the majority of States concurring should also comprize a majority of the inhabitants of the U. States." This motion was not much deliberated on nor approved in the Committee. A similar proviso had been proposed in the debates on the articles of Confederation in 1777, to the articles giving certain powers to " nine States." See Journals of Cong? for 1777, p. 462.

---

[1] The word " who " is substituted in the transcript for " he."

M? WILSON was for a division of the question: otherwise it w? be a leap in the dark.

M? MADISON. could not regard the exclusive [1] privilege of originating money bills as any concession on the side of the small States. Experience proved that it had no effect. If seven States in the upper branch wished a bill to be originated, they might surely find some member from some of the same States in the lower branch who would originate it. The restriction as to amendments was of as little consequence. Amendments could be handed privately by the Senate to members in the other house. Bills could be negatived that they might be sent up in the desired shape. If the Senate should yield to the obstinacy of the 1?t branch the use of that body as a check would be lost. If the 1?t branch should yield to that of the Senate, the privilege would be nugatory. Experience had also shewn both in G. B. and the States having a similar regulation that it was a source of frequent & obstinate altercations. These considerations had produced a rejection of a like motion on a former occasion when judged by its own merits. It could not therefore be deemed any concession on the present, and left in force all the objections which had prevailed ag?t allowing each State an equal voice. He conceived that the Convention was reduced to the alternative of either departing from justice in order to conciliate the smaller States, and the minority of the people of the U. S. or of displeasing these by justly gratifying the larger States and the majority of the people. He could not himself hesitate as to the option he ought to make. The Convention with justice & the majority of the people on their side, had nothing to fear. With injustice and the minority on their side they had every thing to fear. It was in vain to purchase concord in the Convention on terms which would perpetuate discord among their Constituents. The Convention ought to pursue a plan which would bear the test of examination, which would be espoused & supported by the enlightened and impartial part of America, & which they could themselves vindicate and urge. It should be considered that altho' at first many may judge of the system recommended, by their opinion of the Convention, yet finally all will judge of the Convention by the System. The merits of the System alone can finally & effectually obtain the public suffrage. He was not apprehensive that the people of the small States would obstinately refuse to accede to a Gov? founded on just principles, and promising them substantial protection. He could not suspect that Delaware would

---

[1] The word " exclusive " is omitted in the transcript.

brave the consequences of seeking her fortunes apart from the other States, rather than submit to such a Gov! much less could he suspect that she would pursue the rash policy of courting foreign support, which the warmth of one of her representatives [M! Bedford] had suggested, or if she sh⁴ that any foreign nation w⁴ be so rash as to hearken to the overture. As little could he suspect that the people of N. Jersey notwithstanding the decided tone of the gentlemen from that State, would choose rather to stand on their own legs, and bid defiance to events, than to acquiesce under an establishment founded on principles the justice of which they could not dispute, and absolutely necessary to redeem them from the exactions levied on them by the commerce of the neighbouring States. A review of other States would prove that there was as little reason to apprehend an inflexible opposition elsewhere. Harmony in the Convention was no doubt much to be desired. Satisfaction to all the States, in the first instance still more so. But if the principal States comprehending a majority of the people of the U. S. should concur in a just & judicious plan, he had the firmest hopes, that all the other States would by degrees accede to it.

M! BUTLER said he could not let down his idea of the people, of America so far as to believe they would from mere respect to the Convention adopt a plan evidently unjust. He did not consider the privilege concerning money bills as of any consequence. He urged that the 2⁴ branch ought to represent the States according to their property.

M! Gov! MORRIS. thought the form as well as the matter of the Report objectionable. It seemed in the first place to render amendments impracticable. In the next place, it seemed to involve a pledge to agree to the 2⁴ part if the 1ˢᵗ sh⁴ be agreed to. He conceived the whole aspect of it to be wrong. He came here as a Representative of America; he flattered himself he came here in some degree as a Representative of the whole human race; for the whole human race will be affected by the proceedings of this Convention. He wished gentlemen to extend their views beyond the present moment of time; beyond the narrow limits of place from which they derive their political origin. If he were to believe some things which he had heard, he should suppose that we were assembled to truck and bargain for our particular States. He can-not descend to think that any gentlemen are really actuated by these views. We must look forward to the effects of what we do. These alone ought to guide us. Much has been said of the sentiments of the people. They were unknown. They could not be known. All that we can infer is that if the plan we recommend be reasonable & right; all who have reasonable minds and sound intentions will embrace it, notwithstanding what had been said by some gentlemen. Let us suppose that the larger States shall agree; and that the smaller refuse: and let us trace the consequences. The opponents of the system in the smaller States will no doubt make a party, and a noise for a time, but the ties of interest, of kindred & of common habits which connect them with the other States will be too strong to be easily broken. In N. Jersey particularly he was sure a great many would follow the sentiments of Pen⁸ & N. York. This Country must be united. If persuasion does not unite it, the sword will. He begged that ¹ this consideration might have its due weight. The scenes of horror attending civil commotion can not be described, and the conclusion of them will be worse than the term of their continuance. The stronger party will then make traytors of the weaker; and the Gallows & Halter will finish the work of the sword. How far foreign powers would be ready to take part in the confusions he would not say. Threats that they will be invited have it seems been thrown out. He drew the melancholy picture of foreign intrusions as exhibited in the History of Germany, & urged it as a standing lesson to other nations. He trusted that the Gentlemen who may have hazarded such expressions, did not entertain them till they reached their own lips. But returning to the Report he could not think it in any respect calculated for the public good. As the 2ᵈ branch is now constituted, there will be constant disputes & appeals to the States which will undermine the Genˡ Government & controul & annihilate the 1ˢᵗ branch. Suppose that the delegates from Massᵗˢ & Rho I. in the Upper House disagree, and that the former are outvoted. What Results? they will immediately declare that their State will not abide by the decision, and make such representations as will produce that effect. The same may happen as to Virgᵃ & other States. Of what avail then will be what is on paper. State attachments, and State importance have been the bane of this Country. We can not annihilate; but we may perhaps take out the teeth of the serpents. He wished our ideas to be enlarged to the true interest of man, instead of being circumscribed within the narrow compass of a particular Spot. And after all how little can be the motive yielded by selfishness for such a policy. Who can say whether he himself, much less whether his children, will the next year be an inhabitant of this or that State.

---

¹ The word "that" is omitted in the transcript.

M! Bedford. He found that what he had said as to the small States being taken by the hand, had been misunderstood; and he rose to explain. He did not mean that the small States would court the aid & interposition of foreign powers. He meant that they would not consider the federal compact as dissolved untill it should be so by the Acts of the large States. In this case The consequence of the breach of faith on their part, and the readiness of the small States to fulfill their engagements, would be that foreign Nations having demands on this Country would find it their interest to take the small States by the hand, in order to do themselves justice. This was what he meant. But no man can foresee to what extremities the small States may be driven by oppression. He observed also in apology that some allowance ought to be made for the habits of his profession in which warmth was natural & sometimes necessary. But is there not an apology in what was said by [M! Gov! Morris] that the sword is to unite: by M! Ghorum that Delaware must be annexed to Penn! and N. Jersey divided between Pen! and N. York. To hear such language without emotion, would be to renounce the feelings of a man and the duty of a Citizen—As to the propositions of the Committee, the lesser States have thought it necessary to have a security somewhere. This has been thought necessary for the Executive Magistrate of the proposed Gov! who has a sort of negative on the laws; and is it not of more importance that the States should be protected, than that the Executive branch of the Gov! sh⁴ be protected. In order to obtain this, the smaller States have conceded as to the constitution of the first branch, and as to money bills. If they be not gratified by correspondent concessions as to the 2⁴ branch is it to be supposed they will ever accede to the plan; and what will be the consequence if nothing should be done! The condition of the U. States requires that something should be immediately done. It will be better that a defective plan should be adopted, than that none should be recommended. He saw no reason why defects might not be supplied by meetings 10, 15, or 20 years hence.

M! Elseworth said he had not attended the proceedings of the Committee, but was ready to accede to the compromise they had reported. Some compromise was necessary; and he saw none more convenient or reasonable.

M! Williamson hoped that the expressions of individuals would not be taken for the sense of their colleagues, much less of their States which was not & could not be known. He hoped also that the meaning of those expressions would not be misconstrued or exaggerated. He did not conceive that [M! Gov! Morris] meant that the sword ought to be drawn ag.ᵗ the smaller States. He only pointed out the probable consequences of anarchy in the U. S. A similar exposition ought to be given of the expressions [of Mʳ Ghorum]. He was ready to hear the Report discussed; but thought the propositions contained in it, the most objectionable of any he had yet heard.

Mʳ PATTERSON said that he had when the Report was agreed to in the Comᵉ reserved to himself the right of freely discussing it. He acknowledged that the warmth complained of was improper; but he thought the Sword & the Gallows as [1] little calculated to produce conviction. He complained of the manner in which Mʳ M— & Mʳ Govʳ Morris had treated the small States.

Mʳ GERRY. Tho' he had assented to the Report in the Committee, he had very material objections to it. We were however in a peculiar situation. We were neither the same Nation nor different Nations. We ought not therefore to pursue the one or the other of these ideas too closely. If no compromise should take place what will be the consequence. A secession he foresaw would take place; for some gentlemen seem decided on it; two different plans will be proposed; and the result no man could foresee. If we do not come to some agreement among ourselves some foreign sword will probably do the work for us.

Mʳ MASON. The Report was meant not as specific propositions to be adopted; but merely as a general ground of accomodation. There must be some accomodation on this point, or we shall make little further progress in the work. Accomodation was the object of the House in the appointment of the Committee; and of the Committee in the Report they had made. And however liable the Report might be to objections, he thought it preferable to an appeal to the world by the different sides, as had been talked of by some Gentlemen. It could not be more inconvenient to any gentleman to remain absent from his private affairs, than it was for him: but he would bury his bones in this City rather than expose his Country to the Consequences of a dissolution of the Convention without any thing being done.

The 1.ˢᵗ proposition in the report for fixing the representation in the 1.ˢᵗ branch, one member for every 40,000 inhabitants, being taken up.

Mʳ Govʳ MORRIS objected to that scale of apportionment. He thought property ought to be taken into the estimate as well as the number of inhabitants. Life & liberty were generally said to be of

---

[1] The word " as " is crossed out in the transcript.

more value, than property. An accurate view of the matter would nevertheless prove that property was the main object of Society. The savage State was more favorable to liberty than the Civilized; and sufficiently so to life. It was preferred by all men who had not acquired a taste for property; it was only renounced for the sake of property which could only be secured by the restraints of regular Government. These ideas might appear to some new, but they were nevertheless just. If property then was the main object of Gov! certainly it ought to be one measure of the influence due to those who were to be affected by the Governm! He looked forward also to that range of New States which w⁴ soon be formed in the West. He thought the rule of representation ought to be so fixed as to secure to the Atlantic States a prevalence in the National Councils. The new States will know less of the public interest than these, will have an interest in many respects different, in particular will be little scrupulous of involving the Community in wars the burdens & operations of which would fall chiefly on the maritime States. Provision ought therefore to be made to prevent the maritime States from being hereafter outvoted by them. He thought this might be easily done by irrevocably fixing the number of representatives which the Atlantic States should respectively have, and the number which each new State will have. This w⁴ not be unjust, as the Western settlers w⁴ previously know the conditions on which they were to possess their lands. It would be politic as it would recommend the plan to the present as well as future interest of the States which must decide the fate of it.

M! Rutlidge. The gentleman last up had spoken some of his sentiments precisely. Property was certainly the principal object of Society. If numbers should be made the rule of representation, the Atlantic States will [1] be subjected to the Western. He moved that the first proposition in the report be postponed in order to take up the following viz " that the suffrages of the several States be regulated and proportioned according to the sums to be paid towards the general revenue by the inhabitants of each State respectively. that an apportionment of suffrages, according to the ratio aforesaid shall be made and regulated at the end of   years from the 1ˢᵗ meeting of the Legislature of the U. S. and at the end of every   years but that for the present, and until the period above mentioned, the suffrages shall be for N. Hampshire   [2] Massach¹¹   &c.—

---

[1] The word " would " is substituted in the transcript for " will."
[2] The word " for " is here inserted in the transcript.

Col. MASON said the case of new States was not unnoticed in the Committee; but it was thought and he was himself decidedly of opinion that if they made a part of the Union, they ought to be subject to no unfavorable discriminations. Obvious considerations required it.

M: RADOLPH concurred with Col.[1] Mason.

On [2] Question on M: Rutlidges motion.

Mas:[ts] no. Con: no. N. Y. no. N. J. no. P: no. Del. no. Mary:[d] no. V: no. N. C. no. S. C. ay. Geo. not on floor.[3]

Adj:[d]

FRIDAY JULY 6TH IN CONVENTION

M: GOV: MORRIS moved to commit so much of the Report as relates to "1 member for every 40,000 inhabitants" His view was that they might absolutely fix the number for each State in the first instance; leaving the Legislature at liberty to provide for changes in the relative importance of the States, and for the case of new States.

M: WILSON 2[ded] the motion; but with a view of leaving the Committee under no implied shackles.

M: GHORUM apprehended great inconveniency [4] from fixing directly the number of Representatives to be allowed to each State. He thought the number of Inhabitants the true guide; tho' perhaps some departure might be expedient from the full proportion. The States also would vary in their relative extent by separations of parts of the largest States. A part of Virg: is now on the point of a separation. In the province of Mayne a Convention is at this time deliberating on a separation from Mas:[ts] In such events the number of representatives ought certainly to be reduced. He hoped to see all the States made small by proper divisions, instead of their becoming formidable as was apprehended, to the Small States. He conceived that let the Gen:[l] [5] Government be modified as it might, there would be a constant tendency in the State Governm:[ts] to

---

[1] The word "Mr." is substituted in the transcript for "Col."

[2] The word "the" is here inserted in the transcript.

[3] In the transcript the vote reads: "South Carolina, aye—1; Massachusetts, Connecticut, New York, New Jersey, Pennsylvania, Delaware, Maryland, Virginia, North Carolina, no—9; Georgia not on the floor."

[4] The word "inconveniency" is changed to "inconvenience" in the transcript.

[5] The word "Gen:" is omitted in the transcript.

encroach upon it: it was of importance therefore that the extent of the States sh⁴ be reduced as much & as fast as possible. The stronger the Gov⁴ shall be made in the first instance the more easily will these divisions be effected; as it will be of less consequence in the opinion of the States whether they be of great or small extent.

M⁵ GERRY did not think with his Colleague that the large States ought to be cut up. This policy has been inculcated by the middling and smaller States, ungenerously & contrary to the spirit of the Confederation. Ambitious men will be apt to solicit needless divisions, till the States be reduced to the size of Counties. If this policy should still actuate the small States, the large ones cou'd not confederate safely with them; but would be obliged to consult their safety by confederating only with one another. He favored the Commitment and thought that Representation ought to be in the Combined ratio of numbers of Inhabitants and of wealth, and not of either singly.

M⁵ KING wished the clause to be committed chiefly in order to detach it from the Report with which it had no connection. He thought also that the Ratio of Representation proposed could not be safely fixed, since in a century & a half our computed increase of population would carry the number of representatives to an enormous excess; that y⁵ number of inhabitants was not the proper index of ability & wealth; that property was the primary object of Society; and that in fixing a ratio this ought not to [1] be excluded from the estimate. With regard to new States, he observed that there was something peculiar in the business which had not been noticed. The U. S. were now admitted to be proprietors of the Country N. West of the Ohio. Cong⁵ by one of their ordinances have impoliticly laid it out into ten States, and have made it a fundamental article of compact with those who may become settlers, that as soon as the number in any one State shall equal that of the smallest of the 13 original States, it may claim admission into the union. Delaware does not contain it is computed more than 35,000 souls, and for obvious reasons will not increase much for a considerable time. It is possible then that if this plan be persisted in by Cong⁵ 10 new votes may be added, without a greater addition of inhabitants than are represented by the single vote of Pen⁵ The plan as it respects one of the new States is already irrevocable, the sale of the lands having commenced, and the purchasers & settlers will immediately become entitled to all the privileges of the compact.

M⁵ BUTLER agreed to the Commitment if the Committee were to

---

[1] The word " to " is omitted in the transcript.

be left at liberty. He was persuaded that the more the subject was examined, the less it would appear that the number of inhabitants would be a proper rule of proportion. If there were no other objection the changeableness of the standard would be sufficient. He concurred with those who thought some balance was necessary between the old & new States. He contended strenuously that property was the only just measure of representation. This was the great object of Govern[t]: the great cause of war; the great means of carrying it on.

M[r] PINKNEY saw no good reason for committing. The value of land had been found on full investigation to be an impracticable rule. The contributions of revenue including imports & exports, must be too changeable in their amount; too difficult to be adjusted; and too injurious to the non-commercial States. The number of inhabitants appeared to him the only just & practicable rule. He thought the blacks ought to stand on an equality with [1] whites: But w[d] agree to the ratio settled by Cong[s] He contended that Cong[s] had no right under the articles of Confederation to authorize the admission of new States; no such case having been provided for.

M[r] DAVY, was for committing the clause in order to get at the merits of the question arising on the Report. He seemed to think that wealth or property ought to be represented in the 2[d] branch; and numbers in the 1st branch.

On the Motion for committing as made by M[r] Gov[r] Morris.

Mas[ts] ay. Con[t] ay. N. Y. no. N. J. no, P[a] ay. Del. no. M[d] div[d] V[a] ay. N. C. ay. S. C. ay. Geo. ay.[2]

The members app[d] by Ballot were M[r] Gov[r] Morris, M[r] Gorham M[r] Randolph, M[r] Rutlidge, M[r] King.

M[r] WILSON signified that his view in agreeing to the commitm[t] was that the Com[e] might consider the propriety of adopting a scale similar to that established by the Constitution of Mast[s] which w[d] give an advantage to y[e] small States without substantially departing from a [3] rule of proportion.

M[r] WILSON & M[r] MASON moved to postpone the clause relating to money bills in order to take up the clause relating, to an equality of votes in the second branch.

---

[1] The word "the" is here inserted in the transcript.

[2] In the transcript the vote reads: "Massachusetts, Connecticut, Pennsylvania, Virginia, North Carolina, South Carolina, Georgia, aye—7; New York, New Jersey, Delaware, no—3; Maryland, divided."

[3] The word "the" is substituted in the transcript for the word "a."

On the question ¹ Mas⁺: no. Con⁺ no. N. Y. ay. N. J. ay. P⁺: ay. Del. ay. M⁴ ay. V⁺ ay. N. C. no. S. C. ay. Geo. ay.

The clause relating to equality of votes being under consideration,

Doc⁺ FRANKLIN observed that this question could not be properly put by itself, the Committee having reported several propositions as mutual conditions of each other. He could not vote for it if separately taken, but should vote for the whole together.

Col. MASON perceived the difficulty & suggested a reference of the rest of the Report to y⁺ Committee just appointed, that the whole might be brought into one view.

M⁺ RANDOLPH disliked y⁺ reference to that Committee, as it consisted of members from States opposed to the wishes of the smaller States, and could not therefore be acceptable to the latter.

M⁺ MARTIN & M⁺ JENIFER moved to postpone the clause till the Com⁺ last appointed should report.

M⁺ MADISON observed that if the uncommitted part of the Report was connected with the part just committed, it ought also to be committed; if not connected, it need not be postponed till report should be made.

On the question for postponing moved by M⁺ Martin & M⁺ Jennifer   Con⁺ N. J. Del. M⁴ V⁺ Geo., ay ²
P⁺ N. C. S. C...............no ³
Mas. N. Y.............divided

The 1ˢᵗ clause relating to the originating of money bills was then resumed.

M⁺ GOVERN⁺ MORRIS was opposed to a restriction of this right in either branch, considered merely in itself and as unconnected with the point of representation in the 2⁴ branch. It will disable the 2⁴ branch from proposing its own money plans, and giving the people an opportunity of judging by comparison of the merits of those proposed by the 1ˢᵗ branch.

M⁺ WILSON could see nothing like a concession here on the part of the smaller States. If both branches were to say yes ⁴ or no,⁴ it was of little consequence which should say yes ⁴ or no ⁴ first, which last. If either was indiscriminately to have the right of originating, the reverse of the Report, would he thought be most proper; since it

---

¹ The words "of postponement" are here inserted in the transcript and the vote reads: "New York, New Jersey, Pennsylvania, Delaware, Maryland, Virginia, South Carolina, Georgia, aye—8; Massachusetts, Connecticut, North Carolina, no—3."
² The figure "6" is here inserted in the transcript.
³ The figure "3" is here inserted in the transcript.
⁴ The transcript italicizes the words "yes" and "no."

was a maxim that the least numerous body was the fittest for deliberation; the most numerous for decision. He observed that this discrimination had been transcribed from the British into several American constitutions. But he was persuaded that on examination of the American experiments it would be found to be a trifle light as air. Nor could he ever discover the advantage of it in the Parliamentary history of G. Britain. He hoped if there was any advantage in the privilege, that it would be pointed out.

M! WILLIAMSON thought that if the privilege were not common to both branches it ought rather to be confined to the 2ᵈ as the bills in that case would be more narrowly watched, than if they originated with the branch having most of the popular confidence.

M! MASON. The consideration which weighed with the Committee was that the 1ˢᵗ branch would be the immediate representatives of the people, the 2ᵈ would not. Should the latter have the power of giving away the people's money, they might soon forget the source from whence they received it. We might soon have an aristocracy. He had been much concerned at the principles which had been advanced by some gentlemen, but had the satisfaction to find they did not generally prevail. He was a friend to proportional representation in both branches; but supposed that some points must be yielded for the sake of accomodation.

M! WILSON. If he had proposed that the 2ᵈ branch should have an independent disposal of public money, the observations ʼof [Col Mason] would have been a satisfactory answer. But nothing could be farther from what he had said. His question was how is the power of the 1ˢᵗ branch increased or that of the 2ᵈ diminished by giving the proposed privilege to the former? Where is the difference, in which branch it begins if both must concur, in the end?

M! GERRY would not say that the concession was a sufficient one on the part of the small States. But he could not but regard it in the light of a concession. It wᵈ make it a constitutional principle that the 2ᵈ branch were not possessed of the Confidence of the people in money matters, which wᵈ lessen their weight & influence. In the next place if the 2ᵈ branch were dispossessed of the privilege, they wᵈ be deprived of the opportunity which their continuance in office 3 times as long as the 1ˢᵗ branch would give them of makig three successive essays in favor of a particular point.

M! PINKNEY thought it evident that the Concession was wholly on one side, that of the large States, the privilege of originating money bills being of no account.

M! Gov! MORRIS had waited to hear the good effects of the restriction. As to the alarm sounded, of an aristocracy, his creed was that there never was, nor ever will be a civilized Society without an aristocracy. His endeavor was to keep it as much as possible from doing mischief. The restriction if it has any real operation will deprive us of the services of the 2ᵈ branch in digesting & proposing money bills of which it will be more capable than the 1ˢᵗ branch. It will take away the responsibility of the 2ᵈ branch, the great security for good behavior. It will always leave a plea, as to an obnoxious money bill that it was disliked, but could not be constitutionally amended; nor safely rejected. It will be a dangerous source of disputes between the two Houses. We should either take the British Constitution altogether or make one for ourselves. The Executive there has dissolved two Houses as the only cure for such disputes. Will our Executive be able to apply such a remedy? Every law directly or indirectly takes money out of the pockets of the people. Again What use may be made of such a privilege in case of great emergency? Suppose an Enemy at the door, and money instantly & absolutely necessary for repelling him, may not the popular branch avail itself of this duress, to extort concessions from the Senate destructive of the Constitution itself. He illustrated this danger by the example of the Long Parliament's expedᵗˢ for subverting the H. of Lords; concluding on the whole that the restriction would be either useless or pernicious.

Docᵗ FRANKLIN did not mean to go into a justification of the Report; but as it had been asked what would be the use of restraining the 2ᵈ branch from medling with money bills, he could not but remark that it was always of importance that the people should know who had disposed of their money, & how it had been disposed of. It was a maxim that those who feel, can best judge. This end would, he thought, be best attained, if money affairs were to be confined to the immediate representatives of the people. This was his inducement to concur in the report. As to the danger or difficulty that might arise from a negative in the 2ᵈ[1] where the people wᵈ not be proportionally represented, it might easily be got over by declaring that there should be no such Negative: or if that will not do, by declaring that there shall be no such branch at all.

Mʳ MARTIN said that it was understood in the Committee that the difficulties and disputes which had been apprehended, should be guarded agˢᵗ in the detailing of the plan.

Mʳ WILSON. The difficulties & disputes will increase with the

---

[1] The word " branch " is here inserted in the transcript.

attempts to define & obviate them. Queen Anne was obliged to dissolve her Parliam.ᵗ in order to terminate one of these obstinate disputes between the two Houses. Had it not been for the mediation of the Crown, no one can say what the result would have been. The point is still *sub judice* in England. He approved of the principles laid down by the Hon'ble President [1] [Doct.ʳ Franklin] his Colleague, as to the expediency of keeping the people informed of their money affairs. But thought they would know as much, and be as well satisfied, in one way as in the other.

Gen.ˡ PINKNEY was astonished that this point should have been considered as a concession. He remarked that the restriction [2] to money bills had been rejected on the merits singly considered, by 8 States ag.ˢᵗ 3. and that the very States which now called it a concession, were then ag.ˢᵗ it as nugatory or improper in itself.

On the Question whether the clause relating to money bills in the Report of the Com.ᵉ consisting of a member from each State, sh.ᵈ stand as part of the Report—

Mass.ᵗˢ divid.ᵈ Con.ᵗ ay. N. Y. div.ᵈ N. J. ay. P.ᵃ no. Del. ay. M.ᵈ ay. V.ᵃ no. N. C. ay. S. C. no. Geo. div.ᵈ [3]

A Question was then raised whether the question was carried in the affirmative: there being but 5 ays out of 11. States present. The words of the rule are [4] (see May 28). [5]

On the [6] question: Mas. Con.ᵗ N. J. P.ᵃ Del. M.ᵈ N. C. S. C. Geo ay [7]
N. Y. V.ᵃ.............................no [8]

[In several preceding instances like votes had *sub silentio* been entered as decided in the affirmative.]

Adjourned

---

[1] In the transcript after the word "President" reference is made to a footnote which reads: "He was at that time President of the State of Pennsylvania."

[2] The word "as" is here inserted in the transcript.

[3] In the transcript the vote reads: "Connecticut, New Jersey, Delaware, Maryland, North Carolina, aye—5; Pennsylvania, Virginia, South Carolina, no—3; Massachusetts, New York, Georgia, divided."

[4] The phrase "For the words of the Rule" is substituted in the transcript for "The words of the rule are."

[5] A House to do business shall consist of the Deputies of not less than seven States; and all questions shall be decided by the greater number of these which shall be fully represented: but a less number than seven may adjourn from day to day. See *ante*, p. 19.

[6] The word "this" is substituted in the transcript for "the."

[7] The figure "9" is here added in the transcript.

[8] The figure "2" is here added in the transcript.

END OF VOLUME ONE

THE DEBATES IN
THE FEDERAL CONVENTION OF 1787
WHICH FRAMED THE CONSTITUTION
OF THE UNITED STATES OF AMERICA

REPORTED BY

JAMES MADISON
A Delegate from the State of Virginia

THE DEBATES IN
THE FEDERAL CONVENTION OF 1787
WHICH FRAMED THE CONSTITUTION
OF THE UNITED STATES OF AMERICA

REPORTED BY

JAMES MADISON
A Delegate from the State of Virginia

VOLUME TWO

GAILLARD HUNT AND JAMES BROWN SCOTT
EDITORS

I send you enclos'd the propos'd new Federal Constitution for these States. I was engag'd 4 Months of the last Summer in the Convention that form'd it. It is now sent by Congress to the several States for their Confirmation. If it succeeds, I do not see why you might not in Europe carry the Project of good Henry the 4th into Execution, by forming a Federal Union and One Grand Republick of all its different States & Kingdoms; by means of a like Convention; for we had many Interests to reconcile. (Benjamin Franklin to Mr. Grand, October 22, 1787. *Documentary History of the Constitution*, Vol. IV, pp. 341-342.)

JAMES MADISON MEMORIAL COMMITTEE

v

TABLE OF CONTENTS

PART II

THE FEDERAL CONVENTION OF 1787

(continued)

vii

PART III.

THE CONSTITUTION, ITS RATIFICATION AND AMENDMENTS.

---

[1] The Index is only to Madison's Notes of Debates and the Appendix thereto. The Table of Contents is believed to be sufficient for Part I, Antecedents of the Federal Convention of 1787, and Part III, The Constitution, its Ratification and Amendments.

PART II

THE FEDERAL CONVENTION OF 1787

(continued)

SATURDAY, JULY 7. IN CONVENTION

[1] " Shall the clause allowing each State one vote in the 2.ᵈ branch, stand as part of the Report"? being taken up—

M.ʳ GERRY. This is the critical question. He had rather agree to it than have no accomodation. A Govern.ᵗ short of a proper national plan, if generally acceptable, would be preferable to a proper one which if it could be carried at all, would operate on discontented States. He thought it would be best to suspend the [2] question till the Comm.ᵉ yesterday appointed,[3] should make report.

M.ʳ SHERMAN Supposed that it was the wish of every one that some Gen.ˡ Gov.ᵗ should be established. An equal vote in the 2.ᵈ branch would, he thought, be most likely to give it the necessary vigor. The small States have more vigor in their Gov.ᵗˢ than the large ones, the more influence therefore the large ones have, the weaker will be the Gov.ᵗ In the large States it will be most difficult to collect the real & fair sense of the people. Fallacy & undue influence will be practiced with most success: and improper men will most easily get into office. If they vote by States in the 2.ᵈ branch, and each State has an equal vote, there must be always a majority of States as well as a majority of the people on the side of public measures, & the Gov.ᵗ will have decision and efficacy. If this be not the case in the 2.ᵈ branch there may be a majority of the [4] States ag.ᵗᵗ public measures, and the difficulty of compelling them to abide by the public determination, will render the Government feebler than it has ever yet been.

M.ʳ WILSON was not deficient in a conciliating temper, but firmness was sometimes a duty of higher obligation. Conciliation was also misapplied in this instance. It was pursued here rather among the Representatives, than among the Constituents; and it w.ᵈ be of little consequence, if not established among the latter; and there could be little hope of its being established among them if the foundation should not be laid in justice and right.

On [5] Question shall the words stand as part of the Report?

---

[1] The words " The question " are here inserted in the transcript.
[2] The word "this" is substituted in the transcript for "the."
[3] The words "yesterday appointed" are transposed to read "appointed yesterday" in the transcript.
[4] The word "the" is omitted in the transcript.
[5] The word "the" is here inserted in the transcript.

Mass^{ts} div^d Con^t ay. N. Y. ay. N. J. ay. P^a no. Del. ay. M^d ay. V^a no. N. C. ay. S. C. no. Geo. div^d [1]

[Note. Several votes were given here in the affirmative or were div^d because another final question was to be taken on the whole report.]

Mr GERRY thought it would be proper to proceed to enumerate & define the powers to be vested in the Genl Gov^t before a question on the report should be taken, as to the rule of representation in the 2^d branch.

Mr MADISON, observed that it w^d be impossible to say what powers could be safely & properly vested in the Gov^t before it was known, in what manner the States were to be represented in it. He was apprehensive that if a just representation were not the basis of the Gov^t it would happen, as it did when the Articles of Confederation were depending, that every effectual prerogative would be withdrawn or withheld, and the New Gov^t w^d be rendered as impotent and as shortlived as the old.

Mr PATTERSON would not decide whether the privilege concerning money bills were a valuable consideration or not: But he considered the mode & rule of representation in the 1st branch as fully so. and that after the establishment of that point, the small States would never be able to defend themselves without an equality of votes in the 2^d branch. There was no other ground of accomodation. His resolution was fixt. He would meet the large States on that Ground and no other. For himself he should vote agst the Report, because it yielded too much.

Mr Govr MORRIS. He had no resolution unalterably fixed except to do what should finally appear to him right. He was agst the Report because it maintained the improper Constitution of the 2^d branch. It made it another Congress, a mere whisp of straw. It had been s^d [by Mr Gerry] that the new Govern^t would be partly national, partly federal; that it ought in the first quality to protect individuals; in the second, the States. But in what quality was it to protect the aggregate interest of the whole. Among the many provisions which had been urged, he had seen none for supporting the dignity and splendor of the American Empire. It had been one of our greatest misfortunes that the great objects of the nation had been sacrificed constantly to local views; in like manner as the general interests of States had been sacrificed to those of

---

[1] In the transcript the vote reads: "Connecticut, New York, New Jersey, Delaware, Maryland, North Carolina, aye—6; Pennsylvania, Virginia, South Carolina, no—3; Massachusetts, Georgia, divided."

the Counties. What is to be the check in the Senate? none; unless it be to keep the majority of the people from injuring particular States. But particular States ought to be injured for the sake of a majority of the people, in case their conduct should deserve it. Suppose they should insist on claims evidently unjust, and pursue them in a manner detrimental to the whole body. Suppose they should give themselves up to foreign influence. Ought they to be protected in such cases. They were originally nothing more than colonial corporations. On the declaration of Independence, a Governmᵗ was to be formed. The small States aware of the necessity of preventing anarchy, and taking advantage of the moment, extorted from the large ones an equality of votes. Standing now on that ground, they demand under the new system greater rights as men, than their fellow Citizens of the large States. The proper answer to them is that the same necessity of which they formerly took advantage, does not now exist, and that the large States are at liberty now to consider what is right, rather than what may be expedient. We must have an efficient Govᵗ and if there be an efficiency in the local Govᵗˢ the former is impossible. Germany alone proves it. Notwithstanding their common diet, notwithstanding the great prerogatives of the Emperor as head of the Empire, and his vast resources, as sovereign of his particular dominions, no union is maintained: foreign influence disturbs every internal operation, & there is no energy whatever in the general Governmᵗ Whence does this proceed? From the energy of the local authorities; from its being considered of more consequence to support the Prince of Hesse, than the Happiness of the people of Germany. Do Gentlemen wish this to be yᵉ case here. Good God, Sir, is it possible they can so delude themselves. What if all the Charters & Constitutions of the States were thrown into the fire, and all their demagogues into the ocean. What would it be to the happiness of America. And will not this be the case here if we pursue the train in wᶜʰ the business lies. We shall establish an Aulic Council without an Emperor to execute its decrees. The same circumstances which unite the people here, unite them in Germany. They have there a᷍ common language, a common law, common usages and manners, and a common interest in being united; yet their local jurisdictions destroy every tie. The case was the same in the Grecian States. The United Netherlands are at this time torn in factions. With these examples before our eyes shall we form establishments which must necessarily produce the same effects. It is of no consequence from what districts the 2ᵈ branch shall be drawn, if it be so constituted as to yield an asylum ag.ᵗ these evils. As it is now constituted he must be ag.ᵗ its being drawn from the States in equal portions. But shall he was [1] ready to join in devising such an amendment of the plan, as will be most likely to secure our liberty & happiness.

M.ʳ Sʜᴇʀᴍᴀɴ & M.ʳ Eʟsᴇᴡᴏʀᴛʜ moved to postpone the Question on the Report from the Committee of a member from each State, in order to wait for the Report from the Com.ᵉ of 5 last appointed.

Mas.ᵗˢ ay. Con.ᵗ ay. N. Y. no. N. J. ay. P.ᵃ ay. Del. ay. Maryland ay. V.ᵃ no. N. C. no. S. C. no. Geo. no.[2]

Adj.ᵈ

MONDAY JULY 9ᵀᴴ IN CONVENTION

M.ʳ Daniel Carroll from Maryland took his Seat.

M.ʳ Gov.ʳ Mᴏʀʀɪs delivered a report from the Com.ᵉ of 5 members to whom was committed the clause in the Report of the Com.ᵉ consisting of a member from each State, stating the proper ratio of Representatives in the 1.ˢᵗ branch, to be as 1 to every 40,000 inhabitants, as follows viz

"The Committee to whom was referred the 1.ˢᵗ clause of the 1.ˢᵗ proposition reported from the grand Committee, beg leave to report

I.[3] that in the 1.ˢᵗ meeting of the Legislature the 1.ˢᵗ branch thereof consist of 56. members of which Number, N. Hamshire shall have 2. Mass.ᵗˢ 7. R. I.ᵈ 1. Con.ᵗ 4. N. Y. 5. N. J. 3. P.ᵃ 8. Del. 1. M.ᵈ 4. V.ᵃ 9. N. C. 5. S. C. 5. Geo. 2.—

II.[3] But as the present situation of the States may probably alter as well in point of wealth as in the number of their inhabitants, that the Legislature be authorized from time to time to augment y.ᵉ number of Representatives. And in case any of the States shall hereafter be divided, or any two or more States united, or any new States created within the limits of the United States, the Legislature shall possess authority to regulate the number of Representatives in any of the foregoing cases, upon the principles of their wealth and number of inhabitants."

M.ʳ Sʜᴇʀᴍᴀɴ wished to know on what principles or calculations the Report was founded. It did not appear to correspond with any

---

[1] The words "shall be" are substituted in the transcript for "shall he was."

[2] In the transcript the vote reads: "Massachusetts, Connecticut, New Jersey, Pennsylvania, Delaware, Maryland, aye—6; New York, Virginia, North Carolina, South Carolina, Georgia, no—5."

[3] The Roman numerals "I" and "II" are omitted in the transcript.

rule of numbers, or of any requisition hitherto adopted by Cong?

M? GORHAM. Some provision of this sort was necessary in the outset. The number of blacks & whites with some regard to supposed wealth was the general guide Fractions could not be observed. The Legisl? is to make alterations from time to time as justice & propriety may require. Two objections prevailed ag:t the rate[1] of 1 member for every 40,000. inh:t The 1:t was that the Representation would soon be too numerous: the 2.d that the West? States who may have a different interest, might if admitted on that principle by degrees, outvote the Atlantic. Both these objections are removed. The number will be small in the first instance and may be continued so; and the Atlantic States having y? Gov:t in their own hands, may take care of their own interest, by dealing out the right of Representation in safe proportions to the Western States. These were the views of the Committee.

M? L MARTIN wished to know whether the Com? were guided in the ratio, by the wealth or number of inhabitants, of the States, or by[2] both; noting its variations from former apportionments by Cong?

M? Gov? MORRIS & M? RUTLIDGE moved to postpone the 1:t paragraph relating to the number of members to be allowed each State in the first instance, and to take up the 2.d paragraph authorizing the Legisl? to alter the number from time to time according to wealth & inhabitants. The motion was agreed to nem. con.

On[3] Question on the 2.d parag:h taken without any debate

Mas:s ay. Con:t ay. N. Y. no. N. J. no. P? ay. Del. ay. M.d ay. V? ay. N. C. ay. S. C. ay. Geo. ay.[4]

M? SHERMAN moved to refer the 1:t part apportioning the Representatives, to a Comm? of a member from each State.

M? Gov? MORRIS seconded the motion; observing that this was the only case in which such Committees were useful.

M? WILLIAMSON. thought it would be necessary to return to the rule of numbers, but that the Western States stood on different footing. If their property shall[5] be rated as high as that of the Atlantic States, then their representation ought to hold a like proportion. Otherwise if their property was not to be equally rated.

M? Gov? MORRIS. The Report is little more than a guess. Wealth

---

[1] The word "rule" is substituted in the transcript for "rate."
[2] The word "by" is omitted in the transcript.
[3] The word "the" is here inserted in the transcript.
[4] In the transcript the vote reads: "Massachusetts, Connecticut, Pennsylvania, Delaware, Maryland, Virginia, North Carolina, South Carolina, Georgia, aye—9; New York, New Jersey, no—2."
[5] The word "should" is substituted in the transcript for "shall."

was not altogether disregarded by the Com? Where it was apparently in favor of one State, whose n.ᵒˢ were superior to the numbers of another, by a fraction only, a member extraordinary was allowed to the former: and so vice versa. The Committee meant little more than to bring the matter to a point for the consideration of the House.

M: REED asked why Georgia was allowed 2 members, when her number of inhabitants had stood below that of Delaware.

M: Govʳ MORRIS. Such is the rapidity of the population of that State, that before the plan takes effect, it will probably be entitled to 2 Representatives

M: RANDOLPH. disliked the report of the Com? but had been unwilling to object to it. He was apprehensive that as the number was not to be changed till the Natˡ Legislature should please, a pretext would never be wanting to postpone alterations, and keep the power in the hands of those possessed of it. He was in favor of the commitmᵗ to a member from each State

M: PATTERSON considered the proposed estimate for the future according to the Combined rule [1] of numbers and wealth, as too vague. For this reason N. Jersey was agˢᵗ it. He could regard negroes [2] slaves in no light but as property. They are no free agents, have no personal liberty, no faculty of ᷠcquiring property, but on the contrary are themselves property, & like other property entirely at the will of the Master. Has a man in Virgª a number of votes in proportion to the number of his slaves? And if Negroes are not represented in the States to which they belong, why should they be represented in the Genˡ Govᵗ What is the true ᵖrinciple of Representation? It is an expedient by which an assembly of certain individˡˢ chosen by the people is substituted in place of the inconvenient meeting of the people themselves. If such a meeting of the people was actually to take place, would the slaves vote? They would not. Why then shᵈ they be represented. He was also agˢᵗ such an indirect encouragemᵗ of the slave trade; observing that Congˢ in their act relating to the change of the 8 art: of Confedⁿ had been ashamed to use the term " slaves " & had substituted a description.

M: MADISON, reminded M: Patterson that his doctrine of Representation which was in its principle the genuine one, must for ever silence the pretensions of the small States to an equality of votes with the large ones. They ought to vote in the same proportion in which

---

[1] The transcript uses the word " rule " in the plural.
[2] The transcript uses the word " negroes " in the singular.

their citizens would do, if the people of all the States were collectively met. He suggested as a proper ground of compromise, that in the first branch the States should be represented according to their number of free inhabitants; and in the 2ᵈ which had for one of its primary objects the guardianship of property, according to the whole number, including slaves.

Mʳ BUTLER urged warmly the justice & necessity of regarding wealth in the apportionment of Representation.

Mʳ KING had always expected that as the Southern States are the richest, they would not league themselves with the Northⁿ unless some respect were paid to their superior wealth. If the latter expect those preferential distinctions in Commerce & other advantages which they will derive from the connection they must not expect to receive them without allowing some advantages in return. Eleven out of 13 of the States had agreed to consider Slaves in the apportionment of taxation; and taxation and Representation ought to go together.

On the question for committing the first paragraph of the Report to a member from each State.

Masᵗˢ ay. Conᵗ ay. N. Y. no. N. J. ay. Pᵃ ay. Del. ay. Mᵈ ay. Vᵃ ay. N. C. ay. S. C. no. Geo. ay.[1]

The Comᵉ appointed were Mʳ King. Mʳ Sherman, Mʳ Yates, Mʳ Brearly, Mʳ Govʳ Morris, Mʳ Reed, Mʳ Carrol, Mʳ Madison, Mʳ Williamson, Mʳ Rutledge, Mʳ Houston.

Adjᵈ

TEUSDAY. JULY 10 IN CONVENTION

Mʳ KING reported from the Comᵉ yesterday appointed that the States at the 1ˢᵗ meeting of the General Legislature, should be represented by 65 members in the following proportions, to wit. N. Hamshire by 3. Masᵗˢ 8. R. Isᵈ 1. Conᵗ 5. N. Y. 6. N. J. 4. Pᵃ 8. Del. 1. Mᵈ 6. Vᵃ 10. N. C. 5. S. C. 5. Georgia 3.

Mʳ RUTLIDGE moved that N. Hampshire be reduced from 3 to 2. members. Her numbers did not entitle her to 3 and it was a poor State.

Genˡ PINKNEY seconds the motion.

Mʳ KING. N. Hamshire has probably more than 120,000 Inhabᵗˢ and has an extensive Country of tolerable fertility. Its inhabts

---

[1] In the transcript the vote reads: "Massachusetts, Connecticut, New Jersey, Pennsylvania, Delaware, Maryland, Virginia, North Carolina, Georgia, aye—9; New York, South Carolina, no—2."

therefore may [1] be expected to increase fast. He remarked that the four Eastern States having 800,000 souls, have ⅓ fewer representatives than the four Southern States, having not more than 700,000 souls rating the blacks, as 5 for 3. The Eastern people will advert to these circumstances, and be dissatisfied. He believed them to be very desirous of uniting with their Southern brethren, but did not think it prudent to rely so far on that disposition as to subject them to any gross inequality. He was fully convinced that the question concerning a difference of interests did not lie where it had hitherto been discussed, between the great & small States; but between the Southern & Eastern. For this reason he had been ready to yield something in the proportion of representatives for the security of the Southern. No principle would justify the giving them a majority. They were brought as near an equality as was possible. He was not averse to giving them a still greater security, but did not see how it could be done.

Gen! PINKNEY. The Report before it was committed was more favorable to the S. States than as it now stands. If they are to form so considerable a minority, and the regulation of trade is to be given to the Gen! Government, they will be nothing more than overseers for the Northern States. He did not expect the S. States to be raised to a majority of representatives, but wished them to have something like an equality. At present by the alterations of the Com? in favor of the N. States they are removed farther from it than they were before. One member had indeed [2] been added to Virg? which he was glad of as he considered her as a Southern State. He was glad also that the members of Georgia were increased.

M? WILLIAMSON was not for reducing N. Hamshire from 3 to 2. but for reducing some others. The South? Interest must be extremely endangered by the present arrangement. The North? States are to have a majority in the first instance and the means of perpetuating it.

M? DAYTON observed that the line between the [3] North? & Southern interest had been improperly drawn: that P? was the dividing State, there being six on each side of her.

Gen! PINKNEY urged the reduction, dwelt on the superior wealth of the Southern States, and insisted on its having its due weight in the Government.

---

[1] The words "therefore may" are transposed to read "may therefore" in the transcript.
[2] The words "had indeed" are transposed to read "indeed had" in the transcript.
[3] The word "the" is omitted in the transcript.

M: Gov: Morris regretted the turn of the debate. The States he found had many Representatives on the floor. Few he fears [1] were to be deemed the Representatives of America. He thought the Southern States have by the report more than their share of representation. Property ought to have its weight, but not all the weight. If the South? States are to supply money. The North? States are to spill their blood. Besides, the probable Revenue to be expected from the S. States has been greatly overrated. He was ag:t reducing N. Hamshire.

M: Randolph was opposed to a reduction of N. Hamshire, not because she had a full title to three members: but because it was in his contemplation 1.[2] to make it the duty instead of leaving it in [3] the discretion of the Legislature to regulate the representation by a periodical census. 2.[2] to require more than a bare majority of votes in the Legislature in certain cases, & particularly in commercial cases.

On the question for reducing N. Hamshire from 3 to 2 Represent: it passed in the negative

Mas:: no. Con: no. N. J. no. P: no. Del. no. M:d no. V: no. N. C. ay.* S. C. ay. Geo. no.* [4]

Gen: Pinkney and M: Alex: Martin moved that 6 Rep: instead of 5 be allowed to N. Carolina

On the Question, it passed in the negative.

Mas:: no. Con: no. N. J. no. P: no. Del. no. M:d no. V: no. N. C. ay. S. C. ay. Geo. ay.[5]

Gen: Pinkney & M: Butler made the same motion in favor of S. Carolina.

On the Question it passed in the negative

Mas:: no. Con: no. N. Y. no N. J. no. P: no. Del. ay. M:d no. V: no. N. C. ay. S. C. ay. Geo. ay.[6]

Gen: Pinkney & M: Houston moved that Georgia be allowed 4

* In the printed Journal N. C. no. Georgia ay

---

[1] The word "feared" is substituted in the transcript for "fears."
[2] The figures "1" and "2" are changed to "first" and "secondly" in the transcript.
[3] The word "to" is substituted in the transcript for "in."
[4] In the transcript the vote reads: "North Carolina,* South Carolina, aye —2; Massachusetts, Connecticut, New Jersey, Pennsylvania, Delaware, Maryland, Virginia, Georgia,* no—8."
[5] In the transcript the vote reads: "North Carolina, South Carolina, Georgia, aye—3; Massachusetts, Connecticut, New Jersey, Pennsylvania, Delaware, Maryland, Virginia, no—7."
[6] In the transcript the vote reads: "Delaware, North Carolina, South Carolina, Georgia, aye—4; Massachusetts, Connecticut, New York, New Jersey, Pennsylvania, Maryland, Virginia, no—7."

instead of 3 Rep: urging the unexampled celerity of its population.
On the Question, it passed in the Negative

Mas: no. Con: no. N. Y no N. J. no. P: no. Del. no. M⁴ no.
V: ay. N. C. ay. S. C. ay. Geo. ay.[1]

M: MADISON, moved that the number allowed to each State be
doubled. A *majority* of a *Quorum* of 65 members, was too small a
number to represent the whole inhabitants of the U. States; They
would not possess enough of the confidence of the people, and w⁴
be too sparsely taken from the people, to bring with them all the
local information which would be frequently wanted. Double the
number will not be too great, even with the future additions from
New States. The additional expence was too inconsiderable to be
regarded in so important a case. And as far as the augmentation
might be unpopular on that score, the objection was overbalanced
by its effect on the hopes of a greater number of the popular Candidates.

M: ELSEWORTH urged the objection of expence, & that the greater
the number, the more slowly would the business proceed; and the
less probably be decided as it ought, at last. He thought the number
of Representatives too great in most of the State Legislatures: and
that a large number was less necessary in the Gen! Legislature than
in those of the States,—as its business would relate to a few great,
national Objects only.

M: SHERMAN would have preferred 50 to 65. The great distance
they will have to travel will render their attendance precarious and
will make it difficult to prevail on a sufficient number of fit men
to undertake the service. He observed that the expected increase
from New States also deserved consideration.

M: GERRY was for increasing the number beyond 65. The larger
the number, the less the danger of their being corrupted. The people
are accustomed to & fond of a numerous representation, and will
consider their rights as better secured by it. The danger of excess
in the number may be guarded agᵗ by fixing a point within which
the number shall always be kept.

Col. MASON admitted that the objection drawn from the consideration of expence, had weight both in itself, and as the people
might be affected by it. But he thought it outweighed by the objections agᵗ the smallness of the number. 38, will he supposes, as being
a majority of 65, form a quorum. 20 will be a majority of 38. This

---

[1] In the transcript the vote reads: "Virginia, North Carolina, South Carolina, Georgia, aye—4; Massachusetts, Connecticut, New York, New Jersey,
Pennsylvania, Delaware, Maryland, no—7."

was certainly too small a number to make laws for America. They would neither bring with them all the necessary information relative to various local interests, nor possess the necessary confidence of the people. After doubling the number, the laws might still be made by so few as almost to be objectionable on that account.

Mʳ READ was in favor of the Motion. Two of the States [Del. & R. I.] would have but a single member if the aggregate number should remain at 65. and in case of accident to either of these one State wᵈ have no representative present to give explanations or informations of its interests or wishes. The people would not place their confidence in so small a number. He hoped the objects of the Genˡ Govᵗ would be much more numerous than seemed to be expected by some gentlemen, and that they would become more & more so. As to ¹ New States the highest number of Repˢ for the whole might be limited, and all danger of excess thereby prevented.

Mʳ RUTLIDGE opposed the motion. The Representatives were too numerous in all the States. The full number allotted to the States may be expected to attend & the lowest possible quorum shᵈ not therefore be considered. The interests of their Constituents will urge their attendance too strongly for it to be omitted: and he supposed the Genˡ Legislature would not sit more than 6 or 8 weeks in the year.

On the Question for doubling the number, it passed in the negative.

Masᵗˢ no. Conᵗ no. N. Y. no. N. J. no. Pˢ no. Del. ay. Mᵈ no. Vˢ ay. N. C. no. S. C. no. Geo. no.²

On the question for agreeing to the apportionment of Repˢ as amended by the last committee, it passed in the affirmative

Mas. ay. Conᵗ ay. N. Y. ay. N. J. ay. Pˢ ay. Del. ay. Mᵈ ay. Vˢ ay. N. C. ay. S. C. no. Geo. no.³

Mʳ BROOM gave notice to the House that he had concurred with a reserve to himself of an intention to claim for his State an equal voice in the 2ᵈ branch: which he thought could not be denied after this concession of the small States as to the first branch.

Mʳ RANDOLPH moved as an amendment to the report of the Commᵗ of five " that in order to ascertain the alterations in the

---

¹ The word "the" is here inserted in the transcript.
² In the transcript the vote reads: "Delaware, Virginia, aye—2; Massachusetts, Connecticut, New York, New Jersey, Pennsylvania, Maryland, North Carolina, South Carolina, Georgia, no—9."
³ In the transcript the vote reads: "Massachusetts, Connecticut, New York, New Jersey, Pennsylvania, Delaware, Maryland, Virginia, North Carolina, aye—9; South Carolina, Georgia, no—2."

population & wealth of the several States the Legislature should be required to cause a census, and estimate to be taken within one year after its first meeting; and every   years thereafter—and that the Legisl: arrange the Representation accordingly.''

M: Gov: Morris opposed it as fettering the Legislature too much. Advantage may be taken of it in time of war or the apprehension of it, by new States to extort particular favors. If the mode was to be fixed for taking a census, it might certainly be extremely inconvenient: if unfixt the Legislature may use such a mode as will defeat the object: and perpetuate the inequality. He was always ag:t such Shackles on the Legisl: They had been found very pernicious in most of the State Constitutions. He dwelt much on the danger of throwing such a preponderancy [1] into the Western Scale, suggesting that in time the Western people w:d outnumber the Atlantic States. He wished therefore to put it in the power of the latter to keep a majority of votes in their own hands. It was objected he said that if the Legisl: are left at liberty, they will never readjust the Representation. He admitted that this was possible; but he did not think it probable unless the reasons ag:t a revision of it were very urgent & in this case, it ought not to be done.

It was moved to postpone the proposition of M: Randolph in order to take up the following, viz. '' that the Committee of Eleven, to whom was referred the report of the Committee of five on the subject of Representation, be requested to furnish the Convention with the principles on which they grounded the Report,'' which was disagreed to: S. C. only [2] voting in the affirmative.

Adjourned

WEDNESDAY JULY 11. IN CONVENTION

M: Randolph's motion requiring the Legisl: to take a periodical census for the purpose of redressing inequalities in the Representation, was resumed.

M: Sherman was ag:t shackling the Legislature too much. We ought to choose wise & good men, and then confide in them.

M: Mason. The greater the difficulty we find in fixing a proper rule of Representation, the more unwilling ought we to be, to throw the task from ourselves, on the Gen: Legisl: He did not object to

---

[1] The word '' preponderancy '' is changed to '' preponderance '' in the transcript.
[2] The word '' alone '' is substituted in the transcript for '' only.''

the conjectural ratio which was to prevail in the outset; but considered a Revision from time to time according to some permanent & precise standard as essential to ẙ fair representation required in the 1ˢᵗ branch. According to the present population of America, the Northⁿ part of it had a right to preponderate, and he could not deny it. But he wished it not to preponderate hereafter when the reason no longer continued. From the nature of man we may be sure, that those who have power in their hands will not give it up while they can retain it. On the contrary we know they will always when they can rather increase it. If the S. States therefore should have ¾ of the people of America within their limits, the Northern will hold fast the majority of Representatives. ¼ will govern the ¾. The S. States will complain: but they may complain from generation to generation without redress. Unless some principle therefore which will do justice to them hereafter shall be inserted in the Constitution, disagreeable as the declaration was to him, he must declare he could neither vote for the system here, nor support it, in his State. Strong objections had been drawn from the danger to the Atlantic interests from new Western States. Ought we to sacrifice what we know to be right in itself, lest it should prove favorable to States which are not yet in existence. If the Western States are to be admitted into the Union, as they arise, they must, he wᵈ repeat, be treated as equals, and subjected to no degrading discriminations. They will have the same pride & other passions which we have, and will either not unite with or will speedily revolt from the Union, if they are not in all respects placed on an equal footing with their brethern. It has been said they will be poor, and unable to make equal contributions to the general Treasury. He did not know but that in time they would be both more numerous & more wealthy than their Atlantic brethren. The extent & fertility of their soil, made this probable; and though Spain might for a time deprive them of the natural outlet for their productions, yet she will, because she must, finally yield to their demands. He urged that numbers of inhabitants; though not always a precise standard of wealth was sufficiently so for every substantial purpose.

Mʳ WILLIAMSON was for making it the duty of the Legislature to do what was right & not leaving it at liberty to do or not[1] do it. He moved that Mʳ Randolph's proposition be postponᵈ in order to consider the following " that in order to ascertain the alterations that may happen in the population & wealth of the several

---

[1] The word " to " is here inserted in the transcript.

States, a census shall be taken of the free white inhabitants and
¾ths of those of other descriptions on the 1st year after this Government shall have been adopted and every   year thereafter;
and that the Representation be regulated accordingly.''

M᷉ RANDOLPH agreed that M᷉ Williamson's proposition should
stand in the place of his. He observed that the ratio fixt for the
1st meeting was a mere conjecture, that it placed the power in the
hands of that part of America, which could not always be entitled
to it, that this power would not be voluntarily renounced; and that
it was consequently the duty of the Convention to secure its renuncia-
tion when justice might so require; by some constitutional provisions.
If equality between great & small States be inadmissible, because in
that case unequal numbers of Constituents wd be ˙represented by
equal number¹ of votes; was it not equally inadmissible that a
larger & more populous district of America should hereafter have
less representation, than a smaller & less populous district. If a fair
representation of the people be not secured, the injustice of the Govt
will shake it to its foundations. What relates to suffrage is justly
stated by the celebrated Montesquieu, as a fundamental article in
Republican Govt? If the danger suggested by M᷉ Govᵣ Morris be
real, of advantage being taken of the Legislature in pressing moments, it was an additional reason, for tying their hands in such a
manner that they could not sacrifice their trust to momentary considerations. Congᵗ have pledged the public faith to New States,
that they shall be admitted on equal terms. They never would nor
ought to accede on any other. The census must be taken under the
direction of the General Legislature. The States will be too much
interested to take an impartial one for themselves.

M᷉ BUTLER & Genᶦ PINKNEY insisted that blacks be included in
the rule of Representation, *equally* with the Whites: and for that
purpose moved that the words '' three fifths '' be struck out.

M᷉ GERRY thought that ¾ of them was to say the least the full
proportion that could be admitted.

M᷉ GHORUM. This ratio was fixed by Congᵗ as a rule of taxation. Then it was urged by the Delegates representing the States
having slaves that the blacks were still more inferior to freemen.
At present when the ratio of representation is to be established,
we are assured that they are equal to freemen. The arguments on
yᵉ former occasion had convinced him that ¾ was pretty near the
just proportion and he should vote according to the same opinion
now.

---

¹ The transcript uses the word '' number '' in the plural.

M: Butler insisted that the labour of a slave in S. Carol: was as productive & valuable as that of a freeman in Mass:, that as wealth was the great means of defence and utility to the Nation they were equally valuable to it with freemen; and that consequently an equal representation ought to be allowed for them in a Government which was instituted principally for the protection of property, and was itself to be supported by property.

M: Mason, could not agree to the motion, notwithstand it was favorable to Virg: because he thought it unjust. It was certain that the slaves were valuable, as they raised the value of land, increased the exports & imports, and of course the revenue, would supply the means of feeding & supporting an army, and might in cases of emergency become themselves soldiers. As in these important respects they were useful to the community at large, they ought not to be excluded from the estimate of Representation. He could not however regard them as equal to freemen and could not vote for them as such. He added as worthy of remark, that the Southern States have this peculiar species of property, over & above the other species of property common to all the States.

M: Williamson reminded M: Ghorum that if the South: States contended for the inferiority of blacks to whites when taxation was in view, the Eastern States on the same occasion contended for their equality. He did not however either then or now, concur in either extreme, but approved of the ratio of ⅗.

On M: Butlers motion for considering blacks as equal to Whites in the apportionm: of Representation.

Mass: no. Con: no. [N. Y. not on floor.] N. J. no. P: no. Del. ay. M: no. V: no N. C. no. S. C. ay. Geo. ay.[1]

M: Gov: Morris said he had several objections to the proposition of M: Williamson. 1.[2] It fettered the Legislature too much. 2.[3] it would exclude some States altogether who would not have a sufficient number to entitle them to a single Representative. 3.[4] it will not consist with the Resolution passed on Saturday last authorising the Legislature to adjust the Representation from time to time on the principles of population & wealth or [5] with the principles of equity. If slaves were to be considered as inhabitants, not as wealth, then

---

[1] In the transcript the vote reads: "Delaware, South Carolina, Georgia, aye—3; Massachusetts, Connecticut, New Jersey, Pennsylvania, Maryland, Virginia, North Carolina, no—7; New York not on the floor."
[2] The figure "1" is changed to "In the first place" in the transcript.
[3] The figure "2" is changed to "In the second place" in the transcript.
[4] The figure "3" is changed to "In the third place" in the transcript.
[5] The word "or" is changed to "nor" in the transcript.

the s^d Resolution would not be pursued: If as wealth, then why is no other wealth but slaves included? These objections may perhaps be removed by amendments. His great objection was that the number of inhabitants was not a proper standard of wealth. The amazing difference between the comparative numbers & wealth of different Countries, rendered all reasoning superfluous on the subject. Numbers might with greater propriety be deemed a measure of stregth, than of wealth, yet the late defence made by G. Britain, agst her numerous enemies proved in the clearest manner, that it is entirely fallaciòus even in this respect.

Mr KING thought there was great force in the objections of Mr Govr Morris: he would however accede to the proposition for the sake of doing something.

Mr RUTLIDGE contended for the admission of wealth in the estimate by which Representation should be regulated. The Western States will not be able to contribute in proportion to their numbers; they sh^d not therefore be represented in that proportion. The Atlantic States will not concur in such a plan. He moved that " at the end of   years after the 1st meeting of the Legislature, and of every   years thereafter, the Legislature shall proportion the Representation according to the principles of wealth & population"

Mr SHERMAN thought the number of people alone the best rule for measuring wealth as well as representation; and that if the Legislature were to be governed by wealth, they would be obliged to estimate it by numbers. He was at first for leaving the matter wholly to the discretion of the Legislature; but he had been convinced by the observations of [Mr Randolph & Mr Mason,] that the *periods* & the *rule*, of revising the Representation ought to be fixt by the Constitution

Mr REID thought the Legislature ought not to be too much shackled. It would make the Constitution like Religious Creeds, embarrassing to those bound to conform to them & more likely to produce dissatisfaction and scism, than harmony and union.

Mr MASON objected to (Mr Rutlidge motion, as requiring of the Legislature something too indefinite & impracticable, and leaving them a pretext for doing nothing.

Mr WILSON had himself no objection to leaving the Legislature entirely at liberty. But considered wealth as an impracticable rule.

Mr GHORUM. If the Convention who are comparatively so little biassed by local views are so much perplexed, How can it be expected that the Legislature hereafter under the full biass of those views, will be able to settle a standard. He was convinced by the arguments of others & his own reflections, that the Convention ought to fix some standard or other.

Mͬ Govͬ Morris. The argͭˢ of others & his own reflections had led him to a very different conclusion. If we can't agree on a rule that will be just at this time, how can we expect to find one that will be just in all times to come. Surely those who come after us will judge better of things present, than we can of things future. He could not persuade himself that numbers would be a just rule at any time. The remarks of [Mͬ Mason] relative to the Western Country had not changed his opinion on that head. Among other objections it must be apparent they would not be able to furnish men equally enlightened, to share in the administration of our common interests. The Busy haunts of men not the remote wilderness, was the proper school of political Talents. If the Western people get the power into their hands they will ruin the Atlantic interests. The Back members are always most averse to the best measures. He mentioned the case of Penᵃ formerly. The lower part of the State had yᵉ power in the first instance. They kept it in yͬ own hands & the Country was yᵉ better for it. Another objection with him agˢͭ admitting the blacks into the census, was that the people of Penᵃ would revolt at the idea of being put on a footing with slaves. They would reject any plan that was to have such an effect. Two objections had been raised agˢͭ leaving the adjustment of the Representation from time, to time, to the discretion of the Legislature. The 1.¹ was they would be unwilling to revise it at all. The 2.¹ that by referring to *wealth* they would be bound by a rule which if willing, they would be unable to execute. The 1ˢͭ objⁿ distrusts their fidelity. But if their duty, their honor & their oaths will not bind them, let us not put into their hands our liberty, and all our other great interests: let us have no Govͭ at all. 2.² If these ties will bind them, we need not distrust the practicability of the rule. It was followed in part by the Comᵉ in the apportionment of Representatives yesterday reported to the House. The best course that could be taken would be to leave the interests of the people to the Representatives of the people.

Mͬ Madison, was not a little surprised to hear this implicit confidence urged by a member who on all occasions, had inculcated so strongly, the political depravity of men, and the necessity of check-

---

¹ The figures " 1 " and " 2 " are changed to " first " and " second " in the transcript.
² The figure " 2 " is changed to " In the second place " in the transcript.

ing one vice and interest by opposing to them another vice & interest. If the Representatives of the people would be bound by the ties he had mentioned, what need was there of a Senate? What of a Revisionary power? But his reasoning was not only inconsistent with his former reasoning, but with itself. At the same time that he recommended this implicit confidence to the Southern States in the Northern Majority, he was still more zealous in exhorting all to a jealousy of [1] Western Majority. To reconcile the gentl? with himself, it it must be imagined that he determined the human character by the points of the compass. The truth was that all men having power ought to be distrusted to a certain degree. The case of Pen? had been mentioned where it was admitted that those who were possessed of the power in the original settlement, never admitted the new settlem? to a due share of it. England was a still more striking example. The power there had long been in the hands of the boroughs, of the minority; who had opposed & defeated every reform which had been attempted. Virg? was in a lesser [2] degree another example. With regard to the Western States, he was clear & firm in opinion, that no unfavorable distinctions were admissible either in point of justice or policy. He thought also that the hope of contributions to the Treas? from them had been much underrated. Future contributions it seemed to be understood on all hands would be principally levied on imports & exports. The extent and and fertility of the Western Soil would for a long time give to agriculture a preference over manufactures. Trials would be repeated till some articles could be raised from it that would bear a transportation to places where they could be exchanged for imported manufactures. Whenever the Mississpi should be opened to them, which would of necessity be y? case, as soon as their population would subject them to any considerable share of the public burdin, imposts on their trade could be collected with less expence & greater certainty, than on that of the Atlantic States. In the mean time, as their supplies must pass thro' the *Atlantic States*, their contributions would be levied in the same manner with those of the Atlantic States.—He could not agree that any substantial objection lay ag?t fixi? numbers for the perpetual standard of Representation. It was said that Representation & taxation were to go together; that taxation and wealth ought to go together, that population & wealth were not measures of each other. He admitted that in different climates, under different forms of Gov? and in different stages of civilization the inference was per-

---

[1] The word " a " is here inserted in the transcript.
[2] The word " lesser " is changed to " less " in the transcript.

fectly just. He would admit that in no situation, numbers of inhabitants were an accurate measure of wealth. He contended however that in the U. States it was sufficiently so for the object in contemplation. Altho' their climate varied considerably, yet as the Gov'ᵗ the laws, and the manners of all were nearly the same, and the intercourse between different parts perfectly free, population, industry, arts, and the value of labour, would constantly tend to equalize themselves. The value of labour, might be considered as the principal criterion of wealth and ability to support taxes; and this would find its level in different places where the intercourse should be easy & free, with as much certainty as the value of money or any other thing. Wherever labour would yield most, people would resort, till the competition should destroy the inequality. Hence it is that the people are constantly swarming from the more to the less populous places—from Europe to Amᵃ from the Northⁿ & Middle parts of the U. S. to the Southern & Western. They go where land is cheaper, because there labour is dearer. If it be true that the same quantity of produce raised on the banks of the Ohio is of less value, than on the Delaware, it is also true that the same labor will raise twice or thrice, the quantity in the former, that it will raise in the latter situation.

Col. MASON. Agreed with Mʳ Govʳ Morris that we ought to leave the interests of the people to the Representatives of the people: but the objection was that the Legislature would cease to be the Representatives of the people. It would continue so no longer than the States now containing a majority of the people should retain that majority. As soon as the Southern & Western population should predominate, which must happen in a few years, the power wᵈ be in the hands of the minority, and would never be yielded to the majority, unless provided for by the Constitution

On the Question for postponing Mʳ Williamson's motion, in order to consider that of Mʳ Rutlidge it passed in the negative. Massᵗˢ ay. Conᵗ no. N. J. no. Pᵃ ay. Del. ay. Mᵈ no. Vᵃ no. N. C. no. S. C. ay. Geo. ay.[1]

On the question on the first clause of Mʳ Williamson's motion as to taking a census of the *free* inhabitants; it passed in the affirmative Masᵗˢ ay. Conᵗ ay. N. J. ay. Pᵃ ay. Del. no. Mᵈ no. Vᵃ ay. N. C. ay. S. C. no. Geo. no.[2]

---

[1] In the transcript the vote reads: "Massachusetts, Pennsylvania, Delaware, South Carolina, Georgia, aye—5; Connecticut, New Jersey, Maryland, Virginia, North Carolina, no—5."
[2] In the transcript the vote reads: "Massachusetts, Connecticut, New

the next clause as to ¾ of the negroes [1] considered.

M͚ KING. being much opposed to fixing numbers as the rule of representation, was particularly so on account of the blacks. He thought the admission of them along with Whites at all, would excite great discontents among the States having no slaves. He had never said as to any particular point that he would in no event acquiesce in & support it; but he w⁴ say that if in any case such a declaration was to be made by him, it would be in this. He remarked that in the temporary allotment of Representatives made by the Committee, the Southern States had received more than the number of their white & three fifths of their black inhabitants entitled them to.

M͚ SHERMAN. S. Carol͚ had not more beyond her proportion than N. York & N. Hampshire, nor either of them more than was necessary in order to avoid fractions or reducing them below their proportion. Georgia had more; but the rapid growth of that State seemed to justify it. In general the allotment might not be just, but considering all circumstances, he was satisfied with it.

M͚ GHORUM. supported the propriety of establishing numbers as the rule. He said that in Mass͚ estimates had been taken in the different towns, and that persons had been curious enough to compare these estimates with the respective numbers of people; and it had been found even including Boston, that the most exact proportion prevailed between numbers & property. He was aware that there might be some weight in what had fallen from his colleague, as to the umbrage which might be taken by the people of the Eastern States. But he recollected that when the proposition of Cong͚ for changing the 8ᵗʰ art: of Confed͚ was before the Legislature of Mass͚ the only difficulty then was to satisfy them that the negroes ought not to have been counted equally with [2] whites instead of being counted in the ratio of three fifths only.*

M͚ WILSON did not well see on what principle the admission of blacks in the proportion of three fifths could be explained. Are they admitted as Citizens? then why are they not admitted on an equality with White Citizens? are they admitted as property? then why is not other property admitted into the computation? These

* They were then to have been a rule of taxation only.

Jersey, Pennsylvania, Virginia, North Carolina, aye—6; Delaware, Maryland, South Carolina, Georgia, no—4."
    [1] The word "being" is here inserted in the transcript.
    [2] The word "the" is here inserted in the transcript.

were difficulties however which he thought must be overruled by the necessity of compromise. He had some apprehensions also from the tendency of the blending of the blacks with the whites, to give disgust to the people of Pen⁰ as had been intimated by his Colleague [Mᴿ. Govᴿ Morris]. But he differed from him in thinking numbers of inhabᵗˢ so incorrect a measure of wealth. He had seen the Western settlemᵗˢ of Pⁿ and on a comparison of them with the City of Philadⁿ could discover little other difference, than that property was more unequally divided among individuals [1] here than there. Taking the same number in the aggregate in the two situations he believed there would be little difference in their wealth and ability to contribute to the public wants.

Mᴿ Govᴿ Morris was compelled to declare himself reduced to the dilemma of doing injustice to the Southern States or to human nature, and he must therefore do it to the former. For he could never agree to give such encouragement to the slave trade as would be given by allowing them a representation for their negroes, and he did not believe those States would ever confederate on terms that would deprive them of that trade.

On [2] Question for agreeing to include ¾ of the blacks

Massᵗˢ no. Conᵗ ay. N. J. no. Pⁿ no. Del. no. Mardⁿ* no. Vⁿ ay. N. C. ay. S. C. no. Geo. ay [4]

On the question as to taking [2] census " the first year after [2] meeting of the Legislature "

Masᵗˢ ay. Conᵗ no. N. J. ay. Pⁿ ay. Del. ay. Mᵈ no. Vⁿ ay. N. C. ay. S. ay. Geo. no. [5]

On filling the blank for the periodical census, with 15 years." Agreed to nem. con.

Mᴿ Madison moved to add after " 15 years," the words " at least " that the Legislature might anticipate when circumstances were likely to render a particular year inconvenient.

* [Mʳ Carrol sᵈ in explanation of the vote of Mᵈ that he wished the phraseology [3] to be so altered as to obviate if possible the danger which had been expressed of giving umbrage to the Eastern & Middle States.]

---

[1] The words " among individuals " are omitted in the transcript.
[2] The word " the " is here inserted in the transcript.
[3] The transcript italicizes the word " phraseology."
[4] In the transcript the vote reads: " Connecticut, Virginia, North Carolina, Georgia, aye—4; Massachusetts, New Jersey, Pennsylvania, Delaware, Maryland,* South Carolina, no—6."
[5] In the transcript the vote reads: " Massachusetts, New Jersey, Pennsylvania, Delaware, Virginia, North Carolina, South Carolina, aye—7; Connecticut, Maryland, Georgia, no—3."

On this motion for adding " at least," it passed in the negative the States being equally divided.

Mas. ay. Con⁺ no. N. J. no. P⁂ no. Del. no. M⁴ no. V⁂ ay. N. C. ay. S. C. ay. Geo. ay.¹

A Change of ² the phraseology of the other clause so as to read; " and the Legislature shall alter or augment the representation accordingly " was agreed to nem. con.

On the question on the whole resolution of M⁺ Williamson as amended.

Mas. no. Con⁺ no. N. J. no. Del. no. M⁴ no. V⁂ no. N. C. no. S. C. no. Geo. no.³, ⁴

THURSDAY. JULY 12. IN CONVENTION

M⁺ Gov⁺ MORRIS moved to add to the clause empowering the Legislature to vary the Representation according to the principles of wealth & number ⁵ of inhab⁺⁂ a " proviso that taxation shall be in proportion to Representation."

M⁺ BUTLER contended again that Representation s⁴ be according to the full number of inhab⁺⁂ including all the blacks; admitting the justice of M⁺ Gov⁺ Morris's motion.

M⁺ MASON also admitted the justice of the principle, but was afraid embarrassments might be occasioned to the Legislature by it. It might drive the Legislature to the plan of Requisitions.

M⁺ Gov⁺ MORRIS, admitted that some objections lay ag⁺⁺ his motion, but supposed they would be removed by restraining the rule to *direct* taxation. With regard to indirect taxes on *exports* & imports & on consumption, the rule would be inapplicable. Notwithstanding what had been said to the contrary he was persuaded that the imports & consumption were pretty nearly equal throughout the Union.

General PINKNEY liked the idea. He thought it so just that it could not be objected to. But foresaw that if the revision of the

---

¹ In the transcript the vote reads: " Massachusetts, Virginia, North Carolina, South Carolina, Georgia, aye—5; Connecticut, New Jersey, Pennsylvania, Delaware, Maryland, no—5."

² The word " in " is substituted in the transcript for " of."

³ In the transcript the vote reads: " Massachusetts, Connecticut, New Jersey, Delaware, Maryland, Virginia, North Carolina, South Carolina, Georgia, no—9; so it was rejected unanimously."

⁴ The word " Adjourned " is here inserted in the transcript.

⁵ The transcript uses the word " number " in the plural.

census was left to the discretion of the Legislature, it would never be carried into execution. The rule must be fixed, and the execution of it enforced by the Constitution. He was alarmed at what was said yesterday,[*] concerning the negroes. He was now again alarmed at what had been thrown out concerning the taxing of exports. S. Carol! has in one year exported to the amount of £600,000 Sterling all which was the fruit of the labor of her blacks. Will she be represented in proportion to this amount? She will not. Neither ought she then to be subject to a tax on it. He hoped a clause would be inserted in the system, restraining the Legislature from a[1] taxing Exports.

M! WILSON approved the principle, but could not see how it could be carried into execution; unless restrained to direct taxation.

M! Gov! MORRIS having so varied his Motion by inserting the word "direct." It pass! nem. con. as follows—"provided always that direct taxation ought to be proportioned to representation."

M! DAVIE, said it was high time now to speak out. He saw that it was meant by some gentlemen to deprive the Southern States of any share of Representation for their blacks. He was sure that N. Carol! would never confederate on any terms that did not rate them at least as ⅗. If the Eastern States meant therefore to exclude them altogether the business was at an end.

D! JOHNSON, thought that wealth and population were the true, equitable rule[2] of representation; but he conceived that these two principles resolved themselves into one; population being the best measure of wealth. He concluded therefore that ye. number of people ought to be established as the rule, and that all descriptions including blacks *equally* with the whites, ought to fall within the computation. As various opinions had been expressed on the subject, he would move that a Committee might be appointed to take them into consideration and report thereon.

M! Gov! MORRIS. It has[3] been said that it is high time to speak out, as one member, he would candidly do so. He came here to form a compact for the good of America. He was ready to do so with all the States. He hoped & believed that all would enter into such a Compact. If they would not he was ready to join with any States that would. But as the Compact was to be voluntary, it is in vain

---

[*] By M! Gov! Morris.

[1] The word "a" is omitted in the transcript.
[2] The transcript uses the word "rule" in the plural.
[3] The word "had" is substituted in the transcript for "has."

for the Eastern States to insist on what the South.ⁿ States will never agree to. It is equally vain for the latter to require what the other States can never admit; and he verily believed the people of Pen^a. will never agree to a representation of Negroes. What can be desired by these States more than has been already proposed; that the Legislature shall from time to time regulate Representation according to population & wealth.

Genl PINKNEY desired that the rule of wealth should be ascertained and not left to the pleasure of the Legislature; and that property in slaves should not be exposed to danger under a Gov.^t instituted for the protection of property.

The first clause in the Report of the first Grand Committee was postponed.

Mr ELSEWORTH. In order to carry into effect the principle established, moved to add to the last clause adopted by the House the words following " and that the rule of contribution by direct taxation for the support of the Government of the U. States shall be the number of white inhabitants, and three fifths of every other description in the several States, until some other rule that shall more accurately ascertain the wealth of the several States can be devised and adopted by the Legislature."

Mr BUTLER seconded the motion in order that it might be committed.

Mr RANDOLPH was not satisfied with the motion. The danger will be revived that the ingenuity of the Legislature may evade or pervert the rule so as to perpetuate the power where it shall be lodged in the first instance. He proposed in lieu of Mr Elseworth's motion, " that in order to ascertain the alterations in Representation that may be required from time to time by changes in the relative circumstances of the States, a census shall be taken within two years from the 1st meeting of the Genl Legislature of the U. S., and once within the term of every   year afterwards, of all the inhabitants in the manner & according to the ratio recommended by Congress in their resolution of the 18th day of Ap.^l 1783; [rating the blacks at ⅗ of their number] and, that the Legislature of the U. S. shall arrange the Representation accordingly."- He urged strenuously that express security ought to be provided for including slaves in the ratio of Representation. He lamented that such a species of property existed. But as it did exist the holders of it would require this security. It was perceived that the design was entertained by some of excluding slaves altogether; the Legislature therefore ought not to be left at liberty.

M: ELSEWORTH withdraws his motion & seconds that of M: Randolph.

M: WILSON observed that less umbrage would perhaps be taken, ag:ᵗ an admission of the slaves into the Rule of representation, if it should be so expressed as to make them indirectly only an ingredient in the rule, by saying that they should enter into the rule of taxation: and as representation was to be according to taxation, the end would be equally attained. He accordingly moved & was 2ᵈᵉᵈ so to alter the last clause adopted by the House, that together with the amendment proposed the whole should read as follows—provided always that the representation ought to be proportioned according to direct taxation, and in order to ascertain the alterations in the direct taxation which may be required from time to time by the changes in the relative circumstances of the States. Resolved that a census be taken within two years from the first meeting of the Legislature of the U. States, and once within the term of every   years afterwards of all the inhabitants of the U. S. in the manner and according to the ratio recommended by Congress in their Resolution of April 18.[1] 1783; and that the Legislature of the U. S. shall proportion the direct taxation accordingly.''

M: KING. Altho' this amendment varies the aspect somewhat, he had still two powerful objections ag:ᵗ tying down the Legislature to the rule of numbers. 1.[2] they were at this time an uncertain index of the relative wealth of the States. 2.[2] if they were a just index at this time it can not be supposed always to continue so. He was far from wishing to retain any unjust advantage whatever in one part of the Republic. If justice was not the basis of the connection it could not be of long duration. He must be shortsighted indeed who does not foresee that whenever the Southern States shall be more numerous than the Northern, they can & will hold a language that will awe them into justice. If they threaten to separate now in case injury shall be done them, will their threats be less urgent or effectual, when force shall back their demands. Even in the intervening period, there will [3] no point of time at which they will not be able to say, do us justice or we will separate. He urged the necessity of placing confidence to a certain degree in every Gov:ᵗ and did not conceive that the proposed confidence as to a periodical readjustment, of the representation exceeded that degree.

---

[1] The date "April 18" is changed to "the eighteenth day of April" in the transcript.

[2] The figures "1" and "2" are changed to "first" and "secondly" in the transcript.

[3] The word "be" is here inserted in the transcript.

M: PINKNEY moved to amend M: Randolph's motion so as to make "blacks equal to the whites in the ratio of representation." This he urged was nothing more than justice. The blacks are the labourers, the peasants of the Southern States: they are as productive of pecuniary resources as those of the Northern States. They add equally to the wealth, and considering money as the sinew of war, to the strength of the nation. It will also be politic with regard to the Northern States, as taxation is to keep pace with Representation.

Gen! PINKNEY moves to insert 6 years instead of two, as the period computing from [1] 1.st meeting of y.e Legis– within which the first census should be taken. On this question for inserting six [2] instead of "two" in the proposition of M: Wilson, it passed in the affirmative

Masts. no. C:t ay. N. J. ay. P:a ay. Del. div:d May:d ay. V:a no. N. C. no. S. C. ay. Geo. no.[3]

On a [4] question for filling the blank for y.e periodical census with 20 years, it it passed in the negative.

Mas:t no. C:t ay. N. J. ay. P. ay. Del. no. M:d no. V:a no. N. C. no. S. C. no. Geo. no.[5]

On a [4] question for 10 years, it passed in the affirmative.

Mas. ay. Con:t no. N. J. no. P. ay. Del. ay. M:d ay. V:a ay. N. C. ay. S. C. ay. Geo. ay.[6]

On M: Pinkney's motion for rating blacks as equal to Whites instead of as ⅗—

Mas. no. Con:t no. [D:r Johnson ay] N. J. no. P:a no. [3 ag:st 2.] Del. no. M:d no. V:a no. N. C. no. S. C. ay. Geo—ay.[7]

M: Randolph's proposition as varied by M: Wilson being read for [8] question on the whole.

M: GERRY, urged that the principle of it could not be carried

---

[1] The word "the" is here inserted in the transcript.
[2] The word "years" is here inserted in the transcript.
[3] In the transcript the vote reads: "Connecticut, New Jersey, Pennsylvania, Maryland, South Carolina, aye—5; Massachusetts, Virginia, North Carolina, Georgia, no—4; Delaware, divided."
[4] The word "the" is substituted in the transcript for "a."
[5] In the transcript the vote reads: "Connecticut, New Jersey, Pennsylvania, aye—3; Massachusetts, Delaware, Maryland, Virginia, North Carolina, South Carolina, Georgia, no—7."
[6] In the transcript the vote reads: "Massachusetts, Pennsylvania, Delaware, Maryland, Virginia, North Carolina, South Carolina, Georgia, aye—8; Connecticut, New Jersey, no—2."
[7] In the transcript the vote reads: "South Carolina, Georgia, aye—2; Massachusetts, Connecticut, [Doctor Johnson, aye], New Jersey, Pennsylvania, [3 against 2] Delaware, Maryland, Virginia, North Carolina, no—8."
[8] The words "taking the" are here inserted in the transcript.

into execution as the States were not to be taxed as States. With regard to taxes in [1] imports, he conceived they would be more productive. Where there were no slaves than where there were; the consumption being greater—

Mʳ ELSEWORTH. In case of a poll tax there wᵈ be no difficulty. But there wᵈ probably be none. The sum allotted to a State may be levied without difficulty according to the plan used by the State in raising its own supplies. On the question on yᵉ whole proposition; as proportioning representation to direct taxation & both to the white & ¾ of [2] black inhabitants, & requiring a Census within six years—& within every ten years afterwards.

Mas. divᵈ Conᵗ ay. N. J. no. Pᵃ ay. Del. no. Mᵈ ay. Vᵃ ay. N. C. ay. S. C. divᵈ Geo. ay.[3, 4]

FRIDAY. JULY 13.   IN CONVENTION

It being moved to postpone the clause in the Report of the Committee of Eleven as to the originating of money bills in the [5] *first* branch, in order to take up the following—"that in the 2ᵈ branch each State shall have an equal voice."

Mʳ GERRY, moved to add as an amendment to the last clause agreed to by the House, "that from the first meeting of the Legislature of the U. S. till a census shall be taken all monies to be raised for supplying the public Treasury by direct taxation, shall be assessed on the inhabitants of the several States according to the number of their Representatives respectively in the 1ˢᵗ branch." He said this would be as just before as after the Census: according to the general principle that taxation & Representation ought to go together.

Mʳ WILLIAMSON feared that N. Hamshire will have reason to complain. 3 members were allotted to her as a liberal allowance, for this reason among others, that she might not suppose any advantage to have been taken of her absence. As she was still absent, and had no opportunity of deciding whether she would chuse to retain the number on the condition, of her being taxed in proportion

---

[1] The word " on " is substituted in the transcript for " in."
[2] The word " the " is here inserted in the transcript.
[3] In the transcript the vote reads: " Connecticut, Pennsylvania, Maryland, Virginia, North Carolina, Georgia, aye—6; New Jersey, Delaware, no—2; Massachusetts, South Carolina, divided."
[4] The word " Adjourned " is here inserted in the transcript.
[5] The word " *the* " is not italicized in the transcript.

to it, he thought the number ought to be reduced from three to two, before the question [1] on M�r G's motion.

M�r READ could not approve of the proposition. He had observed he said in the Committee a backwardness in some of the members from the large States, to take their full proportion of Representatives. He did not then see the motive. He now suspects it was to avoid their due share of taxation. He had no objection to a just & accurate adjustment of Representation & taxation to each other.

M⁰ Gov⁰ MORRIS & M⁰ MADISON answered that the charge itself involved an acquittal, since notwithstanding the augmentation of the number of members allotted to Mas⁰ & V⁰ the motion for proportioning the burdens thereto was made by a member from the former State & was approved by M⁰- M from the latter who was on the Com⁰ M⁰ Gov⁰ Morris said that he thought P⁰ had her due share in 8 members; and he could not in candor ask for more. M⁰ M. said that having always conceived that the difference of interest in the U. States lay not between the large & small, but the N. & South⁰ States, and finding that the number of members allotted to the N. States was greatly superior, he should have preferred, an addition of two members to the S. States, to wit one to N. & 1 to S. Carl⁰ rather than of one member to Virg⁰ He liked the present motion, because it tended to moderate the views both of the opponents & advocates for rating very high, the negroes.

M⁰ ELSEWORTH hoped the proposition would be withdrawn. It entered too much into detail. The general principle was already sufficiently settled. As fractions can not be regarded in apportioning the N⁰ of representatives, the rule will be unjust, until an actual census shall be made. after that taxation may be precisely proportioned according to the principle established, to the number of inhabitants.

M⁰ WILSON hoped the motion would not be withdrawn. If it sh⁰ it will be made from another quarter. The rule will be as reasonable & just before, as after a Census. As to fractional numbers, the Census will not distroy, but ascertain them. And they will have the same effect after as before the Census: for as he understands the rule, it is to be adjusted not to the number of inhabitants, but of Representatives.

M⁰ SHERMAN opposed the motion. He thought the Legislature ought to be left at liberty: in which case they would probably conform to the principles observed by Cong⁰

---

[1] The words " was taken " are here inserted in the transcript.

Mr Mason did not know that Virg^a would be a loser by the proposed regulation, but had some scruple as to the justice of it. He doubted much whether the conjectural rule which was to precede the Census, would be as just, as it would be rendered by an actual census.

Mr Elseworth & Mr Sherman moved to postpone the motion of Mr Gerry, on ye question, it passed in the negative.

Mas. no. Con^t ay. N. J. ay. P^a no. Del. ay. M^d ay. V^a no. N. C. no. S. C. no. Geo. no.[1]

[2] Question on Mr Gerry's motion; it passed in the negative, the States being equally divided.

Mas. ay. Con^t no. N. J. no. P^a ay. Del. no. M^d no. [V^a no. N. C. ay. S. C. ay. Geo. ay.[3]

Mr Gerry finding that the loss of the question had proceeded from an objection with some, to the proposed assessment of direct taxes on the *inhabitants* of the States, which might restrain the Legislature to a poll tax, moved his proposition again, but so varied as to authorise the assessment on the *States*, which w^d leave [4] the mode to the Legislature, at this caret insert the words interlined [5] viz " that from the 1st meeting of the Legislature of the U. S. untill a census shall be taken, all monies for supplying the public Treasury by direct taxation shall be raised from the said several States according to the number of their representatives respectively in the 1st branch."

On this varied question, it passed in the affirmative

Mas. ay. Con^t no. N. J. no. P^a div^d Del. no. M^d no. V^a ay. N. C. ay. S. C. ay. Geo. ay.[6]

On the motion of Mr Randolph, the vote of saturday [7] last authorising the Legisl^{re} to adjust from time to time, the representation upon the principles of *wealth* & numbers of inhabitants was reconsidered by common consent in order to strike out " Wealth [8]" and adjust the resolution to that requiring periodical revisions according to the number of whites & three fifths of the blacks: the

---

[1] In the transcript the vote reads: "Connecticut, New Jersey, Delaware, Maryland, aye—4; Massachusetts, Pennsylvania, Virginia, North Carolina, South Carolina, Georgia, no—6."

[2] The words " On the " are here inserted in the transcript.

[3] In the transcript the vote reads: "Massachusetts, *Pennsylvania*, North Carolina, South Carolina, Georgia, aye—5; Connecticut, New Jersey, Delaware, Maryland, *Virginia*, no—5."

[4] The word " leaves " is substituted in the transcript for " w^d leave."

[5] Madison's direction concerning the interlined words is omitted in the transcript.

[6] In the transcript the vote reads: "Massachusetts, *Virginia*, North Carolina, South Carolina, Georgia, aye—5; Connecticut, New Jersey, Delaware, Maryland, no—4; *Pennsylvania*, divided."

[7] The word " saturday " is changed to " Monday " in the transcript.

[8] The transcript italicizes the word " Wealth."

motion was in the words following—"But as the present situation
of the States may probably alter in the number of their inhabitants,
that the Legislature of the U. S. be authorized from time to time to
apportion the number of representatives: and in case any of the
States shall hereafter be divided or any two or more States united
or new States created within the limits of the U. S. the Legislature
of[1] U. S. shall possess authority to regulate the number of Representatives in any of the foregoing cases, upon the principle of their
number of inhabitants; according to the provisions hereafter mentioned."

M.ʳ Gov.ʳ Morris opposed the alteration as leaving still an inco-
herence. If Negroes were to be viewed as inhabitants, and the
revision was to proceed on the principle of numbers of inhab.ᵗˢ they
ought to be added in their entire number, and not in the proportion of
³⁄₅. If as property, the word wealth was right, and striking it out,
would produce the very inconsistency which it was meant to get rid
of.—The train of business & the late turn which it had taken, had led
him he said, into deep meditation on it, and He w.ᵈ candidly state
the result. A distinction had been set up & urged, between the
N.ⁿ & South.ⁿ States. He had hitherto considered this doctrine as
heretical. He still thought the distinction groundless. He sees
however that it is persisted in, and that the South.ⁿ Gentlemen will not
be satisfied unless they see the way open to their gaining a majority
in the public Councils. The consequence of such a transfer of power
from the maritime to the interior & landed interest will he foresees be
such an oppression of[2] commerce, that he shall be obliged to vote for
y.ᵉ vicious principle of equality in the 2.ᵈ branch in order to provide
some defence for the N. States ag.ˢᵗ it. But to come more to the
point; either this distinction is fictitious or real; if fictitious let it
be dismissed & let us proceed with due confidence. If it be real,
instead of attempting to blend incompatible things, let us at once take
a friendly leave of each other. There can be no end of demands
for security if every particular interest is to be entitled to it. The
Eastern States may claim it for their fishery, and for other objects,
as the South.ⁿ States claim it for their peculiar objects. In this
struggle between the two ends of the Union, what part ought the
middle States in point of policy to take: to join their Eastern
brethren according to his ideas. If the South.ⁿ States get the power
into their hands, and be joined as they will be with the interior

---

[1] The word "the" is here inserted in the transcript.
[2] The word "to" is substituted in the transcript for "of."

Country, they will inevitably bring on a war with Spain for the Mississippi. This language is already held. The interior Country having no property nor interest exposed on the sea, will be little affected by such a war. He wished to know what security the North? & middle States will have ag:t this danger. It has been said that N. C. S. C., and Georgia only will in a little time have a majority of the people of America. They must in that case include the great interior Country, and every thing was to be apprehended from their getting the power into their hands.

M: BUTLER. The security the South? States want is that their negroes may not be taken from them, which some gentlemen within or without doors, have a very good mind to do. It was not supposed that N. C. S. C. & Geo. would have more people than all the other States, but many more relatively to the other States than they now have. The people & strength of America are evidently bearing Southwardly & S. westw:ly

M: WILSON. If a general declaration would satisfy any gentleman he had no indisposition to declare his sentiments. Conceiving that all men wherever placed have equal rights and are equally entitled to confidence, he viewed without apprehension the period when a few States should contain the superior number of people. The majority of people wherever found ought in all questions to govern the minority. If the interior Country should acquire this majority, it will not only have the right, but will avail themselves [1] of it whether we will or no. This jealousy misled the policy of G. Britain with regard to America. The fatal maxims espoused by her were that the Colonies were growing too fast, and that their growth must be stinted in time. What were the consequences? first. enmity on our part, then actual separation. Like consequences will result on the part of the interior settlements, if like jealousy & policy be pursued on ours. Further, if numbers be not a proper rule, why is not some better rule pointed out. No one has yet ventured to attempt it. Cong? have never been able to discover a better. No State as far as he had heard, has suggested any other. In 1783, after elaborate discussion of a measure of wealth all were satisfied then as they are now that the rule of numbers, does not differ much from the combined rule of numbers & wealth. Again he could not agree that property was the sole or the [2] primary object of Govern:t & society. The cultivation & improvement of the human mind was the most noble object. With respect to this object, as well as to other *personal*

---

[1] The word "itself" is substituted in the transcript for "themselves."
[2] The word "the" is omitted in the transcript.

rights, numbers were surely the natural & precise measure of Representation. And with respect to property, they could not vary much from the precise measure. In no point of view however could the establishm.ᵗ of numbers as the rule of representation in the 1.ˢᵗ branch vary his opinion as to the impropriety of letting a vicious principle into the 2.ᵈ branch.—On the Question to strike out *wealth*, & to make the change as moved by M.ʳ Randolph, it passed in the affirmative—

Mas. ay. Con.ᵗ ay. N. J. ay. P.ᵃ ay. Del. div.ᵈ M.ᵈ ay. V.ᵃ ay. N. C. ay. S. C. ay. Geo. ay.¹

M.ʳ Reed moved to insert after the word– "divided," "or enlarged by addition of territory" which was agreed to nem. con. [his object probably was to provide for such cases as an enlargem.ᵗ of Delaware by annexing to it the Peninsula on the East side of ² Chesapeak]

Adjourned.

SATURDAY. JULY 14.   IN CONVENTION

M.ʳ L. MARTIN called for the question on the whole report, including the parts relating to the origination of money bills, and the equality of votes in the 2.ᵈ branch.

M.ʳ GERRY. wished before the question should be put, that the attention of the House might be turned to the dangers apprehended from Western States. He was for admitting them on liberal terms, but not for putting ourselves into their hands. They will if they acquire power like all men, abuse it. They will oppress commerce, and drain our wealth into the Western Country. To guard ag.ˢᵗ these consequences, he thought it necessary to limit the number of new States to be admitted into the Union, in such a manner, that they should never be able to outnumber the Atlantic States. He accordingly moved " that in order to secure the liberties of the States already confederated, the number of Representatives in the 1.ˢᵗ branch, of the States which shall hereafter be established, shall never exceed in number, the Representatives from such of the States as shall accede to this confederation.

M.ʳ KING. seconded the motion.

---

¹ In the transcript the vote reads: "Massachusetts, Connecticut, New Jersey, Pennsylvania, Maryland, Virginia, North Carolina, South Carolina, Georgia, aye—9; Delaware, divided."
² The word "the" is here inserted in the transcript; and the sentence in brackets is a footnote.

M: SHERMAN, thought there was no probability that the number of future States would exceed that of the Existing States. If the event should ever happen, it was too remote to be taken into consideration at this time. Besides We are providing for our posterity, for our children & our grand Children, who would be as likely to be citizens of new Western States, as of the old States. On this consideration alone, we ought to make no such discrimination as was proposed by the motion.

M: GERRY. If some of our children should remove, others will stay behind, and he thought it incumbent on us to provide for their interests. There was a rage for emigration from the Eastern States to the Western Country, and he did not wish those remaining behind to be at the mercy of the Emigrants. Besides foreigners are resorting to that country, and it is uncertain what turn things may take there.—On the question for agreeing to the Motion of M: Gerry, it passed in the negative.

Mas. ay. Con: ay. N. J. no. P: div⁴ Del: ay. M⁴ ay. V: no. N. C. no. S. C. no. Geo. no.[1]

M: RUTLIDGE proposed to reconsider the two propositions touching the originating of money bills in the first & the equality of votes in the second branch.

M: SHERMAN was for the question on the whole at once. It was he said a conciliatory plan, it had been considered in all its parts, a great deal of time had been spent on[2] it, and if any part should now be altered, it would be necessary to go over the whole ground again.

M: L. MARTIN urged the question on the whole. He did not like many parts of it. He did not like having two branches, nor the inequality of votes in the 1ˢᵗ branch. He was willing however to make trial of the plan, rather than do nothing.

M: WILSON traced the progress of the report through its several stages, remarking yᵗ when on the question concerning an equality of votes, the House was divided, our Constituents had they voted as their representatives did, would have stood as ⅔ agˢᵗ the equality, and ⅓ only in favor of it. This fact would ere long be known, and it will[3] appear that this fundamental point has been carried by ⅓ agˢᵗ ⅔. What hopes will our Constituents entertain when they find

---

[1] In the transcript the vote reads: "Massachusetts, Connecticut, Delaware, Maryland, aye—4; New Jersey, Virginia, North Carolina, South Carolina, Georgia, no—5; Pennsylvania, divided."
[2] The word "upon" is substituted in the transcript for "on."
[3] The word "would" is substituted in the transcript for "will."

that the essential principles of justice have been violated in the outset of the Governm.[t] As to the privilege of originating money bills, it was not considered by any as of much moment, and by many as improper in itself. He hoped both clauses w.[d] be reconsidered. The equality of votes was a point of such critical importance, that every opportunity ought to be allowed, for discussing and collecting the mind of the Convention on [1] it.

M.[r] L. MARTIN denies that there were ⅔ ag.[st] the equality of votes. The States that please to call themselves large, are the weekest in the Union. Look at Mas.[ts] Look at Virg.[a] Are they efficient States? He was for letting a separation take place if they desired it. He had rather there should be two Confederacies, than one founded on any other principle than an equality of votes in the 2.[d] branch at least.

M.[r] WILSON was not surprised that those who say that a minority is [2] more than the [3] majority should say that [4] the minority is stronger than the majority. He supposed the next assertion will be that they are richer also; though he hardly expected it would be persisted in when the States shall be called on for taxes & troops—

M.[r] GERRY. also animadverted on M.[r] L. Martins remarks on the weakness of Mast.[s] He favored the reconsideration with a view not of destroying the equality of votes; but of providing that the States should vote per capita, which he said would prevent the delays & inconveniences that had been experienced in Cong.[s] and would give a national aspect & Spirit to the management of business. He did not approve of a reconsideration of the clause relating to money bills. It was of great consequence. It was the corner stone of the accomodation. If any member of the Convention had the exclusive privilege of making propositions, would any one say that it would give him no advantage over other members. The Report was not altogether to his mind. But he would agree to it as it stood rather than throw it out altogether.

The reconsideration being tacitly agreed to

M.[r] PINKNEY moved that instead of an equality of votes, the States should be represented in the 2.[d] branch as follows: N. H. by. 2. members. Mas. 4. R. I. 1. Con.[t] 3. N. Y. 3. N. J. 2. P.[a] 4. Del 1. M.[d] 3. Virg.[a] 5. N. C. 3. S. C. 3. Geo. 2. making in the whole 36.

---

[1] The word " upon " is substituted in the transcript for " on."
[2] The word " does " is substituted in the transcript for " is."
[3] The word " a " is substituted in the transcript for " the."
[4] The word " that " is omitted in the transcript.

M.ʳ WILSON seconds the motion

M.ʳ DAYTON. The smaller States can never give up their equality. For himself he would in no event yield that security for their rights.

M.ʳ SHERMAN urged the equality of votes not so much as a security for the small States; as for the State Gov.ᵗˢ which could not be preserved unless they were represented & had a negative in the Gen.ˡ Government. He had no objection to the members in the 2.ᵈ b. voting per capita, as had been suggested by [M.ʳ Gerry]

M.ʳ MADISON concurred in this motion of M.ʳ Pinkney as a reasonable compromise.

M.ʳ GERRY said he should like the motion, but could see no hope of success. An accomodation must take place, and it was apparent from what had been seen that it could not do so on the ground of the motion. He was utterly against a partial confederacy, leaving other States to accede or not accede; as had been intimated.

M.ʳ KING said it was always with regret that he differed from his colleagues, but it was his duty to differ from [M.ʳ Gerry] on this occasion. He considered the proposed Government as substantially and formally, a General and National Government over the people of America. There never will be a case in which it will act as a federal Government on the States and not on the individual Citizens. And is it not a clear principle that in a free Gov.ᵗ those who are to be the objects of a Gov.ᵗ ought to influence the operations of it? What reason can be assigned why the same rule of representation s.ᵈ not prevail in the 2.ᵈ branch [1] as in the 1.ˢᵗ? He could conceive none. On the contrary, every view of the subject that presented itself, seemed to require it. Two objections had been raised ag.ˢᵗ it: drawn 1.[2] from the terms of the existing compact 2.[2] from a supposed danger to the smaller States.—As to the first objection he thought it inapplicable. According to the existing confederation, the rule by which the public burdens is to be apportioned is *fixed,* and must be pursued. In the proposed Goverm.ᵗ it can not be fixed, because indirect taxation is to be substituted. The Legislature therefore will have full discretion to impose taxes in such modes & proportions as they may judge expedient. As to the 2.ᵈ objection, he thought it of as little weight. The Gen.ˡ Goverm.ᵗ can never wish to intrude on the State Govern.ᵗˢ There could be no temptation. None had been pointed out. In order to prevent the interference of

---

[1] In the transcript the word "branch" is transposed, making the phrase read: "second, as in the first, branch."

[2] The figures "1" and "2" are changed to "first" and "secondly" in the transcript.

measures which seemed most likely to happen, he would have no objection to throwing all the State debts into the federal debt, making one aggregate debt of about 70,000,000 of dollars, and leaving it to be discharged by the Gen! Gov!—According to the idea of securing the State Gov!² there ought to be three distinct legislative branches. The 2ᵈ was admitted to be necessary, and was actually meant, to check the 1ˢᵗ branch, to give more wisdom, system, & stability to the Gov! and ought clearly as it was to operate on the people to be proportioned to them. For the third purpose of securing the States, there ought then to be a 3ᵈ branch, representing the States as such, and guarding by equal votes their rights & dignities. He would not pretend to be as thoroughly acquainted with his immediate Constituents as his colleagues, but it was his firm belief that Mas!² would never be prevailed on to yield to an equality of votes. In N. York (he was sorry to be obliged to say any thing relative to that State in the absence of its representatives, but the occasion required it), in N. York he had seen that the most powerful argument used by the considerate opponents to the grant of the Impost to Congress, was pointed ag!ᵗ the viccious constitution of Cong! with regard to representation & suffrage. He was sure that no Gov! could ¹ last that was not founded on just principles. He prefer'd the doing of nothing, to an allowance of an equal vote to all the States. It would be better he thought to submit to a little more confusion & convulsion, than to submit to such an evil. It was difficult to say what the views of different Gentlemen might be. Perhaps there might be some who thought no Governm! co-extensive with the U. States could be established with a hope of its answering the purpose. Perhaps there might be other fixed opinions incompatible with the object we were ² pursuing. If there were, he thought it but candid that Gentlemen would ³ speak out that we might understand one another.

M! STRONG. The Convention had been much divided in opinion. In order to avoid the consequences of it, an accomodation had been proposed. A Committee had been appointed: and though some of the members of it were averse to an equality of votes, a Report has ⁴ been made in favor of it. It is agreed on all hands that Congress are nearly at an end. If no Accomodation takes place, the Union itself must soon be dissolved. It has been suggested that if

---

¹ The word "would" is substituted in the transcript for "could."
² The word "are" is substituted in the transcript for "were."
³ The word "should" is substituted in the transcript for "would."
⁴ The word "had" is substituted in the transcript for "has."

we can not come to any general agreement, the principal States may form & recommend a scheme of Government. But will the small States in that case ever accede [1] it. Is it probable that the large States themselves will under such circumstances embrace and ratify it. He thought the small States had made a considerable concession in the article of money bills; and that they might naturally expect some concessions on the other side. From this view of the matter he was compelled to give his vote for the Report taken all together.

M: MADISON expressed his apprehensions that if the proper foundation of Govenm^t was destroyed, by substituting an equality in place of a proportional Representation, no proper superstructure would be raised. If the small States really wish for a Government armed with the powers necessary to secure their liberties, and to enforce obedience on the larger members as well as on [2] themselves he could not help thinking them extremely mistaken in their [3] means. He reminded them of the consequences of laying the existing confederation [4] on improper principles. All the principal parties to its compilation, joined immediately in mutilating & fettering the Governm^t in such a manner that it has disappointed every hope placed on it. He appealed to the doctrine & arguments used by themselves on a former occasion. It had been very properly observed by [M: Patterson] that Representation was an expedient by which the meeting of the people themselves was rendered unnecessary; and that the representatives ought therefore to bear a proportion to the votes which their constituents if convened, would respectively have. Was not this remark as applicable to one branch of the Representation as to the other? But it had been said that the Govern^t would in its operation be partly federal, partly national; that altho' in the latter respect the Representatives of the people ought to be in proportion to the people: yet in the former it ought to be according to the number of States. If there was any solidity in this distinction he was ready to abide by it, if there was none it ought to be abandoned. In all cases where the Genl Governm^t is to act on the people, let the people be represented and the votes be proportional. In all cases where the Govern^t is to act on the States as such, in like manner as Cong^s now act on them, let the States be represented & the votes be equal. This was the true ground of compromise if there was any ground at all. But he denied that there was any ground. He called for a single instance in which the

---

[1] The word "to" is here inserted in the transcript.
[2] The word "on" is omitted in the transcript.
[3] The word "the" is substituted in the transcript for "their."
[4] The transcript italicizes the words "existing confederation."

Gen! Gov! was not to operate on the people individually. The practicability of making laws, with coercive sanctions, for the States as Political bodies, had been exploded on all hands. He observed that the people of the large States would in some way or other secure to themselves a weight proportioned to the importance accruing from their superior numbers. If they could not effect it by a proportional representation in the Gov! they would probably accede to no Gov! which did not in [1] great measure depend for its efficacy on their voluntary cooperation; in which case they would indirectly secure their object. The existing confederacy proved that where the Acts of the Gen! Gov! were to be executed by the particular Gov!? the latter had a weight in proportion to their importance. No one would say that either in Cong? or out of Cong? Delaware had equal weight with Pensylv! If the latter was to supply ten times as much money as the former, and no compulsion could be used, it was of ten times more importance, that she should voluntarily furnish the supply. In the Dutch confederacy the votes of the Provinces were equal. But Holland which supplies about half the money, governs [2] the whole republic. He enumerated the objections agst an equality of votes in the 2^d branch, notwithstanding the proportional representation in the first. 1. the minority could negative the will of the majority of the people. 2. they could extort measures by making them a condition of their assent to other necessary measures. 3. they could obtrude measures on the majority by virtue of the peculiar powers which would be vested in the Senate. 4. the evil instead of being cured by time, would increase with every new State that should be admitted, as they must all be admitted on the principle of equality. 5. the perpetuity it would give to the preponderance of the North^n agst the South^n Scale was a serious consideration. It seemed now to be pretty well understood that the real difference of interests lay, not between the large & small but between the N. & South^n States. The institution of slavery & its consequences formed the line of discrimination. There were 5 States on the South,[3] 8 on the North^n side of this line. Should a proport! representation take place it was true, the N. side [4] would still outnumber the other; but not in the same degree, at this time; and every day would tend towards an equilibrium.

Mr WILSON would add a few words only. If equality in the 2^d

---

[1] The word " a " is here inserted in the transcript.
[2] The word " governed " is substituted in the transcript for " governs."
[3] The word " Southern " is substituted in the transcript for " South."
[4] The word " side " is omitted in the transcript.

branch was an error that time would correct, he should be less anxious to exclude it being sensible that perfection was unattainable in any plan; but being a fundamental and a perpetual error, it ought by all means to be avoided. A vice in the Representation, like an error in the first concoction, must be followed by disease, convulsions, and finally death itself. The justice of the general principle of proportional representation has not in argument at least been yet contradicted. But it is said that a departure from it so far as to give the States an equal vote in one branch of the Legislature is essential to their preservation. He had considered this position maturely, but could not see its application. That the States ought to be preserved he admitted. But does it follow that an equality of votes is necessary for the purpose? Is there any reason to suppose that if their preservation should depend more on the large than on the small States the security of the States ag.ᵗ the Gen.ˡ Government would be diminished? Are the large States less attached to their existence, more likely to commit suicide, than the small? An equal vote then is not necessary as far as he can conceive: and is liable among other objections to this insuperable one: The great fault of the existing confederacy is its inactivity. It has never been a complaint ag.ᵗ Cong.ˢ that they governed overmuch. The complaint has been that they have governed too little. To remedy this defect we were sent here. Shall we effect the cure by establishing an equality of votes as is proposed? no: this very equality carries us directly to Congress: to the system which it is our duty to rectify. The small States cannot indeed act, by virtue of this equality, but they may controul the Gov.ˢ as they have done in Cong.ˢ This very measure is here prosecuted by a minority of the people of America. Is then the object of the Convention likely to be accomplished in this way? Will not our Constituents say? we sent you to form an efficient Gov.ˢ and you have given us one more complex indeed, but having all the weakness of the former Govern.ˢ He was anxious for uniting all the States under one Govern.ˢ He knew there were some respectable men who preferred three confederacies, united by offensive & defensive alliances. Many things may be plausibly said, some things may be justly said, in favor of such a project. He could not however concur in it himself; but he thought nothing so pernicious as bad first principles.

M.ʳ ELSEWORTH asked two questions one of M.ʳ Wilson, whether he had ever seen a good measure fail in Cong.ˢ for want of a majority of States in its favor? He had himself never known such an instance: the other of M.ʳ Madison whether a negative lodged with the majority of the States even the smallest, could be more dangerous than the qualified negative proposed to be lodged in a single Executive Magistrate, who must be taken from some one State?

M: SHERMAN, signified that his expectation was that the Gen! Legislature would in some cases act on the *federal principle,* of requiring quotas. But he thought it ought to be empowered to carry their own plans into execution, if the States should fail to supply their respective quotas.

On the question for agreeing to M: Pinkney's motion for allowing N. H. 2. Mas. 4. &c—it passed in the negative

Mas. no. M: King ay. M: Ghorum absent. Con: no. N. J. no. P: ay. Del. no, M: ay. V: ay. N. C. no. S. C. ay Geo. no.[1]

Adjourned.

MONDAY. JULY 16. IN CONVENTION

On the question for agreeing to the whole Report as amended & including the equality of votes in the 2ᵈ branch. it passed in the Affirmative.

Mas. divided M: Gerry, M: Strong, ay. M: King M: Ghorum no. Con: ay. N. J. ay. Pen: no. Del. ay. M: ay. V: no. N. C. ay. M: Spaight no. S. C. no. Geo. no.[2]

[Here enter the whole in the words entered in the Journal July 16][3]

The whole, thus passed is in the words following viz

" Resolved that in the original formation of the Legislature of the U. S. the first branch thereof shall consist of sixty five members, of which number N. Hampshire shall send 3. Mass:ᵇ 8. Rh. I. 1. Conn: 5. N. Y. 6. N. J. 4. Pen: 8. Del. 1. Mary: 6. Virg: 10. N. C. 5. S. C. 5. Geo. 3.—But as the present situation of the States may probably alter in the number of their inhabitants, the Legislature of the U. S. shall be authorized from time to time to apportion the number of Rep:; and in case any of the States shall hereafter be divided, or enlarged by, addition of territory, or any two or more States united, or any new States created with[4] the limits of the

---

[1] In the transcript the vote reads: "Pennsylvania, Maryland, Virginia, South Carolina, aye—4; Massachusetts, [Mr. King, aye, Mr. Gorham, absent], Connecticut, New Jersey, Delaware, North Carolina, Georgia, no—6."

[2] In the transcript the vote reads: "Connecticut, New Jersey, Delaware, Maryland, North Carolina [Mr. Spaight, no], aye—5; Pennsylvania, Virginia, South Carolina, Georgia, no—4; Massachusetts, divided, [Mr. Gerry, Mr. Strong, aye; Mr. King, Mr. Gorham, no.] "

[3] Madison's direction is omitted in the transcript.

[4] The word "within" is substituted in the transcript for the word "with."

U. S. the Legislature of the U. S. shall possess authority to regulate the number of Rep! in any of the foregoing cases, upon the principle of their number of inhabitants, according to the provisions hereafter mentioned, namely [1]—provided always that representation ought to be proportioned according to direct taxation; and in order to ascertain the alteration in the direct taxation, which may be required from time to time by the changes in the relative circumstances of the States—

Resolved, that a Census be taken within six years from the 1ˢᵗ meeting of the Legislature of the U. S. and once within the term of every 10 years afterwards of all the inhabitants of the U. S. in the manner and according to the ratio recommended by Congress in their Resolution of April 18.[2] 1783, and that the Legislature of the U. S. shall proportion the direct taxation accordingly—

" Resolved, that all bills for raising or appropriating money, and for fixing the salaries of officers of the Govᵗ of the U. S. shall originate in the first branch of the Legislature of the U. S. and shall not be altered or amended in the 2ᵈ branch: and that no money shall be drawn from the public Treasury, but in pursuance of appropriations to be originated in the 1ˢᵗ branch.

" Resolvᵈ that in the 2ᵈ branch of the Legislature of the U. S. each State shall have an equal vote."

The 6ᵗʰ Resol: in the Report from the Comᵉ of the whole House, which had been postponed in order to consider the 7 & 8ᵗʰ Resolⁿˢ: was now resumed. see the Resolⁿ

The 1ˢᵗ member [3] " That the Natᶦ Legislature ought to possess the Legislative Rights vested in Congˢ by the Confederation." was agreed to nem. Con.

The next,[4] " And moreover to legislate in all cases to which the separate States are incompetent; or in which the harmony of the U. S. may be interrupted by the exercise of individual legislation," being read for a question

Mᵣ Butler calls for some explanation of the extent of this power: particularly of the word *incompetent*. The vagueness of the terms rendered it impossible for any precise judgment to be formed.

Mᵣ Ghorum. The vagueness of the terms constitutes the propriety of them. We are now establishing general principles, to be extended hereafter into details which will be precise & explicit.

Mᵣ Rutlidge, urged the objection started by Mᵣ Butler and moved that the clause should be committed to the end that a specification

---

[1] The word " namely " is omitted in the transcript.
[2] The date " April 18 " is changed to " the eighteenth of April " in the transcript.
[3] The words " The 1ˢᵗ member " are omitted in the transcript.
[4] The words " The next " are omitted in the transcript.

of the powers comprised in the general terms, might be reported.

On the question for a[1] commitment, the States[2] were equally divided

Mas. no. Con! ay. N. J. no. P? no. Del. no. M? ay. V? ay. N. C. no. S. C. ay. Geo. ay:[3] So it was lost.

M? RANDOLPH. The vote of this morning [involving an equality of suffrage in 2? branch] had embarrassed the business extremely. All the powers given in the Report from the Com? of the whole, were founded on the supposition that a Proportional representation was to prevail in both branches of the Legislature. When he came here this morning his purpose was to have offered some propositions that might if possible have united a great majority of votes, and particularly might provide ag?t the danger suspected on the part of the smaller States, by enumerating the cases in which it might lie, and allowing an equality of votes in such cases.* But finding from the preceding vote that they persist in demanding an equal vote in all cases, that they have succeeded in obtaining it, and that N. York if present would probably be on the same side, he could not but think we were unprepared to discuss this subject further. It will probably be in vain to come to any final decision with a bare majority on either side. For these reasons he wished the Convention might[6] adjourn, that the large States might consider the steps proper to be taken in the present solemn crisis of the business, and that the small States might also deliberate on the means of conciliation.

M? PATTERSON, thought with M? R. that it was high time for the Convention to adjourn that the rule of secrecy ought to be rescinded, and that our Constituents should be consulted. No conciliation could be admissible on the part of the smaller States on any other ground than that of an equality of votes in the 2? branch. If M? Randolph would reduce to form his motion for an adjournment sine die, he would second it with all his heart.

Gen! PINKNEY wished to know of M? R. whether he meant an adjournment sine die, or only an adjournment for the day. If the former was meant, it differed much from his idea. He could not think of going to S. Carolina and returning again to this place. Be-

---

* See the paper in[4] appendix communicated by M? R. to J. M. July 10.[5]

[1] The word " a " is omitted in the transcript.
[2] The word " votes " is substituted in the transcript for " States."
[3] In the transcript the vote reads: " Connecticut, Maryland, Virginia, South Carolina, Georgia, aye—5; Massachusetts, New Jersey, Pennsylvania, Delaware, North Carolina, no—5."
[4] The word " the " is here inserted in the transcript.
[5] The transcript here inserts "No.—" For the text of this paper see Appendix to Debates, VI, p. 618.
[6] The word " to " is substituted in the transcript for " might."

sides it was chimerical to suppose that the States if consulted would ever accord separately, and beforehand.

M.ʳ RANDOLPH, had never entertained an idea of an adjournment sine die; & was sorry that his meaning had been so readily & strangely misinterpreted. He had in view merely an adjournment till to-morrow, in order that some conciliatory experiment might if possible be devised, and that in case the smaller States should continue to hold back, the larger might then take such measures, he would not say what, as might be necessary.

M.ʳ PATTERSON seconded the adjournment till tomorrow, as an opportunity seemed to be wished by the larger States to deliberate further on conciliatory expedients.

On the question for adjourning till tomorrow, the States were equally divided.

Mas. no. Conᵗ no. N. J. ay. P.ᵃ ay. Del. no. M.ᵈ ay. V.ᵃ ay. N. C. ay. S. C. no. Geo. no.¹ So it was lost.

M.ʳ BROOME thought it his duty to declare his opinion agᵗ an adjournment sine die, as had been urged by M.ʳ Patterson. Such a measure he thought would be fatal. Something must be done by the Convention, tho' it should be by a bare majority.

M.ʳ GERRY observed that Mas.ᵗˢ was opposed to an adjournment, because they saw no new ground of compromise. But as it seemed to be the opinion of so many States that a trial sh.ᵈ- be made, the State would now concur in the adjournmᵗ

M.ʳ RUTLIDGE could see no need of an adjournᵗ because he could see no chance of a compromise. The little States were fixt. They had repeatedly & solemnly declared themselves to be so. All that the large States then had to do, was to decide whether they would yield or not. For his part he conceived that altho' we could not do what we thought best, in itself, we ought to do something. Had we not better keep the Govᵗ up a little longer, hoping that another Convention will supply our omissions, than abandon every thing to hazard. Our Constituents will be very little satisfied with us if we take the latter course.

M.ʳ RANDOLPH & M.ʳ KING renewed the motion to adjourn till tomorrow.

On the question. Mas. ay. Conᵗ no. N. J. ay. P.ᵃ ay. Del. no. M.ᵈ ay. V.ᵃ ay. N. C. ay. S. C. ay. Geo. divᵈ²

Adjourned

---

¹ In the transcript the vote reads: "New Jersey, Pennsylvania, Maryland, Virginia, North Carolina, aye—5; Massachusetts, Connecticut, Delaware, South Carolina, Georgia, no—5."

² In the transcript the vote reads: "Massachusetts, New Jersey, Pennsylvania, Maryland, Virginia, North Carolina, South Carolina, aye—7; Connecticut, Delaware, no—2; Georgia, divided."

On the morning following before the hour of the convention a number of the members from the larger States, by common agreement met for the purpose of consulting on the proper steps to be taken in consequence of the vote in favor of an equal Representation in the 2ᵈ branch, and the apparent inflexibility of the smaller States on that point. Several members from the latter States also attended. The time was wasted in vague conversation on the subject, without any specific proposition or agreement. It appeared indeed that the opinions of the members who disliked the equality of votes differed so [1] much as to the importance of that point, and as to the policy of risking a failure of any general act of the Convention, by inflexibly opposing it. Several of them supposing that no good Governnᵗ could or would be built on that foundation, and that as a division of the Convention into two opinions was unavoidable; it would be better that the side comprising the principal States, and a majority of the people of America, should propose a scheme of Govᵗ to the States, than that a scheme should be proposed on the other side, would have concurred in a firm opposition to the smaller States, and in a separate recommendation, if eventually necessary. Others seemed inclined to yield to the smaller States, and to concur in such an act however imperfect & exceptionable, as might be agreed on by the Convention as a body, tho' decided by a bare majority of States and by a minority of the people of the U. States. It is probable that the result of this consultation satisfied the smaller States that they had nothing to apprehend from a union of the larger, in any plan whatever agˢᵗ the equality of votes in the 2ᵈ branch.

TUESDAY JULY 17.   IN CONVENTION

Mᵣ Governᵣ Morris. moved to reconsider the whole Resolution agreed to yesterday concerning the constitution of the 2 branches of the Legislature. His object was to bring the House to a consideration in the abstract of the powers necessary to be vested in the general Government. It had been said, Let us know how the Govᵗ is to be modelled, and then we can determine what powers can be properly given to it. He thought the most eligible course was, first to determine on the necessary powers, and then so to modify the Governᵗ as that it might be justly & properly enabled to administer them. He feared if we proceeded to a consideration of the powers,

---

[1] The word " so " is omitted in the transcript.

whilst the vote of yesterday including an equality of the States in the 2ᵈ branch, remained in force, a reference to it, either mental or expressed, would mix itself with the merits of every question concerning the powers.—this motion was not seconded. [It was probably approved by several members, who either despaired of success, or were apprehensive that the attempt would inflame the jealousies of the smaller States.]

The 6ᵗʰ Resolⁿ in the Report of the Comᵉ of the Whole relating to the powers, which had been postponed in order to consider the 7 & 8ᵗʰ relating to the constitution of the Natˡ Legislature, was now resumed.

Mʳ SHERMAN observed that it would be difficult to draw the line between the powers of the Genˡ Legislatures, and those to be left with the States; that he did not like the definition contained in the Resolution, and proposed in [1] place of [2] the words " of [3] individual Legislation " line 4.[4] inclusive, to insert " to make laws binding on the people of the United States in all cases which may concern the common interests of the Union; but not to interfere with the Government of the individual States in any matters of internal police which respect the Govᵗ of such States only, and wherein the general welfare of the U. States is not concerned."

Mʳ WILSON 2ᵈᵉᵈ the amendment as better expressing the general principle.

Mʳ Govʳ MORRIS opposed it. The internal police, as it would be called & understood by the States ought to be infringed in many cases, as in the case of paper money & other tricks by which Citizens of other States may be affected.

Mʳ SHERMAN, in explanation of his idea read an enumeration of powers, including the power of levying taxes on trade, but not the power of *direct taxation*.

Mʳ Govʳ MORRIS remarked the omission, and inferred that for the deficiencies of taxes on consumption, it must have been the meaning of Mʳ Sherman, that the Genˡ Govᵗ should recur to quotas & requisitions, which are subversive of the idea of Govᵗ

Mʳ SHERMAN acknowledged that his enumeration did not include direct taxation. Some provision he supposed must be made for supplying the deficiency of other taxation, but he had not formed any.

On [5] Question of Mʳ Sherman's motion, it passed in the negative

---

[1] The word " its " is here inserted in the transcript.
[2] The word " of " is crossed out in the transcript and " to " is written above it.
[3] The word " of " is omitted in the transcript.
[4] The word and figure " line 4 " are crossed out in the transcript.
[5] The word " the " is here inserted in the transcript.

Mas. no. Con⁺ ay. N. J. no. P⁺ no. Del. no. M⁴ ay. V⁺ no.
N. C. no. S. C. no. Geo. no.¹

M⁺ BEDFORD moved that the 2⁴ member of Resolution 6.² be so
altered as to read "and moreover to legislate in all cases for the
general interests of the Union, and also in those to which the States
are separately ³ incompetent," or in which the harmony of the U.
States may be interrupted by the exercise of individual Legislation."

M⁺ Gov⁺ MORRIS 2ᵈˢ the motion

M⁺ RANDOLPH. This is a formidable idea indeed. It involves the
power of violating all the laws and constitutions of the States, and
of intermeddling with their police. The last member of the sentence
is also superfluous, being included in the first.

M⁺ BEDFORD. It is not more extensive or formidable than the
clause as it stands: *no State* being *separately* competent to legislate
for the *general interest* of the Union.

On ⁴ question for agreeing to M⁺ Bedford's motion, it passed in
the affirmative.

Mas. ay. Con⁺ no. N. J. ay. P⁺ ay. Del. ay. M⁴ ay. V⁺ no.
N. C. ay. S. C. no. Geo. no.⁵

On the sentence as amended, it passed in the affirmative.

Mas. ay. Con⁺ ay. N. J. ay. P⁺ ay. Del. ay. M⁴ ay. V⁺ ay.
N. C. ay. S. C. no. Geo. no.⁶

The next.⁷ " To negative all laws passed by the several States
contravening in the opinion of the Nat: Legislature the articles of
Union, or any treaties subsisting under the authority of y⁺ Union "⁸

M⁺ Gov⁺ MORRIS opposed this power as likely to be terrible to the
States, and not necessary, if sufficient Legislative authority should
be given to the Gen¹ Government.

M⁺ SHERMAN thought it unnecessary, as the Courts of the States
would not consider as valid any law contravening the Authority of
the Union, and which the legislature would wish to be negatived.

---

¹ In the transcript the vote reads: " Connecticut, Maryland, aye—2; Massachusetts, New Jersey, Pennsylvania, Delaware, Virginia, North Carolina, South
Carolina, Georgia, no—8."
² The words " the sixth Resolution " are substituted in the transcript for
" Resolution 6."
³ The word " severally " is substituted in the transcript for " separately."
⁴ The word " the " is here inserted in the transcript.
⁵ In the transcript the vote reads: " Massachusetts, New Jersey, Pennsylvania, Delaware, Maryland, North Carolina, aye—6; Connecticut, Virginia, South
Carolina, Georgia, no—4."
⁶ In the transcript the vote reads: " Massachusetts, Connecticut, New
Jersey, Pennsylvania, Delaware, Maryland, Virginia, North Carolina, aye—8;
South Carolina, Georgia, no—2."
⁷ The word " clause ' is here inserted in the transcript.
⁸ The phrase " was then taken up " is here inserted in the transcript.

M⁞ L. MARTIN considered the power as improper & inadmissible. Shall all the laws of the States be sent up to the Gen⁝ Legislature before they shall be permitted to operate?

M⁞ MADISON, considered the negative on the laws of the States as essential to the efficacy & security of the Gen⁝ Gov⁝ The necessity of a general Gov⁝ proceeds from the propensity of the States to pursue their particular interests in opposition to the general interest. This propensity will continue to disturb the system, unless effectually controuled. Nothing short of a negative on their laws will controul it. They can [1] pass laws which will accomplish their injurious objects before they can be repealed by the Gen⁝ Legisl⁝ or be [2] set aside by the National Tribunals. Confidence can not be put in the State Tribunals as guardians of the National authority and interests. In all the States these are more or less depend⁝ on the Legislatures. In Georgia they are appointed annually by the Legislature. In R. Island the Judges who refused to execute an unconstitutional law were displaced, and others substituted, by the Legislature who would be [3] willing instruments of the wicked & arbitrary plans of their masters. A power of negativing the improper laws of the States is at once the most mild & certain means of preserving the harmony of the system. Its utility is sufficiently displayed in the British System. Nothing could maintain the harmony & subordination of the various parts of the empire, but the prerogative by which the Crown, stifles in the birth every Act of every part tending to discord or encroachment. It is true the prerogative is sometimes misapplied thro' ignorance or a partiality to one particular part of y⁝ empire; but we have not the same reason to fear such misapplications in our System. As to the sending all laws up to the Nat⁝ Legisl: that might be rendered unnecessary by some emanation of the power into the States, so far at least, as to give a temporary effect to laws of immediate necessity.

M⁞ Gov⁝ MORRIS was more & more opposed to the negative. The proposal of it would disgust all the States. A law that ought to be negatived will be set aside in the Judiciary departm⁝ and if that security should fail; may be repealed by a Nation⁝ law.

M⁞ SHERMAN. Such a power involves a wrong principle, to wit, that a law of a State contrary to the articles of the Union, would if not negatived, be valid & operative.

M⁞ PINKNEY urged the necessity of the Negative.

---

[1] The word "will" is substituted in the transcript for "can."
[2] The word "be" is omitted in the transcript.
[3] The word "the" is here inserted in the transcript.

On the question for agreeing to the power of negativing laws of States &c " it passed in the negative.

Mas. ay. C͞t no. N. J. no. P͞a no. Del. no. M͞d no. V͞a ay. N. C. ay. S. C. no. Geo. no.[1]

M͞r LUTHER MARTIN moved the following resolution " that the Legislative acts of the U. S. made by virtue & in pursuance of the articles of Union, and all Treaties made & ratified under the authority of the U. S. shall be the supreme law of the respective States, as far as those acts or treaties shall relate to the said States, or their Citi͞zens and inhabitants—& that the Judiciaries of the several States shall be bound thereby in their decisions, any thing in the respective laws of the individual States to the contrary notwithstanding " which was agreed to nem: con:

9͞th Resol: " that Nat͞l Executive consist of a single person." 'Ag͞d to nem. con.[2]

[3] " To be chosen by the National Legisl: "[4]

M͞r GOVERN͞r MORRIS was pointedly ag͞st his being so chosen. He will be the mere creature of the Legisl: if appointed & impeachable by that body. He ought to be elected by the people at large, by the freeholders of the Country. That difficulties attend this mode, he admits. But they have been found superable in N. Y. & in Con͞t and would he believed be found so, in the case of an Executive for the U. States. If the people should elect, they will never fail to prefer some man of distinguished character, or services; some man, if he might so speak, of continental reputation.—If the Legislature elect, it will be the work of intrigue, of cabal, and of faction; it will be like the election of a pope by a conclave of cardinals; real merit will rarely be the title to the appointment. He moved to strike out " National Legislature " & insert " citizens of [5] U. S."

M͞r SHERMAN thought that the sense of the Nation would be better expressed by the Legislature, than by the people at large. The latter will never be sufficiently informed of characters, and besides will never give a majority of votes to any one man. They will generally vote for some man in their own State, and the largest State will have the best chance for the appointment. If the choice be

---

[1] In the transcript the vote reads: "Massachusetts, Virginia, North Carolina, aye—3; Connecticut, New Jersey, Pennsylvania, Delaware, Maryland, South Carolina, Georgia, no—7."

[2] In the transcript this sentence reads as follows: "The ninth Resolution being taken up, the first clause, 'That a National Executive be instituted, to consist of a single person,' was agreed to, nem. con."

[3] The words "The next clause" are here inserted in the transcript.

[4] The words "being considered" are here inserted in the transcript.

[5] The word "the" is here inserted in the transcript.

made by the Legisl⟨re⟩? A majority of voices may be made necessary to constitute an election.

M⟨r⟩ WILSON. two arguments have been urged ag⟨st⟩ an election of the Executive Magistrate by the people. 1 [1] the example of Poland where an Election of the supreme Magistrate is attended with the most dangerous commotions.   The cases he observed were totally dissimilar.   The Polish nobles have resources & dependents which enable them to appear in force, and to threaten the Republic as well as each other.   In the next place the electors all assemble in [2] one place: which would not be the case with us.   The 2⟨d⟩ arg⟨t⟩ is that a *majority* [3] of the people would never concur.   It might be answered that the concurrence of a majority of [4] people is not a necessary principle of election, nor required as such in any of the States.   But allowing the objection all its force, it may be obviated by the expedient used in Mas⟨ts⟩ where the Legislature by [5] majority of voices, decide in case a majority of people do not concur in favor of one of the candidates.   This would restrain the choice to a good nomination at least, and prevent in a great degree intrigue & cabal.   A particular objection with him ag⟨st⟩ an absolute election by the Legisl⟨re⟩? was that the Exec: in that case would be too dependent to stand the mediator between the intrigues & sinister views of the Representatives and the general liberties & interests of the people.

M⟨r⟩ PINKNEY did not expect this question would again have been brought forward; An Election by the people being liable to the most obvious & striking objections.   They will be led by a few active & designing men.   The most populous States by combining in favor of the same individual will be able to carry their points.   The Nat⟨l⟩ Legislature being most immediately interested in the laws made by themselves, will be most attentive to the choice of a fit man to carry them properly into execution.

M⟨r⟩ Gov⟨r⟩ MORRIS.   It is said that in case of an election by the people the populous States will combine & elect whom they please. Just the reverse.   The people of such States cannot combine.   If their be any combination it must be among their representatives in the Legislature.   It is said the people will be led by a few designing men.   This might happen in a small district.   It can never happen throughout the continent.   In the election of a Gov⟨r⟩ of N. York, it sometimes is the case in particular spots, that the activity & intrigues

---

[1] The figure " 1 " is changed to " The first is " in the transcript.
[2] The word " at " is substituted in the transcript for " in."
[3] The transcript does not italicize the word " *majority*."
[4] The word " the " is here inserted in the transcript.
[5] The word " a " is here inserted in the transcript.

of little partizans are successful, but the general voice of the State
is never influenced by such artifices. It is said the multitude will
be uninformed. It is true they would be uninformed of what passed
in the Legislative Conclave, if the election were to be made there;
but they will not be uninformed of those great & illustrious characters which have merited their esteem & confidence. If the Executive be chosen by the Nat! Legislature, he will not be independent
on [1] it; and if not independent, usurpation & tyranny on the
part of the Legislature will be the consequence. This was the case
in England in the last Century. It has been the case in Holland,
where their Senates have engrossed all power. It has been the case
every where. He was surprised that an election by the people at
large should ever have been likened to the polish election of the
first Magistrate. An election by the Legislature will bear a real likeness to the election by the Diet of Poland. The great must be the
electors in both cases, and the corruption & cabal wch are known to
characterise the one would soon find their way into the other. Appointments made by numerous bodies, are always worse than those
made by single responsible individuals, or by the people at large.

Col. MASON. It is curious to remark the different language held
at different times. At one moment we are told that the Legislature is entitled to thorough confidence, and to indifinite power. At
another, that it will be governed by intrigue & corruption, and cannot be trusted at all. But not to dwell on this inconsistency he
would observe that a Government which is to last ought at least to be
practicable. Would this be the case if the proposed election should
be left to the people at large. He conceived it would be as un-
natural to refer the choice of a proper character for chief Magistrate to the people, as it would, to refer a trial of colours to a
blind man. The extent of the Country renders it impossible that
the people can have the requisite capacity to judge of the respective
pretensions of the Candidates.

Mr WILSON. could not see the contrariety stated [by Col. Mason]
The Legisl^{re} might deserve confidence in some respects, and distrust
in others. In acts which were to affect them & y^r Constituents precisely alike confidence was due. In others jealousy was warranted.
The appointment to great offices, where the Legisl^{re} might feel many
motives, not common to the public confidence was surely misplaced.
This branch of business it was notorious was [2] most corruptly managed of any that had been committed to legislative bodies.

---

[1] In the transcript the word "on" is crossed out and "of" is written
above it.
[2] The word "the" is here inserted in the transcript.

M! WILLIAMSON, conceived that there was the same difference between an election in this case, by the people and by the legisla. ture, as between an app! by lot, and by choice. There are at present distinguished characters, who are known perhaps to almost every man. This will not always be the case. The people will be sure to vote for some man in their own State, and the largest State will be sure to succeed. This will not be Virg! however. Her slaves will have no suffrage. As the Salary of the Executive will be fixed, and he will not be eligible a 2ᵈ time, there will not be such a dependence on the Legislature as has been imagined.

[1] Question on an election by the people instead of the Legislature; which [2] passed in the negative.

Mas. no. Con! no. N. J. no. P! ay. Del. no. Mᵈ no. V! no. N. C. no. S. C. no. Geo. no.[3]

M! L. MARTIN moved that the Executive be chosen [1]by Electors appointed by the several Legislatures of the individual States.

M! BROOME 2ᵈˢ On the Question, it passed in the negative.

Mas. no. Con! no. N. J. no. P! no. Del. ay. Mᵈ ay. V! no. N. C. no. S. C. no. Geo. no.[4]

On the question on the words " to be chosen by the Nation! Legislature " it passed unanimously in the affirmative.

" For the term of seven years "—postponed nem. con. on motion of M! Houston & [5] Gov. Morris.

" to carry into execution the nation! laws "—agreed to nem. con.

" to appoint to offices in cases not otherwise provided for."— agreed to nem. con.

" to be ineligible a second time "—M! HOUSTON moved to strike out this clause.

M! SHERMAN 2ᵈˢ the motion.

M! Gov! MORRIS espoused the motion. The ineligibility proposed by the clause as it stood tended to destroy the great motive to good behavior, the hope of being rewarded by a re-appointment. It was saying to him, make hay while the sun shines.

---

[1] The words "On the" are here inserted in the transcript.
[2] The word "which" is crossed out and "it" is written above it in the transcript.
[3] In the transcript the vote reads: "Pennsylvania, aye—1; Massachusetts, Connecticut, New Jersey, Delaware, Maryland, Virginia, North Carolina, South Carolina, Georgia, no—9."
[4] In the transcript the vote reads: "Delaware, Maryland, aye—2; Massachusetts, Connecticut, New Jersey, Pennsylvania, Virginia, North Carolina, South Carolina, Georgia, no—8."
[5] The word "Mr." is here inserted in the transcript.

On the question for striking out as moved by M: Houston, it passed in the affirmative

Mas. ay. Con: ay. N. J. ay. P: ay. Del. no. M: ay. V: no. N. C. no. S. C. no. Geo. ay.[1]

[2] "For the term of 7 years"[3] resumed

M: Broom was for a shorter term since the Executive Magistrate was now to be re-eligible. Had he remained ineligible a 2: time, he should have preferred a longer term.

Doc: M:Clurg moved * to strike out 7 years, and insert "during good behavior." By striking out the words declaring him not re-eligible, he was put into a situation that would keep him dependent for ever on the Legislature; and he conceived the independence of the Executive to be equally essential with that of the Judiciary department.

M: Gov: Morris 2:ded the motion. He expressed great pleasure in hearing it. This was the way to get a good Government. His fear that so valuable an ingredient would not be attained had led him to take the part he had done. He was indifferent how the Executive should be chosen, provided he held his place by this tenure.

M: Broome highly approved the motion. It obviated all his difficulties

M: Sherman considered such a tenure as by no means safe or admissible. As the Executive Magistrate is now re-eligible, he will be on good behavior as far as will be necessary. If he behaves well he will be continued; if otherwise, displaced, on a succeeding election.

M: Madison † If it be essential to the preservation of liberty that the Legisl: Execut: & Judiciary powers be separate, it is essential to a maintenance of the separation, that they should be independent of each other. The Executive could not be independent of the Legislure, if dependent on the pleasure of that branch for a re-appointment. Why was it determined that the Judges should not hold their places by such a tenure? Because they might be tempted

* The probable object of this motion was merely to enforce the argument against the re-eligibility of the Executive Magistrate, by holding out a tenure during good behaviour as the alternative for keeping him independent of the Legislature.

† The view here taken of the subject was meant to aid in parrying the animadversions likely to fall on the motion of D: M:Clurg, for whom J. M. had a particular regard. The Doc: though possessing talents of the highest order, was modest & unaccustomed to exert them in public debate.

---

[1] In the transcript the vote reads: "Massachusetts, Connecticut, New Jersey, Pennsylvania, Maryland, Georgia, aye—6; Delaware, Virginia, North Carolina, South Carolina, no—4."

[2] The words "The clause" are here inserted in the transcript.

[3] The word "being" is here inserted in the transcript.

to cultivate the Legislature, by an undue complaisance, and thus render the Legislature the virtual expositor, as well [1] the maker of the laws. In like manner a dependence of the Executive on the Legislature, would render it the Executor as well as the maker of laws; & then according to the observation of Montesquieu, tyrannical laws may be made that they may be executed in a tyrannical manner. There was an analogy between the Executive & Judiciary departments in several respects. The latter executed the laws in certain cases as the former did in others. The former expounded & applied them for certain purposes, as the latter did for others. The difference between them seemed to consist chiefly in two circumstances— 1.[2] the collective interest & security were much more in the power belonging to the Executive than to the Judiciary department. 2.[2] in the administration of the former much greater latitude is left to opinion and discretion than in the administration of the latter. But if the 2^d consideration proves that it will be more difficult to establish a rule sufficiently precise for trying the Execut: than the Judges, & forms an objection to the same tenure of office, both considerations prove that it might be more dangerous to suffer a union between the Executive & Legisl: powers, than between the Judiciary & Legislative powers. He conceived it to be absolutely necessary to a well constituted Republic that the two first sh^d be kept distinct & independent of each other. Whether the plan proposed by the motion was a proper one was another question, as it depended on the practicability of instituting a tribunal for impeachm^{ts} as certain & as adequate in the one case as in the other. On the other hand, respect for the mover entitled his proposition to a fair hearing & discussion, until a less objectionable expedient should be applied for guarding agst a dangerous union of the Legislative & Executive departments.

Col. MASON. This motion was made some time ago, & negatived by a very large majority. He trusted that it w^d be again negatived. It w^d be impossible to define the misbehaviour in such a manner as to subject it to a proper trial; and perhaps still more impossible to compel so high an offender holding his office by such a tenure to submit to a trial. He considered an Executive during good behavior as a softer name only for an Executive for life. And that the next would be an easy step to hereditary Monarchy. If the motion should finally succeed, he might himself live to see such a Revolu-

---

[1] The word "as" is here inserted in the transcript.
[2] The figures "1" and "2" are changed to "first" and "secondly" in the transcript.

tion. If he did not it was probable his children or grand children would. He trusted there were few men in that House who wished for it. No state he was sure had so far revolted from Republican principles as to have the least bias in its favor.

M: MADISON, was not apprehensive of being thought to favor any step towards monarchy. The real object with him was to prevent its introduction. Experience had proved a tendency in our governments to throw all power into the Legislative vortex. The Executives of the States are in general little more than Cyphers; the legislatures omnipotent. If no effectual check be devised for restraining the instability & encroachments of the latter, a revolution of some kind or other would be inevitable. The preservation of Republican Gov! therefore required some expedient for the purpose, but required evidently at the same time that in devising it, the genuine principles of that form should be kept in view.

M: Gov! MORRIS was as little a friend to monarchy as any gentleman. He concurred in the opinion that the way to keep out monarchical Gov! was to establish such a Repub. Gov! as w! make the people happy and prevent a desire of change.

Doc! McCLURG was not so much afraid of the shadow of monarchy as to be unwilling to approach it; nor so wedded to Republican Gov! as not to be sensible of the tyrannies that had been & may be exercised under that form. It was an essential object with him to make the Executive independent of the Legislature; and the only mode left for effecting it, after the vote destroying his ineligibility a second time, was to appoint him during good behavior.

On the question for inserting " during good behavior " in place of 7 years [with a re-eligibility] it passed in the negative.

Mas. no. C! no. N. J. ay. P: ay. Del. ay. M! no. V: ay. N. C. no. S. C. no. Geo. no.* [1]

* Transfer the above notes hither.[2]

[* This vote is not [3] be considered as any certain index of opinion, as a number in the affirmative probably had it chiefly in view to alarm those attached to a dependence of the Executive on the Legislature, & thereby facilitate some final arrangement of a contrary tendency. The avowed friends of an Executive, "during good behaviour" were not more than three or four, nor is it certain they would finally [4] have adhered to such a tenure. An independence of the three great departments of each other, as far as possible, and the responsibility of all to the will of the community seemed to be generally admitted as the true basis of a well constructed government.]

---

[1] In the transcript the vote reads: "New Jersey, Pennsylvania, Delaware, Virginia, aye—4; Massachusetts, Connecticut, Maryland, North Carolina, South Carolina, Georgia, no—6.* "
[2] Madison's direction concerning the footnotes is omitted in the transcript.
[3] The word "to" is here inserted in the transcript.
[4] The word "finally" is omitted in the transcript.

On the motion " to strike out seven years " it passed in the negative.

Mas. ay. C. no. N. J. no. P. ay. Del. ay. M. no. V. no. N. C. ay. S. C. no. Geo. no.* [1]

It was now unanimously agreed that the vote which had struck out the words " to be ineligible a second time " should be reconsidered to-morrow.

Adj.

WEDNESDAY JULY 18. IN CONVENTION

On motion of M. L. Martin to fix tomorrow for reconsidering the vote concerning " eligibility of Exec. [2] a 2. time " it passed in the affirmative.

Mas. ay. Con. ay. N. J. absent. P. ay. Del. ay. M. ay. V. ay. N. C. ay. S. C. ay. Geo. absent. [3]

The residue of Resol. 9. [4] concerning the Executive was postp. till tomorrow.

Resol. 10. [5] that Executive sh. have a right to negative legislative acts not afterwards passed by ⅔ of each branch. [6] Agreed to nem. con.

Resol. 11. [7] " that a Nat. Judiciary [8] be estab. to consist of one supreme tribunal." ag. to nem. con.

[9] " The Judges of which to be appoint. by the 2. branch of the Nat. Legislature."

M. GHORUM, w. prefer an appointment by the 2. branch to an appointm. by the whole Legislature; but he thought even that branch

[* There was no debate on this motion, the apparent object of many in the affirmative was to secure the re-eligibility by shortening the term, and of many in the negative to embarrass the plan of referring the appointment & dependence of the Executive to the Legislature.]

---

[1] In the transcript the vote reads: " Massachusetts, Pennsylvania, Delaware, North Carolina, aye—4; Connecticut, New Jersey, Maryland, Virginia, South Carolina, Georgia, no—6.* "

[2] The words " eligibility of Executive " are changed to " the ineligibility of the Executive " in the transcript.

[3] In the transcript the vote reads: " Massachusetts, Connecticut, Pennsylvania, Delaware, Maryland, Virginia, North Carolina, South Carolina, aye—8; New Jersey, Georgia, absent."

[4] The words " the ninth Resolution " are substituted in the transcript for " Resol. 9."

[5] The words " The tenth Resolution " are substituted in the transcript for " Resol. 10."

[6] The word " was " is here inserted in the transcript.

[7] The words " The Eleventh Resolution " are substituted in the transcript for " Resol. 11."

[8] The word " shall " is here inserted in the transcript.

[9] The words " On the clause " are here inserted in the transcript.

too numerous, and too little personally responsible, to ensure a good choice. He suggested that the Judges be appointed by the Execu.^{ve} with the advice & consent of the 2^d branch, in the mode prescribed by the constitution of Mas^{ts}. This mode had been long practised in that country, & was found to answer perfectly well.

Mr WILSON, still w^d [1] prefer an appointm^t by the Executive; but if that could not be attained, w^d prefer in the next place, the mode suggested by Mr Ghorum. He thought it his duty however to move in the first instance " that the Judges be appointed by the Executive." Mr Govr MORRIS 2^{ded} the motion.

Mr L. MARTIN was strenuous for an app^t by the 2^d branch. Being taken from all the States it w^d be best informed of characters & most capable of making a fit choice.

Mr SHERMAN concurred in the observations of Mr Martin, adding that the Judges ought to be diffused, which would be more likely to be attended to by the 2^d branch, than by the Executive.

Mr MASON. The mode of appointing the Judges may depend in some degree on the mode of trying impeachments of the Executive. If the Judges were to form a tribunal for that purpose, they surely ought not to be appointed by the Executive. There were insuperable objections besides agst referring the appointment to the Executive. He mentioned as one, that as the Seat of Gov^t must be in some one State, and [2] the Executive would remain in office for a considerable time, for 4, 5, or 6 years at least, he would insensibly form local & personal attachments within the particular State that would deprive equal merit elsewhere, of an equal chance of promotion.

Mr GHORUM. As the Executive will be responsible in point of character at least, for a judicious and faithful discharge of his trust, he will be careful to look through all the States for proper characters. The Senators will be as likely to form their attachments at the seat of Gov^t where they reside, as the Executive. If they can not get the man of the particular State to which they may respectively belong, they will be indifferent to the rest. Public bodies feel no personal responsibly, and give full play to intrigue & cabal. Rh. Island is a full illustration of the insensibility to character, produced by a participation of numbers, in dishonorable measures, and of the length to which a public body may carry wickedness & cabal.

Mr Govr MORRIS supposed it would be improper for an impeachm^t

---

[1] The words " still w^d " are transposed to read " would still " in the transcript.

[2] The word " as " is here inserted in the transcript.

of the Executive to be tried before the Judges. The latter would in such case be drawn into intrigues with the Legislature and an impartial trial would be frustrated. As they w⁴ be much about the Seat of Gov⁴ they might even be previously consulted & arrangements might be made for a prosecution of the Executive. He thought therefore that no argument could be drawn from the probability of such a plan of impeachments ag⁵ᵗ the motion before the House.

M⁵ MADISON, suggested that the Judges might be appointed by the Executive with the concurrence of ⅓ at least, of the 2ᵈ branch. This would unite the advantage of responsibility in the Executive with the security afforded in the 2ᵈ branch ag⁵ᵗ any incautious or corrupt nomination by the Executive.

M⁵ SHERMAN, was clearly for an election by the Senate. It would be composed of men nearly equal to the Executive, and would of course have on the whole more wisdom. They would bring into their deliberations a more diffusive knowledge of characters. It would be less easy for candidates to intrigue with them, than with the Executive Magistrate. For these reasons he thought there would be a better security for a proper choice in the Senate than in the Executive.

M⁵ RANDOLPH. It is true that when the app⁴ of the Judges was vested in the 2ᵈ branch an equality of votes had not been given to it. Yet he had rather leave the appointm⁴ there than give it to the Executive. He thought the advantage of personal responsibility might be gained in the Senate by requiring the respective votes of the members to be entered on the Journal. He thought too that the hope of receiving app⁴ˢ would be more diffusive if they depended on the Senate, the members of which w⁴ be diffusively known, than if they depended on a single man who could not be personally known to a very great extent; and consequently that opposition to the System, would be so far weakened.

M⁵ BEDFORD thought there were solid reasons ag⁵ᵗ leaving the appointment to the Executive. He must trust more to information than the Senate. It would put it in his power to gain over the larger States, by gratifying them with a preference of their Citizens. The responsibility of the Executive so much talked of was chimerical. He could not be punished for mistakes.

M⁵ GHORUM remarked that the Senate could have no better information than the Executive. They must like him, trust to information from the members belonging to the particular State where the Candidates resided. The Executive would certainly be more answerable for a good appointment, as the whole blame of a bad one would fall on him alone. He did not mean that he would be answerable under any other penalty than that of public censure, which with honorable minds was a sufficient one.

On the question for referring the appointment of the Judges to the Executive, instead of the 2ᵈ branch

Mas. ay. Conᵗ no. Pᵃ ay. Del. no. Mᵈ no. Vᵃ no. N. C. no. S. C. no.—Geo. absent.[1]

Mʳ Ghorum moved " that the Judges be nominated and appointed by the Executive, by & with the advice & consent of the 2ᵈ branch & every such nomination shall be made at least   days prior to such appointment." This mode he said had been ratified by the experience of 140 years in Massachussᵗˢ If the appᵗ should be left to either branch of the Legislature, it will be a mere piece of jobbing.

Mʳ Govʳ Morris 2ᵈᵉᵈ & supported the motion.

Mʳ Sherman thought it less objectionable than an absolute appointment by the Executive; but disliked it as too much fettering the Senate.

[2] Question on Mʳ Ghorum's motion

Mas. ay. Conᵗ no. Pᵃ ay. Del. no. Mᵈ ay. Vᵃ ay. N. C. no. S. C. no. Geo. absent.[3]

Mʳ Madison moved that the Judges should be nominated by the Executive, & such nomination should become an appointment if not disagreed to within   days by ⅔ of the 2ᵈ branch. Mʳ Govʳ Morris 2ᵈᵉᵈ the motion. By common consent the consideration of it was postponed till tomorrow.

" To hold their offices during good behavior " & " to receive fixed salaries " agreed to nem: con:

" In which [salaries of Judges] no increase or diminution shall be made so as to affect the persons at the time in office."[4]

Mʳ Govʳ Morris moved to strike out " or increase." He thought the Legislature ought to be at liberty to increase salaries as circumstances might require, and that this would not create any improper dependence in the Judges.

Docʳ Franklin was in favor of the motion. Money may not

[1] In the transcript the vote reads: " Massachusetts, Pennsylvania, aye—2; Connecticut, Delaware, Maryland, Virginia, North Carolina, South Carolina, no —6; Georgia, absent."

[2] The words " On the " are here inserted in the transcript.

[3] In the transcript the vote reads: " Massachusetts, Pennsylvania, Maryland, Virginia, aye—4; Connecticut, Delaware, North Carolina, South Carolina, no—4; Georgia, absent."

[4] The phrase " actually in office at the time " is substituted in the transcript for " at the time in office."

only become plentier, but the business of the department may increase as the Country becomes more populous.

Mᴿ MADISON. The dependence will be less if the *increase alone* should be permitted, but it will be improper even so far to permit a dependence Whenever an increase is wished by the Judges, or may be in agitation in the legislature, an undue complaisance in the former may be felt towards the latter. If at such a crisis there should be in Court suits, to which leading members of the Legislature may be parties, the Judges will be in a situation which ought not to [1] suffered, if it can be prevented. The variations in the value of money, may be guarded agˢᵗ by taking for a standard wheat or some other thing of permanent value. The increase of business will be provided for by an increase of the number who are to do it. An increase of salaries may be easily so contrived as not to affect persons in office.

Mᴿ Govᴿ MORRIS. The value of money may not only alter but the State of Society may alter. In this event the same quantity of wheat, the same value would not be the same compensation. The Amount of salaries must always be regulated by the manners & the style of living in a Country. The increase of business can not, be provided for in the supreme tribunal in the way that has been mentioned. All the business of a certain description whether more or less must be done in that single tribunal. Additional labor alone in the Judges can provide for additional business. Additional compensation therefore ought not to be prohibited.

On the question for striking out " or increase "

Mas. ay. Conᵗ ay. Pᵃ ay. Del. ay. Mᵈ ay. Vᵃ no. N. C. no. S. C. ay. Geo. absent.[2]

The whole clause as amended was then agreed to nem: con:

12. Resol: [3] " that [4] Natᴸ Legislature be empowered to appoint inferior tribunals " [5]

Mᴿ BUTLER could see no necessity for such tribunals. The State Tribunals might do the business.

Mᴿ L. MARTIN concurred. They will create jealousies & oppositions in the State tribunals, with the jurisdiction of which they will interfere.

---

[1] The word " be " is here inserted in the transcript.
[2] In the transcript the vote reads: " Massachusetts, Connecticut, Pennsylvania, Delaware, Maryland, South Carolina, aye—6; Virginia, North Carolina, no—2; Georgia, absent."
[3] The words " The twelfth Resolution " are substituted in the transcript for " 12. Resol."
[4] The word " the " is here inserted in the transcript.
[5] The words " being taken up " are here inserted in the transcript.

M⸴ GHORUM. There are in the States already federal Courts with jurisdiction for trial of piracies &c. committed on the Seas. No complaints have been made by the States or the Courts of the States. Inferior tribunals are essential to render the authority of the Nat! Legislature effectual

M⸴ RANDOLPH observed that the Courts of the States can not be trusted with the administration of the National laws. The objects of jurisdiction are such as will often place the General & local policy at variance.

M⸴ Gov⸴ MORRIS urged also the necessity of such a provision

M⸴ SHERMAN was willing to give the power to the Legislature but wished them to make use of the State Tribunals whenever it could be done, with safety to the general interest.

Col. MASON thought many circumstances might arise not now to be foreseen, which might render such a power absolutely necessary.

On[1] question for agreeing to 12. Resol:[2] empowering the National Legislature to appoint " inferior tribunals."[3] Ag⸴ to nem. con.

[4] 13. Resol: " Impeachments of national officers " were struck out " on motion for the purpose. " The jurisdiction of Nat! Judiciary." Several criticisms having been made on the definition; it was proposed by M⸴ Madison so to alter[5] as to read thus—" that the jurisdiction shall extend to all cases arising under the Nat! laws: And to such other questions as may involve the Nat! peace & harmony," which was agreed to nem. con.

Resol. 14.[6] providing for the admission of new States[7] Agreed to nem. con.

Resol. 15.[8] that provision ought to be made for the continuance of Cong⸴ &c. & for the completion of their engagements.[9]

M⸴ Gov⸴ MORRIS thought the assumption of their engagements might as well be omitted; and that Cong⸴ ought not to be continued till all the States should adopt the reform; since it may become ex-

---

[1] The word " the " is here inserted in the transcript.

[2] The words " the twelfth Resolution " are substituted in the transcript for " 12. Resol."

[3] The words " it was " are here inserted in the transcript.

[4] This paragraph is changed in the transcript to read as follows: " The clause of ' Impeachments of national officers,' was struck out, on motion for the purpose. The thirteenth Resolution, ' The jurisdiction of the National Judiciary, &c.' being then taken up, several . . ."

[5] The word " it " is here inserted in the transcript.

[6] The words " The fourteenth Resolution " are substituted in the transcript for " Resol. 14."

[7] The word " was " is here inserted in the transcript.

[8] The words " The fifteenth Resolution " are substituted in the transcript for " Resol. 15."

[9] The words " being considered " are here inserted in the transcript.

pedient to give effect to it whenever a certain number of States shall adopt it.

M! MADISON the clause can mean nothing more than that provision ought to be made for preventing an interregnum; which must exist in the interval between the adoption of the New Gov! and the commencement of its operation, if the old Gov! should cease on the first of these events.

M! WILSON did not entirely approve of the manner in which the clause relating to the engagements of Cong! was expressed; but he thought some provision on the subject would be proper in order to prevent any suspicion that the obligations of the Confederacy might be dissolved along with the Govern! under which they were contracted.

On the question on the 1st part—relating to [1] continuance of Cong!:"

Mas. no. Con! no. P[a] no. Del. no. M[d] no. V[a] ay. N. C. ay. S. C.* ay. Geo. no.[2]

The 2[d] part as to [1] completion of their engagements,[3] disag[d] to. nem. con.

Resol. 16.[4] " That a Republican Constitution & its. existing laws ought to be guarantied to each State by the U. States."[5]

M! Gov! MORRIS—thought the Resol: very objectionable. He should be very unwilling that such laws as exist in R. Island should be guaranteid.

M! WILSON. The object is merely to secure the States ag!t dangerous commotions, insurrections and rebellions.

Col. MASON. If the Gen! Gov! should have no right to suppress rebellions ag!t particular States, it will be in a bad situation indeed. As Rebellions ag!t itself originate in & ag!t individual States, it must remain a passive Spectator of its own subversion.

M! RANDOLPH. The Resol[n] has 2. objects. 1.[6] to secure Republican Government. 2.[6] to suppress domestic commotions. He urged the necessity of both these provisions.

* In the printed Journal, S. Carolina—no.

---

[1] The word "the" is here inserted in the transcript.
[2] In the transcript the vote reads: "Virginia, North Carolina, South Carolina,* aye—3; Massachusetts, Connecticut, Pennsylvania, Delaware, Maryland, Georgia, no—6."
[3] The word "was" is here inserted in the transcript.
[4] The words "The sixteenth Resolution" are substituted in the transcript for "Resol. 16."
[5] The words "being considered" are here added in the transcript.
[6] The figures "1" and "2" are changed to "first" and "secondly" in the transcript.

Mᵣ MADISON moved to substitute "that the Constitutional authority of the States shall be guarantied to them respectively agˢᵗ domestic as well as foreign violence."

Docᵗ MᶜCLURG seconded the motion.

Mʳ HOUSTON was afraid of perpetuating the existing Constitutions of the States. That of Georgia was a very bad one, and he hoped would be revised & amended. It may also be difficult for the Genˡ Govᵗ to decide between contending parties each of which claim the sanction of the Constitution.

Mʳ L. MARTIN was for leaving the States to suppress Rebellions themselves.

Mʳ GHORUM thought it strange that a Rebellion should be known to exist in the Empire, and the Genˡ Govᵗ shᵈ be restrained from interposing to subdue it. At this rate an enterprising Citizen might erect the standard of Monarchy in a particular State, might gather together partizans from all quarters, might extend his views from State to State, and threaten to establish a tyranny over the whole & the Genˡ Govᵗ be compelled to remain an inactive witness of its own destruction. With regard to different parties in a State; as long as they confine their disputes to words, they will be harmless to the Genˡ Govᵗ & to each other. If they appeal to the sword, it will then be necessary for the Genˡ Govᵗ, however difficult it may be to decide on the merits of their contest, to interpose & put an end to it.

Mʳ CARROL. Some such provision is essential. Every State ought to wish for it. It has been doubted whether it is a casus federis at present. And no room ought to be left for such a doubt hereafter.

Mʳ RANDOLPH moved to add as [1] amendᵗ to the motion; "and that no State be at liberty to form any other than a Republican Govᵗ Mʳ MADISON seconded the motion

Mʳ RUTLIDGE thought it unnecessary to insert any guarantee. No doubt could be entertained but that Congˢ had the authority if they had the means to co-operate with any State in subduing a rebellion. It was & would be involved in the nature of the thing.

Mʳ WILSON moved as a better expression of the idea, "that a Republican form of Governmᵗ shall be guarantied to each State & that each State shall be protected agˢᵗ foreign & domestic violence.

This seeming to be well received, Mʳ MADISON & Mʳ RANDOLPH withdrew their propositions & on the Question for agreeing to Mʳ Wilson's motion, it passed nem. con.

Adjᵈ

---

[1] The word "an" is here inserted in the transcript.

THURSDAY. JULY. 19. IN CONVENTION.

On reconsideration of the vote rendering the Executive re-eligible a 2ᵈ time, Mʳ MARTIN moved to reinstate the words, " to be ineligible a 2ᵈ time."

Mʳ GOVERNEUR MORRIS. It is necessary to take into one view all that relates to the establishment of the Executive; on the due formation of which must depend the efficacy & utility of the Union among the present and future States. It has been a maxim in Political Science that Republican Government is not adapted to a large extent of Country, because the energy of the Executive Magistracy can not reach the extreme parts of it. Our Country is an extensive one. We must either then renounce the blessings of the Union, or provide an Executive with sufficient vigor to pervade every part of it. This subject was of so much importance that he hoped to be indulged in an extensive view of it. One great object of the Executive is to controul the Legislature. The Legislature will continually seek to aggrandize & perpetuate themselves; and will sieze those critical moments produced by war, invasion or convulsion for that purpose. It is necessary then that the Executive Magistrate should be the guardian of the people, even of the lower classes, agˢᵗ Legislative tyranny, against the Great & the wealthy who in the course of things will necessarily compose the Legislative body. Wealth tends to corrupt the mind &¹ to nourish its love of power, and to stimulate it to oppression. History proves this to be the spirit of the opulent. The check provided in the 2ᵈ branch was not meant as a check on Legislative usurpations of power, but on the abuse of lawful powers, on the propensity in ² the 1ˢᵗ branch to legislate too much to run into projects of paper money & similar expedients. It is no check on Legislative tyranny. On the contrary it may favor it, and if the 1ˢᵗ branch can be seduced may find the means of success. The Executive therefore ought to be so constituted as to be the great protector of the Mass of the people.—It is the duty of the Executive to appoint the officers & to command the forces of the Republic: to appoint 1.³ ministerial officers for the administration of public affairs. 2.³ officers for the dispensation of Justice. Who will be the best Judges whether these appointments be well made? The people at large, who will know, will see, will feel the effects of them. Again who can judge

---

¹ The word " and " is crossed out in the transcript.
² The word " of " is substituted in the transcript for " in."
³ The figures " 1 " and " 2 " are changed to " first " and " secondly " in the transcript.

so well of the discharge of military duties for the protection &
security of the people, as the people themselves who are to be protected & secured?—He finds too that the Executive is not to be
re-eligible. What effect will this have? 1.[1] it will destroy the great
incitement to merit public esteem by taking away the hope of being
rewarded with a reappointment. It may give a dangerous turn to
one of the strongest passions in the human breast. The love of fame
is the great spring to noble & illustrious actions. Shut the Civil road
to Glory & he may be compelled to seek it by the sword. 2.[2] It will
tempt him to make the most of the short space of time allotted him,
to accumulate wealth and provide for his friends. 3.[3] It will produce violations of the very constitution it is meant to secure. In
moments of pressing danger the tried abilities and established character of a favorite Magistrate will prevail over respect for the forms
of the Constitution. The Executive is also to be impeachable. This
is a dangerous part of the plan. It will hold him in such dependence that he will be no check on the Legislature, will not be a firm
guardian of the people and of the public interest. He will be the
tool of a faction, of some leading demagogue in the Legislature.
These then are the faults of the Executive establishment as now proposed. Can no better establishm! be devised? If he is to be the
Guardian of the people let him be appointed by the people? If he
is to be a check on the Legislature let him not be impeachable. Let
him be of short duration, that he may with propriety be re-eligible.
It has been said that the candidates for this office will not be known
to the people. If they be known to the Legislature, they must have
such a notoriety and eminence of Character, that they cannot possibly
be unknown to the people at large. It cannot be possible that a
man shall have sufficiently distinguished himself to merit this high
trust without having his character proclaimed by fame throughout
the Empire. As to the danger from an unimpeachable magistrate he
could not regard it as formidable. There must be certain great
officers of State; a minister of finance, of war, of foreign affairs &c.
These he presumes will exercise their functions in subordination to
the Executive, and will be amenable by impeachment to the public
Justice. Without these ministers the Executive can do nothing of
consequence. He suggested a biennial election of the Executive at
the time of electing the 1st branch, and the Executive to hold over,
so as to prevent any interregnum in the administration. An election

---

[1] The figure " 1 " is changed to " In the first place " in the transcript.
[2] The figure " 2 " is changed to " In the second place " in the transcript.
[3] The figure " 3 " is changed to " In the third place " in the transcript.

by the people at large throughout so great an extent of country could not be influenced, by those little combinations and those momentary lies which often decide popular elections within a narrow sphere. It will probably, be objected that the election will be influenced by the members of the Legislature; particularly of the 1ˢᵗ branch, and that it will be nearly the same thing with an election by the Legislature itself. It could not be denied that such an influence would exist. But it might be answered that as the Legislature or the candidates for it would be divided, the enmity of one part would counteract the friendship of another: that if the administration of the Executive were good, it would be unpopular to oppose his reelection, if bad it ought to be opposed & a reappointmᵗ prevented; and lastly that in every view this indirect dependence on the favor of the Legislature could not be so mischievous as a direct dependence for his appointment. He saw no alternative for making the Executive independent of the Legislature but either to give him his office for life, or make him eligible by the people—Again, it might be objected that two years would be too short a duration. But he believes that as long as he should behave himself well, he would be continued in his place. The extent of the Country would secure his re-election agˢᵗ the factions & discontents of particular States. It deserved consideration also that such an ingredient in the plan would render it extremely palatable to the people. These were the general ideas which occurred to him on the subject, and which led him to wish & move that the whole constitution of the Executive might undergo reconsideration.

Mʳ Randolph urged the motion of Mʳ. L. Martin for restoring the words making the Executive ineligible a 2ᵈ time. If he ought to be independent, he should not be left under a temptation to court a re-appointment. If he should be re-appointable by the Legislature, he will be no check on it. His revisionary power will be of no avail. He had always thought & contended as he still did that the danger apprehended by the little States was chimerical; but those who thought otherwise ought to be peculiarly anxious for the motion. If the Executive be appointed, as has been determined, by the Legislature, he will probably be appointed either by joint ballot of both houses, or be nominated by the 1ˢᵗ and appointed by the 2ᵈ branch. In either case the large States will preponderate. If he is to court the same influence for his re-appointment, will he not make his revisionary power, and all the other functions of his administration, subservient to the views of the large States. Besides, is there not great reason to apprehend that in case he should be re-eligible, a false complaisance in the Legislature might lead them to continue an unfit man in office in preference to a fit one. It has been said that a constitutional bar to reappointment will inspire unconstitutional endeavours to perpetuate himself. It may be answered that his endeavous can have no effect unless the people be corrupt to such a degree as to render all precautions hopeless: to which may be added that this argument supposes him to be more powerful & dangerous, than other arguments which have been used, admit, and consequently calls for stronger fetters on his authority. He thought an election by the Legislature with an incapacity to be elected a second time would be more acceptable to the people that[1] the plan suggested by M: Gov: Morris.

M: KING. did not like the ineligibility. He thought there was great force in the remark[2] of M: Sherman, that he who has proved himself to be[3] most fit for an Office, ought not to be excluded by the constitution from holding it. He would therefore prefer any other reasonable plan that could be substituted. He was much disposed to think that in such cases the people at large would chuse wisely. There was indeed some difficulty arising from the improbability of a general concurrence of the people in favor of any one man. On the whole he was of opinion that an appointment by electors chosen by the people for the purpose, would be liable to fewest objections.

M: PATTERSON's ideas nearly coincided he said with those of M: King. He proposed that the Executive should be appointed by Electors to be chosen by the States in a ratio that would allow one elector to the smallest and three to the largest States.

M: WILSON. It seems to be the unanimous sense that the Executive should not be appointed by the Legislature, unless he be rendered in-eligible a 2ᵈ time: he perceived with pleasure that the idea was gaining ground, of an election mediately or immediately by the people.

M: MADISON If it be a fundamental principle of free Gov: that the Legislative, Executive & Judiciary powers should be *separately* exercised, it is equally so that they be *independently* exercised. There is the same & perhaps greater reason why the Executive sh: be independent of the Legislature, than why the Judiciary should: A coalition of the two former powers would be more immediately & certainly dangerous to public liberty. It is essential then that the appointment of the Executive should either be drawn from some source, or held by some tenure, that will give him a free agency with

---

[1] The word "that" is changed to "than" in the transcript.
[2] The word "remark" is used in the plural in the transcript.
[3] The words "to be" are omitted in the transcript.

regard to the Legislature. This could not be if he was to be appointable from time to time by the Legislature. It was not clear that an appointment in the 1ˢᵗ instance even with an ineligibility afterwards would not establish an improper connection between the two departments. Certain it was that the appointment would be attended with intrigues and contentions that ought not to be unnecessarily admitted. He was disposed for these reasons to refer the appointment to some other source. The people at large was in his opinion the fittest in itself. It would be as likely as any that could be devised to produce an Executive Magistrate of distinguished Character. The people generally could only know & vote for some Citizen whose merits had rendered him an object of general attention & esteem. There was one difficulty however of a serious nature attending an immediate choice by the people. The right of suffrage was much more diffusive in the Northern than the Southern States; and the latter could have no influence in the election on the score of the Negroes. The substitution of electors obviated this difficulty and seemed on the whole to be liable to fewest objections.

Mʳ. GERRY. If the Executive is to be elected by the Legislature he certainly ought not to be re-eligible. This would make him absolutely dependent. He was agˢᵗ a popular election. The people are uninformed, and would be misled by a few designing men. He urged the expediency of an appointment of the Executive by Electors to be chosen by the State Executives. The people of the States will then choose the 1ˢᵗ branch: The legislatures of the States the 2ᵈ branch of the National Legislature, and the Executives of the States, the National Executive. This he thought would form a strong attachnᵗ in the States to the National System. The popular mode of electing the chief Magistrate would certainly be the worst of all. If he should be so elected & should do his duty, he will be turned out for it like Govʳ. Bowdoin in Massᵗˢ; & President Sullivan in N. Hamshire.

On the question on Mʳ Govʳ Morris motion to reconsider gen erally the constitution of the Executive.

Mas. ay. Cᵗ ay. N. J. ay & all the others ay.[1]

Mʳ. ELSEWORTH moved to strike out the appointmᵗ by the Natˡ Legislature, and [2] insert " to be chosen by electors appointed, by the Legislatures of the States in the following ratio; towit—one for each State not exceeding 200,000 inhabᵗˢ two for each above yᵗ

---

[1] In the transcript the vote reads: " Massachusetts, Connecticut, New Jersey, and all the others, aye."

[2] The word " to " is here inserted in the transcript.

number & not exceeding 300,000. and three for each State exceeding 300,000.—M: Broome 2ᵈᵉᵈ the motion

M: Rutlidge was opposed to all the modes except the appointm! by the Nat! Legislature. He will be sufficiently independent, if he be not re-eligible.

M: Gerry preferred the motion of M: Elseworth to an appointm! by the Nat! Legislature, or by the people; tho' not to an app! by the State Executives. He moved that the electors proposed by M: E. should be 25 in number, and allotted in the following proportion. to N. H. 1. to Mas. 3. to R. I. 1. to Con! 2. to N. Y. 2.[1] N. J. 2. [1] P: 3. [1] Del. 1. [1] M⁴ 2. [1] V: 3. [1] N. C. 2. [1] S. C. 2. [1] Geo. 1.

The question as moved by M: Elseworth being divided, on the 1ˢᵗ part shall y: Nat! Executive be appointed by Electors?

Mas. div⁴ Con! ay. N. J. ay. P: ay. Del. ay. M⁴ ay. V: ay. N. C. no. S. C. no. Geo. no.[2]

On[3] 2⁴ part shall the Electors be chosen by[3] State Legislatures? Mas. ay. Con! ay. N. J. ay. P: ay. Del. ay. M⁴ ay. V: no. N. C. ay. S. C. no. Geo. ay.[4]

The part relating to the ratio in which the States s⁴ chuse electors was postponed nem. con.

M: L. Martin moved that the Executive be ineligible a 2⁴ time.

M: Williamson 2ᵈˢ the motion. He had no great confidence in the Electors to be chosen for the special purpose. They would not be the most respectable citizens; but persons not occupied in the high offices of Gov! They would be liable to undue influence, which might the more readily be practised as some of them will probably be in appointment 6 or 8 months before the object of it comes on.

M: Elseworth supposed any persons might be appointed Electors, excepting[5] solely, members of the Nat! Legislature.

On the question shall he be ineligible a 2⁴ time? Mas. no. C! no. N. J. no. P: no. Del. no. M⁴ no. V: no. N. C ay. S. C. ay. Geo. no.[6]

---

[1] The word "to" is here inserted in the transcript.
[2] In the transcript the vote reads: "Connecticut, New Jersey, Pennsylvania, Delaware, Maryland, Virginia, aye—6; North Carolina, South Carolina, Georgia, no—3; Massachusetts, divided."
[3] The word "the" is here inserted in the transcript.
[4] In the transcript the vote reads: "Massachusetts, Connecticut, New Jersey, Pennsylvania, Delaware, Maryland, North Carolina, Georgia, aye—8; Virginia, South Carolina, no—2."
[5] The word "except" is substituted in the transcript for "excepting."
[6] In the transcript the vote reads: "North Carolina, South Carolina, aye—2; Massachusetts, Connecticut, New Jersey, Pennsylvania, Delaware, Maryland, Virginia, Georgia, no—8."

On the question Shall the Executive continue for 7 years? It passed in the negative

Mas. div⁴ Con⁴ ay.* N. J. no.* Pᵃ no. Del. no. M⁴ no. Vᵃ no. N. C. div⁴ S. C. ay. Geo. ay.¹

Mʳ KING was afraid we sh⁴ shorten the term too much.

Mʳ Govʳ MORRIS was for a short term, in order to avoid impeach⁴ᵗ which w⁴ be otherwise necessary.

Mʳ BUTLER was agˢᵗ a ² frequency of the elections. Geo. & S. C. were too distant to send electors often.

Mʳ ELSEWORTH was for 6. years. If the elections be too frequent, the Executive will not be firm eno'. There must be duties which will make him unpopular for the moment. There will be *outs* as well as *ins*. His administration therefore will be attacked and misrepresented.

Mʳ WILLIAMSON was for 6 years. The expence will be considerable & ought not to be unnecessarily repeated. If the Elections are too frequent, the best men will not undertake the service and those of an inferior character will be liable to be corrupted.

On ³ question for 6 years?

Mas. ay. Con⁴ ay. N. J. ay. Pᵃ ay. Del. no. M⁴ ay. Vᵃ ay. N. C. ay. S. C. ay. Geo. ay.⁴

Adjourned

FRIDAY JULY 20. IN CONVENTION

The postponed ⁵ Ratio of Electors for appointing the Executive; to wit 1 for each State whose inhabitants do not exceed 100,000,⁶ &c. being taken up.

Mʳ MADISON observed that this would make in time all or nearly all the States equal. Since there were few that would not in time contain the number of inhabitants intitling them to 3 Electors: that this ratio ought either to be made temporary, or so varied as that it would adjust itself to the growing population of the States.

* in the printed Journal Con⁴, no: N. Jersey ay

---

¹ In the transcript the vote reads: "Connecticut,* South Carolina, Georgia, aye—3; New Jersey,* Pennsylvania, Delaware, Maryland, Virginia, no—5; Massachusetts, North Carolina, divided."
² The word "the" is substituted in the transcript for "a."
³ The word "the" is here inserted in the transcript.
⁴ In the transcript the vote reads: "Massachusetts, Connecticut, New Jersey, Pennsylvania, Maryland, Virginia, North Carolina, South Carolina, Georgia, aye—9; Delaware, no."
⁵ The word "proposed" is substituted in the transcript for "postponed."
⁶ In the figure "100,000" the "1" is crossed out and a figure "2" is written above it in the transcript.

M: GERRY moved that in the *1st instance* the Electors should be allotted to the States in the following ratio: to N. H. 1. Mas. 3. R. I. 1. Con: 2. N. Y. 2. N. J. 2. P: 3. Del. 1. M: 2. V: 3. N. C. 2. S. C. 2. Geo. 1.

On the question to postpone in order to take up this motion of M: Gerry. It passed in the affirmative

Mas. ay. Con: no. N. J. no. P: ay. Del. no. M: no. V: ay. N. C. ay. S. C. ay. Geo. ay.[1]

M: ELSEWORTH moved that 2 Electors be allotted to N. H. Some rule ought to be pursued; and N. H. has more than 100,000 inhabitants. He thought it would be proper also to allot 2. to Georgia

M: BROOM & M: MARTIN moved to postpone M: Gerry's allotment of Electors, leaving a fit ratio to be reported by the Committee to be appointed for detailing the Resolutions.

On this motion.

Mas. no. C: no. N. J. ay. P: no. Del. ay. M: ay. V: no. N. C. no. S. C. no. Geo. no.[2]

M: HOUSTON 2:ded the motion of M: Elseworth to add another Elector to N. H. & Georgia. On the Question:

Mas. no. C: ay. N. J. no. P: no. Del. no. M: no. V: no. N. C. no. S. C. ay. Geo. ay.[3]

M: WILLIAMSON moved as an amendment to M: Gerry's allotment of Electors in the 1st instance that in future elections of the Nat: Executive, the number of Electors to be appointed by the several States shall be regulated by their respective numbers of Representatives in the 1st branch pursuing as nearly as may be the present proportions.

On question on M: Gerry's ratio of Electors

Mas. ay. C: ay. N. J. no. P: ay. Del. no. M: no. V: ay. N. C. ay. S. C. ay. Geo. no.[4]

[5] " to be removeable on impeachment and conviction for mal practice or neglect of duty." see Resol: 9.[6]

---

[1] In the transcript the vote reads: "Massachusetts, Pennsylvania, Virginia, North Carolina, South Carolina, Georgia, aye—6; Connecticut, New Jersey, Delaware, Maryland, no—4."

[2] In the transcript the vote reads: "New Jersey, Delaware, Maryland, aye—3; Massachusetts, Connecticut, Pennsylvania, Virginia, North Carolina, South Carolina, Georgia, no—7."

[3] In the transcript the vote reads: "Connecticut, South Carolina, Georgia, aye—3; Massachusetts, New Jersey, Pennsylvania, Delaware, Maryland, Virginia, North Carolina, no—7."

[4] In the transcript the vote reads: "Massachusetts, Connecticut, Pennsylvania, Virginia, North Carolina, South Carolina, aye—6; New Jersey, Delaware, Maryland, Georgia, no—4."

[5] The words "On the clause" are here inserted in the transcript.

[6] The words "the ninth Resolution" are substituted in the transcript for "Resol: 9."

M! Pinkney & M! Gov! Morris moved to strike out this part of the Resolution. M! P. observ⁴ he ought not to be impeachable whilst in office

M! Davie. If he be not impeachable whilst in office, he will spare no efforts or means whatever to get himself re-elected. He considered this as an essential security for the good behaviour of the Executive.

M! Wilson concurred in the necessity of making the Executive impeachable whilst in office.

M! Gov! Morris. He can do no criminal act without Coadjutors who may be punished. In case he should be re-elected, that will be [1] sufficient proof of his innocence. Besides who is to impeach? Is the impeachment to suspend his functions. If it is not the mischief will go on. If it is the impeachment will be nearly equivalent to a displacement, and will render the Executive dependent on those who are to impeach

Col. Mason. No point is of more importance than that the right of impeachment should be continued. Shall any man be above Justice? Above all shall that man be above it, who can commit the most extensive injustice? When great crimes were committed he was for punishing the principal as well as the Coadjutors. There had been much debate & difficulty as to the mode of chusing the Executive. He approved of that which had been adopted at first, namely of referring the appointment to the Nat! Legislature. One objection ag⁵ᵗ Electors was the danger of their being corrupted by the Candidates; & this furnished a peculiar reason in favor of impeachments whilst in office. Shall the man who has practised corruption & by that means procured his appointment in the first instance, be suffered to escape punishment, by repeating his guilt?

Doc! Franklin was for retaining the clause as favorable to the Executive. History furnishes one example only of a first Magistrate being formally brought to public Justice. Every body cried out ag⁵ᵗ this as unconstitutional. What was the practice before this in cases where the chief Magistrate rendered himself obnoxious? Why recourse was had to assassination in wᶜʰ he was not only deprived of his life but of the opportunity of vindicating his character. It w⁴ be the best way therefore to provide in the Constitution for the regular punishment of the Executive where his misconduct should deserve it, and for his honorable acquittal when [2] he should be unjustly accused.

---

[1] The word " a " is here inserted in the transcript.
[2] The word " where " is substituted in the transcript for " when."

M: Gov: Morris admits corruption & some few other offences to be such as ought to be impeachable; but thought the cases ought to be enumerated & defined:

M: Madison thought it indispensable that some provision should be made for defending the Community ag:t the incapacity, negligence or perfidy of the chief Magistrate. The limitation of the period of his service, was not a sufficient security. He might lose his capacity after his appointment. He might pervert his administration into a scheme of peculation or oppression. He might betray his trust to foreign powers. The case of the Executive Magistracy was very distinguishable, from that of the Legislature or of any other public body, holding offices of limited duration. It could not be presumed that all or even a majority of the members of an Assembly would either lose their capacity for discharging, or be bribed to betray, their trust. Besides the restraints of their personal integrity & honor, the difficulty of acting in concert for purposes of corruption was a security to the public. And if one or a few members only should be seduced, the soundness of the remaining members, would maintain the integrity and fidelity of the body. In the case of the Executive Magistracy which was to be administered by a single man, loss of capacity or corruption was more within the compass of probable events, and either of them might be fatal to the Republic.

M: Pinkney did not see the necessity of impeachments. He was sure they ought not to issue from the Legislature who would in that case hold them as a rod over the Executive and by that means effectually destroy his independence. His revisionary power in particular would be rendered altogether insignificant.

M: Gerry urged the necessity of impeachments. A good magistrate will not fear them. A bad one ought to be kept in fear of them. He hoped the maxim would never be adopted here that the chief magistrate could do no wrong.

M: King expressed his apprehensions that an extreme caution in favor of liberty might enervate the Government we were forming. He wished the House to recur to the primitive axiom that the three great departments of Gov:t should be separate & independent: that the Executive & Judiciary should be so as well as the Legislative: that the Executive should be so equally with the Judiciary. Would this be the case, if the Executive should be impeachable? It had been said that the Judiciary would be impeachable. But it should have been remembered at the same time that the Judiciary hold their places not for a limited time, but during good behaviour. It is necessary therefore that a forum should be established for trying misbehaviour. Was the Executive to hold his place during good behaviour? The Executive was to hold his place for a limited term like the members of the Legislature: Like them particularly the Senate whose members would continue in appointmᵗ the same term of 6 years he would periodically be tried for his behaviour by his electors, who would continue or discontinue him in trust according to the manner in which he had discharged it. Like them therefore, he ought to be subject to no intermediate trial, by impeachment. He ought not to be impeachable unless he held his office during good behavior, a tenure which would be most agreeable to him; provided an independent and effectual forum could be devised. But under no circumstances ought he to be impeachable by the Legislature. This would be destructive of his independence and of the principles of the Constitution. He relied on the vigor of the Executive as a great security for the public liberties.

Mʳ RANDOLPH. The propriety of impeachments was a favorite principle with him. Guilt wherever found ought to be punished. The Executive will have great opportunitys of abusing his power; particularly in time of war when the military force, and in some respects the public money will be in his hands. Should no regular punishment be provided, it will be irregularly inflicted by tumults & insurrections. He is aware of the necessity of proceeding with a cautious hand, and of excluding as much as possible the influence of the Legislature from the business. He suggested for consideration an idea which had fallen [from Col Hamilton] of composing a forum out of the Judges belonging to the States: and even of requiring some preliminary inquest whether just grounds [1] of impeachment existed.

Doctʳ FRANKLIN mentioned the case of the Prince of Orange during the late war. An agreement was made between France & Holland; by which their two fleets were to unite at a certain time & place. The Dutch fleet did not appear. Every body began to wonder at it. At length it was suspected that the Statholder was at the bottom of the matter. This suspicion prevailed more & more. Yet as he could not be impeached and no regular examination took place, he remained in his office, and strengtheing his own party, as the party opposed to him became formidable, he gave birth to the most violent animosities & contentions. Had he been impeachable, a regular & peaceable enquiry would have taken place and he would

---

[1] The transcript uses the word "grounds" in the singular.

if guilty have been duly punished, if innocent restored to the confidence of the public.

M: KING remarked that the case of the Statholder was not applicable. He held his place for life, and was not periodically elected. In the former case impeachments are proper to secure good behaviour. In the latter they are unnecessary; the periodical responsibility to the electors being an equivalent security.

M: WILSON observed that if the idea were to be pursued, the Senators who are to hold their places during the same term with the Executive, ought to be subject to impeachment & removal.

M: PINKNEY apprehended that some gentlemen reasoned on a supposition that the Executive was to have powers which would not be committed to him: He presumed that his powers would be so circumscribed as to render impeachments unnecessary.

M: Gov: MORRIS's opinion had been changed by the arguments used in the discussion. He was now sensible of the necessity of impeachments, if the Executive was to continue for any [1] time in office. Our Executive was not like a Magistrate having a life interest, much less like one having an hereditary interest in his office. He may be bribed by a greater interest to betray his trust; and no one would say that we ought to expose ourselves to the danger of seeing the first Magistrate in forign pay, without being able to guard ag:t it by displacing him. One would think the King of England well secured ag:t bribery. He has as it were a fee simple in the whole Kingdom. Yet Charles II was bribed by Louis XIV. The Executive ought therefore to be impeachable for treachery; Corrupting his electors, and incapacity were other causes of impeachment. For the latter he should be punished not as a man, but as an officer, and punished only by degradation from his office. This Magistrate is not the King but the prime-Minister. The people are the King. When we make him amenable to Justice however we should take care to provide some mode that will not make him dependent on the Legislature.

It was moved & 2:ded to postpone the question of impeachments which was negatived. Mas. & S. Carolina only being ay.

On y: Question, Shall the Executive be removeable on impeachments &c.?

Mas. no. C:t ay. N. J. ay. P:a ay. Del ay. M:d ay. V:a ay. N. C. ay. S. C. no. Geo. ay.[2]

---

[1] The words "length of" are here inserted in the transcript.

[2] In the transcript the vote reads: "Connecticut, New Jersey, Pennsylvania, Delaware, Maryland, Virginia, North Carolina, Georgia, aye—8; Massachusetts, South Carolina, no—2."

" [1] Executive to receive fixed compensation." Agreed to nem. con.

" to be paid out of the National Treasury " agreed to, N. Jersey only in the negative.

M: GERRY & [2] Gov: MORRIS moved " that the Electors of the Executive shall not be members of the Nat! Legislature, nor officers of the U. States, nor shall the Electors themselves be eligible to the supreme magistracy." Agreed to nem. con.

Doc: M:CLURG asked whether it would not be necessary, before a Committee for detailing the Constitution should be appointed, to determine on the means by which the Executive is to carry the laws into effect, and to resist combinations ag:t them. Is he to have a military force for the purpose, or to have the command of the Militia, the only existing force that can be applied to that use? As the Resolutions now stand the Committee will have no determinate directions on this great point.

M: WILSON thought that some additional directions to the Committee w:d be necessary.

M: KING. The Committee are to provide for the end. Their discretionary power to provide for the means is involved according to an established axiom.

Adjourned

SATURDAY JULY 21 IN CONVENTION

M: WILLIAMSON moved that the Electors of the Executive should be paid out of the National Treasury for the Service to be performed by them." Justice required this: as it was a national service they were to render. The motion was agreed to Nem. Con.

M: WILSON moved as an amendment to Resol: 10.[3] that the supreme Nat! Judiciary should be associated with the Executive in the Revisionary power." This proposition had been before made and failed: but he was so confirmed by reflection in the opinion of its utility, that he thought it incumbent on him to make another effort: The Judiciary ought to have an opportunity of remonstrating ag:t projected encroachments on the people as well as on themselves. It had been said that the Judges, as expositors of the Laws would have an opportunity of defending their constitutional rights. There was weight in this observation; but this power of the Judges did not go far

---

[1] The word " The " is here inserted in the transcript.
[2] The word " Mr." is here inserted in the transcript.
[3] The words " the tenth Resolution " are substituted for " Resol: 10."

enough. Laws may be unjust, may be unwise, may be dangerous, may be destructive; and yet may not be so unconstitutional as to justify the Judges in refusing to give them effect. Let them have a share in the Revisionary power, and they will have an opportunity of taking notice of these [1] characters of a law, and of counteracting, by the weight of their opinions the improper views of the Legislature.—

M[r] MADISON 2[ded] the motion

M[r] GHORUM did not see the advantage of employing the Judges in this way. As Judges they are not to be presumed to possess any peculiar knowledge of the mere policy of public measures. Nor can it be necessary as a security for their constitutional rights. The Judges in England have no such additional provision for their defence, yet their jurisdiction is not invaded. He thought it would be best to let the Executive alone be responsible, and at most to authorize him to call on [2] Judges for their opinions.

M[r] ELSEWORTH approved heartily of the motion. The aid of the Judges will give more wisdom & firmness to the Executive. They will possess a systematic and accurate knowledge of the Laws, which the Executive can not be expected always to possess. The law of Nations also will frequently come into question. Of this the Judges alone will have competent information.

M[r] MADISON considered the object of the motion as of great importance to the meditated Constitution. It would be useful to the Judiciary departm[t] by giving it an additional opportunity of defending itself ag[st] Legislative encroachments; It would be useful to the Executive, by inspiring additional confidence & firmness in exerting the revisionary power: It would be useful to the Legislature by the valuable assistance it would give in preserving a consistency, conciseness, perspicuity & technical propriety in the laws, qualities peculiarly necessary; & yet shamefully wanting in our republican Codes. It would moreover be useful to the Community at large as an additional check ag[st] a pursuit of those unwise & unjust measures which constituted so great a portion of our calamities. If any solid objection could be urged ag[st] the motion, it must be on the supposition that it tended to give too much strength either to the Executive or Judiciary. He did not think there was the least ground for this apprehension. It was much more to be apprehended that notwithstanding this co-operation of the two departments, the Legislature would still be an overmatch for them. Experience in all the States had evinced a powerful tendency in the Legislature to absorb

---

[1] The word "those" is substituted in the transcript for "these."
[2] The word "the" is here inserted in the transcript.

all power into its vortex. This was the real source of danger to the American Constitutions; & suggested the necessity of giving every defensive authority to the other departments that was consistent with republican principles.

M: Mason said he had always been a friend to this provision. It would give a confidence to the Executive, which he would not otherwise have, and without which the Revisionary power would be of little avail.

M: Gerry did not expect to see this point which had undergone full discussion, again revived. The object he conceived of the Revisionary power was merely to secure the Executive department agst legislative encroachment. The Executive therefore who will best know and be ready to defend his rights ought alone to have the defence of them. The motion was liable to strong objections. It was combining & mixing together the Legislative & the other departments. It was establishing an improper coalition between the Executive & Judiciary departments. It was making Statesmen of the Judges; and setting them up as the guardians of the Rights of the people. He relied for his part on the Representatives of the people as the guardians of their Rights & interests. It was making the Expositors of the Laws, the Legislators which ought never to be done. A better expedient for correcting the laws, would be to appoint as had been done in Pen^a a person or persons of proper skill, to draw bills for the Legislature.

M: Strong thought with M: Gerry that the power of making ought to be kept distinct from that of expounding, the laws. No maxim was better established. The Judges in exercising the function of expositors might be influenced by the part they had taken, in framing [1] the laws.

M: Gov: Morris. Some check being necessary on the Legislature, the question is in what hands it should be lodged. On one side it was contended that the Executive alone ought to exercise it. He did not think that an Executive appointed for 6 years, and impeachable whilst in office w^d be a very effectual check. On the other side it was urged that he ought to be reinforced by the Judiciary department. Agst this it was objected that Expositors of laws ought to have no hand in making them, and arguments in favor of this had been drawn from England. What weight was due to them might be easily determined by an attention to facts. The truth was that the Judges in England had a great share in ye Legislation. They are consulted

---

[1] The word "passing" is substituted in the transcript for "framing."

in difficult & doubtful cases. They may be & some of them are members of the Legislature. They are or may be members of the privy Council, and can there advise the Executive as they will do with us if the motion succeeds. The influence the English Judges may have in the latter capacity in strengthening the Executive check can not be ascertained, as the King by his influence in a manner dictates the laws. There is one difference in the two Cases however which disconcerts all reasoning from the British to our proposed Constitution. The British Executive has so great an interest in his prerogatives and such powerful means of defending them that he will never yield any part of them. The interest of our Executive is so inconsiderable & so transitory, and his means of defending it so feeble, that there is the justest ground to fear his want of firmness in resisting incroachments. He was extremely apprehensive that the auxiliary firmness & weight of the Judiciary would not supply the deficiency. He concurred in thinking the public liberty in greater danger from Legislative usurpations than from any other source. It had been said that the Legislature ought to be relied on as the proper Guardians of liberty. The answer was short and conclusive. Either bad laws will be pushed or not. On the latter supposition no check will be wanted. On the former a strong check will be necessary: And this is the proper supposition. Emissions of paper money, largesses to the people—a remission of debts and similar measures, will at some times be popular, and will be pushed for that reason At other times such measures will coincide with the interests of the Legislature themselves, & that will be a reason not less cogent for pushing them. It may be thought that the people will not be deluded and misled in the latter case. But experience teaches another lesson. The press is indeed a great means of diminishing the evil, yet it is found to be unable to prevent it altogether.

M: L. MARTIN. Considered the association of the Judges with the Executive as a dangerous innovation; as well as one which [1] could not produce the particular advantage expected from it. A knowledge of Mankind, and of Legislative affairs cannot be presumed to belong in a higher deger degree to the Judges than to the Legislature. And as to the Constitutionality of laws, that point will come before the Judges in their proper [2] official character. In this character they have a negative on the laws. Join them with the Executive in the Revision and they will have a double negative. It is necessary that the Supreme Judiciary should have the confidence of the people. This will

[1] The word "that" is substituted in the transcript for "which."
[2] The word "proper" is omitted in the transcript.

soon be lost, if they are employed in the task of remonstrating ag.ᵗ popular measures of the Legislature. Besides in what mode & proportion are they to vote in the Council of Revision?

Mʳ MADISON could not discover in the proposed association of the Judges with the Executive in the Revisionary check on the Legislature any violation of the maxim which requires the great departments of power to be kept separate & distinct. On the contrary he thought it an auxiliary precaution in favor of the maxim. If a Constitutional discrimination of the departments on paper were a sufficient security to each ag.ᵗ encroachments of the others, all further provisions would indeed be superfluous. But experience had taught us a distrust of that security; and that it is necessary to introduce such a balance of powers and interests, as will guarantee the provisions on paper. Instead therefore of contenting ourselves with laying down the Theory in the Constitution that each department ought to be separate & distinct, it was proposed to add a defensive power to each which should maintain the Theory in practice. In so doing we did not blend the departments together. We erected effectual barriers for keeping them separate. The most regular example of this theory was in the British Constitution. Yet it was not only the practice there to admit the Judges to a seat in the legislature, and in the Executive Councils, and to submit to their previous examination all laws of a certain description, but it was a part of their Constitution that the Executive might negative any law whatever; a part of *their* Constitution which had been universally regarded as calculated for the preservation of the whole. The objection ag.ᵗ a union of the Judiciary & Executive branches in the revision of the laws, had either no foundation or was not carried far enough. If such a Union was an improper mixture of powers, or such a Judiciary check on the laws, was inconsistent with the Theory of a free Constitution, it was equally so to admit the Executive to any participation in the making of laws; and the revisionary plan ought to be discarded altogether.

Col. MASON Observed that the defence of the Executive was not the sole object of the Revisionary power. He expected even greater advantages from it. Notwithstanding the precautions taken in the Constitution of the Legislature, it would still so much resemble that of the individual States, that it must be expected frequently to pass unjust and pernicious laws. This restraining power was therefore essentially necessary. It would have the effect not only of hindering the final passage of such laws; but would discourage demagogues from attempting to get them passed. It had been said [by Mʳ L.

Martin] that if the Judges were joined in this check on the laws, they would have a double negative, since in their expository capacity of Judges they would have one negative. He would reply that in this capacity they could impede in one case only, the operation of laws. They could declare an unconstitutional law void. But with regard to every law however unjust oppressive or pernicious, which [1] did not come plainly under this description, they would be under the necessity as Judges to give it a free course. He wished the further use to be made of the Judges, of giving aid in preventing every improper law. Their aid will be the more valuable as they are in the habit and practice of considering laws in their true principles, and in all their consequences.

M! Wilson. The separation of the departments does not require that they should have separate objects but that they should act separately tho' on the same objects. It is necessary that the two branches of the Legislature should be separate and distinct, yet they are both to act precisely on the same object.

M! Gerry had rather give the Executive an absolute negative for its own defence than thus to blend together the Judiciary & Executive departments. It will bind them together in an offensive and defensive alliance ag.st the Legislature, and render the latter unwilling to enter into a contest with them.

M! Gov.r Morris was surprised that any defensive provision for securing the effectual separation of the departments should be considered as an improper mixture of them. Suppose that the three powers, were to be vested in three persons, by compact among themselves; that one was to have the power of making, another of executing, and a third of judging, the laws. Would it not be very natural for the two latter after having settled the partition on paper, to observe, and would not candor oblige the former to admit, that as a security ag.st legislative acts of the former which might easily be so framed as to undermine the powers of the two others, the two others ought to be armed with a veto for their own defence, or at least to have an opportunity of stating their objections ag.st acts of encroachment? And would any one pretend that such a right tended to blend & confound powers that ought to be separately exercised? As well might it be said that If three neighbours had three distinct farms, a right in each to defend his farm ag.st his neighbours, tended to blend the farms together.

M! Ghorum. All agree that a check on the Legislature is neces-

---

[1] The word "that" is substituted in the transcript for "which."

sary. But there are two objections agst admitting the Judges to share
in it which no observations on the other side seem to obviate. the
1st is that the Judges ought to carry into the exposition of the laws
no prepossessions with regard to them. [1] 2^d that as the Judges will
outnumber the Executive, the revisionary check would be thrown
entirely out of the Executive hands, and instead of enabling him to
defend himself, would enable the Judges to sacrifice him.

Mr WILSON. The proposition is certainly not liable to all the
objections which have been urged agst it. According [to Mr Gerry]
it will unite the Executive & Judiciary in an offensive & defensive
alliance agst the Legislature. According to Mr Ghorum it will lead
to a subversion of the Executive by the Judiciary influence. To
the first gentleman the answer was obvious; that the joint weight
of the two departments was necessary to balance the single weight
of the Legislature. To the 1st objection stated by the other Gentleman it might be answered that supposing the prepossion to mix
itself with the exposition, the evil would be overbalanced by the
advantages promised by the expedient. To the 2^d objection, that such
a rule of voting might be provided in the detail as would guard
agst it.

Mr RUTLIDGE thought the Judges of all men the most unfit to
be concerned in the revisionary Council. The Judges ought never to
give their opinion on a law till it comes before them. He thought it
equally unnecessary. The Executive could advise with the officers
of State, as of war, finance &c. and avail himself of their information & opinions.

On [1] Question on Mr Wilson's motion for joining the Judiciary in
the Revision of laws it passed in the negative—

Mas. no. Con^t ay. N. J. not present. P^a div^d Del. no. M^d ay.
V^a ay. N. C. no. S. C. no. Geo. div^d [2]

Resol. 10, giving the Ex. a qualified veto, without the amend^t
was then ag^d to nem. con.[3]

The motion made by Mr Madison July 18.[4] & then postponed,
"that the Judges sh^d be nominated by the Executive & such nomina-

---

[1] The word "the" is here inserted in the transcript.
[2] In the transcript the vote reads: "Connecticut, Maryland, Virginia,
aye—3; Massachusetts, Delaware, North Carolina, South Carolina, no—4; Pennsylvania, Georgia, divided; New Jersey, not present."
[3] This sentence has been changed in the transcript to read as follows: ". The
tenth Resolution, giving the Executive a qualified veto, requiring two-thirds of
each branch of the Legislature to overrule it was then agreed to *nem. con.*"
[4] The date "July 18" is changed in the transcript to "on the eighteenth
of July."

tions become appointments unless disagreed to by ⅔ of the 2ᵈ branch of the Legislature," was now resumed.

Mʳ MADISON stated as his reasons for the motion. 1.¹ that it secured the responsibility of the Executive who would in general be more capable & likely to select fit characters than the Legislature, or even the 2ᵈ b. of it, who might hide their selfish motives under the number concerned in the appointment.— 2.¹ that in case of any flagrant partiality or error, in the nomination it might be fairly presumed that ⅔ of the 2ᵈ branch would join in putting a negative on it. 3.¹ that as the 2ᵈ b. was very differently constituted when the appointment of the Judges was formerly referred to it, and was now to be composed of equal votes from all the States, the principle of compromise which had prevailed in other instances required in this that their shᵈ be a concurrence of two authorities, in one of which the people, in the other the States, should be represented. The Executive Magistrate wᵈ be considered as a national officer, acting for and equally sympathising with every part of the U. States. If the 2ᵈ branch alone should have this power, the Judges might be appointed by a minority of the people, tho' by a majority, of the States, which could not be justified on any principle as their proceedings were to relate to the people, rather than to the States: and as it would moreover throw the appointments entirely into the hands of yᵉ Northern States, a perpetual ground of jealousy & discontent would be furnished to the Southern States.

Mʳ PINKNEY was for placing the appointmᵗ in the 2ᵈ b. exclusively. The Executive will possess neither the requisite knowledge of characters, nor confidence of the people for so high a trust.

Mʳ RANDOLPH wᵈ have preferred the mode of appointmᵗ proposed formerly by Mʳ Ghorum, as adopted in the Constitution of Massᵗᵗ. but thought the motion depending so great an improvement of the clause as it stands, that he anxiously wished it success. He laid great stress on the responsibility of the Executive as a security for fit appointments. Appointments by the Legislatures have generally resulted from cabal, from personal regard, or some other consideration than a title derived from the proper qualifications. The same inconveniencies will proportionally prevail, if the appointments be be referred to either branch of the Legislature or to any other authority administered by a number of individuals.

Mʳ ELSEWORTH would prefer a negative in the Executive on a

---

¹ The figures "1," "2" and "3" are changed to "first," "Secondly" and "Thirdly" in the transcript.

nomination by the 2ᵈ branch, the negative to be overruled by a concurrence of ⅔ of the 2ᵈ b. to the mode proposed by the motion; but preferred an absolute appointment by the 2ᵈ branch to either. The Executive will be regarded by the people with a jealous eye. Every power for augmenting unnecessarily his influence will be disliked. As he will be stationary it was not to be supposed he could have a better knowledge of characters. He will be more open to caresses & intrigues than the Senate. The right to supersede his nomination will be ideal only. A nomination under such circumstances will be equivalent to an appointment.

Mʳ Govʳ MORRIS supported the motion. 1.[1] The States in their corporate capacity will frequently have an interest staked on the determination of the Judges. As in the Senate the States are to vote the Judges ought not to be appointed by the Senate. Next to the impropriety of being Judge in one's own cause, is the appointment of the Judge. 2.[1] It had been said the Executive would be uninformed of characters. The reverse was yᵉ truth. The Senate will be so. They must take the character of candidates from the flattering pictures drawn by their friends. The Executive in the necessary intercourse with every part of the U. S. required by the nature of his administration, will or may have the best possible information. 3.[1] It had been said that a jealousy would be entertained of the Executive. If the Executive can be safely trusted with the command of the army, there cannot surely be any reasonable ground of Jealousy in the present case. He added that if the objections agˢᵗ an appointment of the Executive by the Legislature, had the weight that had been allowed there must be some weight in the objection to an appointment of the Judges by the Legislature or by any part of it.

Mʳ GERRY. The appointment of the Judges like every other part of the Constitution shᵈ be so modelled as to give satisfaction both to the people and to the States. The mode under consideration will give satisfaction to neither. He could not conceive that the Executive could be as well informed of characters throughout the Union, as the Senate. It appeared to him also a strong objection that ⅔ of the Senate were required to reject a nomination of the Executive. The Senate would be constituted in the same manner as Congress. And the appointments of Congress have been generally good.

Mʳ MADISON, observed that he was not anxious that ⅔ should be necessary to disagree to a nomination. He had given this form to

---

[1] The figures "1," "2" and "3" are changed to "First," "Secondly" and "Thirdly" in the transcript.

his motion chiefly to vary it the more clearly from one which had just been rejected. He was content to obviate the objection last made, and accordingly so varied the motion as to let a majority reject.

Col. MASON found it his duty to differ from his colleagues in their opinions & reasonings on this subject. Notwithstanding the form of the proposition by which the appointment seemed to be divided between the Executive & Senate, the appointment was substantially vested in the former alone. The false complaisance which usually prevails in such cases will prevent a disagreement to the first nominations. He considered the appointment by the Executive as a dangerous prerogative. It might even give him an influence over the Judiciary department itself. He did not think the difference of interest between the Northern and Southern States could be properly brought into this argument. It would operate & require some precautions in the case of regulating navigation, commerce & imposts; but he could not see that it had any connection with the Judiciary department.

On the question, the motion now being [1] that the executive should nominate, & such nominations should become appointments unless disagreed to by the Senate "

Mas. ay. C! no. P! ay. Del. no. M! no. V! ay. N. C. no. S. C. no. Geo. no.[2]

On [3] question for agreeing to the clause as it stands by which the Judges are to be appointed by [3] 2! branch

Mas. no. C! ay. P! no. Del. ay. M! ay. V! no. N. C. ay. S. C. ay. Geo. ay.[4]

Adjourned

MONDAY. JULY. 23. IN CONVENTION.

M! John Langdon & M! Nicholas Gilman from N. Hampshire, took their seats.

---

[1] The words "now being" are transposed to read "being now" in the transcript.

[2] In the transcript the vote reads: "Massachusetts, Pennsylvania, Virginia, aye—3; Connecticut, Delaware, Maryland, North Carolina, South Carolina, Georgia, no—6."

[3] The word "the" is here inserted in the transcript.

[4] In the transcript the vote reads: "Connecticut, Delaware, Maryland, North Carolina, South Carolina, Georgia, aye—6; Massachusetts, Pennsylvania, Virginia, no—3; so it passed in the affirmative."

Resol[n]: 17.[1] that provision ought to be made for future amendments of the articles of Union,[2] agreed to, nem. con.

Resol[n] 18.[3] " requiring the Legis: Execut: & Jud? of the States to be bound by oath to support the articles of Union,"[2] taken into consideration.

M[r] WILLIAMSON suggests that a reciprocal oath should be required from the National officers, to support the Governments of the States.

M[r] GERRY moved to insert as an amendm[t] that the oath of the officers of the National Government also should extend to the support of the Nat! Gov? which was agreed to nem. con.

M[r] WILSON said he was never fond of oaths. considering them as a left handed security only. A good Gov? did not need them, and a bad one could not or ought not to be supported. He was afraid they might too much trammel the members of the Existing Gov[t]- in case future alterations should be necessary; and prove an obstacle to Resol: 17.[1] just ag[d] to.

M[r] GHORUM did not know that oaths would be of much use; but could see no inconsistency between them and the 17. Resol: or any regular amend[t] of the Constitution. The oath could only require fidelity to the existing Constitution. A constitutional alteration of the Constitution, could never be regarded as a breach of the Constitution, or of any oath to support it.

M[r] GERRY thought with M[r] Ghorum there could be no shadow of inconsistency in the case. Nor could he see any other harm that could result from the Resolution. On the other side he thought one good effect would be produced by it. Hitherto the officers of the two Governments had considered them as distinct from,[4] not as parts of the General System, & had in all cases of interference given a preference to the State Gov[ts] The proposed oaths will cure that error.

The Resol[n] [18[5]] was agreed to nem. con.—

Resol: 19.[6] referring the new Constitution to Assemblies to be chosen by the people for the express purpose of ratifying it" was next taken into consideration.

---

[1] The words " The seventeenth Resolution " are substituted in the transcript for " Resol[n] 17."
[2] The word " was " is here inserted in the transcript.
[3] The words " The eighteenth Resolution " are substituted in the transcript for " Resol[n] 18."
[4] The word " and " is here inserted in the transcript.
[5] The words " the eighteenth " are substituted in the transcript for " 18."
[6] The words " The nineteenth Resolution " are substituted in the transcript for " Resol: 19."

M: ELSEWORTH moved that it be referred to the Legislatures of the States for ratification. M: PATTERSON 2^{ded} the motion.

Col. MASON considered a reference of the plan to the authority of the people as one of the most important and essential of the Resolutions. The Legislatures have no power to ratify it. They are the mere creatures of the State Constitutions, and can not be greater than their creators. And he knew of no power in any of the Constitutions, he knew there was no power in some of them, that could be competent to this object. Whither then must we resort? To the people with whom all power remains that has not been given up in the Constitutions derived from them. It was of great moment he observed that this doctrine should be cherished as the basis of free Government. Another strong reason was that admitting the Legislatures to have a competent authority, it would be wrong to refer the plan to them, because succeeding Legislatures having equal authority could undo the acts of their predecessors; and the National Gov: would stand in each State on the weak and tottering foundation of an Act of Assembly. There was a remaining consideration of some weight. In some of the States the Gov^{ts} were not derived from the clear & undisputed authority of the people. This was the case in Virginia Some of the best & wisest citizens considered the Constitution as established by an assumed authority. A National Constitution derived from such a source would be exposed to the severest criticisms.

M: RANDOLPH. One idea has pervaded all our proceedings, to wit, that opposition as well from the States as from individuals, will be made to the System to be proposed. Will it not then be highly imprudent, to furnish any unnecessary pretext by the mode of ratifying it. Added to other objections agst a ratification by Legislative authority only, it may be remarked that there have been instances in which the authority of the Common law has been set up in particular States agst that of the Confederation which has had no higher sanction than Legislative ratification.—Whose opposition will be most likely to be excited agst the System? That of the local demagogues who will be degraded by it from the importance they now hold. These will spare no efforts to impede that progress in the popular mind which will be necessary to the adoption of the plan, and which every member will find to have taken place in his own, if he will compare his present opinions with those brought with him into the Convention. It is of great importance therefore that the consideration of this subject should be transferred from the Legislatures where this class of men, have their full influence to a field in which their efforts can be less mischeivous. It is moreover worthy of consideration that some of the States are averse to any change in their Constitution, and will not take the requisite steps, unless expressly called upon to refer the question to the people.

M: GERRY. The arguments of Col. Mason & M: Randolph prove too much. they prove an unconstitutionality in the present federal system even in some of the State Goṽt̃: Inferences drawn from such a source must be inadmissible. Both the State Goṽt̃: & the federal Goṽ: have been too long acquiesced in, to be now shaken. He considered the Confederation to be paramount to any State Constitution. The last article of it authorizing alterations must consequently be so as well as the others, and every thing done in pursuance of the article must have the same high authority with the article.—Great confusion he was confident would result from a recurrence to the people. They would never agree on any thing. He could not see any ground to suppose that the people will do what their rulers will not. The rulers will either conform to, or influence the sense of the people.

M: GHORUM was ag:t referring the plan to the Legislatures. 1. Men chosen by the people for the particular purpose, will discuss the subject more candidly than members of the Legislature who are to lose the power which is to be given up to the Gen! Gov: 2. Some of the Legislatures are composed of several branches. It will consequently be more difficult in these cases to get the plan through the Legislatures, than thro' a Convention. 3. in the States many of the ablest men are excluded from the Legislatures, but may be elected into a Convention. Among these may be ranked many of the Clergy who are generally friends to good Government. Their services were found to be valuable in the formation & establishment of the Constitution of Massach̃t̃: 4. the Legislatures will be interrupted with a variety of little business, by artfully pressing which, designing men will find means to delay from year to year, if not to frustrate altogether, the national system. 5. If the last art: of the Confederation is to be pursued the unanimous concurrence of the States will be necessary. But will any one say, that all the States are to suffer themselves to be ruined, if Rho. Island should persist in her opposition to general measures. Some other States might also tread in her steps. The present advantage which N. York seems to be so much attached to, of taxing her neighbours by the regulation of her trade, makes it very probable, that she will be of the number. It would therefore deserve serious consideration whether provision ought not to be made for giving effect to the System without waiting for the unanimous concurrence of the States.

M�r ELSEWORTH. If there be any Legislatures who should find themselves incompetent to the ratification, he should be content to let them advise with their constituents and pursue such a mode as w⁴ be competent. He thought more was to be expected from the Legislatures than from the people. The prevailing wish of the people in the Eastern States is to get rid of the public debt; and the idea of strengthening the Nat¹ Gov⁺ carries with it that of strengthening the public debt. It was said by Col. Mason 1.¹ that the Legislatures have no authority in this case. 2.² that their successors having equal authority could rescind their acts. As to the 2⁴ point he could not admit it to be well founded. An Act to which the States by their Legislatures, make themselves parties, becomes a compact from which no one of the parties can recede of itself. As to the 1⁺ point, he observed that a new sett of ideas seemed to have crept in since the articles of Confederation were established. Conventions of the people, or with power derived expressly from the people, were not then thought of. The Legislatures were considered as competent. Their ratification has been acquiesced in without complaint. To whom have Cong⁺ applied on subsequent occasions for further powers? To the Legislatures; not to the people. The fact is that we exist at present, and we need not enquire how, as a federal Society, united by a charter one article of which is that alterations therein may be made by the Legislative authority of the States. It has been said that if the confederation is to be observed, the States must *unanimously* concur in the proposed innovations. He would answer that if such were the urgency & necessity of our situation as to warrant a new compact among a part of the States, founded on the consent of the people; the same pleas would be equally valid in favor of a partial compact, founded on the consent of the Legislatures.

M⁺ WILLIAMSON thought the Resol⁰: [19 ³] so expressed as that it might be submitted either to the Legislatures or to Conventions recommended by the Legislatures. He observed that some Legislatures were evidently unauthorized to ratify the system. He thought too that Conventions were to be preferred as more likely to be composed of the ablest men in the States.

M⁺ Gov⁺ MORRIS considered the inference of M⁺ Elseworth from the plea of necessity as applied to the establishment of a new System on y⁰ consent of the people of a part of the States, in favor of a like establishn⁺ on the consent of a part of the Legislatures as a non

---

¹ The figure " 1 " is changed to " in the first place " in the transcript.
² The figure " 2 " is changed to " and in the second " in the transcript.
³ The words " the nineteenth " are substituted in the transcript for " 19."

sequitur. If the Confederation is to be pursued no alteration can be made without the unanimous consent of the Legislatures: Legislative alterations not conformable to the federal compact, would clearly not be valid. The Judges would consider them as null & void. Whereas in case of an appeal to the people of the U. S., the supreme authority, the federal compact may be altered by a *majority of them;* in like manner as the Constitution of a particular State may be altered by a majority of the people of the State. The amendm⁺ moved by M⁺ Elseworth erroneously supposes that we are proceeding on the basis of the Confederation. This Convention is unknown to the Confederation.

M⁺ KING thought with M⁺ Elseworth that the Legislatures had a competent authority, the acquiescence of the people of America in the Confederation, being equivalent to a formal ratification by the people. He thought with M⁺ E— also that the plea of necessity was as valid in the one case as in [1] the other. At the same time he preferred a reference to the authority of the people expressly delegated to Conventions, as the most certain means of obviating all disputes & doubts concerning the legitimacy of the new Constitution; as well as the most likely means of drawing forth the best men in the States to decide on it. He remarked that among other objections made in the State of N. York to granting powers to Cong⁺ one had been that such powers as would operate within the State,[2] could not be reconciled to the Constitution; and therefore were not grantible by the Legislative authority. He considered it as of some consequence also to get rid of the scruples which some members of the State Legislatures might derive from their oaths to support & maintain the existing Constitutions.

M⁺ MADISON thought it clear that the Legislatures were incompetent to the proposed changes. These changes would make essential inroads on the State Constitutions, and it would be a novel & dangerous doctrine that a Legislature could change the constitution under which it held its existence. There might indeed be some Constitutions within the Union, which had given a power to the Legislature to concur in alterations of the federal Compact. But there were certainly some which had not; and in the case of these, a ratification must of necessity be obtained from the people. He considered the difference between a system founded on the Legislatures only, and one founded on the people, to be the true difference between a *league* or *treaty,* and a *Constitution.* The former in point of *moral obligation* might be as inviolable as the latter. In point of *political opera-*

---

[1] The word " in " is omitted in the transcript.
[2] The transcript uses the word " State " in the plural.

tion, there were two important distinctions in favor of the latter. 1.[1] A law violating a treaty ratified by a pre-existing law, might be respected by the Judges as a law, though an unwise or perfidious one. A law violating a constitution established by the people themselves, would be considered by the Judges as null & void. 2.[1] The doctrine laid down by the law of Nations in the case of treaties is that a breach of any one article by any of the parties, frees the other parties from their engagements. In the case of a union of people under one Constitution, the nature of the pact has always been understood to exclude such an interpretation. Comparing the two modes in point of expediency he thought all the considerations which recommended this Convention in preference to Congress for proposing the reform were in favor of State Conventions in preference to the Legislatures for examining and adopting it.

On [2] question on M: Elseworth's motion to refer the plan to the Legislatures of the States

N. H. no. Mas. no. C. ay. no.[3] P. no. Del. ay. M. ay. V. no. N. C. no. S. C. no. Geo. no.[4]

M: Gov: Morris moved that the reference of the plan be made to one general Convention, chosen & authorized by the people to consider, *amend,* & establish the same.—Not seconded.

On [2] question for agreeing to Resolution 19.[5] touching the mode of Ratification as reported from the Committee of the Whole; viz, to refer the Const. after the approbation of Cong: to assemblies chosen by the people:

N. H. ay. Mas. ay. C. ay. P. ay. Del. no. M. ay. V. ay. N. C. ay. S. C. ay. Geo. ay.[6]

M: Gov: Morris & M: King moved that the representation in the second branch consist of   members from each State, who shall vote per capita.

M: Elseworth said he had always approved of voting in that mode.

---

[1] The figures "1" and "2" are changed to "First" and "Secondly" in the transcript.
[2] The word "the" is here inserted in the transcript.
[3] The entry in the notes was originally "N. J. no." Madison struck out "N. J." but inadvertently let "no" remain.
[4] In the transcript the vote reads: "Connecticut, Delaware, Maryland, aye—3; New Hampshire, Massachusetts, Pennsylvania, Virginia, North Carolina, South Carolina, Georgia, no—7."
[5] The words "the nineteenth Resolution" are substituted in the transcript for "Resolution 19."
[6] In the transcript the vote reads: "New Hampshire, Massachusetts, Connecticut, Pennsylvania, Maryland, Virginia, North Carolina, South Carolina, Georgia, aye—9; Delaware, no—1."

M: Gov: Morris moved to fill the *blank* [1] with *three*. He wished the Senate to be a pretty numerous body. If two members only should be allowed to each State, and a majority be made a quorum, the power would be lodged in 14 members, which was too small a number for such a trust.

M: Ghorum preferred two to three members for the blank. A small number was most convenient for deciding on peace & war &c. which he expected would be vested in the 2ᵈ branch. The number of States will also increase. Kentucky, Vermont, the Province of Mayne & Franklin will probably soon be added to the present number. He presumed also that some of the largest States would be divided. The strenghth of the General Gov: will lie not in the largeness, but in the smallness of the States.

Col. Mason thought 3 from each State including new States would make the 2ᵈ branch too numerous. Besides other objections, the additional expence ought always to form one, where it was not absolutely necessary:

M: Williamson. If the number be too great, the distant States will not be on an equal footing with the nearer States. The latter can more easily send & support their ablest Citizens. He approved of the voting per capita.

On the question for filling the blank with " *three* "

N. H. no. Mas. no. Con: no. P: ay. Del. no. V: no. N. C. no. S. C. no. Geo. no.[2]

On [3] question for filling it with " two." Agreed to nem. con.

M: L Martin was opposed to voting per Capita, as departing from the idea of the *States* being represented in the 2ᵈ branch.

M: Carrol, was not struck with any particular objection ag:ᵗ the mode; but he did not wish so hastily to make so material an innovation.

On the question on the whole motion viz. the 2ᵈ b. to consist of 2 members from each State and to vote per capita."

N. H. ay. Mas. ay. C: ay. P: ay. Del. ay. M:ᵈ no. V: ay. N. C. ay. S. C. ay. Geo. ay.[4]

M: Houston & M: Spaight moved " that the appointment of the Executive by Electors chosen by the Legislatures of the States, be re-

---

[1] The transcript does not italicize the word " *blank.*"
[2] In the transcript the vote reads: " Pennsylvania, aye—1; New Hampshire, Massachusetts, Connecticut, Delaware, Virginia, North Carolina, South Carolina, Georgia, no—8."
[3] The word " the " is here inserted in the transcript.
[4] In the transcript the vote reads: " New Hampshire, Massachusetts, Connecticut, Pennsylvania, Delaware, Virginia, North Carolina, South Carolina, Georgia, aye—9; Maryland, no—1."

considered." M: Houston urged the extreme inconveniency & the considerable expence, of drawing together men from all the States for the single purpose of electing the Chief Magistrate.

On the question which was put without any [1] debate.

N. H. ay. Mas. ay. C: ay. P: no. Del. ay. M: no. Virg: no. N. C. ay. S. C. ay. Geo. ay.[2]

Ordered that tomorrow be assigned for the reconsideration.

Con: & Pen: no—all the rest ay.

M: Gerry moved that the proceedings of the Convention for the establishment of a Nat! Gov! (except the part relating to the Executive), be referred to a Committee to prepare & report a Constitution conformable thereto.

Gen! Pinkney reminded the Convention that if the Committee should fail to insert some security to the Southern States ag:t an emancipation of slaves, and taxes on exports, he sh: be bound by duty to his State to vote ag:t their Report— The app: of a Com: as moved by M: Gerry.[3] Ag:d to nem. con.

[4] Shall the Com: consist of 10 members one from each State pres:? All the States were no, except Delaware ay.

Shall it consist of 7. members.

N. H. ay. Mas. ay. C: ay. P: no. Del. no. M: ay. V: no. N. C. no. S. C. ay. Geo. no.[5] The question being lost by an equal division of Votes.

It was agreed nem- con- that the Comttee[6] consist of 5 members, to be appointed tomorrow.

Adjourned

TUESDAY JULY 24.   IN CONVENTION

The appointment of the Executive by Electors[7] reconsidered.

M: Houston moved that he be appointed by the " Nat! Legislature," instead of " Electors appointed by the State Legislatures "

---

[1] The word "any" is omitted in the transcript.
[2] In the transcript the vote reads: "New Hampshire, Massachusetts, Connecticut, Delaware, North Carolina, South Carolina, Georgia, aye—7; Pennsylvania, Maryland, Virginia, no—3."
[3] The word "was" is here inserted in the transcript.
[4] The words "On the question" are here inserted in the transcript.
[5] In the transcript the vote reads: "New Hampshire, Massachusetts, Connecticut, Maryland, South Carolina, aye—5; Pennsylvania, Delaware, Virginia, North Carolina, Georgia, no—5."
[6] The word "should" is here inserted in the transcript.
[7] The word "being" is here inserted in the transcript.

according to the last decision of the mode. He dwelt chiefly on the improbability, that capable men would undertake the service of Electors from the more distant States.

M: Spaight seconded the motion.

M: Gerry opposed it. He thought there was no ground to apprehend the danger urged by M: Houston. The election of the Executive Magistrate will be considered as of vast importance and will excite [1] great earnestness. The best men, the Governours of the States will not hold it derogatory from their character to be the electors. If the motion should be agreed to, it will be necessary to make the Executive ineligible a 2^d time, in order to render him independent of the Legislature; which was an idea extremely repugnant to his way of thinking.

M: Strong supposed that there would be no necessity, if the Executive should be appointed by the Legislature, to make him ineligible a 2^d time; as new elections of the Legislature will have intervened; and he will not depend for his 2^d appointment on the same sett of men as [2] his first was rec^d from. It had been suggested that *gratitude* for his past appointment w^d produce the same effect as dependence for his future appointment. He thought very differently. Besides this objection would lie agst the Electors who would be objects of gratitude as well as the Legislature. It was of great importance not to make the Gov^t too complex which would be the case if a new sett of men like the Electors should be introduced into it. He thought also that the first characters in the States would not feel sufficient motives to undertake the office of Electors.

M: Williamson was for going back to the original ground; to elect the Executive for 7 years and render him ineligible a 2^d time. The proposed Electors would certainly not be men of the 1st nor even of the 2^d grade in the States. These would all prefer a seat either [3] in the Senate or the other branch of the Legislature. He did not like the Unity in the Executive. He had wished the Executive power to be lodged in three men taken from three districts into which the States should be divided. As the Executive is to have a kind of veto on the laws, and there is an essential difference of interests between the N. & S. States, particularly in the carrying trade, the power will be dangerous, if the Executive is to be taken from part of the Union, to the part from which he is not taken. The case is different here from what it is in England; where there is a

---

[1] The word "create" is substituted in the transcript for "excite."
[2] The word "that" is substituted in the transcript for "as."
[3] The word "either" is omitted in the transcript.

sameness of interests throughout the Kingdom. Another objection ag.ᵗ a single Magistrate is that he will be an elective King, and will feel the spirit of one. He will spare no pains to keep himself in for life, and will then lay a train for the succession of his children. It was pretty certain he thought that we should at some time or other have a King; but he wished no precaution to be omitted that might postpone the event as long as possible.—Ineligibility a 2ᵈ time appeared to him to be the best precaution. With this precaution he had no objection to a longer term than 7 years. He would go as far as 10 or 12 years.

M.ʳ GERRY moved that the Legislatures of the States should vote by ballot for the Executive in the same proportions as it had been proposed they should chuse electors; and that in case a majority of the votes should not center on the same person, the 1.ˢᵗ branch of the Nat.ˡ Legislature should chuse two out of the 4 candidates having most votes, and out of these two, the 2.ᵈ branch should chuse the Executive.

M.ʳ KING seconded the motion—and on the Question to postpone in order to take it into consideration. The *noes* were so predominant, that the States were not counted.

¹ Question on M.ʳ Houston's motion that the Executive be app.ᵈ by ² Na.ˡ Legislature

N. H. ay. Mas. ay. C.ᵗ no. N. J. ay. P.ᵃ no. Del. ay. M.ᵈ no. V.ᵃ no. N. C. ay. S. C. ay. Geo. ay.³

M.ʳ L. MARTIN & M.ʳ GERRY moved to re-instate the ineligibility of the Executive a 2ᵈ time.

M.ʳ ELSEWORTH. With many this appears a natural consequence of his being elected by the Legislature. It was not the case with him. The Executive he thought should be reelected if his conduct proved him worthy of it. And he will be more likely to render himself, worthy of it if he be rewardable with it. The most eminent characters also will be more willing to accept the trust under this condition, than if they foresee a necessary degradation at a fixt period.

M.ʳ GERRY. That the Executive sh.ᵈ be independent of the Legislature is a clear point. The longer the duration of his appointment the more will his dependence be diminished. It will be better then for him to continue 10, 15, or even 20, years and be ineligible afterwards.

---

¹ The words " On the " are here inserted in the transcript.
² The word " the " is here inserted in the transcript.
³ In the transcript the vote reads: " New Hampshire, Massachusetts, New Jersey, Delaware, North Carolina, South Carolina, Georgia, aye—7; Connecticut, Pennsylvania, Maryland, Virginia, no—4."

M: KING was for making him re-eligible. This is too great an advantage to be given up for the small effect it will have on his dependence, if impeachments are to lie. He considered these as rendering the tenure during pleasure.

M: L. MARTIN, suspending his motion as to the ineligibility, moved "that the appointm.t of the Executive shall continue for Eleven years.

M: GERRY suggested fifteen years

M: KING twenty years. This is the medium life of princes.*

M: DAVIE Eight years

M: WILSON. The difficulties & perplexities into which the House is thrown proceed from the election by the Legislature which he was sorry had been reinstated. The inconveniency[2] of this mode was such that he would agree to almost any length of time in order to get rid of the dependence which must result from it. He was persuaded that the longest term would not be equivalent to a proper mode of election; unless indeed it should be during good behaviour. It seemed to be supposed that at a certain advance of life, a continuance in office would cease to be agreeable to the officer, as well as desireable to the public. Experience had shewn in a variety of instances that both a capacity & inclination for public service existed—in very advanced stages. He mentioned the instance of a Doge of Venice who was elected after he was 80 years of age. The popes have generally been elected at very advanced periods, and yet in no case had a more steady or a better concerted policy been pursued than in the Court of Rome. If the Executive should come into office at 35. years of age, which he presumes may happen & his continuance should be fixt at 15 years. at the age of 50. in the very prime of life, and with all the aid of experience, he must be cast aside like a useless hulk. What an irreparable loss would the British Jurisprudence have sustained, had the age of 50. been fixt there as the ultimate limit of capacity or readiness to serve the public. The great luminary [L.d Mansfield] held his seat for thirty years after his arrival at that age. Notwithstanding what had been done he could not but hope that a better mode of election would yet be adopted; and one that would be more agreeable to the general sense of the House. That time might be

* This might possibly be meant as a carricature of the previous motions in order to defeat the object of them.

* Transfer hither.[1]

---

[1] Madison's direction concerning the footnote is omitted in the transcript.

[2] The word "inconveniency" is changed to "inconvenience" in the transcript.

given for further deliberation he w⁴ move that the present question
be postponed till tomorrow.

M⁺ BROOM seconded the motion to postpone.

M⁺ GERRY. We seem to be entirely at a loss on this head. He
would suggest whether it would not be adviseable to refer the clause
relating to the Executive to the Committee of detail to be appointed.
Perhaps they will be able to hit on something that may unite the
various opinions which have been thrown out.

M⁺ WILSON. As the great difficulty seems to spring from the
mode of election, he w⁴ suggest a mode which had not been mentioned. It was that the Executive be elected for 6 years by a small
number, not more than 15 of the Nat⁵ Legislature, to be drawn from
it, not by ballot, but by lot and who should retire immediately and
make the election without separating. By this mode intrigue would
be avoided in the first instance, and the dependence would be
diminished. This was not he said a digested idea and might be
liable to strong objections.

M⁺ Gov⁵ MORRIS. Of all possible modes of appointment that by
the Legislature is the worst. If the Legislature is to appoint, and
to impeach or to influence the impeachment, the Executive will be
the mere creature of it. He had been opposed to the impeachment
but was now convinced that impeachments must be provided for,
if the app⁵ was to be of any duration. No man w⁴ say, that an
Executive known to be in the pay of an Enemy, should not be
removeable in some way or other. He had been charged heretofore [by
Col. Mason] with inconsistency in pleading for confidence in the
Legislature on some occasions, & urging a distrust on others. The
charge was not well founded. The Legislature is worthy of unbounded confidence in some respects, and liable to equal distrust in
others. When their interest coincides precisely with that of their
Constituents, as happens in many of their Acts, no abuse of trust
is to be apprehended. When a strong personal interest happens to
be opposed to the general interest, the Legislature can not be too much
distrusted. In all public bodies there are two parties. The Executive
will necessarily be more connected with one than with the other.
There will be a personal interest therefore in one of the parties to
oppose as well as in the other to support him. Much had been said
of the intrigues that will be practised by the Executive to get into
office. Nothing had been said on the other side of the intrigues to
get him out of office. Some leader of ¹ party will always covet his

---

¹ The word " a " is here inserted in the transcript.

seat, will perplex his administration, will cabal with the Legislature, till he succeeds in supplanting him. This was the way in which the King of England was got out, he meant the real King, the Minister. This was the way in which Pitt [L⁴ Chatham] forced himself into place. Fox was for pushing the matter still farther. If he had carried his India bill, which he was very near doing, he would have made the Minister, the King in form almost as well as in substance. Our President will be the British Minister, yet we are about to make him appointable by the Legislature. Something had been said of the danger of Monarchy. If a good government should not now be formed, if a good organization of the Execuve should not be provided, he doubted whether we should not have something worse than a limited Monarchy. In order to get rid of the dependence of the Executive on the Legislature, the expedient of making him ineligible a 2ᵈ time had been devised. This was as much as to say we sh⁴ give him the benefit of experience, and then deprive ourselves of the use of it. But make him ineligible a 2ᵈ time—and prolong his duration even to 15– years, will he by any wonderful interposition of providence at that period cease to be a man? No he will be unwilling to quit his exaltation, the road to his object thro' the Constitution will be shut; he will be in possession of the sword, a civil war will ensue, and the Commander of the victorious army on which ever side, will be the despot of America. This consideration renders him particularly anxious that the Executive should be properly constituted. The vice here would not, as in some other parts of the system be curable. It is the most difficult of all rightly to balance the Executive. Make him too weak: The Legislature will usurp his powers: Make him too strong. He will usurp on the Legislature. He preferred a short period, a re-eligibility, but a different mode of election. A long period would prevent an adoption of the plan: it ought to do so. He sh⁴ himself be afraid to trust it. He was not prepared to decide on Mʳ Wilson's mode of election just hinted by him. He thought it deserved consideration It would be better that chance sᵈ decide than intrigue.

On a¹ question to postpone the consideration of the Resolution on the subject of the Executive

N. H. no. Mas. no. Cᵗ ay. N. J. no. Pᵃ ay. Del. div⁴ M⁴ ay. Vᵃ ay. N. C. no. S. C. no. Geo. no.²

---

¹ The word "the" is substituted in the transcript for "a."
² In the transcript the vote reads: "Connecticut, Pennsylvania, Maryland, Virginia, aye—4; New Hampshire, Massachusetts, New Jersey, North Carolina, South Carolina, Georgia, no—6."

M�r WILSON then moved that the Executive be chosen every
      years by   Electors to be taken by lot from the Nat¹
Legislature who shall proceed immediately to the choice of the
Executive and not separate until it be made.''

M�r CARROL 2ᵈˢ the motion

M�r GERRY. this is committing too much to chance. If the lot
should fall on a sett of unworthy men, an unworthy Executive must
be saddled on the Country. He thought it had been demonstrated
that no possible mode of electing by the Legislature could be a good
one.

M�r KING. The lot might fall on a majority from the same State
which wᵈ ensure the election of a man from that State. We ought to
be governed by reason, not by chance. As nobody seemed to be
satisfied, he wished the matter to be postponed

M⁵ WILSON did not move this as the best mode. His opinion
remained unshaken that we ought to resort to the people for the
election. He seconded the postponement.

M⁵ Govʳ MORRIS observed that the chances were almost infinite
agˢᵗ a majority of electors from the same State.

On a question whether the last motion was in order, it was
determined in the affirmative; 7. ays. 4 noes.

On the question of postponenᵗ it was agreed to nem. con.

M⁵ CARROL took occasion to observe that he considered the clause
declaring that direct taxation on the States should be in proportion
to representation, previous to the obtaining an actual census, as very
objectionable, and that he reserved to himself the right of opposing
it, if the Report of the Committee of detail should leave it in the
plan.

M⁵ Govʳ MORRIS hoped the Committee would strike out the whole
of the clause proportioning direct taxation to representation. He
had only meant it as a* bridge to assist us over a certain gulph;
having passed the gulph the bridge may be removed. He thought
the principle laid down with so much strictness, liable to strong
objections

On a ballot for a Committee to report a Constitution conformable
to the Resolutions passed by the Convention, the members chosen
were

* The object was to lessen the eagerness on one side,¹ & the opposition on
the other, to the share of representation claimed by the S. Sothern States on
account of the Negroes.
* The N. B. to be transferred hither without the N. B.²

¹ The word "for" is here inserted in the transcript.
² Madison's direction concerning the footnote is omitted in the transcript.

M. Rutlidge, M. Randolph, M. Ghorum, M. Elseworth, M. Wilson—

On motion to discharge the Com? of the whole from the propositions submitted to the Convention by M. C. Pinkney as the basis of a constitution, and to refer them to the Committee of detail just appointed, it was ag^d to nem: con.

A like motion was then made & agreed to nem: con: with respect to the propositions of M. Patterson

Adjourned.

WEDNESDAY JULY 25. IN CONVENTION

[1] Clause relating to the Executive [2] again under consideration.

M. ELSEWORTH moved "that the Executive be appointed by the Legislature," except when the magistrate last chosen shall have continued in office the whole term for which he was chosen, & be reeligible, in which case the choice shall be by Electors appointed by the Legislatures of the States for that purpose." By this means a deserving magistrate may be reelected without making him dependent on the Legislature.[3]

M. GERRY repeated his remark that an election at all by the Nat! Legislature was radically and incurably wrong; and moved that the Executive be appointed by the Governours & Presidents of the States, with advice of their Councils, and where there are no Councils by Electors chosen by the Legislatures. The executives to vote in the following proportions: viz—

M. MADISON. There are objections agst every mode that has been, or perhaps can be proposed. The election must be made either by some existing authority under the Nat! or State Constitutions—or by some special authority derived from the people—or by the people themselves.—The two Existing authorities under the Nat! Constitution w^d be the Legislative & Judiciary. The latter he presumed was out of the question. The former was in his Judgment liable to in-superable objections. Besides the general influence of that mode on the independence of the Executive, 1.[4] the election of the Chief Magistrate would agitate & divide the legislature so much that the public interest would materially suffer by it. Public bodies are

---

[1] The word " The " is here inserted in the transcript.
[2] The word " being " is here inserted in the transcript.
[3] The transcript italicizes the phrase " making him dependent on the Legislature."
[4] The figure " 1 " is changed to " In the first place " in the transcript.

always apt to be thrown into contentions, but into more violent ones by such occasions than by any others. 2.[1] the candidate would intrigue with the Legislature, would derive his appointment from the predominant faction, and be apt to render his administration subservient to its views. 3.[2] The Ministers of foreign powers would have and [3] make use of, the opportunity to mix their intrigues & influence with the Election. Limited as the powers of the Executive are, it will be an object of great moment with the great rival powers of Europe who have American possessions, to have at the head of our Governm.[t] a man attached to their respective politics & interests. No pains, nor perhaps expence, will be spared, to gain from the Legislature an appointm.[t] favorable to their wishes. Germany & Poland are witnesses of this danger. In the former, the election of the Head of the Empire, till it became in a manner hereditary, interested all Europe, and was much influenced by foreign interference. In the latter, altho' the elective Magistrate has very little real power, his election has at all times produced the most eager interference of forign princes, and has in fact at length slid entirely into foreign hands. The existing authorities in the States are the Legislative, Executive & Judiciary. The appointment of the Nat.[l] Executive by the first, was objectionable in many points of view, some of which had been already mentioned. He would mention one which of itself would decide his opinion. The Legislatures of the States had betrayed a strong propensity to a variety of pernicious measures. One object of the Nat.[l] Legisl.[re] was to controul this propensity. One object of the Nat.[l] Executive, so far as it would have a negative on the laws, was to controul the Nat.[l] Legislature, so far as it might be infected with a similar propensity. Refer the appointm.[t] of the Nat.[l] Executive to the State Legislatures, and this controuling purpose may be defeated. The Legislatures can & will act with some kind of regular plan, and will promote the appointm.[t] of a man who will not oppose himself to a favorite object. Should a majority of the Legislatures at the time of election have the same object, or different objects of the same kind, The Nat.[l] Executive would be rendered subservient to them.—An appointment by the State Executives, was liable among other objections to this insuperable one, that being standing bodies, they could & would be courted, and intrigued with by the Candidates, by their partizans, and by the Ministers of foreign powers. The State Judiciarys had not [4] & he pre-

---

[1] The figure " 2 " is changed to " In the second place " in the transcript.
[2] The figure " 3 " is changed to " In the third place " in the transcript.
[3] The word "would " is here inserted in the transcript.
[4] The word "been " is here inserted in the transcript.

sumed w^d not be proposed as a proper source of appointment. The option before us then lay between an appointment by Electors chosen by the people—and an immediate appointment by the people. He thought the former mode free from many of the objections which had been urged agst it, and greatly preferable to an appointment by the Nat^l Legislature. As the electors would be chosen for the occasion, would meet at once, & proceed immediately to an appointment, there would be very little opportunity for cabal, or corruption. As a farther precaution, it might be required that they should meet at some place, distinct from the seat of Gov^t and even that no person within a certain distance of the place at the time sh^d be eligible. This Mode however had been rejected so recently & by so great a majority that it probably would not be proposed anew. The remaining mode was an election by the people or rather by the qualified part of them, at large: With all its imperfections he liked this best. He would not repeat either the general argum^{ts} for or the objections agst this mode. He would only take notice of two difficulties which he admitted to have weight. The first arose from the disposition in the people to prefer a Citizen of their own State, and the disadvantage this w^d throw on the smaller States. Great as this objection might be he did not think it equal to such as lay agst every other mode which had been proposed. He thought too that some expedient might be hit upon that would obviate it. The second difficulty arose from the disproportion of qualified voters in the N. & S. States, and the disadvantages which this mode would throw on the latter. The answer to this objection was 1.[1] that this disproportion would be continually decreasing under the influence of the Republican laws introduced in the S. States, and the more rapid increase of their population. 2.[2] That local considerations must give way to the general interest. As an individual from the S. States he was willing to make the sacrifice.

Mr ELSEWORTH. The objection drawn from the different sizes of the States, is unanswerable. The Citizens of the largest States would invariably prefer the Candidate within the State; and the largest States w^d invariably have the man.

[3] Question on Mr Elseworth's motion as above.

N. H. ay. Mas. no. C^t ay. N. J. no. P^a ay. Del. no. M^d ay. V^a no. N. C. no. S. C. no. Geo. no.[4]

---

[1] The figure " 1 " is changed to " in the first place " in the transcript.
[2] The figure " 2 " is changed to " in the second place " in the transcript.
[3] The words " On the " are here inserted in the transcript.
[4] In the transcript the vote reads: " New Hampshire, Connecticut, Pennsylvania, Maryland, aye—4; Massachusetts, New Jersey, Delaware, Virginia, North Carolina, South Carolina, Georgia, no—7."

M: PINKNEY moved that the election by the Legislature be qualified with a proviso that no person be eligible for more than 6 years in any twelve years. He thought this would have all the advantage & at the same time avoid in some degree the inconveniency,[1] of an absolute ineligibility a 2ᵈ time.

Col. MASON approved the idea. It had the sanction of experience in the instance of Cong: and some of the Executives of the States. It rendered the Executive as effectually independent, as an ineligibility after his first election, and opened the way at the same time for the advantage of his future services. He preferred on the whole the election by the Nat! Legislature: Tho' Candor obliged him to admit, that there was great danger of foreign influence, as had been suggested. This was the most serious objection with him that had been urged.

M: BUTLER. The two great evils to be avoided are cabal at home, & influence from abroad. It will be difficult to avoid either if the Election be made by the Nat! Legislature. On the other hand: The Gov: should not be made so complex & unwieldy as to disgust the States. This would be the case, if the election shᵈ be referred to the people. He liked best an election by Electors chosen by the Legislatures of the States. He was ag�st a re-eligibility at all events. He was also ag�st a ratio of votes in the States. An equality should prevail in this case. The reasons for departing from it do not hold in the case of the Executive as in that of the Legislature.

M: GERRY approved of M: Pinkney's motion as lessening the evil.

Mr Gov: MORRIS was ag�st a rotation in every case. It formed a political School, in wᶜʰ we were always governed by the scholars, and not by the Masters. The evils to be guarded ag�st in this case are 1.[2] the undue influence of the Legislature. 2.[2] instability of Councils. 3.[2] misconduct in office. To guard agᵗ the first, we run into the second evil. We adopt a rotation which produces instability of Councils. To avoid Sylla we fall into Charibdis. A change of men is ever followed by a change of measures We see this fully exemplified in the vicissitudes among ourselves, particularly in the State of Pen: The self-sufficiency of a victorious party scorns to tread in the paths of their predecessors. Rehoboam will not imitate Soloman. 2.[3] the Rotation in office will not prevent intrigue and depend-

---

[1] The word "inconveniency" is changed to "inconvenience" in the transcript.

[2] The figures "1," "2" and "3" are changed to "first," "secondly" and "thirdly" in the transcript.

[3] The figure "2" is changed to "Secondly" in the transcript.

ence on the Legislature. The man in office will look forward to the period at which he will become re-eligible. The distance of the period, the improbability of such a protraction of his life will be no obstacle. Such is the nature of man, formed by his benevolent author no doubt for wise ends, that altho' he knows his existence to be limited to a span, he takes his measures as if he were to live for ever. But taking another supposition, the inefficacy of the expedient will be manifest. If the magistrate does not look forward to his re-election to the Executive, he will be pretty sure to keep in view the opportunity of his going into the Legislature itself. He will have little objection then to an extension of power on a theatre where he expects to act a distinguished part; and will be very unwilling to take any step that may endanger his popularity with the Legislature, on his influence over which the figure he is to make will depend. 3.[1] To avoid the third evil, impeachments will be essential, and hence an additional reason ag^{st} an election by the Legislature. He considered an election by the people as the best, by the Legislature as the worst, mode. Putting both these aside, he could not but favor the idea of M^r. Wilson, of introducing a mixture of lot. It will diminish, if not destroy both cabal & dependence.

Mr WILLIAMSON was sensible that strong objections lay ag^{st} an election of the Executive by the Legislature, and that it opened a door for foreign influence. The principal objection ag^{st} an election by the people seemed to be, the disadvantage under which it would place the smaller States. He suggested as a cure for this difficulty, that each man should vote for 3 candidates, One of these[2] he observed would be probably of his own State, the other 2. of some other States; and as probably of a small as a large one.

Mr Govr MORRIS liked the idea, suggesting as an amendment that each man should vote for two persons one of whom at least should not be of his own State.

Mr MADISON also thought something valuable might be made of the suggestion with the proposed amendment of it. The second best man in this case would probably be the first, in fact. The only objection which occurred was that each Citizen after hav^g given his vote for his favorite fellow Citizen, w^d throw away his second on some obscure Citizen of another State, in order to ensure the object of his first choice. But it could hardly be supposed that the Citizens of many States would be so sanguine of having their favorite elected, as not to give their second vote with sincerity to the next object of

---

[1] The figure " 3 " is changed to " Finally " in the transcript.
[2] The word " them " is substituted in the transcript for " these."

their choice. It might moreover be provided in favor of the smaller States that the Executive should not be eligible more than   times in   years from the same State.

M: GERRY. A popular election in this case is radically vicious. The ignorance of the people would put it in the power of some one set of men dispersed through the Union & acting in Concert to delude them into any appointment. He observed that such a Society of men existed in the Order of the Cincinnati. They are respectable, United, and influencial. They will in fact elect the chief Magistrate in every instance, if the election be referred to the people. His respect for the characters composing this Society could not blind him to the danger & impropriety of throwing such a power into their hands.

M: DICKENSON. As far as he could judge from the discussions which had taken place during his attendance, insuperable objections lay ag:t an election of the Executive by the Nat: Legislature; as also by the Legislatures or Executives of the States. He had long leaned towards an election by the people which he regarded as the best & purest source. Objections he was aware lay ag:t this mode, but not so great he thought as ag:t the other modes. The greatest difficulty in the opinion of the House seemed to arise from the partiality of the States to their respective Citizens. But, might not this very partiality be turned to a useful purpose. Let the people of each State chuse its best Citizen. The people will know the most eminent characters of their own States, and the people of different States will feel an emulation in selecting those of which [1] they will have the greatest reason to be proud. Out of the thirteen names thus selected, an Executive Magistrate may be chosen either by the Nat: Legislature, or by Electors appointed by it.

On a Question which was moved for postponing M: Pinkney's motion; in order to make way for some such proposition as had been hinted by M: Williamson & others: it passed in the negative.

N. H. no. Mas. no. C: ay. N. J. ay. P: ay. Del. no. M: ay. V: ay. N. C. no. S. C. no. Geo. no.[2]

On M: Pinkney's motion that no person shall serve in the Executive more than 6 years in 12. years, it passed in the negative.

---

[1] The word " whom " is substituted in the transcript for " which."

[2] In the transcript the vote reads: " Connecticut, New Jersey, Pennsylvania, Maryland, Virginia, aye—5; New Hampshire, Massachusetts, Delaware, North Carolina, South Carolina, Georgia, no—6."

N. H. ay. Mas. ay. C: no. N. J. no. P: no. Del. no. M⁴ no. V: no. N. C. ay. S. C. ay. Geo. ay.[1]

On a motion that the members of the Committee be furnished with copies of the proceedings it was so determined; S. Carolina alone being in the negative.

It was then moved that the members of the House might take copies of the Resolions which had been agreed to; which passed in the negative.

N. H. no. Mas. no. Con: ay. N. J. ay. P: no. Del. ay. Mary⁴ no. V: ay. N. C. ay. S. C. no Geo. no.[2]

M: Gerry & M: Butler moved to refer the resolution relating to the Executive (except the clause making it consist of a single person) to the Committee of detail

M: Wilson hoped that so important a branch of the System w⁴ not be committed untill a general principle sh⁴ be fixed by a vote of the House.

M: Langdon, was for the Commitment—Adj⁴

Thursday July. 26. in Convention.

Col.[3] Mason. In every Stage of the Question relative to the Executive, the difficulty of the subject and the diversity of the opinions concerning it have appeared. Nor have any of the modes of constituting that department been satisfactory. 1.[4] It has been proposed that the election should be made by the people at large; that is that an act which ought to be performed by those who know most of Eminent characters, & qualifications, should be performed by those who know least. 2.[4] that the election should be made by the Legislatures of the States. 3.[4] by the Executives of the States. Ag:ᵗ these modes also strong objections have been urged. 4.[4] It has been proposed that the election should be made by Electors chosen by the people for that purpose. This was at first agreed to: But on further consideration has been rejected. 5.[4] Since which, the mode of M: Wil-

---

[1] In the transcript the vote reads: "New Hampshire, Massachusetts, North Carolina, South Carolina, Georgia, aye—5; Connecticut, New Jersey, Pennsylvania, Delaware, Maryland, Virginia, no—6."

[2] In the transcript the vote reads: "Connecticut, New Jersey, Delaware, Virginia, North Carolina, aye—5; New Hampshire, Massachusetts, Pennsylvania, Maryland, South Carolina, Georgia, no—6."

[3] The word "Mr." is substituted in the transcript for "Col."

[4] The figures "1," "2," "3," "4" and "5" are changed to "First," "Secondly," "Thirdly," etc. in the transcript.

liamson, requiring each freeholder to vote for several candidates has been proposed. This seemed like many other propositions, to carry a plausible face, but on closer inspection is liable to fatal objections. A popular election in any form, as M� Gerry has observed, would throw the appointment into the hands of the Cincinnati, a Society for the members of which he had a great respect; but which he never wished to have a preponderating influence in the Govᵗ 6.[1] Another expedient was proposed by M⁺ Dickenson, which is liable to so palpable & material an inconvenience that he had little doubt of its being by this time rejected by himself. It would exclude every man who happened not to be popular within his own State; tho' the causes of his local unpopularity might be of such a nature as to recommend him to the States at large. 7.[1] Among other expedients, a lottery has been introduced. But as the tickets do not appear to be in much demand, it will probably, not be carried on, and nothing therefore need be said on that subject. After reviewing all these various modes, he was led to conclude, that an election by the Natˡ Legislature as originally proposed, was the best. If it was liable to objections, it was liable to fewer than any other. He conceived at the same time that a second election ought to be absolutely prohibited. Having for his primary object, for the pole[2] -star of his political conduct, the preservation of the rights of the people, he held it as an essential point, as the very palladium of Civil liberty, that the great officers of State, and particularly the Executive should at fixed periods return to that mass from which they were at first taken, in order that they may feel & respect those rights & interests, which are again to be personally valuable to them. He concluded with moving that the constitution of the Executive as reported by the Comᵉ of the whole be re-instated, viz. " that the Executive be appointed for seven years, & be ineligible a 2ᵈ time "

M⁺ DAVIE seconded the motion

Docᵗ FRANKLIN. It seems to have been imagined by some that the returning to the mass of the people was degrading the magistrate. This he thought was contrary to republican principles. In free Governments the rulers are the servants, and the people their superiors & sovereigns. For the former therefore to return among the latter was not to *degrade* but to *promote* them. And it would be imposing an unreasonable burden on them, to keep them always in a State of servitude, and not allow them to become again one of the Masters.

---

[1] The figures " 6 " and " 7 " are changed to " Sixthly " and " Seventhly " in the transcript.

[2] The word " polar " is substituted in the transcript for the word " pole."

¹ Question on Col. Masons motion as above; which ² passed in the affirmative

N. H. ay. Mas!ᵗˢ not on floor. Cᵗ no. N. J. ay. Pᵃ no. Del. no. Mᵈ ay. Vᵃ ay. N. C. ay. S. C. ay. Geo. ay.³

Mᵣ Govʳ Morris was now agˢᵗ the whole paragraph. In answer to Col. Mason's position that a periodical return of the great officers of the State into the mass of the people, was the palladium of Civil liberty he wᵈ observe that on the same principle the Judiciary ought to be periodically degraded; certain it was that the Legislature ought on every principle, yet no one had proposed, or conceived that the members of it should not be re-eligible. In answer to Docᵗ Franklin, that a return into the mass of the people would be a promotion, instead of a degradation, he had no doubt that our Executive like most others would have too much patriotism to shrink from the burden of his office, and too much modesty not to be willing to decline the promotion.

On the question on the whole resolution as amended in the words following—" that a National Executive be instituted—to consist of a single person—to be chosen by the Natl legislature—for the term of seven years—to be ineligible a 2ᵈ time—with power to carry into execution the natl laws—to appoint to offices in cases not otherwise provided for—to be removeable on impeachment & conviction of malpractice or neglect of duty—to receive a fixt compensation for the devotion of his time to the public service, to be paid out of the Natl treasury "—it passed in the affirmative

N. H. ay. Mas. not on floor. Cᵗ ay. N. J. ay. Pᵃ no. Del. no. Mᵈ no. Vᵃ divᵈ Mᵣ Blair & Col. Mason ay. Genl Washington & Mᵣ Madison no. Mᵣ Randolph happened to be out of the House. N. C. ay. S. C. ay. Geo. ay.⁴

Mᵣ Mason moved " that the Committee of detail be instructed to receive a clause requiring certain qualifications of landed property & citizenship of the U. States in members of the ⁵ Legislature, and disqualifying persons having unsettled Accᵗˢ with or being indebted to the

---

¹ The words " On the " are here inserted in the transcript.
² The word " which " is crossed out in the transcript and " it " is written above it.
³ In the transcript the vote reads: " New Hampshire, New Jersey, Maryland, Virginia, North Carolina, South Carolina, Georgia, aye—7; Connecticut, Pennsylvania, Delaware, no—3; Massachusetts not on the floor."
⁴ In the transcript the vote reads: " New Hampshire, Connecticut, New Jersey, North Carolina, South Carolina, Georgia, aye—6; Pennsylvania, Delaware, Maryland, no—3; Massachusetts not on the floor; Virginia, divided [Mr. Blair and Col. Mason, aye. General Washington and Mr. Madison no, Mr. Randolph happened to be out of the House.] "
⁵ The word " National " is here inserted in the transcript.

U. S. from being members of the Nat! Legislature ''—He observed that persons of the latter descriptions had frequently got into the State Legislatures, in order to promote laws that might shelter their delinquencies; and that this evil had crept into Cong? if Report was to be regarded.

M? PINCKNEY seconded the motion

M? Gov? MORRIS. If qualifications are proper, he w? prefer them in the electors rather than the elected. As to debtors of the U. S. they are but few. As to persons having unsettled accounts he believed them to be pretty many. He thought however that such a discrimination would be both odious & useless, and in many instances unjust & cruel. The delay of settlem? had been more the fault of the public than of the individuals. What will be done with those patriotic Citizens who have lent money, or services or property to their Country, without having been yet able to obtain a liquidation of their claims? Are they to be excluded?

M? GHORUM was for leaving to the Legislature, the providing ag?? such abuses as had been mentioned.

Col. MASON mentioned the parliamentary qualifications adopted in the Reign of Queen Anne, which he said had met with universal approbation

M? MADISON had witnessed the zeal of men having acc?? with the public, to get into the Legislatures for sinister purposes. He thought however that if any precaution were to be [1] taken for excluding them, the one proposed, by Col. Mason ought to be new [2] modelled. It might be well to limit the exclusion to persons who had rec? money from the public, and had not accounted for it.

M? Gov? MORRIS. It was a precept of great antiquity as well as [3] high authority that we should not be righteous overmuch. He thought we ought to be equally on our guard ag?? being wise over much. The proposed regulation would enable the Goven? to exclude particular persons from office as long as they pleased He mentioned the case of the Commander in Chief's presenting his account for secret services, which he said was so moderate that every one was astonished at it; and so simple that no doubt could arise on it. Yet had the Auditor been disposed to delay the settlement, how easily might he [4] have effected it, & how cruel w? it be in such a case to keep a

---

[1] The words "to be" are omitted in the transcript.
[2] The word "new" is crossed out and the syllable "re" is written above it.
[3] The word "of" is here inserted in the transcript.
[4] The words "might he" are transposed to read "he might" in the transcript.

distinguished & meritorious Citizen under a temporary disability & disfranchisement. He mentioned this case merely to illustrate the objectionable nature of the proposition. He was opposed to such minutious regulations in a Constitution. The parliamentary qualifications quoted by Col. Mason, had been disregarded in practice; and was but a scheme of the landed ag.ᵗ the monied interest.

M.ʳ Pinckney & Gen.ˡ Pinckney moved to insert by way of amendm.ᵗ the words Judiciary & Executive so as to extend the qualifications to those departments which was agreed to nem. con.

M.ʳ Gerry thought the inconveniency [1] of excluding a few worthy individuals who might be public debtors or have unsettled acc.ᵗˢ ought not to be put in the scale ag.ˢᵗ the public advantages of the regulation, and that the motion did not go far enough.

M.ʳ King observed that there might be great danger in requiring landed property as a qualification since it would [2] exclude the monied interest, whose aids may be essential in particular emergencies to the public safety.

M.ʳ Dickenson, was ag.ˢᵗ any recital of qualifications in the Constitution. It was impossible to make a compleat one, and a partial one w.ᵈ by implication tie up the hands of the Legislature from supplying the omissions, The best defence lay in the freeholders who were to elect the Legislature. Whilst this Source [3] should remain pure, the public interest would be safe. If it ever should be corrupt, no little expedients would repel the danger. He doubted the policy of interweaving into a Republican constitution a veneration for wealth. He had always understood that a veneration for poverty & virtue, were the objects of republican encouragement. It seemed improper that any man of merit should be subjected to disabilities in a Republic where merit was understood to form the great title to public trust, honors & rewards.

M.ʳ Gerry if property be one object of Government, provisions for securing [4] it cannot be improper.

M.ʳ Madison moved to strike out the word *landed*, before the word "qualifications." If the proposition s.ᵈ be agreed to he wished the Committee to be at liberty to report the best criterion they could devise. Landed possessions were no certain evidence of real wealth.

---

[1] The word "inconveniency" is changed to "inconvenience" in the transcript.

[2] The word "might" is substituted in the transcript for the word "would."

[3] The word "resource" is erroneously substituted in the transcript for the word "source."

[4] The words "to secure" are substituted for "for securing," in the transcript.

Many enjoyed them to a great extent who were more in debt than they were worth. The unjust laws of the States had proceeded more from this class of men, than any others. It had often happened that men who had acquired landed property on credit, got into the Legislatures with a view of promoting an unjust protection agst their Creditors. In the next place, if a small quantity of land should be made the standard, it would be no security; if a large one, it would exclude the proper representatives of those classes of Citizens who were not landholders. It was politic as well as just that the interests & rights of every class should be duly represented & understood in the public Councils. It was a provision every where established that the Country should be divided into districts & representatives taken from each, in order that the Legislative Assembly might equally understand & sympathise, with the rights of the people in every part of the Community. It was not less proper that every class of Citizens should have an opportunity of making their rights be felt & understood in the public Councils. The three principal classes into which our citizens were divisible, were the landed the commercial, & the manufacturing. The 2^d & 3^d class, bear as yet a small proportion to the first. The proportion however will daily increase. We see in the populous Countries in [1] Europe now, what we shall be hereafter. These classes understand much less of each others interests & affairs, than men of the same class inhabiting different districts. It is particularly requisite therefore that the interests of one or two of them should not be left entirely to the care, or the [2] impartiality of the third. This must be the case if landed qualifications should be required; few of the mercantile, & scarcely any of the manufacturing class, chusing whilst they continue in business to turn any part of their Stock into landed property. For these reasons he wished if it were possible that some other criterion than the mere possession of land should be devised. He concurred with Mr Govr Morris in thinking that qualifications in the Electors would be much more effectual than in the elected. The former would discriminate between real & ostensible property in the latter; But he was aware of the difficulty of forming any uniform standard that would suit the different circumstances & opinions prevailing in the different States.

Mr Govr Morris 2^{ded} the motion.

On the Question for striking out " landed "

---

[1] The word " of " is substituted in the transcript for " in."

[2] The word " the " is omitted in the transcript.

N. H. ay. Mas. ay. C^t ay. N. J. ay. P^a ay. Del. ay. M^d no. V^a ay. N. C. ay. S. C. ay. Geo. ay.[1]

On [2] Question on [2] 1st part of Col. Masons proposition as to qualification of property & citizenship," as so amended

N. H. ay. Mas^{ts} ay. C^t no. N. J. ay. P^a no. Del. no. M^d ay. V^a ay. N. C. ay. S. C. ay. Geo. ay.[3]

" The 2^d part, for disqualifying debtors, and persons having unsettled accounts," being under consideration

Mr CARROL moved to strike out " having unsettled accounts "

Mr GHORUM seconded the motion; observing that it would put the commercial & manufacturing part of the people on a worse footing than others as they would be most likely to have dealings with the public.

Mr L. MARTIN. if these words should be struck out, and the remaining words concerning debtors retained, it will be the interest of the latter class to keep their accounts unsettled as long as possible.

Mr WILSON was for striking them out. They put too much power in the hands of the Auditors, who might combine with rivals in delaying settlements in order to prolong the disqualifications of particular men. We should consider that we are providing a Constitution for future generations, and not merely for the peculiar circumstances of the moment. The time has been, and will again be, when the public safety may depend on the voluntary aids of individuals which will necessarily open acc^{ts} with the public, and when such acc^{ts} will be a characteristic of patriotism. Besides a partial enumeration of cases will disable the Legislature from disqualifying odious & dangerous characters.

Mr LANGDON was for striking out the whole clause for the reasons given by Mr Wilson. So many exclusions he thought too would render the system unacceptable to the people.

Mr GERRY. If the argum^{ts} used to day were to prevail, we might have a Legislature composed of public debtors, pensioners, placemen & contractors. He thought the proposed qualifications would be pleasing to the people. They will be considered as a security agst unnecessary or undue burdens being imposed on them. He moved to add " pensioners " to the disqualified characters which was negatived.

---

[1] In the transcript the vote reads: "New Hampshire, Massachusetts, Connecticut, New Jersey, Pennsylvania, Delaware, Virginia, North Carolina, South Carolina, Georgia, aye—10; Maryland, no."

[2] The word "the" is here inserted in the transcript.

[3] In the transcript the vote reads: "New Hampshire, Massachusetts, New Jersey, Maryland, Virginia, North Carolina, South Carolina, Georgia, aye—8; Connecticut, Pennsylvania, Delaware, no—3."

N. H. no   Mas. ay.   Con. no.   N. J. no.   P. no.   Del. no.   Mary.
ay.   V. no.   N. C. divided.   S. C. no.   Geo. ay.[1]

M. Gov. MORRIS. The last clause, relating to public debtors will
exclude every importing merchant. Revenue will be drawn it is
foreseen as much as possible, from trade. Duties of course will be
bonded, and the Merch. will remain debtors to the public. He repeated that it had not been so much the fault of individuals as of
the public that transactions between them had not been more generally liquidated & adjusted. At all events to draw from our short &
scanty experience rules that are to operate through succeeding ages,
does not savour much of real wisdom.

On[2] question for striking out, "persons having unsettled accounts
with the U. States."

N. H. ay.   Mas. ay.   C. ay.   N. J. no.   P. ay.   Del. ay.   M. ay.
V. ay.   N. C. ay.   S. C. ay.   Geo. no.[3]

M. ELSEWORTH was for disagreeing to the remainder of the clause
disqualifying public debtors; and for leaving to the wisdom of the
Legislature and the virtue of the Citizens, the task of providing
ag. such evils. Is the smallest as well[4] largest debtor to be excluded? Then every arrear of taxes will disqualify. Besides how
is it to be known to the people when they elect who are or are not
public debtors. The exclusion of pensioners & placemen in Engl.
is founded on a consideration not existing here. As persons of that
sort are dependent on the Crown, they tend to increase its influence.

M. PINKNEY s. he was at first a friend to the proposition, for the
sake of the clause relating to qualifications of property; but he disliked the exclusion of public debtors; it went too far. It w. exclude
persons who had purchased confiscated property or should purchase
Western territory of the public, and might be some obstacle to the
sale of the latter.

On the question for agreeing to the clause disqualifying public
debtors

N. H. no.   Mas. no.   C. no.   N. J. no.   P. no.   Del. no.   M. no.
V. no.   N. C. ay.   S. C. no.   Geo. ay.[5]

---

[1] In the transcript the vote reads: "Massachusetts, Maryland, Georgia,
aye—3; New Hampshire, Connecticut, New Jersey, Pennsylvania, Delaware,
Virginia, South Carolina, no—7; North Carolina, divided."
[2] The word "the" is here inserted in the transcript.
[3] In the transcript the vote reads: "New Hampshire, Massachusetts, Connecticut, Pennsylvania, Delaware, Maryland, Virginia, North Carolina, South
Carolina, aye—9; New Jersey, Georgia, no—2."
[4] The words "as the" are here inserted in the transcript.
[5] In the transcript the vote reads: "North Carolina, Georgia, aye—2; New
Hampshire, Massachusetts, Connecticut, New Jersey, Pennsylvania, Delaware,
Maryland, Virginia, South Carolina, no—9."

Col. Mason. observed that it would be proper, as he thought, that some provision should be made in the Constitution ag.ᵗ choosing for the seat of the Gen.ˡ Gov.ᵗ the City or place at which the seat of any State Gov.ᵗ might be fixt.   There were 2 objections ag.ˢᵗ having them at the same place, which without mentioning others, required some precaution on the subject.   The 1.ˢᵗ was that it tended to produce disputes concerning jurisdiction.   The 2.ᵈ & principal one was that the intermixture of the two Legislatures tended to give a provincial tincture to yᵉ Nat.ˡ deliberations.   He moved that the Com.ᵉ be instructed to receive a clause to prevent the seat of the Nat.ˡ Gov.ᵗ being in the same City or town with the Seat of the Gov.ᵗ of any State longer than untill the necessary public buildings could be erected.

M.ʳ Alex. Martin 2ᵈᵉᵈ the motion.

M.ʳ Gov.ʳ Morris did not dislike the idea, but was apprehensive that such a clause might make enemies of Phild.ᵃ & N. York which had expectations of becoming the Seat of the Gen.ˡ Gov.ᵗ

M.ʳ Langdon approved the idea also: but suggisted the case of a State moving its seat of Gov.ᵗ to the nat.ˡ seat after the erection of the public buildings.

M.ʳ Ghorum.   The precaution may be evaded by the Nat.ˡ Legisl.ʳᵉ by delaying to erect the public buildings

M.ʳ Gerry conceived it to be the gene.ˡ sense of America, that neither the Seat of a State Gov.ᵗ nor any large commercial City should be the seat of the Gen.ˡ Gov.ᵗ

M.ʳ Williamson liked the idea, but knowing how much the passions of men were agitated by this matter, was apprehensive of turning them ag.ˢᵗ the System.   He apprehended also that an evasion might be practiced in the way hinted by M.ʳ Ghorum.

M.ʳ Pinkney thought the seat of a State Gov.ᵗ ought to be avoided; but that a large town or its vicinity would be proper for the Seat of the Gen.ˡ Gov.ᵗ

Col. Mason did not mean to press the motion at this time, nor to excite any hostile passions ag.ˢᵗ the system.   He was content to withdraw the motion for the present.

M.ʳ Butler was for fixing by the Constitution the place, & a central one, for the seat of the Nat.ˡ Gov.ᵗ

The proceedings since Monday last were referred unanimously [1] to the Com.ᵉ of detail, and the Convention then unanimously Adjourned till Monday, Aug.ˢᵗ 6. that the Com.ᵉ of detail might have time to

---

[1] The words "referred unanimously" are transposed to read "unanimously referred" in the transcript.

prepare & report the Constitution.   The whole proceedings[1] as referred are as follow: " [here copy them from the Journal p. 207[2]

[June 20.[3]	I.	RESOLVED, That the Government of the United States ought to consist of a supreme legislative, judiciary, and executive.
June 21.	II.	RESOLVED, That the legislature consist of two branches.
	III.	RESOLVED, That the members of the first branch of the legislature ought to be elected by the people of the several states,
June 22.		for the term of two years; to be paid out of the publick treasury; to receive an adequate compensation for their services; to
June 23.		be of the age of twenty-five years at least; to be ineligible[4] and incapable of holding any office under the authority of the United States (except those peculiarly belonging to the functions of the first branch) during the term of service of the first branch.
June 25.	IV.	RESOLVED, That the members of the second branch of the legislature of the United States ought to be chosen by the individual
June 26.		legislatures; to be of the age of thirty years at least; to hold their offices for six years, one third to go out biennally; to receive a compensation for the devotion of their time to the publick service; to be ineligible to and incapable of holding any office, under the authority of the United States (except those peculiarly belonging to the functions of the second branch) during the term for which they are elected, and for one year thereafter.
	V.	RESOLVED, That each branch ought to possess the right of originating acts.
Postponed 27.	VI.	RESOLVED, That the national legislature
July 16.		ought to possess the legislative rights
July 17.		vested in Congress by the confederation; and moreover, to legislate in all cases for the general interests of the union, and also

---

[1] The word "proceedings" is crossed out in the transcript and "Resolutions" is written above it.

[2] Madison's direction is omitted in the transcript.

[3] The printed Journal says, page 11, that these 23 Resolutions are "collected from the proceedings of the convention, as they are spread over the journal from June 19th to July 26th." The dates in the margin show when the respective Resolutions were adopted. They are omitted in the transcript.

[4] The word "to" is here inserted in the transcript.

in those to which the states are separately incompetent, or in which the harmony of the United States may be interrupted by the exercise of individual legislation.

VII. RESOLVED, That the legislative acts of the United States, made by virtue and in pursuance of the articles of union, and all treaties made and ratified under the authority of the United States, shall be the supreme law of the respective states, as far as those acts or treaties shall relate to the said states, or their citizens and inhabitants; and that the judiciaries of the several states shall be bound thereby in their decisions, any thing in the respective laws of the individual states to the contrary, notwithstanding.

16.   VIII. RESOLVED, That in the original formation of the legislature of the United States, the first branch thereof shall consist of sixty-five members; of which number

New Hampshire shall send	three,
Massachusetts . . .	eight,
Rhode Island . . .	one,
Connecticut . . .	five,
New York	six,
New Jersey . . .	four,
Pennsylvania . . .	eight,
Delaware	one,
Maryland	six,
Virginia	ten,
North Carolina . .	five,
South Carolina . .	five,
Georgia	three.

But as the present situation of the states may probably alter in the number of their inhabitants, the legislature of the United States shall be authorized, from time to time, to apportion the number of representatives; and in case any of the states shall hereafter be divided, or enlarged by addition of territory, or any two or more states united, or any new states created within the limits of the United States, the legislature of the United States shall possess authority to regulate the number of representatives, in any of the foregoing cases, upon the principle of their number of inhabitants according to the provisions hereafter mentioned, namely—Provided always, that representation ought to be proportioned according [1] to direct taxation. And in order to ascertain the alteration in the direct taxation, which may be required from time to time by the changes in the relative circumstances of the states—

IX. RESOLVED, That a census be taken within six years from the first meeting of the legisletur of the United States, and once within the term of every ten years afterwards, of all the inhabitants of the United States, in the manner and according to the ratio recommended by Congress in their resolution of April 18, 1783; and that the legislature of the United States shall proportion the direct taxation accordingly.

X. RESOLVED, That all bills for raising or appropriating money, and for fixing the salaries of the officers of the government of the United States, shall originate in the first branch of the legislature of the United States, and shall not be altered or amended by the second branch; and that no money shall be drawn from the publick treasury, but in pursuance of appropriations to be originated by the first branch.

XI. RESOLVED, That in the second branch of the legislature of the United States, each state shall have an equal vote.

July 26.   XII. RESOLVED, That a national executive be instituted, to consist of a single person; to be chosen by the national legislature, for the term of seven years; to be ineligible a second time; with power to carry into execution the national laws; to appoint to offices in cases not otherwise provided for; to be removable on impeachment, and conviction of mal-practice or neglect of duty; to receive a fixed compensation for the devotion of his time to [2] publick service; to be paid out of the publick treasury.

July 21.   XIII. RESOLVED, That the national executive shall have a right to negative any legislative act, which shall not be afterwards passed, unless by two third parts of each branch of the national legislature.

---

[1] The word "according" is omitted in the transcript.
[2] The word "the" is here inserted in the transcript.

18.

July 21.

18.

XIV. RESOLVED, That a national judiciary be established, to consist of one supreme tribunal, the judges of which shall be appointed by the second branch of the national legislature; to hold their offices during good behaviour; to receive punctually, at stated times, a fixed compensation for their services, in which no diminution shall be made, so as to affect the persons actually in office at the time of such diminution.

XV. RESOLVED, That the national legislature be empowered to appoint inferior tribunals.

XVI. RESOLVED, That the jurisdiction of the national judiciary shall extend to cases arising under laws passed by the general legislature; and to such other questions as involve the national peace and harmony.

XVII. RESOLVED, That provision ought to be made for the admission of states lawfully arising within the limits of the United States, whether from a voluntary junction of government and territory, or otherwise, with the consent of a number of voices in the national legislature less than the whole.

XVIII. RESOLVED, That a republican form of government shall be guarantied to each state; and that each state shall be protected against foreign and domestick violence.

23.

XIX. RESOLVED, That provision ought to be made for the amendment of the articles of union, whensoever it shall seem necessary.

XX. RESOLVED, That the legislative, executive, and judiciary powers, within the several states, and of the national government, ought to be bound, by oath, to support the articles of union.

XXI. RESOLVED, That the amendments which shall be offered to the confederation by the convention ought, at a proper time or times after the approbation of Congress, to be submitted to an assembly or assemblies of representatives, recommended by the several legislatures, to be expressly chosen by the people to consider and decide thereon.

XXII. RESOLVED, That the representation in the second branch of the legislature of the United States [1] consist of two members from each state, who shall vote per capita.

---

[1] The word " shall " is here inserted in the transcript.

26.   **XXIII.** RESOLVED, That it be an instruction to the committee, to whom were referred the proceedings of the convention for the establishment of a national government, to receive a clause or clauses, requiring certain qualifications of property and citizenship, in the United States, for the executive, the judiciary, and the members of both branches of the legislature of the United States.]

With the above resolutions were referred the propositions offered by M: C. Pinckney on the 29.th of May, & by M: Patterson on the 15th of June.[1]

MONDAY AUGUST 6TH IN CONVENTION

M: John Francis Mercer from Maryland took his seat.

M: RUTLIDGE delivered in the Report of the Committee of detail as follows: a printed copy being at the same time furnished to each member: [2]

" We the people of the States of New Hampshire, Massachussetts, Rhode-Island and Providence Plantations, Connecticut, New-York, New-Jersey, Pennsylvania, Delaware, Maryland, Virginia, North-Carolina, South-Carolina, and Georgia, do ordain, declare, and establish the following Constitution for the Government of Ourselves and our Posterity.

ARTICLE I

The stile of the Government shall be, "The United States of America "

[3] II

The Government shall consist of supreme legislative, executive; and judicial powers.

---

[1] The word " Adjourned " is here inserted in the transcript.

[2] Madison's printed copy is marked: " As Reported by Com^e of Detail viz of five. Aug. 6. 1787." It is a large folio of seven pages. In the enumeration of the Articles by a misprint VI. was repeated, and the alterations in Article VII. and succeeding articles were made by Madison. In Sec. 11 of Article VI., as it was printed, it appeared: " The enacting stile of the laws of the United States shall be. ' Be it enacted, and it is hereby enacted by the House of Representatives, and by the Senate of the United States, in Congress assembled.' " which Madison altered to read: " The enacting stile of the laws of the United States shall be. ' Be it enacted by the Senate & representatives in Congress assembled.' " The printed copy among the Madison papers is a duplicate of the copy filed by General Washington with the papers of the Constitution, and Sec. 11 is there given as actually printed.

Madison accurately transcribed the report for his notes and it is this copy which is used in the text.

[3] The word " Article " is here inserted in the transcript.

[1] III

The legislative power shall be vested in a Congress, to consist of two separate and distinct bodies of men, a House of Representatives and a Senate; each of which shall in all cases have a negative on the other. The Legislature shall meet on the first Monday in December [2] every year.

IV

Sect. 1. The members of the House of Representatives shall be chosen every second year, by the people of the several States comprehended within this Union. The qualifications of the electors shall be the same, from time to time, as those of the electors in the several States, of the most numerous branch of their own legislatures.

Sect. 2. Every member of the House of Representatives shall be of the age of twenty five years at least; shall have been a citizen in the United States for at least three years before his election; and shall be, at the time of his election, a resident of the State in which he shall be chosen.

Sect. 3. The House of Representatives shall, at its first formation, and until the number of citizens and inhabitants shall be taken in the manner herein after described, consist of sixty five Members, of whom three shall be chosen in New-Hampshire, eight in Massachusetts, one in Rhode-Island and Providence Plantations, five in Connecticut, six in New-York, four in New-Jersey, eight in Pennsylvania, one in Delaware, six in Maryland, ten in Virginia, five in North-Carolina, five in South-Carolina, and three in Georgia.

Sect. 4. As the proportions of numbers in different States will alter from time to time; as some of the States may hereafter be divided; as others may be enlarged by addition of territory; as two or more States may be united; as new States will be erected within the limits of the United States, the Legislature shall, in each of these cases, regulate the number of representatives by the number of inhabitants, according to the provisions herein after made, at the rate of one for every forty thousand.

Sect. 5. All bills for raising or appropriating money, and for fixing the salaries of the officers of Government, shall originate in the House of Representatives, and shall not be altered or amended by the Senate. No money shall be drawn from the Public Treasury, but in pursuance of appropriations that shall originate in the House of Representatives.

Sect. 6. The House of Representatives shall have the sole power of impeachment. It shall choose its Speaker and other officers.

Sect. 7. Vacancies in the House of Representatives shall be supplied by writs of election from the executive authority of the State, in the representation from which it [3] shall happen.

---

[1] The word " Article " is here inserted in the transcript.
[2] The word " in " is here inserted in the transcript.
[3] The word " it " is crossed out and the word " they " is written above it in the transcript.

[1] V

Sect 1. The Senate of the United States shall be chosen by the Legislatures of the several States. Each Legislature shall chuse two members. Vacancies may be supplied by the Executive until the next meeting of the Legislature. Each member shall have one vote.

Sect. 2. The Senators shall be chosen for six years; but immediately after the first election they shall be divided, by lot, into three classes, as nearly as may be, numbered one, two and three. The seats of the members of the first class shall be vacated at the expiration of the second year, of the second class at the expiration of the fourth year, of the third class at the expiration of the sixth year, so that a third part of the members may be chosen every second year.

Sect. 3. Every member of the Senate shall be of the age of thirty years at least; shall have been a citizen in the United States for at least four years before his election; and shall be, at the time of his election, a resident of the State for which he shall be chosen.

Sect. 4. The Senate shall chuse its own President and other officers.

[1] VI

Sect. 1. The times and places and manner of holding the elections of the members of each House shall be prescribed by the Legislature of each State; but their provisions concerning them may, at any time, be altered by the Legislature of the United States.

Sect. 2. The Legislature of the United States shall have authority to establish such uniform qualifications of the members of each House, with regard to property, as to the said Legislature shall seem expedient.

Sect. 3. In each House a majority of the members shall constitute a quorum to do business; but a smaller number may adjourn from day to day.

Sect. 4. Each House shall be the judge of the elections, returns and qualifications of its own members.

Sect. 5. Freedom of speech and debate in the Legislature shall not be impeached or questioned in any Court or place out of the Legislature; and the members of each House shall, in all cases, except treason felony and breach of the peace, be privileged from arrest during their attendance at Congress, and in going to and returning from it.

Sect. 6. Each House may determine the rules of its proceedings; may punish its members for disorderly behaviour; and may expel a member.

Sect. 7. The House of Representatives, and the Senate, when it shall be acting in a legislative capacity, shall keep a journal of their proceedings, and shall, from time to time, publish them: and the yeas and nays of the members of each House, on any question, shall at the desire of one-fifth part of the members present, be entered on the journal.

---

[1] The word " Article " is here inserted in the transcript.

Sect. 8. Neither House, without the consent of the other, shall adjourn for more than three days, nor to any other place than that at which the two Houses are sitting. But this regulation shall not extend to the Senate, when it shall exercise the powers mentioned in the   article.

Sect. 9. The members of each House shall be ineligible to, and incapable of holding any office under the authority of the United States, during the time for which they shall respectively be elected: and the members of the Senate shall be ineligible to, and incapable of holding any such office for one year afterwards.

Sect. 10. The members of each House shall receive a compensation for their services, to be ascertained and paid by the State, in which they shall be chosen.

[1] Sect. 11. The enacting stile of the laws of the United States shall be. "Be it enacted by the Senate and Representatives in Congress assembled."

Sect. 12. Each House shall possess the right of originating bills, except in the cases beforementioned.

Sect. 13. Every bill, which shall have passed the House of Representatives and the Senate, shall, before it become [2] a law, be presented to the President of the United States for his revision: if, upon such revision, he approve of it, he shall signify his approbation by signing it: But if, upon such revision, it shall appear to him improper for being passed into a law, he shall return it, together with his objections against it, to that House in which it shall have originated, who shall enter the objections at large on their journal and proceed to reconsider the bill. But if after such reconsideration, two thirds of that House shall, notwithstanding the objections of the President, agree to pass it, it shall together with his objections, be sent to the other House, by which it shall likewise be reconsidered, and if approved by two thirds of the other House also, it shall become a law. But in all such cases, the votes of both Houses shall be determined by yeas and nays; and the names of the persons voting for or against the bill shall be entered on the journal of each House respectively. If any bill shall not be returned by the President within seven days after it shall have been presented to him, it shall be a law, unless the legislature, by their adjournment, prevent its return; in which case it shall not be a law.

[3] VII

Sect. 1. The Legislature of the United States shall have the power to lay and collect taxes, duties, imposts and excises;

To regulate commerce with foreign nations, and among the several States;

To establish an uniform rule of naturalization throughout the United States;

---

[1] Section 11 is copied in the transcript as originally printed. See footnote [2] on p. 337.

[2] The word "becomes" is substituted in the transcript for "become."

[3] The word "Article" is here inserted in the transcript.

To coin money;

To regulate the value of foreign coin;

To fix the standard of weights and measures;

To establish Post-offices;

To borrow money, and emit bills on the credit of the United States;

To appoint a Treasurer by ballot;

To constitute tribunals inferior to the Supreme Court;

To make rules concerning captures on land and water;

To declare the law and punishment of piracies and felonies committed on the high seas, and the punishment of counterfeiting the coin of the United States, and of offences against the law of nations;

To subdue a rebellion in any State, on the application of its legislature;

To make war;

To raise armies;

To build and equip fleets;

To call forth the aid of the militia, in order to execute the laws of the Union, enforce treaties, suppress insurrections, and repel invasions;

And to make all laws that shall be necessary and proper for carrying into execution the foregoing powers, and all other powers vested, by this Constitution, in the government of the United States, or in any department or officer [1] thereof;

Sect. 2.   Treason against the United States shall consist only in levying war against the United States, or any of them; and in adhering to the enemies of the United States, or any of them.   The Legislature of the United States shall have power to declare the punishment of treason.   No person shall be convicted of treason, unless on the testimony of two witnesses.   No attainder of treason shall work corruption of blood, nor forfeiture, except during the life of the person attainted.

Sect. 3.   The proportions of direct taxation shall be regulated by the whole number of white and other free citizens and inhabitants, of every age, sex and condition, including those bound to servitude for a term of years, and three fifths of all other persons not comprehended in the foregoing description, (except Indians not paying taxes) which number shall, within six years after the first meeting of the Legislature, and within the term of every ten years afterwards, be taken in such [2] manner as the said Legislature shall direct.

Sect. 4.   No tax or duty shall be laid by the Legislature on articles exported from any State; nor on the migration or importation of such persons as the several States shall think proper to admit; nor shall such migration or importation be prohibited.

Sect. 5.   No capitation tax shall be laid, unless in proportion to the Census hereinbefore directed to be taken.

Sect. 6.   No navigation act shall be passed without the assent of two thirds of the members present in the each House.

---

[1] The letter " r " is stricken from the word " officer " in the transcript.

[2] The word " a " is here inserted in the transcript.

Sect. 7.   The United States shall not grant any title of Nobility.

[1] VIII

The Acts of the Legislature of the United States made in pursuance of this Constitution, and all treaties made under the authority of the United States shall be the supreme law of the several States, and of their citizens and inhabitants; and the judges in the several States shall be bound thereby in their decisions; any thing in the Constitutions or laws of the several States to the contrary notwithstanding.

[1] IX

Sect 1.   The Senate of the United States shall have power to make treaties, and to appoint Ambassadors, and Judges of the Supreme Court.

Sect. 2.   In all disputes and controversies now subsisting, or that may hereafter subsist between two or more States, respecting jurisdiction or territory, the Senate shall possess the following powers. Whenever the Legislature, or the Executive authority, or lawful agent of any State, in controversy with another, shall by memorial to the Senate, state the matter in question, and apply for a hearing; notice of such memorial and application shall be given by order of the Senate, to the Legislature or the Executive authority of the other State in Controversy. The Senate shall also assign a day for the appearance of the parties, by their agents, before the [2] House. The Agents shall be directed to appoint, by joint consent, commissioners or judges to constitute a Court for hearing and determining the matter in question. But if the Agents cannot agree, the Senate shall name three persons out of each of the several States; and from the list of such persons each party shall alternately strike out one, until the number shall be reduced to thirteen; and from that number not less than seven nor more than nine names, as the Senate shall direct, shall in their presence, be drawn out by lot; and the persons whose names shall be so drawn, or any five of them shall be commissioners or Judges to hear and finally determine the controversy; provided a majority of the Judges, who shall hear the cause, agree in the determination. If either party shall neglect to attend at the day assigned, without shewing sufficient reasons for not attending, or being present shall refuse to strike, the Senate shall proceed to nominate three persons out of each State, and the Clerk of the Senate shall strike in behalf of the party absent or refusing. If any of the parties shall refuse to submit to the authority of such Court; or shall not appear to prosecute or defend their claim or cause, the Court shall nevertheless proceed to pronounce judgment. The judgment shall be final and conclusive. The proceedings shall be transmitted to the President of the Senate, and shall be lodged among the public records, for the security of the parties concerned. Every Commis-

---

[1] The word " Article " is here inserted in the transcript.
[2] The word " the " is changed to " that " in the transcript.

sioner shall, before he sit in judgment, take an oath, to be administred by one of the Judges of the Supreme or Superior Court of the State where the cause shall be tried, "well and truly to hear and determine the matter in question according to the best of his judgment, without favor, affection, or hope of reward.'"

Sect. 3. All controversies concerning lands claimed under different grants of two or more States, whose jurisdictions, as they respect such lands shall have been decided or adjusted subsequent [1] to such grants, or any of them, shall, on application to the Senate, be finally determined, as near as may be, in the same manner as is before prescribed for deciding controversies between different States.

[2] X

Sect. 1. The Executive Power of the United States shall be vested in a single person. His stile shall be, "The President of the United States of America;" and his title shall be, "His Excellency." He shall be elected by ballot by the Legislature. He shall hold his office during the term of seven years; but shall not be elected a second time.

Sect. 2. He shall, from time to time, give information to the Legislature, of the state of the Union: he may recommend to their consideration such measures as he shall judge necessary, and expedient: he may convene them on extraordinary occasions. In case of disagreement between the two Houses, with regard to the time of adjournment, he may adjourn them to such time as he thinks proper: he shall take care that the laws of the United States be. duly and faithfully executed: he shall commission all the officers of the United States; and shall appoint officers in all cases not otherwise provided for by this Constitution. He shall receive Ambassadors, and may correspond with the supreme Executives of the several States. He shall have power to grant reprieves and pardons; but his pardon shall not be pleadable in bar of an impeachment. He shall be commander in chief of the Army and Navy of the United States, and of the Militia of the several States. He shall, at stated times, receive for his services, a compensation, which shall neither be increased nor diminished during his continuance in office. Before he shall enter on the duties of his department, he shall take the following oath or affirmation, "I ——— solemnly swear (or affirm) that that [3] I will faithfully execute the office of Pres   t of the United States of America." He shall be removed from his office on impeachment by the House of Representatives, and conviction in the supreme Court, of treason, bribery, or corruption. Ir case of his removal as aforesaid, death, resignation,. or disability to discharge the powers and duties of his office, the President of the Senate shall exercise those powers and duties, until another President of the United States be chosen, or until the disability of the President be removed.

---

[1] The syllable "ly" is added in the transcript to the word "subsequent."
[2] The word "Article" is here inserted in the transcript.
[3] The word "that" is omitted in the transcript.

[1] XI

Sect. 1. The Judicial Power of the United States shall be vested in one Supreme Court, and in such inferior Courts as shall, when necessary, from time to time, be constituted by the Legislature of the United States.

Sect. 2. The Judges of the Supreme Court, and of the Inferior Courts, shall hold their offices during good behaviour. They shall, at stated times, receive for their services, a compensation, which shall not be diminished during their continuance in office.

Sect. 3. The Jurisdiction of the Supreme Court shall extend to all cases arising under laws passed by the Legislature of the United States; to all cases affecting Ambassadors, other Public Ministers and Consuls; to the trial of impeachments of officers of the United States; to all cases of Admiralty and maritime jurisdiction; to controversies between two or more States, (except such as shall regard Territory or Jurisdiction) between a State and Citizens of another State, between Citizens of different States, and between a State or the Citizens thereof and foreign States, citizens or subjects. In cases of impeachment, cases affecting Ambassadors, other Public Ministers and Consuls, and those in which a State shall be party, this jurisdiction shall be original. In all the other cases beforementioned, it shall be appellate, with such exceptions and under such regulations as the Legislature shall make. The Legislature may assign any part of the jurisdiction abovementioned (except the trial of the President of the United States) in the manner, and under the limitations which it shall think proper, to such Inferior Courts, as it shall constitute from time to time.

Sect. 4. The trial of all criminal offences (except in cases of impeachments) shall be in the State where they shall be committed; and shall be by Jury.

Sect. 5. Judgment, in cases of Impeachment, shall not extend further than to removal from office, and disqualification to hold and enjoy any office of honour, trust or profit, under the United States. But the party convicted shall, nevertheless be liable and subject to indictment, trial, judgment and punishment according to law.

[1] XII

No State shall coin money; nor grant letters of marque and reprisal; nor enter into any Treaty, alliance, or confederation; nor grant any title of Nobility.

[1] XIII

No State, without the consent of the Legislature of the United States, shall emit bills of credit, or make any thing but specie a tender in payment of debts; nor lay imposts or duties on imports; nor keep troops or ships of war in time of peace; nor enter into any agreement or compact with another State, or with any foreign power;

---

[1] The word "Article" is here inserted in the transcript.

nor engage in any war, unless it shall be actually invaded by enemies, or the danger of invasion be so imminent, as not to admit of delay, until the Legislature of the United States can be consulted.

[1] XIV

The Citizens of each State shall be entitled to all privileges and immunities of citizens in the several States.

[1] XV

Any person charged with treason, felony or high misdemeanor in any State, who shall flee from justice, and shall be found in any other State, shall, on demand of the Executive power of the State from which he fled, be delivered up and removed to the State having jurisdiction of the offence.

[1] XVI

Full faith shall be given in each State to the acts of the Legislatures, and to the records and judicial proceedings of the Courts and magistrates of every other State.

[1] XVII

New States lawfully constituted or established within the limits of the United States may be admitted, by the Legislature, into this Government; but to such admission the consent of two thirds of the members present in each House shall be necessary. If a new State shall arise within the limits of any of the present States, the consent of the Legislatures of such States shall be also necessary to its admission. If the admission be consented to, the new States shall be admitted on the same terms with the original States. But the Legislature may make conditions with the new States, concerning the public debt which shall be then subsisting.

[1] XVIII

The United States shall guaranty to each State a Republican form of Government; and shall protect each State against foreign invasions, and, on the application of its Legislature, against domestic violence.

[1] XIX

On the application of the Legislatures of two thirds of the States in the Union, for an amendment of this Constitution, the Legislature of the United States shall call a Convention for that purpose.

[1] XX

The members of the Legislatures, and the Executive and Judicial officers of the United States, and of the several States, shall be bound by oath to support this Constitution.

---

[1] The word " Article " is here inserted in the transcript.

[1] XXI

The ratifications of the Conventions of   States shall be sufficient for organizing this Constitution.

[1] XXII

This Constitution shall be laid before the United States in Congress assembled, for their approbation; and it is the opinion of this Convention, that it should be afterwards submitted to a Convention chosen,[2] under the recommendation of its legislature, in order to receive the ratification of such Convention.

[1] XXIII

To introduce this government, it is the opinion of this Convention, that each assenting Convention should notify its assent and ratification to the United States in Congress assembled; that Congress, after receiving the assent and ratification of the Conventions of States, should appoint and publish a day, as early as may be, and appoint a place for commencing proceedings under this Constitution; that after such publication, the Legislatures of the several States should elect members of the Senate, and direct the election of members of the House of Representatives; and that the members of the Legislature should meet at the time and place assigned by Congress, and should, as soon as may be, after their meeting, choose the President of the United States, and proceed to execute this Constitution.''

A motion was made to adjourn till Wednesday, in order to give leisure to examine the Report; which passed in the negative— N. H. no. Mas. no. C^t no. P^a ay. M^d ay. Virg. ay. N. C. no. S. C. no.[3]

The House then adjourned till to morrow [4] 11 OC.

TEUSDAY AUGUST 7TH IN CONVENTION

The Report of the Committee of detail being taken up,

Mr PINKNEY moved that it be referred to a Committee of the whole. This was strongly opposed by Mr GHORUM & several others, as likely to produce unnecessary delay; and was negatived. Delaware Mary^d & Virg^a only being in the affirmative.

---

[1] The word " Article " is here inserted in the transcript.
[2] The phrase " in each State " is here inserted in the transcript.
[3] In the transcript the vote reads: " Pennsylvania, Maryland, Virgini.., aye—3; New Hampshire, Massachusetts, Connecticut, North Carolina, South Carolina, no—5."
[4] The word " at " is here inserted in the transcript.

The preamble of the Report was agreed to nem. con. So were Art: I & II.[1]

Art: III. [2, 3] considered. Col. MASON doubted the propriety of giving each branch a negative on the other " in all cases." There were some cases in which it was he supposed not intended to be given as in the case of balloting for appointments.

M: Gov: MORRIS moved to insert " legislative acts " instead of "all cases"

M: WILLIAMSON 2ds him.

M: SHERMAN. This will restrain the operation of the clause too much. It will particularly exclude a mutual negative in the case of ballots, which he hoped would take place.

M: GHORUM contended that elections ought to be made by *joint ballot*. If separate ballots should be made for the President, and the two branches should be each attached to a favorite, great delay contention & confusion may ensue. These inconveniences have been felt in Mast: in the election of officers of little importance compared with the Executive of the U. States. The only objection ag:t a joint ballot is that it may deprive the Senate of their due weight; but this ought not to prevail over the respect due to the public tranquility & welfare.

M: WILSON was for a joint ballot in several cases at least; particularly in the choice of the President, and was therefore for the amendment. Disputes between the two Houses during & concern: the vacancy of the Executive might have dangerous consequences.

Col. MASON thought the amendment of M: Gov: Morris extended too far. Treaties are in a subsequent part declared to be laws, they will be therefore [4] subjected to a negative; altho' they are to be made as proposed by the Senate alone. He proposed that the mutual negative should be restrained to " cases requiring the distinct assent " of the two Houses.

M: Gov: MORRIS thought this but a repetition of the same thing; the mutual negative and distinct assent, being equavalent expressions. Treaties he thought were not laws.

M: MADISON moved to strike out the words " each of which shall in all cases, have a negative on the other; the idea being sufficiently expressed in the preceding member of the article; vesting the "legislative power" in "distinct bodies," especially as the respective

---

[1] See page 337.
[2] See page 338.
[3] The word " being " is here inserted in the transcript.
[4] The words " be therefore " are changed in the transcript to "therefore be."

powers and mode of exercising them were fully delineated in a subsequent article.

Gen! PINKNEY 2^{ded} the motion

On[1] question for inserting legislative Acts as moved by Mr Govr Morris.[2]

N. H. ay. Mas. ay. C^t ay. P^a ay. Del. no. M^d no. V^a no. N. C. ay. S. C. no. Geo. no.[3]

On[1] question for agreeing to M^r M's motion to strike out &c.— N. H. ay. Mas. ay. C^t no. P^a ay. Del. ay. M^d no. V^a ay. N. C. no. S. C. ay. Geo. ay.[4]

Mr MADISON wished to know the reasons of the Com^e for fixing by ye Constitution the time of Meeting for the Legislature; and suggested, that it be required only that one meeting at least should be held every year leaving the time to be fixed or varied by law.

Mr Govr MORRIS moved to strike out the sentence. It was improper to tie down the Legislature to a particular time, or even to require a meeting every year. The public business might not require it.

Mr PINKNEY concurred with Mr Madison.

Mr GHORUM. If the time be not fixed by the Constitution, disputes will arise in the Legislature; and the States will be at a loss to adjust thereto, the times of their elections. In the N. England States the annual time of meeting had been long fixed by their Charters & Constitutions, and no inconveniency[5] had resulted. He thought it necessary that there should be one meeting at least every year as a check on the Executive department.

Mr ELSEWORTH was agst striking out the words. The Legislature will not know till they are met whether the public interest required their meeting or not. He could see no impropriety in fixing the day, as the Convention could judge of it as well as the Legislature.

Mr WILSON thought on the whole it would be best to fix the day.

Mr KING could not think there would be a necessity for a meeting every year. A great vice in our system was that of legislating too much. The most numerous objects of legislation belong to the States.

---

[1] The word "the" is here inserted in the transcript.

[2] The phrase "it passed in the negative, the votes being equally divided," is here inserted in the transcript.

[3] In the transcript the vote reads: "New Hampshire, Massachusetts, Connecticut, Pennsylvania, North Carolina, aye—5; Delaware, Maryland, Virginia, South Carolina, Georgia, no—5."

[4] In the transcript the vote reads: "New Hampshire, Massachusetts, Pennsylvania, Delaware, Virginia, South Carolina, Georgia, aye—7; Connecticut, Maryland, North Carolina, no—3."

[5] The word "inconveniency" is changed in the transcript to "inconvenience."

Those of the Nat! Legislature were but few. The chief of them were commerce & revenue. When these should be once settled, alterations would be rarely necessary & easily made.

M! MADISON thought if the time of meeting should be fixed by a law it w.ᵈ be sufficiently fixed & there would be no difficulty then as had been suggested, on the part of the States in adjusting their elections to it. One consideration appeared to him to militate strongly ag.ˢᵗ fixing a time by the Constitution. It might happen that the Legislature might be called together by the public exigencies & finish their Session but a short time before the annual period. In this case it would be extremely inconvenient to reassemble so quickly & without the least necessity. He thought one annual meeting ought to be required; but did not wish to make two unavoidable.

Col. MASON thought the objections against fixing the time insuperable: but that an annual meeting ought to be required as essential to the preservation of the Constitution. The extent of the Country will supply business. And if it should not, the Legislature, besides *legislative*, is to have *inquisitorial* powers, which can not safely be long kept in a state of suspension.

M! SHERMAN was decided for fixing the time, as well as for frequent meetings of the Legislative body. Disputes and difficulties will arise between the two Houses, & between both & the States, if the time be changeable—frequent meetings of Parliament were required at the Revolution in England as an essential safeguard of liberty. So also are annual meetings in most of the American charters & constitutions. There will be business eno' to require it. The Western Country, and the great extent and varying state of our affairs in general will supply objects.

M! RANDOLPH was ag.ˢᵗ fixing any day irrevocably; but as there was no provision made any where in the Constitution for regulating the periods of meeting, and some precise time must be fixed, untill the Legislature shall make provision, he could not agree to strike out the words altogether. Instead of which he moved to add the words following—" unless a different day shall be appointed by law."

M! MADISON 2ᵈᵉᵈ the motion, & on the question

N. H. no. Mas. ay. C.ᵗ no. P.ᵃ ay. Del. ay. M.ᵈ ay. V.ᵃ ay. N. C. ay. S. C. ay. Geo. ay.[1]

M! Gov.ʳ MORRIS moved to strike out Dec.ʳ & insert May. It might frequently happen that our measures ought to be influenced by those

---

[1] In the transcript the vote reads: " Massachusetts, Pennsylvania, Delaware, Maryland, Virginia, North Carolina, South Carolina, Georgia, aye—8; New Hampshire, Connecticut, no—2."

in Europe, which were generally planned during the Winter and of which intelligence would arrive in the Spring.

M⁺ MADISON 2ᵈᵉᵈ the motion. he preferred May to Dec⁺ because the latter would require the travelling to & from the seat of Gov⁺ in the most inconvenient seasons of the year.

M⁺ WILSON. The Winter is the most convenient season for business.

M⁺ ELSEWORTH. The summer will interfere too much with private business, that of almost all the probable members of the Legislature being more or less connected with agriculture.

M⁺ RANDOLPH. The time is of no great moment now, as the Legislature can vary it. On looking into the Constitutions of the States, he found that the times of their elections with which the election [1] of the Nat⁺ Representatives would no doubt be made to co-incide, would suit better with Dec⁺ than May. And it was adviseable to render our innovations as little incommodious as possible.

On [2] question for " May " instead of " Dec⁺ "

N. H. no. Mas. no. C⁺ no. P⁺ no. Del. no. M⁺ no. V⁺ no. N. C. no. S. C. ay. Geo. ay.[3]

M⁺ READ moved to insert after the word " Senate " the words, " subject to the Negative to be hereafter provided." His object was to give an absolute negative to the Executive—He considered this as so essential to the Constitution, to the preservation of liberty, & to the public welfare, that his duty compelled him to make the motion.

M⁺ Gov⁺ MORRIS 2ᵈᵉᵈ him. And on the question

N. H. no. Mas. no. C⁺ no. P⁺ no. Del. ay. M⁺ no. V⁺ no. N. C. no. S. C. no. Geo. no.[4]

M⁺ RUTLIDGE. Altho' it is agreed on all hands that an annual meeting of the Legislature should be made necessary, yet that point seems not to be freed from doubt as the clause stands. On this suggestion, " Once at least in every year," were inserted, nem. con.

Art. III with the foregoing alterations was ag⁺ to nem. con. and

---

[1] The word " election " is used in the plural in the transcript.

[2] The word " the " is here inserted in the transcript.

[3] In the transcript the vote reads: " South Carolina, Georgia, aye—2; New Hampshire, Massachusetts, Connecticut, Pennsylvania, Delaware, Maryland, Virginia, North Carolina, no—8."

[4] In the transcript the vote reads: " Delaware, aye—1; New Hampshire, Massachusetts, Connecticut, Pennsylvania, Maryland, Virginia, North Carolina, South Carolina, Georgia, no—9."

is as follows '' The Legislative power shall be vested in a Congress to consist of 2 separate & distinct bodies of men; a House of Rep? & a Senate The Legislature shall meet at least once in every year, and such meeting shall be on the 1ˢᵗ monday in Dec? unless a different day shall be appointed by law.''

'' Art IV. Sect. 1.¹ˏ ² taken up.''

Mᴿ Govᴿ Morris moved to strike out the last member of the section beginning with the words '' qualifications '' of Electors,'' in order that some other provision might be substituted which wᵈ restrain the right of suffrage to freeholders.

Mᴿ Fitzimmons 2ᵈᵉᵈ the motion

Mᴿ Williamson was opposed to it.

Mᴿ Wilson. This part of the Report was well considered by the Committee, and he did not think it could be changed for the better. It was difficult to form any uniform rule of qualifications for all the States. Unnecessary innovations he thought too should be avoided. It would be very hard & disagreeable for the same persons at the same time, to vote for representatives in the State Legislature and to be excluded from a vote for those in the Natˡ Legislature.

Mᴿ Govᴿ Morris. Such a hardship would be neither great nor novel. The people are accustomed to it and not dissatisfied with it, in several of the States. In some the qualifications are different for the choice of the Govᴿ & ³ Representatives; In others for different Houses of the Legislature. Another objection agˢᵗ the clause as it stands is that it makes the qualifications of the Natˡ Legislature depend on the will of the States, which he thought not proper.

Mᴿ Elseworth. thought the qualifications of the electors stood on the most proper footing. The right of suffrage was a tender point, and strongly guarded by most of the State Constitutions. The people will not readily subscribe to the Natˡ Constitution if it should subject them to be disfranchised. The States are the best Judges of the circumstances & temper of their own people.

Col. Mason. The force of habit is certainly not attended to by those gentlemen who wish for innovations on this point. Eight or nine States have extended the right of suffrage beyond the freeholders, what will the people there say, if they should be disfranchised. A power to alter the qualifications would be a dangerous power in the hands of the Legislature.

Mᴿ Butler. There is no right of which the people are more

---

¹ See page 338.
² The words " was then " are here inserted in the transcript.
³ The words " of the " are here inserted in the transcript.

jealous than that of suffrage Abridgments of it tend to the same revolution as in Holland where they have at length thrown all power into the hands of the Senates, who fill up vacancies themselves, and form a rank aristocracy.

M: DICKENSON. had a very different idea of the tendency of vesting the right of suffrage in the freeholders of the Country. He considered them as the best guardians of liberty; And the restriction of the right to them as a necessary defence ag:t the dangerous influence of those multitudes without property & without principle with which our Country like all others, will in time abound. As to the unpopularity of the innovation it was in his opinion chemirical. The great mass of our Citizens is composed at this time of freeholders, and will be pleased with it.

M: ELSEWORTH. How shall the freehold be defined? Ought not every man who pays a tax, to vote for the representative who is to levy & dispose of his money? Shall the wealthy merchants & manufacturers, who will bear a full share of the public burdens be not allowed a voice in the imposition of them—taxation & representation ought to go together.

M: Gov: MORRIS. He had long learned not to be the dupe of words. The sound of Aristocracy therefore had no effect on [1] him. It was the thing, not the name, to which he was opposed, and one of his principal objections to the Constitution as it is now before us, is that it threatens this [2] Country with an Aristocracy. The aristocracy will grow out of the House of Representatives. Give the votes to people who have no property, and they will sell them to the rich who will be able to buy them. We should not confine our attention to the present moment. The time is not distant when this Country will abound with mechanics & manufactures [3] who will receive their bread from their employers. Will such men be the secure & faithful Guardians of liberty? Will they be the impregnable barrier ag:t aristocracy?—He was as little duped by the association of the words " taxation & Representation." The man who does not give his vote freely is not represented. It is the man who dictates the vote. Children do not vote. Why? because they want prudence, because they have no will of their own. The ignorant & the dependent can be as little trusted with the public interest. He did not conceive the difficulty of defining " freeholders " to be insuperable. Still less

---

[1] The word "upon" is substituted in the transcript for "on."
[2] The word "the" is substituted in the transcript for "this."
[3] The word "manufacturers" is substituted in the transcript for "manufactures."

that the restriction could be unpopular. 9/10 of the people are at present freeholders and these will certainly be pleased with it. As to Merchᵗˢ &c. if they have wealth & value the right they can acquire it. If not they don't deserve it.

Col. MASON. We all feel too strongly the remains of antient prejudices, and view things too much through a British medium. A Freehold is the qualification in England, & hence it is imagined to be the only proper one. The true idea in his opinion was that every man having evidence of attachment to & permanent common interest with the Society ought to share in all its rights & privileges. Was this qualification restrained to freeholders? Does no other kind of property but land evidence a common interest in the proprietor? does nothing besides property mark a permanent attachment. Ought the merchant, the monied man, the parent of a number of children whose fortunes are to be pursued in his own Country, to be viewed as suspicious characters, and unworthy to be trusted with the common rights of their fellow Citizens

Mʳ MADISON. the right of suffrage is certainly one of the fundamental articles of republican Government, and ought not to be left to be regulated by the Legislature. A gradual abridgment of this right has been the mode in which Aristocracies have been built on the ruins of popular forms. Whether the Constitutional qualification ought to be a freehold, would with him depend much on the probable reception such a change would meet with in [1] States where the right was now exercised by every description of people. In several of the States a freehold was now the qualification. Viewing the subject in its merits alone, the freeholders of the Country would be the safest depositories of Republican liberty. In future times a great majority of the people will not only be without landed, but any other sort of, property. These will either combine under the influence of their common situation; in which case, the rights of property & the public liberty, will not be secure in their hands: or which [2] is more probable, they will become the tools of opulence & ambition, in which case there will be equal danger on another side. The example of England had been misconceived [by Col Mason]. A very small proportion of the Representatives are there chosen by freeholders. The greatest part are chosen by the Cities & boroughs, in many of which the qualification of suffrage is as low as it is in any one of the U. S. and it was in the boroughs & Cities rather than the Counties, that bribery

---

[1] The word " the " is here inserted in the transcript.
[2] The word " which " is crossed out in the transcript and " what " is written above it.

most prevailed, & the influence of the Crown on elections was most dangerously exerted.[1]

Doc[r] FRANKLIN. It is of great consequence that we sh[d] not depress the virtue & public spirit of our common people; of which they displayed a great deal during the war, and which contributed principally to the favorable issue of it. He related the honorable refusal of the American seamen who were carried in great numbers into the British Prisons during the war, to redeem themselves from misery or to seek their fortunes, by entering on board the Ships of the Enemies to their Country; contrasting their patriotism with a contemporary instance in which the British seamen made prisoners by the Americans, readily entered on the ships of the latter on being promised a share of the prizes that might be made out of their own Country. This proceeded he said from the different manner in which the common people were treated in America & G. Britain. He did not think that the elected had any right in any case to narrow the privileges of the electors. He quoted as arbitrary the British Statute setting forth the danger of tumultuous meetings, and under that pretext narrowing the right of suffrage to persons having freeholds of a certain value; observing that this Statute was soon followed by another under the succeeding Parliam[t] subjecting the people who had no votes to peculiar labors & hardships. He was persuaded also that such a restriction as was proposed would give great uneasiness in the populous States. The sons of a substantial farmer, not being themselves freeholders, would not be pleased at being disfranchised, and there are a great many persons of that description.

M[r] MERCER. The Constitution is objectionable in many points, but in none more than the present. He objected to the footing on which the qualification was put, but particularly to the *mode of election* by the people. The people can not know & judge of the characters of Candidates. The worse possible choice will be made. He quoted the case of the Senate in Virg[a] as an example in point. The people in Towns can unite their votes in favor of one favorite; & by that means always prevail over the people of the Country, who being dispersed will scatter their votes among a variety of candidates.

M[r] RUTLIDGE thought the idea of restraining the right of suffrage to the freeholders a very unadvised one. It would create division among the people & make enemies of all those who should be excluded.

---

[1] In the transcript the following footnote is here added: " See Appendix No. — for ᵣ note of Mr. Madison to this speech." See Appendix to Debates VII, Nos. 1 and 2, p. 619, for notes concerning Madison's speech of August 7, 1787.

On the question for striking out as moved by M! Gov! Morris, from the word " qualifications " to the end of the III article

N. H. no. Mas. no. C! no. P! no. Del. ay. M! div! V! no. N. C. no. S. C. no. Geo. not pres! [1]

Adjourned

WEDNESDAY AUG^ST 8. IN CONVENTION

Art: IV. Sect. 1.[2, 3]—M! MERCER expressed his dislike of the whole plan, and his opinion that it never could succeed.

M! GHORUM. he had never seen any inconveniency[4] from allowing such as were not freeholders to vote, though it had long been tried. The elections in Phil! N. York & Boston where the Merchants, & Mechanics vote are at least as good as those made by freeholders only. The case in England was not accurately stated yesterday [by M! Madison] The Cities & large towns are not the seat of Crown influence & corruption. These prevail in the Boroughs, and not on account of the right which those who are not freeholders have to vote, but of the smallness of the number who vote. The people have been long accustomed to this right in various parts of America, and will never allow it to be abridged. We must consult their rooted prejudices if we expect their concurrence in our propositions.

M! MERCER did not object so much to an election by the people at large including such as were not freeholders, as to their being left to make their choice without any guidance. He hinted that Candidates ought to be nominated by the State Legislatures.

On[5] question for agreeing to Art: IV- Sect. 1 it pass! nem. con. Art IV. Sect. 2.[2, 6] taken up.

Col. MASON was for opening a wide door for emigrants; but did not chuse to let foreigners and adventurers make laws for us & govern us. Citizenship for three years was not enough for ensuring that local knowledge which ought to be possessed by the Representative. This was the principal ground of his objection to so short a term. It might also happen that a rich foreign Nation, for example

---

[1] In the transcript the vote reads: "Delaware, aye—1; New Hampshire, Massachusetts, Connecticut, Pennsylvania, Virginia, North Carolina, South Carolina, no—7; Maryland, divided; Georgia, not present."

[2] See page 338.

[3] The words "being under consideration" are here inserted in the transcript.

[4] The word "inconveniency" is changed to "inconvenience" in the transcript.

[5] The word "the" is here inserted in the transcript.

[6] The words "was then" are here inserted in the transcript.

Great Britain, might send over her tools who might bribe their way into the Legislature for insidious purposes. He moved that "seven" years instead of "three," be inserted.

M⸰ Gov⸰ Morris 2⸰ded the Motion, & on the question, all the States agreed to it except Connecticut.

M⸰ Sherman moved to strike out the word "resident" and insert "inhabitant," as less liable to misconstruction.

M⸰ Madison 2⸰ded the motion, both were vague, but the latter least so in common acceptation, and would not exclude persons absent occasionally for a considerable time on public or private business. Great disputes had been raised in Virg⸰ concerning the meaning of residence as a qualification of Representatives which were determined more according to the affection or dislike to the man in question, than to any fixt interpretation of the word.

M⸰ Wilson preferred "inhabitant."

M⸰ Gov⸰ Morris, was opposed to both and for requiring nothing more than a freehold. He quoted great disputes in N. York occasioned by these terms, which were decided by the arbitrary will of the majority. Such a regulation is not necessary. People rarely chuse a nonresident—It is improper as in the 1⸰st branch, *the people at large,* not the *States,* are represented.

M⸰ Rutlidge urged & moved that a residence of 7 years sh⸰d be required in the State Wherein the Member sh⸰d be elected. An emigrant from N. England to S. C. or Georgia would know little of its affairs and could not be supposed to acquire a thorough knowledge in less time.

M⸰ Read reminded him that we were now forming a *Nat⸰l* Gov⸰ and such a regulation would correspond little with the idea that we were one people.

M⸰ Wilson. enforced the same consideration.

M⸰ Madison suggested the case of new States in the West, which could have perhaps no representation on that plan.

M⸰ Mercer. Such a regulation would present a greater alienship among the States [1] than existed under the old federal system. It would interweave local prejudices & State distinctions in the very Constitution which is meant to cure them. He mentioned instances of violent disputes raised in Maryland concerning the term "residence"

M⸰ Elseworth thought seven years of residence was by far too long a term: but that some fixt term of previous residence would be

---

[1] The phrase "among the States" is omitted in the transcript.

proper. He thought one year would be sufficient, but seemed to have no objection to three years.

M͏ͬ DICKENSON proposed that it should read " inhabitant actually resident for   year.[1]" This would render the meaning less indeterminate.

M͏ͬ WILSON. If a short term should be inserted in the blank, so strict an expression might be construed to exclude the members of the Legislature, who could not be said to be actual residents in their States whilst at the Seat of the Gen͏�l Government.

M͏ͬ MERCER. It would certainly exclude men, who had once been inhabitants, and returning from residence elsewhere to resettle in their original State; although a want of the necessary knowledge could not in such case[2] be presumed.

M͏ͬ MASON thought 7 years too long, but would never agree to part with the principle. It is a valuable principle. He thought it a defect in the plan that the Representatives would be too few to bring with them all the local knowledge necessary. If residence be not required, Rich men of neighbouring States, may employ with success the means of corruption in some particular district and thereby get into the public Councils after having failed in their own State.[3] This is the practice in the boroughs of England.

On the question for postponing in order to consider M͏ͬ Dickensons motion

N. H. no. Mas. no. C͏ͭ no. N. J. no. P͏ᵃ no. Del. no. M͏ᵈ ay. V͏ᵃ no. N. C. no. S. C. ay. Geo. ay.[4]

On the question for inserting " inhabitant " in place of " resident "—ag͏ᵈ to nem. con.

M͏ͬ ELSEWORTH & Col. MASON move to insert " one year " for previous inhabitancy

M͏ͬ WILLIAMSON liked the Report as it stood. He thought " resident " a good eno' term. He was ag͏ᵗ requiring any period of previous residence. New residents if elected will be most zealous to Conform to the will of their constituents, as their conduct will be watched with a more jealous eye.

M͏ͬ BUTLER & M͏ͬ RUTLIDGE moved " three years " instead of " one year " for previous inhabitancy.

On the question for 3 years—

---

[1] The transcript uses the word " year " in the plural.
[2] The transcript uses the word " case " in the plural.
[3] The transcript uses the word " State " in the plural.
[4] In the transcript the vote reads: " Maryland, South Carolina, Georgia, aye—3; New Hampshire, Massachusetts, Connecticut, New Jersey, Pennsylvania, Delaware, Virginia, North Carolina, no—8."

N. H. no. Mas. no. C⸞ no. N. J. no. P⸞ no. Del. no. M⸞ no. V⸞ no. N. C. no. S. C. ay. Geo. ay.[1]

On the question for "1 year"

N. H. no—Mas. no. C⸞ no. N. J. ay. P⸞ no. Del. no. M⸞ div⸞ V⸞ no. N. C. ay. S. C. ay. Geo. ay.[2]

Art. IV. Sect. 2. As amended in manner preceding, was agreed to nem. con.

Art: IV. Sect. 3."[3, 4] taken up.

Gen⸞ PINKNEY & M⸞ PINKNEY moved that the number of representatives allotted to S. Carol⸞ be "six" on the question,

N. H. no. Mas. no. C⸞ no. N. J. no. P⸞ no. Delaware ay M⸞ no. V⸞ no. N. C. ay. S. C. ay. Geo. ay.[5]

The 3. Sect. of Art: IV was then agreed to.

Art: IV. Sect. 4.[3, 4] taken up.

M⸞ WILLIAMSON moved to strike out " according to the provisions hereinafter after made " and to insert the words " according " to the rule hereafter to be provided for direct taxation "—See Art. VII. sect. 3.[6]

On the question for agreeing to M⸞ Williamson's amendment

N. H. ay. Mas. ay. C⸞ ay. N. J. no. P⸞ ay. Del. no. M⸞ ay. V⸞ ay. N. C. ay. S. C. ay. Geo. ay.[7]

M⸞ KING wished to know what influence the vote just passed was meant[8] have on the succeeding part of the Report, concerning the admission of slaves into the rule of Representation. He could not reconcile his mind to the article if it was to prevent objections to the latter part. The admission of slaves was a most grating circumstance to his mind, & he believed would be so to a great part of the people of America. He had not made a strenuous opposition to it heretofore because he had hoped that this concession would have produced a readiness which had not been manifested, to

---

[1] In the transcript the vote reads: "South Carolina, Georgia, aye—2; New Hampshire, Massachusetts, Connecticut, New Jersey, Pennsylvania, Delaware, Maryland, Virginia, North Carolina, no—9."

[2] In the transcript the vote reads: "New Jersey, North Carolina, South Carolina, Georgia, aye—4; New Hampshire, Massachusetts, Connecticut, Pennsylvania, Delaware, Virginia, no—6; Maryland, divided."

[3] See page 338.

[4] The words "was then" are here inserted in the transcript.

[5] In the transcript the vote reads: "Delaware, North Carolina, South Carolina, Georgia, aye—4; New Hampshire, Massachusetts, Connecticut, New Jersey, Pennsylvania, Maryland, Virginia, no—7."

[6] See page 341.

[7] In the transcript the vote reads: "New Hampshire, Massachusetts, Connecticut, Pennsylvania, Maryland, Virginia, North Carolina, South Carolina, Georgia, aye—9; New Jersey, Delaware, no—2."

[8] The word " to " is here inserted in the transcript.

strengthen the Gen! Gov! and to mark a full confidence in it. The Report under consideration had by the tenor of it, put an end to all those hopes. In two great points the hands of the Legislature were absolutely tied. The importation of slaves could not be prohibited—exports could not be taxed. Is this reasonable? What are the great objects of the Gen! System? 1.[1] defence ag.[st] foreign invasion. 2.[1] ag.[st] internal sedition. Shall all the States then be bound to defend each; & shall each be at liberty to introduce a weakness which will render defence more difficult? Shall one part of the U. S. be bound to defend another part, and that other part be at liberty not only to increase its own danger, but to withhold the compensation for the burden? If slaves are to be imported shall not the exports produced by their labor, supply a revenue the better to enable the Gen! Gov! to defend their masters?—There was so much inequality & unreasonableness in all this, that the people of the Northern States could never be reconciled to it. No candid man could undertake to justify it to them. He had hoped that some accomodation w.[d] have taken place on this subject; that at least a time w.[d] have been limited for the importation of slaves. He never could agree to let them be imported without limitation & then be represented in the Nat! Legislature. Indeed he could so little persuade himself of the rectitude of such a practice, that he was not sure he could assent to it under any circumstances. At all events, either slaves should not be represented, or exports should be taxable.

M.[r] Sherman regarded the slave trade as iniquitous; but the point of representation having been settled after much difficulty & deliberation, he did not think himself bound to make opposition; especially as the present article as amended did not preclude any arrangement whatever on that point in another place of the Report.

M.[r] Madison objected to 1 for every 40,000, inhabitants as a perpetual rule. The future increase of population if the Union sh.[d] be permanent, will render the number of Representatives excessive.

M.[r] Ghorum. It is not to be supposed that the Gov! will last so long as to produce this effect. Can it be supposed that this vast Country including the Western territory will 150 years hence remain one nation?

M.[r] Elseworth. If the Gov! should continue so long, alterations may be made in the Constitution in the manner proposed in a subsequent article.

M.[r] Sherman & M.[r] Madison moved to insert the words " not

---

[1] The figures " 1 " and " 2 " are changed to " First " and " Secondly " in the transcript.

exceeding " before the words " 1 for every 40,000, which was agreed to nem. con.

M: Gov: MORRIS moved to insert " free " before the word inhabitants. Much he said would depend on this point. He never would concur in upholding domestic slavery. It was a nefarious institution. It was the curse of heaven on the States where it prevailed. Compare the free regions of the Middle States, where a rich & noble cultivation marks the prosperity & happiness of the people, with the misery & poverty which overspread the barren wastes of V: Mary: & the other States having slaves. Travel thro' y: whole Continent & you behold the prospect continually varying with the appearance & disappearance of slavery. The moment you leave y: E. Sts. & enter N. York, the effects of the institution become visible, passing thro' the Jerseys & entering P: every criterion of superior improvement witnesses the change. Proceed southw^dly & every step you take thro' y: great region of slaves presents a desert increasing, with y: increasing proportion proportion of these wretched beings. Upon what principle is it that the slaves shall be computed in the representation? Are they men? Then make them Citizens and let them vote. Are they property? Why then is no other property included? The Houses in this city [Philad:] are worth more than all the wretched slaves which cover the rice swamps of South Carolina. The admission of slaves into the Representation when fairly explained comes to this: that the inhabitant of Georgia and S. C. who goes to the Coast of Africa, and in defiance of the most sacred laws of humanity tears away his fellow creatures from their dearest connections & damns them to the most cruel bondages,[1] shall have more votes in a Gov: instituted for protection of the rights of mankind, than the Citizen of P: or N. Jersey who views with a laudable horror, so nefarious a practice. He would add that Domestic slavery is the most prominent feature in the aristocratic countenance of the proposed Constitution. The vassalage of the poor has ever been the favorite offspring of Aristocracy. And What is the proposed compensation to the Northern States for a sacrifice of every principle of right, of every impulse of humanity. They are to bind themselves to march their militia for the defence of the S. States; for their defence ag:st those very slaves of whom they complain. They must supply vessels & seamen in case of foreign Attack. The Legislature will have indefinite power to tax them by excises, and duties on imports: both of which will fall heavier on them than on the Southern inhabi-

---

[1] The transcript uses the word " bondages " in the singular.

tants; for the bohea tea used by a Northern freeman, will pay more tax than the whole consumption of the miserable slave, which consists of nothing more than his physical subsistence and the rag that covers his nakedness. On the other side the Southern States are not to be restrained from importing fresh supplies of wretched Africans, at once to increase the danger of attack, and the difficulty of defence; nay they are to be encouraged to it by an assurance of having their votes in the Nat! Gov! increased in proportion, and are at the same time to have their exports & their slaves exempt from all contributions for the public service. Let it not be said that direct taxation is to be proportioned to representation. It is idle to suppose that the Gen! Gov! can stretch its hand directly into the pockets of the people scattered over so vast a Country. They can only do it through the medium of exports imports & excises. For what then are all these sacrifices to be made? He would sooner submit himself to a tax for paying for all the negroes in the U. States, than saddle posterity with such a Constitution.

M? DAYTON 2^{ded} the motion. He did it he said that his sentiments on the subject might appear whatever might be the fate of the amendment.

M? SHERMAN. did not regard the admission of the Negroes into the ratio of representation, as liable to such insuperable objections. It was the freemen of the South? States who were in fact to be represented according to the taxes paid by them, and the Negroes are only included in the Estimate of the taxes. This was his idea of the matter.

M? PINKNEY, considered the fisheries & the Western frontier as more burdensome to the U. S. than the slaves. He thought this could be demonstrated if the occasion were a proper one.

M? WILSON. thought the motion premature. An agreement to the clause would be no bar to the object of it.

[1] Question On [2] motion to insert " free " before " inhabitants."

N. H. no. Mas. no. C! no. N. J. ay. P? no. Del. no. M? no. V? no. N. C. no. S. C. no. Geo. no.[3]

On the suggestion of M? DICKENSON the words, " provided that each State shall have one representative at least."—were added nem. con.

Art. IV. Sect. 4. as amended was agreed to nem. con.

---

[1] The words " On the " are here inserted in the transcript.
[2] The word " the " is here inserted in the transcript.
[3] In the transcript the vote reads: "New Jersey, aye—1; New Hampshire, Massachusetts, Connecticut, Pennsylvania, Delaware, Maryland, Virginia, North Carolina, South Carolina, Georgia, no—10."

Art. IV. Sect. 5.[1,2] taken up

M: PINKNEY moved to strike out Sect. 5. As giving no peculiar advantage to the House of Representatives, and as clogging the Gov: If the Senate can be trusted with the many great powers proposed, it surely may be trusted with that of originating money bills.

M: GHORUM. was ag:st allowing the Senate to *originate;* but [3] only to *amend.*

M: Gov: MORRIS. It is particularly proper that the Senate sh:d have the right of originating money bills. They will sit constantly, will consist of a smaller number, and will be able to prepare such bills with due correctness; and so as to prevent delay of business in the other House.

Col. MASON was unwilling to travel over this ground again. To strike out the section, was to unhinge the compromise of which it made a part. The duration of the Senate made it improper. He does not object to that duration. On the Contrary he approved of it. But joined with the smallness of the number, it was an argument against adding this to the other great powers vested in that body. His idea of an Aristocracy was that it was the govern: of the few over the many. An aristocratic body, like the screw in mechanics, worki:g its way by slow degrees, and holding fast whatever it gains, should ever be suspected of an encroaching tendency. The purse strings should never be put into its hands.

M: MERCER. considered the exclusive power of originating Money bills as so great an advantage, that it rendered the equality of votes in the Senate ideal & of no consequence.

M: BUTLER was for adhering to the principle which had been settled.

M: WILSON was opposed to it on its merits without regard to the compromise

M: ELSEWORTH did not think the clause of any consequence, but as it was thought of consequence by some members from the larger States, he was willing it should stand.

M: MADISON was for striking it out: considering it as of no advantage to the large States as fettering the Gov: and as a source of injurious altercations between the two Houses.

On the question for striking out " Sect. 5. Art. IV "

---

[1] See page 338.
[2] The words " was then " are here inserted in the transcript.
[3] The words " was for allowing it " are here inserted in the transcript.

N. H. no.   Mas. no.   C! no.   N. J. ay.   P. ay.   Del. ay.   M. ay.
V. ay.   N. C. no.   S. C. ay.   Geo. ay.[1]

Adj.

Thursday. Aug. 9. in Convention

Art: IV. Sect. 6.[2,3]   M. Randolph expressed his dissatisfaction at the disagreement yesterday to Sect. 5. concerning money bills, as endangering the success of the plan, and extremely objectionable in itself; and gave notice that he should move for a reconsideration of the vote.

M. Williamson said he had formed a like intention.

M. Wilson, gave notice that he sh. move to reconsider the vote, requiring seven instead of three years of Citizenship as a qualification of candidates for the House of Representatives.

Art. IV. Sect. 6 & 7.[2,4] Agreed to nem. con.

Art. V. Sect 1.[5,6] taken up.

M. Wilson objected to vacancies in the Senate being supplied by the Executives of the States. It was unnecessary as the Legislatures will meet so frequently. It removes the appointment too far from the people; the Executives in most of the States being elected by the Legislatures. As he had always thought the appointment of the Executives[7] by the Legislative department wrong: so it was still more so that the Executive should elect into the Legislative department.

M. Randolph thought it necessary in order to prevent inconvenient chasms in the Senate. In some States the Legislatures meet but once a year. As the Senate will have more power & consist of a smaller number than the other House, vacancies there will be of more consequence. The Executives might be safely trusted he thought with the appointment for so short a time.

M. Elseworth. It is only said that the Executive *may* supply the[8] vacancies. When the Legislative meeting happens to be near, the

---

[1] In the transcript the vote reads: "New Jersey, Pennsylvania, Delaware, Maryland, Virginia, South Carolina, Georgia, aye—7; New Hampshire, Massachusetts, Connecticut, North Carolina, no—4."
[2] See page 338.
[3] The words "was taken up" are here inserted in the transcript.
[4] The word "were" is here inserted in the transcript.
[5] See page 339.
[6] The words "was then" are here inserted in the transcript.
[7] The word "Executives" is in the singular in the transcript.
[8] The word "the" is omitted in the transcript.

power will not be exerted. As there will be but two members from a State vacancies may be of great moment.

M⁷ WILLIAMSON. Senators may resign or not accept. This provision is therefore absolutely necessary.

On the question for striking out " vacancies shall be supplied by ¹ Executives

N. H. no. Mas. no. C⁺ no. N. J. no. P⁴ ay. M⁴ div⁴ V⁴ no. N. C. no. S. C. no. Geo. no.²

M⁷ WILLIAMSON moved to insert after " vacancies shall be supplied by the Executives," the following ³ words " unless other provision shall be made by the Legislature " [of the State].

M⁷ ELSEWORTH. He was willing to trust the Legislature, or the Executive of a State, but not to give the former a discretion to refer appointments for the Senate to whom they pleased.

⁴ Question on M⁷ Williamson's motion

N. H. no. Mas. no. C⁺ no. N. J. no. P⁴ no. M⁴ ay. V⁴ no. N. C. ay. S. C. ay. Geo. ay.⁵

M⁷ MADISON in order to prevent doubts whether resignations could be made by Senators, or whether they could refuse to accept, moved to strike out the words after " vacancies," & insert the words " happening by refusals to accept, resignations or otherwise may be supplied by the Legislature of the State in the representation of which such vacancies shall happen, or by the Executive thereof until the next meeting of the Legislature "

M⁷ GOV⁷ MORRIS this is absolutely necessary, otherwise, as members chosen into the Senate are disqualified from being appointed to any office by Sect. 9. of this art: it will be in the power of a Legislature by appointing a man a Senator ag⁵ᵗ his consent, to deprive the U. S. of his services.

The motion of M⁷ Madison was agreed to nem. con.

M⁷ RANDOLPH called for division of the Section, so as to leave a distinct question on the last words " each member shall have one vote." He wished this last sentence to be postponed until the reconsideration should have taken place on Sect. 5. Art. IV. concerning

---

¹ The word "the" is here inserted in the transcript.
² In the transcript the vote reads: "Pennsylvania, aye—1; New Hampshire, Massachusetts, Connecticut, New Jersey, Virginia, North Carolina, South Carolina, Georgia, no—8; Maryland, divided."
³ The word "following" is omitted in the transcript.
⁴ The words "On the" are here inserted in the transcript.
⁵ In the transcript the vote reads: "Maryland, North Carolina, South Carolina, Georgia, aye—4; New Hampshire, Massachusetts, Connecticut, New Jersey, Pennsylvania, Virginia, no—6."

money bills. If that section should not be reinstated his plan would be to vary the representation in the Senate.

M: Strong concurred in M: Randolphs ideas on this point

M: Read did not consider the section as to money bills of any advantage to the larger States and had voted for striking it out as being viewed in the same light by the larger States. If it was considered by them as of any value, and as a condition of the equality of votes in the Senate, he had no objection to its being re-instated.

M: Wilson—M: Elseworth & M: Madison urged that it was of no advantage to the larger States, and that it might be a dangerous source of contention between the two Houses. All the principal powers of the Nat! Legislature had some relation to money.

Doc: Franklin, considered the two clauses, the originating of money bills, and the equality of votes in the Senate, as essentially connected by the compromise which had been agreed to.

Col. Mason said this was not the time for discussing this point. When the originating of money bills shall be reconsidered, he thought it could be demonstrated that it was of essential importance to restrain the right to the House of Representatives the immediate choice of the people.

M: Williamson. The State of N. C. had agreed to an equality in the Senate, merely in consideration that money bills should be confined to the other House: and he was surprised to see the Smaller States forsaking the condition on which they had received their equality.

[1] Question on the Section 1.[2] down to the last sentence

N. H. ay. Mas. no. C: ay. N. J. ay. P: no* Del. ay. M: ay. Virg: ay N. C. no. S. C. div: Geo. ay.[3]

M: Randolph moved that the last sentence "each member shall have one vote." be postponed

It was observed that this could not be necessary; as in case the section as to originating[4] bills should not be reinstated, and a revision of the Constitution should ensue, it w: still be proper that the members should vote per Capita. A postponement of the pre-

* In the printed Journal Pensylvania. ay.

---

[1] The words "On the" are here inserted in the transcript.
[2] The words "first section" are substituted for "Section 1" in the transcript.
[3] In the transcript the vote reads: "New Hampshire, Connecticut, New Jersey, Delaware, Maryland, Virginia, Georgia, aye—7; Massachusetts, Pennsylvania,* North Carolina, no—3; South Carolina, divided."
[4] The word "money" is here inserted in the transcript.

ceding sentence allowing to each State 2 members w̱ have been more proper

M͟ʳ Mason, did not mean to propose a change of this mode of voting per capita in any event. But as there might be other modes proposed, he saw no impropriety in postponing the sentence. Each State may have two members, and yet may have unequal votes. He said that unless the exclusive [1] originating of money bills should be restored to the House of Representatives, he should, not from obstinacy, but duty and conscience, oppose throughout the equality of Representation in the Senate.

M͟ʳ Gov͟ʳ Morris. Such declarations were he supposed, addressed to the smaller States in order to alarm them for their equality in the Senate, and induce them ag͟ˢᵗ their judgments, to concur in restoring the section concerning money bills. He would declare in his turn that as he saw no prospect of amending the Constitution of the Senate & considered the section relating to money bills as intrinsically bad, he would adhere to the section establishing the equality at all events.

M͟ʳ Wilson. It seems to have been supposed by some that the section concerning money bills is desirable to the large States. The fact was that two of those States [P͟ᵃ & V͟ᵃ] had uniformly voted ag͟ˢᵗ it without reference to any other part of the system.

M͟ʳ Randolph, urged as Col. Mason had done that the sentence under consideration was connected with that relating to Money bills, and might possibly be affected by the result of the motion for reconsidering the latter. That the postponement was therefore not improper.

[2] Question for postponing " each member shall have one vote."

N. H. div̱ Mas. no. C͟ᵗ no. N. J. no. P͟ᵃ no. Del. no. M͟ᵈ no. V͟ᵃ ay. N. C. ay. S. C. no. Geo. no.[3]

The words were then agreed to as part of the section.

M͟ʳ Randolph then gave notice that he should move to reconsider this whole Sect: 1. Art. V. as connected with the 5. Sect. art. IV. as to which he had already given such notice.

Art. V. Sect. 2ᵈ [4,5] taken up.

M͟ʳ Gov͟ʳ Morris moved to insert after the words " immediately

---

[1] The words " right of " are here inserted in the transcript.
[2] The words " On the " are here inserted in the transcript.
[3] In the transcript the vote reads: " Virginia, North Carolina, aye—2; Massachusetts, Connecticut, New Jersey, Pennsylvania, Delaware, Maryland, South Carolina, Georgia, no—8; New Hampshire, divided."
[4] See page 339.
[5] The words " was then " are here inserted in the transcript.

after," the following " they shall be assembled in consequence of—" which was agreed to nem. con. as was then the whole Sect. 2.[1]

Art: V. Sect. 3.[2,3] taken up.

M[r] Gov[r] MORRIS moved to insert 14 instead of 4 years citizenship as a qualification for Senators: urging the danger of admitting strangers into our public Councils. M[r] PINKNEY 2[ds] him

M[r] ELSEWORTH. was opposed to the motion as discouraging meritorious aliens from emigrating to this Country.

M[r] PINKNEY. As the Senate is to have the power of making treaties & managing our foreign affairs, there is peculiar danger and impropriety in opening its door to those who have foreign attachments. He quoted the jealousy of the Athenians on this subject who made it death for any stranger to intrude his voice into their Legislative proceedings.

Col. MASON highly approved of the policy of the motion. Were it not that many not natives of this Country had acquired great merit[4] during the revolution, he should be for restraining the eligibility into the Senate, to natives.

M[r] MADISON, was not averse to some restrictions on this subject; but could never agree to the proposed amendment. He thought any restriction however in the *Constitution* unnecessary, and improper. unnecessary; because the Nat[l] Legisl[re]. is to have the right of regulating naturalization, and can by virtue thereof fix different periods of residence as conditions of enjoying different privileges of Citizenship: Improper; because it will give a tincture of illiberality to the Constitution: because it will put it out of the power of the Nat[l] Legislature even by special acts of naturalization to confer the full rank of Citizens on meritorious strangers & because it will discourage the most desireable class of people from emigrating to the U. S. Should the proposed Constitution have the intended effect of giving stability & reputation to our Gov[ts]. great numbers of respectable Europeans: men who love liberty and wish to partake its blessings, will be ready to transfer their fortunes hither. All such would feel the mortification of being marked with suspicious incapacitations though they s[d] not covet the public honors He was not apprehensive that any dangerous number of strangers would be appointed by the State Legislatures, if they were left at liberty to do so: nor that foreign powers would make use of strangers as instruments for

---

[1] The figure " 2 " is omitted in the transcript.
[2] See page 339.
[3] The words " was then " are here inserted in the transcript.
[4] The word " credit " is substituted in the transcript for " merit."

their purposes. Their bribes would be expended on men whose circumstances would rather stifle than excite jealousy & watchfulness in the public.

Mᶦ BUTLER was decidedly opposed to the admission of foreigners without a long residence in the Country. They bring with them, not only attachments to other Countries; but ideas of Govᵗ so distinct from ours that in every point of view they are dangerous. He acknowledged that if he himself had been called into public life within a short time after his coming to America, his foreign habits opinions & attachments would have rendered him an improper agent in public affairs. He mentioned the great strictness observed in Great Britain on this subject.

Docᵗ FRANKLIN was not agᵗᵗ a reasonable time, but should be very sorry to see any thing like illiberality inserted in the Constitution. The people in Europe are friendly to this Country. Even in the Country with which we have been lately at war, we have now & had during the war, a great many friends not only among the people at large but in both houses of Parliament. In every other Country in Europe all the people are our friends. We found in the course of the Revolution that many strangers served us faithfully– and that many natives took part agᵗᵗ their Country. When foreigners after looking about for some other Country in which they can obtain more happiness, give a preference to ours, it is a proof of attachment which ought to excite our confidence & affection.

Mᶦ RANDOLPH did not know but it might be problematical whether emigrations to this Country were on the whole useful or not: but be could never agree to the motion for disabling them for 14 years to participate in the public honours. He reminded the Convention of the language held by our patriots during the Revolution, and the principles laid down in all our American Constitutions. Many foreigners may have fixed their fortunes among us under the faith of these invitations. All persons under this description, with all others who would be affected by such a regulation, would enlist themselves under the banners of hostility to the proposed System. He would go as far as seven years, but no farther.

Mᶦ WILSON said he rose with feelings which were perhaps peculiar; mentioning the circumstance of his not being a native, and the possibility, if the ideas of some gentlemen should be pursued, of his being incapacitated from holding a place under the very Constitution, which he had shared in the trust of making. He remarked the illiberal complexion which the motion would give to the System, & the effect which a good system would have in inviting meritorious foreigners among us, and the discouragement & mortification they must feel from the degrading discrimination, now proposed. He had himself experienced this mortification. On his removal into Maryland, he found himself, from defect of residence, under certain legal incapacities which never ceased to produce chagrin, though he assuredly did not desire & would not have accepted the offices to which they related. To be appointed to a place may be matter of indifference. To be incapable of being appointed, is a circumstance grating and mortifying.

M᠄ Gov᠄ Morris. The lesson we are taught is that we should be governed as much by our reason, and as little by our feelings as possible. What is the language of Reason on this subject? That we should not be polite at the expence of prudence. There was a moderation in all things. It is said that some tribes of Indians, carried their hospitality so far as to offer to strangers their wives & daughters. Was this a proper model for us? He would admit them to his house, he would invite them to his table, would provide for them comfortable lodgings; but would not carry the complaisance so far as, to bed them with his wife. He would let them worship at the same altar, but did not choose to make Priests of them. He ran over the privileges which emigrants would enjoy among us, though they should be deprived of that of being eligible to the great offices of Government; observing that they exceeded the privileges allowed to foreigners in any part of the world; and that as every Society from a great nation down to a club had the right of declaring the conditions on which new members should be admitted, there could be no room for complaint. As to those philosophical gentlemen, those Citizens of the World as they call themselves, He owned he did not wish to see any of them in our public Councils. He would not trust them. The men who can shake off their attachments to their own Country can never love any other. These attachments are the wholesome prejudices which uphold all Governments, Admit a Frenchman into your Senate, and he will study to increase the commerce of France: an Englishman,[1] he will feel an equal biass in favor of that of England. It has been said that The Legislatures will not chuse foreigners, at least improper ones. There was no knowing what Legislatures would do. Some appointments made by them, proved that every thing ought to be apprehended from the cabals practised on such occasions. He mentioned the case of a foreigner who left this State in disgrace, and worked himself into an appointment from another to Congress.

---

[1] The word " and " is here inserted in the transcript.

[1] Question on the motion of M�r Gov�r Morris to insert 14 in place of 4 years

N. H. ay. Mas. no. C⁺ no. N. J. ay. P⁺ no. Del. no. M⁴ no. V⁺ no. N. C. no. S. C. ay. Geo. ay.[2]

On 13 years, moved M�r Gov⁺ Morris[3]

N. H. ay. Mas. no. C⁺ no. N. J. ay. P⁺ no. Del. no. M⁴ no. V⁺ no. N. C. no. S. C. ay. Geo. ay.

On 10 years moved by Gen⁺ PINKNEY[4]

N. H. ay. Mas. no. C⁺ no. N. J. ay. P⁺ no. Del. no. M⁴ no. V⁺ no. N. C. no. S. C. ay. Geo. ay.

D⁺ FRANKLIN reminded the Convention that it did not follow from an omission to insert the restriction in the Constitution that the persons in question w⁴ be actually chosen into the Legislature.

M⁺ RUTLIDGE. 7 years of Citizenship have been required for the House of Representatives. Surely a longer term is requisite for the Senate, which will have more power.

M⁺ WILLIAMSON. It is more necessary to guard the Senate in this case than the other House. Bribery & cabal can be more easily practised in the choice of the Senate which is to be made by the Legislatures composed of a few men, than of the House of Represent⁺ who will be chosen by the people.

M⁺ RANDOLPH will agree to 9 years with the expectation that it will be reduced to seven if M⁺ Wilson's motion to reconsider the vote fixing 7 years for the House of Representatives should produce a reduction of that period.

On a[5] question for 9 years.

N. H. ay. Mas. no. C⁺ no. N. J. ay. P⁺ no. Del. ay. M⁴ no. V⁺ ay. N. C. div⁴ S. C. ay. Geo. ay.[6]

The term " Resident " was struck out, & " inhabitant " inserted nem. con.

Art. V Sect. 3, as amended[7] agreed to nem. con.

---

[1] The words " On the " are here inserted in the transcript.

[2] In the transcript the vote reads: " New Hampshire, New Jersey, South Carolina, Georgia, aye—4; Massachusetts, Connecticut, Pennsylvania, Delaware, Maryland, Virginia, North Carolina, no—7."

[3] In the transcript this sentence reads as follows: " On the question for thirteen years, moved by Mr. Gouverneur Morris, it was negatived, as above." The vote by States is omitted.

[4] The phrase " the votes were the same," is here inserted in the transcript, and the vote by States is omitted.

[5] In the transcript the word " a " is stricken out and " the " is written above it.

[6] In the transcript the vote reads: " New Hampshire, New Jersey, Delaware, Virginia, South Carolina, Georgia, aye—6; Massachusetts, Connecticut, Pennsylvania, Maryland, no—4; North Carolina, divided."

[7] The words " was then " are here inserted in the transcript.

Sect. 4.[1] agreed to nem. con.[2]

Art. VI. sect. 1.[1, 3] taken up.

M: MADISON & M: GOV: MORRIS moved to strike out " each House " & to insert " the House of Representatives "; the right of the Legislatures to regulate the times & places &c in the election of Senators being involved in the right of appointing them, which was disagreed to.

[4] Division of the question being called,[5] it was taken on the first part down to "but their provisions concerning &c"

The first part was agreed to nem. con.

M: PINKNEY & M: RUTLIDGE moved to strike out the remaining part viz but their provisions concerning them may at any time be altered by the Legislature of the United States." The States they contended could & must be relied on in such cases.

M: GHORUM. It would be as improper [6] take this power from the Nat[l] Legislature, as to Restrain the British Parliament from regulating the circumstances of elections, leaving this business to the Counties themselves—

M: MADISON. The necessity of a Gen[l] Gov[t] supposes that the State Legislatures will sometimes fail or refuse to consult the common interest at the expence of their local conveniency [7] or prejudices. The policy of referring the appointment of the House of Representatives to the people and not to the Legislatures of the States, supposes that the result will be somewhat influenced by the mode. This view of the question seems to decide that the Legislatures of the States ought not to have the uncontrouled right of regulating the times places & manner of holding elections. These were words of great latitude. It was impossible to foresee all the abuses that might be made of the discretionary power. Whether the electors should vote by ballot or viva voce, should assemble at this place or that place; should be divided into districts or all meet at one place, sh[d] all vote for all the representatives; or all in a district vote for a number allotted to the district; these & many other points would depend on the Legislatures, and might materially affect the appointments. Whenever the State Legislatures had a favorite measure to

---

[1] See page 339.
[2] In the transcript this sentence reads as follows: " Article 5, Sect. 4 was agreed to *nem. con.*"
[3] The words "was then" are here inserted in the transcript.
[4] The word " A " is here inserted in the transcript.
[5] The word "for" is here inserted in the transcript.
[6] The word "to" is here inserted in the transcript.
[7] The word " conveniency " is changed to " convenience " in the transcript.

carry, they would take care so to mould their regulations as to favor the candidates they wished to succeed. Besides, the inequality of the Representation in the Legislatures of particular States, would produce a like inequality in their representation in the Nat! Legislature, as it was presumable that the Counties having the power in the former case would secure it to themselves in the latter. What danger could there be in giving a controuling power to the Nat! Legislature? Of whom was it to consist? 1.[1] of a Senate to be chosen by the State Legislatures. If the latter therefore could be trusted, their representatives could not be dangerous. 2.[1] of Representatives elected by the same people who elect the State Legislatures; surely then if confidence is due to the latter, it must be due to the former. It seemed as improper in principle, though it might be less inconvenient in practice, to give to the State Legislatures this great authority over the election of the Representatives of the people in the Gen! Legislature, as it would be to give to the latter a like power over the election of their Representatives in the State Legislatures.

M! KING. If this power be not given to the Nat! Legislature, their right of judging of the returns of their members may be frustrated. No probability has been suggested of its being abused by them. Altho this scheme of erecting the Gen! Gov! on the authority of the State Legislatures has been fatal to the federal establishment, it would seem as if many gentlemen, still foster the dangerous idea.

M! Gov! MORRIS— observed that the States might make false returns and then make no provisions for new elections

M! SHERMAN did not know but it might be best to retain the clause, though he had himself sufficient confidence in the State Legislatures. The motion of M! P. & M! R. did not prevail—

The word "respectively" was inserted after the word "State"

On the motion of M! Read the word " their " was struck out, & " regulations in such cases " inserted in place of " provisions concerning them." the clause then reading—" but regulations in each of the foregoing cases may at any time, be made or altered by the Legislature of the U. S " This was meant to give the Nat! Legislature a power not only to alter the provisions of the States, but to make regulations in case the States should fail or refuse altogether.

Art. VI. Sect. 1. as thus amended was agreed to nem. con.

Adjourned.

---

[1] The figures " 1 " and " 2 " are changed to " First " and " Secondly " in the transcript.

FRIDAY AUG.ST 10.   IN CONVENTION

Art. VI. Sect. 2.[1,2] taken up.

M.r PINKNEY. The Committee as he had conceived were instructed to report the proper qualifications of property for the members of the Nat.l Legislature; instead of which they have referred the task to the Nat.l Legislature itself. Should it be left on this footing, the first Legislature will meet without any particular qualifications of property: and if it should happen to consist of rich men they might fix such such qualifications as may be too favorable to the rich; if of poor men, an opposite extreme might be run into. He was opposed to the establishment of an undue aristocratic influence in the Constitution but he thought it essential that the members of the Legislature, the Executive, and the Judges, should be possessed of competent property to make them independent & respectable. It was prudent when such great powers were to be trusted to connect the tie of property with that of reputation in securing a faithful administration. The Legislature would have the fate of the Nation put into their hands. The President would also have a very great influence on it. The Judges would have not only [3] important causes between Citizen & Citizen but also, where foreigners are concerned. They will even be the Umpires between the U. States and individual States as well as between one State & another. Were he to fix the quantum of property which should be required, he should not think of less than one hundred thousand dollars for the President, half of that sum for each of the Judges, and in like proportion for the members of the Nat.l Legislature. He would however leave the sums blank. His motion was that the President of the U. S. the Judges, and members of the Legislature should be required to swear that they were respectively possessed of a cleared [4] unincumbered Estate to the amount of   in the case of the President &c &c.

M.r RUTLIDGE seconded the motion; observing that the Committee had reported no qualifications because they could not agree on any among themselves, being embarrassed by the danger on one side of displeasing the people by making them high, and on the other of rendering them nugatory by making them low.

---

[1] See page 339.
[2] The word " was " is here inserted in the transcript.
[3] The words " have not only " are transposed in the transcript to read "not only have."
[4] The word " clear " is substituted in the transcript for " cleared."

M: ELSEWORTH. The different circumstances of different parts of the U. S. and the probable difference between the present and future circumstances of the whole, render it improper to have either *uniform* or *fixed* qualifications. Make them so high as to be useful in the S. States, and they will be inapplicable to the E. States. Suit them to the latter, and they will serve no purpose in the former. In like manner what may be accomodated to the existing State of things among us, may be very inconvenient in some future state of them. He thought for these reasons that it was better to leave this matter to the Legislative discretion than to attempt a provision for it in the Constitution.

Doct? FRANKLIN expressed his dislike of [1] every thing that tended to debase the spirit of the common people. If honesty was often the companion of wealth, and if poverty was exposed to peculiar temptation, it was not less true that the possession of property increased the desire of more property. Some of the greatest rogues he was ever acquainted with, were the richest rogues. We should remember the character which the Scripture requires in Rulers, that they should be men hating covetousness. This Constitution will be much read and attended to in Europe, and if it should betray a great partiality to the rich, will not only hurt us in the esteem of the most liberal and enlightened men there, but discourage the common people from removing into [2] this Country.

The Motion of M: Pinkney was rejected by so general a *no*, that the States were not called.

M: MADISON was opposed to the Section as vesting an improper & dangerous power in the Legislature. The qualifications of electors and elected were fundamental articles in a Republican Gov: and ought to be fixed by the Constitution. If the Legislature could regulate those of either, it can by degrees subvert the Constitution. A Republic may be converted into an aristocracy or oligarchy as well by limiting the number capable of being elected, as the number authorised to elect. In all cases where the representatives of the people will have a personal interest distinct from that of their Constituents, there was the same reason for being jealous of them, as there was for relying on them with full confidence, when they had a common interest. This was one of the former cases. It was as improper as to allow them to fix their own wages, or their own privileges. It was a power also which might be made subservient to the views of one faction ag:t another. Qualifications founded on

---

[1] The word "to" is substituted in the transcript for "of."
[2] The word "to" is substituted in the transcript for "into."

artificial distinctions may be devised, by the stronger in order to keep out partizans of a weaker faction.

Mᵣ ELSEWORTH, admitted that the power was not unexceptionable; but he could not view it as dangerous. Such a power with regard to the electors would be dangerous because it would be much more liable to abuse.

Mᵣ GOVᵣ MORRIS moved to strike out " with regard to property " in order to leave the Legislature entirely at large.

Mᵣ WILLIAMSON. This could [1] surely never be admitted. Should a majority of the Legislature be composed of any particular description of men, of lawyers for example, which is no improbable supposition, the future elections might be secured to their own body.

Mᵣ MADISON observed that the British Parliamᵗ possessed the power of regulating the qualifications both of the electors, and the elected; and the abuse they had made of it was a lesson worthy of our attention. They had made the changes in both cases subservient to their own views, or to the views of political or Religious parties.

[2] Question on the motion to strike out with regard to property
N. H. no. Mas. no. Cᵗ ay. N. J. ay. Pᵃ ay. Del. no.* Mᵈ no. Vᵃ no. N. C. no. S. C. no. Geo. ay.[3]

Mᵣ RUTLIDGE was opposed to leaving the power to the Legislature. He proposed that the qualifications should be the same as for members of the State Legislatures.

Mᵣ WILSON thought it would be best on the whole to let the Section go out. A uniform rule would probably be never [4] fixed by the Legislature, and this particular power would constructively exclude every other power of regulating qualifications.

On the question for agreeing to Art. VI. Sect. 2ᵈ–
N. H. ay. Mas. ay. Cᵗ no. N. J. no. Pᵃ no. Mᵈ no. Vᵃ no. N. C. no. S. C. no. Geo. ay.[5]

On Motion of Mᵣ Wilson to reconsider Art: IV. Sect. 2; so as to restore 3 in place of seven years of citizenship as a qualification for being elected into the House of Representᵗ

* In the printed Journal Delaware did not vote.

---

[1] The word "would" is substituted in the transcript for "could."
[2] The words "On the" are here inserted in the transcript.
[3] In the transcript the vote reads: "Connecticut, New Jersey, Pennsylvania, Georgia, aye—4; New Hampshire, Massachusetts, Delaware,* Maryland, Virginia, North Carolina, South Carolina, no—7."
[4] In the transcript the words "be never" are transposed to read "never be."
[5] In the transcript the vote reads: "New Hampshire, Massachusetts, Georgia, aye—3; Connecticut, New Jersey, Pennsylvania, Maryland, Virginia, North Carolina, South Carolina, no—7."

N. H. no. Mas. no. C⁺ ay. N. J. no. P⁺ ay. Del. ay. M⁺ ay. V⁺ ay. N. C. ay. S. C. no. Geo. no.[1]

Monday next was then assigned for the reconsideration: all the States being ay. except Mass⁺⁺ & Georgia

Art: VI. Sect. 3.[2,3] taken up.

M⁺ GHORUM contended that less than a Majority in each House should be made of[4] Quorum, otherwise great delay might happen in business, and great inconvenience from the future increase of numbers.

M⁺ MERCER was also for less than a majority. So great a number will put it in the power of a few by seceding at a critical moment to introduce convulsions, and endanger the Governm⁺ Examples of secession have already happened in some of the States. He was for leaving it to the Legislature to fix the Quorum, as in Great Britain, where the requisite number is small & no inconveniency[5] has been experienced.

Col. MASON. This is a valuable & necessary part of the plan. In this extended Country, embracing so great a diversity of interests, it would be dangerous to the distant parts to allow a small number of members of the two Houses to make laws. The Central States could always take care to be on the Spot and by meeting earlier than the distant ones, or wearying their patience, and outstaying them, could carry such measures as they pleased. He admitted that inconveniences might spring from the secession of a small number: But he had also known good produced by an apprehension, of it. He had known a paper emission prevented by that cause in Virginia. He thought the Constitution as now moulded was founded on sound principles, and was disposed to put into it extensive powers. At the same time he wished to guard ag⁺ abuses as much as possible. If the Legislature should be able to reduce the number at all, it might reduce it as low as it pleased & the U. States might be governed by a Juncto—A majority of the number which had been agreed on, was so few that he feared it would be made an objection ag⁺ the plan.

M⁺ KING admitted there might be some danger of giving an ad-

---

[1] In the transcript the vote reads: "Connecticut, Pennsylvania, Delaware, Maryland, Virginia, North Carolina, aye—6; New Hampshire, Massachusetts, New Jersey, South Carolina, Georgia, no—5."

[2] See page 339.

[3] The words "was then" are here inserted in the transcript.

[4] In the transcript the word "of" is crossed out and "a" is written above it.

[5] The word "inconveniency" is changed to "inconvenience" in the transcript.

vantage to the Central States; but was of opinion that the public inconveniency [1] on the other side was more to be dreaded.

M: Gov: Morris moved to fix the quorum at 33 members in the H. of Rep: & 14 in the Senate. This is a majority of the present number, and will be a bar to the Legislature: fix the number low and they will generally attend knowing that advantage may be taken of their absence. the Secession of a small number ought not to be suffered to break a quorum. Such events in the States may have been of little consequence. In the national Councils, they may be fatal. Besides other mischiefs, if a few can break up a quorum, they may seize a moment when a particular part of the Continent may be in need of immediate aid, to extort, by threatening a secession, some unjust & selfish measure.

M: Mercer 2^{ded} the motion

M: King said he had just prepared a motion which instead of fixing the numbers proposed by M: Gov: Morris as Quorums, made those the lowest numbers, leaving the Legislature at liberty to increase them or not. He thought the future increase of members would render a majority of the whole extremely cumbersome.

M: Mercer agreed to substitute M: Kings motion in place of M: Morris's.

M: Elseworth was opposed to it. It would be a pleasing ground of confidence to the people that no law or burden could be imposed on them, by a few men. He reminded the movers that the Constitution proposed to give such a discretion with regard to the number of Representatives that a very inconvenient number was not to be apprehended. The inconveniency [1] of secessions may be guarded agst by giving to each House an authority to require the attendance of absent members.

M: Wilson concurred in the sentiments of M: Elseworth.

M: Gerry seemed to think that some further precautions than merely fixing the quorum might be necessary. He observed that as 17 w^d be a majority of a quorum of 33, and 8 of 14, questions might by possibility be carried in the H. of Rep: by 2 large States, and in the Senate by the same States with the aid of two small ones.—He proposed that the number for a quorum in the H. of Rep: should not exceed 50 nor be less than 33, leaving the intermediate discretion to the Legislature.

M: King, as the quorum could not be altered with^t the concurrence

---

[1] The word "inconveniency" is changed to "inconvenience" in the transcript.

of the President by less than ⅔ of each House, he thought there could be no danger in trusting the Legislature.

M⸬ CARROL this will be no security ag⸬ᵗ a continuance of the quorums at 33 & 14. when they ought to be increased.

On [1] question on M⸬ Kings motion "that not less than 33 in the H. of Rep⸬ nor less than 14 in the Senate sh⸬ᵈ constitute a Quorum, which may be increased by a law, on additions to [1] members in either House.

N. H. no. Mas. ay. C⸬ no. N. J. no. P⸬ no. Del. ay. M⸬ᵈ no. V⸬ no. N. C. no. S. C. no. Geo. no.[2]

M⸬ RANDOLPH & M⸬ MADISON moved to add to the end of Art. VI. Sect 3. "and may be authorised to compel the attendance of absent members in such manner & under such penalties as each House may provide." Agreed to by all except Pen⸬ which was divided.

Art: VI. Sect. 3.[3] agreed to as amended Nem. con.

Sect. 4.[4] ⎫
Sect. 5.[4] ⎬ Agreed to nem. con.[5]
            ⎭

M⸬ MADISON observed that the right of expulsion (Art. VI. Sect. 6.) [4] was too important to be exercised by a bare majority of a quorum: and in emergencies of faction might be dangerously abused. He moved that "with the concurrence of ⅔ " might be inserted between may & expel.

M⸬ RANDOLPH & M⸬ MASON approved the idea.

M⸬ GOV⸬ MORRIS. This power may be safely trusted to a majority. To require more may produce abuses on the side of the minority. A few men from factious motives may keep in a member who ought to be expelled.

M⸬ CARROL thought that the concurrence of ⅔ at least ought to be required.

On the question for [6] requiring ⅔ in cases of expelling a member.[7]

N. H. ay. Mas. ay. C⸬ ay. N. J. ay. P⸬ div⸬ᵈ Del. ay. M⸬ᵈ ay. V⸬ ay. N. C. ay. S. C. ay. Geo. ay.[7]

---

[1] The word "the" is here inserted in the transcript.

[2] In the transcript the vote reads: "Massachusetts, Delaware, aye—2; New Hampshire, Connecticut, New Jersey, Pennsylvania, Maryland, Virginia, North Carolina, South Carolina, Georgia, no—9."

[3] The word "was" is here inserted in the transcript.

[4] See page 339.

[5] In the transcript this reads as follows: "Sections 4 and 5, of Article 6, were then agreed to, *nem. con.*"

[6] The word "for" is omitted in the transcript.

[7] In the transcript the vote by States is omitted and the following sentence is inserted: "ten States were in the affirmative, Pennsylvania, divided."

Art. VI. Sect. 6. as thus amended [1] agreed to nem. con.

Art: VI. Sect. 7 [1, 2] taken up.

M[r] Gov[r] Morris urged that if the yeas & nays were proper at all any individual ought to be authorised to call for them: and moved an amendment to that effect.– The small States may otherwise be under a disadvantage, and find it difficult, to get a concurrence of ⅙

M[r] Randolph 2[ded] y[e] motion.

M[r] Sherman had rather strike out the yeas & nays altogether. They never have done any good, and have done much mischief. They are not proper as the reasons governing the voter never appear along with them.

M[r] Elseworth was of the same opinion

Col. Mason liked the Section as it stood. it was a middle way between the two extremes.

M[r] Ghorum was opposed to the motion for allowing a single member to call the yeas & nays, and recited the abuses of it, in Mass[ts]. 1 [3] in stuffing the journals with them on frivolous occasions. 2 [3] in misleading the people who never know the reasons determining the votes.

The motion for allowing a single member to call the yeas & nays was disag[d] to nem. con.

M[r] Carrol. & M[r] Randolph moved   Here insert the motion at the bottom of page * [4]

* to strike out the words " each House " and to insert the words " the House of Representatives " in Sect. 7. Art. 6. and to add to the Section the words " and any member of the Senate shall be at liberty to enter his dissent."

M[r] Gov[r] Morris & M[r] Wilson observed that if the minority were to have a right to enter their votes & reasons, the other side would have a right to complain, if it were not extended to them: & to allow it to both, would fill the Journals, like the records of a Court, with replications, rejoinders &c.

[5] Question on M[r] Carrols motion to allow a member to enter his dissent

---

[1] The words " was then " are here inserted in the transcript.
[2] See page 339.
[3] The figures " 1 " and " 2 " are changed to " first " and " secondly " in the transcript.
[4] Madison's direction is omitted in the transcript.
[5] The words " On the " are here inserted in the transcript.

N. H. no. Mas. no. Con! no. N. J. no. P? no. Del. no. M? ay. V? ay. N. C. no. S. C. ay. Geo. no.[1]

M? Gerry moved to strike out the words " when it shall be acting in its legislative capacity " in order to extend the provision to the Senate when exercising its peculiar authorities and to insert " except such parts thereof as in their judgment require secrecy " after the words " publish them."—[It was thought by others that provision should be made with respect to these when that part came under consideration which proposed to vest those additional authorities in the Senate.]

On this question for striking out the words " when acting in its Legislative capacity "

N. H. div? Mas. ay. C! no. N. J. no. P? no. Del. ay. M? ay. V? ay. N. C. ay. S. C. ay. Geo. ay.[2]

Adjourned

SATURDAY AUG?T 11.   IN CONVENTION

M? Madison & M? Rutlidge moved "that each House shall keep a journal of its proceeding,[3] & shall publish the same from time to time; except such part of the proceedings of the Senate, when acting not in its Legislative capacity as may be judged by that House to require secrecy."

M? Mercer. This implies that other powers than legislative will be given to the Senate which he hoped would not be given.

M? Madison & M? R's motion. was disag? to by all the States except Virg?

M? Gerry & M? Sharman moved to insert after the words " publish them " the following " except such as relate to treaties & military operations." Their object was to give each House a discretion in such cases.—On this question

N. H. no. Mas. ay. C! ay. N. J. no. P? no. Del. no. V? no. N. C. no. S. C. no. Geo. no.[4]

---

[1] In the transcript the vote reads: "Maryland, Virginia, South Carolina, aye—3; New Hampshire, Massachusetts, Connecticut, New Jersey, Pennsylvania, Delaware, North Carolina, Georgia, no—8."

[2] In the transcript the vote reads: "Massachusetts, Delaware, Maryland, Virginia, North Carolina, South Carolina, Georgia, aye—7; Connecticut, New Jersey, Pennsylvania, no—3; New Hampshire, divided."

[3] The transcript uses the word "proceeding" in the plural.

[4] In the transcript the vote reads: "Massachusetts, Connecticut, aye—2; New Hampshire, New Jersey, Pennsylvania, Delaware, Virginia, North Carolina, South Carolina, Georgia, no—8."

M̲ͬ ELSEWORTH. As the clause is objectionable in so many shapes, it may as well be struck out altogether. The Legislature will not fail to publish their proceedings from time to time. The people will call for it if it should be improperly omitted.

M̲ͬ WILSON thought the expunging of the clause would be very improper. The people have a right to know what their Agents are doing or have done, and it should not be in the option of the Legislature to conceal their proceedings. Besides as this is a clause in the existing confederation, the not retaining it would furnish the adversaries of the reform with a pretext by which week & suspicious minds may be easily misled.

M̲ͬ MASON thought it would give a just alarm to the people, to make a conclave of their Legislature.

M̲ͬ SHERMAN thought the Legislature might be trusted in this case if in any.

[1] Question on [2] 1.ˢᵗ part of the section down to *"publish them"* inclusive: [3] Agreed to nem. con.

[1] Question on the words to follow, to wit except such parts thereof as may in their Judgment require secrecy." N. H. div̲ᵈ Mas. ay. C̲ᵗ ay. N. J. ay. P̲ᵃ no. Del. no. M̲ᵈ no. V̲ᵃ ay. N. C. ay. S. C. no. Geo. ay.[4]

The remaining part as to yeas & nays,— [5] agreed to nem. con.

Art VI. Sect. 8.[6,7] taken up.

M̲ͬ KING remarked that the section authorized the 2 Houses to adjourn to a new place. He thought this inconvenient. The mutability of place had dishonored the federal Gov̲ᵗ and would require as strong a cure as we could devise. He thought a law at least should be made necessary to a removal of the Seat of Gov̲ᵗ

M̲ͬ MADISON, viewed the subject in the same light, and joined with M̲ͬ King in a motion requiring a law.

M̲ͬ GOVERN̲ͬ MORRIS proposed the additional alteration by inserting the words "during the Session" &c."

M̲ͬ SPAIGHT. this will fix the seat of Gov̲ᵗ at N. Y. The present Congress will convene them there in the first instance, and they will

---

[1] The words " On the " are here inserted in the transcript.
[2] The word " the " is here inserted in the transcript.
[3] The words " it was " are here inserted in the transcript.
[4] In the transcript the vote reads: "Massachusetts, Connecticut, New Jersey, Virginia, North Carolina, Georgia, aye—6; Pennsylvania, Delaware, Maryland, South Carolina, no—4; New Hampshire, divided."
[5] The word " was " is here inserted in the transcript.
[6] See page 340.
[7] The words " was then " are here inserted in the transcript.

never be able to remove; especially if the Presid! should be [1] Northern Man.

M! Gov! Morris such a distrust is inconsistent with all Gov!

M! Madison supposed that a central place for the seat of Gov! was so just and w? be so must insisted on by the H. of Representatives, that though a law should be made requisite for the purpose, it could & would be obtained. The necessity of a central residence of the Gov! w? be much greater under the new than old Gov! The members of the new Gov! w? be more numerous. They would be taken more from the interior parts of the States; they w? not like members of y? present Cong? come so often from the distant States by water. As the powers & objects of the new Gov! would be far greater y? heretofore, more private individuals w? have business calling them to the seat of it, and it was more necessary that the Gov! should be in that position from which it could contemplate with the most equal eye, and sympathize most equally with, every part of the nation. These considerations he supposed would extort a removal even if a law were made necessary. But in order to quiet suspicions both within & without doors, it might not be amiss to authorize the 2 Houses by a concurrent vote to adjourn at their first meeting to the most proper place, and to require thereafter, the sanction of a law to their removal.

The motion was accordingly moulded into the following form— " the Legislature shall at their first assembling determine on a place at which their future sessions shall be held; neither House shall afterwards, during the session of the House of Rep! without the consent of the other, adjourn for more than three days, nor shall they adjourn to any other place than such as shall have been fixt by law"

M! Gerry thought it would be wrong to let the Presid! check the will of the 2 Houses on this subject at all

M! Williamson supported the ideas of M! Spaight

M! Carrol was actuated by the same apprehensions

M! Mercer, it will serve no purpose to require the two Houses at their first meeting to fix on a place. They will never agree.

After some further expressions from others denoting an apprehension that the seat of Gov! might be continued at an improper place if a law should be made necessary to a removal, and [2] the motion above stated with another for recommitting the section had been negatived, the section was left in the shape it which it was reported as to this point. The words "during the session of the Legislature

---

[1] The word "a" is here inserted in the transcript.
[2] The word "after" is here inserted in the transcript.

were prefixed to the 8th section—and the last sentence "But this regulation shall not extend to the Senate when it shall exercise the powers mention [1] in the   article " struck struck out. The 8th section as amended was then agreed to.

M[r] RANDOLPH moved according to notice to reconsider Art: IV. Sect. 5.[2] concerning money-bills which had been struck out. He argued 1.[3] that he had not wished for this privilege whilst a proportional Representation in the Senate was in contemplation, but since an equality had been fixed in that house, the large States would require this compensation at least. 2.[3] that it would make the plan more acceptable to the people, because they will consider the Senate as the more aristocratic body, and will expect that the usual guards ag[st] its influence [4] be provided according to the example in [5] G. Britain. 3.[3] the privilege will give some advantage to the House of Rep[s] if it extends to the originating only—but still more, if it restrains the Senate from amend[g] 4.[3] he called on the smaller States to concur in the measure, as the condition by which alone the compromise had entitled them to an equality in the Senate. He signified that he should propose instead of the original Section, a clause specifying that the bills in question should be for the purpose of Revenue, in order to repel y[e] objection ag[st] the extent of the words "raising money," which might happen incidentally, and that the Senate should not so amend or alter as to increase or diminish the sum; in order to obviate the inconveniences urged ag[st] a restriction of the Senate to a simple affirmative or negative.

M[r] WILLIAMSON 2[ded] the motion

M[r] PINKNEY was sorry to oppose the opportunity gentlemen asked to have the question again opened for discussion, but as he considered it a mere waste of time he could not bring himself to consent to it. He said that notwithstanding what had been said as to the compromise, he always considered this section as making no part of it. The rule of Representation in the 1st branch was the true condition of that in the 2[d] branch.—Several others spoke for & ag[st] the reconsideration, but without going into the merits—On the Question to reconsider

N. H. ay. Mas. ay. C[t] ay. N. J.* ay. P[a] ay. Del. ay. M[d] no.

* In the printed Journal N. Jersey—no.

---

[1] The word " mentioned " is substituted in the transcript for " mention."
[2] See page 338.
[3] The figures " 1," " 2," " 3 " and " 4 " are changed in the transcript t[o] " first," " Secondly " etc.
[4] The word " will " is here inserted in the transcript.
[5] The word " of " is substituted in the transcript for " in."

V⁹ ay. N. C. ay. S. C. div⁴ Geo. ay.—¹ Monday was then assigned—²

Adj⁴

MONDAY AUG⁸ᵀ 13. IN CONVENTION

Art. IV. Sect. 2 ³, ⁴ reconsidered—

M⁹ WILSON & M⁹ RANDOLPH moved to strike out " 7 years " and insert " 4 years," as the requisite term of Citizenship to qualify for the House of Rep⁹ M⁹ Wilson said it was very proper the electors should govern themselves by this consideration; but unnecessary & improper that the Constitution should chain them down to it.

M⁹ GERRY wished that in future the eligibility might be confined to Natives. Foreign powers will intermeddle in our affairs, and spare no expence to influence them. Persons having foreign attachments will be sent among us & insinuated into our councils, in order to be made instruments for their purposes. Every one knows the vast sums laid out in Europe for secret services. He was not singular in these ideas. A great many of the most influencial men in Mass⁹ reasoned in the same manner.

M⁹ WILLIAMSON moved to insert 9 years instead of seven. He wished this Country to acquire as fast as possible national habits. Wealthy emigrants do more harm by their luxurious examples, than good, by the money, they bring with them.

Col. HAMILTON was in general ag⁹ᵗ embarrassing the Gov⁹ with minute restrictions. There was on one side the possible danger that had been suggested. On the other side, the advantage of encouraging foreigners was obvious & admitted. Persons in Europe of moderate fortunes will be fond of coming here where they will be on a level with the first Citizens. He moved that the section be so altered as to require merely citizenship & inhabitancy. The right of determining the rule of naturalization will then leave a discretion to the Legislature on this subject which will answer every purpose.

M⁹ MADISON seconded the motion. He wished to maintain the character of liberality which had been professed in all the Constitutions & publications of America. He wished to invite foreigners of

---

¹ In the transcript the vote reads: " New Hampshire, Massachusetts, Connecticut, New Jersey,* Pennsylvania, Delaware, Virginia, North Carolina, Georgia, aye—9; Maryland, no—1; South Carolina, divided."
² The words " for the reconsideration " are here inserted in the transcript.
³ See page 338.
⁴ The word " being " is here inserted in the transcript.

merit & republican principles among us.   America was indebted to emigrations for her settlement & Prosperity.   That part of America which had encouraged them most had advanced most rapidly in population, agriculture & the arts.   There was a possible danger he admitted that men with foreign predilections might obtain appointments but it was by no means probable that it would happen in any dangerous degree.   For the same reason that they would be attached to their native Country, our own people w^d prefer natives of this Country to them.   Experience proved this to be the case.   Instances were rare of a foreigner being elected by the people within any short space after his coming among us.   If bribery was to be practised by foreign powers, it would not be attempted among the electors but among the elected; and among natives having full Confidence of the people not among strangers who would be regarded with a jeoulous eye.

Mr WILSON, cited Pennsylv^a as a proof of the advantage of encouraging emigrations.   It was perhaps the youngest [except Georgia] settlem^t on the Atlantic; yet it was at least among the foremost in population & prosperity.   He remarked that almost all the Genl officers of the Pen^a line of the late army were foreigners. And no complaint had ever been made against their fidelity or merit. Three of her deputies to the Convention [Mr R. Morris, Mr Fitzimmons & himself] were also not natives.   He had no objection to Col. Hamiltons motion & would withdraw the one made by himself.

Mr BUTLER was strenuous agst admitting foreigners into our public Councils.

[1] Question on Col. Hamilton's Motion

N. H. no. Mas. no. C^t ay. N. J. no. P^a ay. Del. no. M^d ay. V^a ay. N. C. no. S. C. no. Geo. no.[2]

[1] Question on Mr Williamson's moution to insert 9 years instead of seven.

N. H. ay. Mas^{ts} no. C^t no. N. J. no. P^a no. Del. no. M^d no. V^a no. N. C. no. S. C. ay. Geo. ay.[3]

Mr WILSON's renewed the motion for 4 years instead' of 7. & on [4] question

---

[1] The words " On the " are here inserted in the transcript.

[2] In the transcript the vote reads: " Connecticut, Pennsylvania, Maryland, Virginia, aye—4; New Hampshire, Massachusetts, New Jersey, Delaware, North Carolina, South Carolina, Georgia, no—7."

[3] In the transcript the vote reads: " New Hampshire, South Carolina, Georgia, aye—3; Massachusetts, Connecticut, New Jersey, Pennsylvania, Delaware, Maryland, Virginia, North Carolina, no—8."

[4] The word " the " is here inserted in the transcript.

N. H. no. Mas. no. C̣ ay. N. J. no. Pạ no. Del. no. Ṃᵈ ay.
Ṿ ay. N. C. no. S. C. no. Geo. no.[1]

Ṃ Goṿ Morris moved to add to the end of the section [art IV.
S. 2] a proviso that the limitation of seven years should not affect
the rights of any person now a Citizen.

Ṃ Mercer 2ᵈᵉᵈ the motion. It was necessary he said to prevent
a disfranchisement of persons who had become Citizens under and
on[2] the faith & according to the laws & Constitution from being on
a[3] level in all respects with natives.

Ṃ Rutlidge. It might as well bẹ said that all qualifications are
disfranchiseṃᵗ and that to require the age of 25 years was a disfranchisement. The policy of the precaution was as great with regard
to foreigners now Citizens; as to those who are to be naturalized in
future.

Ṃ Sherman. The U. States have not invited foreigners nor
pledged their faith that they should enjoy equal privileges with
native Citizens. The Individual States alone have done this. The
former therefore are at liberty to make any discriminations they may
judge requisite.

Ṃ Ghorum. When foreigners are naturalized it ẉ seem as if
they stand on an equal footing with natives. He doubted then the
propriety of giving a retrospective force to the restriction.

Ṃ Madison animadverted on the peculiarity of the doctrine of
Ṃ Sharman. It was a subtilty by which every national engagement
might be evaded. By parity of reason, wherever our public debts,
or foreign treaties become inconvenient nothing more would be necessary to relieve us from them, than to new[4] model the Constitution. It
was said that the *U. S.* as such have not pledged their faith to the
naturalized foreigners, & therefore are not bound. Be it so, & that
the States alone are bound. Who are to form the New Constitution
by which the condition of that class of citizens is to be made worse
than the other class? Are not the States ỵ Agents? will they not
be the members of it? Did they not appoint this Convention? Are
not they to ratify its proceedings? Will not the new Constitution
be their Act? If the new Constitution then violates the faith pledged
to any description of people will not the makers of it, will not the

---

[1] In the transcript the vote reads: "Connecticut, Maryland, Virginia,
aye—3; New Hampshire, Massachusetts, New Jersey, Pennsylvania, Delaware,
North Carolina, South Carolina, Georgia, no—8."

[2] The words "and on" are omitted in the transcript.

[3] The words "their actual" are substituted in the transcript for "being
on a."

[4] In the transcript the word "new" is crossed out and the syllable "re" is
written above it.

States, be the violators. To justify the doctrine it must be said that the States can get rid of their [1] obligation by revising the Constitution, though they could not do it by repealing the law under which foreigners held their privileges. He considered this a matter of real importance. It woud expose us to the reproaches of all those who should be affected by it, reproaches which w^d soon be ecchoed from the other side of the Atlantic; and would unnecessarily enlist among the Adversaries of the reform a very considerable body of Citizens: We should moreover reduce every State to the dilemma of rejecting it or of violating the faith pledged to a part of its Citizens.

Mr Govr MORRIS considered the case of persons under 25 years,[2] as very different from that of foreigners. No faith could be pleaded by the former in bar of the regulation. No assurance had ever been given that persons under that age should be in all cases on a level with those above it. But with regard to foreigners among us, the faith had been pledged that they should enjoy the privileges of Citizens. If the restriction as to age had been confined to natives, & had left foreigners under 25 years,[2] eligible in this case, the discrimination w^d have been an equal injustice on the other side.

Mr PINKNEY remarked that the laws of the States had varied much the terms of naturalization in different parts of America; and contended that the U. S. could not be bound to respect them on such an occasion as the present. It was a sort of recurrence to first principles.

Col. MASON was struck not like [Mr Madison] with the *peculiarity*, but the *propriety* of the doctrine of Mr Sharman. The States have formed different qualifications themselves, for enjoying different rights of citizenship. Greater caution w^d be necessary in the outset of the Gov^t than afterwards. All the great objects w^d be then [3] provided for. Everything would be then set in Motion. If persons among us attached to G. B. should work themselves into our Councils, a turn might be given to our affairs & particularly to our Commercial regulations which might have pernicious consequences. The great Houses of British Merchants will spare no pains to insinuate the instruments of their views into the Gov^t

Mr WILSON read the clause in the Constitution of Pen^a giving to foreigners after two years residence all the rights whatsoever of citizens, combined it with the article of Confederation making the Citizens of one State Citizens of all, inferred the obligation Pen^a was under to maintain the faith thus pledged to her citizens of foreign

---

[1] The word "the" is substituted in the transcript for "their."

[2] The words "of age" are here inserted in the transcript.

[3] The words "be then" are transposed in the transcript to read "then be."

birth, and the just complaints which her failure would authorize: He observed likewise that the Princes & States of Europe would avail themselves of such breach of faith to deter their subjects from emigrating to the U. S.

M⸳ MERCER enforced the same idea of a breach of faith.

M⸳ BALDWIN could not enter into the force of the arguments ag⸳ᵗ extending the disqualification to foreigners now Citizens. The discrimination of the place of birth, was not more objectionable than that of age which all had concurred in the propriety of.

[1] Question on the proviso of M⸳ Gov⸳ Morris in favor of foreigners now Citizens

N. H. no. Mas. no. C⸳ ay. N. J. ay. P⸳ ay. Del. no. Mary⸳ ay. V⸳ ay. N. C. no. S. C. no. Geo. no.[2]

M⸳ CARROL moved to insert "5 years" instead "of seven," in Section 2⸳ Art: IV

N. H. no. Mas. no. C⸳ ay. N. J. no. P⸳ div⸳ Del. no. M⸳ ay. V⸳ ay. N. C. no. S. C. no. Geo. no.[3]

The Section [Art IV. Sec. 2.] as formerly amended was then agreed to nem. con.

M⸳ WILSON moved that [in Art: V. Sect. 3.[4]] 9 years be reduced to seven, which was disag⸳ to and the 3⸳ section [Art. V.] confirmed by the following vote.

N. H. ay. Mas. ay. C⸳ no. N. J. ay. P⸳ no. Del. ay. M⸳ no. V⸳ ay. N. C. ay. S. C. ay. Geo. ay.[5]

Art. IV. Sec 5.[6] being reconsidered.

M⸳ RANDOLPH moved that the clause be altered so as to read— " Bills for raising money for the *purpose of revenue* or for appropriating the same shall originate in the House of Representatives and shall not be so amended or altered by the Senate as to increase or diminish the sum to be raised, or change the mode of levying it, or the objects of its appropriation."—He would not repeat his reasons, but barely remind the members from the smaller States of the compromise by which the larger States were entitled to this privilege.

---

[1] The words "On the" are here inserted in the transcript.

[2] In the transcript the vote reads: "Connecticut, New Jersey, Pennsylvania, Maryland, Virginia, aye—5; New Hampshire, Massachusetts, Delaware, North Carolina, South Carolina, Georgia, no—6."

[3] In the transcript the vote reads: "Connecticut, Maryland, Virginia, aye—3; New Hampshire, Massachusetts, New Jersey, Delaware, North Carolina, South Carolina, Georgia, no—7; Pennsylvania, divided."

[4] See page 339.

[5] In the transcript the vote reads: "New Hampshire, Massachusetts, New Jersey, Delaware, Virginia, North Carolina, South Carolina, Georgia, aye—8; Connecticut, Pennsylvania, Maryland, no—3."

[6] See page 338.

Col. MASON. This amendment removes all the objections urged ag.ʳᵗ the section as it stood at first. By specifying *purposes of revenue*, it obviated the objection that the Section extended to all bills under which money might incidentally arise. By authorising amendments in the Senate it got rid of the objections that the Senate could not correct errors of any sort, & that it would introduce into the House of Rep.ᵗ the practice of tacking foreign matter to money bills. These objections being removed, the arguments in favor of the proposed restraint on the Senate ought to have their full force. 1.[1] the Senate did not represent the *people*, but the *States* in their political character. It was improper therefore that it should tax the people. The reason was the same ag.ᵗ their doing it; as it had been ag.ᵗ Cong.ᵗ doing it. [2] Nor was it in any respect necessary in order to cure the evils of our Republican system. He admitted that notwithstanding the superiority of the Republican form over every other, it had its evils. The chief ones, were the danger of the majority oppressing the minority, and the mischievous influence of demagogues. The Gen.ˡ Government of itself will cure these.[3] As the States will not concur at the same time in their unjust & oppressive plans, the General Gov.ᵗ will be able to check & defeat them, whether they result from the wickedness of the majority, or from the misguidance of demagogues. Again, the Senate is not like the H. of Rep.ᵗ chosen frequently and obliged to return frequently among the people. They are to be chosen by the Sts for 6 years, will probably settle themselves at the seat of Gov.ᵗ will pursue schemes for their own aggrandizement—will be able by weary.ᵍ out the H. of Rep.ᵗ and taking advantage of their impatience at the close of a long Session, to extort measures for that purpose. If they should be paid as he expected would be yet determined & wished to be so, out of the Nat.ˡ Treasury, they will particularly extort an increase of their wages. A bare negative was a very different thing from that of originating bills. The practice in Engl.ᵈ was in point. The House of Lords does not represent nor tax the people, because not elected by the people. If the Senate can originate, they will in the recess of the Legislative Sessions, hatch their mischievous projects, for their own purposes, and have their money bills ready[4] cut & dried, (to use a common phrase) for the meeting of the H. of Rep.ᵗ He compared the case to Poyning's law—and signified that the House of Rep.ᵗ might be

---

[1] The figure " 1 " is changed to " First " in the transcript.
[2] The word " Secondly " is here inserted in the transcript.
[3] The word " them " is substituted in the transcript for " these."
[4] The word " ready " is omitted in the transcript.

rendered by degrees like the Parliament of Paris, the mere depository
of the decrees of the Senate. As to the compromise so much had
passed on that subject that he would say nothing about it. He did
not mean by what he had said to oppose the permanency of the
Senate. On the contrary he had no repugnance to an increase of
it—nor to allowing it a negative, though the Senate was not by its
present constitution entitled to it. But in all events he would contend that the purse strings should be in the hands of the Representatives of the people.

M! WILSON was himself directly opposed to the equality of votes
granted to the Senate by its present Constitution. At the same time
he wished not to multiply the vices of the system. He did not mean
to enlarge on a subject which had been so much canvassed, but
would remark as an insuperable objection ag.st the proposed restriction of money bills to the H. of Rep! that it would be a source
of perpetual contentions where there was no mediator to decide them.
The Presid! here could not like the Executive Magistrate in England
interpose by a prorogation, or dissolution. This restriction had been
found pregnant with altercation in every State where the Constitution had established it. The House of Rep! will insert other things
in money bills, and by making them conditions of each other, destroy
the deliberative liberty of the Senate. He stated the case of a Preamble to a money bill sent up by the House of Commons in the reign
of Queen Anne, to the H. of Lords, in which the conduct of the displaced Ministry, who were to be impeached before the Lords, was
condemned; the Commons thus extorting a premature judgm! without
any hearing of the Parties to be tried, and the H. of Lords being thus
reduced to the poor & disgraceful expedient of opposing to the
authority of a law, a protest on their Journals ag.st its being drawn
into precedent. If there was any thing like Poynings law in the
present case, it was in the attempt to vest the exclusive right of
originating in the H. of Rep! and so far he was agst it. He should
be equally so if the right were to be exclusively vested in the Senate.
With regard to the purse strings, it was to be observed that the
purse was to have two strings, one of which was in the hands of
the H. of Rep! the other in those of the Senate. Both houses must
concur in untying, and of what importance could it be which untied
first, which last. He could not conceive it to be any objection to the
Senate's preparing the bills, that they would have leisure for that
purpose and would be in the habits of business. War, Commerce, &
Revenue were the great objects of the Gen! Government. All of them

are connected with money. The restriction in favor of the H. of Represt�!̣ would exclude the Senate from originating any important bills whatever—

Mᣵ Gᴇʀʀʏ considered this as a part of the plan that would be much scrutinized. Taxation & representation are strongly associated in the minds of the people, and they will not agree that any but their immediate representatives shall meddle with their purses. In short the acceptance of the plan will inevitably fail, if the Senate be not restrained from originating Money bills.

Mᣴ Gᴏᴠᴇʀɴᣵ Mᴏʀʀɪs All the arguments suppose the right to originate money [1] & to tax, to be exclusively vested in the Senate.—The effects commented on may be produced by a Negative only in the Senate. They can tire out the other House, and extort their concurrence in favorite measures, as well by withholding their negative, as by adhering to a bill introduced by themselves.

Mᣴ Mᴀᴅɪsᴏɴ thought If the substitute offered by Mᣴ Randolph for the original section is to be adopted it would be proper to allow the Senate at least so to amend as to *diminish* the sum [2] to be raised. Why should they be restrained from checking the extravagance of the other House? One of the greatest evils incident to Republican Govᣴ was the spirit of contention & faction. The proposed substitute, which in some respects lessened the objections agᣵᵗ the section, had a contrary effect with respect to this particular. It laid a foundation for new difficulties and disputes between the two houses. The word *revenue* was ambiguous. In many acts, particularly in the regulations of trade, the object would be twofold. The raising of revenue would be one of them. How could it be determined which was the primary or predominant one; or whether it was necessary that revenue shᣵ be the sole object, in exclusion even of other incidental effects. When the Contest was first opened with G. B. their power to regulate trade was admitted. Their power to raise revenue rejected. An accurate investigation of the subject afterward proved that no line could be drawn between the two cases. The words *amend or alter*, form an equal source of doubt & altercation. When an obnoxious paragraph shall be sent down from the Senate to the House of Repˢ—it will be called an origination under the name of an amendment. The Senate may actually couch extraneous matter

---

[1] The word "money" is omitted in the transcript. In Madison's notes it is written above the words "originate" and "&" without a caret indicating its position. It appears to have been omitted in all previous editions.

[2] The transcript uses the word "sum" in the plural.

under that name. In these cases, the question will turn on the *degree* of connection between the matter & object of the bill and the alteration or amendment offered to it. Can there be a more fruitful source of dispute, or a kind of dispute more difficult to be settled? His apprehensions on this point were not conjectural. Disputes had actually flowed from this source in Virg? where the Senate can originate no bill. The words "so as to *increase or diminish* the sum to be raised," were liable to the same objections. In levying indirect taxes, which it seemed to be understood were to form the principal revenue of the new Gov? the sum to be raised, would be increased or diminished by a variety of collateral circumstances influencing the consumption, in general, the consumption of foreign or of domestic articles—of this or that particular species of articles, and even by the mode of collection which may be closely connected with the productiveness of a tax.—The friends of the section had argued its necessity from the permanency of the Senate. He could not see how this argum? applied. The Senate was not more permanent now than in the form it bore in the original propositions of M? Randolph and at the time when no objection whatever was hinted ag? its originating money bills. Or if in consequence of a loss of the present question, a proportional vote in the Senate should be reinstated as has been urged as the indemnification the permanency of the Senate will remain the same.—If the right to originate be vested exclusively in the House of Rep? either the Senate must yield ag? its judgment to that House, in which case the Utility of the check will be lost— or the Senate will be inflexible & the H. of Rep? must adapt its money bill to the views of the Senate, in which case, the exclusive right will be of no avail.—As to the Compromise of which so much had been said, he would make a single observation. There were 5 States which had opposed the equality of votes in the Senate, viz. Mas? Penn? Virg? N. Carolina & S. Carol? As a compensation for the sacrifice extorted from them on this head, the exclusive origination of money bills in the other House had been tendered. Of the five States a majority viz. Penn? Virg? & S. Carol? have uniformly voted ag? the proposed compensation, on its own merits, as rendering the plan of Gov? still more objectionable. Mass? has been divided. N. Carolina alone has set a value on the compensation, and voted on that principle. What obligation then can the small States be under to concur ag? their judgments in reinstating the section?

M? DICKENSON. Experience must be our only guide. Reason may mislead us. It was not Reason that discovered the singular & admirable mechanism of the English Constitution. It was not Reason

that discovered or ever could have discovered the odd & in the eye
of those who are governed by reason, the absurd mode of trial by
Jury. Accidents probably produced these discoveries, and experience
has give a sanction to them. This is then our guide. And has
not experience verified the utility of restraining money bills to the
immediate representatives of the people. Whence the effect may have
proceeded he could not say; whether from the respect with which
this privilege inspired the other branches of Gov:t to the H. of
Commons, or from the turn of thinking it gave to the people at large
with regard to their rights, but the effect was visible & could not be
doubted—Shall we oppose to this long experience, the short experience of 11 years which we had ourselves, on this subject. As to disputes, they could not be avoided any way. If both Houses should
originate, each would have a different bill to which it would be attached, and for which it would contend.—He observed that all the
prejudices of the people would be offended by refusing this exclusive
privilege to the H. of Repres: and these prejudices sh:d never be disregarded by us when no essential purpose was to be served. When
this plan goes forth it will be attacked by the popular leaders. Aristocracy will be the watchword; the Shibboleth among its adversaries.
Eight States have inserted in their Constitutions the exclusive
right of originating money bills in favor of the popular branch
of the Legislature. Most of them however allowed the other
branch to amend. This he thought would be proper for us to
do.

Mr RANDOLPH regarded this point as of such consequence, that
as he valued the peace of this Country, he would press the adoption
of it. We had numerous & monstrous difficulties to combat. Surely
we ought not to increase them. When the people behold in the Senate,
the countenance of an aristocracy; and in the president, the form
at least of a little monarch, will not their alarms be sufficiently raised
without taking from their immediate representatives, a right which
has been so long appropriated to them.—The Executive will have
more influence over the Senate, than over the H. of Rep: Allow the
Senate to originate in this case, & that influence will be sure to mix
itself in their deliberations & plans. The Declaration of War he conceived ought not to be in the Senate composed of 26 men only, but
rather in the other House. In the other House ought to be placed
the origination of the means of war. As to Commercial regulations
which may involve revenue, the difficulty may be avoided by restraining the definition to bills, for the *mere* or *sole*, purpose of raising
revenue. The Senate will be more likely to be corrupt than the

H. of Rep: and should therefore have less to do with money matters. His principal object however was to prevent popular objections against the plan, and to secure its adoption.

M: RUTLIDGE. The friends of this motion are not consistent in their reasoning. They tell us that we ought to be guided by the long experience of G. B. & not our own experience of 11 years: and yet they themselves propose to depart from it. The *H. of Commons* not only have the exclusive right of originating, but the *Lords* are not allowed to alter or amend a money bill. Will not the people say that this restriction is but a mere tub to the whale. They cannot but see that it is of no real consequence; and will be more likely to be displeased with it as an attempt to bubble them, than to impute it to a watchfulness over their rights. For his part, he would prefer giving the exclusive right to the Senate, if it was to be given exclusively at all. The Senate being more conversant in business, and having more leisure, will digest the bills much better, and as they are to have no effect, till examined & approved by the H. of Rep: there can be no possible danger. These clauses in the Constitutions of the States had been put in through a blind adherence to the British model. If the work was to be done over now, they would be omitted. The experiment in S. Carolina, where the Senate cannot originate or amend money bills, has shewn that it answers no good purpose; and produces the very bad one of continually dividing & heating the two houses. Sometimes indeed if the matter of the amendment of the Senate is pleasing to the other House they wink at the encroachment; if it be displeasing, then the Constitution is appealed to. Every Session is distracted by altercations on this subject. The practice now becoming frequent is for the Senate not to make formal amendments; but to send down a schedule of the alterations which will procure the bill their assent.

M: CARROL. The most ingenious men in Mary⁴ are puzzled to define the case of money bills, or explain the Constitution on that point; tho' it seemed to be worded with all possible plainness & precision. It is a source of continual difficulty & squabble between the two houses.

M: M⁰HENRY mentioned an instance of extraordinary subterfuge, to get rid of the apparent force of the Constitution.

On [1] Question on the first part of the motion as to the exclusive originating of Money bills in [1] H. of Rep:

N. H. ay. Mas. ay. C: no. N. J. no. P: no. Del. no. M⁴ no. Virg:

---

[1] The word "the" is here inserted in the transcript.

ay. M⁛ Blair & M⁛ M. no.   M⁛ R. Col. Mason and * Gen! Washington
ay N. C. ay. S. C. no. Geo. no.¹

² Question on Originating by ³ H. of Rep⁑ & *amending* by ³ Senate, as reported Art. IV. Sect. 5.

N. H. ay. Mas. ay. C⁑ no. N. J. no. P⁑ no. Del. no. M⁑ no.
V⁑ † ay. N. C. ay. S. C. no. Geo. no.⁴

² Question on the last clause of Sect: 5—Art. IV—viz " No money shall be drawn from the Public Treasury, but in pursuance of *appropriations* that shall originate in the House of Rep⁑ It passed in the negative

N. H. no. Mas. ay Con. no. N. J. no. P⁑ no Del. no. M⁑ no.
V⁑ no. N. C. no. S. C. no. Geo. no.⁵

Adj⁑

TUESDAY AUG. 14. IN CONVENTION

Article VI. Sect. 9.⁶, ⁷ taken up.

M⁑ PINKNEY argued that the making the members ineligible to offices was *degrading* to them, and the more improper as their election into the Legislature implied that they had the confidence of the people; that it was *inconvenient,* because the Senate might be supposed to contain the fittest men.   He hoped to see that body become a School of public Ministers, a nursery of Statesmen: that it was *impolitic,* because the Legislature would cease to be a magnet to the first talents and abilities.   He moved to postpone the section in order to take up the following proposition viz—" the members of each House shall be incapable of holding any office under the U. S.

* he disapproved & till now voted ag⁑t the exclusive privilege, he gave up his judgment he said because it was not of very material weight with him & was made an essential point with others who if disappointed, might be less cordial in other points of real weight.
† In the printed Journ Virg⁑—no.

---

¹ In the transcript the vote reads: " New Hampshire, Massachusetts, Virginia [Mr. Blair and Mr. Madison no, Mr. Randolph, Colonel Mason and General Washington,* aye], North Carolina, aye—4; Connecticut, New Jersey, Pennsylvania, Delaware, Maryland, South Carolina, Georgia, no—7."
² The words " On the " are here inserted in the transcript.
³ The word " the " is here inserted in the transcript.
⁴ In the transcript the vote reads: " New Hampshire, Massachusetts, Virginia,† North Carolina, aye—4; Connecticut, New Jersey, Pennsylvania, Delaware, Maryland, South Carolina, Georgia, no—7."
⁵ In the transcript the vote reads: " Massachusetts, aye—1; New Hampshire, Connecticut, New Jersey, Pennsylvania, Delaware, Maryland, Virginia, North Carolina, South Carolina, Georgia, no—10."
⁶ See page 340.
⁷ The word " was " is here inserted in the transcript.

for which they or any of [1] others for their benefit receive any salary, fees, or emoluments of any kind—and the acceptance of such office shall vacate their seats respectively''

Gen! MIFFLIN 2^{ded} the motion.

Col. MASON ironically proposed to strike out the whole section, as a more effectual expedient for encouraging that exotic corruption which might not otherwise thrive so well in the American Soil- for compleating that Aristocracy which was probably in the contemplation of some among us, and for inviting into the Legislative Service, those generous & benevolent characters who will do justice to each other's merit, by carving out offices & rewards for it. In the present state of American morals & manners, few friends it may be thought will be lost to the plan, by the opportunity of giving premiums to a mercenary & depraved ambition.

M: MERCER. It is a first principle in political science, that wherever the rights of property are secured, an aristocracy will grow out of it. Elective Governments also necessarily become aristocratic, because the rulers being few can & will draw emoluments for themselves from the many. The Governments of America will become aristocracies. They are so already. The public measures are calculated for the benefit of the Governors, not of the people. The people are dissatisfied & complain. They change their rulers, and the public measures are changed, but it is only a change of one scheme of emolument to the rulers, for another. The people gain nothing by it, but an addition of instability & uncertainty to their other evils.— Governm^{ts} can only be maintained by *force* or *influence*. The Executive has not *force*, deprive him of influence [2] by rendering the members of the Legislature ineligible to Executive offices, and he becomes a mere phantom of authority. The aristocratic part will not even let him in for a share of the plunder. The Legislature must & will be composed of wealth & abilities, and the people will be governed by a Junto. The Executive ought to have a Council, being members of both Houses. Without such an influence, the war will be between the aristocracy & the people. He wished it to be between the Aristocracy & the Executive. Nothing else can protect the people agst those speculating Legislatures which are now plundering them throughout the U. States.

M: GERRY read a Resolution of the Legislature of Mass^{ts} passed before the Act of Cong^s recommending the Convention, in which her deputies were instructed not to depart from the rotation established

---

[1] The word " of " is omitted in the transcript.
[2] The transcript italicizes the word " influence."

in the 5.ᵗʰ art: of [1] Confederation, nor to agree in any case to give to the members of Cong: a capacity to hold offices under the Government. This he said was repealed in consequence of the Act of Cong: with which the State thought it proper to comply in an unqualified manner. The Sense of the State however was still the same. He could not think with M. Pinkney that the disqualification was degrading. Confidence is the road to tyranny. As to Ministers & Ambassadors few of them were necessary. It is the opinion of a great many that they ought to be discontinued, on our part; that none may be sent among us, & that source of influence be [2] shut up. If the Senate were to appoint Ambassadors as seemed to be intended, they will multiply embassies for their own sakes. He was not so fond of those productions as to wish to establish nurseries for them. If they are once appointed, the House of Rep: will be obliged to provide salaries for them, whether they approve of the measures or not. If men will not serve in the Legislature without a prospect of such offices, our situation is deplorable indeed. If our best Citizens are actuated by such mercenary views, we had better chuse a single despot at once. It will be more easy to satisfy the rapacity of one than of many. According to the idea of one Gentleman [M. Mercer] our Government it seems is to be a Gov: of plunder. In that case it certainly would be prudent to have but one rather than many to be employed in it. We cannot be too circumspect in the formation of this System. It will be examined on all sides and with a very suspicious eye. The People who have been so lately in arms ag.ˢᵗ G. B. for their liberties, will not easily give them up. He lamented the evils existing at present under our Governments, but imputed them to the faults of those in office, not to the people. The misdeeds of the former will produce a critical attention to the opportunities afforded by the new system to like or greater abuses. As it now stands it is as compleat an aristocracy as ever was framed   If great powers should be given to the Senate we shall be governed in reality by a Junto as has been apprehended. He remarked that it would be very differently constituted from Cong⁸- 1.[3] there will be but 2 deputies from each State, in Cong: there may be 7. and are generally 5.—2.[4] they are chosen for six years, those of Cong: annually.   3.[5] they are not subject to recall; those of Cong: are.   4. In Cong: 9 *States* [6] are necessary

---

[1] The word " the " is here inserted in the transcript.
[2] The word " be " is omitted in the transcript.
[3] The figure " 1 " is changed to " In the first place." in the transcript.
[4] The figure " 2 " is changed to " In the second place " in the transcript.
[5] The figure " 3 " is changed to " In the third place " in the transcript.
[6] The phrase " And finally, in Congress *nine* States " is substituted in the transcript for " 4. In Cong: 9 *States*."

for all great purposes—here 8 *persons* will suffice. Is it to be presumed that the people will ever agree to such a system? He moved to render the members of the H. of Rep! as well as of the Senate ineligible not only during, but for one year after the expiration of their terms.—If it should be thought that this will injure the Legislature by keeping out of it men of abilities who are willing to serve in other offices it may be required as a qualification for other offices, that the Candidate shall have served a certain time in the Legislature.

M! Gov! Morris. Exclude the officers of the army & navy, and you form a band having a different interest from & opposed to the civil power: you stimulate them to despise & reproach those " talking Lords who dare not face the foe." Let this spirit be roused at the end of a war, before your troops shall have laid down their arms, and though the Civil authority " be intrenched in parchment to the teeth " they will cut their way to it. He was ag!t rendering the members of the Legislature ineligible to offices. He was for rendering them eligible ag! after having vacated their Seats by accepting office. Why should we not avail ourselves of their services if the people chuse to give them their confidence. There can be little danger of corruption either among the people or the Legislatures who are to be the Electors. If they say, we see their merits, we honor the men, we chuse to renew our confidence in them, have they not a right to give them a preference; and can they be properly abridged of it.

M! Williamson; introduced his opposition to the motion by referring to the question concerning " money bills." That clause he said was dead. Its ghost he was afraid would notwithstanding haunt us. It had been a matter of conscience with him, to insist upon [1] it as long as there was hope of retaining it. He had swallowed the vote of rejection, with reluctance. He could not digest it. All that was said on the other side was that the restriction was not *convenient*. We have now got a House of Lords which is to originate money-bills.—To avoid another *inconveniency*,[2] we are to have a whole Legislature at liberty to cut out offices for one another. He thought a self-denying ordinance for ourselves would be more proper. Bad as the Constitution has been made by expunging the restriction on the Senate concerning money bills he did not wish to make it worse by expunging the present Section. He had scarcely seen a single corrupt measure in the Legislature of N. Carolina, which could not be traced up to office hunting.

M! Sherman. The Constitution sh! lay as few temptations as

---

[1] The word " on " is substituted in the transcript for " upon."
[2] The word " *inconveniency* " is changed to " *inconvenience* " in the transcript.

possible in the way of those in power. Men of abilities will increase as the Country grows more populous and, and [1] the means of education are more diffused.

M.ʳ PINKNEY. No State has rendered the members of the Legislature ineligible to offices. In S. Carolina the Judges are eligible into the Legislature. It can not be supposed then that the motion will be offensive to the people. If the State Constitutions should be revised he believed restrictions of this sort w.ᵈ be rather diminished than multiplied.

M.ʳ WILSON could not approve of the Section as it stood, and could not give up his judgment to any supposed objections that might arise among the people. He considered himself as acting & responsible for the welfare of millions not immediately represented in this House. He had also asked himself the serious question what he should say to his constituents in case they should call upon him to tell them why he sacrificed his own Judgment in a case where they authorised him to exercise it? Were he to own to them that he sacrificed it in order to flatter their prejudices, he should dread the retort: did you suppose the people of Penn.ᵃ had not good sense enough to receive a good Government? Under this impression he should certainly follow his own Judgment which disapproved of the section. He would remark in addition to the objections urged ag.ˢᵗ it, that as one branch of the Legislature was to be appointed by the Legislatures of the States, the other by the people of the States, as both are to be paid by the States, and to be appointable to State offices, nothing seemed to be wanting to prostrate the Nat.ˡ Legislature, but to render its members ineligible to Nat.ˡ offices, & by that means take away its power of attracting those talents which were necessary to give weight to the Govern.ᵗ and to render it useful to the people. He was far from thinking the ambition which aspired to Offices of dignity and trust, an ignoble or culpable one. He was sure it was not politic to regard it in that light, or to withold from it the prospect of those rewards, which might engage it in the career of public service. He observed that the State of Penn.ᵃ which had gone as far as any State into the policy of fettering power, had not rendered the members of the Legislature ineligible to offices of Gov.ᵗ

M.ʳ ELSWORTH did not think the mere postponement of the reward would be any material discouragement of merit. Ambitious minds will serve 2 years or 7 years in the Legislature for the sake of qualifying themselves for other offices. This he thought a sufficient security for obtaining the services of the ablest men in the Legis-

---

[1] The word "as" is substituted in the transcript for "and."

lature, although whilst members they should be ineligible to Public offices. Besides, merit will be most encouraged, when most impartially rewarded. If rewards are to circulate only within the Legislature, merit out of it will be discouraged.

M⁺ MERCER was extremely anxious on this point. What led to the appointment of this Convention? The corruption & mutability of the Legislative Councils of the States. If the plan does not remedy these, it will not recommend itself; and we shall not be able in our private capacities to support & enforce it: nor will the best part of our Citizens exert themselves for the purpose.—It is a great mistake to suppose that the paper we are to propose will govern the U. States? It is The men whom it will bring into the Govern⁺ and interest in maintaining it that is [1] to govern them. The paper will only mark out the mode & the form. Men are the substance and must do the business. All Gov⁺ must be by force or influence. It is not the King of France—but 200,000 janisaries of power that govern that Kingdom. There will be no such force here; influence then must be substituted; and he would ask whether this could be done, if the members of the Legislature should be ineligible to offices of State; whether such a disqualification would not determine all the most influencial men to stay at home, and & prefer appointments within their respective States.

M⁺ WILSON was by no means satisfied with the answer given by M⁺ Elseworth to the argument as to the discouragement of merit. The members must either go a second time into the Legislature, and disqualify themselves—or say to their Constituents, we served you before only from the mercenary view of qualifying ourselves for offices, and have⁺ answered this purpose we do not chuse to be again elected.

M⁺ Gov⁺ MORRIS put the case of a war, and the Citizen the [2] most capable of conducting it, happening to be a member of the Legislature. What might have been the consequence of such a regulation at the commencement, or even in the Course of the late contest for our liberties?

On [3] question for postponing in order to take up M⁺ Pinkneys motion, it was lost.

N. H. ay. Mas. no. C⁺ no. N. J. no. P⁺ ay. Del. ay. M⁺ ay. V⁺ ay. N. C. no. S. C. no. Geo. div⁺ [4]

---

[1] The word "are" is substituted in the transcript for "is."
[2] The word "the" is omitted in the transcript.
[3] The word "the" is here inserted in the transcript.
[4] In the transcript the vote reads: "New Hampshire, Pennsylvania, Delaware, Maryland, Virginia, aye—5; Massachusetts, Connecticut, New Jersey, North Carolina, South Carolina, no—5; Georgia, divided."

M: Gov: Morris moved to insert, after "office," except offices in the army or navy: but in that case their offices shall be vacated. M: Broom 2ᵈˢ him.

M: Randolph had been & should continue uniformly opposed to the striking out of the clause; as opening a door for influence & corruption. No arguments had made any impression on him, but those which related to the case of war, and a co-existing incapacity of the fittest commanders to be employed. He admitted great weight in these, and would agree to the exception proposed by M: Gov: Morris.

M: Butler & M: Pinkney urged a general postponem: of 9 Sect. Art. VI. till it should be seen what powers would be vested in the Senate, when it would be more easy to judge of the expediency of allowing the officers of State to be chosen out of that body.—a general postponement was agreed to nem. con.

Art: VI. sect. 10.¹, ² taken up—"that members be paid by their respective States."

M: Elseworth said that in reflecting on this subject he had been satisfied that too much dependence on the States would be produced by this mode of payment. He moved to strike ³ out and insert " that they should " be paid out of the Treasury of the U. S. an allowance not exceeding (blank) dollars per day or the present value thereof.

M: Gov: Morris, remarked that if the members were to be paid by the States it would throw an unequal burden on the distant States, which would be unjust as the Legislature was to be a national Assembly. He moved that the payment be out of the Nat: Treasury; leaving the quantum to the discretion of the Nat: Legislature. There could be no reason to fear that they would overpay themselves.

M: Butler contended for payment by the States; particularly in the case of the Senate, who will be so long out of their respective States, that they will lose sight of their Constituents unless dependent on them for their support.

M: Langdon was ag: payment by the States. There would be some difficulty in fixing the sum; but it would be unjust to oblige the distant States to bear the expence of their members in travelling to and from the Seat of Gov:

M: Madison If the H. of Rep: is to be chosen *biennially*—and the Senate to be *constantly* dependent on the Legislatures which are

---

¹ See page 340.
² The words " was then " are here inserted in the transcript.
³ The word " it " is here inserted in the transcript.

chosen *annually*, he could not see any chance for that stability in the Gen! Gov! the want of which was a principal evil in the State Gov!! His fear was that the organization of the Gov! supposing the Senate to be really independ! for six years, would not effect our purpose. It was nothing more than a combination of the peculiarities of two of the State Gov!! which separately had been found insufficient. The Senate was formed on the model of that of Maryl! The Revisionary check, on that of N. York. What the effect of a union of these provisions might be, could not be foreseen. The enlargement of the sphere of the Government was indeed a circumstance which he thought would be favorable as he had on several occasions undertaken to shew. He was however for fixing at least two extremes not to be exceeded by the Nat! Legisl!! in the payment of themselves.

M! GERRY. There are difficulties on both sides. The observation of M! Butler has weight in it. On the other side, the State Legislatures may turn out the Senators by reducing their salaries. Such things have been practised.

Col. MASON. It has not yet been noticed that the clause as it now stands makes the House of Represent! also dependent on the State Legislatures; so that both houses will be made the instruments of the politics of the States whatever they may be.

M! BROOM could see no danger in trusting the Gen! Legislature with the payment of themselves. The State Legislatures had this power, and no complaint had been made of it.

M! SHERMAN was not afraid that the Legislature would make their own wages too high; but too low, so that men ever so fit could not serve unless they were at the same time rich. He thought the best plan would be to fix a moderate allowance to be paid out of the Nat! Treas! and let the States make such additions as they might judge fit. He moved that 5 dollars per day be the sum, any further emoluments to be added by the States.

M! CARROL had been much surprised at seeing this clause in the Report. The dependence of both Houses on the State Legislatures is compleat; especially as the members of the former are eligible to State offices. The States can now say': if you do not comply with our wishes, we will starve you: if you do we will reward you. The new Gov! in this form was nothing more than a second edition of Congress in two volumes, instead of one, and perhaps with very few amendments—

M! DICKENSON took it for granted that all were convinced of the necessity of making the Gen! Gov! independent of the prejudices, passions, and improper views of the State Legislatures. The contrary of This was effected by the section as it stands. On the other hand there were objections ag⁸ᵗ taking a permanent standard as wheat which had been suggested on a former occasion, as well as against leaving the matter to the pleasure of the Nat! Legislature. He proposed that an Act should be passed every 12 years by the Nat! Legisl⁹ settling the quantum of their wages. If the Gen! Gov! should be left dependent on the State Legislatures, it would be happy for us if we had never met in this Room.

M⁹ ELSEWORTH was not unwilling himself to trust the Legislature with authority to regulate their own wages, but well knew that an unlimited discretion for that purpose would produce strong, tho' perhaps not insuperable objections. He thought changes in the value of money, provided for by his motion in the words, " or the present value thereof."

M⁹ L. MARTIN. As the Senate is to represent the States, the members of it ought to be paid by the States.

M⁹ CARROL. The Senate was to represent & manage the affairs of the whole, and not to be the advocates of State interests. They ought then not to be dependent on nor paid by the States.

On the question for paying the Members of the Legislature out of the Nat! Treasury,

N. H. ay. Mas. no. C! ay. N. J. ay. P⁹ ay. Del. ay. M⁹ ay. V⁹ ay. N. C. ay. S. C. no. Geo. ay.[1]

M⁹ ELSEWTH moved that the pay be fixed at 5 doll⁹ or the present value thereof per day during their attendance & for every thirty miles in travelling to & from Congress.

M⁹ STRONG preferred 4 dollars, leaving the Sts. at liberty to make additions.

On[2] question for fixing the pay at 5 dollars.

N. H. no. Mas. no. C! ay. N. J. no. P⁹ no. Del. no. M⁹ no. V⁹ ay. N. C. no. S. C. no. Geo. no.[3]

M⁹ DICKENSON proposed that the wages of the members of both houses s⁹ be required to be the same.

M⁹ BROOME seconded him.

M⁹ GHORUM. this would be unreasonable. The Senate will be detained longer from home, will be obliged to remove their families,

---

[1] In the transcript the vote reads: " New Hampshire, Connecticut, New Jersey, Pennsylvania, Delaware, Maryland, Virginia, North Carolina, Georgia, aye—9; Massachusetts, South Carolina, no—2."

[2] The word " the " is here inserted in the transcript.

[3] In the transcript the vote reads: " Connecticut, Virginia, aye—2; New Hampshire, Massachusetts, New Jersey, Pennsylvania, Delaware, Maryland, North Carolina, South Carolina, Georgia, no—9."

and in time of war perhaps to sit constantly. Their allowance should certainly be higher. The members of the Senates in the States are allowed more, than those of the other house.

M! DICKENSON withdrew his motion

It was moved & agreed to amend the Section by adding—" to be ascertained by law."

The Section [Art VI. Sec. 10] as amended, agreed to nem. con.

Adj�ᵈ

WEDNESDAY AUGUST 15. IN CONVENTION

Art: VI. Sect. 11.[1, 2] Agreed to nem. con.

Art: VI Sect. 12.[1, 3] taken up.

M! STRONG moved to amend the article so as to read—" Each House shall possess the right of originating all bills, except bills for raising money for the purposes of revenue, or for appropriating the same and for fixing the salaries of the officers of the Gov! which shall originate in the House of Representatives; but the Senate may propose or concur with amendments as in other cases "

Col. MASON, 2ᵈˢ the motion. He was extremely earnest to take this power from the Senate, who he said could already sell the whole Country by means of Treaties.

M! GHORUM urged the amendment as of great importance. The Senate will first acquire the habit of preparing money bills, and then the practice will grow into an exclusive right of preparing them.

M! GOVERN! MORRIS opposed it as unnecessary and inconvenient.

M! WILLIAMSON. some think this restriction on the Senate essential to liberty, others think it of no importance. Why should not the former be indulged. he was for an efficient and stable Gov! but many would not strengthen the Senate if not restricted in the case of money bills. The friends of the Senate would therefore lose more than they would gain by refusing to gratify the other side. He moved to postpone the subject till the powers of the Senate should be gone over.

M! RUTLIDGE 2ᵈˢ the motion.

M! MERCER should hereafter be ag!ᵗ returning to a reconsideration of this section. He contended, (alluding to M! Mason's observa-

---

[1] See page 340.
[2] The word "was" is here inserted in the transcript.
[3] The words "was then" are here inserted in the transcript.

tions) that the Senate ought not to have the power of treaties. This power belonged to the Executive department; adding that Treaties woula not be final so as to alter the laws of the land, till ratified by legislative authority. This was the case of Treaties in Great Britain; particularly the late Treaty of Commerce with France.

Col. MASON. did not say that a Treaty would repeal a law; but that the Senate by means of treaty[1] might alienate territory &c, without legislative sanction. The cessions of the British Islands in[2] W- Indies by Treaty alone were an example. If Spain should possess herself of Georgia therefore the Senate might by treaty dismember the Union. He wished the motion to be decided now, that the friends of it might know how to conduct themselves.

On[2] question for postponing Sec: 12. it passed in the affirmative.

N. H. ay. Mas. ay C[t] no. N. J. no Pen[a] no. Del. no Mary[d] no. V[a] ay. N. C. ay. S. C. ay. Geo. ay.—[3]

M[r] MADISON moved that all acts before they become laws should be submitted both to the Executive and Supreme Judiciary Departments, that if either of these should object ⅔ of each House, if both should object, ¾ of each House, should be necessary to overrule the objections and give to the acts the force of law—[4]

See the motion at large in the Journal of this date, page 253, & insert it here."[5]

[" Every bill which shall have passed the two houses, shall, before it become a law, be severally presented to the President of the United States, and to the judges of the supreme court for the revision of each. If, upon such revision, they shall approve of it, they shall respectively signify their approbation by signing it; but if, upon such revision, it shall appear improper to either, or both, to be passed into a law, it shall be returned, with the objections against it, to that house, in which it shall have originated, who shall enter the objections at large on their journal, and proceed to reconsider the bill: but if, after such reconsideration, two thirds of that house, when either the President, or a majority of the judges shall object, or three fourths, where

---

[1] The transcript uses the word "treaty" in the plural.
[2] The word "the" is here inserted in the transcript.
[3] In the transcript the vote reads: "New Hampshire, Massachusetts, Virginia, North Carolina, South Carolina, Georgia, aye—6; Connecticut, New Jersey, Pennsylvania, Delaware, Maryland, no—5."
[4] This paragraph is stricken out in the transcript.
[5] Madison's direction concerning the motion is omitted in the transcript and the following sentence is inserted: "Mr. Madison moved the following amendment of Article 6, Section 13."[6]
[6] See page 340.

both shall object, shall agree to pass it, it shall, together with the objections, be sent to the other house, by which it shall likewise be reconsidered; and, if approved by two thirds, or three fourths of the other house, as the case may be, it shall become a law."]

M͞r Wilson seconds the motion

M͞r Pinkney opposed the interference of the Judges in the Legislative business: it will involve them in parties, and give a previous tincture to their opinions.

M͞r Mercer heartily approved the motion. It is an axiom that the Judiciary ought to be separate from the Legislative: but equally so that it ought to be independent of that department. The true policy of the axiom is that legislative usurpation and oppression may be obviated. He disapproved of the Doctrine that the Judges as expositors of the Constitution should have authority to declare a law void. He thought laws ought to be well and cautiously made, and then to be uncontroulable.

M͞r Gerry. This motion comes to the same thing with what has been already negatived.

[1] Question on the motion of M͞r Madison.

N. H. no. Mass. no. C͞t no. N. J. no. P͞a no. Del. ay. Mary͞d ay. Virg͞a ay. N. C. no. S. C. no. Geo. no.[2]

M͞r Gov͞r Morris regretted that something like the proposed check could not be agreed to. He dwelt on the importance of public credit, and the difficulty of supporting it without some strong barrier against the instability of legislative Assemblies. He suggested the idea of requiring three fourths of each house to *repeal* laws where the President should not concur. He had no great reliance on the revisionary power as the Executive was now to be constituted [elected by the [3] Congress]. The legislature will contrive to soften down the President. He recited the history of paper emissions, and the perseverance of the legislative assemblies in repeating them, with all the distressing effects of such measures before their eyes. Were the National legislature formed, and a war was now to break out, this ruinous expedient would be again resorted to, if not guarded against. The requiring ¾ to repeal would, though not a compleat remedy, prevent the hasty passage of laws, and the frequency of those repeals which destroy faith in the public, and which are among our greatest calamities.–

---

[1] The words "On the" are here inserted in the transcript.
[2] In the transcript the vote reads: "Delaware, Maryland, Virginia, aye—3; New Hampshire, Massachusetts, Connecticut, New Jersey, Pennsylvania, North Carolina, South Carolina, Georgia, no—8."
[3] The word "the" is omitted in the transcript.

M: DICKENSON was strongly impressed with the remark of M: Mercer as to the power of the Judges to set aside the law. He thought no such power ought to exist. He was at the same time at a loss what expedient to substitute. The Justiciary of Arragon he observed became by degrees, the lawgiver.

M: Gov: MORRIS, suggested the expedient of an absolute negative in the Executive. He could not agree that the Judiciary which was part of the Executive, should be bound to say that a direct violation of the Constitution was law. A controul over the legislature might have its inconveniences. But view the danger on the other side. The most virtuous Citizens will often as members of a legislative body concur in measures which afterwards in their private capacity they will be ashamed of. Encroachments of the popular branch of the Government ought to be guarded ag:t The Ephori at Sparta became in the end absolute. The Report of the Council of Censors in Pennsylv: points out the many invasions of the legislative department on the Executive numerous as the latter * is, within the short term of seven years, and in a State where a strong party is opposed to the Constitution, and watching every occasion of turning the public resentments ag:t it. If the Executive be overturned by the popular branch, as happened in England, the tyranny of one man will ensue. In Rome where the Aristocracy overturned the throne, the consequence was different. He enlarged on the tendency of the legislative Authority to usurp on the Executive and wished the section to be postponed, in order to consider of some more effectual check than requiring ⅔ only to overrule the negative of the Executive.

M: SHERMAN. Can one man be trusted better than all the others if they all agree? This was neither wise nor safe. He disapproved of Judges meddling in politics and parties. We have gone far enough in forming the negative as it now stands.

M: CARROL- when the negative to be overruled by ⅔ only was agreed to, the *quorum* was not fixed. He remarked that as a majority was now to be the quorum, 17. in the larger, and 8 in the smaller house might carry points. The advantage that might be taken of this seemed to call for greater impediments to improper laws. He thought the controuling power however of the Executive could not be well decided, till it was seen how the formation of that department would be finally regulated. He wished the consideration of the matter to be postponed.

* The Executive consists at this time [1] of ab:t 20 members.

<hr>

[1] The phrase " consisted at that time " is substituted in the transcript for " consists at this time."

M: GHORUM saw no end to these difficulties and postponements. Some could not agree to the form of Government before the powers were defined. Others could not agree to the powers till it was seen how the Government was to be formed. He thought a majority as large a quorum as was necessary. It was the quorum almost every where fixt in the U. States.

M: WILSON; after viewing the subject with all the coolness and attention possible was most apprehensive of a dissolution of the Gov: from the legislature swallowing up all the other powers. He remarked that the prejudices ag:t the Executive resulted from a misapplication of the adage that the parliament was the palladium of liberty. Where the Executive was really formidable, *King* and *Tyrant,* were naturally associated in the minds of people; not *legislature* and *tyranny.* But where the Executive was not formidable, the two last were most properly associated. After the destruction of the King in Great Britain, a more pure and unmixed tyranny sprang up in the parliament than had been exercised by the monarch. He insisted that we had not guarded ag:t the danger on this side by a sufficient self-defensive power either to the Executive or Judiciary department.

M: RUTLIDGE was strenuous ag:t postponing; and complained much of the tediousness of the proceedings.

M: ELSEWORTH held the same language. We grow more & more skeptical as we proceed. If we do not decide soon, we shall be unable to come to any decision.

The question for postponement passed in the negative: Del: & Mary: only being in the affirmative.

M: WILLIAMSON moved to change " ⅔ of each House " into " ¾ " as requisite to overrule the dissent of the President. He saw no danger in this, and preferred giving the power to the Presid: alone, to admitting the Judges into the business of legislation.

M: WILSON 2:ds the motion; referring to and repeating the ideas of M: Carroll.

On this motion for ¾. instead of two thirds; it passed in the affirmative

N. H. no. Mas. no. C:t ay. N. J. no. Pen: div: Del. ay. M:d ay. V:a ay. N. C. ay. S. C. ay. Geo. no.[1]

M: MADISON, observing that if the negative of the President was confined to *bills;* it would be evaded by acts under the form and

---

[1] In the transcript the vote reads: " Connecticut, Delaware, Maryland, Virginia, North Carolina, South Carolina, aye—6; New Hampshire, Massachusetts, New Jersey, Georgia, no—4; Pennsylvania, divided."

name of Resolutions, votes &c, proposed that or resolve" should be added after " *bill* " in the beginning of sect 13. with an exception as to votes of adjournment &c.— after a short and rather confused conversation on the subject, the question was put & rejected, the States [1] being as follows,

N. H. no. Mas. ay. C⁺ no. N. J. no. Pen⁺ no. Del. ay. M⁴ no. V⁺ no. N. C. ay. S. C. no. Geo. no.[2]

" *Ten* [3] days (Sundays excepted)" instead of " *seven* " were allowed to the President for returning bills with his objections N. H. & Mas: only voting ag⁺ it.

The 13 Sect: of art. VI as amended was then agreed to.

Adjourned.

THURSDAY. AUGUST 16. IN CONVENTION.

M⁺ RANDOLPH having thrown into a new form the motion, putting votes, Resolutions &c. on a footing with *Bills*, renewed it as follows " Every order resolution or vote, to which the concurrence of the Senate & House of Rep⁺ may be necessary (except on a question of adjournment and in the cases hereinafter mentioned) shall be presented to the President for his revision; and before the same shall have force shall be approved by him, or being disapproved by him shall be repassed by the Senate & House of Rep⁺ according to the rules & limitations prescribed in the case of a Bill."

M⁺ SHERMAN thought it unnecessary, except as to votes taking money out of the Treasury which might be provided for in another place.

On [4] Question as moved by M⁺ Randolph [5]

N. H. ay. Mas: not present, C⁺ ay. N. J. no. P⁺ ay. Del. ay. M⁴ ay. V⁺ ay. N. C. ay. S. C. ay. Geo. ay.[6]

The Amendment was made a Section 14. of Art VI.

Art: VII. Sect. 1.[7, 8] taken up.

M⁺ L. MARTIN asked what was meant by the .Committee of detail

---

[1] The word "votes" is substituted in the transcript for "States."

[2] In the transcript the vote reads: "Massachusetts, Delaware, North Carolina, aye—3; New Hampshire, Connecticut, New Jersey, Pennsylvania, Maryland, Virginia, South Carolina, Georgia, no—8."

[3] The transcript does not italicize the word " *Ten*."

[4] The word "the" is here inserted in the transcript.

[5] The phrase "it was agreed to" is here inserted in the transcript.

[6] In the transcript the vote reads: "New Hampshire, Connecticut, Pennsylvania, Delaware, Maryland, Virginia, North Carolina, South Carolina, Georgia, aye—9; New Jersey, no—1; Massachusetts, not present."

[7] See page 340.

[8] The words "was then" are here inserted in the transcript.

in the expression " *duties* " and " *imposts.*" If the meaning were the same, the former was unnecessary; if different, the matter ought to be made clear.

M! Wilson, *duties* are applicable to many objects to which the word *imposts* does not relate. The latter are appropriated to commerce; the former extend to a variety of objects, as stamp duties &c.

M! Carroll reminded the Convention of the great difference of interests among the States, and doubts the propriety in that point of view of letting a majority be a quorum.

M! Mason urged the necessity of connecting with the power of levying taxes duties &c, the prohibition in Sect 4 of art VI that no tax should be laid on exports. He was unwilling to trust to its being done in a future article. He hoped the North? States did not mean to deny the Southern this security. It would hereafter be as desirable to the former when the latter should become the most populous. He professed his jealousy for the productions of the Southern or as he called them, the staple States. He moved to insert the following amendment " provided that no tax duty or imposition shall be laid by the Legislature of the U. States on articles exported from any State "

M! Sherman had no objection to the proviso here, other than [1] it would derange the parts of the report as made by the Committee, to take them in such an order.

M! Rutlidge. It being of no consequence in what order points are decided, he should vote for the clause as it stood, but on condition that the subsequent part relating to negroes should also be agreed to.

M! Governeur Morris considered such a proviso as inadmissible any where. It was so radically objectionable, that it might cost the whole system the support of some members. He contended that it would not in some cases be equitable to tax imports without taxing exports; and that taxes on exports would be often the most easy and proper of the two.

M! Madison 1.[2] the power of taxing [3] exports is proper in itself, and as the States can not with propriety exercise it separately, it ought to be vested in them collectively. 2.[2] it might with particular advantage be exercised with regard to articles in which America was not rivalled in foreign markets, as Tob? &c. The contract between the

---

[1] The word "that" is here inserted in the transcript.

[2] The figures "1" and "2" are changed in the transcript to "First" and "Secondly."

[3] The words "laying taxes on" are substituted in the transcript for "taxing."

French Farmers Genl and Mr Morris stipulating that if taxes s.^d be laid in America on the export of Tob.^o they s.^d be paid by the Farmers, shewed that it was understood by them, that the price would be thereby raised in America, and consequently the taxes be paid by the European Consumer. 3.[1] it would be unjust to the States whose produce was exported by their neighbours, to leave it subject to be taxed by the latter. This was a grievance which had already filled N. H. Con.^t N. Jer.^y Del: and N. Carolina with loud complaints, as it related to imports, and they would be equally authorised by taxes by the States on exports. 4.[1] The South.ⁿ States being most in danger and most needing naval protection, could the less complain if the burden should be somewhat heaviest on them. 5.[2] we are not providing for the present moment only, and time will equalize the situation of the States in this matter. He was for these reasons ag.st the motion

Mr WILLIAMSON considered the clause proposed ag.st taxes on exports as reasonable and necessary.

Mr ELSEWORTH was ag.st Taxing exports; but thought the prohibition stood in the most proper place, and was ag.st deranging the order reported by the Committee

Mr WILSON was decidedly ag.st prohibiting general taxes on exports. He dwelt on the injustice and impolicy of leaving N. Jersey Connecticut &c any longer subject to the exactions of their commercial neighbours.

Mr GERRY thought the legislature could not be trusted with such a power. It might ruin the Country. It might be exercised partially, raising one and depressing another part of it.

Mr Govr MORRIS. However the legislative power may be formed, it will if disposed be able to ruin the Country. He considered the taxing of exports to be in many cases highly politic. Virginia has found her account in taxing Tobacco. All Countries having peculiar articles tax the exportation of them; as France her wines and brandies. A tax here on lumber, would fall on the W. Indies & punish their restrictions on our trade. The same is true of livestock and in some degree of flour. In case of a dearth in the West Indies, we may extort what we please. Taxes on exports are a necessary source of revenue. For a long time the people of America will not have money to pay direct taxes. Seize and sell their effects and you push them into Revolts.

---

[1] The figures " 3 " and " 4 " are changed in the transcript to " Thirdly " and " Fourthly."

[2] The figure " 5 " is changed in the transcript to " And finally."

M⸿ MERCER was strenuous against giving Congress power to tax exports. Such taxes were [1] impolitic, as encouraging the raising of articles not meant for exportation. The States had now a right where their situation permitted, to tax both the imports and exports of their uncommercial neighbours. It was enough for them to sacrifice one half of it. It had been said the Southern States had most need of naval protection. The reverse was the case. Were it not for promoting the carrying trade of the North⸿ States, the South⸿ States could let their trade go into foreign bottoms, where it would not need our protection. Virginia by taxing her tobacco had given an advantage to that of Maryland.

M⸿ SHERMAN. To examine and compare the States in relation to imports and exports will be opening a boundless field. He thought the matter had been adjusted, and that imports were to be subject, and exports not, to be taxed. He thought it wrong to tax exports except it might be such articles as ought not to be exported. The complexity of the business in America would render an equal tax on exports impracticable. The ˙oppression of the uncommercial States was guarded ag⸿ by the power to regulate trade between the States. As to compelling foreigners, that might be done by regulating trade in general. The Government would not be trusted with such a power. Objections are most likely to be excited by considerations relating to taxes & money. A power to tax exports would shipwreck the whole.

M⸿ CARROL was surprised that any objection should be made to an exception of exports from the power of taxation.

It was finally agreed that the question concerning exports sh⸿ lie over for the place in which the exception stood in the report: Mary⸿ alone voting ag⸿ it

Sect: 1. [art. VII][2, 3] agreed to: M⸿ GERRY alone answering no.

[4] Clause for regulating commerce with foreign nations &c.[5] agreed to nem. con.

[6] for coining money. ag⸿ to nem. con.

[6] for regulating foreign coin. d⸿   d⸿

[6] for fixing the standard of weights & measures. d⸿   d⸿

---

[1] The word " are " is substituted in the transcript for " were."

[2] This phrase was erroneously copied in the transcript as " Article 1, Section 1," but was corrected when printed.

[3] The words " was then " are here inserted in the transcript.

[4] The word " The " is here inserted in the transcript.

[5] The word " was " is here inserted in the transcript.

[6] In the transcript these three lines are changed to read as follows: " Several clauses,—for coining money—for regulating foreign coin,—for fixing the standard of weights and measures,—were agreed to, *nem. oon.*"

[1] " To establish post-offices.'' M᙮ GERRY moved to add, and post-roads. M᙮ MERCER 2ᵈᵉᵈ & on [2] question

N. H. no. Mas. ay. Cᵗ no. N. J. no. Penᵃ no. Del. ay. Mᵈ ay. Vᵃ ay. N. C. no. S. C. ay. Geo. ay.[3]

M᙮ Govᵗ MORRIS moved to strike out " and emit bills on the credit of the U. States ''—If the United States had credit such bills would be unnecessary: if they had not, unjust & useless.

M᙮ BUTLER, 2ᵈˢ the motion.

M᙮ MADISON, will it not be sufficient to prohibit the making them a *tender?* This will remove the temptation to emit them with unjust views. And promissory notes in that shape may in some emergencies be best.

M᙮ Govᵗ MORRIS. striking out the words will leave room still for notes of a *responsible* minister which will do all the good without the mischief. The Monied interest will oppose the plan of Government, if paper emissions be not prohibited.

M᙮ GHORUM was for striking out, without inserting any prohibition. if the words stand they may suggest and lead to the measure.

Col.[4] MASON had doubts on the subject. Congˢ he thought would not have the power unless it were expressed. Though he had a mortal hatred to paper money, yet as he could not foresee all emergences, he was unwilling to tie the hands of the Legislature. He observed that the late war could not have been carried on, had such a prohibition existed.

M᙮ GHORUM. The power as far as it will be necessary or safe, is involved in that of borrowing.

M᙮ MERCER was a friend to paper money, though in the present state & temper of America, he should neither propose nor approve of such a measure. He was consequently opposed to a prohibition of it altogether. It will stamp suspicion on the Government to deny it a discretion on this point. It was impolitic also to excite the opposition of all those who were friends to paper money. The people of property would be sure to be on the side of the plan, and it was impolitic to purchase their further attachment with the loss of the opposite class of Citizens

M᙮ ELSEWORTH thought this a favorable moment to shut and bar the door against paper money. The mischiefs of the various experi-

---

[1] The words " The clause " are here inserted in the transcript.

[2] The word " the " is here inserted in the transcript.

[3] In the transcript the vote reads: " Massachusetts, Delaware, Maryland, Virginia, South Carolina. Georgia, aye—6; New Hampshire, Connecticut, New Jersey, Pennsylvania, North Carolina, no—5."

[4] The word " Mr." is substituted in the transcript for " Col."

ments which had been made, were now fresh in the public mind and had excited the disgust of all the respectable part of America. By witholding the power from the new Govern! more friends of influence would be gained to it than by almost any thing else. Paper money can in no case be necessary. Give the Government credit, and other resources will offer. The power may do harm, never good.

M⁚ RANDOLPH, notwithstanding his antipathy to paper money, could not agree to strike out the words, as he could not foresee all the occasions which ¹ might arise.

M⁚ WILSON. It will have a most salutary influence on the credit of the U. States to remove the possibility of paper money. This expedient can never succeed whilst its mischiefs are remembered, and as long as it can be resorted to, it will be a bar to other resources.

M⁚ BUTLER. remarked that paper was a legal tender in no Country in Europe. He was urgent for disarming the Government of such a power.

M⁚ MASON was still averse to tying the hands of the Legislature *altogether*. If there was no example in Europe as just remarked, it might be observed on the other side, that there was none in which the Government was restrained on this head.

M⁚ READ, thought the words, if not struck out, would be as alarming as the mark of the Beast in Revelations.

M⁚ LANGDON had rather reject the whole plan than retain the three words "(and emit bills")

On the motion for striking out

N. H. ay. Mas. ay. C⁚ ay. N. J. no. P⁚ ay. Del. ay. M⁴ no. V⁚ ay.* N. C. ay. S. C. ay. Geo. ay.²

The clause for borrowing money,⁴ agreed to nem. con.

Adj⁴

* This vote in the affirmative by Virg⁚ was occasioned by the acquiescence of M⁚ Madison who became satisfied that striking out the words would not disable the Gov⁚ from the use of public notes as far as they could be safe & proper; & would only cut off the pretext for a paper currency,* and particularly for making the bills a tender * either for public or private debts.

---

¹ The word "that" is substituted in the transcript for "which."
² In the transcript the vote reads: "New Hampshire, Massachusetts, Connecticut, Pennsylvania, Delaware, Virginia,* North Carolina, South Carolina, Georgia, aye—9; New Jersey, Maryland, no—2."
³ The transcript italicizes the words "paper currency" and "a tender."
⁴ The word "was" is here inserted in the transcript.

FRIDAY AUGUST 17ᵀᴴ IN CONVENTION

Art VII. Sect. 1.[1, 2] resumed. on the clause " to appoint[3] Treasurer by ballot."

Mʳ GHORUM moved to insert " joint " before ballot, as more convenient as well as reasonable, than to require the separate concurrence of the Senate.

Mʳ PINKNEY 2ᵈˢ the motion. Mʳ SHERMAN opposed it as favoring the larger States.

Mʳ READ moved to strike out the clause, leaving the appointment of the Treasurer as of other officers to the Executive. The Legislature was an improper body for appointments. Those of the State legislatures were a proof of it. The Executive being responsible would make a good choice.

Mʳ MERCER 2ᵈˢ the motion of Mʳ Read.

On the motion for inserting the word " joint " before ballot

N. H. ay. Mas. ay. Cᵗ no. N. J. no. Pᵃ ay. Mᵈ no. Vᵃ ay. N. C. ay. S. C. ay. Geo. ay.[4]

Col. MASON in opposition to Mʳ Reads motion desired it might be considered to whom the money would belong; if to the people, the legislature representing the people ought to appoint the keepers of it.

On striking out the clause as amended by inserting " Joint "

N. H. no. Mas. no. Cᵗ no Pᵃ ay. Del. ay. Mᵈ ay. Vᵃ no. N. C. no. S. C. ay. Geo. no.[5]

[6]" To constitute inferior tribunals "[7] agreed to nem. con.[8]

" To make rules as to captures on land & water "- dᵒ dᵒ[9]

[6]" To declare the law and punishment of piracies and felonies &c " &c[10] considered.

Mʳ MADISON moved to strike out " and punishment " &c.[11]

Mʳ MASON doubts the safety of it, considering the strict rule of

---

[1] See page 340.
[2] The word " was " is here inserted in the transcript.
[3] The word " a " is here inserted in the transcript.
[4] In the transcript the vote reads: " New Hampshire, Massachusetts, Pennsylvania, Virginia, North Carolina, South Carolina, Georgia, aye—7; Connecticut, New Jersey, Maryland, no—3."
[5] In the transcript the vote reads: " Pennsylvania, Delaware, Maryland, South Carolina, aye—4; New Hampshire, Massachusetts, Connecticut, Virginia, North Carolina, Georgia, no—6."
[6] The words " The clause " are here inserted in the transcript.
[7] The word " was " is here inserted in the transcript.
[8] The phrase " as also the clause " is here inserted in the transcript.
[9] The words " do. do." are omitted in the transcript.
[10] The word " being " is here inserted in the transcript.
[11] In the transcript the following phrase is here added: " after the words, ' To declare the law.' "

construction in criminal cases. He doubted also the propriety of
taking the power in all these cases wholly from the States.

M: Govern: Morris thought it would be necessary to extend the
authority farther, so as to provide for the punishment of counterfeiting in general. Bills of exchange for example might be forged
in one State and carried into another:

It was suggested by some other member that *foreign* paper might
be counterfeited by Citizens; and that it might be politic to provide
by national authority for the punishment of it.

M: Randolph did not conceive that expunging " the punishment " would be a constructive exclusion of the power. He doubted
only the efficacy of the word " declare."

M: Wilson was in favor of the motion. Strictness was not necessary in giving authority to enact penal laws; though necessary in
enacting & expounding them.

On motion [1] for striking out " and punishment " as moved by
M: Madison

N. H. no. Mas. ay. C: no. P: ay. Del. ay. M: no. V: ay.
N. C. ay. S. C. ay. Geo. ay.[2]

M: Gov: Morris moved to strike out " declare the law " and
insert "punish" before "piracies." and on the question

N. H. ay. Mas. ay. C: no. P: ay. Del. ay. M: ay. V: no.
N. C. no. S. C. ay. Geo. ay.[3]

M: Madison, and M: Randolph moved to insert, " define &," before " punish."

M: Wilson, thought " felonies " sufficiently defined by common
law.

M: Dickenson concurred with M: Wilson.

M: Mercer was in favor of the amendment.

M: Madison. felony at common law is vague. It is also defective.
One defect is supplied by Stat: of Anne as to running away with
vessels which at common law was a breach of trust only. Besides no
foreign law should be a standard farther than [4] is expressly adopted—
If the laws of the States were to prevail on this subject, the citizens
of different States would be subject to different punishments for
the same offence at sea. There would be neither uniformity nor

---

[1] The words "the question" are substituted in the transcript for "motion."
[2] In the transcript the vote reads: "Massachusetts, Pennsylvania, Delaware,
Virginia, North Carolina, South Carolina, Georgia, aye—7; New Hampshire,
Connecticut, Maryland, no—3."
[3] In the transcript the vote reads: "New Hampshire, Massachusetts, Pennsylvania, Delaware, Maryland, South Carolina, Georgia, aye—7; Connecticut,
Virginia, North Carolina, no—3."
[4] The word "it" is here inserted in the transcript.

stability in the law—The proper remedy for all these difficulties was to vest the power proposed by the term " define " in the Nat! legislature.

M! Gov! Morris would prefer *designate* to *define,* the latter being as he he conceived, limited to the preexisting meaning.—

It was said by others to be applicable to the creating of offences also, and therefore suited the case both of felonies & of piracies. The motion of M! M. & M! R was agreed to.

M! Elseworth enlarged the motion so as to read " to define and punish piracies and felonies committed on the high seas, counterfeiting the securities and current coin of the U. States, and offences ag! the law of Nations " which was agreed to nem. con.

[1] " To subdue a rebellion in any State, on the application of its legislature." [2]

M! Pinkney moved to strike out " on the application of its legislature "

M! Gov! Morris 2ᵈˢ

M! L. Martin opposed it as giving a dangerous & unnecessary power. The consent of the State ought to precede the introduction of any extraneous force whatever.

M! Mercer supported the opposition of M! Martin.

M! Elseworth proposed to add after " legislature " " or Executive."

M! Gov! Morris. The Executive may possibly be at the head of the Rebellion. The Gen! Gov! should enforce obedience in all cases where it may be necessary.

M! Elseworth. In many cases The Gen! Gov! ought not to be able to interpose, unless called upon. He was willing to vary his motion so as to read, " or without it when the legislature cannot meet."

M! Gerry was ag! letting loose the myrmidons of the U. States on a State without its own consent. The States will be the best Judges in such cases. More blood would have been spilt in Mass!ˢ in the late insurrection, if the Gen! authority had intermeddled.

M! Langdon was for striking out as moved by M! Pinkney. The apprehension of the national force, will have a salutary effect in preventing insurrections.

M! Randolph. If the Nat! Legislature is to judge whether the State legislature can or cannot meet, that amendment would make the clause as objectionable as the motion of M! Pinkney.

---

[1] The words " The clause " are here inserted in the transcript.
[2] The phrase " was next considered " is here inserted in the transcript.

M: Gov: Morris. We are acting a very strange part. We first form a strong man to protect us, and at the same time wish to tie his hands behind him, The legislature may surely be trusted with such a power to preserve the public tranquility.

On the motion to add " or without it [application] when the legislature cannot meet "[1]

N. H. ay. Mas. no. C: ay. P: div? Del. no. M? no. V: ay. N. C. div? S. C. ay. Geo. ay.[2] So agreed to—[3]

M: Madison and M: Dickenson moved to insert as explanatory, after " State "—" against the Government thereof " There might be a rebellion ag:t the U. States—which[4] was Agreed to nem. con.

On the clause as amended

N. H. ay. Mas * abs: C: ay. Pen. abs: Del. no. M? no. V: ay. N. C. no. S. C. no. Georg. ay—so it was lost.[5]

[6] " To make war "

M: Pinkney opposed the vesting this power in the Legislature. Its proceedings were too slow. It w? meet but once a year. The H: of Rep: would be too numerous for such deliberations. The Senate would be the best depository, being more acquainted with foreign affairs, and most capable of proper resolutions. If the States are equally represented in[7] Senate, so as to give no advantage to[7] large States, the power will notwithstanding be safe, as the small have their all at stake in such cases as well as the large States. It would be singular for one authority to make war, and another peace.

M: Butler. The objections ag:t the Legislature lie in[8] great degree ag:t the Senate. He was for vesting the power in the President, who will have all the requisite qualities, and will not make war but when the Nation will support it.

M: Madison and M: Gerry moved to insert " declare," striking out " make " war; leaving to the Executive the power to repel sudden attacks.

M: Sharman thought it stood very well. The Executive sh? be

* In the printed Journal, Mas. no.

---

[1] The phrase " it was agreed to " is here added in the transcript.
[2] In the transcript the vote reads: "New Hampshire, Connecticut, Virginia, South Carolina, Georgia, aye—5; Massachusetts, Delaware, Maryland, no—3; Pennsylvania, North Carolina, divided."
[3] The words "So agreed to " are omitted in the transcript.
[4] The words "The motion " are substituted in the transcript for " which."
[5] In the transcript the vote reads: "New Hampshire, Connecticut, Virginia, Georgia, aye—4; Delaware, Maryland, North Carolina, South Carolina, no—4; Massachusetts,* Pennsylvania, absent. So it was lost."
[6] The words "The clause " are here inserted in the transcript.
[7] The word " the " is here inserted in the transcript.
[8] The word " a " is here inserted in the transcript.

able to repel and not to commence war. "Make "[1] better than "declare" the latter narrowing the power too much.

M: GERRY never expected to hear in a republic a motion to empower the Executive alone to declare war.

M: ELSWORTH. there is a material difference between the cases of making *war* and making *peace*. It sh.ᵈ be more easy to get out of war, than into it. War also is a simple and overt declaration. peace attended with intricate & secret negociations.

M: MASON was ag.ˢᵗ giving the power of war to the Executive, because not safely to be trusted with it; or to the Senate, because not so constructed as to be entitled to it. He was for clogging rather than facilitating war; but for facilitating peace. He preferred "*declare*" to "*make.*"

On the motion to insert *declare*—in place of *make*, it was agreed to.

N. H. no. Mas. abs.ᵗ. Con.ᵗ no.* P.ᵃ ay. Del. ay. M.ᵈ ay. V.ᵃ ay. N. C. ay. S. C. ay. Geo. ay.[4]

M: PINKNEY's motion to strike out[5] whole clause,[6] disag.ᵈ to without call of States.

M: BUTLER moved to give the Legislature[5] power of peace, as they were to have that of war.

M: GERRY 2.ᵈˢ him. 8 Senators may possibly exercise the power if vested in that body, and 14 if all should be present; and may consequently give up part of the U. States. The Senate are more liable to be corrupted by an Enemy than the whole Legislature.

On the motion for adding "and peace" after "war "[7]

N. H. no. Mas. no. C.ᵗ no. P.ᵃ no. Del. no. M.ᵈ no. V.ᵃ no. N. C. no S. C. no. Geo. no.[8]

Adjourned

* [2] On the remark by M: King that "*make*" war might be understood to "conduct" it which was an Executive function, M: Elseworth gave up his objection, and the vote of Con.ᵗ [3] was changed to—ay.

---

[1] The word "is" is here inserted in the transcript.
[2] The transcript here inserts the following: "Connecticut voted in the negative; but."
[3] The words "of Con.ᵗ" are omitted in the transcript.
[4] In the transcript the vote reads: "Connecticut,* Pennsylvania, Delaware, Maryland, Virginia, North Carolina, South Carolina, Georgia, aye—8; New Hampshire, no—1; Massachusetts, absent."
[5] The word "the" is here inserted in the transcript.
[6] The word "was" is here inserted in the transcript.
[7] The transcript here adds the following: "it was unanimously negatived."
[8] The vote by States is omitted.

SATURDAY AUGUST 18.   IN CONVENTION

M: MADISON submitted in order to be referred to the Committee
of detail the following powers as proper to be added to those of
the General Legislature

"To dispose of the unappropriated lands of the U. States"
"To institute temporary Governments for New States arising
therein"
"To regulate affairs with the Indians as well within as with-
out the limits of the U. States
"To exercise exclusively Legislative authority at the Seat of the
General Government, and over a district around the same, not ex-
eeeding   square miles; the Consent of the Legislature of the
State or States comprizing the same, being first obtained"
"To grant charters of incorporation in cases where the public
good may require them, and the authority of a single State may be
incompetent"
"To secure to literary authors their copy rights for a limited
time"
"To establish an University"
"To encourage by premiums & provisions, the advancement of
useful knowledge and discoveries"
"To authorize the Executive to procure and hold for the use
of the U. S. landed property for the erection of Forts, Magazines,
and other necessary buildings"

These propositions were referred to the Committee of detail
which had prepared the Report and at the same time the following
which were moved by M: Pinkney: in both cases unanimously.

"To fix and permanently establish the seat of Government of
the U. S. in which they shall possess the exclusive right of soil &
jurisdiction"
"To establish seminaries for the promotion of literature and the
arts & sciences"
"To grant charters of incorporation"
"To grant patents for useful inventions"
"To secure to Authors exclusive rights for a certain time"
"To establish public institutions, rewards and immunities for
the promotion of agriculture, commerce, trades and manufactures"
"That funds which shall be appropriated for [1] payment of public Creditors, shall not during the time of such appropriation, be
diverted or applied to any other purpose and that the Committee prepare a clause or clauses for restraining the Legislature of the U. S.
from establishing a perpetual revenue"

---

[1] The word " the " is here inserted in the transcript.

"To secure the payment of the public debt"

"To secure all creditors under the New Constitution from a violation of the public faith when pledged by the authority of the Legislature"

"To grant letters of mark and reprisal"

"To regulate Stages on the post roads"

M: Mason introduced the subject of regulating the militia. He thought such a power necessary to be given to the Gen! Government. He hoped there would be no standing army in time of peace, unless it might be for a few garrisons. The Militia ought therefore to be the more effectually prepared for the public defence. Thirteen States will never concur in any one system, if the displining of the Militia be left in their hands. If they will not give up the power over the whole, they probably will over a part as a select militia. He moved as an addition to the propositions just referred to the Committee of detail, & to be referred in like manner, " a power to regulate the militia."

M: Gerry remarked that some provision ought to be made in favor of public Securities, and something inserted concerning letters of marque, which he thought not included in the power of war. He proposed that these subjects should also go to a Committee.

M: Rutlidge moved to refer a clause " that funds appropriated to public creditors should not be diverted to other purposes."

M: Mason was much attached to the principle, but was afraid such a fetter might be dangerous in time of war. He suggested the necessity of preventing the danger of perpetual revenue which must of necessity subvert the liberty of any Country. If it be objected to on the principle of M: Rutlidge's motion that public credit may require perpetual provisions, that case might be excepted: it being declared that in other cases, no taxes should be laid for a longer term than   years. He considered the caution observed in Great Britain on this point as the paladium of the public liberty.

M: Rutlidge's motion was referred—He then moved that a Grand Committee be appointed to consider the necessity and expediency of the U. States assuming all the State debts—A regular settlement between the Union & the several States would never take place. The assumption would be just as the State debts were contracted in the common defence. It was necessary, as the taxes on imports the only sure source of revenue were to be given up to the Union. It was politic, as by disburdening the people of the State debts it would conciliate them to the plan.

M: King and M: Pinkney seconded the motion

[Col. MASON interposed a motion that the Committee prepare a clause for restraining perpetual revenue, which was agreed to nem. con.]

M⁀ SHERMAN thought it would be better to authorise the Legislature to assume the State debts, than to say positively it should be done. He considered the measure as just and that it would have a good effect to say something about the Matter.

M⁀ ELSEWORTH differed from M⁀ Sherman- As far as the State debts ought in equity to be assumed, he conceived that they might and would be so.

M⁀ PINKNEY observed that a great part of the State debts were of such a nature that although in point of policy and true equity they ought,[1] yet would they not be viewed in the light of fœderal expenditures.

M⁀ KING thought the matter of more consequence than M⁀ Elseworth seemed to do; and that it was well worthy of commitment. Besides the considerations of justice and policy which had been mentioned, it might be remarked that the State Creditors an active and formidable party would otherwise be opposed to a plan which transferred to the Union the best resources of the States without transferring the State debts at the same time. The State Creditors had generally been the strongest foes to the impost-plan. The State debts probably were of greater amount than the fœderal. He would not say that it was practicable to consolidate the debts, but he thought it would be prudent to have the subject considered by a Committee.

On M⁀ Rutlidge's motion, that[2] Com⁀ be appointed to consider of the assumption &c[3]

N. H. no. Mas. ay. C⁀ ay. N. J. no. P⁀ div⁀ Del. no. M⁀ no. V⁀ ay. N. C. ay. S. C. ay. Geo. ay.[4]

M⁀ Gerry's motion to provide for public securities, for stages on post-roads, and for letters of marque & reprisal, were[5] committed nem. con.

M⁀ KING suggested that all unlocated lands of particular States ought to be given up if State debts were to be assumed:—M⁀ Williamson concurred in the idea.

---

[1] The words "to be" are here inserted in the transcript.
[2] The word "a" is here inserted in the transcript.
[3] The transcript here adds the following: "it was agreed to."
[4] In the transcript the vote reads: "Massachusetts, Connecticut, Virginia, North Carolina, South Carolina, Georgia, aye—6; New Hampshire, New Jersey, Delaware, Maryland, no—4; Pennsylvania, divided."
[5] In the transcript the word "were" is crossed out and "was" is written above it.

A Grand Committee was appointed consisting of * transfer hither the appointment & names of the Committee.[1] [The Com: appointed by ballot were [2] M: Langdon, M: King, M: Sherman, M: Livingston, M: Clymer, M: Dickenson, M: M:Henry, M: Mason, M: Williamson, M: C. C. Pinkney,[3] M: Baldwin.]

M: RUTLIDGE remarked on the length of the Session, the probable impatience of the public and the extreme anxiety of many members of the Convention to bring the business to an end; concluding with a motion that the Convention meet henceforward precisely at 10 OC. A. M. and that precisely at 4 OC. P. M. the President adjourn the House without motion for the purpose. and that no motion to adjourn sooner be allowed

On this question

N. H. ay. Mas. ay. C: ay. N. J. ay. P: no. Del. ay. M: no. V: ay. N. C. ay. S. C. ay. Geo. ay.[4]

M: ELSEWORTH observed that a Council had not yet been provided for the President. He conceived there ought to be one. His proposition was that it should be composed of the President of the Senate—the Chief-Justice, and the ministers as they might be estab: for the departments of foreign & domestic affairs, war finance and marine, who should advise but not conclude the President.

M: PINKNEY wished the proposition to lie over, as notice had been given for a like purpose by M: Gov: Morris who was not then on the floor. His own idea was that the President sh: be authorised to call for advice or not as he might chuse. Give him an able Council and it will thwart him; a weak one and he will shelter himself under their sanction.

M: GERRY was ag:st letting the heads of the departments, particularly of finance have any thing to do in business connected with legislation. He mentioned the Chief Justice also as particularly exceptionable. These men will also be so taken up with other matters as to neglect their own proper duties.

M: DICKENSON urged that the great appointments should be made by the Legislature, in which case they might properly be consulted by the Executive, but not if made by the Executive himself—This subject by general consent lay over; & the House proceeded to the clause " To raise armies."

---

[1] Madison's direction is omitted in the transcript.
[2] The phrase " The Com: appointed by ballot were " is omitted in the transcript.
[3] The word " and " is here inserted in the transcript.
[4] In the transcript the vote reads: " New Hampshire, Massachusetts, Connecticut, New Jersey, Delaware, Virginia, North Carolina, South Carolina, Georgia, aye—9; Pennsylvania, Maryland, no—2."

Mͬ GHORUM moved to add "and support" after "raise." Agreed to nem. con. and then the clause [1] agreed to nem. con. as amended

Mͬ GERRY took notice that there was no check here agͦͭ standing armies in time of peace. The existing Congͦ is so constructed that it cannot of itself maintain an army. This wᵈ not be the case under the new system. The people were jealous on this head, and great opposition to the plan would spring from such an omission. He suspected that preparations of force were now making agͦͭ it. [he seemed to allude to the activity of the Govͬ of N. York at this crisis in disciplining the militia of that State.] He thought an army dangerous in time of peace & could never consent to a power to keep up an indefinite number. He proposed that there shall [2] not be kept up in time of peace more than   thousand troops. His idea was that the blank should be filled with two or three thousand.

Instead of "to build and equip fleets"—"to provide & maintain a navy" [3] agreed to nem. con. as a more convenient definition of the power.

[4] " To make rules for the Government and regulation of the land & naval forces," [3] added from the existing Articles of Confederation.

Mͬ L. MARTIN and Mͬ GERRY now regularly moved " provided that in time of peace the army shall not consist of more than   thousand men."

Gen�128 PINKNEY asked whether no troops were ever to be raised untill an attack should be made on us?

Mͬ GERRY. if there be no restriction, a few States may establish a military Govͭ

Mͬ WILLIAMSON, reminded him of Mͬ Mason's motion for limiting the appropriation of revenue as the best guard in this case.

Mͬ LANGDON saw no room for Mͬ Gerry's distrust of the Representatives of the people.

Mͬ DAYTON. preparations for war are generally made in [5] peace; and a standing force of some sort may, for ought we know, become unavoidable. He should object to no restrictions consistent with these ideas.

The motion of Mͬ Martin & Mͬ Gerry was disagreed to nem. con.

Mͬ MASON moved as an additional power " to make laws for the regulation and discipline of the militia of the several States, reserving

---

[1] The word "was" is here inserted in the transcript.
[2] The word "should" is substituted in the transcript for "shall."
[3] The word "was" is here inserted in the transcript.
[4] The words "A clause" are here inserted in the transcript.
[5] The words "time of" are here inserted in the transcript.

to the States the appointment of the officers." He considered uniformity as necessary in the regulation of the Militia throughout the Union.

Gen! PINKNEY mentioned a case during the war in which a dissimilarity in the militia of different States had produced the most serious mischiefs. Uniformity was essential. The States would never keep up a proper discipline of their militia.

M! ELSEWORTH was for going as far in submitting the militia to the Gen! Government as might be necessary, but thought the motion of M! Mason went too far. He moved that the militia should have the same arms & exercise and be under rules established by the Gen! Gov! when in actual service of the U. States and when States neglect to provide regulations for militia, it sh⁴ be regulated & established by the Legislature of ¹ U. S. The whole authority over the Militia ought by no means to be taken away from the States whose consequence would pine away to nothing after such a sacrifice of power. He thought the Gen! Authority could not sufficiently pervade the Union for such a purpose, nor could it accomodate itself to the local genius of the people. It must be vain to ask the States to give the Militia out of their hands.

M! SHERMAN 2ᵈˢ the motion.

M! DICKENSON. We are come now to a most important matter, that of the sword. His opinion was that the States never would nor ought to give up all authority over the Militia. He proposed to restrain the general power to one fourth part at a time, which by rotation would discipline the whole Militia.

M! BUTLER urged the necessity of submitting the whole Militia to the general Authority, which had the care of the general defence.

M! MASON. had suggested the idea of a select militia. He was led to think that would be in fact as much as the Gen! Gov! could advantageously be charged with. He was afraid of creating insuperable objections to the plan. He withdrew his original motion, and moved a power " to make laws for regulating and disciplining the militia, not exceeding one tenth part in any one year, and reserving the appointment of officers to the States."

Gen! PINKNEY, renewed M! Mason's original motion. For a part to be under the Gen! and ² part under the State Gov⁺ˢ w⁴ be an incurable evil. he saw no room for such distrust of the Gen! Gov!

M! LANGDON 2ᵈˢ Gen! Pinkney's renewal. He saw no more reason to be afraid of the Gen! Gov! than of the State Gov⁺ˢ He was

---

¹ The word " the " is here inserted in the transcript.
² The word " a " is here inserted in the transcript.

more apprehensive of the confusion of the different authorities on this subject, than of either.

M![r] MADISON thought the regulation of the Militia naturally appertaining to the authority charged with the public defence. It did not seem in its nature to be divisible between two distinct authorities. If the States would trust the Gen![l] Gov![t] with a power over the public treasure, they would from the same consideration of necessity grant it the direction of the public force. Those who had a full view of the public situation w![d] from a sense of the danger, guard ag![st] it: the States would not be separately impressed with the general situation, nor have the due confidence in the concurrent exertions of each other.

M![r] ELSEWORTH. considered the idea of a select militia as impracticable; & if it were not it would be followed by a ruinous declension of the great body of the Militia. The States will [1] never submit to the same militia laws. Three or four shilling's as a penalty will enforce obedience better in New England, than forty lashes in some other places.

M![r] PINKNEY thought the power such an one as could not be abused, and that the States would see the necessity of surrendering it. He had however but a scanty faith in Militia. There must be also a real military force. This alone can effectually answer the purpose. The United States had been making an experiment without it, and we see the consequence in their rapid approaches towards anarchy.*

M![r] SHERMAN, took notice that the States might want their Militia for defence ag![st] invasions and insurrections, and for enforcing obedience to their laws. They will not give up this point. In giving up that of taxation, they retain a concurrent power of raising money for their own use.

M![r] GERRY thought this the last point remaining to be surrendered. If it be agreed to by the Convention, the plan will have as black a mark as was set on Cain. He had no such confidence in the Gen![l] Gov![t] as some gentlemen professed, and believed it would be found that the States have not.

Col. MASON. thought there was great weight in the remarks of M![r] Sherman, and moved an exception to his motion " of such part of the Militia as might be required by the States for their own use."

M![r] READ doubted the propriety of leaving the appointment of the

---

* This had reference to the disorders particularly which had occurred in Massach![ts] which had called for the interposition of the federal troops.

[1] The word "would" is substituted in the transcript for "will."

Militia officers in [1] the States. In some States they are elected by the legislatures; in others by the people themselves. He thought at least an appointment by the State Executives ought to be insisted on.

On [2] committing to the grand Committee last appointed, the latter motion of Col. Mason, & the original one revived by Ge! Pinkney

N. H. ay. Mas. ay. C? no. N. J. no. P? ay. Del. ay. M? div?
V? ay. N. C. ay. S. C. ay. Geo. ay.[3]

Adjourned

MONDAY AUGUST 20. IN CONVENTION.

M? PINKNEY submitted to the House, in order to be referred to the Committee of detail, the following propositions—

"Each House shall be the Judge of its own privileges, and shall have authority to punish by imprisonment every person violating the same; or who, in the place where the Legislature may be sitting and during the time of its Session, shall threaten any of its members for any thing said or done on the House—or who shall assault any of them therefor—or who shall assault or arrest any witness or other person ordered to attend either of the Houses in his way going or returning; or who shall rescue any person arrested by their order."

"Each branch of the Legislature, as well as the supreme Executive shall have authority to require the opinions of the supreme Judicial Court upon important questions of law, and upon solemn occasions"

"The privileges and benefit of the Writ of Habeas corpus shall be enjoyed in this Government in the most expeditious and ample manner; and shall not be suspended by the Legislature except upon the most urgent and pressing occasions, and for a limited time not exceeding   months."

"The liberty of the Press shall be inviolably preserved"

"No troops shall be kept up in time of peace, but by consent of the Legislature"

"The military shall always be subordinate to the Civil power, and no grants of money shall be made by the Legislature for supporting military Land forces, for more than one year at a time"

"No soldier shall be quartered in any House in time of peace without consent of the owner."

"No person holding the office of President of the U. S., a Judge of their supreme Court, Secretary for the department of Foreign Affairs, of Finance, of Marine, of War, or of   , shall be capable

---

[1] The word " in " is crossed out in the transcript and " to " is written above it.
[2] The words " the question for " are here inserted in the transcript.
[3] In the transcript the vote reads: " New Hampshire, Massachusetts, Pennsylvania, Delaware, Virginia, North Carolina, South Carolina, Georgia, aye—8; Connecticut, New Jersey, no—2; Maryland, divided."

of holding at the same time any other office of Trust or Emolument under the U. S. or an individual State''

"No religious test or qualification shall ever be annexed to any oath of office under the authority of the U. S.''

"The U. S. shall be for ever considered as one Body corporate and politic in law, and entitled to all the rights privileges and immunities, which to Bodies corporate do or ought to appertain''

"The Legislature of the U. S. shall have the power of making the great seal which shall be kept by the President of the U. S. or in his absence by the President of the Senate, to be used by them as the occasion may require.—It shall be called the great Seal of the U. S. and shall be affixed to all laws.''

"All Commissions and writs shall run in the name of the U. S.''

"The Jurisdiction of the supreme Court shall be extended to all controversies between the U. S. and an individual State, or the U. S. and the Citizens of an individual State''

These propositions were referred to the Committee of detail without debate or consideration of them, by the House.

M: Gov: MORRIS 2^{ded} by M: PINKNEY submitted the following propositions which were in like manner referred to the Committee of Detail.

"To assist the President in conducting the public affairs there shall be a council of State composed of the following officers—   1. The Chief Justice of the Supreme Court, who shall from time to time recommend such alterations of and additions to the laws of the U. S. as may in his opinion, be necessary to the due administration of Justice, and such as may promote useful learning and inculcate sound morality throughout the Union: He shall be President of the Council in the absence of the President

2. The Secretary of Domestic Affairs who shall be appointed by the President and hold his office during pleasure. It shall be his duty to attend to matters of general police, the State of Agriculture and manufactures, the opening of roads and navigations, and the facilitating communications thro' the U. States; and he shall from time to time recommend such measures and establishments as may tend to promote those objects.

3. The Secretary of Commerce and Finance who shall also be appointed by the President during pleasure. It shall be his duty to superintend all matters relating to the public finances, to prepare & report plans of revenue and for the regulation of expenditures, and also to recommend such things as may in his Judgment promote the commercial interests of the U. S.

4.   The Secretary of foreign affairs who shall also be appointed by the President during pleasure. It shall be his duty to correspond with all foreign Ministers, prepare plans of Treaties, & consider such as may be transmitted from abroad; and generally to attend to the interests of the U. S. in their connections with foreign powers.

5. The Secretary of War who shall also be appointed by the President during pleasure. It shall be his duty to superintend every thing relating to the war-Department, such as the raising and equipping of troops, the care of military stores, public fortifications, arsenals & the like—also in time of war to prepare & recommend plans of offence and Defence.

6. The Secretary of the Marine who shall also be appointed during pleasure—It shall be his duty to superintend every thing relating to the Marine-Department, the public Ships, Dock-Yards, Naval-Stores & arsenals—also in[1] time of war, to prepare and recommend plans of offence and defence.

The President shall also appoint a Secretary of State to hold his office during pleasure; who shall be Secretary to the Council of State, and also public Secretary to the President. It shall be his duty to prepare all public despatches from the President which he shall countersign

The President may from time to time submit any matter to the discussion of the Council of State, and he may require the written opinions of any one or more of the members: But he shall in all cases exercise his own judgment, and either Conform to such opinions or not as he may think proper; and every officer abovementioned shall be responsible for his opinion on the affairs relating to his particular Department.

Each of the officers abovementioned shall be liable to impeachment. & removal from office for neglect of duty malversation, or corruption"

Mr GERRY moved " that the Committee be instructed to report proper qualifications for the President, and[2] mode of trying the Supreme Judges in cases of impeachment.

The clause " to call forth the aid of the Militia &c. was postponed till report should be made as to the power over the Militia referred yesterday to the Grand Committee of eleven.

Mr MASON moved to enable Congress " to enact sumptuary laws." No Government can be maintained unless the manners be made consonant to it. Such a discretionary power may do good and can do no harm. A proper regulation of excises & of trade may do a great deal but it is best to have an express provision. It was objected to sumptuary laws that they were contrary to nature. This was a vulgar error. The love of distinction it is true is natural; but the object of sumptuary laws is not to extinguish this principle but to give it a proper direction.

Mr ELSEWORTH. The best remedy is to enforce taxes & debts.

---

[1] The word " the " is here inserted in the transcript.
[2] The word " a " is here inserted in the transcript.

As far as the regulation of eating & drinking can be reasonable, it is provided for in the power of taxation.

M⸢ Gov⸣ Morris argued that sumptuary laws tended to create a landed Nobility, by fixing in the great-landholders and their posterity their present possessions.

M⸢ Gerry. the law of necessity is the best sumptuary law.

On [1] Motion of M⸢ Mason " as to Sumptuary laws "

N. H. no. Mas. no. C⸢ no. N. J. no. P⸢ no. Del. ay. M⸢ ay. V⸢ no. N. C. no. S. C. no. Geo. ay.[2]

[3] " And to make all laws necessary and proper for carrying into execution the foregoing powers, and all other powers vested, by this Constitution, in the Government of the U. S. or any department or officer thereof."

M⸢ Madison and M⸢ Pinkney moved to insert between " laws " and " necessary " " and establish all offices," it appearing to them liable to cavil that the latter was not included in the former.

M⸢ Gov⸣ Morris, M⸢ Wilson, M⸢ Rutlidge and M⸢ Elseworth urged that the amendment could not be necessary.

On the motion for inserting " and establish all offices "

N. H. no. Mas. ay. C⸢ no. N. J. no. P⸢ no. Del. no. M⸢ ay. V⸢ no. N. C. no. S. C. no. Geo. no.[4]

The clause as reported was then agreed to nem. con.

Art: VII sect. 2.[5] concerning Treason which see.[6]

M⸢ Madison, thought the definition too narrow. It did not appear to go as far as the Stat. of Edw⸢ III. He did not see why more latitude might not be left to the Legislature. It w⸢ be as safe as in the hands of State legislatures; and it was inconvenient to bar a discretion which experience might enlighten, and which might be applied to good purposes as well as be abused.

M⸢ Mason was for pursuing the Stat: of Edw⸢ III

M⸢ Gov⸣ Morris was for giving to the Union an exclusive right to declare what sh⸢ be treason. In case of a contest between the U. S. and a particular State, the people of the latter must, under the disjunctive terms of the clause, be traitors to one or other authority.

---

[1] The word "the" is here inserted in the transcript.

[2] In the transcript the vote reads: "Delaware, Maryland, Georgia, aye—3; New Hampshire, Massachusetts, Connecticut, New Jersey, Pennsylvania, Virginia, North Carolina, South Carolina, no—8."

[3] The words "On the clause" are here inserted in the transcript.

[4] In the transcript the vote reads: "Massachusetts, Maryland, aye—2; New Hampshire, Connecticut, New Jersey, Pennsylvania, Delaware, Virginia, North Carolina, South Carolina, Georgia, no—9."

[5] See page 341.

[6] In the transcript the words "which see" are crossed out and the phrase "was then taken up" is written above them.

M? RANDOLPH thought the clause defective in adopting the words " in adhering " only. The British Stat: adds, " giving them aid and comfort " which had a more extensive meaning.

M? ELSEWORTH considered the definition as the same in fact with that of the Statute.

M? Gov? MORRIS " adhering " does not go so far as " giving aid and Comfort" or the latter words may be restrictive of "adhering," in either case the Statute is not pursued.

M? WILSON held " giving aid and comfort " to be explanatory, not operative words; and that it was better to omit them.

M? DICKENSON, thought the addition of " giving aid & comfort " unnecessary & improper; being too vague and extending too far. He wished to know what was meant by the " testimony of two witnesses" whether they were to be witnesses to the same overt act or to different overt acts. He thought also that proof of an overt-act ought to be expressed as essential in the case.

Doc? JOHNSON considered " giving aid & comfort " as explanatory of " adhering " & that something should be inserted in the definition concerning overt-acts. He contended that Treason could not be both ag.st the U. States—and individual States; being an offence ag.st the Sovereignty which can be but one in the same community.

M? MADISON remarked that " and " before " in adhering " should be changed into " or " otherwise both offences viz of levying war, & of adhering to the Enemy might be necessary to constitute Treason. He added that as the definition here was of treason against *the U. S.* it would seem that the individual States w.d be left in possession of a concurrent power so far as to define & punish treason particularly ag.st themselves; which might involve double punishm.t

It was moved that the whole clause be recommitted which was lost, the votes being equally divided.

N. H. no. Mas. no. C.t no. N. J. ay. P.a ay. Del. no. M.d ay. V.a ay. N. C. div.d S. C. no. Geo. ay.— [1]

M? WILSON & Doc? JOHNSON moved, that " or any of them " after " United States " be struck out in order to remove the embarrassment: which was agreed to nem. con.

M? MADISON. This had [2] not removed the embarrassment. The

---

[1] In the transcript the vote reads: "New Jersey, Pennsylvania, Maryland, Virginia, Georgia, aye—5; New Hampshire, Massachusetts, Connecticut, Delaware, South Carolina, no—5; North Carolina, divided."

[2] The word "has" is substituted in the transcript for "had."

same Act might be treason agst the United States as here defined—and agst a particular State according to its laws.

Mr ELSEWORTH. There can be no danger to the gen^l authority from this; as the laws of the U. States are to be paramount.

Doc^r JOHNSON was still of opinion there could be no Treason agst a particular State. It could not even at present, as the Confederation now stands, the Sovereignty being in the Union; much less can it be under the proposed system.

Col. MASON. The United States will have a qualified sovereignty only. The individual States will retain a part of the Sovereignty. An Act may be treason agst a particular State which is not so agst the U. States. He cited the Rebellion of Bacon in Virginia as an illustration of the doctrine.

Doc^r JOHNSON: That case would amount to Treason agst the Sovereign, the Supreme Sovereign, the United States.

Mr KING observed that the controversy relating to Treason might be of less magnitude than was supposed; as the Legislature might punish capitally under other names than Treason.

Mr Govr MORRIS and Mr RANDOLPH wished to substitute the words of the British Statute and moved to postpone Sect 2. art VII in order to consider the following substitute—" Whereas it is essential to the preservation of liberty to define precisely and exclusively what shall constitute the crime of Treason, it is therefore ordained, declared & established, that if a man do levy war agst the U. S., within their territories, or be adherent to the enemies of the U. S. within the said territories, giving them aid and comfort within their territories or elsewhere, and thereof be provably attainted of open deed by the people of his condition, he shall be adjudged guilty of Treason."

On this question

N. H.   Mas. no. C^t no. N. J. ay. P^a no. Del. no. M^d no. V^a ay. N. C. no. S. C. no. Geo. no.[1]

It was[2] moved to strike out " agst [3] United States " after " treason " so as to define treason generally, and on this question

Mas. ay. C^t ay. N. J. ay. P^a ay. Del. ay. M^d ay. V^a no. N. C. no. S. C. ay. Geo. ay.[4]

---

[1] In the transcript the vote reads: " New Jersey, Virginia, aye—2; Massachusetts, Connecticut, Pennsylvania, Delaware, Maryland, North Carolina, South Carolina, Georgia, no—8."

[2] The word " then " is here inserted in the transcript.

[3] The word " the " is here inserted in the transcript.

[4] In the transcript the vote reads: " Massachusetts, Connecticut, New Jersey, Pennsylvania, Delaware, Maryland, South Carolina, Georgia, aye—8; Virginia, North Carolina, no—2."

It was then moved to insert after " two witnesses " the words " to the same overt act."

Doc! FRANKLIN wished this amendment to take place– prosecutions for treason were generally virulent; and perjury too easily made use of against innocence.

M! WILSON. much may be said on both sides. Treason may sometimes be practised in such a manner, as to render proof extremely difficult—as in a traitorous correspondence with an Enemy.

On the question—as to same overt act

N. H. ay. Mas. ay. C! ay. N. J. no. P! ay. Del. ay. M! ay. V! no. N. C. no. S. C. ay. Geo. ay.[1]

M! KING moved to insert before the word " power " the word " sole," giving the U. States the exclusive right to declare the punishment of Treason.

M! BROOM 2ds the motion.

M! WILSON in cases of a general nature, treason can only be agst the U— States. and in such they shd have the sole right to declare the punishment—yet in many cases it may be otherwise. The subject was however intricate and he distrusted his present judgment on it.

M! KING this amendment results from the vote defining, treason generally by striking out agst the U. States; which excludes any treason agst particular States. These may however punish offences as high misdemesnors.

On [2] inserting the word " sole." It passed in the negative

N. H. ay. Mas. ay. C! no. N. J. no. P! ay. Del. ay. M! no. V! no. N. C. no. S. C. ay. Geo. no.— [3]

M! WILSON. the clause is ambiguous now. " Sole " ought either to have been inserted- or "against the U. S." to be re-instated.

M! KING no line can be drawn between levying war and adhering to [4] enemy- agst the U. States and agst an individual State— Treason agst the latter must be so agst the former.

M! SHERMAN, resistance agst the laws of the U. States as distinguished from resistance agst the laws of a particular State, forms the line.

---

[1] In the transcript the vote reads: "New Hampshire, Massachusetts, Connecticut, Pennsylvania, Delaware, Maryland, South Carolina, Georgia, aye—8; New Jersey, Virginia, North Carolina, no—3."

[2] The words " the question for " are here inserted in the transcript.

[3] In the transcript the vote reads: "New Hampshire, Massachusetts, Pennsylvania, Delaware, South Carolina, aye—5; Connecticut, New Jersey, Maryland, Virginia, North Carolina, Georgia, no—6."

[4] The word " the " is here inserted in the transcript.

M⸢ᴿ⸣ Eʟsᴇᴡᴏʀᴛʜ. the U. S. are sovereign on their [1] side of the line dividing the jurisdictions—the States on the other—each ought to have power to defend their respective Sovereignties.

M⸢ᴿ⸣ Dɪᴄᴋᴇɴsᴏɴ, war or insurrection ag⸢st⸣ a member of the Union must be so ag⸢st⸣ the whole body; but the Constitution should be made clear on this point.

The clause was reconsidered nem. con—& then, M⸢ᴿ⸣ Wɪʟsᴏɴ & M⸢ᴿ⸣ Eʟsᴇᴡᴏʀᴛʜ moved to reinstate " ag⸢st⸣ the U. S." after " Treason "—on which question

N. H. no. Mᴀs. no. C⸢t⸣ ay. N. J. ay. P⸢a⸣ no. Del. no. M⸢d⸣ ay. V⸢a⸣ ay. N. C. ay. S. C. no. Geo. ay.[2]

M⸢ᴿ⸣ Mᴀᴅɪsᴏɴ was not satisfied with the footing on which the clause now stood. As Treason ag⸢st⸣ the U. States involves treason ag⸢st⸣ particular States, and vice versa, the same act may be twice tried & punished by the different authorities. M⸢ᴿ⸣ Gov⸢r⸣ Mᴏʀʀɪs viewed the matter in the same light—

It was moved & 2⸢ded⸣ to amend the sentence to read—" Treason ag⸢st⸣ the U. S. shall consist only in levying war against them, or in adhering to their enemies" which was agreed to.

Col. Mᴀsᴏɴ moved to insert the words " giving them aid [3] comfort," as restrictive of " adhering to their Enemies &c." the latter he thought would be otherwise too indefinite—This motion was agreed to: Con⸢t⸣ Del: & Georgia only being in the Negative.

M⸢ᴿ⸣ L. Mᴀʀᴛɪɴ moved to insert after conviction &c—" or on confession in open court"—and on the question, (the negative States thinking the words superfluous) it was agreed to

N. H: ay. Mᴀs. no. C⸢t⸣ ay. N. J. ay. P. ay. Del. ay. M⸢d⸣ ay. V⸢a⸣ ay. N. C. div⸢d⸣ S. C. no. Geo. no.[4]

Art: VII. Sect. 2, as amended was then agreed to nem. con.

[5] Sect. 3 [6] taken up " white & other " struck out nem. con. as superfluous.

M⸢ᴿ⸣ Eʟsᴇᴡᴏʀᴛʜ moved to require the first census to be taken

---

[1] The word " one " is substituted in the transcript for " their."

[2] In the transcript the vote reads: " Connecticut, New Jersey, Maryland, Virginia, North Carolina, Georgia, aye—6; New Hampshire, Massachusetts, Pennsylvania, Delaware, South Carolina, no—5."

[3] The word " and " is here inserted in the transcript.

[4] In the transcript the vote reads: " New Hampshire, Connecticut, New Jersey, Pennsylvania, Delaware, Maryland, Virginia, aye—7; Massachusetts, South Carolina, Georgia, no—3; North Carolina, divided."

[5] In the transcript this sentence reads as follows: " Article 7, Sect. 3 was taken up. The words 'white and others,' were struck out ". . .

[6] See page 341.

within "three" instead of "six" years from the first meeting of the Legislature—and on [1] question

N. H. ay. Mas. ay. C^t ay. N. J. ay. P^a ay. Del. ay. M^d ay V^a ay. N. C. ay. S. C. no. Geo. no.[2]

Mr KING asked what was the precise meaning of *direct* taxation? No one answ^d

Mr GERRY moved to add to the [3] 3^d Sect. art. VII, the following clause "That from the first meeting, of the Legislature of the U. S. until a Census shall be taken all monies for supplying the public Treasury by direct taxation shall be raised from the several States according to the number of their Representatives respectively in the first branch "

Mr LANGDON. This would bear unreasonably hard on N: H. and he must be agst it.

Mr CARROL. opposed it. The number of Rep^s did not admit of a proportion exact enough for a rule of taxation.

Before any question the House

Adjourned

TUESDAY AUGUST 21.   IN CONVENTION

Governour LIVINGSTON from the Committee of Eleven to whom was referred the propositions respecting the debts of the several States and also the Militia entered on the 18th inst: delivered the following report:

"The Legislature of the U. S. shall have power to fulfil the engagements which have been entered into by Congress, and to discharge as well the debts of the U. S. as the debts incurred by the several States during the late war, for the common defence and general welfare"

"To make laws for organizing arming and disciplining the militia, and for governing such part of them as may be employed in the service of the U. S. reserving to the States respectively, the appointment of the officers, and the authority of training the Militia according to the discipline prescribed by the U. States"

Mr GERRY considered giving the power only, without adopting the obligation, as destroying the security now enjoyed by the public

---

[1] The word "the" is here inserted in the transcript.
[2] In the transcript the vote reads: "New Hampshire, Massachusetts, Connecticut, New Jersey, Pennsylvania, Delaware, Maryland, Virginia, North Carolina, aye—9; South Carolina, Georgia, no—2."
[3] The word "the" is omitted in the transcript.

creditors of the U— States. He enlarged on the merit of this class of citizens, and the solemn faith which had been pledged under the existing Confederation. If their situation should be changed as here proposed great opposition would be excited ag⁻ᵗ the plan. He urged also that as the States had made different degrees of exertion to sink their respective debts, those who had done most would be alarmed, if they were now to be saddled with a share of the debts of States which had done least.

M⁻ Sherman. It means neither more nor less than the confederation as it relates to this subject.

M⁻ Elseworth moved that the Report delivered in by Gov⁻ Livingston should lie on the table.[1] Agreed to nem. con.

Art: VII. Sect. 3.[2] resumed.—M⁻ Dickenson moved to postpone this in order to reconsider Art: IV. Sect. 4. and to *limit* the number of representatives to be allowed to the large States. Unless this were done the small States would be reduced to entire insignificancy,[3] and encouragement given to the importation of slaves.

M⁻ Sherman would agree to such a reconsideration, but did not see the necessity of postponing the section before the House.—M⁻ Dickenson withdrew his motion.

Art: VII. Sect. 3.[4] then agreed to 10 ays. Delaware alone being[5] no.

M⁻ Sherman moved to add to Sect. 3. the following clause "and all accounts of supplies furnished, services performed, and monies advanced by the several States to the U. States, or by the U. S. to the several States shall be adjusted by the same rule "

M⁻ Govern⁻ Morris 2ᵈˢ the motion.

M⁻ Ghorum, thought it wrong to insert this in the Constitution. The Legislature will no doubt do what is right. The present Congress have such a power and are now exercising it.

M⁻ Sherman unless some rule be expressly given none will exist under the new system.

M⁻ Elseworth. Though The contracts of Congress will be binding, there will be no rule for executing them on the States; and one ought to be provided.

M⁻ Sherman withdrew his motion to make way for one of M⁻ Williamson to add to Sect. 3. "By this rule the several quotas of the States shall be determined in Settling the expences of the late war."

---

[1] The words "which was" are here inserted in the transcript.
[2] The words "was then" are here inserted in the transcript.
[3] The word "insignificancy" is changed to "insignificance" in the transcript.
[4] The word "was" is here inserted in the transcript.
[5] The word "being" is omitted in the transcript.

M: CARROL brought into view the difficulty that might arise on this subject from the establishment of the Constitution as intended without the *unanimous* consent of the States

M: Williamson's motion was postponed nem- con-

Art: VI Sect. 12.[1] which had been postponed Aug: 15.[2] was now called for by Col. MASON, who wished to know how the proposed amendment as to money bills would be decided, before he agreed to any further points.

M: Gerry's motion of yesterday that previous to a census, direct taxation be proportioned on the States according to the number of Representatives, was taken up. He observed that the principal acts of Government would probably take place within that period, and it was but reasonable that the States should pay in proportion to their share in them.

M: ELSEWORTH thought such a rule unjust. there was a great difference between the number of Represent:, and the number of inhabitants as a rule in this case. Even if the former were proportioned as nearly as possible to the latter, it would be a very inaccurate rule. A State might have one Representative only that had inhabitants enough for 1½ or more, if fractions could be applied, &c—. He proposed to amend the motion by adding the words "subject to a final liquidation by the foregoing rule when a census shall have been taken."

M: MADISON. The last apportionment of Cong:, on which the number of Representatives was founded, was conjectural and meant only as a temporary rule till a Census should be established.

M: READ. The requisitions of Cong: had been accomodated to the the impoverishments produced by the war; and to other local and temporary circumstances—

M: WILLIAMSON opposed M: Gerry's motion

M: LANGDON was not here when N. H. was allowed three members. If [3] it was more than her share; he did not wish for them.

M: BUTLER contended warmly for M: Gerry's motion as founded in reason and equity.

M: ELSEWORTH's proviso to M: Gerry's motion was agreed to nem. con.

M: KING thought the power of taxation given to the Legislature rendered the motion of M: Gerry altogether unnecessary.

---

[1] See page 340.
[2] The words "on the fifteenth of August" are substituted in the transcript for "Aug: 15."
[3] The word "if" is omitted in the transcript.

On Mʳ Gerry's motion as amended

N. H. no. Mas. ay. Cᵗ no. N. J. no. Pᵃ no. Del. no. Mᵈ no. Vᵃ no. N. Ci. divᵈ S. C. ay. Geo. no.[1]

On a question, Shall Art: VI Sect. 12. with the amendment to it proposed & entered on the 15 instant, as called for by Col. Mason be now taken up? it passed in the Negative.

N. H. ay. Mas no. Cᵗ ay. N. J. no. Pᵃ no. Del. no. Mᵈ ay. Vᵃ ay. N. C. ay. S. C. no. Geo. no[2]

Mʳ L. MARTIN. The power of taxation is most likely to be criticised by the public. Direct taxation should not be used but in case of absolute necessity; and then the States will be best Judges of the mode. He therefore moved the following addition to Sect: 3. Art: VII "And whenever the Legislature of the U: S: shall find it necessary that revenue should be raised by direct taxation, having apportioned the same, according to the above rule on the several States, requisitions shall be made of the respective States to pay into the Continental Treasury their respective quotas within a time in the said requisitions specified, and in case of any of the States failing to comply with such requisitions, then and then only to devise and pass acts directing the mode, and authorizing the collection of the same"

Mʳ MᶜHENRY 2ᵈᵉᵈ the motion—there was no debate, and on the question

N. H. no. Cᵗ no. N. J. ay. Penᵃ no. Del. no. Mᵈ divᵈ (Jenifer & Carrol no). Vᵃ no. N. C. no. S. C. no. Geo. no.[3]

Art. VII. Sect. 4.[4, 5]—Mʳ LANGDON. by this section the States are left at liberty to tax exports. N. H. therefore with other non-exporting States, will be subject to be taxed by the States exporting its produce. This could not be admitted. It seems to be feared that the Northern States will oppress the trade of the Southⁿ This may be guarded agᵗ by requiring the concurrence of ⅔ or ¾ of the legislature in such cases.

Mʳ ELSEWORTH. It is best as it stands. The power of regulating trade between the States will protect them agᵗ each other. Should this not be the case, the attempts of one to tax the produce of another

---

[1] In the transcript the vote reads "Massachusetts, South Carolina, aye—2; New Hampshire, Connecticut, New Jersey, Pennsylvania, Delaware, Maryland, Virginia, Georgia, no—8; North Carolina, divided."

[2] In the transcript the vote reads: "New Hampshire, Connecticut, Virginia, Maryland, North Carolina, aye—5; Massachusetts, New Jersey, Pennsylvania, Delaware, South Carolina, Georgia, no—6."

[3] In the transcript the vote reads: "New Jersey, aye—1; New Hampshire, Connecticut, Pennsylvania, Delaware, Virginia, North Carolina, South Carolina, Georgia, no—8; Maryland, divided [Jenifer and Carroll, no]."

[4] See page 341.

[5] The words "was then taken up" are here inserted in the transcript.

passing through its hands, will force a direct exportation and defeat themselves. There are solid reasons ag:t Cong: taxing exports. 1.[1] it will discourage industry, as taxes on imports discourage luxury. 2.[1] The produce of different States is such as to prevent uniformity in such taxes. There are indeed but a few articles that could be taxed at all; as Tob: rice & indigo, and a tax on these alone would be partial & unjust. 3.[1] The taxing of exports would engender incurable jealousies.

M: WILLIAMSON. Tho' N. C. has been taxed by Virg: by a duty on 12,000 Hhs of her Tob: exported thro' Virg: yet he would never agree to this power. Should it take take place, it would distroy the last hope of an adoption of the plan.

M: Gov: MORRIS. These local considerations ought not to impede the general interest. There is great weight in the argument, that the exporting States will tax the produce of their uncommercial neighbours. The power of regulating the trade between P: & N. Jersey will never prevent the former from taxing the latter. Nor will such a tax force a direct exportation from N. Jersey. The advantages possessed by a large trading City, outweigh the disadvantage of a moderate duty; and will retain the trade in that channel.- If no tax can be laid on exports, an embargo cannot be laid though in time of war such a measure may be of critical importance. Tobacco, lumber and live-stock are three objects belonging to different States, of which great advantage might be made by a power to tax exports. To these may be added Ginseng and Masts for Ships by which a tax might be thrown on other nations. The idea of supplying the West Indies with lumber from Nova Scotia is one of the many follies of lord Sheffield's pamphlets. The State of the Country also will change, and render duties on exports, as skins, beaver & other peculiar raw materials, politic in the view of encouraging American Manufactures.

M: BUTLER was strenuously opposed to a power over exports; as unjust and alarming to the Staple-States.

M: LANGDON suggested a prohibition on the States from taxing the produce of other States exported from their harbours.

M: DICKENSON. The power of taxing exports may be inconvenient at present; but it must be of dangerous consequence to prohibit it with respect to all articles and for ever. He thought it would be better to except particular articles from the power.

M: SHERMAN. It is best to prohibit the National legislature in all cases. The States will never give up all power over trade. An

---

[1] The figures " 1," " 2 " and " 3 " are changed in the transcript to " First," " Secondly " and " Thirdly."

enumeration of particular articles would be difficult invidious and improper.

M. MADISON As we aught to be governed by national and permanent views, it is a sufficient argument for giving y.º power over exports that a tax, tho' it may not be expedient at present, may be so hereafter. A proper regulation of exports may & probably will be necessary hereafter, and for the same purposes as the regulation of imports; viz, for revenue—domestic manufactures—and procuring equitable regulations from other nations. An Embargo may be of absolute necessity, and can alone be effectuated by the Gen! authority. The regulation of trade between State and State can not effect more than indirectly to hinder a State from taxing its own exports; by authorizing its Citizens to carry their commodities freely into a neighbouring State which might decline taxing exports in order to draw into its channel the trade of its neighbours. As to the fear of disproportionate burdens on the more exporting States, it might be remarked that it was agreed on all hands that the revenue w.ª principally be drawn from trade, and as only a given revenue would be needed, it was not material whether all should be drawn wholly from imports—or half from those, and half from exports. The imports and exports must be pretty nearly equal in every State—and relatively the same among the different States.

M. ELSEWORTH did not conceive an embargo by the Congress interdicted by this section.

M. MᶜHENRY conceived that power to be included in the power of war.

M. WILSON. Pennsylvania exports the produce of Mary.ª N. Jersey, Delaware & will by & by when the River Delaware is opened, export for N- York. In favoring the general power over exports therefore, he opposed the particular interest of his State. He remarked that the power had been attacked by reasoning which could only have held good in case the Gen¹ Gov.ᵗ had been *compelled*, instead of *authorized*, to lay duties on exports. To deny this power is to take from the Common Gov.ᵗ half the regulation of trade. It was his opinion that a power over exports might be more effectual than that over imports in obtaining beneficial treaties of commerce

M. GERRY was strenuously opposed to the power over exports. It might be made use of to compel the States to comply with the will of the Gen! Government, and to grant it any new powers which might be demanded. We have given it more power already than we know how will be exercised. It will enable the Gen! Gov.ᵗ to oppress the States as much as Ireland is oppressed by Great Britain.

M: FITZIMMONS would be ag:t a tax on exports to be laid immediately; but was for giving a power of laying the tax when a proper time may call for it. This would certainly be the case when America should become a manufacturing Country. He illustrated his argument by the duties in G. Britain on wool &c.

Col. MASON. If he were for reducing the States to mere corporations as seemed to be the tendency of some arguments, he should be for subjecting their exports as well as imports to a power of general taxation. He went on a principle often advanced & in which he concurred, that " a majority when interested will oppress the minority." This maxim had been verified by our own Legislature [of Virginia]. If we compare the States in this point of view the 8 Northern States have an interest different from the five South? States; and have in one branch of the legislature 36 votes ag:t 29. and in the other, in the proportion of 8 ag:t 5. The Southern States had therefore good ground for their suspicions. The case of Exports was not the same with that of imports. The latter were the same throughout the States: The former very different. As to Tobacco other nations do raise it, and are capable of raising it as well as Virg? &c. The impolicy of taxing that article had been demonstrated by the experiment of Virginia.

M: CLYMER remarked that every State might reason with regard to its particular productions, in the same manner as the Southern States. The middle States may apprehend an oppression of their wheat flour, provisions &c. and with more reason, as these articles were exposed to a competition in foreign markets not incident to Tob? rice &c. They may apprehend also combinations ag:t them between the Eastern & Southern States as much as the latter can apprehend them between the Eastern & middle. He moved as a qualification of the power of taxing Exports that it should be restrained to regulations of trade, by inserting after the word " duty " Sect 4 art VII the words, " for the purpose of revenue."

On [1] Question on M: Clymer's motion

N. H. no. Mas. no. C: no. N. J. ay. P: ay. Del. ay. M: no. V: no. N. C. no. S. C. no. Geo. no.[2]

M: MADISON. In order to require ⅔ of each House to tax exports —as a lesser evil than a total prohibition moved to insert the words " unless by consent of two thirds of the Legislature."

M: WILSON 2:ds and on this question, it passed in the Negative.

---

[1] The word " the " is here inserted in the transcript.
[2] In the transcript the vote reads: " New Jersey, Pennsylvania, Delaware, aye—3; New Hampshire, Massachusetts, Connecticut, Maryland, Virginia, North Carolina, South Carolina, Georgia, no—8."

N. H. ay. Mas. ay. C! no. N. J. ay. P? ay. Del. ay. M! no.
V? no [Col. Mason, M? Randolph, M? Blair no. Gen! Washington &
J. M. ay.] N. C. no. S. C. no. Geo. no.[1]

[2] Question on Sect: 4. art VII. as far as to " no tax sh! be laid
on exports—It passed in the affirmative.

N. H. no. Mas. ay. C! ay. N. J. no. P? no. Del. no. M! ay.
V? ay (Gen! W. & J. M. no) N. C. ay. S. C. ay. Geo. ay.[3]

M? L. MARTIN, proposed to vary the Sect: 4. art VII. so as to
allow a prohibition or tax on the importation of slaves. 1.[4] as five
slaves are to be counted as 3 free men in the apportionment of Representatives; such a clause w? leave an encouragement to this trafic.
2.[5] slaves weakened one part of the Union which the other parts were
bound to protect: the privilege of importing them was therefore
unreasonable. 3.[6] it was inconsistent with the principles of the revolution and dishonorable to the American character to have such a
feature in the Constitution.

M? RUTLIDGE did not see how the importation of slaves could be
encouraged by this Section. He was not apprehensive of insurrections and would readily exempt the other States from the obligation
to protect the Southern against them.— Religion & humanity had
nothing to do with this question. Interest alone is the governing
principle with nations. The true question at present is whether the
South? States shall or shall not be parties to the Union. If the
Northern States consult their interest, they will not oppose the increase of Slaves which will increase the commodities of which they
will become the carriers.

M? ELSEWORTH was for leaving the clause as it stands. let every
State import what it pleases. The morality or wisdom of slavery are
considerations belonging to the States themselves. What enriches a
part enriches the whole, and the States are the best judges of their
particular interest. The old confederation had not meddled with
this point, and he did not see any greater necessity for bringing it
within the policy of the new one:

---

[1] In the transcript the vote reads: "New Hampshire, Massachusetts, New
Jersey, Pennsylvania, Delaware, aye—5; Connecticut, Maryland, Virginia [Col.
Mason, Mr. Randolph, Mr. Blair, no; General Washington, Mr. Madison, aye]
North Carolina, South Carolina, Georgia, no—6."
[2] The words "On the" are here inserted in the transcript.
[3] In the transcript the vote reads: "Massachusetts, Connecticut, Maryland,
Virginia [Genl. Washington and Mr. Madison, no] North Carolina, South Carolina, Georgia, aye—7; New Hampshire, New Jersey, Pennsylvania, Delaware,
no—4."
[4] The figure "1" is changed in the transcript to "In the first place."
[5] The figure "2" is changed in the transcript to "In the second place."
[6] The figure "3" is changed in the transcript to "And in the third place."

M: PINKNEY. South Carolina can never receive the plan if it prohibits the slave trade. In every proposed extension of the powers of the Congress, that State has expressly & watchfully excepted that of meddling with the importation of negroes. If the States be all left at liberty on this subject, S. Carolina may perhaps by degrees do of herself what is wished, as Virginia & Maryland have already [1] done.

Adjourned

WEDNESDAY AUGUST 22. IN CONVENTION.

Art VII sect 4.[2, 3] resumed. M: SHERMAN was for leaving the clause as it stands. He disapproved of the slave trade; yet as the States were now possessed of the right to import slaves, as the public good did not require it to be taken from them, & as it was expedient to have as few objections as possible to the proposed scheme of Government, he thought it best to leave the matter as we find it. He observed that the abolition of Slavery seemed to be going on in the U. S. & that the good sense of the several States would probably by degrees compleat it. He urged on the Convention the necessity of despatching its business.

Col. MASON. This infernal trafic originated in the avarice of British Merchants. The British Gov: constantly checked the attempts of Virginia to put a stop to it. The present question concerns not the importing States alone but the whole Union. The evil of having slaves was experienced during the late war. Had slaves been treated as they might have been by the Enemy, they would have proved dangerous instruments in their hands. But their folly dealt by the slaves, as it did by the Tories. He mentioned the dangerous insurrections of the slaves in Greece and Sicily; and the instructions given by Cromwell to the Commissioners sent to Virginia, to arm the servants & slaves, in case other means of obtaining its submission should fail. Maryland & Virginia he said had already prohibited the importation of slaves expressly. N. Carolina had done the same in substance. All this would be in vain if S. Carolina & Georgia be at liberty to import. The Western people are already calling out for slaves for their new lands, and will fill that Country with slaves if they can be got thro' S. Carolina & Georgia. Slavery discourages

---

[1] The words "have already" are transposed in the transcript to read "already have."

[2] See page 341.

[3] The word "was" is here inserted in the transcript.

arts & manufactures. The poor despise labor when performed by slaves. They prevent the immigration of Whites, who really enrich & strengthen a Country. They produce the most pernicious effect on manners. Every master of slaves is born a petty tyrant. They bring the judgment of heaven on a Country. As nations can not be rewarded or punished in the next world they must be in this. By an inevitable chain of causes & effects providence punishes national sins, by national calamities. He lamented that some of our Eastern brethren had from a lust of gain embarked in this nefarious traffic. As to the States being in possession of the Right to import, this was the case with many other rights, now to be properly given up. He held it essential in every point of view that the Genˡ Govᵗ should have power to prevent the increase of slavery.

Mʳ ELSWORTH. As he had never owned a slave could not judge of the effects of slavery on character: He said however that if it was to be considered in a moral light we ought to go farther and free those already in the Country.—As slaves also multiply so fast in Virginia & & Maryland that it is cheaper to raise than import them; whilst in the sickly rice swamps foreign supplies are necessary, if we go no farther than is urged, we shall be unjust towards S. Carolina & Georgia. Let us not intermeddle. As population increases poor laborers will be so plenty as to render slaves useless. Slavery in time will not be a speck in our Country. Provision is already made in Connecticut for abolishing it. And the abolition has already taken place in Massachussets. As to the danger of insurrections from foreign influence, that will become a motive to kind treatment of the slaves.

Mʳ PINKNEY. If slavery be wrong, it is justified by the example of all the world. He cited the case of Greece Rome & other antient States; the sanction given by France England, Holland & other modern States. In all ages one half of mankind have been slaves. If the S. States were let alone they will probably of themselves stop importations. He wᵈ himself as a Citizen of S. Carolina vote for it. An attempt to take away the right as proposed will produce serious objections to the Constitution which he wished to see adopted.

General PINKNEY declared it to be his firm opinion that if himself & all his colleagues were to sign the Constitution & use their personal influence, it would be of no avail towards obtaining the assent of their Constituents. S. Carolina & Georgia cannot do without slaves. As to Virginia she will gain by stopping the importations. Her slaves will rise in value, & she has more than she wants. It would be unequal to reauire S. C. & Georgia to confederate on such unequal terms. He said the Royal assent before the Revolution had never been refused to S. Carolina as to Virginia. He contended that the importation of slaves would be for the interest of the whole Union. The more slaves, the more produce to employ the carrying trade; The more consumption also, and the more of this, the more of revenue for the common treasury. He admitted it to be reasonable that slaves should be dutied like other imports, but should consider a rejection of the clause as an exclusion of S. Carol: from the Union.

M͞ʳ BALDWIN had conceived national objects alone to be before the Convention, not such as like the present were of a local nature. Georgia was decided on this point. That State has always hitherto supposed a Gen͞l Governm͞t to be the pursuit of the central States who wished to have a vortex for every thing—that her distance would preclude her from equal advantage—& that she could not prudently purchase it by yielding national powers. From this it might be understood in what light she would view an attempt to abridge one of her favorite prerogatives. If left to herself, she may probably put a stop to the evil. As one ground for this conjecture, he took notice of the sect of   which he said was a respectable class of people, who carried their ethics beyond the mere *equality of men*, extending their humanity to the claims of the whole animal creation.

M͞ʳ WILSON observed that if S. C. & Georgia were themselves disposed to get rid of the importation of slaves in a short time as had been suggested, they would never refuse to Unite because the importation might be prohibited. As the Section now stands all articles imported are to be taxed. Slaves alone are exempt. This is in fact a bounty on that article.

M͞ʳ GERRY thought we had nothing to do with the conduct of the States as to Slaves, but ought to be careful not to give any sanction to it.

M͞ʳ DICKENSON considered it as inadmissible on every principle of honor & safety that the importation of slaves should be authorised to the States by the Constitution. The true question was whether the national happiness would be promoted or impeded by the importation, and this question ought to be left to the National Gov͞t not to the States particularly interested. If Eng͞d & France permit slavery, slaves are at the same time excluded from both those Kingdoms. Greece and Rome were made unhappy by their slaves. He could not believe that the South͞n States would refuse to confederate on the account apprehended; especially as the power was not likely to be immediately exercised by the Gen͞l Government.

M⸱ WILLIAMSON stated the law of N. Carolina on the subject, to wit that it did not directly prohibit the importation of slaves. It imposed a duty of £5. on each slave imported from Africa. £10 on each from elsewhere, & £50 on each from a State licensing manumission. He thought the S. States could not be members of the Union if the clause sh⸱ be rejected, and that it was wrong to force any thing down, not absolutely necessary, and which any State must disagree to.

M⸱ KING thought the subject should be considered in a political light only. If two States will not agree to the Constitution as stated on one side, he could affirm with equal belief on the other, that great & equal opposition would be experienced from the other States. He remarked on the exemption of slaves from duty whilst every other import was subjected to it, as an inequality that could not fail to strike the commercial sagacity of the North⸱ & middle States.

M⸱ LANGDON was strenuous for giving the power to the Gen⸱ Gov⸱ He c⸱ not with a good conscience leave it with the States who could then go on with the traffic, without being restrained by the opinions here given that they will themselves cease to import slaves.

Gen⸱ PINKNEY thought himself bound to declare candidly that he did not think S. Carolina would stop her importations of slaves in any short time, but only stop them occasionally as she now does. He moved to commit the clause that slaves might be made liable to an equal tax with other imports which he he thought right & w⸱ᶜʰ w⸱ remove one difficulty that had been started.

M⸱ RUTLIDGE. If the Convention thinks that N. C. S. C. & Georgia will ever agree to the plan, unless their right to import slaves be untouched, the expectation is vain. The people of those States will never be such fools as to give up so important an interest. He was strenuous ag⸱ᵗ striking out the Section, and seconded the motion of Gen⸱ Pinkney for a commitment.

M⸱ Gov⸱ MORRIS wished the whole subject to be committed including the clauses relating to taxes on exports & to a navigation-act. These things may form a bargain among the Northern & Southern States.

M⸱ BUTLER declared that he never would agree to the power of taxing exports.

M⸱ SHERMAN said it was better to let the S. States import slaves than to part with them, if they made that a sine qua non. He was opposed to a tax on slaves imported as making the matter worse, because it implied they were *property*. He acknowledged that if the power of prohibiting the importation should be given to the Gen⸱

Government that it would be exercised. He thought it would be its duty to exercise the power.

Mͬ READ was for the commitment provided the clause concerning taxes on exports should also be committed.

Mͭ SHERMAN observed that that clause had been agreed to & therefore could not [1] committed.

Mͬ RANDOLPH was for committing in order that some middle ground might, if possible, be found. He could never agree to the clause as it stands. He wᵈ sooner risk the constitution. He dwelt on the dilemma to which the Convention was exposed. By agreeing to the clause, it would revolt the Quakers, the Methodists, and many others in the States having no slaves. On the other hand, two States might be lost to the Union. Let us then, he said, try the chance of a commitment.

On the question for committing the remaining part of Sect. 4 & 5.[2] of art: 7. N. H. no. Mas. absͭ Conͭ ay N. J. ay Pᵃ no. Del. no Maryᵈ ay. Vᵃ ay. N. C. ay S. C. ay. Geo. ay.[3]

Mͭ PINKNEY & Mͬ LANGDON moved to commit Sect. 6.[2] as to [4] navigation act by two thirds of each House

Mͭ GORHAM did not see the propriety of it. Is it meant to require a greater proportion of votes? He desired it to be remembered that the Eastern States had no motive to Union but a commercial one. They were able to protect themselves. They were not afraid of external danger, and did not need the aid of the Southͫ States.

Mͭ WILSON wished for a commitment in order to reduce the proportion of votes required.

Mͭ ELSWORTH was for taking the plan as it is. This widening of opinions has [5] a threatening aspect. If we do not agree on this middle & moderate ground he was afraid we should lose two States, with such others as may be disposed to stand aloof, should fly into a variety of shapes & directions, and most probably into several confederations and not without bloodshed.

On [6] Question for committing 6 Sect. as to [4] navigation act to a

---

[1] The word " be " is here inserted in the transcript.
[2] See page 341.
[3] In the transcript the vote reads: " Connecticut, New Jersey, Maryland, Virginia, North Carolina, South Carolina, Georgia, aye—7; New Hampshire, Pennsylvania, Delaware, no—3; Massachusetts, absent."
[4] The word " a " is here inserted in the transcript.
[5] The word " had " is substituted in the transcript for " has."
[6] The word " the " is here inserted in the transcript.

member from each State—N. H. ay. Mas. ay. C^t no. N. J. no. P^a ay. Del. ay. M^d ay. V^a ay. N. C. ay. S. C. ay. Geo. ay.[1]

The Committee appointed were Mr Langdon, King, Johnson, Livingston, Clymer, Dickenson, L. Martin, Madison, Williamson, C. C. Pinkney, & Baldwin.

To this committee were referred also the two clauses abovementioned, of the 4 & 5. Sect: of Art. 7.

Mr RUTLIDGE, from the Committee to whom were referred on the 18 & 20th instant the propositions of Mr Madison & Mr Pinkney, made the Report following.—

[Here insert the Report from the Journal of the Convention of this date.] [2]

["The committee report, that in their opinion the following additions should be made to the report now before the convention namely,

"At the end of the first clause of the first section of the seventh article add, 'for payment of the debts and necessary expenses of the United States; provided that no law for raising any branch of revenue, except what may be specially appropriated for the payment of interest on debts or loans, shall continue in force for more than   years.'

"At the end of the second clause, second section, seventh article, add, 'and with Indians, within the limits of any state, not subject to the laws thereof.'

"At the end of the sixteenth clause of the second section, seventh article, add, 'and to provide, as may become necessary, from time to time, for the well managing and securing the common property and general interests and welfare of the United States in such manner as shall not interfere with the governments of individual states, in matters which respect only their internal police, or for which their individual authorities [3] may be competent.'

"At the end of the first section, tenth article, add, 'he shall be of the age of thirty five years, and a citizen of the United States, and shall have been an inhabitant thereof for twenty one years.'

"After the second section of the tenth article, insert the following as a third section:

" 'The President of the United States shall have a privy council, which shall consist of the president of the senate, the speaker of the house of representatives, the chief justice of the supreme court, and the principal officer in the respective departments of foreign affairs, domestic affairs, war, marine, and finance, as such departments of office shall from time to time be established, whose duty it

---

[1] In the transcript the vote reads: "New Hampshire, Massachusetts, Pennsylvania, Delaware, Maryland, Virginia, North Carolina, South Carolina, Georgia, aye—9; Connecticut, New Jersey, no—2."

[2] Madison's direction is omitted in the transcript.

[3] The transcript uses the word "authorities" in the singular.

shall be to advise him in matters respecting the execution of his
office, which he shall think proper to lay before them: but their
advice shall not conclude him, nor affect his responsibility for the
measures which he shall adopt.'

"At the end of the second section of the eleventh article, add,
'the judges of the supreme court shall be triable by the senate, on
impeachment by the house of representatives.'

"Between the fourth and fifth lines of the third section of the
eleventh article, after the word 'controversies,' insert 'between the
United States and an individual state, or the United States and an
individual person.' "] [1]

A motion to rescind the order of the House respecting the hours
of meeting & adjourning, was negatived:

Mass: P? Del. Mar^d .... ay [2]

N. H. Con: N. J. V? N. C. S. C. Geo. no [3]

M? GERRY & M? M?HENRY moved to insert after the 2^d sect.[4]
Art: 7, the Clause following, to wit, "The Legislature shall pass
no bill of attainder nor any ex post facto law." *

M? GERRY urged the necessity of this prohibition, which he said
was greater in the National than the State Legislature, because the
number of members in the former being fewer [5] were on that account
the more to be feared.

M? Gov? MORRIS thought the precaution as to ex post facto laws
unnecessary; but essential as to bills of attainder

M? ELSEWORTH contended that there was no lawyer, no civilian
who would not say that ex post facto laws were void of themselves.
It can not then be necessary to prohibit them.

M? WILSON was against inserting any thing in the Constitution
as to ex post facto laws. It will bring reflexions on the Constitution—
and proclaim that we are ignorant of the first principles of Legislation, or are constituting a Government which [6] will be so.

The question being divided, The first part of the motion relating
to bills of attainder was agreed to nem. contradicente.

On the second part relating to ex post facto laws—

M? CARROL remarked that experience overruled all other calcula-

---

* The proceedings on this motion involving the two questions on "attainders
& ex post facto laws," are not so fully stated in the Printed Journal.

---

[1] *Journal, Acts and Proceedings of the Convention . . . which formed the
Constitution of the United States* (1819), p. 277.

[2] The figure " 4 " is here inserted in the transcript.

[3] The figure " 7 " is here inserted in the transcript.

[4] The word " of " is here inserted in the transcript.

[5] The word " they " is here inserted in the transcript.

[6] The word " that " is substituted in the transcript for " which."

tions. It had proved that in whatever light they might be viewed by civilians or others, the State Legislatures had passed them, and they had taken effect.

M: WILSON. If these prohibitions in the State Constitutions have no effect, it will be useless to insert them in this Constitution. Besides, both sides will agree to the principle, &[1] will differ as to its application.

M: WILLIAMSON. Such a prohibitory clause is in the Constitution of N. Carolina, and tho it has been violated, it has done good there & may do good here, because the Judges can take hold of it.

Doc: JOHNSON thought the clause unnecessary, and implying an improper suspicion of the National Legislature.

M: RUTLIDGE was in favor of the clause.

On the question for inserting the prohibition of ex post facto laws.

N. H. ay. Mas. ay. Con: no. N. J. no. P: no. Del. ay. M: ay. Virg: ay N. C. div: S. C. ay. Geo. ay.[2]

The report of the committee of 5. made by M: Rutlidge, was taken up & then postponed that each member might furnish himself with a copy.

The Report of the Comittee of Eleven delivered in & entered on the Journal of the 21st inst. was then taken up. and the first clause containing the words " The Legislature of the U. S. *shall have power to fulfil the engagements which have been entered into by Congress* " being under consideration,

M: ELSWORTH argued that they were unnecessary. The U. S. heretofore entered into Engagements by Cong: who were their agents. They will hereafter be bound to fulfil them by their new agents.

M: RANDOLPH thought such a provision necessary: for though the U. States will be bound, the new Gov: will have no authority in the case unless it be given to them.

M: MADISON thought it necessary to give the authority in order to prevent misconstruction. He mentioned the attempts made by the Debtors to British subjects to shew that contracts under the old Government, were dissolved by the Revolution which destroyed the political identity of the Society.

M: GERRY thought it essential that some explicit provision should

---

[1] The word " but " is substituted in the transcript for " &."
[2] In the transcript the vote reads: " New Hampshire, Massachusetts, Delaware, Maryland, Virginia, South Carolina, Georgia, aye—7; Connecticut, New Jersey, Pennsylvania, no—3; North Carolina, divided."

be made on this subject, so that no pretext might remain for getting rid of the public engagements.

M̃ Goṽᵗ Morris moved by way of amendment to substitute— "The Legislature *shall* discharge the debts & fulfil the engagements, of the U. States."

It was moved to vary the amendment by striking out " discharge the debts " & to insert " liquidate the claims," which being negatived,

The amendment moved by M̃ᵗ Goṽᵗ Morris was agreed to all the States being in the affirmative.

It was moved & 2ᵈᵉᵈ to strike the following words out of the 2ᵈ clause of the report "and the authority of training the Militia according to the discipline prescribed by the U. S." Before a question was taken

The House adjourned

IN CONVENTION THURSDAY AUG: 23. 1787 [1]

The Report of the Committee of Eleven made Aug: 21.[2] being taken up, and the following clause being under consideration to wit " To make laws for organizing, arming & disciplining the Militia, and for governing such part [3] of them as may be employed in the service of the U. S. reserving to the States respectively, the appointment of the officers, and authority of training the militia according to the discipline prescribed—"

M̃ᵗ Sherman moved to strike out the last member— "and authority of training &c. He thought it unnecessary. The States will have this authority of course if not given up.

M̃ᵗ Elsworth doubted the propriety of striking out the sentence. The reason assigned applies as well to the other reservation of the appointment to offices. He remarked at the same time that the term discipline was of vast extent and might be so expounded as to include all power on the subject.

M̃ᵗ King, by way of explanation, said that by *organizing*, the Committee meant, proportioning the officers & men—by *arming,* specifying the kind size & caliber of arms—& by *disciplining* prescribing the manual exercise evolutions &c.

---

[1] The year " 1787 " is omitted in the transcript.
[2] The words " the twenty-first of August " are substituted in the transcript for " Aug: 21."
[3] The transcript uses the word "part" in the plural.

M⸢ SHERMAN withdrew his motion

M⸢ GERRY. This power in the U. S. as explained is making the States drill-sergeants. He had as lief let the Citizens of Massachussets be disarmed, as to take the command from the States, and subject them to the Gen⸥ Legislature. It would be regarded as a system of Despotism.

M⸢ MADISON observed that *"arming"* as explained did not did not extend to furnishing arms; nor the term "disciplining" to penalties & Courts Martial for enforcing them.

M⸢ KING added, to his former explanation that *arming* meant not only to provide for uniformity of arms, but included [1] authority to regulate the modes of furnishing, either by the Militia themselves, the State Governments, or the National Treasury: that *laws* for disciplining, must involve penalties and every thing necessary for enforcing penalties.

M⸢ DAYTON moved to postpone the paragraph, in order to take up the following proposition

" To establish an uniform & general system of discipline for the Militia of these States, and to make laws for organizing, arming, disciplining & governing *such part of them as may be employed in the service of the U. S.,* reserving to the States respectively the appointment of the officers, and all authority over the Militia not herein given to the General Government"

On the question to postpone in favor of this proposition: it passed in the Negative

N. H. no. Mas no. C⸥ no. N. J. ay. P. no. Del. no. Mary⸤ ay. V⸤ no. N. C. no. S. C. no. Geo. ay.[2]

M⸢ ELSWORTH & M⸢ SHERMAN moved to postpone the 2⸤ clause in favor of the following "To establish an uniformity of arms, exercise & organization for the Militia, and to provide for the Government of them when called into the service of the U. States" The object of this proposition was to refer the plan for the Militia to the General Gov⸤ but [3] leave the execution of it to the State Gov⸤⸣

M⸢ LANGDON said He could not understand the jealousy expressed by some Gentleman.[4] The General & State Gov⸤⸣ were not enemies to each other, but different institutions for the good of the people of America. As one of the people he could say, the National Gov⸤

---

[1] The word "the" is here inserted in the transcript.
[2] In the transcript the vote reads: "New Jersey, Maryland, Georgia, aye—3; New Hampshire, Massachusetts, Connecticut, Pennsylvania, Delaware, Virginia, North Carolina, South Carolina, no—8."
[3] The word "to" is here inserted in the transcript.
[4] The word "gentleman" is used in the plural in the transcript.

is mine, the State Gov.̱ is mine. In transferring power from one to the other, I only take out of my left hand what it can not so well use, and put it into my right hand where it can be better used.

M.̱ GERRY thought it was rather taking out of the right hand & putting it into the left. Will any man say that liberty will be as safe in the hands of eighty or a hundred men taken from the whole continent, as in the hands of two or three hundred taken from a single State.

M.̱ DAYTON was against so absolute a uniformity. In some States there ought to be a greater proportion of cavalry than in others. In some places rifles would be most proper, in others muskets &c.

Gen.̱ PINKNEY preferred the clause reported by the Committee, extending the meaning of it to the case of fines &c.

M.̱ MADISON. The primary object is to secure an effectual discipline of the Militia. This will no more be done if left to the States separately than the requisitions have been hitherto paid by them. The States neglect their Militia now, and the more they are consolidated into one nation, the less each will rely on its own interior provisions for its safety & the less prepare its Militia for that purpose; in like manner as the militia of a State would have been still more neglected than it has been if each County had been independently charged with the care of its Militia. The Discipline of the Militia is evidently a *National* concern, and ought to be provided for in the *National* Constitution.

M.̱ L. MARTIN was confident that the States would never give up the power over the Militia; and that, if they were to do so the militia would be less attended to by the Gen.̱ than by the State Governments.

M.̱ RANDOLPH asked what danger there could be that the Militia could be brought into the field and made to commit suicide on themselves. This is a power that can not from its nature be abused, unless indeed the whole mass should be corrupted. He was for trammelling the Gen.̱ Gov.̱ wherever there was danger, but here there could be none. He urged this as an essential point; observing that the Militia were every where neglected by the State Legislatures, the members of which courted popularity too much to enforce a proper discipline. Leaving the appointment of officers to the States protects the people ag.ˢᵗ every apprehension that could produce murmur.

On [1] Question on M.̱ Elsworth's Motion

---

[1] The word "the" is here inserted in the transcript.

N. H. no. Mas. no. C! ay. N. J. no. P? no. Del. no. M⁴ no.
V? no. N. C. no. S. C. no. Geo. no.¹

A motion was then made to recommit the 2ᵈ clause which was negatived.

On the question to agree to the 1ˢᵗ part of the clause, namely

"To make laws for organizing arming & disciplining the Militia, and for governing such part of them as may be employed in the service of the U. S."

N. H ay. Mas. ay. C! no. N. J. ay. P? ay. Del. ay. M⁴ no.
V? ay. N. C. ay. S. C. ay. Geo. ay.²

M! MADISON moved to amend the next part of the clause so as to read " reserving to the States respectively, the appointment of the officers, *under the rank of General officers* "

M! SHERMAN considered this as absolutely inadmissible. He said that if the people should be so far asleep as to allow the most influential officers of the militia to be appointed by the Gen! Government, every man of discernment would rouse them by sounding the alarm to them.

M! GERRY. Let us at once destroy the State Gov⁺ have an Executive for life or hereditary, and a proper Senate, and then there would be some consistency in giving full powers to the Gen! Gov⁺ but as the States are not to be abolished, he wondered at the attempts that were made to give powers inconsistent with their existence. He warned the Convention ag⁺ pushing the experiment too far. Some people will support a plan of vigorous Government at every risk. Others of a more democratic cast will oppose it with equal determination, and a Civil war may be produced by the conflict.

M! MADISON. As the greatest danger is that of disunion of the States, it is necessary to guard ag⁺ it by sufficient powers to the Common Gov⁺ and as the greatest danger to liberty is from large standing armies, it is best to prevent them, by an effectual provision for a good Militia.

On the Question to agree to M! Madison's motion

N. H. ay. Mas. no. C! no. N. J. no. P? no. Del. no. M⁴ no.
V? no. N. C. no. S. C. ay. Geo.* ay.³

* In the printed Journal, Geo: no.

---

¹ In the transcript the vote reads: " Connecticut, aye; the other ten States, no."
² In the transcript the vote reads: "New Hampshire, Massachusetts, New Jersey, Pennsylvania, Delaware, Virginia, North Carolina, South Carolina, Georgia, aye—9; Connecticut, Maryland, no—2."
³ In the transcript the vote reads: "New Hampshire, South Carolina, Georgia,* aye—3; Massachusetts, Connecticut, New Jersey, Pennsylvania, Delaware, Maryland, Virginia, North Carolina, no—8."

On the question to agree to the "reserving to the States the appointment of the officers." It was agreed to nem: contrad:

On the question on the clause "and the authority of training the Militia according to the discipline prescribed by the U. S—"

N. H. ay. Mas. ay. C! ay. N. J. ay. P! ay. Del. no. M⁴ ay. V! no. N. C. ay. S. C. no. Geo. no.[1]

On the question to agree to Art. VII. Sect. 7.[2] as reported It passed nem. contrad:

M! PINKNEY urged the necessity of preserving foreign Ministers & other officers of the U. S. independent of external influence and moved to insert, after Art VII Sect 7. the clause following—"No person holding any office of profit or trust[3] under the U. S. shall without the consent of the Legislature, accept of any present, emolument, office or title of any kind whatever, from any King, Prince or foreign State which passed nem: contrad.

M! RUTLIDGE moved to amend Art: VIII[2] to read as follows,

"This Constitution & the laws of the U. S. made in pursuance thereof, and all Treaties made under the authority of the U. S. shall be the supreme law of the several States and of their citizens and inhabitants; and the Judges in the several States shall be bound thereby in their decisions, any thing in the Constitutions or laws of the several States, to the contrary notwithstanding."

which was agreed to nem: contrad:

Art: IX[2] being next for consideration,

M! Gov! MORRIS argued ag!ᵗ the appointment of officers by the Senate. He considered the body as too numerous for the[4] purpose; as subject to cabal; and as devoid of responsibility. If Judges were to be tried by the Senate according to a late report of a Committee it was particularly wrong to let the Senate have the filling of vacancies which its own decrees were to create.

M! WILSON was of the same opinion & for like reasons.

The[5] art IX being waived and art VII. sect 1.[6] resumed,

M! Gov! MORRIS moved to strike the following words out of the

---

[1] In the transcript the vote reads: "New Hampshire, Massachusetts, Connecticut, New Jersey, Pennsylvania, Maryland, North Carolina, aye—7; Delaware, Virginia, South Carolina, Georgia, no—4."

[2] See page 342.

[3] The words "profit or trust" are transposed to read "trust or profit" in the transcript.

[4] The word "that" is substituted in the transcript for "the."

[5] The word "the" is crossed out in the transcript.

[6] See page 340.

18 clause " enforce treaties " as being superfluous, since treaties were to be " laws "— which was agreed to nem: contrad:

M: Gov: Morris moved to alter [1] 1.st part. of [1] 18. clause sect. 1. art. VII [2] so as to read " to provide for calling forth the Militia to execute the laws of the Union, suppress insurrections and repel invasions."

which was agreed to nem: contrad

On the question then to agree to the 18 clause of Sect. 1. art: 7. as amended it passed in the affirmative nem: contradicente.

M: C- Pinkney moved to add as an additional power to be vested in the Legislature of the U. S. " To negative all laws passed by the several States interfering in the opinion of the Legislature with the general interests and harmony of the Union; provided that two thirds of the members of each House assent to the same"

This principle he observed had formerly been agreed to. He considered the precaution as essentially necessary: The objection drawn from the predominance of the large States had been removed by the equality established in the Senate. M: Broome 2.ded the proposition.

M: Sherman thought it unnecessary; the laws of the General Government being Supreme & paramount to the State laws according to the plan, as it now stands.

M: Madison proposed that it should be committed. He had been from the beginning a friend to the principle; but thought the modification might be made better.

M: Mason wished to know how the power was to be exercised. Are all laws whatever to be brought up? Is no road nor bridge to be established without the Sanction of the General Legislature? Is this to sit constantly in order to receive & revise the State Laws? He did not mean by these remarks to condemn the expedient, but he was apprehensive that great objections would lie ag.st it.

M: Williamson thought it unnecessary, & having been already decided, a revival of the question was a waste of time.

M: Wilson considered this as the key-stone wanted to compleat the wide arch of Government, we are raising. The power of self-defence had been urged as necessary for the State Governments. It was equally necessary for the General Government. The firmness of Judges is not of itself sufficient. Something further is requisite. It will be better to prevent the passage of an improper law, than to declare it void when passed.

---

[1] The word " the " is here inserted in the transcript.
[2] The transcript omits " sect. 1. art. VII."

M.ʳ RUTLIDGE. If nothing else, this alone would damn and ought to damn the Constitution. Will any State ever agree to be bound hand & foot in this manner. It is worse than making mere corporations of them whose bye laws would not be subject to this shackle.

M.ʳ ELSEWORTH observed that the power contended for w.ᵈ require either that all laws of the State Legislatures should previously to their taking effect be transmitted to the Gen.ˡ Legislature, or be repealable by the Latter; or that the State Executives should be appointed by the Gen.ˡ Government, and have a controul over the State laws. If the last was meditated let it be declared.

M.ʳ PINKNEY declared that he thought the State Executives ought to be so appointed with such a controul, & that it would be so provided if another Convention should take place.

M.ʳ GOVERN.ᵗ MORRIS did not see the utility or practicability of the proposition of M.ʳ Pinkney, but wished it to be referred to the consideration of a Committee.

M.ʳ LANGDON was in favor of the proposition. He considered it as resolvable into the question whether the extent of the National Constitution was to be judged of by the Gen.ˡ or the State Governments.

On the question for commitment, it passed in the negative.

N. H. ay. Mas.ᵗˢ no. Con.ᵗ no. N. J. no. P.ᵃ ay. Del: ay. M.ᵈ ay. V.ᵃ ay. N. C. no. S. C. no. Geo. no.[1]

M.ʳ PINKNEY then withdrew his proposition.

The 1.ˢᵗ sect. of art: VII [2] being so amended as to read " The Legislature *shall* fulfil the engagements and discharge the debts of the U. S. & shall have the power to lay & collect taxes duties imposts & excises," was agreed to.

M.ʳ BUTLER expressed his dissatisfaction lest it should compel payment as well to the Blood-suckers who had speculated on the distresses of others, as to those who had fought & bled for their country. He would be ready he said tomorrow to vote for a discrimination between those classes of people, and gave notice that he should [3] move for a reconsideration.

Art IX. sect. 1.[4] being resumed, to wit " The Senate of the U. S. shall have power to make treaties, and to appoint Ambassadors, and Judges of the Supreme Court."

---

[1] In the transcript the vote reads: "New Hampshire, Pennsylvania, Delaware, Maryland, Virginia, aye—5; Massachusetts, Connecticut, New Jersey, North Carolina, South Carolina, Georgia, no—6."

[2] The phrase "The first clause of article 7. section 1" is substituted in the transcript for "The 1ˢᵗ sect. of art: VII."

[3] The word "would" is substituted in the transcript for "should."

[4] See page 342.

M.̷ MADISON observed that the Senate represented the States alone, and that for this as well as other obvious reasons it was proper that the President should be an agent in Treaties.

M.̷ GOV.̷ MORRIS did not know that he should agree to refer the making of Treaties to the Senate at all, but for the present w.̷ move to add, as an amendment to the section after "Treaties"—[1] "but no Treaty shall be binding on the U. S. which is not ratified by a law."

M.̷ MADISON suggested the inconvenience of requiring a legal *ratification* of treaties of alliance for the purposes of war &c &c

M.̷ GHORUM. Many other disadvantages must be experienced if treaties of peace & all negociations are to be previously ratified— and if not previously, the Ministers would be at a loss how to proceed. What would be the case in G. Britain if the King were to proceed in this manner. American Ministers must go abroad not instructed by the same Authority (as will be the case with other Ministers) which is to ratify their proceedings.

M.̷ GOV.̷ MORRIS. As to treaties of alliance, they will oblige foreign powers to send their Ministers here, the very thing we should wish for. Such treaties could not be otherwise made, if his amendment sh.̷ succeed. In general he was not solicitous to multiply & facilitate Treaties. He wished none to be made with G. Britain, till she should be at war. Then a good bargain might be made with her. So with other foreign powers. The more difficulty in making treaties, the more value will be set on them.

M.̷ WILSON. In the most important Treaties, the King of G Britain being obliged to resort to Parliament for the execution of them, is under the same fetters as the amendment of M.̷ Morris will impose on the Senate. It was refused yesterday to permit even the Legislature to lay duties on exports. Under the clause, without the amendment, the Senate alone can make a Treaty, requiring all the Rice of S. Carolina to be sent to some one particular port.

M.̷ DICKINSON concurred in the amendment, as most safe and proper, tho' he was sensible it was unfavorable to the little States; w.̷ would otherwise have an *equal* share in making Treaties.

Doc.̷ JOHNSON thought there was something of solecism in saying that the acts of a Minister with plenipotentiary powers from one Body, should depend for ratification on another Body. The Example of the King of G. B. was not parellel. Full & compleat power was vested in him. If the Parliament should fail to provide the necessary means of execution, the Treaty would be violated.

---

[1] The words "the following" are here inserted in the transcript.

M: GHORUM in answer to M: Gov: MORRIS, said that negociations on the spot were not to be desired by us, especially if the whole Legislature is to have any thing to do with Treaties. It will be generally influenced by two or three men, who will be corrupted by the Ambassadors here. In such a Government as ours, it is necessary to guard against the Government itself being seduced.

M: RANDOLPH observing that almost every Speaker had made objections to the clause as it stood, moved in order to a further consideration of the subject, that the Motion of M: Gov: Morris should be postponed, and on this question It was lost the States being equally divided.

Mass.ᵗˢ no. Con.ᵗ no. N. J. ay. Pen.ᵃ ay. Del. ay. M.ᵈ ay. V.ᵃ ay. N. C. no. S. C. no. Geo. no.[1]

On M: Gov: Morris Motion

Mas.ᵗˢ no. Con.ᵗ no. N. J. no. P.ᵃ ay. Del. no. M.ᵈ no. V.ᵃ no. N. C. div.ᵈ S. C. no. Geo. no.[2]

The several clauses of Sect: 1. Art IX, were then separately postponed after inserting " and other public Ministers " next after "Ambassadors."

M: MADISON hinted for consideration, whether a distinction might not be made between different sorts of Treaties—Allowing the President & Senate to make Treaties eventual and of Alliance for limited terms—and requiring the concurrence of the whole Legislature in other Treaties.

The 1ˢᵗ Sect art IX. was finally referred nem: con: to the committee of Five, and the House then

Adjourned

FRIDAY AUGUST 24. 1787.[3] IN CONVENTION

Governour LIVINGSTON, from the Committee of Eleven, to whom were referred the two remaining clauses of the 4ᵗʰ Sect & the 5 & 6 Sect: of the 7ᵗʰ art:[4] delivered in the following Report:

"Strike out so much of the 4ᵗʰ Sect: as was referred to the Committee and insert—"The migration or importation of such per-

---

[1] In the transcript the vote reads: "New Jersey, Pennsylvania, Delaware, Maryland, Virginia, aye—5; Massachusetts, Connecticut, North Carolina, South Carolina, Georgia, no—5."

[2] In the transcript the vote reads: "Pennsylvania, aye—1; Massachusetts, Connecticut, New Jersey, Delaware, Maryland, Virginia, South Carolina, Georgia, no—8."

[3] The year "1787" is omitted in the transcript.

[4] See page 341.

sons as the several States now existing shall think proper to admit, shall not be prohibited by the Legislature prior to the year 1800, but a tax or duty may be imposed on such migration or importation at a rate not exceeding the average of the duties laid on imports."

" The 5 Sect: to remain as in the Report "

" The 6 Sect to be stricken out "

Mʳ BUTLER, according to notice, moved that clause 1ˢᵗ sect. 1. of Art VII, as to the discharge of debts, be reconsidered tomorrow. He dwelt on the division of opinion concerning the domestic debts, and the different pretensions of the different classes of holders. Genˡ PINKNEY 2ᵈᵉᵈ him.

Mʳ RANDOLPH wished for a reconsideration in order to better the expression, and to provide for the case of the State debts as is done by Congress.

On the question for reconsidering

N. H. no. Mas: ay. Conᵗ ay N. J. ay. Penᵃ absent. Del. ay Mᵈ no. Vᵃ ay. N. C. absent, S. C. ay. Geo. ay.[1]—and tomorrow assigned for the reconsideration.

Sect: 2 & 3 of art: IX [2] being taken up,

Mʳ RUTLIDGE said this provision for deciding controversies between the States was necessary under the Confederation, but will be rendered unnecessary by the National Judiciary now to be established, and moved to strike it out.

Docʳ JOHNSON 2ᵈᵉᵈ the Motion

Mʳ SHERMAN concurred: so did Mʳ DAYTON.

Mʳ WILLIAMSON was for postponing instead of striking out, in order to consider whether this might not be a good provision, in cases where the Judiciary were interested or too closely connected with the parties.

Mʳ GHORUM had doubts as to striking out. The Judges might be connected with the States being parties—He was inclined to think the mode proposed in the clause would be more satisfactory than to refer such cases to the Judiciary.

On the Question for postponing the 2ᵈ & 3ᵈ Section, it passed in the negative

N. H. ay. Masᵗˢ no. Conᵗ no N. J. no. Penᵃ absᵗ Del. no. Mᵈ no. Vᵃ no. N. C. ay. S. C. no. Geo. ay.[3]

---

[1] In the transcript the vote reads: "Massachusetts, Connecticut, New Jersey, Delaware, Virginia, South Carolina, Georgia, aye—7; New Hampshire, Maryland, no—2; Pennsylvania, North Carolina, absent."

[2] See pages 342 and 343.

[3] In the transcript the vote reads: "New Hampshire, North Carolina, Georgia, aye—3; Massachusetts, Connecticut, New Jersey, Delaware, Maryland, Virginia, South Carolina, no—7; Pennsylvania, absent."

M⁺ WILSON urged the striking out, the Judiciary being a better provision.

On Question for striking out [1] 2 & 3 Sections [2] Art: IX

N. H. ay. Mas. ay. C⁺ ay. N. J. ay. P⁺ abs⁺ Del. ay. M⁴ ay. V⁺ ay. N. C. no. S. C. ay. Geo. no.[3]

Art X. sect. 1.[4] " The executive power of the U. S. shall be vested in a single person. His stile shall be " The President of the U. S. of America " and his title shall be " His Excellency." He shall be elected by ballot by the Legislature. He shall hold his office during the term of seven years; but shall not be elected a second time.

On the question for vesting the power in a *single person*. It was agreed to nem: con: So also on the *Stile* and *title*.

M⁺ RUTLIDGE moved to insert " joint " before the word " ballot," as the most convenient mode of electing.

M⁺ SHERMAN objected to it as depriving the *States* represented in the *Senate* of the negative intended them in that house.

M⁺ GHORUM said it was wrong to be considering at every turn whom the Senate would represent. The public good was the true object to be kept in view. Great delay and confusion would ensue if the two Houses sh⁴ vote separately, each having a negative on the choice of the other.

M⁺ DAYTON. It might be well for those not to consider how the Senate was constituted, whose interest it was to keep it out of sight.— If the amendment should be agreed to, a *joint* [5] ballot would in fact give the appointment to one House. He could never agree to the clause with such an amendment. There could be no doubt of the two Houses separately concurring in the same person for President. The importance & necessity of the case would ensure a concurrence.

M⁺ CARROL moved to strike out " by the Legislature " and insert "by the people." M⁺ WILSON 2ᵈᵉᵈ him & on the question

N. H. no. Mass⁺ no. Con⁺ no. N. J. no. P⁺ ay. Del. ay. M⁴ no. V⁺ no N. C. no. S. C. no. Geo. no.[6]

M⁺ BREARLY was opposed to the motion for [7] inserting the word

---

[1] The word " the " is here inserted in the transcript.
[2] The word " of " is here inserted in the transcript.
[3] In the transcript the vote reads: " New Hampshire, Massachusetts, Connecticut, New Jersey, Delaware, Maryland, Virginia, South Carolina, aye—8; North Carolina, Georgia, no—2; Pennsylvania, absent."
[4] See page 343.
[5] The transcript does not italicize the word " *joint.* "
[6] In the transcript the vote reads: " Pennsylvania, Delaware, aye—2; New Hampshire, Massachusetts, Connecticut, New Jersey, Maryland, Virginia, North Carolina, South Carolina, Georgia, no—9."
[7] The words " the motion for " are omitted in the transcript.

" joint." The argument that the small States should not put their hands into the pockets of the large ones did not apply in this case.

M.ʳ WILSON urged the reasonableness of giving the larger States a larger share of the appointment, and the danger of delay from a disagreement of the two Houses. He remarked also that the Senate had peculiar powers balancing the advantage given by a joint balot in this case to the other branch of the Legislature.

M.ʳ LANGDON. This general officer ought to be elected by the joint & general voice. In N. Hampshire the mode of separate votes by the two Houses was productive of great difficulties. The negative of the Senate would hurt the feelings of the man elected by the votes of the other branch. He was for inserting " joint " tho' unfavorable to N. Hampshire as a small State.

M.ⁱ WILSON remarked that as the President of the Senate was to be President of the U. S. that Body in cases of vacancy might have an interest in throwing dilatory obstacles in the way, if its separate concurrence should be required.

M.ʳ MADISON. If the amendment be agreed to the rule of voting will give to the largest State, compared with the smallest, an influence as 4 to 1 only, altho the population is as 10 to 1. This surely can not be unreasonable as the President is to act for the *people* not for the *States*. The President of the *Senate* also is to be occasionally President of the U. S. and by his negative alone can make ¾ of the other branch necessary to the passage of a law. This is another advantage enjoyed by the Senate.

On the question for inserting " joint," it passed in the affirmative

N. H. ay. Mas.ᵗˢ ay. C.ᵗ no. N. J. no. P.ᵃ ay. Del. ay. M.ᵈ no. V.ᵃ ay. N. C. ay. S. C. ay. Geo. no.[1]

M.ʳ DAYTON then moved to insert, after the word " Legislatures "[2] the words "each State having one vote" M.ʳ BREARLEY 2.ᵈᵉᵈ him, and on the question it passed in the negative

N. H. no. Mas. no. C.ᵗ ay. N. J. ay. P.ᵃ no. Del. ay. M.ᵈ ay. V.ᵃ no. N. C. no. S. C. no. Geo. ay.[3]

M.ʳ PINKNEY moved to insert after the word " Legislature " the words " to which election a majority of the votes of the members present shall be required" &

---

[1] In the transcript the vote reads: " New Hampshire, Massachusetts, Pennsylvania, Delaware, Virginia, North Carolina, South Carolina, aye—7; Connecticut, New Jersey, Maryland, Georgia, no—4."

[2] In the transcript the word " Legislatures " is in the singular.

[3] In the transcript the vote reads: " Connecticut, New Jersey, Delaware, Maryland, Georgia, aye—5; New Hampshire, Massachusetts, Pennsylvania, Virginia, North Carolina, South Carolina, no—6."

On this question, it passed in the affirmative

N. H. ay. Mas. ay. C: ay. N. J. no. P: ay. Del. ay. M⁴ ay. V: ay. N. C. ay. S. C. ay. Geo. ay.¹

M: READ moved " that in case the numbers for the two highest in votes should be equal, then the President of the Senate shall have an additional casting vote," which was disagreed to by a general negative.

M: Gov: MORRIS opposed the election of the President by the Legislature. He dwelt on the danger of rendering the Executive uninterested in maintaining the rights of his Station, as leading to Legislative tyranny. If the Legislature have the Executive dependent on them, they can perpetuate & support their usurpations by the influence of tax-gatherers & other officers, by fleets armies &c. Cabal & corruption are attached to that mode of election: so also² is ineligibility a second time. Hence the Executive is interested in Courting popularity in the Legislature by sacrificing his Executive Rights; & then he can go into that Body, after the expiration of his Executive office, and enjoy there the fruits of his policy. To these considerations he added that rivals would be continually intrigueing to oust the President from his place. To guard against all these evils he moved that the President "shall be chosen by Electors to be chosen by the People of the several States" M: CARROL 2ᵈᵉᵈ him & on the question it passed in the negative.

N. H. no. Mas. no. C: ay. N. J. ay. P: ay. Del. ay. M⁴ no. V: ay. N. C. no. S. C. no. Geo. no.³

M: DAYTON moved to postpone the consideration of the two last clauses of Sect. 1. art. X. which was disagreed to without a count of the States.

M: BROOME moved to refer the two clauses to a Committee of a member from each State, & on the question, it failed the States being equally divided

N. H. no. Mas. no. C: div⁴ N. J. ay. P: ay. Del. ay. M⁴ ay. V: ay. N. C. no. S. C. no. Geo. no.⁴

On the question taken on the first part of M: Gov: Morris's

---

¹ In the transcript the vote reads: "New Hampshire, Massachusetts, Connecticut, Pennsylvania, Delaware, Maryland, Virginia, North Carolina, South Carolina, Georgia, aye—10; New Jersey, no—1."

² The word "also" is omitted in the transcript.

³ In the transcript the vote reads: "Connecticut, New Jersey, Pennsylvania, Delaware, Virginia, aye—5; New Hampshire, Massachusetts, Maryland North Carolina, South Carolina, Georgia, no—6."

⁴ In the transcript the vote reads: "New Jersey, Pennsylvania, Delaware, Maryland, Virginia, aye—5; New Hampshire, Massachusetts, North Carolina, South Carolina, Georgia, no—5; Connecticut, divided."

Motion towit "shall be chosen by electors" as an abstract question, it failed the States being equally divided.

N. H. no. Mas. abs! C! div! N. Jersey ay. P! ay. Del. ay. M! div! V! ay. N. C. no. S. C. no. Geo. no.[1]

The consideration of the remaining clauses of Sect 1. art X. was then postponed till tomorrow at the instance of the Deputies of New Jersey.

Sect. 2. Art: X[2] being taken up, the word information was transposed & inserted after " Legislature "

On motion of M! Gov! Morris, " he may " was struck out, & "and" inserted before "recommend" in clause 2! sect 2! art: X. in order to make it the *duty* of the President to recommend, & thence prevent umbrage or cavil at his doing it.

M! Sherman objected to the sentence " and shall appoint officers in all cases not otherwise provided for by[3] this Constitution." He admitted it to be proper that many officers in the Executive Department should be so appointed—but contended that many ought not, as general officers in the army in time of peace &c. Herein lay the corruption in G. Britain. If the Executive can model the army, he may set up an absolute Government; taking advantage of the close of a war and an army commanded by his creatures. James 2! was not obeyed by his officers because they had been appointed by his predecessors not by himself. He moved to insert " or by law " after the word " Constitution."

On Motion of M! Madison "officers" was struck out and "to offices " inserted, in order to obviate doubts that he might appoint officers without a previous creation of the offices by the Legislature.

On the question for inserting "or by law as moved by M! Sherman

N. H. no. Mas. no. C! ay. N. J. no. Pen! no. Del. no. M! no. V! no. N. C. absent. S. C. no. Geo. no.[4]

M! Dickinson moved to strike out the words " and shall appoint to offices in all cases not otherwise provided for by this Constitution" and insert—" and shall appoint to all offices established by this Constitution, except in cases herein otherwise provided for, and to all offices which may hereafter be created by law."

M! Randolph observed that the power of appointments was a

---

[1] In the transcript the vote reads: " New Jersey, Pennsylvania, Delaware, Virginia, aye—4; New Hampshire, North Carolina, South Carolina, Georgia, no—4; Connecticut, Maryland, divided; Massachusetts, absent."

[2] See page 343.

[3] The word " in " is substituted in the transcript for " by."

[4] In the transcript the vote reads: " Connecticut, aye—1; New Hampshire, Massachusetts, New Jersey, Pennsylvania, Delaware, Maryland, Virginia, South Carolina, Georgia, no—9; North Carolina, absent."

formidable one both in the Executive & Legislative hands—and suggested whether the Legislature should not be left at liberty to refer appointments in some cases, to some State authority.

Mr DICKENSON's motion, it [1] passed in the affirmative

N. H. no. Mas. no. C^t ay. N. J. ay. P^a ay. Del. no. M^d ay. V^a ay. N. C. abs^t S. C. no. Geo. ay.[2]

Mr DICKINSON then moved to annex to his last amendment " except where by law the appointment shall be vested in the Legislatures or Executives of the several States." Mr RANDOLPH 2^{ded} the motion

Mr WILSON— If this be agreed to it will soon be a standing instruction from the State Legislatures to pass no law creating offices, unless the app^{ts} be referred to them.

Mr SHERMAN objected to " Legislatures " in the motion, which was struck out by consent of the movers.

M^r GOV^r MORRIS. This would be putting it in the power of the States to say, " You shall be viceroys but we will be viceroys over you "—

The Motion was negatived without a Count of the States—

Ordered unanimously that the order respecting the adjournment at 4 OClock be repealed, & that in future the House assemble at 10 OC. & adjourn at 3 OC.[3]

Adjourned

SATURDAY AUGUST. 25. 1787.[4] IN CONVENTION

The 1st clause of 1 Sect. of art: VII [5] being reconsidered

Col. MASON objected to the term " *shall* "—fullfil the engagements & discharge the debts &c as too strong. It may be impossible to comply with it. The Creditors should be kept in the same plight. They will in one respect be necessarily and properly in a better. The Government will be more able to pay them. The use of the term *shall* will beget speculations and increase the pestilent practice of stock-jobbing. There was a great distinction between original creditors & those who purchased fraudulently of the ignorant and distressed. He did not mean to include those who have bought

---

[1] The word " it " is omitted in the transcript.
[2] In the transcript the vote reads: " Connecticut, New Jersey, Pennsylvania, Maryland, Virginia, Georgia, aye—6; New Hampshire, Massachusetts, Delaware, South Carolina, no—4; North Carolina, absent."
[3] The letters " OC " are omitted in the transcript.
[4] The year " 1787 " is omitted in the transcript.
[5] See page 340.

Stock in open market. He was sensible of the difficulty of drawing the line in this case, but He did not wish to preclude the attempt. Even fair purchasers at 4. 5. 6. 8 for 1 did not stand on the same footing with [1] first Holders, supposing them not to be blameable. The interest they receive even in paper is equal to their purchase money. What he particularly wished was to leave the door open for buying up the securities, which he thought would be precluded by the term " shall " as requiring *nominal payment*, & which was not inconsistent with his ideas of public faith. He was afraid also the word *shall*, might extend to all the old continental paper.

M: LANGDON wished to do no more than leave the Creditors in statu quo.

M: GERRY said that for himself he had no interest in the question being not possessed of more of the securities than would, by the interest, pay his taxes. He would observe however that as the public had received the value of the literal amount, they ought to pay that value to some body. The frauds on *the soldiers* ought to have been foreseen. These poor & ignorant people could not but part with their securities. There are other creditors who will part with any thing rather than be cheated of the capital of their advances. The interest of the States he observed was different on this point, some having more, others less than their proportion of the paper. Hence the idea of a scale for reducing its value had arisen. If the public faith would admit, of which he was not clear, he would not object to a revision of the debt so far as to compel restitution to the ignorant & distressed, who have been defrauded. As to Stock-jobbers he saw no reason for the censures thrown on them. They keep up the value of the paper. Without them there would be no market.

M: BUTLER said he meant neither to increase nor diminish the security of the creditors.

M: RANDOLPH moved to postpone the clause in favor of the following " All debts contracted & engagements entered into, by or under the authority of Cong: shall be as valid ag:t the U. States under this constitution as under the Confederation."

Doc: JOHNSON. The debts are debts of the U- S- of the great Body of America. Changing the Government can not change the obligation of the U- S- which devolves of course on the New Government. Nothing was in his opinion necessary to be said. If any thing, it should be a mere declaration as moved by M: Randolph.

M: Gov: MORRIS, said he never had become a public Creditor that

---

[1] The word " the " is here inserted in the transcript.

he might urge with more propriety the compliance with public faith. He had always done so and always would, and preferr'd the term *shall* as most explicit. As to *buying up* the debt, the term *shall* was not inconsistent with it, if provision be first made for paying the interest: if not, such an expedient was a mere evasion. He was content to say nothing as the New Government would be bound of course—but would prefer the clause with the term "*shall,* because it would create many friends to the plan.

On M�500 Randolph's Motion

N. H. ay. Mas. ay. Cᵗ ay. N. J. ay. Pᵃ no Del. ay. Maryᵈ ay Vᵃ ay. N. C. ay. S. C. ay. Geo ay.[1]

M�500 SHERMAN thought it necessary to connect with the clause for laying taxes duties &c an express provision for the object of the old debts &c—and moved to add to the 1ˢᵗ clause of 1ˢᵗ sect. art VII " for the payment of said debts and for the defraying the expences that shall be incurred for the common defence and general welfare."

The proposition, as being unnecessary was disagreed to, Connecticut alone, being in the affirmative.

The Report of the Committee of eleven [see friday the 24ᵗʰ instant] being taken up,

Genˡ PINKNEY moved to strike out the words "the year eighteen hundred " as the year limiting the importation of slaves, and to insert the words " the year eighteen hundred and eight "

M�500 GHORUM 2ᵈᵉᵈ the motion

M�500 MADISON. Twenty years will produce all the mischief that can be apprehended from the liberty to import slaves. So long a term will be more dishonorable to the National [2] character than to say nothing about it in the Constitution.

On the motion; which passed in the affirmative.

N. H. ay. Mas. ay. Cᵗ ay. N. J. no. Pᵃ no. Del. no. Mᵈ ay. Vᵃ no. N. C. ay. S. C. ay. Geo. ay.[3]

M�500 Govʳ MORRIS was for making the clause read at once, " [4] importation of slaves into N. Carolina, S. Carolina & Georgia shall not be prohibited &c." This he said would be most fair and would avoid the ambiguity by which, under the power with regard to

---

[1] In the transcript the vote reads: "New Hampshire, Massachusetts, Connecticut, New Jersey, Delaware, Maryland, Virginia, North Carolina, South Carolina, Georgia, aye—10; Pennsylvania, no—1."

[2] The word "American" is substituted in the transcript for "National."

[3] In the transcript the vote reads: "New Hampshire, Massachusetts, Connecticut, Maryland, North Carolina, South Carolina, Georgia, aye—7; New Jersey, Pennsylvania, Delaware, Virginia, no—4."

[4] The word "the" is here inserted in the transcript.

naturalization, the liberty reserved to the States might be defeated. He wished it to be known also that this part of the Constitution was a compliance with those States. If the change of language however should be objected to by the members from those States, he should not urge it.

Col: Mason was not against using the term " slaves " but ag^st naming N. C. S. C. & Georgia, lest it should give offence to the people of those States.

Mr Sherman liked a description better than the terms proposed, which had been declined by the old Cong^s & were not pleasing to some people. Mr Clymer concurred with Mr Sherman

Mr Williamson said that both in opinion & practice he was, against slavery; but thought it more in favor of humanity, from a view of all circumstances, to let in S. C. & Georgia on those terms, than to exclude them from the Union.

Mr Govr Morris withdrew his motion.

Mr Dickenson wished the clause to be confined to the States which had not themselves prohibited the importation of slaves, and for that purpose moved to amend the clause so as to read " The importation of slaves into such of the States as shall permit the same shall not be prohibited by the Legislature of the U- S- until the year 1808 "—which was disagreed to nem: cont: *

The first part of the report was then agreed to, amended as follows.

" The migration or importation of such persons as the several States now existing shall think proper to admit, shall not be prohibited by the Legislature prior to the year 1808."

N. H. Mas. Con. M^d N. C. S. C. Geo: ay [1]

N. J. P^a Del. Virg^a ....no [2]

Mr Baldwin in order to restrain & more explicitly define " the average duty " moved to strike out of the 2^d part the words " average of the duties laid on imports " and insert " common impost on articles not enumerated " which was agreed to nem: cont:

Mr Sherman was ag^st this 2^d part, as acknowledging men to be property, by taxing them as such under the character of slaves.

Mr King & Mr Langdon considered this as the price of the 1st part.

Genl Pinkney admitted that it was so.

* In the printed Journal, Con^t Virg^a & Georgia voted in the affirmative.

---

[1] The figure " 7 " is here inserted in the transcript.
[2] The figure " 4 " is here inserted in the transcript.

Col: MASON. Not to tax, will be equivalent to a bounty on the importation of slaves.

Mʳ GHORUM thought that Mʳ Sherman should consider the duty, not as implying that slaves are property, but as a discouragement to the importation of them.

Mʳ Govʳ MORRIS remarked that as the clause now stands it implies that the Legislature may tax freemen imported.

Mʳ SHERMAN in answer to Mʳ Ghorum observed that the smallness of the duty shewed revenue to be the object, not the discouragement of the importation.

Mʳ MADISON thought it wrong to admit in the Constitution the idea that there could be property in men. The reason of duties did not hold, as slaves are not like merchandize, consumed, &c

Col. MASON (in answ⁴ to Govʳ Morris) the provision as it stands was necessary for the case of Convicts in order to prevent the introduction of them.

It was finally agreed nem: contrad: to make the clause read " but a tax or duty may be imposed on such importation not exceeding ten dollars for each person," and then the 2ᵈ part as amended was agreed to.

Sect 5. art. VII was agreed to nem: con: as reported.

Sect. 6. art. VII. in the Report, was postponed.

On motion of Mʳ MADISON 2ᵈᵉᵈ by Mʳ Govʳ MORRIS Art VIII [1] was reconsidered and after the words " all treaties made," were inserted nem: con: the words " or which shall be made " This insertion was meant to obviate all doubt concerning the force of treaties preexisting, by making the words " all treaties made " to refer to them, as the words inserted would refer to future treaties.

Mʳ CARROL & Mʳ L. MARTIN expressed their apprehensions, and the probable apprehensions of their constituents, that under the power of regulating trade the General Legislature, might favor the ports of particular States, by requiring vessels destined to or from other States to enter & clear thereat, as vessels belonging or bound to Baltimore, to enter & clear at Norfolk &c They moved the following proposition

" The Legislature of the U: S: shall not oblige vessels belonging to citizens thereof, or to foreigners, to enter or pay duties or imposts in any other State than in that to which they may be bound, or to clear out in any other than the State in which their cargoes may be laden on board; nor shall any privilege or immunity be granted to

---

[1] See page 342.

any vessels on entering or clearing out, or paying duties or imposts in one State in preference to another "

M! Ghorum thought such a precaution unnecessary; & that the revenue might be defeated, if vessels could run up long rivers, through the jurisdiction of different States without being required to enter, with the opportunity of landing & selling their cargoes by the way.

M! MᶜHenry & Gen! Pinkney made the following propositions

" Should it be judged expedient by the Legislature of the U. S. that one or more ports for collecting duties or imposts other than those ports of entrance & clearance already established by the respective States, should be established, the Legislature of the U. S. shall signify the same to the Executives of the respective States, ascertaining the number of such ports judged necessary; to be laid by the said Executives before the Legislatures of the States at their next Session; and the Legislature of the U. S. shall not have the power of fixing or establishing the particular ports for collecting duties or imposts in any State, except the Legislature of such State shall neglect to fix and establish the same during their first session to be held after such notification by the Legislature of the U. S. to the Executive of such State "

" All duties imposts & excises, prohibitions or restraints laid or made by the Legislature of the U. S. shall be uniform & equal throughout the U. S."

These several propositions were referred, nem: con: to a Committee composed of a member from each State. The committee appointed by ballot were M! Langdon, M! Ghorum, M! Sherman, M! Dayton, M! Fitzimmons, M! Read, M! Carrol, M! Mason, M! Williamson, M! Butler, M! Few.

On The question now taken on M! Dickinson motion of yesterday, allowing appointments to offices, to be referred by the Gen! Legislature to the Executives of the Several States " as a farther amendment to sect. 2, art. X. the votes were,

N. H. no. Mas. no. C! ay. P! no. Del. no. Mᵈ divided. V! ay. N. C. no. S. C. no. Geo. ay.[1]

In amendment of the same section,[2] " other public Ministers " were inserted after " ambassadors."

M! Gov! Morris moved to strike out of the section—" and may correspond with the supreme Executives of the several States " as

---

[1] In the transcript the vote reads: " Connecticut, Virginia, Georgia, aye—3; New Hampshire, Massachusetts, Pennsylvania, Delaware, North Carolina, South Carolina, no—6; Maryland, divided."

[2] The expression " the words " is here inserted in the transcript.

unnecessary and implying that he could not correspond with others. M![?] Broome 2[ded] him.

On the question

N. H. ay. Mas. ay. C![t] ay. P![a] ay. Del. ay. M![d] no. V![a] ay. N. C. ay. S. C. ay. Geo. ay.[1]

[2] " Shall receive ambassadors & other public Ministers," [3] agreed to, nem. con.

M![r] Sherman moved to amend the " power to grant reprieves & pardon [4] " so as to read " to grant reprieves until the ensuing session of the Senate, and pardons with consent of the Senate."

On the question

N. H. no. Mas. no. C![t] ay. P![a] no M![d] no. V![a] no. N. C. no. S. C. no. Geo. no.[5]

[6] " except in cases of impeachment " [7] inserted nem: con: after " pardon " [4]

On the question to agree to —" but his pardon shall not be pleadable in bar " [8]

N. H. ay. Mas. no. C![t] no. P![a] no. Del. no. M![d] ay. V![a] no. N. C. ay. S. C. ay. Geo. no.[9]

Adjourned.

Monday Aug[st] 27th 1787.[10] In Convention

Art X. Sect. 2.[11] being resumed.

M![r] L. Martin moved to insert the words " after conviction " after the words " reprieves and pardons "

M![r] Wilson objected that pardon before conviction might be necessary in order to obtain the testimony of accomplices. He stated

---

[1] In the transcript the vote reads: " New Hampshire, Massachusetts, Connecticut, Pennsylvania, Delaware, Virginia, North Carolina, South Carolina, Georgia, aye—9; Maryland, no—1."

[2] The words " The clause " are here inserted in the transcript.

[3] The word " was " is here inserted in the transcript.

[4] The transcript uses the word " pardon " in the plural.

[5] In the transcript the vote reads: " Connecticut, aye—1; New Hampshire, Massachusetts, Pennsylvania, Maryland, Virginia, North Carolina, South Carolina, Georgia, no—8."

[6] The expression " the words " is here inserted in the transcript.

[7] The word " were " is here inserted in the transcript.

[8] The phrase " It passed in the negative " is here inserted in the transcript.

[9] In the transcript the vote reads: " New Hampshire, Maryland, North Carolina, South Carolina, aye—4; Massachusetts, Connecticut, Pennsylvania, Delaware, Virginia, Georgia, no—6."

[10] The year " 1787 " is omitted in the transcript.

[11] See page 343.

the case of forgeries in which this might particularly happen.—M⸢ L. Martin withdrew his motion.

M⸢ Sherman moved to amend the clause giving the Executive the command of the Militia, so as to read " and of the Militia of the several States, *when called into the actual service of the U. S.*" and on the Question

N. H. ay. Mas. abs⸣ C⸣ ay. N. J. abs⸣ P⸣ ay. Del. no. M⸣ ay. V⸣ ay. N. C. abs⸣ S. C. no. Geo. ay.[1]

The clause for removing the President on impeachment by the House of Rep⸣ and conviction in the supreme Court, of Treason, Bribery or corruption, was postponed nem: con: at the instance of M⸣ Gov⸣ Morris, who thought the Tribunal an improper one, particularly, if the first judge was to be of the privy Council.

M⸣ Gov⸣ Morris objected also to the President of the Senate being provisional successor to the President, and suggested a designation of the Chief Justice.

M⸣ Madison added as a ground of objection that the Senate might retard the appointment of a President in order to carry points whilst the revisionary power was in the President of their own body, but suggested that the Executive powers during a vacancy, be administered by the persons composing the Council to the President.

M⸣ Williamson suggested that the Legislature ought to have power to provide for occasional successors & moved that the last clause [of 2 sect. X art:] relating to a provisional successor to the President be postponed.

M⸣ Dickinson 2⸣ᵈᵉᵈ the postponement, remarking that it was too vague. What is the extent of the term " disability " & who is to be the judge of it?

The postponement was agreed to nem: con:

Col: Mason & M⸣ Madison, moved to add to the oath to be taken by the supreme Executive " and will to the best of my judgment and power preserve protect and defend the Constitution of the U. S."

M⸣ Wilson thought the general provision for oaths of office, in a subsequent place, rendered the amendment unnecessary—

On the question

N. H. ay. Mas. abs⸣ C⸣ ay. P⸣ ay. Del. no. M⸣ ay. V⸣ ay. N. C. abs⸣ S. C. ay. Geo. ay.[2]

---

[1] In the transcript the vote reads: "New Hampshire, Connecticut, Pennsylvania, Maryland, Virginia, Georgia, aye—6; Delaware, South Carolina, no —2; Massachusetts, New Jersey, North Carolina, absent."

[2] In the transcript the vote reads: "New Hampshire, Connecticut, Pennsylvania, Maryland, Virginia, South Carolina, Georgia, aye—7; Delaware, no, Massachusetts, New Jersey, North Carolina, absent."

Art: XI.[1] being [2] taken up.

Doc[r] JOHNSON suggested that the judicial power ought to extend to equity as well as law—and moved to insert the words " both in law and equity " after the words " U. S." in the 1st line, of sect. 1.

M[r] READ objected to vesting these powers in the same Court.

On the question

N. H. ay. Mas. absent. C[t] ay. N. J. abs[t] P. ay. Del. no. M[d] no. Virg[a] ay. N. C. abs[t] S. C. ay. Geo. ay.[3]

On the question to agree to Sect. 1. art. XI. as amended.[4]

N. H. ay. Mas. abs[t] C[t] ay. P[a] ay. N. J. abs[t] Del. no. M[d] no. V[a] ay. N. C. abs[t] S. C. ay. Geo. ay.

M[r] DICKINSON moved as an amendment to sect. 2. art XI [1] after the words " good behavior " the words " provided that they may be removed by the Executive on the application by the Senate and House of Representatives."

M[r] GERRY 2[ded] the motion

M[r] Gov[t] MORRIS thought it a contradiction in terms to say that the Judges should hold their offices during good behavior, and yet be removeable without a trial. Besides it was fundamentally wrong to subject Judges to so arbitrary an authority.

M[r] SHERMAN saw no contradiction or impropriety if this were made part of the constitutional regulation of the Judiciary establishment. He observed that a like provision was contained in the British Statutes.

M[r] RUTLIDGE. If the Supreme Court is to judge between the U. S. and particular States, this alone is an insuperable objection to the motion.

M[r] WILSON considered such a provision in the British Government as less dangerous than here, the House of Lords & House of Commons being less likely to concur on the same occasions. Chief Justice Holt, he remarked, had *successively* offended by his independent conduct, both houses of Parliament. Had this happened at the same time, he would have been ousted. The Judges would be in a bad situation if made to depend on every [5] gust of faction which might prevail in the two branches of our Gov[t]

---

[1] See page 344.
[2] The word " next " is here inserted in the transcript.
[3] In the transcript the vote reads: " New Hampshire, Connecticut, Pennsylvania, Virginia, South Carolina, Georgia, aye—6; Delaware, Maryland, no—2; Massachusetts, New Jersey, North Carolina, absent."
[4] The transcript here inserts the following: " the States were the same as on the preceding question." The vote by States is omitted.
[5] The word " any " is substituted in the transcript for " every."

M͏ͬ RANDOLPH opposed the motion as weakening too much the independence of the Judges.

M͏ͬ DICKINSON was not apprehensive that the Legislature composed of different branches constructed on such different principles, would improperly unite for the purpose of displacing a Judge.

On the question for agreeing to M͏ͬ Dickinson's Motion [1]

N. H. no. Mas. abs͏ͭ C͏ͭ ay. N. J. abs͏ͭ P͏ͣ no. Del. no. M͏ͩ no. V͏ͣ no. N. C. abs͏ͭ S. C. no. Geo. no.

On the question on Sect. 2. art: XI as reported. Del & Mary͏ͩ only no.

M͏ͬ MADISON and M͏ͬ M͏ͨHENRY moved to reinstate the words " increased or " before the word " diminished " in the 2͏ͩ sect. art XI.

M͏ͬ Gov͏ͬ MORRIS opposed it for reasons urged by him on a former occasion—

Col: MASON contended strenuously for the motion. There was no weight he said in the argument drawn from changes in the value of the metals, because this might be provided for by an increase of salaries so made as not to affect persons in office, and this was the only argument on which much stress seemed to have been laid.

Gen͏ͤ PINKNEY. The importance of the Judiciary will require men of the first talents: large salaries will therefore be necessary, larger than the U. S. can allow [2] in the first instance. He was not satisfied with the expedient mentioned by Col: Mason. He did not think it would have a good effect or a good appearance, for new Judges to come in with higher salaries than the old ones.

M͏ͬ Gov͏ͬ MORRIS said the expedient might be evaded & therefore amounted to nothing. Judges might resign, and then be re-appointed to increased salaries.

On the question

N. H. no. C͏ͭ no. P͏ͣ no. Del. no. M͏ͩ div͏ͩ V͏ͣ ay. S. C. no. Geo. abs͏ͭ also Mas͏ͭ͛ N. J. & N. C.[3]

M͏ͬ RANDOLPH & M͏ͬ MADISON then moved to add the following words to sect. 2. art XI. " nor increased by any Act of the Legislature which shall operate before the expiration of three years after the passing thereof "

On this question

---

[1] The transcript here inserts the following: "it was negatived, Connecticut, aye; all the other States present, no." The vote by States is omitted.

[2] The word "afford" is substituted in the transcript for "allow."

[3] In the transcript the vote reads: "Virginia, aye—1; New Hampshire, Connecticut, Pennsylvania, Delaware, South Carolina, no—5; Maryland, divided. Massachusetts, New Jersey, North Carolina, Georgia, absent."

N. H. no. C⁺ no. P⁺ no. Del. no. M⁴ ay. V⁺ ay. S. C. no. Geo. abs⁺ also Mas. N. J. & N. C.¹

Sect. 3. art. XI ² being taken up, the following clause was postponed–viz. " to the trial of impeachments of officers of the U. S." by which the jurisdiction of the supreme Court was extended to such cases.

M⁺ MADISON & M⁺ GOV⁺ MORRIS moved to insert after the word " controversies '" the words " to which the U. S. shall be a party." which was agreed to nem: con:

Doc⁺ JOHNSON moved to insert the words " this Constitution and the " before the word " laws "

M⁺ MADISON doubted whether it was not going too far to extend the jurisdiction of the Court generally to cases arising under the Constitution & whether it ought not to be limited to cases of a Judiciary Nature. The right of expounding the Constitution in cases not of this nature ought not to be given to that Department.

The motion of Doc⁺ Johnson was agreed to nem: con: it being generally supposed that the jurisdiction given was constructively limited to cases of a Judiciary nature.

On motion of M⁺ RUTLIDGE the words " passed by the Legislature " were struck out, and after the words " U. S " were inserted nem. con: the words " and treaties made or which shall be made under their authority " conformably to a preceding amendment in another place.

The clause " in cases of impeachment," was postponed.

M⁺ GOV⁺ MORRIS wished to know what was meant by the words " In all the cases before mentioned it [jursdiction] shall be appellate with such exceptions &c," whether it extended to matters of fact as well as law—and to cases of Common law as well as Civil law.

M⁺ WILSON. The Committee he believed meant facts as well as law & Common as well as Civil law. The jurisdiction of the federal Court of Appeals had he said been so construed.

M⁺ DICKINSON moved to add after the word " appellate " the words both as to law & fact which was agreed to nem: con:

M⁺ MADISON & M⁺ GOV⁺ MORRIS moved to strike out the beginning of the 3⁴ sect. " The jurisdiction of the supreme Court " & to insert the words " the Judicial power " which was agreed to nem: con:

The following motion was disagreed to, to wit to insert " In all

---

¹ In the transcript the vote reads: "Maryland, Virginia, aye—2; New Hampshire, Connecticut, Pennsylvania, Delaware, South Carolina, no—5; Massachusetts, New Jersey, North Carolina, Georgia, absent."

² See page 344.

the other cases before mentioned the Judicial power shall be exercised in such manner as the Legislature shall direct '' Del. Virg: ay [1]

N. H Con. P. M. S. C. G no [2]

On a question for striking out the last sentence of sect. 3. '' The Legislature may assign &c.'' [3]

N. H. ay. C: ay. P: ay. Del. ay. M: ay. V: ay. S. C. ay. Geo. ay. [4]

M: SHERMAN moved to insert after the words '' between Citizens of different States '' the words, '' between Citizens of the same State claiming lands under grants of different States ''—according to the provision in the 9th Art: of the Confederation—which was agreed to nem: con:

Adjourned

TUESDAY AUGUST 28. 1787. [5] IN CONVENTION

M: SHERMAN from the Committee to whom were referred several propositions on the 25th instant, made the following report— [6]

That there be inserted after the 4 clause of [7] 7th section

'' Nor shall any regulation of commerce or revenue give preference to the ports of one State over those of another, or oblige vessels bound to or from any State to enter, clear or pay duties in another and all tonnage, duties, imposts & excises laid by the Legislature shall be uniform throughout the U. S.''

Ordered to lie on the table. [8]

Art XI Sect. 3 [9], [10] It was moved to strike out the words '' it shall be appellate '' & to insert the words '' the supreme Court shall have appellate jurisdiction,''—in order to prevent uncertainty whether '' it '' referred to the *supreme Court*, or to the *Judicial power*.

On the question

N. H ay. Mas. ay. C: ay. N. J. abs: P: ay. Del. ay. M: no. V: ay. N C ay. S. C. ay. Geo. ay. [11]

---

[1] The figure '' 2 '' is here inserted in the transcript.
[2] The figure '' 6 '' is here inserted in the transcript.
[3] The phrase '' it passed *nem. con.*'' is here added in the transcript.
[4] The vote by States is omitted in the transcript.
[5] The year '' 1787 '' is omitted in the transcript.
[6] The phrase '' which was ordered to lie on the table '' is here added in the transcript.
[7] The word '' the '' is here inserted in the transcript.
[8] This sentence is omitted in the transcript.
[9] See page 344.
[10] The words '' being considered '' are here inserted in the transcript.
[11] In the transcript the vote reads: '' New Hampshire, Massachusetts, Connecticut, Pennsylvania, Delaware, Virginia, North Carolina, South Carolina, Georgia, aye—9; Maryland, no—1; New Jersey, absent.''

Sect. 4.[1] was so amended nem: con: as to read " The trial of all crimes (except in cases of impeachment) shall be by jury, and such trial shall be held in the State where the said crimes shall have been committed; but when not committed within any State, then the trial shall be at such place or places as the Legislature may direct." The object of this amendment was to provide for trial by jury of offences committed out of any State.

M.ʳ PINKNEY, urging the propriety of securing the benefit of the Habeas corpus in the most ample manner, moved " that it should not be suspended but on the most urgent occasions, & then only for a limited time, not exceeding twelve months "

M.ʳ RUTLIDGE was for declaring the Habeas Corpus inviolable.[2] He did not conceive that a suspension could ever be necessary at the same time through all the States.

M.ʳ Govʳ MORRIS moved that " The privilege of the writ of Habeas Corpus shall not be suspended; unless where in cases of Rebellion or invasion the public safety may require it."

M.ʳ WILSON doubted whether in any case a suspension could be necessary, as the discretion now exists with Judges, in most important cases to keep in Gaol or admit to Bail.

The first part of M.ʳ Govʳ Morris' motion, to the word " unless " was agreed to nem: con:—on the remaining part;

N. H. ay. Mas. ay. C.ᵗ ay. P.ᵃ ay. Del. ay. M.ᵈ ay. V.ᵃ ay. N. C. no. S. C. no. Geo. no.:[3]

Sec. 5. of art: XI.[1] was agreed to *nem: con:* *

Art: XII.[1] being [4] taken up.

M.ʳ WILSON & M.ʳ SHERMAN moved to insert after the words " coin money " the words " nor emit bills of credit, nor make any thing but gold & silver coin a tender in payment of debts " making these prohibitions absolute, instead of making the measures allowable (as in the XIII art:) *with the consent of the Legislature of the U. S.*

M.ʳ GHORUM thought the purpose would be as well secured by the provision of art: XIII which makes the consent of the Gen.ˡ Legislature necessary, and that in that mode, no opposition would be

---

* The vote on this section as stated in the printed Journal is not unanimous: the statement here is probably the right one.

[1] See page 344.
[2] The word " inviolate " is substituted in the transcript for " inviolable."
[3] In the transcript the vote reads: " New Hampshire, Massachusetts, Connecticut, Pennsylvania, Delaware, Maryland, Virginia, aye—7; North Carolina, South Carolina, Georgia, no—3."
[4] The word " then " is here inserted in the transcript.

excited; whereas an absolute prohibition of paper money would rouse the most desperate opposition from its partizans.

M⁺ SHERMAN thought this a favorable crisis for crushing paper money. If the consent of the Legislature could authorise emissions of it, the friends of paper money, would make every exertion to get into the Legislature in order to licence it.

The question being divided; on the 1ˢᵗ part—" nor emit bills of credit "

N. H. ay. Mas. ay. C⁺ ay. P⁺ ay. Del. ay. M⁺ div⁺ V⁺ no. N. C. ay. S. C. ay. Geo. ay.¹

The remaining part of M⁺ Wilson's & Sherman's motion was agreed to nem: con:

M⁺ KING moved to add, in the words used in the Ordinance of Cong⁺ establishing new States, a prohibition on the States to interfere in private contracts.

M⁺ Gov⁺ MORRIS. This would be going too far. There are a thousand laws, relating to bringing actions—limitations of actions & ² which affect contracts. The Judicial power of the U. S. will be a protection in cases within their jurisdiction; and within the State itself a majority must rule, whatever may be the mischief done among themselves.

M⁺ SHERMAN. Why then prohibit bills of credit?

M⁺ WILSON was in favor of M⁺ King's motion.

M⁺ MADISON admitted that inconveniences might arise from such a prohibition but thought on the whole it would be overbalanced by the utility of it. He conceived however that a negative on the State laws could alone secure the effect. Evasions might and would be devised by the ingenuity of ³ Legislatures.

Col: MASON. This is carrying the restraint too far. Cases will happen that can not be foreseen, where some kind of interference will be proper & essential. He mentioned the case of limiting the period for bringing actions on open account—that of bonds after a certain lapse of time—asking whether it was proper to tie the hands of the States from making provision in such cases?

M⁺ WILSON. The answer to these objections is that *retrospective* ⁴ interferences ⁵ only are to be prohibited.

---

¹ In the transcript the vote reads: "New Hampshire, Massachusetts, Connecticut, Pennsylvania, Delaware, North Carolina, South Carolina, Georgia, aye—8; Virginia, no—1; Maryland, divided."
² The character "&" is changed in the transcript to "&c."
³ The word "the" is here inserted in the transcript.
⁴ The transcript does not italicize the word "*retrospective*."
⁵ The transcript italicizes the word "inferences."

M! MADISON. Is not that already done by the prohibition of ex post facto laws, which will oblige the Judges to declare such interferences null & void.

M! RUTLIDGE moved instead of M! King's Motion to insert—" nor pass bills of attainder nor retrospective * laws " on which motion N. H. ay. C! no. N. J. ay. P! ay. Del. ay. M! no. Virg! no. N. C. ay. S. C. ay. Geo. ay.[1]

M! MADISON moved to insert after the word " reprisal " (art. XII) the words " nor lay embargoes." He urged that such acts by the States would be unnecessary—impolitic—and unjust.

M! SHERMAN thought the States ought to retain this power in order to prevent suffering & injury to their poor.

Col: MASON thought the amendment would be not only improper but dangerous, as the Gen! Legislature would not sit constantly and therefore could not interpose at the necessary moments. He enforced his objection by appealing to the necessity of sudden embargoes during the war, to prevent exports, particularly in the case of a blockade.

M! Gov! MORRIS considered the provision as unnecessary; the power of regulating trade between State & State already vested in the Gen! Legislature, being sufficient.

On the question
N. H. no. Mas. ay. C! no. N. J. no. P! no. Del. ay. M! no. V! no. N. C. no. S. C. ay. Geo. no.[2]

M! MADISON moved that the words " nor lay imposts or duties on imports " be transferred from art: XIII where the consent of the Gen! Legislature may licence the act—into art: XII which will make the prohibition on the States absolute. He observed that as the States interested in this power by which they could tax the imports of their neighbors passing thro' their markets, were a majority, they could give the consent of the Legislature, to the injury of N. Jersey, N. Carolina &c-

M! WILLIAMSON 2ded the motion

M! SHERMAN thought the power might safely be left to the Legislature of the U. States.

Col: MASON, observed that particular States might wish to encour-

* In the printed Journal—" ex post facto."

---

[1] In the transcript the vote reads: " New Hampshire, New Jersey, Pennsylvania, Delaware, North Carolina, South Carolina, Georgia, aye—7; Connecticut, Maryland, Virginia, no—3."

[2] In the transcript the vote reads: " Massachusetts, Delaware, South Carolina, aye—3; New Hampshire, Connecticut, New Jersey, Pennsylvania, Maryland, Virginia, North Carolina, Georgia, no—8."

age by import [1] duties certain manufactures for which they enjoyed natural advantages, as Virginia, the manufacture of Hemp &c.

M: MADISON. The encouragement of Manufactures in that mode requires duties not only on imports directly from foreign Countries, but from the other States in the Union, which would revive all the mischiefs experienced from the want of a Gen! Government over commerce.

On the question

N. H. ay. Mas. no. C: no. N. J. ay. P: no. Del: ay. M: no. V: no. N. C. ay. S. C. no. Geo. no.[2]

Art: XII as amended [3] agreed to nem: con:

Art: XIII [4] being [5] taken up. M: KING moved to insert after the word " imports " the words " or exports " so as to prohibit the states from taxing either,—&

On this question it passed in the affirmative.

N. H. ay. Mas. ay. C: no. N. J. ay. P. ay. Del. ay. M: no. V: no. N. C. ay. S. C. no. Geo. no.[6]

M: SHERMAN moved to add after the word " exports "—the words " nor with such consent but for the use of the U. S."—so as to carry the proceeds of all State duties on imports & [7] exports, into the common Treasury.

M: MADISON liked the motion as preventing all State imposts— but lamented the complexity we were giving to the commercial system.

M: Gov: MORRIS thought the regulation necessary to prevent the Atlantic States from endeavoring to tax the Western States—& promote their interest by opposing the navigation of the Mississippi which would drive the Western people into the arms of G. Britain.

M: CLYMER thought the encouragement of the Western Country was suicide on [8] the old States. If the States have such different interests that they can not be left to regulate their own manufactures without encountering the interests of other States, it is a proof that they are not fit to compose one nation.

---

[1] The word "impost" is substituted in the transcript for "import."

[2] In the transcript the vote reads: "New Hampshire, New Jersey, Delaware, North Carolina, aye—4; Massachusetts, Connecticut, Pennsylvania, Maryland, Virginia, South Carolina, Georgia, no—7."

[3] The words "was then" are here inserted in the transcript.

[4] See page 344.

[5] The words "was then" are substituted in the transcript for "being."

[6] In the transcript the vote reads: "New Hampshire, Massachusetts, New Jersey, Pennsylvania, Delaware, North Carolina, aye—6; Connecticut, Maryland, Virginia, South Carolina, Georgia, no—5."

[7] The word "or" is substituted for "&" in the transcript.

[8] The words "the part of" are here inserted in the transcript.

Mr KING was afraid that the regulation moved by Mr Sherman would too much interfere with a policy of States respecting their manufactures, which may be necessary. Revenue he reminded the House was the object of the general Legislature.

On Mr Sherman's motion

N. H. ay. Mas. no. C^t ay. N. J. ay. P^a ay. Del. ay. M^d no. V^a ay. N. C. ay. S. C. ay. Geo. ay.[1]

Art XIII was then agreed to as amended.

Art. XIV [2] was [3] taken up.

Gen! PINKNEY was not satisfied with it. He seemed to wish some provision should be included in favor of property in slaves.

On the question on Art: XIV.

N. H. ay. Mas. ay. C^t ay. N. J. ay. P^a ay. Del. ay. M^d ay. V^a ay. N. C. ay. S. C. no. Geo. divided.[4]

Art: XV.[2] being taken up, the words " high misdemesnor," were struck out, and [5] " other crime " inserted, in order to comprehend all proper cases: it being doubtful whether " high misdemeanor " had not a technical meaning too limited.

Mr BUTLER and Mr PINKNEY moved " to require fugitive slaves and servants to be delivered up like criminals."

Mr WILSON. This would oblige the Executive of the State to do it at the public expence.

Mr SHERMAN saw no more propriety in the public seizing and surrendering a slave or servant, than a horse.

Mr BUTLER withdrew his proposition in order that some particular provision might be made apart from this article.

Art XV as amended was then agreed to nem: con:

Adjourned

WEDNESDAY AUGUST 29TH 1787.[6] IN CONVENTION

Art: XVI.[2, 7,] taken up.

Mr WILLIAMSON moved to substitute in place of it, the words

---

[1] In the transcript the vote reads: " New Hampshire, Connecticut, New Jersey, Pennsylvania, Delaware, Virginia, North Carolina, South Carolina, Georgia, aye—9; Massachusetts, Maryland, no—2."

[2] See page 345.

[3] The word " then " is here inserted in the transcript.

[4] In the transcript the vote reads: " New Hampshire, Massachusetts, Connecticut, New Jersey, Pennsylvania, Delaware, Maryland, Virginia, North Carolina, aye—9; South Carolina, no—1; Georgia, divided."

[5] The expression " the words " is here inserted in the transcript.

[6] The year " 1787 " is omitted in the transcript.

[7] The word " being " is here inserted in the transcript.

of the Articles of Confederation on the same subject. He did not understand precisely the meaning of the article.

M! WILSON & Doc! JOHNSON supposed the meaning to be that Judgments in one State should be the ground of actions in other States, & that acts of the Legislatures should be included, for the sake of Acts of insolvency &c.

M! PINKNEY moved to commit art XVI, with the following proposition, '' To establish uniform laws upon the subject of bankruptcies, and respecting the damages arising on the protest of foreign bills of exchange ''

M! GHORUM was for agreeing to the article, and committing the proposition.

M! MADISON was for committing both. He wished the Legislature might be authorized to provide for the *execution* of Judgments in other States, under such regulations as might be expedient. He thought that this might be safely done, and was justified by the nature of the Union.

M! RANDOLPH said there was no instance of one nation executing judgments of the Courts of another nation. He moved the following proposition:

'' Whenever the act of any State, whether Legislative, Executive or Judiciary shall be attested & exemplified under the seal thereof, such attestation and exemplification, shall be deemed in other States as full proof of the existence of that act—and its operation shall be binding in every other State, in all cases to which it may relate, and which are within the cognizance and jurisdiction of the State, wherein the said act was done.''

On the question for committing Art: XVI. with M! Pinkney's motion

N. H. no. Mas. no. C! ay. N. J. ay. P! ay. Del. ay. M! ay. V! ay. N. C. ay. S. C. ay. Geo. ay.[1]

The motion of M! Randolph was also committed nem: con:

M! Gov! MORRIS moved to commit also the following proposition on the same subject.

'' Full faith ought to be given in each State to the public acts, records, and judicial proceedings of every other State; and the Legislature shall by general laws, determine the proof and effect of such acts, records, and proceedings,'' and it was committed nem: contrad:

---

[1] In the transcript the vote reads: '' Connecticut, New Jersey, Pennsylvania, Delaware, Maryland, Virginia, North Carolina, South Carolina, Georgia, aye—9; New Hampshire, Massachusetts, no—2.''

The committee appointed for these references, were M�には Rutlidge, M Randolph, M Gorham, M Wilson, & M Johnson.

M DICKENSON mentioned to the House that on examining Blackstone's Commentaries, he found that the terms,[1] " ex post facto " related to criminal cases only; that they would not consequently restrain the States from retrospective laws in civil cases, and that some further provision for this purpose would be requisite.

Art. VII Sect. 6 by yᵉ Committee of eleven reported to be struck out (see the 24 instant) being now taken up,

M PINKNEY moved to postpone the Report in favor of the following proposition—" That no act of the Legislature for the purpose of regulating the commerce of the U- S. with foreign powers, or among the several States, shall be passed without the assent of two thirds of the members of each House." He remarked that there were five distinct commercial interests. 1. the fisheries & W. India trade, which belonged to the N. England States. 2. the interest of N. York lay in a free trade. 3. Wheat & flour the Staples of the two Middle States (N. J. & Penn). 4 Tob the staple of Mary & Virginia & partly of N. Carolina. 5. Rice & Indigo, the staples of S. Carolina & Georgia. These different interests would be a source of oppressive regulations if no check to a bare majority should be provided. States pursue their interests with less scruple than individuals. The power of regulating commerce was a pure concession on the part of the S. States. They did not need the protection of the N. States at present.

M MARTIN 2ᵈᵉᵈ the motion

Gen PINKNEY said it was the true interest of the S. States to have no regulation of commerce; but considering the loss brought on the commerce of the Eastern States by the revolution, their liberal conduct towards the views * of South Carolina, and the interest the weak Southⁿ States had in being united with the strong Eastern States, he thought it proper that no fetters should be imposed on the power of making commercial regulations; and that his constituents though prejudiced against the Eastern States, would be reconciled to this liberality. He had himself, he said, prejudices agᵗ the Eastern States before he came here, but would acknowledge that he had found them as liberal and candid as any men whatever.

* he meant the permission to import slaves. An understanding on the two subjects of *navigation* and *slavery*, had taken place between those parts of the Union, which explains the vote on the motion depending, as well as the language of Gen Pinkney & others.

---

[1] The transcript uses the word "terms" in the singular.

M: CLYMER. The diversity of commercial interests of necessity creates difficulties, which ought not to be increased by unnecessary restrictions. The Northern & middle States will be ruined, if not enabled to defend themselves against foreign regulations.

M: SHERMAN, alluding to M: Pinkney's enumeration of particular interests, as requiring a security ag:t abuse of the power; observed that the diversity was of itself a security, adding that to require more than a majority to decide a question was always embarrassing as had been experienced in cases requiring the votes of nine States in Congress.

M: PINKNEY replied that his enumeration meant the five minute interests. It still left the two great divisions of Northern & Southern Interests.

M: Gov: MORRIS, opposed the object of the motion as highly injurious. Preferences to American ships will multiply them, till they can carry the Southern produce cheaper than it is now carried.—A navy was essential to security, particularly of the S. States, and can only be had by a navigation act encouraging American bottoms & seamen. In those points of view then alone, it is the interest of the S. States that navigation acts should be facilitated. Shipping he said was the worst & most precarious kind of property, and stood in need of public patronage.

M: WILLIAMSON was in favor of making two thirds instead of a majority requisite, as more satisfactory to the Southern people. No useful measure he believed had been lost in Congress for want of nine votes. As to the weakness of the Southern States, he was not alarmed on that account. The sickliness of their climate for invaders would prevent their being made an object. He acknowledged that he did not think the motion requiring ⅔ necessary in itself, because if a majority of [1] Northern States should push their regulations too far, the S. States would build ships for themselves: but he knew the Southern people were apprehensive on this subject and would be pleased with the precaution.

M: SPAIGHT was against the motion. The Southern States could at any time save themselves from oppression, by building ships for their own use.

M: BUTLER differed from those who considered the rejection of the motion as no concession on the part of the S. States. He considered the interests of these and of the Eastern States, to be as different as the interests of Russia and Turkey. Being notwithstand-

---

[1] The word "the" is here inserted in the transcript.

ing desirous of conciliating the affections of the East: States, he should vote ag.ᵗ requiring ⅔ instead of a majority.

Col. MASON. If the Gov.ᵗ is to be lasting, it must be founded in the confidence & affections of the people, and must be so constructed as to obtain these. The *Majority* will be governed by their interests. The Southern States are the *minority* in both Houses. Is it to be expected that they will deliver themselves bound hand & foot to the Eastern States, and enable them to exclaim, in the words of Cromwell on a certain occasion—'' the lord hath delivered them into our hands.

M.ʳ WILSON took notice of the several objections and remarked that if every peculiar interest was to be secured, *unanimity* ought to be required. The majority he said would be no more governed by interest than the minority. It was surely better to let the latter be bound hand and foot than the former. Great inconveniences had, he contended, been experienced in Congress from the article of confederation requiring nine votes in certain cases.

M.ʳ MADISON, went into a pretty full view of the subject. He observed that the disadvantage to the S. States from a navigation act, lay chiefly in a temporary rise of freight, attended however with an increase of South.ⁿ as well as Northern Shipping—with the emigration of Northern Seamen & merchants to the Southern States—& with a removal of the existing & injurious retaliations among the States on each other. The power of foreign nations to obstruct our retaliating measures on them by a corrupt influence would also be less if a majority sh.ᵈ be made competent than if ⅔ of each House sh.ᵈ be required to Legislative acts in this case. An abuse of the power would be qualified with all these good effects. But he thought an abuse was rendered improbable by the provision of 2 branches— by the independence of the Senate, by the negative of the Executive, by the interest of Connecticut & N: Jersey which were agricultural, not commercial States; by the interior interest which was also agricultural in the most commercial States,[1] by the accession of Western States which w.ᵈ be altogether agricultural. He added that the Southern States would derive an essential advantage in the general security afforded by the increase of our maritime strength. He stated the vulnerable situation of them all, and of Virginia in particular. The increase of the coasting trade, and of seamen, would also be favorable to the S. States, by increasing, the consumption of their produce. If the Wealth of the Eastern should in a still greater

---

[1] The word " and " is here inserted in the transcript.

proportion be augmented, that wealth w.^d contribute the more to the public wants, and be otherwise a national benefit.

Mr RUTLIDGE was ag.st the motion of his colleague. It did not follow from a grant of the power to regulate trade, that it would be abused. At the worst a navigation act could bear hard a little while only on the S. States. As we are laying the foundation for a great empire, we ought to take a permanent view of the subject and not look at the present moment only. He reminded the House of the necessity of securing the West India trade to this country. That was the great object, and a navigation Act was necessary for obtaining it.

Mr RANDOLPH said that there were features so odious in the constitution as it now stands, that he doubted whether he should be able to agree to it. A rejection of the motion would compleat the deformity of the system. He took notice of the argument in favor of giving the power over trade to a majority, drawn from the opportunity foreign powers would have of obstructing retaliating [1] measures, if two thirds were made requisite. He did not think there was weight in that consideration. The difference between a majority & two thirds did not afford room for such an opportunity. Foreign influence would also be more likely to be exerted on the President who could require three fourths by his negative. He did not mean however to enter into the merits. What he had in view was merely to pave the way for a declaration which he might be hereafter obliged to make if an accumulation of obnoxious ingredients should take place, that he could not give his assent to the plan.

Mr GORHAM. If the Government is to be so fettered as to be unable to relieve the Eastern States what motive can they have to join in it, and thereby tie their own hands from measures which they could otherwise take for themselves. The Eastern States were not led to strengthen the Union by fear for their own safety. He deprecated the consequences of disunion, but if it should take place it was the Southern part of the Continent that had the [2] most reason to dread them. He urged the improbability of a combination against the interest of the Southern States, the different situations of the Northern & Middle States being a security against it. It was moreover certain that foreign ships would never be altogether excluded especially those of Nations in treaty with us.

On the question to pospone in order to take up Mr Pinkney's Motion

---

[1] The word "retaliatory" is substituted in the transcript for "retaliating."
[2] The word "the" is omitted in the transcript.

N. H. no. Mas. no. C: no. N. J. no. P: no. Del. no. M^d ay.
V: ay. N. C. ay. S. C. no. Geo. ay.[1]

The Report of the Committee for striking out sect: 6. requiring
two thirds of each House to pass a navigation act was then agreed
to, nem: con:

M! BUTLER moved to insert after art: XV. "If any person
bound to service or labor in any of the U. States shall escape into
another State, he or she shall not be discharged from such service
or labor, in consequence of any regulations subsisting in the State
to which they escape, but shall be delivered up to the person
justly claiming their service or labor," which was agreed to
nem: con:

Art: XVII[2] being[3] taken up, M! Gov! MORRIS moved to strike out
the two last sentences, to wit "If the admission be consented to, the
new States shall be admitted on the same terms with the original
States. But the Legislature may make conditions with the new
States, concerning the public debt, which shall be then subsisting."—
He did not wish to bind down the Legislature to admit Western
States on the terms here stated.

M! MADISON opposed the motion, insisting that the Western
States neither would nor ought to submit to a union which degraded
them from an equal rank with[4] other States.

Col: MASON. If it were possible by just means to prevent emigrations to the Western Country, it might be good policy. But go the
people will as they find it for their interest, and the best policy is
to treat them with that equality which will make them friends not
enemies.

M! Gov! MORRIS, did not mean to discourage the growth of the
Western Country. He knew that to be impossible. He did not wish
however to throw the power into their hands.

M! SHERMAN, was ag:t the motion, & for fixing an equality of
privileges by the Constitution.

M! LANGDON was in favor of the Motion, he did not know but
circumstances might arise which would render it inconvenient to
admit new States on terms of equality.

M! WILLIAMSON was for leaving the Legislature free. The existing *small* States enjoy an equality now, and for *that* reason are ad-

---

[1] In the transcript the vote reads: "Maryland, Virginia, North Carolina,
Georgia, aye—4; New Hampshire, Massachusetts, Connecticut, New Jersey,
Pennsylvania, Delaware, South Carolina, no—7."

[2] See page 345.

[3] The word "then" is here inserted in the transcript.

[4] The word "the" is here inserted in the transcript.

mitted to it in the Senate.   This reason is not applicable to new Western States.

On M�r Govr Morris's motion for striking out.

N. H. ay.   Mas. ay.   Cᵗ ay.   N. J. ay.   Pᵃ ay.   Del. ay.   Mᵈ no V⁰ no.   N. C. ay.   S. C. ay.   Geo. ay.[1]

Mr L. Martin & Mr Govr Morris moved to strike out of art XVII. " but to such admission the consent of two thirds of the members present shall be necessary."   Before any question was taken on this motion,

Mr Govt Morris moved the following proposition as a substitute for the XVII art:

" New States may be admitted by the Legislature into this Union: but no new State shall be erected within the limits of any of the present States, without the consent of the Legislature of such State, as well as of the Genⁱ Legislature "

The first part to Union inclusive was agreed to nem: con:

Mr L. Martin opposed the latter part.   Nothing he said would so alarm the limited States as to make the consent of the large States claiming the Western lands, necessary to the establishment of new States within their limits.   It is proposed to guarantee the States. Shall Vermont be reduced by force in favor of the States claiming it?   Frankland & the Western country of Virginia were in a like situation.

On Mr Govr Morris's motion to substitute &c it was agreed to. N. H. no.   Mas. ay.   Cᵗ no.   N. J. no.   Pᵃ ay.   Del. no.   Mᵈ no. V⁰ ay.   N. C. ay.   S. C. ay.   Geo. ay.[2]

Art: XVII—[3] before the House, as amended.

Mr Sherman was against it.   He thought it unnecessary.   The Union can not dismember a State without its consent.

Mr Langdon thought there was great weight in the argument of Mr Luther Martin, and that the proposition substituted by Mr Govt Morris would excite a dangerous opposition to the plan.

Mr Govr Morris thought on the contrary that the small States would be pleased with the regulation, as it holds up the idea of dismembering the large States.

Mr Butler.   If new States were to be erected without the con-

---

[1] In the transcript the vote reads: "New Hampshire, Massachusetts, Connecticut, New Jersey, Pennsylvania, Delaware, North Carolina, South Carolina, Georgia, aye—9; Maryland, Virginia, no—2."

[2] In the transcript the vote reads: "Massachusetts, Pennsylvania, Virginia, North Carolina, South Carolina, Georgia, aye—6; New Hampshire, Connecticut, New Jersey, Delaware, Maryland, no—5."

[3] The word "being" is here inserted in the transcript.

sent of the dismembered States, nothing but confusion would ensue. Whenever taxes should press on the people, demagogues would set up their schemes of new States.

Doc! JOHNSON agreed in general with the ideas of M! Sherman, but was afraid that as the clause stood, Vermont would be subjected to N. York, contrary to the faith pledged by Congress. He was of opinion that Vermont ought to be compelled to come into the Union.

M! LANGDON said his objections were connected with the case of Vermont. If they are not taken in, & remain exempt from taxes, it would prove of great injury to N. Hampshire and the other neighbouring States

M! DICKINSON hoped the article would not be agreed to. He dwelt on the impropriety of requiring the small States to secure the large ones in their extensive claims of territory.

M! WILSON. When the *majority* of a State wish to divide they can do so. The aim of those in opposition to the article, he perceived, was that the Gen! Government should abet the *minority*, & by that means divide a State against its own consent.

M! Gov! MORRIS. If the forced division of States is the object of the new System, and is to be pointed ag!t one or two States, he expected, the Gentleman ¹ from these would pretty quickly leave us.

Adjourned

THURSDAY AUGUST 30ᵀᴴ 1787.² IN CONVENTION

Art XVII ³ resumed for a question on it as amended by M! Gov! Morris's substitutes.⁴

M! CARROL moved to strike out so much of the article as requires the consent of the State to its being divided. He was aware that the object of this prerequisite might be to prevent domestic disturbances, but such was our situation with regard to the Crown lands, and the sentiments of Maryland on that subject, that he perceived we should again be at sea, if no guard was provided for the right of the U. States to the back lands. He suggested that it might be proper to provide that nothing in the Constitution should affect the Right of the U. S. to lands ceded by G. Britain in the Treaty of peace, and proposed a committment to a member from each State. He assured

---

¹ The transcript uses the word " Gentleman " in the plural.
² The year " 1787 " is omitted in the transcript.
³ The word " being " is here inserted in the transcript.
⁴ The transcript uses the word " substitutes " in the singular.

the House that this was a point of a most serious nature. It was desireable above all things that the act of the Convention might be agreed to unanimously. But should this point be disregarded, he believed that all risks would be run by a considerable minority, sooner than give their concurrence.

M�: L. Martin 2ᵈᵉᵈ the motion for a committment.

M⸴ Rutlidge is it to be supposed that the States are to be cut up without their own consent. The case of Vermont will probably be particularly provided for. There could be no room to fear, that Virginia or N. Carolina would call on the U. States to maintain their Government over the Mountains.

M⸴ Williamson said that N. Carolina was well disposed to give up her western lands, but attempts at compulsion was [1] not the policy of the U. S. He was for doing nothing in the constitution in the present case, and for leaving the whole matter in Statu quo.

M⸴ Wilson was against the committment. Unanimity was of great importance, but not to be purchased by the majority's yielding to the minority. He should have no objection to leaving the case of [2] new States as heretofore. He knew of [3] nothing that would give greater or juster alarm than the doctrine, that a political society is to be torne asunder without its own consent.

On M⸴ Carrol's motion for commitment

N. H. no. Mas. no. C⸴ no. N. J. ay. P⸴ no. Del. ay. M⸴ ay. V⸴ no. N. C. no. S. C. no. Geo. no.[4]

M⸴ Sherman moved to postpone the substitute for art: XVII agreed to yesterday in order to take up the following amendment "The Legislature shall have power to admit other States into the Union, and new States to be formed by the division or junction of States now in the Union, with the consent of the Legislature of such States." [The first part was meant for the case of Vermont to secure its admission.]

On the question, it passed in the negative

N. H. ay. Mas. ay. C⸴ ay. N. J. no. P⸴ ay. Del. no. M⸴ no. V⸴ no. N. C. no. S. C. ay. Geo. no.[5]

---

[1] In the transcript the word "was" is crossed out and "were" is written above it.

[2] The word "the" is here inserted in the transcript.

[3] The word "of" is omitted in the transcript.

[4] In the transcript the vote reads: "New Jersey, Delaware, Maryland, aye —3; New Hampshire, Massachusetts, Connecticut, Pennsylvania, Virginia, North Carolina, South Carolina, Georgia, no—8."

[5] In the transcript the vote reads: "New Hampshire, Massachusetts, Connecticut, Pennsylvania, South Carolina, aye—5; New Jersey, Delaware, Maryland, Virginia, North Carolina, Georgia, no—6."

Doc͏ᵗ JOHNSON moved to insert the words " hereafter formed or " after the words " shall be " in the substitute for art: XVII, [the more clearly to save Vermont as being already formed into a State, from a dependence on the consent of N. York to ¹ her admission.] The motion was agreed to Del. & M͏ᵈ only dissenting.

M͏ʳ GOVERN͏ʳ MORRIS moved to strike out the word " limits " in the substitute, and insert the word " jurisdiction " [This also ² meant to guard the case of Vermont, the jurisdiction of N. York not extending over Vermont which was in the exercise of sovereignty, tho' Vermont was within the asserted limits of New York]

On this question

N. H. ay. Mas. ay. C͏ᵗ ay. N. J. no. P͏ᵃ ay. Del. ay. M͏ᵈ ay. V͏ᵃ ay. N. C. no. S. C. no. Geo. no.³

M͏ʳ L. MARTIN, urged the unreasonableness of forcing & guaranteeing the people of Virginia beyond the Mountains, the Western people, of N. Carolina, & of Georgia, & the people of Maine, to continue under the States now governing them, without the consent of those States to their separation. Even if they should become the *majority*, the majority of *Counties*, as in Virginia may still hold fast the dominion over them. Again the majority may place the seat of Government entirely among themselves & for their own conveniency,⁴ and still keep the injured parts of the States in subjection, under the guarantee of the Gen͏ˡ Government ag͏ˢᵗ domestic violence. He wished M͏ʳ Wilson had thought a little sooner of the value of *political* bodies. In the beginning, when the rights of the small States were in question, they were phantoms, ideal beings. Now when the Great States were to be affected, political societies were of a sacred nature. He repeated and enlarged on the unreasonableness of requiring the small States to guarantee the Western claims of the large ones.—It was said yesterday by M͏ʳ Gov͏ʳ Morris, that if the large States were to be split to pieces without their consent, their representatives here would take their leave. If the Small States are to be required to guarantee them in this manner, it will be found that the Representatives of other States will with equal firmness take their leave of the Constitution on the table.

It was moved by M͏ʳ L. MARTIN to postpone the substituted article, in order to take up the following.

---

¹ The word " for " is substituted in the transcript for " to."
² The word " was " is here inserted in the transcript.
³ In the transcript the vote reads: " New Hampshire, Massachusetts, Connecticut, Pennsylvania, Delaware, Maryland, Virginia, aye—7; New Jersey, North Carolina, South Carolina, Georgia, no—4."
⁴ The word " conveniency " is changed to " convenience " in the transcript.

" The Legislature of the U. S. shall have power to erect New States within as well as without the territory claimed by the several States or either of them, and admit the same into the Union: provided that nothing in this constitution shall be construed to affect the claim of the U. S. to vacant lands ceded to them by the late treaty of peace. which passed in the negative: N. J. Del. & M⁹ only ay.

On the question to agree to M⁻ Gov⁻ Morris's substituted article as amended in the words following,

" New States may be admitted by the Legislature into the Union: but no new State shall be hereafter formed or erected within the jurisdiction of any of the present States without the consent of the Legislature of such State as well as of the General Legislature "

N. H. ay. Mas. ay. C⁻ ay. N. J. no. P⁻ ay. Del. no. M⁹ no. V⁻ ay. N. C. ay. S. C. ay. Geo. ay.[1]

M⁻ DICKINSON moved to add the following clause to the last—

" Nor shall any State be formed by the junction of two or more States or parts thereof, without the consent of the Legislatures of such States, as well as of the Legislature of the U. States." which was agreed to without a count of the votes.

M⁻ CARROL moved to add—" Provided nevertheless that nothing in this Constitution shall be construed to affect the claim of the U. S. to vacant lands ceded to them by the Treaty of peace." This he said might be understood as relating to lands not claimed by any particular States, but he had in view also some of the claims of particular States.

M⁻ WILSON was ag⁻ the motion. There was nothing in the Constitution affecting one way or the other the claims of the U. S. & it was best to insert nothing, leaving every thing on that litigated subject in statu quo.

M⁻ MADISON considered the claim of the U. S. as in fact favored by the jurisdiction of the Judicial power of the U. S. over controversies to which they should be parties. He thought it best on the whole to be silent on the subject. He did not view the proviso of M⁻ Carrol as dangerous; but to make it neutral & fair, it ought to go farther & declare that the claims of particular States also should not be affected.

M⁻ SHERMAN thought the proviso harmless, especially with the

---

[1] In the transcript the vote reads: "New Hampshire, Massachusetts, Connecticut, Pennsylvania, Virginia, North Carolina, South Carolina, Georgia, aye —8; New Jersey, Delaware, Maryland, no—3."

addition suggested by M̠ Madison in favor of the claims of particular States.

M̠ BALDWIN did not wish any undue advantage to be given to Georgia. He thought the proviso proper with the addition proposed. It should be remembered that if Georgia has gained much by the cession in the Treaty of peace, she was in danger during the war, of a Uti possidetis.

M̠ RUTLIDGE thought it wrong to insert a proviso where there was nothing which it could restrain, or on which it could operate.

M̠ CARROL withdrew his motion and moved the following.

" Nothing in this Constitution shall be construed to alter the claims of the U. S. or of the individual States to the Western territory, but all such claims shall be examined into & decided upon, by the Supreme Court of the U. States."

M̠ Gov̠ MORRIS moved to postpone this in order to take up the following.

" The Legislature shall have power to dispose of and make all needful rules and regulations respecting the territory or other property belonging to the U. States; and nothing in this constitution contained, shall be so construed as to prejudice any claims either of the U. S. or of any particular State."—The postponem̠ ag̠ to nem. con.

M̠ L. MARTIN moved to amend the proposition of M̠ Gov̠ Morris by adding—" But all such claims may be examined into & decided upon by the supreme Court of the U. States."

M̠ Gov̠ MORRIS. this is unnecessary, as all suits to which the U. S. are parties, are already to be decided by the Supreme Court.

M̠ L. MARTIN, it is propor in order to remove all doubts on this point.

[1] Question on M̠ L. Martin's amendatory motion

N. H. no. Mas. no. C̠ no. N. J. ay. P̠ no. Del. no. M̠ ay. V̠ no—[2] States not farther called the negatives being sufficient & the point [3] given up.

The Motion of M̠ Gov̠ Morris was then agreed to, M̠ alone dissenting.

Art: XVIII [4] being taken up,—the word " foreign " was struck out. nem: con: as superfluous, being implied in the term " invasion."

---

[1] The words "On the" are here inserted in the transcript.
[2] In the transcript the vote reads: "New Jersey, Maryland, aye—2; New Hampshire, Massachusetts, Connecticut, Pennsylvania, Delaware, Virginia, no—6."
[3] The word "being" is here inserted in the transcript.
[4] See page 345.

M: DICKINSON moved to strike out " on the application of its Legislature, against " He thought it of essential importance to the tranquility of the U. S. that they should in all cases suppress domestic violence, which may proceed from the State Legislature itself, or from disputes between the two branches where such exist

M: DAYTON mentioned the Conduct of Rho: Island as shewing the necessity of giving latitude to the power of the U. S. on this subject.

On the question

N. H. no. Mas. no. C: no. N. J. ay. P: ay. Del. ay. M: no. V: no. N. C. no. S. C. no. Geo. no.[1]

On a question for striking out " domestic violence " and insert: " insurrections." It passed in the negative.

N. H. no. Mas. no. C: no. N. J. ay. P: no. Del. no. M: no. V: ay. N. C. ay. S. C. ay. Geo. ay.[2]

M: DICKINSON moved to insert the words, " or Executive " after the words " application of its Legislature "—The occasion itself he remarked might hinder the Legislature from meeting.

On this question

N. H. ay. Mas. no. C: ay. N. J. ay. P: ay. Del. ay. M: div: V: no. N. C. ay. S. C. ay. Geo. ay.[3]

M: L. MARTIN moved to subjoin to the last amendment the words " in the recess of the Legislature " On which question[4]

N. H. no. Mas. no. C: no. P: no. Del. no. M: ay. V: no. N. C. no. S. C. no. Geo. no.

On[5] Question on the last clause as amended

N. H. ay. Mas. ay. C: ay. N. J. ay. P: ay. Del. no. M: no. V: ay. N. C. ay. S. C. ay. Geo. ay.[6]

Art: XIX[7,8] taken up.

M: Gov: MORRIS suggested that the Legislature should be left at liberty to call a Convention, whenever they please.

---

[1] In the transcript the vote reads: "New Jersey, Pennsylvania, Delaware, aye—3; New Hampshire, Massachusetts, Connecticut, Maryland, Virginia, North Carolina, South Carolina, Georgia, no—8."

[2] In the transcript the vote reads: "New Jersey, Virginia, North Carolina, South Carolina, Georgia, aye—5; New Hampshire, Massachusetts, Connecticut, Pennsylvania, Delaware, Maryland, no—6."

[3] In the transcript the vote reads: "New Hampshire, Connecticut, New Jersey, Pennsylvania, Delaware, North Carolina, South Carolina, Georgia, aye —8; Massachusetts, Virginia, no—2; Maryland, divided."

[4] The transcript here adds the words: "Maryland only, aye," and omits the vote by States.

[5] The word "the" is here inserted in the transcript.

[6] In the transcript the vote reads: "New Hampshire, Massachusetts, Connecticut, New Jersey, Pennsylvania, Virginia, North Carolina, South Carolina, Georgia, aye—9; Delaware, Maryland, no—2."

[7] See page 345.

[8] The words "was then" are here inserted in the transcript.

The art: was agreed to nem: con:

Art: XX.[1,2] taken up.—[3] "or affirmation" was[4] added after "oath."

M⸢r⸣ PINKNEY moved to add to the art:—"but no religious test shall ever be required as a qualification to any office or public trust under the authority of the U. States"

M⸢r⸣ SHERMAN thought it unnecessary, the prevailing liberality being a sufficient security ag⸢st⸣ such tests.

M⸢r⸣ Gov⸢r⸣ MORRIS & Gen⸢l⸣ PINKNEY approved the motion.

The motion was agreed to nem: con: and then the whole Article; N. C. only no—& M⸢d⸣ divided

Art: XXI.[5,6] taken up. viz:[7] "The ratifications of the Conventions of   States shall be sufficient for organizing this Constitution."

M⸢r⸣ WILSON proposed to fill the blank with "seven" that being a majority of the whole number & sufficient for the commencement of the plan.

M⸢r⸣ CARROL moved to postpone the article in order to take up the Report of the Committee of Eleven (see Tuesday Aug⸢st⸣ 28)[8]—and on the question

N. H. no. Mas. no. C⸢t⸣ no. N. J. ay. P⸢a⸣ no. Del. ay. M⸢d⸣ ay. V⸢a⸣ no. N. C. no. S. C. no. Geo. no.[9]

M⸢r⸣ Gov⸢r⸣ MORRIS thought the blank ought to be filled in a twofold way, so as to provide for the event of the ratifying States being contiguous which would render a smaller number sufficient, and the event of their being dispersed, which w⸢d⸣ require a greater number for the introduction of the Government.

M⸢r⸣ SHERMAN. observed that the States being now confederated by articles which require unanimity in changes, he thought the ratification in this case of ten States at least ought to be made necessary.

M⸢r⸣ RANDOLPH was for filling the blank with "nine" that being

---

[1] See page 345.
[2] The words "was then" are here inserted in the transcript.
[3] The expression "the words" is here inserted in the transcript.
[4] In the transcript the word "was" is crossed out and "were" is written above it.
[5] See page 346.
[6] The words "being then" are here inserted in the transcript.
[7] The word "viz" is omitted in the transcript.
[8] The words "the twenty-eighth of August" are substituted in the transcript for "Tuesday Aug⸢st⸣ 28."
[9] In the transcript the vote reads: "New Jersey, Delaware, Maryland, aye—3; New Hampshire, Massachusetts, Connecticut, Pennsylvania, Virginia, North Carolina, South Carolina, Georgia, no—8."

a respectable majority of the whole, and being a number made familiar by the constitution of the existing Congress.

Mʳ Wⁱˡˢᴼⁿ mentioned " eight " as preferable.

Mʳ Dⁱᴄᴷⁱⁿˢᴼⁿ asked whether the concurrence of Congress is to be essential to the establishment of the system, whether the refusing States in the Confederacy could be deserted—and whether Congress could concur in contravening the system under which they acted?

Mʳ Mᴀᴅⁱˢᴼⁿ, remarked that if the blank should be filled with " seven " eight, or " nine "—the Constitution as it stands might be put in force over the whole body of the people, tho' less than a majority of them should ratify it.

Mʳ Wⁱˡˢᴼⁿ. As the Constitution stands, the States only which ratify can be bound. We must he said in this case go to the original powers of Society. The House on fire must be extinguished, without a scrupulous regard to ordinary rights.

Mʳ Bᵁᵀˡᴱᴿ was in favor of " nine." He revolted at the idea, that one or two States should restrain the rest from consulting their safety.

Mʳ Cᴀᴿᴿᴼˡ moved to fill the blank with " the thirteen," unanimity being necessary to dissolve the existing confederacy which had been unanimously established.

Mʳ Kⁱⁿᴳ thought this amendᵗ necessary, otherwise as the Constitution now stands it will operate on the whole though ratified by a part only.

Adjourned

Fᴿⁱᴅᴀʸ Aᵁᴳᵁˢᵀ 31ˢᵀ 1787.[1] Iⁿ Cᴼⁿᵛᴱⁿᵀⁱᴼⁿ.

Mʳ Kⁱⁿᴳ moved to add to the end of art: XXI the words " between the said States " so as to confine the operation of the Govᵗ to the States ratifying it.

On the question

N. H. ay. Mas. ay. Cᵗ ay. N. J. ay. Pᵃ ay. Mᵈ no. Virgᵃ ay. N. C. ay. S. C. ay. Geo. ay.[2]

Mʳ Mᴀᴅⁱˢᴼⁿ proposed to fill the blank in the article with " any seven or more States entitled to thirty three members at least in the House of Representatives according to the allotment made in the

---

[1] The year " 1787 " is omitted in the transcript.
[2] In place of the vote by States the transcript reads: " nine States voted in the affirmative; Maryland, no; Delaware, absent."

3 Sect: of art: 4." This he said would require the concurrence of a majority both of the States and [1] people.

M: SHERMAN doubted the propriety of authorizing less than all the States to execute the Constitution, considering the nature of the existing Confederation. Perhaps all the States may concur, and on that supposition it is needless to hold out a breach of faith.

M: CLYMER and M: CARROL moved to postpone the consideration of Art: XXI in order to take up the Reports of Committees not yet acted on. On this question, the States were equally divided.

N. H. ay. Mas. no. C: div.^d N. J. no. P: ay. Del. ay. M^d ay. V: no. N. C no. S. C. no. G. ay.[2]

M: Govr MORRIS moved to strike out "Conventions of the" after "ratifications," leaving the States to pursue their own modes of ratification.

M: CARROL mentioned the mode of altering the Constitution of Maryland pointed out therein, and that no other mode could be pursued in that State.

M: KING thought that striking out "Conventions" as the requisite mode was equivalent to giving up the business altogether. Conventions alone, which will avoid all the obstacles from the complicated formation of the Legislatures, will succeed, and if not positively required by the plan, its enemies will oppose that mode.

M: Govr MORRIS said he meant to facilitate the adoption of the plan, by leaving the modes approved by the several State Constitutions to be followed.

M: MADISON considered it best to require Conventions; among other reasons, for this, that the powers given to the Genl Gov^t being taken from the State Gov^ts the Legislatures would be more disinclined than conventions composed in part at least of other men; and if disinclined, they could devise modes apparently promoting, but really, thwarting the ratification. The difficulty in Maryland was no greater than in other States, where no mode of change was pointed out by the Constitution, and all officers were under oath to support it. The people were in fact, the fountain of all power, and by resorting to them, all difficulties were got over. They could alter constitutions as they pleased. It was a principle in the Bills of rights, that first principles might be resorted to.

M: M^cHENRY said that the officers of Gov^t in Maryland were

---

[1] The word "the" is here inserted in the transcript.
[2] In the transcript the vote reads: "New Hampshire, Pennsylvania, Delaware, Maryland, Georgia, aye—5; Massachusetts, New Jersey, Virginia, North Carolina, South Carolina, no—5; Connecticut, divided."

under oath to support the mode of alteration prescribed by the Constitution.

M! GHORUM, urged the expediency of " Conventions " also M!
PINKNEY, for reasons, formerly urged on a discussion of this question.

M! L. MARTIN insisted on a reference to the State Legislatures.
He urged the danger of commotions from a resort to the people &
to first principles in which the Governments might be on one side
& the people on the other. He was apprehensive of no such consequences however in Maryland, whether the Legislature or the people should be appealed to. Both of them would be generally against
the Constitution. He repeated also the peculiarity in the Maryland
Constitution.

M! KING observed that the Constitution of Massachussets was
made unalterable till the year 1790, yet this was no difficulty with
him. The State must have contemplated a recurrence to first principles before they sent deputies to this Convention.

M! SHERMAN moved to postpone art. XXI [1] & [2] take up art: XXII [1]
on which question,

N. H. no. Mas. no. C! ay. N. J. no. P. ay. Del. ay. M! ay.
V! ay. N. C. no S. C. no. Geo. no.[3]

On M! GOV! Morris's motion to strike out " Conventions of the,"
it was negatived.

N. H. no. Mas. no. C! ay. N. J. no. P! ay. Del. no. M! ay.
V! no. S. C. no. Geo. ay.[4]

On [5] filling the blank in Art: XXI with " thirteen " moved by
M! CARROL & L. MARTIN

N. H. no. Mas. no. C! no—all no. except Maryland.[6]

M! SHERMAN & M! DAYTON moved to fill the blank with " ten "

M! WILSON supported the motion of M! MADISON, requiring a
majority both of the people and of States.

M! CLYMER was also in favor of it.

Col: MASON was for preserving ideas familiar to the people.
Nine States had been required in all great cases under the Confederation & that number was on that account preferable

---

[1] See page 346.
[2] The word " to " is here inserted in the transcript.
[3] In the transcript the vote reads: " Connecticut, Pennsylvania, Delaware,
Maryland, Virginia, aye—5; New Hampshire, Massachusetts, New Jersey, North
Carolina, South Carolina, Georgia, no—6."
[4] In the transcript the vote reads: " Connecticut, Pennsylvania, Maryland,
Georgia, aye—4; New Hampshire, Massachusetts, New Jersey, Delaware, Virginia, South Carolina, no—6."
[5] The words " the question for " are here inserted in the transcript.
[6] In the transcript the vote reads: " all the States were no, except Maryland."

On the question for " ten "

N. H. no. Mas. no. C! ay. N. J. ay. Pᵃ no. Del. no. Mᵈ ay.
V: no. N. C. no. S. C. no. Geo. ay.[1]

On question for " nine "

N. H. ay. Mas. ay. C! ay. N. J. ay. P: ay. Del. ay. Mᵈ ay.
V: no. N. C. no. S. C. no. Geo. ay [2]

Art: XXI. as amended was then agreed to by all the States, Maryland excepted, & M⁺ Jenifer being, ay.

Art. XXII [3, 4] taken up, to wit, " This Constitution shall be laid before the U. S. in Cong⁺ assembled for their approbation; and it is the opinion of this Convention that it should be afterwards submitted to a Convention chosen, in each State under the recommendation of its Legislature, in order to receive the ratification of such Convention "

M⁺ Gov⁺ MORRIS & M⁺ PINKNEY moved to strike out the words " for their approbation " On this question

N. H. ay. Mas. no. C! ay. N. J. ay.* P: ay. Del. ay. Mᵈ no
V: ay. N. C. ay. S. C. ay. Geo. no.[5]

M⁺ Gov⁺ MORRIS & M⁺ PINKNEY then moved to amend the art: so as to read

" This Constitution shall be laid before the U. S. in Congress assembled; and it is the opinion of this Convention that it should afterwards be submitted to a Convention chosen in each State, in order to receive the ratification of such Convention: to which end the several Legislatures ought to provide for the calling Conventions within their respective States as speedily as circumstances will permit."--M⁺ Gov⁺ MORRIS said his object was to impress in stronger terms the necessity of calling Conventions in order to prevent enemies to the plan, from giving it the go by. When it first appears, with the sanction of this Convention, the people will be favorable to it. By degrees the State officers, & those interested in the State Gov⁺ will intrigue & turn the popular current against it.

M⁺ L. MARTIN believed M⁺ Morris to be right, that after a while

* In the printed Journal N. Jersey—no.

---

[1] In the transcript the vote reads: "Connecticut, New Jersey, Maryland, Georgia, aye—4; New Hampshire, Massachusetts, Pennsylvania, Delaware, Virginia, North Carolina, South Carolina, no—7.".

[2] In the transcript the vote reads: "New Hampshire, Massachusetts, Connecticut, New Jersey, Pennsylvania, Delaware, Maryland, Georgia, aye—8; Virginia, North Carolina, South Carolina, no—3."

[3] See page 346.

[4] The words "was then" are here inserted in the transcript.

[5] In the transcript the vote reads: "New Hampshire, Connecticut, New Jersey,* Pennsylvania, Delaware, Virginia, North Carolina, South Carolina, aye—8; Massachusetts, Maryland, Georgia, no—3."

the people would be ag.ˢᵗ it, but for a different reason from that alledged. He believed they would not ratify it unless hurried into it by surprize.

M.ʳ GERRY enlarged on the idea of M.ʳ L. Martin in which he concurred, represented the system as full of vices, and dwelt on the impropriety of distroying the existing Confederation, without the unanimous consent of the parties to it.

[1] Question on M.ʳ Gov.ʳ Morris's & M.ʳ Pinkney's motion

N. H. ay. Mas. ay. C.ᵗ no. N. J. no. P.ª ay. Del. ay. M.ᵈ no. V.ª no. N. C. no. S. C. no. Geo. no.[2]

M.ʳ GERRY moved to postpone art: XXII.

Col: MASON 2.ᵈᵉᵈ the motion, declaring that he would sooner chop off his right hand than put it to the Constitution as it now stands. He wished to see some points not yet decided brought to a decision, before being compelled to give a final opinion on this article. Should these points be improperly settled, his wish would then be to bring the whole subject before another general Convention.

M.ʳ Gov.ʳ MORRIS was ready for a postponement. He had long wished for another Convention, that will have the firmness to provide a vigorous Government, which we are afraid to do.

M.ʳ RANDOLPH stated his idea to be, in case the final form of the Constitution should not permit him to accede to it, that the State Conventions should be at liberty to propose amendments to be submitted to another General Convention which may reject or incorporate them, as shall [3] be judged proper.

On the question for postponing

N. H. no. Mas. no. C.ᵗ no. N. J. ay. P.ª no. Del. no. M.ᵈ ay. V.ª no. N. C. ay. S. C. no. Geo. no.[4]

On the question on Art: XXII

N. H. ay. Mas. ay. C.ᵗ ay. N. J. ay. P.ª ay. Del. ay. M.ᵈ no. V.ª ay. N. C. ay. S. C. ay. Geo. ay.[5]

Art: XXIII [6] being taken up, as far as the words " assigned by Congress " inclusive, was agreed to nem: con: the blank having been first filled with the word " nine " as of course.

---

[1] The words " On the " are here inserted in the transcript.

[2] In the transcript the vote reads: " New Hampshire, Massachusetts, Pennsylvania, Delaware, aye—4; Connecticut, New Jersey, Maryland, Virginia, North Carolina, South Carolina, Georgia, no—7."

[3] The word " may " is substituted in the transcript for " shall."

[4] In the transcript the vote reads: " New Jersey, Maryland, North Carolina, aye—3; New Hampshire, Massachusetts, Connecticut, Pennsylvania, Delaware, Virginia, South Carolina, Georgia, no—8."

[5] In the transcript the vote reads: " ten States aye; Maryland no."

[6] See page 346.

On a motion for postponing the residue of the clause, concerning the choice of the President &c.

N. H. no. Mas. ay. C: no. N. J. no. P: no. Del. ay. M⁰ no. V: ay. N. C. ay. S. C. no. Geo. no.[1]

M: Gov: Morris then moved to strike out the words " choose the President of the U. S. and "—this point, of choosing the President not being yet finally determined, & on this question

N. H. no. Mas. ay. C: ay. N. J. ay. P: ay. Del. ay. M⁰ div⁰ V: ay. N. C. ay. S. C. ay.* Geo. ay [2]

Art: XXIII as amended was then agreed to nem: con:

The Report of the Grand Committee of eleven made by M: Sherman was then taken up (see Aug: 28).[3]

On the question to agree to the following clause, to be inserted after Sect. 4. art: VII. " nor shall any regulation of commerce or revenue give preference to the ports of one State over those of another." Agreed to nem: con:

On the clause " or oblige vessels bound to or from any State to enter clear or pay duties in another "

M: Madison thought the restriction w⁰ be inconvenient, as in the River Delaware, if a vessel cannot be required to make entry below the jurisdiction of Pennsylvania.

M: Fitzimmons admitted that it might be inconvenient, but thought it would be a greater inconveniency [4] to require vessels bound to Philad: to enter below the jurisdiction of the State.

M: Gorham & M: Langdon, contended that the Gov: would be so fettered by this clause, as to defeat the good purpose of the plan. They mentioned the situation of the trade of Mas. & N. Hampshire, the case of Sandy Hook which is in the State of N. Jersey, but where precautions ag:t smuggling into N. York, ought to be established by the Gen: Government.

M: McHenry said the clause would not shreen a vessel from being obliged to take an officer on board as a security for due entry &c.

M: Carrol was anxious that the clause should be agreed to. He assured the House, that this was a tender point in Maryland.

* In printed Journal—S. C.—no.

---

[1] In the transcript the vote reads: " Massachusetts, Delaware, Virginia, North Carolina, aye—4; New Hampshire, Connecticut, New Jersey, Pennsylvania, Maryland, South Carolina, Georgia, no—7."

[2] In the transcript the vote reads: " Massachusetts, Connecticut, New Jersey, Pennsylvania, Delaware, Virginia, North Carolina, South Carolina,* Georgia, aye—9; New Hampshire, no; Maryland, divided."

[3] In the transcript this date reads " the twenty-eighth of August."

[4] The word " inconveniency " is changed to " inconvenience " in the transcript.

M~~r~~ JENNIFER urged the necessity of the clause in the same point of view.

On the question for agreeing to it

N. H. no. C~~t~~ ay. N. J. ay. P~~a~~ ay. Del. ay. M~~d~~ ay. V~~a~~ ay. N. C. ay. S. C. no. Geo. ay.[1]

The word " tonnage " was struck out, nem: con: as comprehended in " duties "

On [2] question on the clause of the Report " and all duties, imposts & excises, laid by the Legislature shall be uniform throughout the U. S." It was agreed to nem: con: *

On motion of M~~r~~ SHERMAN it was agreed to refer such parts of the Constitution as have been postponed, and such parts of Reports as have not been acted on, to a Committee of a member from each State; the Committee appointed by ballot, being—M~~r~~ Gilman, M~~r~~ King, M~~r~~ Sherman, M~~r~~ Brearly, M~~r~~ Gov~~r~~ Morris, M~~r~~ Dickinson, M~~r~~ Carrol, M~~r~~ Madison, M~~r~~ Williamson, M~~r~~ Butler & M~~r~~ Baldwin.

[The House [4] adjourned]

SATURDAY SEP~~R~~ 1. 1787 [5] IN CONVENTION.

M~~r~~ BREARLEY from the Comm~~e~~ of eleven to which were referred yesterday, the postponed parts of the Constitution, & parts of Reports not acted upon, made the following partial report.

That in lieu of the 9~~th~~ Sect: of art: 6. the words following be inserted viz " The members of each House shall be ineligible to any civil office under the authority of the U. S. during the time for which they shall respectively be elected, and no person holding an office under the U. S. shall be a member of either House during his continuance in office."

M~~r~~ RUTLIDGE from the Committee to whom were referred sundry propositions (see Aug: 29), together with art: XVI, reported that the following additions be made to the Report—viz

After the word " States " in the last line on the Margin of the

* In printed Journal N. H. and S. C. entered as * in the negative.

---

[1] In the transcript the vote reads: "Connecticut, New Jersey, Pennsylvania, Delaware, Maryland, Virginia, North Carolina, Georgia, aye—8; New Hampshire, South Carolina, no—2."

[2] The word " the " is here inserted in the transcript.

[3] The word " as " is omitted in the transcript.

[4] The words " The House " are omitted in the transcript.

[5] The year " 1787 " is omitted in the transcript.

3ᵈ page (see the printed Report)—add " to establish uniform laws on the subject of Bankruptcies."

And insert the following as Art: XVI viz

" Full faith and credit ought to be given in each State to the public acts, records, and Judicial proceedings of every other State, and the Legislature shall by general laws prescribe the manner in which such acts, Records, & proceedings shall be proved, and the effect which Judgments obtained in one State, shall have in another."

After receiving these reports

The House adjourned to 10 OC. on Monday next [1]

MONDAY SEPᴿ 3. 1787.[2]   IN CONVENTION

Mʳ Govʳ MORRIS moved to amend the Report concerning the respect to be paid to Acts Records &c of one State, in other States (see Sepᵣ 1.) by striking out " judgments obtained in one State shall have in another " and to insert the word " thereof " after the word " effect "

Col: MASON favored the motion, particularly if the " effect " was to be restrained to judgments & Judicial proceedings

Mʳ WILSON remarked, that if the Legislature were not allowed to *declare the effect* the provision would amount to nothing more than what now takes place among all Independent Nations.

Docʳ JOHNSON thought the amendment as worded would authorise the Genˡ Legislature to declare the effect of Legislative acts of one State, in another State.

Mʳ RANDOLPH considered it as strengthening the general objection agˢᵗ the plan, that its definition of the powers of the Government was so loose as to give it opportunities of usurping all the State powers. He was for not going farther than the Report, which enables the Legislature to provide for the effect of *Judgments*.

On the amendment as moved by Mʳ Govʳ Morris

Mas. ay. Cᵗ ay. N. J. ay. Pᵃ ay. Mᵈ no. Vᵃ no. N. C. ay. S. C. ay. Geo. no.[3]

On motion of Mʳ MADISON,[4] " ought to " was[5] struck out, and

---

[1] The phrase " to 10 OC on Monday next " is omitted in the transcript.

[2] The year " 1787 " is omitted in the transcript.

[3] In the transcript the vote reads: " Massachusetts, Connecticut, New Jersey, Pennsylvania, North Carolina, South Carolina, aye—6; Maryland, Virginia, Georgia, no—3."

[4] The expression " the words " is here inserted in the transcript.

[5] The word " was " is crossed out in the transcript and " were " is written above it.

" shall " inserted; and " shall " between " Legislature " & " by general laws " struck out, and " may " inserted, nem: con:

On the question to agree to the report as amended viz " Full faith & credit shall be given in each State to the public acts, records & judicial proceedings of every other State, and the Legislature may by general laws prescribe the manner in which such acts records & proceedings shall be proved, and the effect thereof "[1] Agreed to with! a count of [2] Sts.

The clause in the Report " To establish uniform laws on the subject of Bankruptcies " being taken up.

M? Sherman observed that Bankruptcies were in some cases punishable with death by the laws of England, & He did not chuse to grant a power by which that might be done here.

M? Gov? Morris said this was an extensive & delicate subject. He would agree to it because he saw no danger of abuse of the power by the Legislature of the U. S.

On the question to agree to the clause

N. H. ay. Mas. ay. C? no. N. J. ay. P? ay. M? ay. V? ay. N. C. ay. S. C. ay. Geo. ay.[3]

M? Pinkney moved to postpone the Report of the Committee of Eleven (see Sep? 1) in order to take up the following,

" The members of each House shall be incapable of holding any office under the U. S. for which they or any other for their benefit, receive any salary, fees or emoluments of any kind, and the acceptance of such office shall vacate their seats respectively." He was strenuously opposed to an ineligibility of members to office, and therefore wished to restrain the proposition to a mere incompatibility. He considered the eligibility of members of the Legislature to the honorable offices of Government, as resembling the policy of the Romans, in making the temple of virtue the road to the temple of fame.

On this question

N. H. no. Mas. no. C? no. N. J. no. P? ay. M? no. V? no. N. C. ay. S. C. no. Geo. no.[4]

M? King moved to insert the word " created " before the word " during " in the Report of the Committee. This he said would

---

[1] The words " it was " are here inserted in the transcript.
[2] The word " the " is here inserted in the transcript.
[3] In place of the vote by States the transcript reads: " Connecticut alone was in the negative."
[4] In the transcript the vote reads: " Pennsylvania, North Carolina, aye—2; New Hampshire, Massachusetts, Connecticut, New Jersey, Maryland, Virginia, South Carolina, Georgia, no—8."

exclude the members of the first Legislature under the Constitution, as most of the offices w^d then be created.

Mr WILLIAMSON 2^{ded} the motion. He did not see why members of the Legislature should be ineligible to *vacancies* happening during the term of their election.

Mr SHERMAN was for entirely incapacitating members of the Legislature. He thought their eligibility to offices would give too much influence to the Executive. He said the incapacity ought at least to be extended to cases where salaries should be *increased,* as well as *created,* during the term of the member. He mentioned also the expedient by which the restriction could be evaded to wit: an existing officer might be translated to an office created, and a member of the Legislature be then put into the office vacated.

Mr Govr MORRIS contended that the eligibility of members to office w^d lessen the influence of the Executive. If they cannot be appointed themselves, the Executive will appoint their relations & friends, retaining the service & votes of the members for his purposes in the Legislature. Whereas the appointment of the members deprives him of such an advantage.

Mr GERRY. thought the eligibility of members would have the effect of opening batteries agst good officers, in order to drive them out & make way for members of the Legislature.

Mr GORHAM was in favor of the amendment. Without it we go further than has been done in any of the States, or indeed any other Country. The experience of the State Governments where there was no such ineligibility, proved that it was not necessary; on the contrary that the eligibility was among the inducements for fit men to enter into the Legislative service

Mr RANDOLPH was inflexibly fixed against inviting men into the Legislature by the prospect of being appointed to offices.

Mr BALDWIN remarked that the example of the States was not applicable. The Legislatures there are so numerous that an exclusion of their members would not leave proper men for offices. The case would be otherwise in the General Government.

Col: MASON. Instead of excluding merit, the ineligibility will keep out corruption, by excluding office-hunters.

Mr WILSON considered the exclusion of members of the Legislature, as increasing the influence of the Executive as observed by Mr Govr Morris at the same time that it would diminish, the general energy of the Government. He said that the legal disqualification for office would be odious to those who did not wish for office, but did not wish either to be marked by so degrading a distinction.

M: PINKNEY. The first Legislature will be composed of the ablest men to be found. The States will select such to put the Government into operation. Should the Report of the Committee or even the amendment be agreed to, The great offices, even those of the Judiciary Department which are to continue for life, must be filled whilst those most capable of filling them will be under a disqualification.

On the question on M: King's motion

N. H. ay. Mas. ay. C: no. N. J. no. P: ay. M: no. V: ay. N. C. ay. S. C. no. Geo. no.[1]

The amendment being thus lost by the equal division of the States, M: WILLIAMSON moved to insert the words " created or the emoluments whereof shall have been increased " before the word " during " in the Report of the Committee

M: KING 2ded the motion, &

On the question

N. H. ay. Mas. ay. C: no. N. J. no. P: ay. M: no. V: ay. N. C. ay. S. C. no. Geo. divided.[2]

The last clause rendering a Seat in the Legislature & an office incompatible was agreed to nem. con:

The Report as amended & agreed to is as follows.

" The members of each House shall be ineligible to any Civil office under the authority of the U. States, created, or the emoluments whereof shall have been increased during the time for which they shall respectively be elected—and no person holding any office under the U. S. shall be a member of either House during his continuance in office."

Adjourned

TUESDAY SEP: 4. 1787.[3] IN CONVENTION

M: BREARLY from the Committee of eleven made a further partial Report as follows

" The Committee of Eleven to whom sundry resolutions &c were referred on the 31st of August, report that in their opinion the

---

[1] In the transcript the vote reads: " New Hampshire, Massachusetts, Pennsylvania, Virginia, North Carolina, aye—5; Connecticut, New Jersey, Maryland, South Carolina, Georgia, no—5."

[2] In the transcript the vote reads: " New Hampshire, Massachusetts, Pennsylvania, Virginia, North Carolina, aye—5; Connecticut, New Jersey, Maryland, South Carolina, aye—4; Georgia, divided."

[3] The year " 1787 " is omitted in the transcript.

following additions and alterations should be made to the Report before the Convention, viz

 * (1.) The first clause of sect: 1. art. 7. to read as follow—' The Legislature shall have power to lay and collect taxes duties imposts & excises, to pay the debts and provide for the common defence & general welfare, of the U. S.'

 (2). At the end of the 2ᵈ clause of sect. 1. art. 7. add ' and with the Indian Tribes.'

 (3) In the place of the 9ᵗʰ art. Sect. 1. to be inserted ' The Senate of the U. S. shall have power to try all impeachments; but no person shall be convicted without the concurrence of two thirds of the members present.'

 (4) After the word ' Excellency ' in sect. 1. art. 10. to be inserted. ' He shall hold his office during the term of four years, and together with the vice-President, chosen for the same term, be elected in the following manner, viz. Each State shall appoint in such manner as its Legislature may direct, a number of electors equal to the whole number of Senators and members of the House of Representatives to which the State may be entitled in the Legislature. The Electors shall meet in their respective States, and vote by ballot for two persons, of whom one at least shall not be an inhabitant of the same State with themselves; and they shall make a list of all the persons voted for, and of the number of votes for each, which list they shall sign and certify and transmit sealed to the Seat of the Genˡ Government, directed to the President of the Senate—The President of the Senate shall in that House open all the certificates; and the votes shall be then & there counted. The Person having the greatest number of votes shall be the President, if such number be a majority of that of the electors; and if there be more than one who have such majority, and have an equal number of votes, then the Senate shall immediately choose by ballot one of them for President: but if no person have a majority, then from the five highest on the list, the Senate shall choose by ballot the President. And in every case after the choice of the President, the person having the greatest number of votes shall be vice-president: but if there should remain two or more who have equal votes, the Senate shall choose from them the vice-President. The Legislature may determine the time of choosing and assembling the Electors, and the manner of certifying and transmitting their votes.'

 (5) ' Sect. 2. No person except a natural born citizen or a Citizen of the U. S. at the time of the adoption of this Constitution shall be eligible to the office of President; nor shall any person be elected to that office, who shall be under the age of thirty five years, and who has not been in the whole, at least fourteen years a resident within the U. S.'

 (6) ' Sect. 3. The vice-president shall be ex officio President of the Senate, except when they sit to try the impeachment of the

---

 * This is an exact copy. The variations in that in the printed Journal are occasioned by its incorporation of subsequent amendments. This remark is appliable to other cases.

President, in which case the Chief Justice shall preside, and excepting also when he shall exercise the powers and duties of President,
in which case & in case of his absence, the Senate shall chuse a
President pro tempore—The vice President when acting as President
of the Senate shall not have a vote unless the House be equally
divided.'

(7) ' Sect. 4. The President by and with the advice and Consent of the Senate, shall have power to make Treaties; and he shall
nominate and by and with the advice and consent of the Senate
shall appoint ambassadors, and other public Ministers, Judges of
the Supreme Court, and all other Officers of the U. S., whose appointments are not otherwise herein provided for. But no Treaty shall
be made without the consent of two thirds of the members present.'

(8) After the words—'' into the service of the U. S.'' in sect. 2.
art: 10. add ' and may require the opinion in writing of the principal officer in each of the Executive Departments, upon any subject
relating to the duties of their respective offices.'

[1] The latter part of Sect. 2. Art: 10. to read as follows.

(9) [1] ' He shall be removed from his office on impeachment by the
House of Representatives, and conviction by the Senate, for Treason,
or bribery, and in case of his removal as aforesaid, death, absence,
resignation or inability to discharge the powers or duties of his office,
the vice-president shall exercise those powers and duties until
another President be chosen, or until the inability of the President
be removed.'

The (1st) clause of the Report was agreed to, nem. con.

The (2) clause was also agreed to nem: con:

The (3) clause was postponed in order to decide previously on
the mode of electing the President.

The (4) clause was accordingly taken up.

M: GORHAM disapproved of making the next highest after the
President, the vice-President, without referring the decision to the
Senate in case the next highest should have less than a majority of
votes. as the regulation stands a very obscure man with very few
votes may arrive at that appointment

M: SHERMAN said the object of this clause of the report of the
Committee was to get rid of the ineligibility, which was attached to
the mode of election by the Legislature, & to render the Executive
independent of the Legislature. As the choice of the President was to
be made out of the five highest, obscure characters were sufficiently
guarded against in that case; and he had no objection to requiring
the vice-President to be chosen in like manner, where the choice
was not decided by a majority in the first instance

---

[1] The figure " 9 " is transposed to precede the sentence beginning " The
latter " . . . in the transcript.

M⸢ MADISON was apprehensive that by requiring both the President & vice President to be chosen out of the five highest candidates, the attention of the electors would be turned too much to making candidates instead of giving their votes in order to a definitive choice. Should this turn be given to the business, the election would, in fact be consigned to the Senate altogether. It would have the effect at the same time, he observed, of giving the nomination of the candidates to the largest States.

M⸢ Gov⸢ MORRIS concurred in, & enforced the remarks of M⸢ Madison.

M⸢ RANDOLPH & M⸢ PINKNEY wished for a particular explanation & discussion of the reasons for changing the mode of electing the Executive.

M⸢ Gov⸢ MORRIS said he would give the reasons of the Committee and his own. The 1ˢᵗ was the danger of intrigue & faction if the appointm⸢ should be made by the Legislature. 2.[1] the inconveniency[2] of an ineligibility required by that mode in order to lessen its evils. 3.[3] The difficulty of establishing a Court of Impeachments, other than the Senate which would not be so proper for the trial nor the other branch for the impeachment of the President, if appointed by the Legislature, 4.[4] No body had appeared to be satisfied with an appointment by the Legislature. 5.[5] Many were anxious even for an immediate choice by the people. 6.[6] the indispensible necessity of making the Executive independent of the Legislature.—As the Electors would vote at the same time throughout the U. S. and at so great a distance from each other, the great evil of cabal was avoided. It would be impossible also to corrupt them. A conclusive reason for making the Senate instead of the Supreme Court the Judge of impeachments, was that the latter was to try the President after the trial of the impeachment.

Col: MASON confessed that the plan of the Committee had removed some capital objections, particularly the danger of cabal and corruption. It was liable however to this strong objection, that nineteen times in twenty the President would be chosen by the Senate, an improper body for the purpose

M⸢ BUTLER thought the mode not free from objections, but much

---

[1] The figure " 2 " is changed in the transcript to " The next was."
[2] The word " inconveniency " is changed in the transcript to " inconvenience."
[3] The figure " 3 " is changed in the transcript to " The third was."
[4] The figure " 4 " is changed in the transcript to " In the fourth place."
[5] The figure "5" is changed in the transcript to " In the fifth place."
[6] The figure " 6 " is changed in the transcript to " And finally, the sixth reason was."

more so than an election by the Legislature, where as in elective monarchies, cabal faction & violence would be sure to prevail.

M! PINKNEY stated as objections to the mode 1.[1] that it threw the whole appointment in fact into the hands of the Senate. 2.[1] The Electors will be strangers to the several candidates and of course unable to decide on their comparative merits. 3.[1] It makes the Executive reeligible which will endanger the public liberty. 4.[1] It makes the same body of men which will in fact elect the President his Judges in case of an impeachment.

M! WILLIAMSON had great doubts whether the advantage of reeligibility would balance the objection to such a dependence of the President on the Senate for his reappointment. He thought at least the Senate ought to be restrained to the *two* highest on the list

M! GOV! MORRIS said the principal advantage aimed at was that of taking away the opportunity for cabal. The President may be made if thought necessary ineligible on this as well as on any other mode of election. Other inconveniences may be no less redressed on this plan than any other.

M! BALDWIN thought the plan not so objectionable when well considered, as at first view. The increasing intercourse among the people of the States, would render important characters less & less unknown; and the Senate would consequently be less & less likely to have the eventual appointment thrown into their hands.

M! WILSON. This subject has greatly divided the House, and will also divide [2] people out of doors. It is in truth the most difficult of all on which we have had to decide. He had never made up an opinion on it entirely to his own satisfaction. He thought the plan on the whole a valuable improvement on the former. It gets rid of one great evil, that of cabal & corruption; & Continental Characters will multiply as we more & more coalesce, so as to enable the electors in every part of the Union to know & judge of them. It clears the way also for a discussion of the question of re-eligibility on its own merits, which the former mode of election seemed to forbid. He thought it might be better however to refer the eventual appointment to the Legislature than to the Senate, and to confine it to a smaller number than five of the Candidates. The eventual election by the Legislature w⁴ not open cabal anew, as it would be restrained to certain designated objects of choice, and as these must have had the previous sanction of a number of the States: and if the election be

---

[1] The figures " 1," " 2," " 3 " and " 4 " are changed in the transcript to " first," " Secondly," etc.

[2] The word " the " is here inserted in the transcript.

made as it ought as soon as the votes of the electors are opened & it is known that no one has a majority of the whole, there can be little danger of corruption. Another reason for preferring the Legislature to the Senate in this business, was that the House of Rep⁴ will be so often changed as to be free from the influence & faction to which the permanence of the Senate may subject that branch.

M⁵ RANDOLPH preferred the former mode of constituting the Executive, but if the change was to be made, he wished to know why the eventual election was referred to the *Senate* and not to the *Legislature?* He saw no necessity for this and many objections to it. He was apprehensive also that the advantage of the eventual appointment would fall into the hands of the States near the Seat of Government.

M⁵ Gov⁵ MORRIS said the *Senate* was preferred because fewer could then, say to the President, you owe your appointment to us. He thought the President would not depend so much on the Senate for his re-appointment as on his general good conduct.

The further consideration of the Report was postponed that each member might take a copy of the remainder of it.

The following motion was referred to the Committee of Eleven— to wit,—" To prepare & report a plan for defraying the expences of the Convention "

* M⁵ PINKNEY moved a clause declaring " that each House should be judge of the privilege² of its own members. M⁵ Gov⁵ MORRIS 2ᵈᵉᵈ the motion

M⁵ RANDOLPH & M⁵ MADISON expressed doubts as to the propriety of giving such a power, & wished for a postponement.

M⁵ Gov⁵ MORRIS thought it so plain a case that no postponement could be necessary.

M⁵ WILSON thought the power involved, and the express insertion of it needless. It might beget doubts as to the power of other public bodies, as Courts &c. Every Court is the judge of its own privileges.

M⁵ MADISON distinguished between the power of Judging of privileges previously & duly established, and the effect of the motion which would give a discretion to each House as to the extent of its own privileges. He suggested that it would be better to make provision for ascertaining by *law*, the privileges of each House, than to

---

* This motion not inserted¹ in the printed Journal.

¹ The words " is not contained " are substituted in the transcript for "not inserted."

² The transcript uses the word "privilege" in the plural.

allow each House to decide for itself. He suggested also the necessity of considering what privileges ought to be allowed to the Executive.

Adjourned

WEDNESDAY SEP.ᴿ 5. 1787.[1] IN CONVENTION.

Mʳ BREARLEY from the Committee of Eleven made a farther report as follows,

(1) To add to the clause "to declare war" the words "and grant letters of marque and reprisal"

(2) To add to the clause "to raise and support armies" the words "but no appropriation of money to that use shall be for a longer term than two years"

(3) Instead of sect: 12. art 6. say—" All bills for raising revenue shall originate in the House of Representatives, and shall be subject to alterations and amendments by the Senate: no money shall be drawn from the Treasury, but in consequence of appropriations made by law."

(4) Immediately before the last clause of sect. 1. art. 7. insert " To exercise exclusive legislation in all cases whatsoever over such district (not exceeding ten miles square) as may by Cession of particular States and the acceptance of the Legislature become the seat of the Government of the U. S. and to exercise like authority over all places purchased for the erection of Forts, Magazines, Arsenals, Dock-Yards, and other needful buildings"

(5) " To promote the progress of Science and[2] useful arts by securing for limited times to authors & inventors, the exclusive right to their respective writings and discoveries"

This report being taken up.—The (1) clause was agreed to nem: con:

To the (2) clause Mʳ GERRY objected that it admitted of appropriations to an army, for two years instead of one, for which he could not conceive a reason. that it implied that[3] there was to be a standing army which he inveighed against as dangerous to liberty, as unnecessary even for so great an extent of Country as this, and if necessary, some restriction on the number & duration ought to be provided: Nor was this a proper time for such an innovation. The people would not bear it.

Mʳ SHERMAN remarked that the appropriations were permitted only, not required to be for two years. As the Legislature is to be

---

[1] The year "1787" is omitted in the transcript.
[2] The word "the" is here inserted in the transcript.
[3] The word "that" is omitted in the transcript.

biennially elected, it would be inconvenient to require appropriations to be for one year, as there might be no Session within the time necessary to renew them. He should himself he said like a reasonable restriction on the number and continuance of an army in time of peace.

The clause (2) was [1] agreed to nem: con:

The (3) clause, M: Gov: MORRIS moved to postpone. It had been agreed to in the Committee on the ground of compromise, and he should feel himself at liberty to dissent to [2] it, if on the whole he should not be satisfied with certain other parts to be settled.—M: PINKNEY 2[ded] the motion

M: SHERMAN was for giving immediate ease to those who looked on this clause as of great moment, and for trusting to their concurrence in other proper measures.

On the question for postponing

N. H. ay. Mas. no. C: ay. N. J. ay. P: ay. Del. ay. M[d] ay. V: no. N. C. ay. S. C. ay. Geo. ay. [3]

So much of the (4) clause as related to the seat of Government was agreed to nem: con:

On the residue, to wit, " to exercise like authority over all places purchased for forts &c.

M: GERRY contended that this power might be made use of to enslave any particular State by buying up its territory, and that the strongholds proposed would be a means of awing the State into an undue obedience to the Gen: Government.

M: KING thought himself the provision unnecessary, the power being already involved: but would move to insert after the word " purchased " the words " by the consent of the Legislature of the State " This would certainly make the power safe.

M: Gov: MORRIS 2[ded] the motion, which was agreed to nem: con: as was then the residue of the clause as amended.

The (5) clause was agreed to nem: con:

The following resolution & order being reported from the Committee of eleven, to wit,

" Resolved that the U. S. in Congress be requested to allow and cause to be paid to the Secretary and other officers of this Convention

---

[1] The word " then " is here inserted in the transcript.

[2] The word " to " is crossed out in the transcript and " from " is written above it.

[3] In the transcript the vote reads: " New Hampshire, Connecticut, New Jersey, Pennsylvania, Delaware, Maryland, North Carolina, South Carolina, Georgia, aye—9; Massachusetts, Virginia, no—2."

such sums in proportion to their respective times of service, as are allowed to the Secretary & similar officers of Congress."

" Ordered that the Secretary make out & transmit to the Treasury office of the U. S. an account for the said Services, & for the incidental expences of this Convention "

The resolution & order were separately agreed to nem: con:

M! GERRY gave notice that he should move to reconsider articles XIX. XX. XXI. XXII.

M! WILLIAMSON gave like notice as to the Article fixing the number of Representatives, which he thought too small. He wished also to allow Rho: Island more than one, as due to her probable number of people, and as proper to stifle any pretext arising from her absence on the occasion.

The Report made yesterday as to the appointment of the Executive being [1] taken up. M! PINKNEY renewed his opposition to the mode, arguing 1.[2] that the electors will not have sufficient knowledge of the fittest men, & will be swayed by an attachment to the eminent men of their respective States. Hence 2dly the dispersion of the votes would leave the appointment with the Senate, and as the President's re-appointment will thus depend on the Senate he will be the mere creature of that body. 3.[2] He will combine with the Senate agst the House of Representatives. 4.[2] This change in the mode of election was meant to get rid of the ineligibility of the President a second time, whereby he will become fixed for life under the auspices of the Senate

M! GERRY did not object to this plan of constituting the Executive in itself, but should be governed in his final vote by the powers that may be given to the President.

M! RUTLIDGE was much opposed to the plan reported by the Committee. It would throw the whole power into the Senate. He was also against a re-eligibility. He moved to postpone the Report under consideration & take up the original plan of appointment by the Legislature, to wit. " He shall be elected by joint ballot by the Legislature to which election a majority of the votes of the members present shall be required: He shall hold his office during the term of seven years; but shall not be elected a second time."

On this motion to postpone

---

[1] The word " then " is here inserted in the transcript.
[2] The figures " 1," " 3 " and " 4 " are changed to " first," " Thirdly " and " Fourthly " in the transcript.

N. H. div⁴ Mas. no. C⁴ no. N. J. no P⁴ no. Del. no. M⁴ no. V⁴ no. N. C. ay. S. C. ay. Geo. no.[1]

Col. MASON admitted that there were objections to an appointment by the Legislature as originally planned. He had not yet made up his mind, but would state his objections to the mode proposed by the Committee. 1.[2] It puts the appointment in fact into the hands of the Senate, as it will rarely happen that a majority of the whole votes will fall on any one candidate: and as the Existing President will always be one of the 5 highest, his re-appointment will of course depend on the Senate. 2.[2] Considering the powers of the President & those of the Senate, if a coalition should be established between these two branches, they will be able to subvert the Constitution—The great objection with him would be removed by depriving the Senate of the eventual election. He accordingly moved to strike out the words '' if such number be a majority of that of the electors.''

M⁴ WILLIAMSON 2ᵈᵉᵈ the motion. He could not agree to the clause without some such modification. He preferred making the highest tho' not having a majority of the votes, President, to a reference of the matter to the Senate. Referring the appointment to the Senate lays a certain foundation for corruption & aristocracy.

M⁴ GOV⁴ MORRIS thought the point of less consequence than it was supposed on both sides. It is probable that a majority of votes will fall on the same man. As each elector is to give two votes, more than ¼ will give a majority. Besides as one vote is to be given to a man out of the State, and as this vote will not be thrown away, ½ the votes will fall on characters eminent & generally known. Again if the President shall have given satisfaction, the votes will turn on him of course, and a majority of them will reappoint him, without resort to the Senate: If he should be disliked, all disliking him, would take care to unite their votes so as to ensure his being supplanted.

Col. MASON those who think there is no danger of there not being a majority for the same person in the first instance, ought to give up the point to those who think otherwise.

M⁴ SHERMAN reminded the opponents of the new mode proposed that if the small states had the advantage in the Senate's deciding among the five highest candidates, the large States would have in fact the nomination of these candidates

---

[1] In the transcript the vote reads: "North Carolina, South Carolina, aye —2; Massachusetts, Connecticut, New Jersey, Pennsylvania, Delaware, Maryland, Virginia, Georgia, no—8; New Hampshire, divided."

[2] The figures "1" and "2" are changed in the transcript to "First" and "Secondly."

On the motion of Col: Mason

N. H. no. Mas. no. Cᵗ no. N. J. no. Pᵃ no. Del. no. Mᵈ ay.*
Vᵃ no. N. C. ay. S. C. no. Geo. no.[1]

Mʳ WILSON moved to strike out " Senate " and insert the word " Legislature "

Mʳ MADISON considered it as[2] a primary object to render an eventual resort to any part of the Legislature improbable. He was apprehensive that the proposed alteration would turn the attention of the large States too much to the appointment of candidates, instead of aiming at an effectual appointment of the officer, as the large States would predominate in the Legislature which would have the final choice out of the Candidates. Whereas if the Senate in which the small States predominate should have this[3] final choice, the concerted effort of the large States would be to make the appointment in the first instance conclusive.

Mʳ RANDOLPH. We have in some revolutions of this plan made a bold stroke for Monarchy. We are now doing the same for an aristocracy. He dwelt on the tendency of such an influence in the Senate over the election of the President in addition to its other powers, to convert that body into a real & dangerous Aristocracy.

Mʳ DICKINSON was in favor of giving the eventual election to the Legislature, instead of the Senate. It was too much influence to be superadded to that body.

On the question moved by Mʳ Wilson

N. H. divᵈ Mas. no. Cᵗ no. N. J. no. Pᵃ ay. Del. no. Mᵈ no.
Vᵃ ay. N. C. no. S. C. ay. Geo. no.[4]

Mʳ MADISON & Mʳ WILLIAMSON moved to strike out the word " majority " and insert " one third " so that the eventual power might not be exercised if less than a majority, but not less than ⅓ of the Electors should vote for the same person.

Mʳ GERRY objected that this would put it in the power of three or four States to put in whom they pleased.

Mʳ WILLIAMSON. There are seven States which do not contain one third of the people. If the Senate are to appoint, less than one sixth of the people will have the power.

* In printed Journal Maryland—no.

---

[1] In the transcript the vote reads: "Maryland,* North Carolina, aye; the other nine States, no."

[2] The word "as" is stricken out in the transcript.

[3] The word "the" is substituted in the transcript for "this."

[4] In the transcript the vote reads: "Pennsylvania, Virginia, South Carolina, aye—3; Massachusetts, Connecticut, New Jersey, Delaware, Maryland, North Carolina, Georgia, no—7; New Hampshire, divided."

On the question

N. H. no. Mas. no. C! no. N. J. no. P? no. Del. no. M⁴ no.
V? ay. N. C. ay. S. C. no. Geo. no.[1]

M⁖ GERRY suggested that the eventual election should be made by six Senators and seven Representatives cnosen by joint ballot of both Houses.

M⁖ KING observed that the influence of the Small States in the Senate was somewhat balanced by the influence of the large States in bringing forward the candidates; * and also by the Concurrence of the small States in the Committee in the clause vesting the exclusive origination of Money bills in the House of Representatives.

Col: MASON moved to strike out the word " five " and insert the word " three " as the highest candidates for the Senate to choose out of.

M⁖ GERRY 2ᵈᵉᵈ the motion

M⁖ SHERMAN would sooner give up the plan. He would prefer seven or thirteen.

On the question moved by Col: Mason & M⁖ Gerry

N. H. no. Mas. no. C! no. N. J. no. P? no. Delaware M⁴ no.
V? ay. N. C. ay. S. C. no. Geo. no.[3]

M⁖ SPAIGHT and M⁖ RUTLIDGE moved to strike out " five " and insert " thirteen "—to which all the States disagreed—except N. C. & S. C.

M⁖ MADISON & M⁖ WILLIAMSON moved to insert after " Electors " the words " who shall have balloted " so that the non voting electors not being counted might not increase the number necessary as a majority of the whole, to decide the choice without the agency of the Senate.

On this question

---

* This explains the compromise mentioned above[2] by M⁖ Gov⁖ Morris. Col. Mason M⁖ Gerry & other members from large States set great value on this privilege of originating money bills. Of this the members from the small States, with some from the large States who wished a high mounted Gov⁖ endeavored to avail themselves, by making that privilege, the price of arrangements in the constitution favorable to the small States, and to the elevation of the Government.

---

[1] In the transcript the vote reads: " Virginia, North Carolina, aye; the other nine States, no."
[2] The words " alluded to " are substituted in the transcript for " mentioned above."
[3] In the transcript the vote reads: " Virginia, North Carolina, aye; nine States, no."

N. H. no. Mas. no. C̤ no. N. J. no. P̤ ay. Del. no. M̤ ay. V̤ ay. N. C. ay. S. C. no. Geo. no.[1]

M̤ Dickinson moved, in order to remove ambiguity from the intention of the clause as explained by the vote, to add, after the words " if such number be a majority of the whole number of the Electors " the word " appointed "

On this motion

N. H. ay. Mas. ay. Con: ay. N. J. ay. P̤ ay. Delaware M̤ ay. V̤ no. N. C. no. S. C. ay. Geo. ay.[2]

Col: Mason. As the mode of appointment is now regulated, he could not forbear expressing his opinion that it is utterly inadmissible. He would prefer the Government of Prussia to one which will put all power into the hands of seven or eight men, and fix an Aristocracy worse than absolute monarchy.

The words " and of their giving their votes " being inserted on motion for that purpose, after the words " The Legislature may determine the time of chusing and assembling the Electors "

The House adjourned.

Thursday Sep̤ 6. 1787.[3] In Convention

M̤ King and M̤ Gerry moved to insert in the (5)[4] clause of the Report (see Sep̤ 4[5]) after the words " may be entitled in the Legislature " the words following—" But no person shall be appointed an elector who is a member of the Legislature of the U. S. or who holds any office of profit or trust under the U. S." which passed nem: con:

M̤ Gerry proposed, as the President was to be elected by the Senate out of the five highest candidates, that if he should not at the end of his term be re-elected by a majority of the Electors, and no other candidate should have a majority, the eventual election should be made by the Legislature. This he said would relieve the

---

[1] In the transcript the vote reads: " Pennsylvania, Maryland, Virginia, North Carolina, aye—4; New Hampshire, Massachusetts, Connecticut, New Jersey, Delaware, South Carolina, Georgia, no—7."

[2] In the transcript the vote reads: " New Hampshire, Massachusetts, Connecticut, New Jersey, Pennsylvania, Delaware, Maryland, South Carolina, Georgia, aye—9; Virginia, North Carolina, no—2."

[3] The year " 1787 " is omitted in the transcript.

[4] The word " fourth " is substituted in the transcript for " (5)," the latter being an error.

[5] In the transcript the date reads: " the fourth of September."

President from his particular dependence on the Senate for his continuance in office.

M⁎ KING liked the idea, as calculated to satisfy particular members & promote unanimity, & as likely to operate but seldom.

M⁎ READ opposed it, remarking that if individual members were to be indulged, alterations would be necessary to satisfy most of them.

M⁎ WILLIAMSON espoused it as a reasonable precaution against the undue influence of the Senate.

M⁎ SHERMAN liked the arrangement as it stood, though he should not be averse to some amendments. He thought he said that if the Legislature were to have the eventual appointment instead of the Senate, it ought to vote in the case by States, in favor of the small States, as the large States would have so great an advantage in nominating the candidates.

M⁎ Gov⁎ MORRIS thought favorably of M⁎ Gerry's proposition. It would free the President from being tempted in naming to Offices, to Conform to the will of the Senate, & thereby virtually give the appointments to office, to the Senate.

M⁎ WILSON said that he had weighed carefully the report of the Committee for remodelling the constitution of the Executive; and on combining it with other parts of the plan, he was obliged to consider the whole as having a dangerous tendency to aristocracy; as throwing a dangerous power into the hands of the Senate. They will have in fact, the appointment of the President, and through his dependence on them, the virtual appointment to offices; among others the offices of the Judiciary Department. They are to make Treaties; and they are to try all impeachments. In allowing them thus to make the Executive & Judiciary appointments, to be the Court of impeachments, and to make Treaties which are to be laws of the land, the Legislative, Executive & Judiciary powers are all blended in one branch of the Government. The power of making Treaties involves the case of subsidies, and here as an additional evil, foreign influence is to be dreaded. According to the plan as it now stands, the President will not be the man of the people as he ought to be, but the Minion of the Senate. He cannot even appoint a tide-waiter without the Senate. He had always thought the Senate too numerous a body for making appointments to office. The Senate, will moreover in all probability be in constant Session. They will have high salaries. And with all those powers, and the President in their interest, they will depress the other branch of the Legislature, and aggrandize themselves in proportion. Add to all this, that the Senate sitting in conclave, can by holding up to their respective States various and improbable candidates, contrive so to scatter their votes, as to bring the appointment of the President ultimately before themselves. Upon the whole, he thought the new mode of appointing the President, with some amendments, a valuable improvement; but he could never agree to purchase it at the price of the ensuing parts of the Report, nor befriend a system of which they make a part.

M: Gov: Morris expressed his wonder at the observations of M: Wilson so far as they preferred the plan in the printed Report to the new modification of it before the House, and entered into a comparative view of the two, with an eye to the nature of M: Wilsons objections to the last. By the first the Senate he observed had a voice in appointing the President out of all the Citizens of the U. S: by this they were limited to five candidates previously nominated to them, with a probability of being barred altogether by the successful ballot of the Electors. Here surely was no increase of power. They are now to appoint Judges nominated to them by the President. Before they had the appointment without any agency whatever of the President. Here again was surely no additional power. If they are to make Treaties as the plan now stands, the power was the same in the printed plan. If they are to try impeachments, the Judges must have been triable by them before. Wherein then lay the dangerous tendency of the innovations to establish an aristocracy in the Senate? As to the appointment of officers, the weight of sentiment in the House, was opposed to the exercise of it by the President alone; though it was not the case with himself. If the Senate would act as was suspected, in misleading the States into a fallacious disposition of their votes for a President, they would, if the appointment were withdrawn wholly from them, make such representations in their several States where they have influence, as would favor the object of their partiality.

M: Williamson. replying to M: Morris: observed that the aristocratic complexion proceeds from the change in the mode of appointing the President which makes him dependent on the Senate.

M: Clymer said that the aristocratic part to which he could never accede was that in the printed plan, which gave the Senate the power of appointing to offices.

M: Hamilton said that he had been restrained from entering into the discussions by his dislike of the Scheme of Gov: in General; but as he meant to support the plan to be recommended, as better than nothing, he wished in this place to offer a few remarks. He liked the new modification, on the whole, better than that in the printed Report. In this the President was a Monster elected for seven years, and ineligible afterwards; having great powers, in appointments to office, & continually tempted by this constitutional disqualification to abuse them in order to subvert the Government. Although he should be made re-eligible, still if appointed by the Legislature, he would be tempted to make use of corrupt influence to be continued in office. It seemed peculiarly desireable therefore that some other mode of election should be devised. Considering the different views of different States, & the different districts Northern Middle & Southern, he concurred with those who thought that the votes would not be concentered, and that the appointment would consequently in the present mode devolve on the Senate. The nomination to offices will give great weight to the President. Here then is a mutual connection & influence, that will perpetuate the President, and aggrandize both him & the Senate. What is to be the remedy? He saw none better than to let the highest number of ballots, whether a majority or not, appoint the President. What was the objection to this? Merely that too small a number might appoint. But as the plan stands, the Senate may take the candidate having the smallest number of votes, and make him President.

Mʳ SPAIGHT & Mʳ WILLIAMSON moved to insert " seven " instead of " four " years for the term of the President— *

On this motion

N. H. ay. Mas. no. Cᵗ no. N. J. no. Pᵃ no. Del. no. Mᵈ no. Vᵃ ay. N. C. ay. S. C. no. Geo. no.[2]

Mʳ SPAIGHT & Mʳ WILLIAMSON, then moved to insert " six " instead of " four."

On which motion

N. H. no. Mas. no. Cᵗ no. N. J. no. Pᵃ no. Del. no. Mᵈ no. Vᵃ no. N. C. ay. S. C. ay. Geo. no[3]

On the term " four " all the States were ay, except N. Carolina, no.

On the question[4] (Clause 4. in the Report) for Appointing[5] Presi-

* Transfer hither what is brackets.[1]
[* An ineligibility wᵈ have followed (tho' it wᵈ seem from the vote not in the opinion of all) this prolongation of the term.]

---

[1] Madison's direction is omitted in the transcript.
[2] In the transcript the vote reads: " New Hampshire, Virginia, North Carolina, aye—3; Massachusetts, Connecticut, New Jersey, Pennsylvania, Delaware, Maryland, South Carolina, Georgia, no—8."
[3] In the transcript the vote reads: " North Carolina, South Carolina, aye—2; New Hampshire, Massachusetts, Connecticut, New Jersey, Pennsylvania, Delaware, Maryland, Virginia, Georgia, no—9."
[4] The words " on the " are here inserted in the transcript.
[5] The word " the " is here inserted in the transcript.

dent by electors—down to the words,—" entitled in the Legislature " inclusive.

N. H. ay. Mas: ay. Con! ay N. J. ay. P? ay. Del. ay. M? ay. V? ay. N. C. no. S. C. no. Geo. ay.[1]

It was moved that the Electors meet at the seat of the Gen! Gov! which passed in the Negative. N. C. only being ay.

It was[2] moved to insert the words " under the seal of the State " after the word " transmit " in[3] 4th clause of the Report which was disagreed to; as was another motion to insert the words " and who shall have given their votes " after the word " appointed " in the 4th Clause of the Report as added yesterday on motion of M? Dickinson.

On several motions, the words " in presence of the Senate and House of Representatives " were inserted after the word " counted " and the word " immediately " before the word " choose "; and the words " of the Electors " after the word " votes."

M? SPAIGHT said if the election by Electors is to be crammed down, he would prefer their meeting altogether and deciding finally without any reference to the Senate and moved " That the Electors meet at the seat of the General Government."

M? WILLIAMSON 2ded the motion, on which all the States were in the negative except N: Carolina.

On motion the words " But the election shall be on the same day throughout the U. S." were added after the words " transmitting their votes "

N. H. ay. Mas. no. C! ay. N. J. no. P? ay. Del. no. M? ay. V? ay. N. C. ay. S. C. ay. Geo—ay.[4]

On a question on the sentence in clause (4). " if such number be a majority of that of the Electors appointed."

N. H. ay. Mas. ay. C! ay. N. J. ay. P? no. Del. ay. M? ay. V? no. N. C. no. S. C. ay. Geo. ay.[5]

On a question on the clause referring the eventual appointment of the President to the Senate

---

[1] In the transcript the vote reads: "New Hampshire, Massachusetts, Connecticut, New Jersey, Pennsylvania, Delaware, Maryland, Virginia, Georgia, aye—9; North Carolina, South Carolina, no—2."

[2] The word "then" is here inserted in the transcript.

[3] The word "the" is here inserted in the transcript.

[4] In the transcript the vote reads: "New Hampshire, Connecticut, Pennsylvania, Maryland, Virginia, North Carolina, South Carolina, Georgia, aye—8; Massachusetts, New Jersey, Delaware, no—3."

[5] In the transcript the vote reads: "New Hampshire, Massachusetts, Connecticut, New Jersey, Delaware, Maryland, South Carolina, Georgia, aye—8; Pennsylvania, Virginia, North Carolina, no—3."

N. H. ay. Mas. ay. C⸱ ay. N. J. ay. P⸱ ay. Del. ay. V⸱ ay. N. C. no.[1] Here the call ceased.

M⸱ MADISON made a motion requiring ⅔ at least of the Senate to be present at the choice of a President. M⸱ PINKNEY 2ᵈᵉᵈ the motion

M⸱ GORHAM thought it a wrong principle to require more than a majority in any case. In the present case [2] it might prevent for a long time any choice of a President. On the question moved by M⸱ M. & M⸱ P.

N. H. ay: Mas. abs⸱ C⸱ no. N. J. no. P⸱ no. Del. no. Mᵈ ay. V⸱ ay. N. C. ay. S. C. ay. Geo. ay.[3]

M⸱ WILLIAMSON suggested as better than an eventual choice by the Senate, that this choice should be made by the Legislature, voting *by States* and not *per capita*.

M⸱ SHERMAN suggested the House of Rep⸱ as preferable to the Legislature, and moved, accordingly,

To strike out the words " The Senate shall immediately choose &c." and insert " The House of Representatives shall immediately choose by ballot one of them for President, the members from each State having one vote."

Col: MASON liked the latter mode best as lessening the aristocratic influence of the Senate.

On the Motion of M⸱ Sherman

N. H. ay. Mas. ay. C⸱ ay. N. J. ay. P⸱ ay. Del. no. Mᵈ ay. V⸱ ay. N. C. ay. S. C. ay. Geo. ay.[4]

M⸱ GOV⸱ MORRIS suggested the idea of providing that in all cases, the President in office, should not be one of the five Candidates; but be only re-eligible in case a majority of the electors should vote for him. [This was another expedient for rendering the President independent of the Legislative body for his continuance in office.]

M⸱ MADISON remarked that as a majority of members wᵈ make a quorum in the H. of Rep⸱ it would follow from the amendment of M⸱ Sherman giving the election to a majority of States, that the

---

[1] In the transcript the vote reads: " New Hampshire, Massachusetts, Connecticut, New Jersey, Pennsylvania, Delaware, Virginia, aye—7; North Carolina, no."

[2] The word " case " is omitted in the transcript.

[3] In the transcript the vote reads: " New Hampshire, Maryland, Virginia, North Carolina, South Carolina, Georgia, aye—6; Connecticut, New Jersey, Pennsylvania, Delaware, no—4; Massachusetts, absent."

[4] In the transcript the vote reads: " New Hampshire, Massachusetts, Connecticut, New Jersey, Pennsylvania, Maryland, Virginia, North Carolina, South Carolina, Georgia, aye—10. Delaware, no—1."

President might be elected by two States only, Virg: & Pen: which have 18 members, if these States alone should be present

On a motion that the eventual election of Presid: in case of *an equality* [1] of the votes of the electors be referred to the House of Rep:

N. H. ay. Mas. ay. N. J. no. P: ay. Del. no. M: no. V: ay. N. C. ay. S. C. ay. Geo. ay.[2]

M: KING moved to add to the amendment of M: Sherman " But a quorum for this purpose shall consist of a member or members from two thirds of the States," and also of a majority of the whole number of the House of Representatives."

Col: MASON liked it as obviating the remark of M: Madison— The motion as far as " States " inclusive was ag: to. On the residue to wit, " and also of a majority of the whole number of the House of Rep: it passed in the Negative.

N. H. no. Mas. ay. C: ay. N. J. no. P: ay. Del. no. M: no. V: ay. N. C. ay. S. C. no. Geo. no.[3]

The Report relating to the appointment of the Executive stands as amended, as follows,

" He shall hold his office during the term of four years, and together with the vice-President, chosen for the same term, be elected in the following manner.

Each State shall appoint in such manner as its Legislature may direct, a number of electors equal to the whole number of Senators and members of the House of Representatives, to which the State may be entitled in the Legislature:

But no person shall be appointed an Elector who is a member of the Legislature of the U. S. or who holds any office of profit or trust under the U. S.

The Electors shall meet in their respective States and vote by ballot for two persons, of whom one at least shall not be an inhabitant of the same State with themselves; and they shall make a list of all the persons voted for, and of the number of votes for each, which list they shall sign and certify, and transmit sealed to the Seat of the General Government, directed to the President of the Senate.

The President of the Senate shall in the presence of the Senate and House of Representatives open all the certificates & the votes shall then be counted.

The person having the greatest number of votes shall be the

---

[1] The transcript does not italicize the words " *an equality*."
[2] In the transcript the vote reads: " New Hampshire, Massachusetts, Pennsylvania, Virginia, North Carolina, South Carolina, Georgia, aye—7; New Jersey, Delaware, Maryland, no—3."
[3] In the transcript the vote reads: " Massachusetts, Connecticut, Pennsylvania, Virginia, North Carolina, aye—5; New Hampshire, New Jersey, Delaware, Maryland, South Carolina, Georgia, no—6."

President (if such number be a majority of the whole number of electors appointed) and if there be more than one who have such majority, and have an equal number of votes, then the House of Representatives shall immediately choose by ballot one of them for President, the Representation from each State having one vote. But if no person have a majority, then from the five highest on the list, the House of Representatives shall in like manner choose by ballot the President. In the choice of a President by the House of Representatives, a Quorum shall consist of a member or members from two thirds of the States [* and the concurrence of a majority of all the States shall be necessary to such choice.]—And in every case after the choice of the President, the person having the greatest number of votes of the Electors shall be the vice-president: But, if there should remain two or more who have equal votes, the Senate shall choose from them the vice-President.

The Legislature may determine the time of choosing the Electors, and of their giving their votes; and the manner of certifying and transmitting their votes—But the election shall be on the same day throughout the U. States."

Adjourned

FRIDAY SEP.ᴿ 7. 1787.³ IN CONVENTION

The mode of constituting the Executive being resumed, M.ʳ RANDOLPH moved, to insert in the first Section of the report made yesterday⁴

" The Legislature may declare by law what officer of the U. S. shall act as President in case of the death, resignation, or disability of the President and Vice-President; and such officer shall act accordingly until the time of electing a President shall arrive."

M.ʳ MADISON observed that this, as worded, would prevent a supply of the vacancy by an intermediate election of the President, and moved to substitute—" until such disability be removed, or a President shall be elected.† M.ʳ GOVERN.ʳ MORRIS 2ᵈᵉᵈ the motion, which was agreed to.

It seemed to be an objection to the provision with some, that according to the process established for chusing the Executive, there would be difficulty in effecting it at other than the fixed periods;

* NOTE. This clause was not inserted on this day, but on the 7ᵗʰ ¹ Sep.ʳ See Friday the 7ᵗʰ ³

† In the printed Journal this amendment is put into the original Motion.

---

¹ The word " of " is here inserted in the transcript.
² The word " inst." is here inserted in the transcript.
³ The year " 1787 " is omitted in the transcript.
⁴ The words " the following " are here inserted in the transcript.

with others, that the Legislature was restrained in the temporary appointment to *" officers "* of the *U. S:* They wished it to be at liberty to appoint others than such.

On the Motion of M? Randolph as amended, it passed in the affirmative

N. H. divided. Mas. no. C? no. N. J. ay. P? ay. Del. no. M? ay. V? ay. N. C. no. S. C. ay. Geo. ay.[1]

M? GERRY moved " that in the election of President by the House of Representatives, no State shall vote by less than three members, and where that number may not be allotted to a State, it shall be made up by its Senators; and a concurrence of a majority of all the States shall be necessary to make such choice." Without some such provision five individuals might possibly be competent to an election; these being a majority of two thirds of the existing number of States; and two thirds being a quorum for this business.

M? MADISON 2^{ded} the motion

M? READ observed that the States having but one member only in the House of Rep? would be in danger of having no vote at all in the election: the sickness or absence either of the Representative or one of the Senators would have that effect.

M? MADISON replied that, if one member of the House of Representatives should be left capable of voting for the State, the states having one Representative only would still be subject to that danger. He thought it an evil that so small a number at any rate should be authorized, to elect. Corruption would be greatly facilitated by it. The mode itself was liable to this further weighty objection that the representatives of a *Minority* of the people, might reverse the choice of a *majority* of the *States* and of the *people.* He wished some cure for this inconveniency[2] might yet be provided.

M? GERRY withdrew the first part of his motion; and on the,— Question on the 2^d part viz. " and a concurrence of a majority of all the States shall be necessary to make such choice " to follow the words " a member or members from two thirds of the States "—It was agreed to nem: con:

The section 2. (see Sep? 4) requiring that the President should be a natural-born Citizen, &c & have been resident for fourteen years, & be thirty five years of age, was agreed to nem: con:

---

[1] In the transcript the vote reads: "New Jersey, Pennsylvania, Maryland, Virginia, South Carolina, Georgia, aye—6; Massachusetts, Connecticut, Delaware, North Carolina, no—4; New Hampshire, divided."

[2] The word " inconveniency " is changed to " inconvenience " in the transcript.

[1] Section 3. (see Sep: 4). " The vice President shall be ex-officio President of the Senate "

M: GERRY opposed this regulation. We might as well put the President himself at the head of the Legislature. The close intimacy that must subsist between the President & vice-president makes it absolutely improper. He was ag:t having any vice President.

M: Gov: MORRIS. The vice president then will be the first heir apparent that ever loved his father. If there should be no vice president, the President of the Senate would be temporary successor, which would amount to the same thing.

M: SHERMAN saw no danger in the case. If the vice-President were not to be President of the Senate, he would be without employment, and some member by being made President must be deprived of his vote, unless when an equal division of votes might happen in the Senate, which would be but seldom.

M: RANDOLPH concurred in the opposition to the clause.

M: WILLIAMSON, observed that such an officer as vice-President was not wanted. He was introduced only for the sake of a valuable mode of election which required two to be chosen at the same time.

Col: MASON, thought the office of vice-President an encroachment on the rights of the Senate; and that it mixed too much the Legislative & Executive, which as well as the Judiciary departments,[2] ought to be kept as separate as possible. He took occasion to express his dislike of any reference whatever of the power to make appointments to either branch of the Legislature. On the other hand he was averse to vest so dangerous a power in the President alone. As a method for avoiding both, he suggested that a privy Council of six members to the president should be established; to be chosen for six years by the Senate, two out of the Eastern two out of the middle, and two out of the Southern quarters of the Union, & to go out in rotation two every second year; the concurrence of the Senate to be required only in the appointment of Ambassadors, and in making treaties, which are more of a legislative nature. This would prevent the constant sitting of the Senate which he thought dangerous, as well as keep the departments separate & distinct. It would also save the expence of constant sessions of the Senate. He had he said always considered the Senate as too unwieldy & ex-

---

[1] This paragraph is changed in the transcript to read as follows: " The third section, ' The Vice-President shall be *ex-officio* President of the Senate ' being then considered."

[2] The letter " s " is stricken from the word " departments " in the transcript.

pensive for appointing officers, especially the smallest, such as tide waiters &c. He had not reduced his idea to writing, but it could be easily done if it should be found acceptable.

On the question shall the vice President be ex officio President of the Senate?

N. H. ay. Mas. ay. Cᵗ ay. N. J. no. Pᵃ ay. Del ay. Mas no. Vᵃ ay. N. C. absᵗ S. C. ay. Geo. ay.[1]

The other parts of the same Section (3) [2] were then agreed to.

The Section 4.—to wit, " The President by & with the advice and consent of the Senate shall have power to make Treaties &c " [3]

Mᵣ WILSON moved to add, after the word " Senate " the words, " and House of Representatives." As treaties he said are to have the operation of laws, they ought to have the sanction of laws also. The circumstance of secrecy in the business of treaties formed the only objection; but this he thought, so far as it was inconsistent with obtaining the Legislative sanction, was outweighed by the necessity of the latter.

Mᵣ SHERMAN thought the only question that could be made was whether the power could be safely trusted to the Senate. He thought it could; and that the necessity of secresy in the case of treaties forbade a reference of them to the whole Legislature.

Mᵣ FITZIMMONS 2ᵈᵉᵈ the motion of Mᵣ Wilson, & on the question N. H. no. Mas. no. Cᵗ no. N. J. no. Pᵃ ay. Del. no. Mᵈ no. Vᵃ no. N. C. no. S. C. no. Geo. no.[4]

The first sentence as to making treaties was then Agreed to: nem: con:

[5] " He shall nominate &c Appoint Ambassadors &c."

Mᵣ WILSON objected to the mode of appointing, as blending a branch of the Legislature with the Executive. Good laws are of no effect without a good Executive; and there can be no good Executive without a responsible appointment of officers to execute. Responsibility is in a manner destroyed by such an agency of the Senate. He would prefer the council proposed by Col: Mason, provided its advice should not be made obligatory on the President.

---

[1] In the transcript the vote reads: " New Hampshire, Massachusetts, Connecticut, Pennsylvania, Delaware, Virginia, South Carolina, Georgia, aye—8; New Jersey, Maryland, no—2; North Carolina, absent."

[2] The figure " 3 " is omitted in the transcript.

[3] The phrase " was then taken up " is here added in the transcript.

[4] In the transcript the vote reads: " Pennsylvania, aye—1; New Hampshire, Massachusetts, Connecticut, New Jersey, Delaware, Maryland, Virginia, North Carolina, South Carolina, Georgia, no—10."

[5] The words " On the clause " are here inserted in the transcript.

M: PINKNEY was against joining the Senate in these appointments, except in the instance of Ambassadors whom [1] he thought ought not to be appointed by the President

M: Gov: MORRIS said that as the President was to nominate, there would be responsibility, and as the Senate was to concur, there would be security. As Congress now make appointments there is no responsibility.

M: GERRY. The idea of responsibility in the nomination to offices is chimerical. The President can not know all characters, and can therefore always plead ignorance.

M: KING. As the idea of a Council proposed by Col. Mason has been supported by M: Wilson, he would remark that most of the inconveniencies charged on the Senate are incident to a Council of Advice. He differed from those who thought the Senate would sit constantly. He did not suppose it was meant that all the minute officers were to be appointed by the Senate, or any other original source, but by the higher officers of the departments to which they belong. He was of opinion also that the people would be alarmed at an unnecessary creation of new Corps which must increase the expence as well as influence of the Government.

On the question on these words in the clause viz—" He shall nominate & by & with the advice and consent of the Senate, shall appoint ambassadors, and other public ministers (and Consuls) [2] Judges of the Supreme Court " [3] Agreed to nem: con: the insertion of " and consuls " having first taken place.

On the question on the following words " And all other officers of [4] U. S."

N. H. ay. Mas. ay. C: ay. N. J. ay. P: no. Del. ay M: ay. V: ay. N. C. ay. S. C. no. Geo. ay.[5]

On motion of M: SPAIGHT—" that the President shall have power to fill up all vacancies that may happen during the recess of the Senate by granting Commissions which shall expire at the end of the next Session of the Senate " It was agreed to nem: con:

[4] Section 4. " The President by and with the advice and consent of the Senate shall have power to make Treaties "—" *But no treaty*

---

[1] The word " who " is substituted in the transcript for " whom."
[2] The word " and " is here inserted in the transcript.
[3] The words " it was " are here inserted in the transcript.
[4] The word " the " is here inserted in the transcript.
[5] In the transcript the vote reads: " New Hampshire, Massachusetts, Connecticut, New Jersey, Delaware, Maryland, Virginia, North Carolina, Georgia, aye—9; Pennsylvania, South Carolina, no—2."

shall be made without the consent of two thirds of the members present "—this last [1] being before the House.

M: WILSON thought it objectionable to require the concurrence of ⅔ which puts it in [2] the power of a minority to controul the will of a majority.

M: KING concurred in the objection; remarking that as the Executive was here joined in the business, there was a check which did not exist in Congress where The concurrence of ⅔ was required.

M: MADISON moved to insert after the word " treaty " the words " except treaties of peace " allowing these to be made with less difficulty than other treaties—It was agreed to nem: con:

M: MADISON then moved to authorise a concurrence of two thirds of the Senate to make treaties of peace, without the concurrence of the President."—The President he said would necessarily derive so much power and importance from a state of war that he might be tempted, if authorised, to impede a treaty of peace. M: BUTLER 2ded the motion

M: GORHAM thought the precaution [3] unnecessary as the means of carrying on the war would not be in the hands of the President, but of the Legislature.

M: GOV: MORRIS thought the power of the President in this case harmless; and that no peace ought to be made without the concurrence of the President, who was the general Guardian of the National interests.

M: BUTLER was strenuous for the motion, as a necessary security against ambitious & corrupt Presidents. He mentioned the late perfidious policy of the Statholder in Holland; and the artifices of the Duke of Marlbro' to prolong the war of which he had the management.

M: GERRY was of opinion that in treaties of peace a greater rather than less proportion of votes was necessary, than in other treaties. In Treaties of peace the dearest interests will be at stake, as the fisheries, territory &c. In treaties of peace also there is more dander to the extremities of the Continent, of being sacrificed, than on any other occasions.

M: WILLIAMSON thought that Treaties of peace should be guarded at least by requiring the same concurrence as in other Treaties.

On the motion of M: Madison & M: Butler

---

[1] The words " being considered, and the last clause " are substituted in the transcript for " this last."
[2] The word " into " is substituted in the transcript for " in."
[3] In the transcript the word " precaution " is stricken out and the word " security " is written above it.

N. H. no. Mas. no. C⁺ no. N. J. no. P⁺ no. Del. no. M⁺ ay.
V⁺ no. N. C. no. S. C. ay. Geo. ay.[1]

On the part of the clause concerning treaties amended by the exception as to Treaties of peace,

N. H. ay. Mas. ay. C⁺ ay. N. J. no. P⁺ no. Del. ay. M⁺ ay.
V⁺ ay. N. C. ay. S. C. ay. Geo. no.[2]

[3] " and may require the opinion in writing of the principal officer in each of the Executive Departments, upon any subject relating to the duties of their respective offices," being before the House

Col: MASON * said that in rejecting a Council to the President we were about to try an experiment on which the most despotic Governments had never ventured. The Grand Signor himself had his Divan. He moved to postpone the consideration of the clause in order to take up the following

" That it be an instruction to the Committee of the States to prepare a clause or clauses for establishing an Executive Council, as a Council of State, for the President of the U. States, to consist of six members, two of which from the Eastern, two from the middle, and two from the Southern States, with a Rotation and duration of office similar to those of the Senate; such Council to be appointed by the Legislature or by the Senate."

Doctor FRANKLIN 2⁺ᵈᵉᵈ the motion. We seemed he said too much to fear cabals in appointments by a number, and to have too much confidence in those of single persons. Experience shewed that caprice, the intrigues of favorites & mistresses, &c[4] were nevertheless the means most prevalent in monarchies. Among instances of abuse in such modes of appointment, he mentioned the many bad Governors appointed in G. B. for the Colonies. He thought a Council would not only be a check on a bad President but be a relief to a good one.

M⁺ Gov⁺ MORRIS. The question of a Council was considered in the Committee, where it was judged that the Presid⁺ by persuading his Council, to concur in his wrong measures, would acquire their protection for them.

---

* In the printed Journal, M⁺ Madison is erroneously substituted for Col: Mason.

---

[1] In the transcript the vote reads: "Maryland, South Carolina, Georgia, aye —3; New Hampshire, Massachusetts, Connecticut, New Jersey, Pennsylvania, Delaware, Virginia, North Carolina, no—8."

[2] In the transcript the vote reads: "New Hampshire, Massachusetts, Connecticut, Delaware, Maryland, Virginia, North Carolina, South Carolina, aye—8; New Jersey, Pennsylvania, Georgia, no—3."

[3] The words "The clause" are here inserted in the transcript.

[4] The character "&c" is omitted in the transcript.

M: WILSON approved of a Council in preference to making the Senate a party to appointm:

M: DICKENSON was for a Council. It w⁴ be a singular thing if the measures of the Executive were not to undergo some previous discussion before the President.

M: MADISON was in favor of the instruction to the Committee proposed by Col: Mason.

The motion of M:[1] Mason was negatived. Mary⁴ ay. S. C. ay. Geo. ay— N. H. no. Mas. no. C: no. N. J. no P: no. Del. no. V: no. N C no.[2]

On the question,[3] " authorising the President to call for the opinions of the Heads of Departments, in writing ": it passed in the affirmative, N. H. only being no.*

The clause was then unanimously agreed to—

M: WILLIAMSON & M: SPAIGHT moved " that no Treaty of Peace affecting Territorial rights sh⁴ be made without the concurrence of two thirds of the members of the Senate present.

M: KING. It will be necessary to look out for securities for some other rights, if this principle be established; he moved to extend the motion—" to all present rights of the U. States."

Adjourned

SATURDAY SEPTEMBER 8ᵀᴴ: IN CONVENTION

The last Report of[4] Committee of Eleven (see Sep: 4) was resumed.

M: KING moved to strike out the " exception of Treaties of peace " from the general clause requiring two thirds of the Senate for making Treaties

M: WILSON wished the requisition of two thirds to be struck out altogether If the majority cannot be trusted, it was a proof, as observed by M: Ghorum, that we were not fit for one Society.

A reconsideration of the whole clause was agreed to.

M: Gov: MORRIS was ag:t striking out the " exception of Treaties

* Not so stated in the Printed Journal; but comformable to the result afterwards appearing.

---

[1] The word " Col." is substituted in the transcript for " Mr."
[2] In the transcript the vote reads: " Maryland, South Carolina, Georgia, aye—3; New Hampshire, Massachusetts, Connecticut, New Jersey, Pennsylvania, Delaware, Virginia, North Carolina, no—8."
[3] The word " for " is here inserted in the transcript.
[4] The word " the " is here inserted in the transcript.

of peace " If two thirds of the Senate should be required for peace, the Legislature will be unwilling, to make war for that reason, on account of the Fisheries or the Mississippi, the two great objects of the Union. Besides, if a majority of the Senate be for peace, and are not allowed to make it, they will be apt to effect their purpose in the more disagreeable mode, of negativing the supplies for the war.

M: WILLIAMSON remarked that Treaties are to be made in the branch of the Gov: where there may be a majority of the States without a majority of the people. Eight men may be a majority of a quorum, & should not have the power to decide the conditions of peace. There would be no danger, that the exposed States, as S. Carolina or Georgia, would urge an improper war for the Western Territory.

M: WILSON If two thirds are necessary to make peace, the minority may perpetuate war, against the sense of the majority.

M: GERRY enlarged on the danger of putting the essential rights of the Union in the hands of so small a number as a majority of the Senate, representing, perhaps, not one fifth of the people. The Senate will be corrupted by foreign influence.

M: SHERMAN was ag:t leaving the rights established by the Treaty of peace, to the Senate, & moved to annex a " proviso that no such rights sh:d be ceded without the sanction of the Legislature.

M: Gov: MORRIS seconded the ideas of M: Sherman.

M: MADISON observed that it had been too easy in the present Congress to make Treaties altho' nine States were required for the purpose.

On the question for striking [1] " except Treaties of peace "

N. H. ay. Mas. ay. C: ay. N. J. no. P: ay. Del. no. M: no V: ay. N. C. ay. S. C. ay. Geo. ay.[2]

M: WILSON & M: DAYTON move to strike out the clause requiring two thirds of the Senate for making Treaties.—on which,

N. H. no. Mas. no. C: div:d N. J. no. P: no Del. ay. M:d no. V: no. N. C. no. S. C. no. Geo. no.[3]

M: RUTLIDGE & M: GERRY move that " no Treaty [4] be made with-

---

[1] The word " out " is here inserted in the transcript.

[2] In the transcript the vote reads: " New Hampshire, Massachusetts, Connecticut, Pennsylvania, Virginia, North Carolina, South Carolina, Georgia, aye —8; New Jersey, Delaware, Maryland, no—3."

[3] In the transcript the vote reads: " Delaware, aye—1; New Hampshire, Massachusetts, New Jersey, Pennsylvania, Maryland, Virginia, North Carolina, South Carolina, Georgia, no—9; Connecticut, divided."

[4] The word " shall " is here inserted in the transcript.

out the consent of ⅔ of all the members of the Senate "—according to the example in the present Cong!

M: GHORUM. There is a difference in the case, as the President's consent will also be necessary in the new Gov!

On the question

N. H. no. Mass. no. (M: Gerry ay) C! no. N. J. no. P! no. Del. no. M! no. V! no. N. C. ay. S. C. ay. Geo. ay.[1]

M: SHARMAN mov! that no Treaty [2] be made without a Majority of the whole number of the Senate. M: GERRY seconded him.

M: WILLIAMSON. This will be less security than ⅔ as now required.

M: SHERMAN. It will be less embarrassing.

On the question, it passed in the negative.

N. H. no. Mas. ay. C! ay. N. J. no. P! no. Del. ay. M! no. V! no. N. C. no. S. C. ay. Geo. ay.[3]

M: MADISON mov! that a Quorum of the Senate consist of ⅔ of all the members.

M: Gov! MORRIS—This will put it in the power of one man to break up a Quorum.

M: MADISON, This may happen to any Quorum.

On the Question it passed in the negative

N. H. no. Mas. no. C! no. N. J. no. P! no. Del. no. M! ay. V! ay. N. C. ay. S. C. ay. Geo. ay.[4]

M: WILLIAMSON & M: GERRY, mov! " that no Treaty sh! be made with! previous notice to the members, & a reasonable time for their attending."

On the Question

All the States no, except N. C. S. C. & Geo. ay.

On a question on [5] clause of the Report of the Com! of Eleven relating to Treaties by ⅔ of the Senate. All the States were ay—except P! N. J. & Geo. no.

M: GERRY mov! that no officer [2] be app! but to offices created by

---

[1] In the transcript the vote reads: " North Carolina, South Carolina, Georgia, aye—3; New Hampshire, Massachusetts (Mr. Gerry, aye), Connecticut, New Jersey, Pennsylvania, Delaware, Maryland, Virginia, no—8."

[2] The word " shall " is here inserted in the transcript.

[3] In the transcript the vote reads: " Massachusetts, Connecticut, Delaware, South Carolina, Georgia, aye—5; New Hampshire, New Jersey, Pennsylvania, Maryland, Virginia, North Carolina, no—6."

[4] In the transcript the vote reads: " Maryland, Virginia, North Carolina, South Carolina, Georgia, aye—5; New Hampshire, Massachusetts, Connecticut, New Jersey, Pennsylvania, Delaware, no—6."

[5] The word " the " is here inserted in the transcript.

the Constitution or by law"—This was rejected as unnecessary by six no's & five ays;[1]

The Ayes. Mas. C! N. J. N. C. Geo.—Noes. N. H. P!: Del. M? V? S. C.[2]

The clause referring to the Senate, the trial of impeachments ag.st the President, for Treason & bribery, was taken up.

Col. MASON. Why is the provision restrained to Treason & bribery only? Treason as defined in the Constitution will not reach many great and dangerous offences. Hastings is not guilty of Treason. Attempts to subvert the Constitution may not be Treason as above defined. As bills of attainder which have saved the British Constitution are forbidden, it is the more necessary to extend: the power of impeachments. He mov? to add after " bribery " " or maladministration." M! GERRY seconded him.

M! MADISON   So vague a term will be equivalent to a tenure during pleasure of the Senate.

M! Gov? MORRIS, it will not be put in force & can do no harm. An election of every four years will prevent maladministration.

Col. MASON withdrew " maladministration " & substitutes " other high crimes & misdemesnors ag.st the State "

On the question thus altered

N. H. ay. Mas. ay. C! ay. N. J. no. P? no. Del. no. M? ay. V? ay. N. C. ay. S. C. ay.* Geo. ay.[3]

M! MADISON, objected to a trial of the President by the Senate, especially as he was to be impeached by the other branch of the Legislature, and for any act which might be called a misdemesnor. The President under these circumstances was made improperly dependent. He would prefer the Supreme Court for the trial of impeachments, or rather a tribunal of which that should form a part.

M! Gov? MORRIS thought no other tribunal than the Senate could be trusted. The supreme Court were too few in number and might be warped or corrupted. He was ag.st a dependence of the Executive on the Legislature, considering the Legislative tyranny the great danger to be apprehended; but there could be no danger that the Senate would say untruly on their oaths that the President was guilty

---

* In the printed Journal, S. Carolina—no.

[1] The words " by six no's & five ayes " are stricken out in the transcript.

[2] In the transcript the vote reads: " Massachusetts, Connecticut, New Jersey, North Carolina, Georgia, aye—5; New Hampshire, Pennsylvania, Delaware, Maryland, Virginia, South Carolina, no—6."

[3] In the transcript the vote reads: " New Hampshire, Massachusetts, Connecticut, Maryland, Virginia, North Carolina, South Carolina,* Georgia, aye—8; New Jersey, Pennsylvania, Delaware, no—3."

of crimes or facts, especially as in four years he can be turned out.

M: PINKNEY disapproved of making the Senate the Court of Impeachments, as rendering the President too dependent on the Legislature. If he opposes a favorite law, the two Houses will combine ag:t him, and under the influence of heat and faction throw him out of office.

M: WILLIAMSON thought there was more danger of too much lenity than [1] too much rigour towards the President, considering the number of cases in which the Senate was associated with the President.

M: SHERMAN regarded the Supreme Court as improper to try the President, because the Judges would be appointed by him.

On motion by M: MADISON to strike out the words—"by the Senate" after the word "conviction"

N. H. no. Mas. no. C: no. N. J. no. P: ay. Del. no. M: no. V: ay. N. C. no. S. C. no. Geo. no.[2]

In the amendment of Col: Mason just agreed to, the word "State" after the words "misdemeanors against" was struck out, and the words "United States" inserted unanimously,[3] in order to remove ambiguity.

On the question to agree to [4] clause as amended,

N. H. ay. Mas. ay. Cont ay N. J. ay. P: no. Del ay M: ay. V: ay. N. C. ay. S. C. ay. Geo. ay.[5]

On motion [6] "The vice-President and other Civil officers of the U. S. shall be removed from office on impeachment and conviction as aforesaid" was added to the clause on the subject of impeachments.

The clause of the report made on the 5th [7] Sep: & postponed was taken up, to wit—"All bills for raising revenue shall originate in the House of Representatives; and shall be subject to alterations and amendments by the Senate. No money shall be drawn from the Treasury but in consequence of appropriations made by law."

It was moved to strike out the words "and shall be subject to alterations and amendments by the Senate" and insert the words

---

[1] The word "of" is here inserted in the transcript.

[2] In the transcript the vote reads: "Pennsylvania, Virginia, aye—2; New Hampshire, Massachusetts, Connecticut, New Jersey, Delaware, Maryland, North Carolina, South Carolina, Georgia, no—9."

[3] The words "inserted unanimously" are transposed in the transcript to read "unanimously inserted."

[4] The word "the" is here inserted in the transcript.

[5] In the transcript the vote reads: "New Hampshire, Massachusetts, Connecticut, New Jersey, Delaware, Maryland, Virginia, North Carolina, South Carolina, Georgia, aye—10; Pennsylvania, no—1."

[6] The words "the following" are here inserted in the transcript.

[7] The word "of" is here inserted in the transcript.

used in the Constitution of Massachussetts on the same subject—[1] " but the Senate may propose or concur with amendments as in other bills "—which was agreed too nem: con:

On the question On the first part of the clause— " All bills for raising revenue shall originate in the house of Representatives "*

N. H. ay. Mas. ay. C^t ay. N. J. ay P^a ay. Del. no. M^d no. V^a ay. N. C. ay. S. C. ay. Geo. ay.[3]

Mr Govr Morris moved to add to clause (3)[4] of the report made on Sep^t 4.[5] the words " and every member shall be on oath " which being agreed to, and a question taken on the clause so amended viz— " The Senate of the U. S. shall have power to try all impeachments; but no person shall be convicted without the concurrence of two thirds of the members present; and every member shall be on oath "

N. H. ay. Mas. ay. C^t ay. N. J. ay. P^a no. Del. ay. M^d ay. V^a no. N. C. ay. S. C. ay. Geo. ay.[6]

Mr Gerry repeated his motion above made on this day, in the form following " The Legislature shall have the sole right of establishing offices not herein[7] provided for," which was again negatived: Mas. Con^t & Geo. only being ay.

M^r McHenry observed that the President had not yet been any where authorised to convene the Senate, and moved to amend Art. X. sect. 2. by striking out the words " he may convene them [the Legislature] on extraordinary occasions " & insert " He may convene both or either of the Houses on extraordinary occasions." This he added would also provide for the case of the Senate being in Session at the time of convening the Legislature.

Mr Wilson said he should vote agst the motion, because it implied that the senate might be in Session, when the Legislature was not, which he thought improper.

* This was a conciliatory vote, the effect of the compromise formerly alluded to. See Note Wednesday Sepr 5.[2]

---

[1] The word " viz " is here inserted in the transcript.

[2] The words "Wednesday, Sepr 5," are stricken out in the transcript and " page —" is inserted in their place.

[3] In the transcript the vote reads: "New Hampshire, Massachusetts, Connecticut, New Jersey, Pennsylvania, Virginia, North Carolina, South Carolina, Georgia, aye—9; Delaware, Maryland, no—2."

[4] The words "the third clause" are substituted in the transcript for "clause (3)."

[5] The words "the fourth of September" are substituted in the transcript for " Sepr 4."

[6] In the transcript the vote reads: "New Hampshire, Massachusetts, Connecticut, New Jersey, Delaware, Maryland, North Carolina, South Carolina, Georgia, aye—9; Pennsylvania, Virginia, no—2."

[7] The word " heretofore " is substituted in the transcript for " herein."

On the question

N. H. ay. Mas. no. C! ay. N. J. ay. P! no. Del. ay. M⁴ ay. V! no. N. C. ay. S. C. no. Geo. ay.¹

A Committee was then appointed by Ballot to revise the stile of and arrange the articles which had been agreed to by the House. The committee consisted of M! Johnson, M! Hamilton, M! Gov! Morris, M! Madison and M! King.

M! WILLIAMSON moved that previous to this work of the Committee the clause relating to the number of the House of Representatives sh⁴ be reconsidered for the purpose of increasing the number.

M! MADISON 2^ded the Motion

M! SHERMAN opposed it. he thought the provision on that subject amply sufficient.

Col: HAMILTON expressed himself with great earnestness and anxiety in favor of the motion. He avowed himself a friend to a vigorous Government, but would declare at the same time, that² he held it essential that the popular branch of it should be on a broad foundation. He was seriously of opinion that the House of Representatives was on so narrow a scale as to be really dangerous, and to warrant a jealousy in the people for their liberties. He remarked that the connection between the President & Senate would tend to perpetuate him, by corrupt influence. It was the more necessary on this account that a numerous representation in the other branch of the Legislature should be established.

On the motion of M! Williamson to reconsider, it was negatived

*N. H. no. Mas. no. C! no. N. J. no. P! ay. Del. ay. M⁴ ay. V! ay. N. C. ay. S. C. no. Geo. no.³

Adj⁴

MONDAY SEP^R 10. 1787 ⁴ IN CONVENTION

M! GERRY moved to reconsider Art XIX. viz. " On the application of the Legislatures of two thirds of the States in the Union, for

* This motion & vote are entered on the Printed journal of the ensuing morning.

---

¹ In the transcript the vote reads: "New Hampshire, Connecticut, New Jersey, Delaware, Maryland, North Carolina, Georgia, aye—7; Massachusetts, Pennsylvania, Virginia, South Carolina, no—4."
² The word "that" is omitted in the transcript.
³ In the transcript the vote reads: "Pennsylvania, Delaware, Maryland, Virginia, North Carolina, aye—5; New Hampshire, Massachusetts, Connecticut, New Jersey, South Carolina, Georgia, no—6."
⁴ The year "1787" is omitted in the transcript.

an amendment of this Constitution, the Legislature of the U. S. shall call a Convention for that purpose." [see Aug. 6.] [1]

This Constitution he said is to be paramount to the State Constitutions. It follows, hence, from this article that two thirds of the States may obtain a Convention, a majority of which can bind the Union to innovations that may subvert the State-Constitutions altogether. He asked whether this was a situation proper to be run into.

M[r] HAMILTON 2[ded] the motion, but he said with a different view from M[r] Gerry. He did not object to the consequence stated by M[r] Gerry. There was no greater evil in subjecting the people of the U. S. to the major voice than the people of a particular State. It had been wished by many and was much to have been desired that an easier mode for [2] introducing amendments had been provided by the articles of [3] Confederation. It was equally desireable now that an easy mode should be established for supplying defects which will probably appear in the New System. The mode proposed was not adequate. The State Legislatures will not apply for alterations but with a view to increase their own powers. The National Legislature will be the first to perceive and will be most sensible to the necessity of amendments, and ought also to be empowered, whenever two thirds of each branch should concur to call a Convention. There could be no danger in giving this power, as the people would finally decide in the case.

M[r] MADISON remarked on the vagueness of the terms, "call a Convention for the purpose," as sufficient reason for reconsidering the article. How was a Convention to be formed? by what rule decide? what the force of its acts?

On the motion of M[r] Gerry to reconsider

N. H. div[d] Mas. ay. C[t] ay. N. J. no. P[a] ay. Del. ay. M[d] ay. V[a] ay. N. C. ay. S. C. ay. Geo. ay. [4]

M[r] SHERMAN moved to add to the article " or the Legislature may propose amendments to the several States for their approbation, but no amendments shall be binding until consented to by the several States."

M[r] GERRY 2[ded] the motion

M[r] WILSON moved to insert " two thirds of " before the words

---

[1] In the transcript the date reads: "the sixth of August."
[2] The word "of" is found in the transcript in place of "for."
[3] The word "the" is here inserted in the transcript.
[4] In the transcript the vote reads: "Massachusetts, Connecticut, Pennsylvania, Delaware, Maryland, Virginia, North Carolina, South Carolina, Georgia, aye—9; New Jersey, no—1; New Hampshire, divided."

"several States"—on which amendment to the motion of M^r
Sherman

N. H. ay. Mas. no. C^t no. N. J. no. P^a ay. Del. ay. M^d ay.
V^a ay. N. C. no. S. C. no. Geo. no.[1]

Mr WILSON then moved to insert " three fourths of " before " the
several Sts " which was agreed to nem: con:

Mr MADISON moved to postpone the consideration of the amended
proposition in order to take up the following,

" The Legislature of the U. S. whenever two thirds of both
Houses shall deem necessary, or on the application of two thirds of
the Legislatures of the several States, shall propose amendments to
this Constitution, which shall be valid to all intents and purposes as
part thereof, when the same shall have been ratified by three fourths
at least of the Legislatures of the several States, or by Conventions
in three fourths thereof, as one or the other mode of ratification may
be proposed by the Legislature of the U S : " *

Mr HAMILTON 2^{ded} the motion.

Mr RUTLIDGE said he never could agree to give a power by which
the articles relating to slaves might be altered by the States not
interested in that property and prejudiced against it. In order to
obviate this objection, these words were added to the proposition : *
" provided that no amendments which may be made prior to the
year 1808, shall in any manner affect the 4 & 5 sections of the VII
article "—The postponement being agreed to,

On the question on the proposition of Mr Madison & Mr Hamilton
as amended

N. H. div^d Mas. ay. C^t ay. N. J. ay. P^a ay. Del. no. M^d ay.
V^a ay. N. C. ay. S. C. ay. Geo ay.[3]

Mr GERRY moved to reconsider art: XXI and XXII. from the
latter of which " for the approbation of Cong^s " had been struck
out. He objected to proceeding to change the Government without
the approbation of Congress, as being improper and giving just
umbrage to that body. He repeated his objections also to an annul-
ment of the confederation with so little scruple or formality.

* The Printed Journal makes the succeeding proviso as to sections 4 & 5.
of art: VII [2] moved by Mr Rutlidge, part of the proposition of Mr Madison.

---

[1] In the transcript the vote reads: " New Hampshire, Pennsylvania, Delaware, Maryland, Virginia, aye—5; Massachusetts, Connecticut, New Jersey,
North Carolina, South Carolina, Georgia, no—6."

[2] The words " the fourth and fifth sections of the seventh article " are substituted in the transcript for " sections 4 & 5. of art: VII."

[3] In the transcript the vote reads: " Massachusetts, Connecticut, New Jersey,
Pennsylvania, Maryland, Virginia, North Carolina, South Carolina, Georgia, aye
—9; Delaware, no—1; New Hampshire, divided."

M⁞ HAMILTON concurred with M⁞ Gerry as to the indecorum of not requiring the approbation of Congress. He considered this as a necessary ingredient in the transaction. He thought it wrong also to allow nine States as provided by art XXI. to institute a new Government on the ruins of the existing one. He w⁙ propose as a better modification of the two articles (XXI & XXII) that the plan should be sent to Congress in order that the same if approved by them, may be communicated to the State Legislatures, to the end that they may refer it to State Conventions; each Legislature declaring that if the Convention of the State should think the plan ought to take effect among nine ratifying States, the same sh⁙ take effect accordingly.

M⁞ GORHAM. Some States will say that nine States shall be sufficient to establish the plan, others will require unanimity for the purpose. And the different and conditional ratifications will defeat the plan altogether.

M⁞ HAMILTON. No Convention convinced of the necessity of the plan will refuse to give it effect on the adoption by nine States. He thought this mode less exceptionable than the one proposed in the article, and [1] would attain the same end.

M⁞ FITZIMMONS remarked that the words " for their approbation " had been struck out in order to save Congress from the necessity of an Act inconsistent with the Articles of Confederation under which they held their authority.

M⁞ RANDOLPH declared, if no change should be made in the [2] this part of the plan, he should be obliged to dissent from the whole of it. He had from the beginning he said been convinced that radical changes in the system of the Union were necessary. Under this conviction he had brought forward a set of republican propositions as the basis and outline of a reform. These Republican propositions had however, much to his regret, been widely, and in his opinion, irreconcileably departed from. In this state of things it was his idea and he accordingly meant to propose, that the State Conventions sh⁙ be at liberty to offer amendments to the plan; and that these should be submitted to a second General Convention, with full power to settle the Constitution finally. He did not expect to succeed in this proposition, but the discharge of his duty in making the attempt, would give quiet to his own mind.

M⁞ WILSON was against a reconsideration for any of the purposes which had been mentioned.

---

[1] The words " while it " are substituted in the transcript for " and."
[2] The word " the " is omitted in the transcript.

M: KING thought it would be more respectful to Congress to submit the plan generally to them; than in such a form as expressly and necessarily to require their approbation or disapprobation. The assent of nine States he considered as sufficient; and that it was more proper to make this a part of the Constitution itself, than to provide for it by a supplemental or distinct recommendation.

M: GERRY urged the indecency and pernicious tendency of dissolving in so slight a manner, the solemn obligations of the articles of confederation. If nine out of thirteen can dissolve the compact, Six out of nine will be just as able to dissolve the new one hereafter.

M: SHERMAN was in favor of M: King's idea of submitting the plan generally to Congress. He thought nine States ought to be made sufficient: but that it would be best [1] to make it a separate act and in some such form as that intimated by Col: Hamilton, than to make it a particular article of the Constitution.

On the question for reconsidering the two articles, XXI & XXII—
N. H. div⁴ Mas. no. C: ay. N. J. ay. P: no. Del. ay. M⁴ ay. V: ay. N. C. ay. S. C. no. Geo. ay.[2]

M: HAMILTON then moved to postpone art XXI in order to take up the following, containing the ideas he had above expressed, viz

Resolved that the foregoing plan of a Constitution be transmitted to the U. S. in Congress assembled, in order that if the same shall be agreed to by them, it may be communicated to the Legislatures of the several States, to the end that they may provide for its final ratification by referring the same to the Consideration of a Convention of Deputies in each State to be chosen by the people thereof, and that it be recommended to the said Legislatures in their respective acts for organizing such convention to declare, that if the said Convention shall approve of the said Constitution, such approbation shall be binding and conclusive upon the State, and further that if the said Convention should be of opinion that the same upon the assent of any nine States thereto, ought to take effect between the States so assenting, such opinion shall thereupon be also binding upon such State, and the said Constitution shall take effect between the States assenting thereto "

M: GERRY 2ᵈᵉᵈ the motion.

M: WILSON. This motion being seconded, it is necessary now to speak freely. He expressed in strong terms his disapprobation of the expedient proposed, particularly the suspending the plan of

---

[1] The word "best" is crossed out in the transcript and "better" is written above it.
[2] In the transcript the vote reads: "Connecticut, New Jersey, Delaware, Maryland, Virginia, North Carolina, Georgia, aye—7; Massachusetts, Pennsylvania. South Carolina, no—3; New Hampshire, divided."

the Convention on the approbation of Congress. He declared it to be worse than folly to rely on the concurrence of the Rhode Island members of Cong? in the plan. Maryland has voted on this floor; for requiring the unanimous assent of the 13 States to the proposed change in the federal System. N. York has not been represented for a long time past in the Convention. Many individual deputies from other States have spoken much against the plan. Under these circumstances can it be safe to make the assent of Congress necessary. After spending four or five months in the laborious & arduous task of forming a Government for our Country, we are ourselves at the close throwing insuperable obstacles in the way of its success.

M? CLYMER thought that the mode proposed by M? Hamilton would fetter & embarrass Cong? as much as the original one, since it equally involved a breach of the articles of Confederation.

M? KING concurred with M? Clymer. If Congress can accede to one mode, they can to the other. If the approbation of Congress be made necessary, and they should not approve, the State Legislatures will not propose the plan to Conventions; or if the States themselves are to provide that nine States shall suffice to establish the System, that provision will be omitted, every thing will go into confusion, and all our labor be lost.

M? RUTLIDGE viewed the matter in the same light with M? King.

On the question to postpone in order to take up Col: Hamilton's motion

N. H. no. Mas. no. C? ay. N. J. no. P? no. Del. no. M? no. V? no. N. C. no. S. C. no. Geo. no.[1]

A Question being then taken on the article XXI. It was agreed to unanimously.

Col: HAMILTON withdrew the remainder of the motion to postpone art XXII, observing that his purpose was defeated by the vote just given;

M? WILLIAMSON & M? GERRY moved to re-instate the words " for the approbation of Congress " in art: XXII which was disagreed to nem: con:

M? RANDOLPH took this opportunity to state his objections to the System. They turned on the Senate's being made the Court of Impeachment for trying the Executive—on the necessity of ¾ instead

---

[1] In the transcript the vote reads: " Connecticut, aye—1; New Hampshire, Massachusetts, New Jersey, Pennsylvania, Delaware, Maryland, Virginia, North Carolina, South Carolina, Georgia, no—10."

of ⅔ of each house to overrule the negative of the President—on the smallness of the number of the Representative branch,—on the want of limitation to a standing army—on the general clause concerning necessary and proper laws—on the want of some particular restraint on navigation acts—on the power to lay duties on exports—on the Authority of the General Legislature to interpose on the application of the *Executives* of the States—on the want of a more definite boundary between the General & State Legislatures—and between the General and State Judiciaries—on the the unqualified power of the President to pardon treasons—on the want of some limit to the power of the Legislature in regulating their own compensations. With these difficulties in his mind, what course he asked was he to pursue? Was he to promote the establishment of a plan which he verily believed would end in Tyranny? He was unwilling he said to impede the wishes and Judgment of the Convention, but he must keep himself free, in case he should be honored with a seat in the Convention of his State, to act according to the dictates of his judgment. The only mode in which his embarrassments could be removed, was that of submitting the plan to Cong? to go from them to the State Legislatures, and from these to State Conventions having power to adopt reject or amend; the process to close with another General Convention with full power to adopt or reject the alterations proposed by the State Conventions, and to establish finally the Government. He accordingly proposed a Resolution to this effect.

Doc? FRANKLIN 2ded the motion

Col: MASON urged & obtained that the motion should lie on the table for a day or two to see what steps might be taken with regard to the parts of the system objected to by M? Randolph.

M? PINKNEY moved " that it be an instruction to the Committee for revising the stile and arrangement of the articles agreed on, to prepare an Address to the People, to accompany the present Constitution, and to be laid with the same before the U. States in Congress."

* The motion itself was referred to the Committee, nem: con:

* M? RANDOLPH moved to refer to the Committee also a motion relating to pardons in cases of Treason—which was agreed to nem: con:

Adjourned

* These motions [1] not entered in the printed Journal.

---

[1] The word " are " is here inserted in the transcript.

TUESDAY SEP.ᴿ 11. 1787.[1] IN CONVENTION

The Report of the Committee of Stile & arrangement not being made & being waited for,

The House Adjourned

WEDNESDAY SEP.ᴿ 12. 1787.[1] IN CONVENTION

Doc.ᵗ JOHNSON from the Committee of stile &c. reported a digest of the plan, of which printed copies were ordered to be furnished to the members. He also reported a letter to accompany the plan, to Congress. (Here insert a transcript of the former from the annexed sheet as *printed* * and of the latter from the draft as finally agreed to.[3]

WE, THE PEOPLE OF THE UNITED STATES, IN ORDER TO FORM a more perfect union, to establish justice, insure domestic tranquility, provide for the common defence, promote the general welfare, and secure the blessings of liberty to ourselves and our posterity, do ordain and establish this Constitution for the United States of America.

ARTICLE I.

Sect. 1. ALL legislative powers herein granted shall be vested in a Congress of the United States, which shall consist of a Senate and House of Representatives.

Sect. 2. The House of Representatives shall be composed of members chosen every second year by the people of the several states, and the electors in each state shall have the qualifications requisite for electors of the most numerous branch of the state legislature.

No person shall be a representative who shall not have attained to the age of twenty-five years, and been seven years a citizen of the United States, and who shall not, when elected, be an inhabitant of that state in which he shall be chosen.

Representatives and direct taxes shall be apportioned among the several states which may be included within this Union, according to their respective numbers, which shall be determined by adding to the whole number of free persons, including those bound to servitude for a term of years, and excluding Indians not taxed, three-fifths of all other persons. The actual enumeration

---

* "This is a literal copy of the printed Report. The Copy in the printed Journal contains some of the alterations subsequently made in the House.[2]

[1] The year " 1787 " is omitted in the transcript.
[2] No transcript of the report was, however, made by Madison, but it was copied by Payne and inserted in this place in the Payne transcript. The text here printed is a copy of the printed report accompanying Madison's notes. The letter is printed at page 553.
[3] Madison's direction concerning the report is omitted in the transcript.

shall be made within three years after the first meeting of the Congress of the United States, and within every subsequent term of ten years, in such manner as they shall by law direct. The number of representatives shall not exceed one for every forty thousand, but each state shall have at least one representative: and until such enumeration shall be made, the state of New-Hampshire shall be entitled to chuse three, Massachusetts eight, Rhode-Island and Providence Plantations one, Connecticut five, New-York six, New-Jersey four, Pennsylvania eight, Deleware one, Maryland six, Virginia ten, North-Carolina five, South-Carolina five, and Georgia three.

When vacancies happen in the representation from any state, the Executive authority thereof shall issue writs of election to fill such vacancies.

The House of Representatives shall choose their Speaker and other officers; and they shall have the sole power of impeachment.

Sect. 3. The Senate of the United States shall be composed of two senators from each state, chosen by the legislature thereof, for six years: and each senator shall have one vote.

Immediately after they shall be assembled in consequence of the first election, they shall be divided * [by lot] as equally as may be into three classes. The seats of the senators of the first class shall be vacated at the expiration of the second year, of the second class at the expiration of the fourth year, and of the third class at the expiration of the sixth year, so that one-third may be chosen every second year: and if vacancies happen by resignation, or otherwise, during the recess of the Legislature of any state, the Executive thereof may make temporary appointments until the next meeting of the Legislature.

No person shall be a senator who shall not have attained to the age of thirty years, and been nine years a citizen of the United States, and who shall not, when elected, be an inhabitant of that state for which he shall be chosen.

The Vice-President of the United States shall be, ex officio [1] President of the senate, but shall have no vote, unless they be equally divided.

The Senate shall choose their other officers, and also a President pro tempore, in the absence of the Vice-President, or when he shall exercise the office of President of the United States.

The Senate shall have the sole power to try all impeachments. When sitting for that purpose, they shall be on oath. When the President of the United States is tried, the Chief Justice shall preside: And no person shall be convicted without the concurrence of two-thirds of the members present.

Judgment in cases of impeachment shall not extend further than to removal from office, and disqualification to hold and enjoy any office of honor, trust or profit under the United States: but the party convicted shall nevertheless be liable and subject to indictment, trial, judgment and punishment, according to law.

Sect. 4. The times, places and manner of holding elections for senators and representatives, shall be prescribed in each state by the legislature thereof: but the Congress may at any time by law make or alter such regulations.

* The words, "by lot," were not in the Report as printed; but were inserted in manuscript, as a typografical error, departing from the text of the Report referred to the Committee of Style & arrangement.

[1] The words "ex officio" are omitted in the transcript.

The Congress shall assemble at least once in every year, and such meeting shall be on the first Monday in December, unless they shall by law appoint a different day.

Sect. 5.   Each house shall be the judge of the elections, returns and qualifications of its own members, and a majority of each shall constitute a quorum to do business: but a smaller number may adjourn from day to day, and may be authorised to compel the attendance of absent members, in such manner, and under such penalties as each house may provide.

Each house may determine the rules of its proceedings; punish its members for disorderly behaviour, and, with the concurrence of two-thirds, expel a member.

Each house shall keep a journal of its proceedings, and from time to time publish the same, excepting such parts as may in their judgment require secrecy; and the yeas and nays of the members of either house on any question shall, at the desire of one-fifth of those present, be entered on the journal.

Neither house, during the session of Congress, shall, without the consent of the other, adjourn for more than three days, nor to any other place than that in which the two houses shall be sitting.

Sect. 6.   The senators and representatives shall receive a compensation for their services, to be ascertained by law, and paid out of the treasury of the United States.   They shall in all cases, except treason, felony and breach of the peace, be privileged from arrest during their attendance at the session of their respective houses, and in going to and returning from the same; and for any speech or debate in either house, they shall not be questioned in any other place.

No senator or representative shall, during the time for which he was elected, be appointed to any civil office under the authority of the United States, which shall have been created, or the emoluments whereof shall have been encreased during such time; and no person holding any office under the United States, shall be a member of either house during his continuance in office.

Sect. 7.   The enacting stile of the laws shall be, " Be it enacted by the senators and representatives in Congress assembled."

All bills for raising revenue shall originate in the house of representatives: but the senate may propose or concur with amendments as on other bills.

Every bill which shall have passed the house of representatives and the senate, shall, before it become a law, be presented to the president of the United States.   If he approve he shall sign it, but if not he shall return it, with his objections to that house in which it shall have originated, who shall enter the objections at large on their journal, and proceed to reconsider it. If after such reconsideration two-thirds of that house shall agree to pass the bill, it shall be sent, together with the objections, to the other house, by which it shall likewise be reconsidered, and if approved by two-thirds of that house, it shall become a law.   But in all such cases the votes of both houses shall be determined by yeas and nays, and the names of the persons voting for and against the bill shall be entered on the journal of each house respectively.   If any bill shall not be returned by the President within ten days (Sundays excepted) after it shall have been presented to him, the same shall be a law, in like manner as if he had signed it, unless the Congress by their adjournment prevent its return, in which case it shall not be a law.

Every order, resolution, or vote to which the concurrence of the Senate and House of Representatives may be necessary (except on a question of adjournment) shall be presented to the President of the United States; and before the same shall take effect, shall be approved by him, or, being disapproved by him, shall be repassed by * three-fourths of the Senate and House of Representatives, according to the rules and limitations prescribed in the case of a bill.

Sect. 8. The Congress may by joint ballot appoint a treasurer. They shall have power

To lay and collect taxes, duties, imposts and excises; to pay the debts and provide for the common defence and general welfare of the United States.

To borrow money on the credit of the United States.

To regulate commerce with foreign nations, among the several states, and with the Indian tribes.

To establish an uniform rule of naturalization, and uniform laws on the subject of bankruptcies throughout the United States.

To coin money, regulate the value thereof, and of foreign coin, and fix the standard of weights and measures.

To provide for the punishment of counterfeiting the securities and current coin of the United States.

To establish post offices and post roads.

To promote the progress of science and useful arts, by securing for limited times to authors and inventors the exclusive right to their respective writings and discoveries.

To constitute tribunals inferior to the supreme court.

To define and punish piracies and felonies committed on the high seas, and † [punish] offences against the law of nations.

To declare war, grant letters of marque and reprisal, and make rules concerning captures on land and water.

To raise and support armies: but no appropriation of money to that use shall be for a longer term than two years.

To provide and maintain a navy.

To make rules for the government and regulation of the land and naval forces.

To provide for calling forth the militia to execute the laws of the union, suppress insurrections and repel invasions.

To provide for organizing, arming and disciplining the militia, and for governing such part of them as may be employed in the service of the United States, reserving to the States respectively, the appointment of the officers, and the authority of training the militia according to the discipline prescribed by Congress.

* In the entry of this Report in the printed Journal " two thirds " are substuted for " three fourths." This change was made after the Report was received.[1]

† [punish] a typographical omission.[2]

---

[1] This is a mistake on Madison's part.

[2] The words " in the printed Report " are here added in the transcript.

To exercise exclusive legislation in all cases whatsoever, over such district (not exceeding ten miles square) as may, by cession of particular States, and the acceptance of Congress, become the seat of the [1] government of the United States, and to exercise like authority over all places purchased by the consent of the legislature of the state in which the same shall be, for the erection of forts, magazines, arsenals, dock-yards, and other needful buildings—And

To make all laws which shall be necessary and proper for carrying into execution the foregoing powers, and all other powers vested by this constitution in the government of the United States, or in any department or officer thereof.

Sect. 9. The migration or importation of such persons as the several states now existing shall think proper to admit, shall not be prohibited by the Congress prior to the year one thousand eight hundred and eight, but a tax or duty may be imposed on such importation, not exceeding ten dollars for each person.

The privilege of the writ of habeas corpus shall not be suspended, unless when in cases of rebellion or invasion the public safety may require it.

No bill of attainder shall be. passed, nor any ex post facto law.

No capitation tax shall be laid, unless in proportion to the census herein before directed to be taken.

No tax or duty shall be laid on articles exported from any state.

No money shall be drawn from the treasury, but in consequence of appropriations made by law.

No title of nobility shall be granted by the United States. And no person holding any office of profit or trust under them, shall, without the consent of the Congress, accept of any present, emolument, office, or title, of any kind whatever, from any king, prince, or foreign state.

Sect. 10. No state shall coin money, nor [2] emit bills of credit, nor [2] make any thing but gold or silver coin a tender in payment of debts, nor [2] pass any bill of attainder, nor [2] ex post facto laws, nor [2] laws altering or impairing the obligation of contracts; nor [2] grant letters of marque and reprisal, nor [2] enter into any treaty, alliance, or confederation, nor [2] grant any title of nobility.

No state shall, without the consent of Congress, lay imposts or duties on imports or exports, nor [2] with such consent, but to the use of the treasury of the United States. Nor [2] keep troops nor [2] ships of war in time of peace, nor [2] enter into any agreement or compact with another state, nor [2] with any foreign power. Nor [2] engage in any war, unless it shall be actually invaded by enemies, or the danger of invasion be so imminent, as not to admit of delay until the Congress can be consulted.

II.

Sect. 1. The executive power shall be vested in a president of the United States of America. He shall hold his office during the term of four years, and, together with the vice-president, chosen for the same term, be elected in the following manner:

---

[1] The word " the " is omitted in the transcript.
[2] The word " or " is substituted in the transcript for " nor," the letter " n " having been crossed off in Madison's printed copy.

Each state shall appoint, in such manner as the legislature thereof may direct, a number of electors, equal to the whole number of senators and representatives to which the state may be entitled in Congress: but no senator or representative shall be appointed an elector, nor any person holding an office of trust or profit under the United States.

The electors shall meet in their respective states, and vote by ballot for two persons, of whom one at least shall not be an inhabitant of the same state with themselves. And they shall make a list of all the persons voted for, and of the number of votes for each; which list they shall sign and certify, and transmit sealed to the seat of the general government, directed to the president of the senate. The president of the senate shall in the presence of the senate and house of representatives open all the certificates, and the votes shall then be counted. The person having the greatest number of votes shall be the president, if such number be a majority of the whole number of electors appointed; and if there be more than one who have such majority, and have an equal number of votes, then the house of representatives shall immediately chuse by ballot one of them for president; and if no person have a majority, then from the five highest on the list the said house shall in like manner choose the president. But in choosing the president, the votes shall be taken by states and not per capita, the representation from each state having one vote. A quorum for this purpose shall consist of a member or members from two-thirds of the states, and a majority of all the states shall be necessary to a choice. In every case, after the choice of the president by the representatives, the person having the greatest number of votes of the electors shall be the vice-president. But if there should remain two or more who have equal votes, the senate shall choose from them by ballot the vice-president.

The Congress may determine the time of chusing the electors, and the time in which they shall give their votes; but the election shall be on the same day throughout the United States.

No person except a natural born citizen, or a citizen of the United States, at the time of the adoption of this constitution, shall be eligible to the office of president; neither shall any person be eligible to that office who shall not have attained to the age of thirty-five years, and been fourteen years a resident within the United States.

In case of the removal of the president from office, or of his death, resignation, or inability to discharge the powers and duties of the said office, the same shall devolve on the vice-president, and the Congress may by law provide for the case of removal, death, resignation or inability, both of the president and vice-president, declaring what officer shall then act as president, and such officer shall act accordingly, until the disability be removed, or the period for chusing another president arrive.

The president shall, at stated times, receive a fixed compensation for his services, which shall neither be encreased nor diminished during the period for which he shall have been elected.

Before he enter on the execution of his office, he shall take the following oath or affirmation: "I ——, do solemnly swear (or affirm) that I will faithfully execute the office of president of the United States, and will to the best of my judgment and power, preserve, protect and defend the constitution of the United States."

Sect. 2.   The president shall be commander in chief of the army and navy of the United States, and of the militia of the several States:[1] he may require the opinion, in writing, of the principal officer in each of the executive departments, upon any subject relating to the duties of their respective offices, when called into the actual service of the United States,[1] and he shall have power to grant reprieves and pardons for offences against the United States, except in cases of impeachment.

He shall have power, by and with the advice and consent of the senate, to make treaties, provided two-thirds of the senators present concur; and he shall nominate, and by and with the advice and consent of the senate, shall appoint ambassadors, other public ministers and consuls, judges of the supreme court, and all other officers of the United States, whose appointments are not herein otherwise provided for.

The president shall have power to fill up all vacancies that may happen during the recess of the senate, by granting commissions which shall expire at the end of their next session.

Sect. 3.   He shall from time to time give to the Congress information of the state of the union, and recommend to their consideration such measures as he shall judge necessary and expedient: he may, on extraordinary occasions, convene both houses, or either of them, and in case of disagreement between them, with respect to the time of adjournment, he may adjourn them to such time as he shall think proper: he shall receive ambassadors and other public ministers: he shall take care that the laws be faithfully executed, and shall commission all the officers of the United States.

Sect. 4.   The president, vice-president and all civil officers of the United States, shall be removed from office on impeachment for, and conviction of treason, bribery, or other high crimes and misdemeanors.

III.

Sect. 1.   The judicial power of the United States, both in law and equity, shall be vested in one supreme court, and in such inferior courts as the Congress may from time to time ordain and establish.   The judges, both of the supreme and inferior courts, shall hold their offices during good behaviour, and shall, at stated times, receive for their services, a compensation, which shall not be diminished during their continuance in office.

Sect. 2.   The judicial power shall extend to all cases, both in law and equity, arising under this constitution, the laws of the United States, and treaties made, or which shall be made, under their authority.   To all cases affecting ambassadors, other public ministers and consuls.   To all cases of admiralty and maritime jurisdiction.   To controversies to which the United States shall be a party.   To controversies between two or more States; between a state and citizens of another state; between citizens of different States; between citizens of the same state claiming lands under grants of different States, and between a state, or the citizens thereof, and foreign States, citizens or subjects.

In cases affecting ambassadors, other public ministers and consuls, and

---

[1] The phrase " when called into the actual service of the United States " is transposed in the transcript so that it follows the words " several States."

those in which a state shall be party, the supreme court shall have original jurisdiction. In all the other cases before mentioned, the supreme court shall have appellate jurisdiction, both as to law and fact, with such exceptions, and under such regulations as the Congress shall make.

The trial of all crimes, except in cases of impeachment, shall be by jury; and such trial shall be held in the state where the said crimes shall have been committed; but when not committed within any state, the trial shall be at such place or places as the Congress may by law have directed.

Sect. 3. Treason against the United States, shall consist only in levying war against them, or in adhering to their enemies, giving them aid and comfort. No person shall be convicted of treason unless on the testimony of two witnesses to the same overt act, or on confession in open court.

The Congress shall have power to declare the punishment of treason, but no attainder of treason shall work corruption of blood nor forfeiture, except during the life of the person attainted.

IV.

Sect. 1. Full faith and credit shall be given in each state to the public acts, records, and judicial proceedings of every other state. And the Congress may by general laws prescribe the manner in which such acts, records and proceedings shall be proved, and the effect thereof.

Sect. 2. The citizens of each state shall be entitled to all privileges and immunities of citizens in the several states.

A person charged in any state with treason, felony, or other crime, who shall flee from justice, and be found in another state, shall on demand of the executive authority of the state from which he fled be delivered up, and removed to the state having jurisdiction of the crime.

No person legally held to service or labour in one state, escaping into another, shall in consequence of regulations subsisting therein be discharged from such service or labor, but shall be delivered up on claim of the party to whom such service or labour may be due.

Sect. 3. New states may be admitted by the Congress into this union; but no new state shall be formed or erected within the jurisdiction of any other state; nor any state be formed by the junction of two or more states, or parts of states, without the consent of the legislatures of the states concerned as well as of the Congress.

The Congress shall have power to dispose of and make all needful rules and regulations respecting the territory or other property belonging to the United States: and nothing in this Constitution shall be so construed as to prejudice any claims of the United States, or of any particular state.

Sect. 4. The United States shall guarantee to every state in this union a Republican form of government, and shall protect each of them against invasion; and on application of the legislature or executive, against domestic violence.

V.

The Congress, whenever two-thirds of both houses shall deem necessary, or on the application of two-thirds of the legislatures of the several states, shall propose amendments to this constitution, which shall be valid to all intents and purposes, as part thereof, when the same shall have been ratified by three-fourths at least of the legislatures of the several states, or by conventions in three-fourths thereof, as the one or the other mode of ratification may be proposed by the Congress: Provided, that no amendment which may be made prior to the year 1808 shall in any manner affect the and   sections of [1]   article

VI.

All debts contracted and engagements entered into before the adoption of this Constitution shall be as valid against the United States under this Constitution as under the confederation.

This constitution, and the laws of the United States which shall be made in pursuance thereof; and all treaties made, or which shall be made, under the authority of the United States, shall be the supreme law of the land; and the judges in every state shall be bound thereby, any thing in the constitution or laws of any state to the contrary notwithstanding.

The senators and representatives beforementioned, and the members of the several state legislatures, and all executive and judicial officers, both of the United States and of the several States, shall be bound by oath or affirmation, to support this constitution; but no religious test shall ever be required as a qualification to any office or public trust under the United States.

VII.

The ratification of the conventions of nine States, shall be sufficient for the establishment of this constitution between the States so ratifying the same.

LETTER.[2]

We have now the honor to submit to the consideration of the United States in Congress assembled, that Constitution which has appeared to us the most adviseable.

The friends of our country have long seen and desired, that the power of making war, peace and treaties, that of levying money and regulating commerce, and the correspondent executive and judicial authorities should

---

[1] The word "the" is here inserted in the transcript.
[2] The draft of the letter accompanied the draft of the Constitution reported on this date, but was not printed with it. The Journal says: "The draft of a letter to Congress being at the same time reported, was read once throughout; and afterwards agreed to by paragraphs." (See *Journal of the Federal Convention* (1819), page 367.) The letter does not appear to have caused debate. Having been accepted September 12th, it was printed with the final Constitution September 17th. The text here used is that of the final print, which was also copied by Payne for the transcript. The letter is printed in full, *infra*, page 639.

be fully and effectually vested in the general government of the Union: but the impropriety of delegating such extensive trust to one body of men is evident—Hence [1] results the necessity of a different organization.

It is obviously impracticable in the fœderal government of these States to secure all rights of independent sovereignty to each, and yet provide for the interest and safety of all—Individuals entering into society must give up a share of liberty to preserve the rest. The magnitude of the sacrifice must depend as well on situation and circumstance, as on the object to be obtained. It is at all times difficult to draw with precision the line between those rights which must be surrendered, and those which may be reserved; and on the present occasion this difficulty was encreased by a difference among the several States as to their situation, extent, habits, and particular interests.

In all our deliberations on this subject we kept steadily in our view, that which appears [2] to us the greatest interest of every true American, the consolidation of our union, in which is involved our prosperity, felicity, safety, perhaps our national existence. This important consideration, seriously and deeply impressed on our minds, led each State in the Convention to be less rigid on [3] points of inferior magnitude, than might have been otherwise expected; and thus the Constitution, which we now present, is the result of a spirit of amity, and of that mutual deference and concession which the peculiarity of our political situation rendered indispensible.

That it will meet the full and entire approbation of every State is not perhaps to be expected; but each will doubtless consider, that had her interest alone been consulted, the consequences might have been particularly disagreeable or [4] injurious to others; that it is liable to as few exceptions as could reasonably have been expected, we hope and believe; that it may promote the lasting welfare of that country so dear to us all, and secure her freedom and happiness, is our most ardent wish.

M⸢r⸣ WILLIAMSON moved to reconsider the clause requiring three fourths of each House to overrule the negative of the President, in order to strike out ¾ and insert ⅔. He had he remarked himself proposed ¾ instead of ⅔, but he had since been convinced that the latter proportion was the best. The former puts too much in the power of the President.

M⸢r⸣ SHERMAN was of the same opinion; adding that the States would not like to see so small a minority and the President, prevailing over the general voice. In making laws regard should be had to the sense of the people, who are to be bound by them, and it was more probable that a single man should mistake or betray this sense than the Legislature

---

[1] The word "Thence" is substituted in the transcript for "Hence."
[2] The word "appeared." is substituted in the transcript for "appears."
[3] The word "in" is substituted in the transcript for "on."
[4] The word "and" is substituted in the transcript for "or."

Mͬ Govͬ Morris. Considering the difference between the two proportions numerically, it amounts in one House to two members only; and in the other to not more than five; according to the numbers of which the Legislature is at first to be composed. It is the interest moreover of the distant States to prefer ¾ as they will be oftenest absent and need the interposing check of the President. The excess rather than the deficiency of laws was to be dreaded. The example of N. York shews that ⅔ is not sufficient to answer the purpose.

Mͬ Hamilton added his testimony to the fact that ⅔ in N. York had been ineffectual either where a popular object, or a legislative faction operated; of which he mentioned some instances.

Mͬ Gerry. It is necessary to consider the danger on the other side also. ⅔ will be a considerable, perhaps a proper security. ¾ puts too much in the power of a few men. The primary object of the revisionary check of the President is not to protect the general interest, but to defend his own department. If ¾ be required, a few Senators having hopes from the nomination of the President to offices, will combine with him and impede proper laws. Making the vice-President Speaker increases the danger.

Mͬ Williamson was less afraid of too few than of too many laws. He was most of all afraid that the repeal of bad laws might be rendered too difficult by requiring ¾ to overcome the dissent of the President.

Col: Mason had always considered this as one of the most exceptionable parts of the System. As to the numerical argument of Mͬ Govͬ Morris, little arithmetic was necessary to understand that ¾ was more than ⅔, whatever the numbers of the Legislature might be. The example of New York depended on the real merits of the laws. The Gentlemen citing it, had no doubt given their own opinions. But perhaps there were others of opposite opinions who could equally paint the abuses on the other side. His leading view was to guard against too great an impediment to the repeal of laws.

Mͬ Govͬ Morris dwelt on the danger to the public interest from the instability of laws, as the most to be guarded against. On the other side there could be little danger. If one man in office will not consent where he ought, every fourth year another can be substituted. This term was not too long for fair experiments. Many good laws are not tried long enough to prove their merit. This is often the case with new laws opposed to old habits. The Inspection laws of Virginia & Maryland to which all are now so much attached were unpopular at first.

M⁚ PINKNEY was warmly in opposition to ¾ as putting a dangerous power in the hands of a few Senators headed by the President.

M⁚ MADISON. When ¾ was agreed to, the President was to be elected by the Legislature and for seven years. He is now to be elected by the people and for four years. The object of the revisionary power is twofold. 1.[1] to defend the Executive Rights 2.[1] to prevent popular or factious injustice. It was an important principle in this & in the State Constitutions to check legislative injustice and incroachments. The Experience of the States had demonstrated that their checks are insufficient. We must compare the danger from the weakness of ⅔ with the danger from the strength of ¾. He thought on the whole the former was the greater. As to the difficulty of repeals, it was probable that in doubtful cases the policy would soon take place of limiting the duration of laws so as to require renewal instead of repeal.

The reconsideration being agreed to. On the question to insert ⅔ in place of ¾.

N. H. div⁴ Mas. no. C⁚ ay. N. J. ay. P⁚ no. Del. no. M⁴ ay. M⁚ M꞉Henry no. V⁚ no. Gen! Washington M⁚ Blair, M⁚ Madison no. Col. Mason, M⁚ Randolph ay. N. C. ay. S. C. ay. Geo. ay.[2]

M⁚ WILLIAMSON, observed to the House that no provision was yet made for juries in Civil cases and suggested the necessity of it.

M⁚ GORHAM. It is not possible to discriminate equity cases from those in which juries are proper. The Representatives of the people may be safely trusted in this matter.

M⁚ GERRY urged the necessity of Juries to guard ag꞉ᵗ corrupt Judges. He proposed that the Committee last appointed should be directed to provide a clause for securing the trial by Juries.

Col: MASON perceived the difficulty mentioned by M⁚ Gorham. The jury cases can not be specified. A general principle laid down on this and some other points would be sufficient. He wished the plan had been prefaced with a Bill of Rights, & would second a Motion if made for the purpose. It would give great quiet to the people; and with the aid of the State declarations, a bill might be prepared in a few hours.

---

[1] The figures "1" and "2" are changed in the transcript to "first" and "secondly."

[2] In the transcript the vote reads: "Connecticut, New Jersey, Maryland [Mr. McHenry, no.], North Carolina, South Carolina, Georgia, aye—6; Massachusetts, Pennsylvania, Delaware, Virginia [General Washington, Mr. Blair, Mr. Madison, no; Col. Mason, Mr. Randolph, aye], no—4; New Hampshire, divided."

M.ʳ GERRY concurred in the idea & moved for a Committee to prepare a Bill of Rights.   Col: MASON 2ᵈᵉᵈ the motion.

M.ʳ SHERMAN, was for securing the rights of the people where requisite.   The State Declarations of Rights are not repealed by this Constitution; and being in force are sufficient.   There are many cases where juries are proper which can not be discriminated.   The Legislature may be safely trusted.

Col: MASON.   The Laws of the U. S. are to be paramount to State Bills of Rights.

On the question for a Com.ᵉ to prepare a Bill of Rights

N. H. no.   Mas. abs.ᵗ   C.ᵗ no.   N. J. no.   P.ᵃ no.   Del. no.   M.ᵈ no. V.ᵃ no.   N. C. no.   S. C. no.   Geo. no.[1]

The Clause relating to exports being reconsidered, at the instance of Col: Mason, who urged that the restriction on the States would prevent the incidental duties necessary for the inspection & safe-keeping of their produce, and be ruinous to the Staple States, as he called the five Southern States, he moved as follows—" provided nothing herein contained shall be construed to restrain any State from laying duties upon exports for the sole purpose of defraying the charges of inspecting, packing, storing and indemnifying the losses, in keeping the commodities in the care of public officers, before exportation."   In answer to a remark which he anticipated, towit, that the States could provide for these expences, by a tax in some other way, he stated the inconveniency[2] of requiring the Planters to pay a tax before the actual delivery for exportation.

M.ʳ MADISON 2ᵈᵉᵈ the motion.   It would at least be harmless; and might have the good effect of restraining the States to bona fide duties for the purpose, as well as of authorising explicitly such duties; tho' perhaps the best guard against an abuse of the power of the States on this subject, was the right in the Gen.ˡ Government to regulate trade between State & State.

M.ʳ Gov.ʳ MORRIS saw no objection to the motion.   He did not consider the dollar per Hhd laid on Tob.ᵒ in Virg.ᵃ as a duty on exportation, as no drawback would be allowed on Tob.ᵒ taken out of the Warehouse for internal consumption.

M.ʳ DAYTON was afraid the proviso w.ᵈ enable Pennsylv.ᵃ to tax

---

[1] In the transcript the vote reads: "New Hampshire, Connecticut, New Jersey, Pennsylvania, Delaware, aye—5; Maryland, Virginia, North Carolina, South Carolina, Georgia, no—5; Massachusetts, absent." This was the copyist's error as Madison's original notes agree with the Journal, which reads: "Which passed unanimously in the negative."

[2] The word "inconveniency" is changed in the transcript to "inconvenience."

N. Jersey under the idea of Inspection duties of which Pen⁶ would Judge.

M⁶ GORHAM & M⁶ LANGDON, thought there would be no security if the proviso sh⁴ be agreed to, for the States exporting thro' other States, ag⁵ᵗ the ¹ oppressions of the latter. How was redress to be obtained in case duties should be laid beyond the purpose expressed?

M⁶ MADISON. There will be the same security as in other cases. The jurisdiction of the supreme Court must be the source of redress. So far only had provision been made by the plan ag⁵ᵗ injurious acts of the States. His own opinion was, that this was insufficient. A negative on the State laws alone could meet all the shapes which these could assume. But this had been overruled.

M⁶ FITZIMMONS. Incidental duties on Tob⁶ & flour, never have been & never can be considered as duties on exports.

M⁶ DICKINSON. Nothing will save ² States in the situation of N. Hampshire N Jersey Delaware &c from being oppressed by their neighbors, but requiring the assent of Cong⁵ to inspection duties. He moved that this assent sh⁴ accordingly be required.

M⁶ BUTLER 2ᵈᵉᵈ the motion.

Adjourned

───────

THURSDAY SEP⁶ 13. 1787.³ IN CONVENTION

Col: MASON. He had moved without success for a power to make sumptuary regulations. He had not yet lost sight of his object. After descanting on the extravagance of our manners, the excessive consumption of foreign superfluities, and the necessity of restricting it, as well with œconomical as republican views, he moved that a Committee be appointed to report articles of association for encouraging by the advice the influence and the example of the members of the Convention, œconomy frugality and american manufactures.

Doc⁶ JOHNSON 2ᵈᵉᵈ the motion which was without debate agreed to, nem: con: and a Committee appointed, consisting of Col: Mason, Doc⁶ Franklin, M⁶ Dickenson, Doc⁶ Johnson, and M⁶ Livingston.*

Col: MASON renewed his proposition of yesterday on the subject

* This motion & appointment of the Comittee, not ⁴ in the printed Journal. No report was made by the Com⁶

---

¹ The word "these" is substituted in the transcript for "the."
² The word "the" is here inserted in the transcript.
³ The year "1787" is omitted in the transcript.
⁴ The words "do not appear" are substituted in the transcript for "not."

of inspection laws, with an additional clause giving to Congress a controul over them in case of abuse—as follows,

" Provided that no State shall be restrained from imposing the usual duties on produce exported from such State, for the sole purpose of defraying the charges of inspecting, packing, storing, and indemnifying the losses on such produce, while in the custody of public officers: but all such regulations shall in case of abuse, be subject to the revision and controul of Congress."

There was no debate & on the question

N. H. ay. Mas. ay. C: ay. P: no. Del. no. M: ay. V: ay. N. C. ay. S. C. no. Geo. ay.[1]

The Report from the Committee of stile & arrangement, was taken up, in order to be compared with the articles of the plan as agreed to by the House & referred to the Committee, and to receive the final corrections and sanction of the Convention.

Art. 1. sect. 2. On motion of M: RANDOLPH the word " servitude " was struck out, and " service "* unanimously inserted, the former being thought to express the condition of slaves, & the latter the obligations of free persons.

M: DICKENSON & M: WILSON moved to strike out " and direct taxes," from sect. 2. art. 1. as improperly placed in a clause relating merely to the Constitution of the House of Representatives.

M: GOV: MORRIS. The insertion here was in consequence of what had passed on this point; in order to exclude the appearance of counting the negroes in *the Representation*. The including of them may now be referred to the object of direct taxes, and incidentally only to that of Representation.

On the motion to strike out " and direct taxes " from this place

N. H. no. Mas. no. C: no. N. J. ay. P: no. Del. ay. M: ay. V: no. N. C. no. S. C. no. Geo. no.[2]

Art. 1. sect. 7 "—if any bill shall not be returned by the president within ten days (Sundays excepted) after it shall have been presented to him &c "

M: MADISON, moved to insert between " after " and " it " in Sect. 7. Art. 1 the words " the day on which," in order to prevent a

* See page 372 of the printed Journal.

---

[1] In the transcript the vote reads: "New Hampshire, Massachusetts, Connecticut, Maryland, Virginia, North Carolina, Georgia, aye—7; Pennsylvania, Delaware, South Carolina, no—3."
[2] In the transcript the vote reads: "New Jersey, Delaware, Maryland, aye —3; New Hampshire, Massachusetts, Connecticut, Pennsylvania, Virginia, North Carolina, South Carolina, Georgia, no—8."

question whether the day on which the bill be presented, ought to be counted or not as one of the ten days.

M: RANDOLPH 2^{ded} the motion.

M: GOVERNU: MORRIS. The amendment is unnecessary. The law knows no fractions of days.

A number of members being very impatient & calling for the question

N. H. no. Mas. no. C: no. N. J. no. P: ay. Del. no. M: ay. V: ay. N. C. no S. C. no. Geo. no— [1]

Doc: JOHNSON made a further report from the Committee of stile &c of the following resolutions to be substituted for 22 & 23 articles

" Resolved that the preceding Constitution be laid before the U. States in Congress assembled, and that it is the opinion of this Convention, that it should afterwards be submitted to a Convention of Delegates chosen in each State by the people thereof; under the recommendation of its Legislature, for their assent & ratification; & that each Convention assenting & ratifying the same should give notice thereof to the U. S. in Cong: assembled.

" Resolved that it is the opinion of this Convention that as soon as the Conventions of nine States, shall have ratified this Constitution, the U. S. in Cong: assembled should fix a day on which electors should be appointed by the States which shall have ratified the same; and a day on which the Electors should assemble to vote for the President; and the time and place for commencing proceedings under this Constitution—That after such publication the Electors should be appointed, and the Senators and Representatives elected: That the Electors should meet on the day fixed for the election of the President, and should transmit their votes certified signed, sealed and directed, as the Constitution requires, to the Secretary of the U. States in Cong: assembled: that the Senators and Representatives should convene at the time & place assigned; that the Senators should appoint a President for the sole purpose of receiving, opening, and counting the votes for President, and that after he shall be chosen, the Congress, together with the President should without delay proceed to execute this Constitution."

Adjourned

FRIDAY SEP^R 14TH 1787.[2] IN CONVENTION

The Report of the Committee of Stile & arrangement being resumed,

---

[1] In the transcript the vote reads: "Pennsylvania, Maryland, Virginia, aye —3; New Hampshire, Massachusetts, Connecticut, New Jersey, Delaware, North Carolina, South Carolina, Georgia, no—8."

[2] The year "1787" is omitted in the transcript.

M⁚ WILLIAMSON moved to reconsider in order to increase the number of Representatives fixed for the first Legislature. His purpose was to make an addition of one half generally to the number allotted to the respective States; and to allow two to the smallest States.

On this motion

N. H. no. Mas. no. C⁚ no. N. J. no. P⁚ ay. Del. ay. M⁚ ay. V⁚ ay. N C. ay. S. C. no. Geo. no.[1]

Art. 1. sect. 3.–the words * " by lot " were struck out nem: con: on motion of M⁚ MADISON, that some rule might prevail in the rotation that would prevent both the members from the same State from going out at the same time.

" Ex officio " struck out of the same section as superfluous: nem: con: and " or affirmation." after " oath " inserted also unanimously.

M⁚ RUTLIDGE and M⁚ GOV⁚ MORRIS moved " that persons impeached be suspended from their office [3] until they be tried and acquitted "

M⁚ MADISON. The President is made too dependent already on the Legislature, by the power of one branch to try him in consequence of an impeachment by the other. This intermediate suspension, will put him in the power of one branch only. They can at any moment, in order to make way for the functions of another who will be more favorable to their views, vote a temporary removal of the existing Magistrate.

M⁚ KING concurred in the opposition to the amendment

On the question to agree to it

N. H. no. Mas. no. Cᵗ ay. N. J. no. P⁚ no. Del. no. M⁚ no. V⁚ no. N. C. no. S. C. ay. Geo. ay.[4]

Art. 1. sect. 4. " except as to the places of choosing Senators " [5] added nem: con: to the end of the first clause, in order to exempt the seats of Gov⁚ in the States from the power of Congress.

* " By lot " had been re-instated from the Report of five made Aug. 6. as a correction of the printed report by the Com⁚ of stile & arrangement.[2]

---

[1] In the transcript the vote reads: " Pennsylvania, Delaware, Maryland, Virginia, North Carolina, aye—5; New Hampshire, Massachusetts, Connecticut, New Jersey, South Carolina, Georgia, no—6."

[2] In the transcript this note reads as follows: " ' By lot,' had been reinstated from the Report of the Committee of five made on the sixth of August, as a correction of the printed Report by the Committee of style, &c."

[3] The transcript uses the word " office " in the plural.

[4] In the transcript the vote reads: " Connecticut, South Carolina, Georgia, aye—3; New Hampshire, Massachusetts, New Jersey, Pennsylvania, Delaware, Maryland, Virginia, North Carolina, no—8."

[5] The word " was " is here inserted in the transcript.

Art. 1. Sect. 5. " Each House shall keep a Journal of its proceedings, and from time to time publish the same, excepting such parts as may in their judgment require secresy."

Col: MASON & Mʳ GERRY moved to insert after the word " parts " the words " of the proceedings of the Senate " so as to require publication of all the proceedings of the House of Representatives.

It was intimated on the other side that cases might arise where secresy might be necessary in both Houses. Measures preparatory to a declaration of war in which the House of Repᵗ was to concur, were instanced.

On the question, it passed in the negative

N. H. no. (Rh. I abs) Mas. no. Con: no. (N. Y. abs) N. J. no. Pen. ay. Del. no. Mary. ay. Virg. no. N. C. ay. S. C. divᵈ Geor. no.[1]

Mʳ BALDWIN observed that the clause, Art. 1. Sect 6. declaring that no member of Congˢ " during the time for which he was elected; shall be appointed to any Civil office under the authority of the U. S. which shall have been created, or the emoluments whereof shall have been increased during such time," would not extend to offices *created by the Constitution;* and the salaries of which would be created, *not increased* by Congˢ at their first session. The members of the first Congˢ consequently might evade the disqualification in this instance.—He was neither seconded nor opposed; nor did any thing further pass on the subject.

Art. 1. Sect. 8. The Congress " may by joint ballot appoint a Treasurer "

Mʳ RUTLIDGE moved to strike out this power, and let the Treasurer be appointed in the same manner with other officers.

Mʳ GORHAM & Mʳ KING said that the motion, if agreed, to would have a mischievous tendency. The people are accustomed & attached to that mode of appointing Treasurers, and the innovation will multiply objections to the System.

Mʳ Govʳ MORRIS remarked that if the Treasurer be not appointed by the Legislature, he will be more narrowly watched, and more readily impeached.

Mʳ SHERMAN. As the two Houses appropriate money, it is best for them to appoint the officer who is to keep it; and to appoint him as they make the appropriation, not by joint but several votes.

Genˡ PINKNEY. The Treasurer is appointed by joint ballot in

---

[1] In the transcript the vote reads: " Pennsylvania, Maryland, North Carolina, aye—3; New Hampshire, Massachusetts, Connecticut, New Jersey, Delaware, Virginia, Georgia, no—7."

South Carolina. The consequence is that bad appointments are made, and the Legislature will not listen to the faults of their own officer.

On the motion to strike out

N. H. ay. Mas. no. Cᵗ ay. N. J. ay. Pᵃ no. Del. ay. Mᵈ ay. Vᵃ no. N. C. ay. S. C. ay. Geo. ay.[1]

Art I. sect. 8.[2] " but all such duties imposts & excises, shall be uniform throughout the U. S." was[3] unanimously annexed to the power of taxation.

[4] To define & punish piracies and felonies on the high seas, and " punish " offences against the law of nations.

Mʳ Govʳ Morris moved to strike out " punish " before the words " offences agˢᵗ the law of nations," so as to let these be *definable* as well as punishable, by virtue of the preceding member of the sentence.

Mʳ Wilson hoped the alteration would by no means be made. To pretend to *define* the law of nations which depended on the authority of all the civilized nations of the world, would have a look of arrogance, that would make us ridiculous.

Mʳ Govʳ[5] The word *define* is proper when applied to *offences* in this case; the law of nations being often too vague and deficient to be a rule.

On the question to strike out the word " punish " it passed in the affirmative

N. H. ay. Mas. no. Cᵗ ay. N. J. ay. Pᵃ no. Del. ay. Mᵈ no. Vᵃ no. N. C. ay. S. C. ay. Geo. no.[6]

Docᵗ Franklin moved * to add after the words " post roads " Art I. Sect. 8. " a power to provide for cutting canals where deemed necessary "

Mʳ Wilson 2ᵈᵉᵈ the motion

Mʳ Sherman objected. The expence in such cases will fall on the U. States, and the benefit accrue to the places where the canals may be cut.

* This motion by Dʳ Franklin not stated in the printed Journal, as are some other motions.

---

[1] In the transcript the vote reads: " New Hampshire, Connecticut, New Jersey, Delaware, Maryland, North Carolina, South Carolina, Georgia, aye—8; Massachusetts, Pennsylvania, Virginia, no—3."
[2] The expression " the words " is here inserted in the transcript.
[3] The word " was " is changed in the transcript to " were."
[4] The words " On the clause " are here inserted in the transcript.
[5] The name " Morris " is here inserted in the transcript.
[6] In the transcript the vote reads: " New Hampshire, Connecticut, New Jersey, Delaware, North Carolina, South Carolina, aye—6; Massachusetts, Pennsylvania, Maryland, Virginia, Georgia, no—5."

M: WILSON. Instead of being an expence to the U. S. they may be made a source of revenue.

M: MADISON suggested an enlargement of the motion into a power " to grant charters of incorporation where the interest of the U. S. might require & the legislative provisions of individual States may be incompetent." His primary object was however to secure an easy communication between the States which the free intercourse now to be opened, seemed to call for. The political obstacles being removed, a removal of the natural ones as far as possible ought to follow. M: RANDOLPH 2^{ded} the proposition

M: KING thought the power unnecessary.

M: WILSON. It is necessary to prevent *a State* from obstructing the *general* welfare.

M: KING. The States will be prejudiced and divided into parties by it. In Philad: & New York, It will be referred to the establishment of a Bank, which has been a subject of contention in those Cities. In other places it will be referred to mercantile monopolies.

M: WILSON mentioned the importance of facilitating by canals, the communication with the Western Settlements. As to Banks he did not think with M: King that the power in that point of view would excite the prejudices & parties apprehended. As to mercantile monopolies they are already included in the power to regulate trade.

Col: MASON was for limiting the power to the single case of Canals. He was afraid of monopolies of every sort, which he did not think were by any means already implied by the Constitution as supposed by M: Wilson.

The motion being so modified as to admit a distinct question specifying & limited to the case of canals,

N. H. no. Mas. no. C: no. N. J. no. P: ay. Del. no. M: no. V: ay. N. C. no. S. C no. Geo. ay.[1]

The other part fell of course, as including the power rejected.

M: MADISON & M: PINKNEY then moved to insert in the list of powers vested in Congress a power—" to establish an University, in which no preferences or distinctions should be allowed on account of Religion."

M: WILSON supported the motion

M: GOV: MORRIS. It is not necessary. The exclusive power at the Seat of Government, will reach the object.

On the question

---

[1] In the transcript the vote reads: " Pennsylvania, Virginia, Georgia, aye—3; New Hampshire, Massachusetts, Connecticut, New Jersey, Delaware, Maryland, North Carolina, South Carolina, no—8."

N. H. no. Mas. no. Con: div? D: Johnson ay. M: Sherman no.
N. J. no. P: ay. Del. no. M? no. V: ay. N. C. ay. S. C. ay.
Geo. no.[1]

Col: MASON, being sensible that an absolute prohibition of standing armies in time of peace might be unsafe, and wishing at the same time to insert something pointing out and guarding against the danger of them, moved to preface the clause (Art I sect. 8) " To provide for organizing, arming and disciplining the Militia &c " with the words " " And that the liberties of the people may be better secured against the danger of standing armies in time of peace " M: RANDOLPH 2^{ded} the motion

M: MADISON was in favor of it. It did not restrain Congress from establishing a military force in time of peace if found necessary; and as armies in time of peace are allowed on all hands to be an evil, it is well to discountenance them by the Constitution, as far as will consist with the essential power of the Gov: on that head.

M: Gov: MORRIS opposed the motion as setting a dishonorable mark of distinction on the military class of Citizens

M: PINKNEY & M: BEDFORD concurred in the opposition.

On the question

N. H. no. Mas. no. C: no. N. J. no. P: no. Del. no. Mary? no V: ay. N. C. no. S. C. no. Geo. ay.[2]

Col: MASON moved to strike out from the clause (art I sect 9.) " No bill of attainder nor any expost facto law shall be passed " the words " nor any ex post facto law." He thought it not sufficiently clear that the prohibition meant by this phrase was limited to cases of a criminal nature, and no Legislature ever did or can altogether avoid them in Civil cases.

M: GERRY 2^{ded} the motion but with a view to extend the prohibition to " Civil cases," which he thought ought to be done.

On the question; all the States were—no

M: PINKNEY & M: GERRY, moved to insert a declaration " that the liberty of the Press should be inviolably observed."

M: SHERMAN. It is unnecessary. The power of Congress does not extend to the Press. On the question, it passed in the negative

---

[1] In the transcript the vote reads: " Pennsylvania, Virginia, North Carolina, South Carolina, aye—4; New Hampshire, Massachusetts, New Jersey, Delaware, Maryland, Georgia, no—6; Connecticut, divided [Dr. Johnson, aye; Mr. Sherman, no].

[2] In the transcript the vote reads: " Virginia, Georgia, aye—2; New Hampshire, Massachusetts, Connecticut, New Jersey, Pennsylvania, Delaware, Maryland, North Carolina, South Carolina, no—9."

N. H. no.* Mas. ay. C! no. N. J. no. P! no. Del. no. M^d ay. V! ay. N. C. no. S. C. ay. Geo. no.[1]

Art. I. Sect. 9. " No capitation tax shall be laid, unless &c "

M! READ moved to insert after " capitation " the words, " or other direct tax " He was afraid that some liberty might otherwise be taken to saddle the States, with a readjustment by this rule, of past requisitions of Cong!—and that his amendment by giving another cast to the meaning would take away the pretext. M! WILLIAMSON 2^{ded} the motion which was agreed to, On motion of Col: MASON [2] " or enumeration " [3] inserted after, as explanatory of " Census " Con. & S. C. only, no.

* Here insert the amendment added in the lateral margin.[4]

* At the end of the clause " no tax or duty shall be laid on articles exported from any State " was added the following amendment conformably to a vote on the   day of [5]   viz—no preference shall be given by any regulation of commerce or revenue to the ports of one State over those of another: nor shall vessels bound to or from one State, be obliged to enter, clear or pay duties in another.

Col. MASON moved a clause requiring " that an Account of the public expenditures should be annually published " M! GERRY 2^{ded} the motion

M! Gov! MORRIS urged that this w^d be impossible in many cases.

M! KING remarked, that the term expenditures went to every minute shilling. This would be impracticable. Cong! might indeed make a monthly publication, but it would be in such general statements as would afford no satisfactory information.

M! MADISON proposed to strike out " annually " from the motion & insert " from time to time," which would enjoin the duty of frequent publications and leave enough to the discretion of the Legislature. Require too much and the difficulty will beget a habit of doing nothing. The articles of Confederation require half-yearly publications on this subject. A punctual compliance being often impossible, the practice has ceased altogether.

* In the printed Journal N. Hampshire ay.

---

[1] In the transcript the vote reads: "Massachusetts, Maryland, Virginia, South Carolina, aye—4; New Hampshire,* Connecticut, New Jersey, Pennsylvania, Delaware, North Carolina, Georgia, no—7."
[2] The expression " the words " is here inserted in the transcript.
[3] The word " were " is here inserted in the transcript.
[4] Madison's direction concerning the amendment is omitted in the transcript.
[5] The date "thirty-first of August " is supplied in the transcript.

M͞: Wilson 2ᵈᵉᵈ & supported the motion. Many operations of finance can not be properly published at certain times.

M͞: Pinkney was in favor of the motion.

M͞: Fitzimmons. It is absolutely impossible to publish expenditures in the full extent of the term.

M͞: Sherman thought " from time to time " the best rule to be given.

" Annual " was struck out—& those words—inserted nem: con:

The motion of Col: Mason so amended was then agreed to nem: con: and added after—" appropriations by law as follows—" and a regular statement and account of the receipts & expenditures of all public money shall be published from time to time "

Here insert the Amendment at the foot of the page ¹

* The first clause of Art. I Sect 10—was altered so as to read— " No State shall enter into any Treaty alliance or confederation; grant letters of marque and reprisal; coin money; emit bills of credit; make any thing but gold & silver coin a tender in payment of debts; pass any bill of attainder, ex post ² law, or law impairing the obligation of contracts, or grant any title of nobility."

M͞: Gerry entered into observations inculcating the importance of public faith, and the propriety of the restraint put on the States from impairing the obligation of contracts, alledging that Congress ought to be laid under the like prohibitions, he made a motion to that effect. He was not 2ᵈᵉᵈ

Adjourned.

Saturday Sepᴿ 15ᵀᴴ 1787.³ In Convention

M͞: Carrol reminded the House that no address to the people had yet been prepared. He considered it of great importance that such an one should accompany the Constitution. The people had been accustomed to such on great occasions, and would expect it on this. He moved that a Committee be appointed for the special purpose of preparing an Address.

M͞: Rutledge objected on account of the delay it would produce and the impropriety of addressing the people before it was known whether Congress would approve and support the plan. Congress,

---

¹ Madison's direction concerning the amendment is omitted in the transcript.
² The word "facto" is here inserted in the transcript.
³ The year "1787" is omitted in the transcript.

if an address be thought proper can prepare as good a one. The members of the Convention can also explain the reasons of what has been done to their respective Constituents.

M: SHERMAN concurred in the opinion that an address was both unnecessary and improper.

On the motion of M: Carrol

N. H. no. Mas. no. C: no. N. J. no. P: ay. Del. ay. M: ay. V: ay. N. C.* abs: S. C.* no. Geo. no [1]

M: LANGDON. Some gentlemen have been very uneasy that no increase of the number of Representatives has been admitted. It has in particular been thought that one more ought to be allowed to N. Carolina. He was of opinion that an additional one was due both to that State & to Rho: Island, & moved to reconsider for that purpose.

M: SHERMAN. When the Committee of eleven reported the apportionment—five Representatives were thought the proper share of N. Carolina. Subsequent information however seemed to entitle that State to another.

On the motion to reconsider

N. H. ay. Mas. no. C: ay. N. J. no. Pen. div: Del. ay. M: ay. V: ay. N. C. ay. S. C. ay. Geo. ay.[2]

M: LANGDON moved to add 1 member to each of the Representations of N. Carolina & Rho: Island.

M: KING was ag:t any change whatever as opening the door for delays. There had been no official proof that the numbers of N. C. are greater than before estimated, and he never could sign the Constitution if Rho: Island is to be allowed two members that is, one fourth of the number allowed to Massts, which will be known to be unjust.

M: PINKNEY urged the propriety of increasing the number of Rep: allotted to N. Carolina.

M: BEDFORD contended for an increase in favor of Rho: Island, and of Delaware also

On the question for allowing two Rep: to Rho: Island, it passed in the negative

* In the printed Journal N. Carolina—no & S. Carol: omitted.

---

[1] In the transcript the vote reads: "Pennsylvania, Delaware, Maryland, Virginia, aye—4; New Hampshire, Massachusetts, Connecticut, New Jersey, South Carolina,* Georgia, no—6; North Carolina,* absent."

[2] In the transcript the vote reads: "New Hampshire, Connecticut, Delaware, Maryland, Virginia, North Carolina, South Carolina, Georgia, aye—8; Massachusetts, New Jersey, no—2; Pennsylvania, divided.

N. H. ay. Mas. no. C⁺ no. N. J. no. P⁺ no. Del. ay. M⁴ ay. V⁺ no. N. C. ay. S. C. no. Geo. ay.[1]

On the question for allowing six to N. Carolina, it passed in the negative.

N. H. no. Mas. no. C⁺ no. N. J. no. P⁺ no. Del. no. M⁴ ay. V⁺ ay. N. C. ay. S. C. ay. Geo. ay.[2]

Art 1. Sect. 10. (paragraph 2). "No State shall, without the consent of Congress lay imposts or duties on imports or exports; nor with such consent, but to the use of the Treasury of the U. States."

In consequence of the proviso moved by Col: Mason: and agreed to on the 13 [3] Sep⁺, this part of the section was laid aside in favor of the following substitute viz. "No State shall, without the consent of Congress, lay any imposts or duties on imports or exports, except what may be absolutely necessary for executing its Inspection laws; and the nett produce of all duties and imposts, laid by any State on imports or exports, shall be for the use of the Treasury of the U. S; and all such laws shall be subject to the revision and controul of the Congress"

On a motion to strike out the last part "and all such laws shall be subject to the revision and controul of the Congress" it passed in the negative.

N. H. no. Mas. no. C⁺ no. N. J. no. P⁺ div⁴ Del. no. M⁴ no. V⁺ ay. N. C. ay. S. C. no. Geo. ay.[4]

The substitute was then agreed to: Virg⁺ alone being in the negative.

The remainder of the paragraph being under consideration— viz—"nor keep troops nor ships of war in time of peace, nor enter into any agreement or compact with another State, nor with any foreign power. Nor engage in any war, unless it shall be actually invaded by enemies, or the danger of invasion be so imminent as not to admit of delay, until Congress can be consulted"

M⁺ M⁰ HENRY & M⁺ CARROL moved that "no State shall be re-

---

[1] In the transcript the vote reads: "New Hampshire, Delaware, Maryland, North Carolina, Georgia, aye—5; Massachusetts, Connecticut, New Jersey, Pennsylvania, Virginia, South Carolina, no—6."

[2] In the transcript the vote reads: "Maryland, Virginia, North Carolina, South Carolina, Georgia, aye—5; New Hampshire, Massachusetts, Connecticut, New Jersey, Pennsylvania, Delaware, no—6."

[3] The word "of" is here inserted in the transcript.

[4] In the transcript the vote reads: "Virginia, North Carolina, Georgia, aye —3; New Hampshire, Massachusetts, Connecticut, New Jersey, Delaware, Maryland, South Carolina, no—7; Pennsylvania, divided."

strained from laying duties of tonnage for the purpose of clearing harbours and erecting light-houses."

Col. Mason in support of this explained and urged the situation of the Chesapeak which peculiarly required expences of this sort.

M: Gov: Morris. The States are not restrained from laying tonnage as the Constitution now Stands. The exception proposed will imply the contrary, and will put the States in a worse condition than the gentleman [Col Mason] wishes.

M: Madison. Whether the States are now restrained from laying tonnage duties depends on the extent of the power "to regulate commerce." These terms are vague, but seem to exclude this power of the States. They may certainly be restrained by Treaty. He observed that there were other objects for tonnage Duties as the support of Seamen &c. He was more & more convinced that the regulation of Commerce was in its nature indivisible and ought to be wholly under one authority.

M: Sherman. The power of the U. States to regulate trade being supreme can controul interferences of the State regulations when [1] such interferences happen; so that there is no danger to be apprehended from a concurrent jurisdiction.

M: Langdon insisted that the regulation of tonnage was an essential part of the regulation of trade, and that the States ought to have nothing to do with it. On motion " that no State shall lay any duty on tonnage without the Consent of Congress "

N. H. ay. Mas. ay. C: div: N. J. ay. P: no. Del. ay. M: ay. V: no. N. C. no. S. C. ay. Geo. no.[2]

The remainder of the paragraph was then remoulded and passed as follows viz—" No State shall without the consent of Congress, lay any duty of tonnage, keep troops or ships of war in time of peace, enter into any agreement or compact with another State, or with a foreign power, or engage in war, unless actually invaded, or in such imminent danger as will not admit of delay."

[3] Art II. sect. 1. (paragraph 6) " or the period for chusing another president arrive " was changed into " or a President shall be elected " conformably to a vote of the   day of

---

[1] In Madison's notes the word "when" is written above "which." The transcript uses "when."

[2] In the transcript the vote reads: "New Hampshire, Massachusetts, New Jersey, Delaware, Maryland, South Carolina, aye—6; Pennsylvania, Virginia, North Carolina, Georgia, no—4; Connecticut, divided."

[3] In the transcript this paragraph reads as follows: "Article 2, sect. 1, (the sixth paragraph) the words ' or the period for choosing another President arrive,' were changed into, ' or a President shall be elected,' conformably to a vote of the seventh of September."

M⸰ RUTLIDGE and Doc⸰ FRANKLIN moved to annex to the end of paragraph 7. Sect. 1. art II—"and he [the President] shall not receive, within that period, any other emolument from the U. S. or any of them," on which question

N. H. ay. Mas. ay. C⸰ no. N. J. no. P⸰ ay. Del. no. M⸰ ay. V⸰ ay. N. C. no. S. C. ay. Geo. ay.[1]

Art: II. Sect. 2. "he shall have power to grant reprieves and pardons for offences against the U. S. &c"

M⸰ RANDOLPH moved to "except cases of treason." The prerogative of pardon in these cases was too great a trust. The President may himself be guilty. The Traytors may be his own instruments.

Col: MASON supported the motion.

M⸰ GOV⸰ MORRIS had rather there should be no pardon for treason, than let the power devolve on the Legislature.

M⸰ WILSON. Pardon is necessary for cases of treason, and is best placed in the hands of the Executive. If he be himself a party to the guilt he can be impeached and prosecuted.

M⸰ KING thought it would be inconsistent with the Constitutional separation of the Executive & Legislative powers to let the prerogative be exercised by the latter. A Legislative body is utterly unfit for the purpose. They are governed too much by the passions of the moment. In Massachussets, one assembly would have hung all the insurgents in that State: the next was equally disposed to pardon them all. He suggested the expedient of requiring the concurrence of the Senate in Acts of Pardon.

M⸰ MADISON admitted the force of objections to the Legislature, but the pardon of treasons was so peculiarly improper for the President that he should acquiesce in the transfer of it to the former, rather than leave it altogether in the hands of the latter. He would prefer to either an association of the Senate as a Council of advice, with the President.

M⸰ RANDOLPH could not admit the Senate into a share of the Power. the great danger to liberty lay in a combination between the President & that body.

Col: MASON. The Senate has already too much power. There can be no danger of too much lenity in legislative pardons, as the Senate must con concur, & the President moreover can require ⅔ of both Houses.

---

[1] In the transcript the vote reads: "New Hampshire, Massachusetts, Pennsylvania, Maryland, Virginia, South Carolina, Georgia, aye—7; Connecticut, New Jersey, Delaware, North Carolina, no—4."

On the motion of Mʳ Randolph

N. H. no. Mas. no. Cᵗ divᵈ N. J. no. Pᵃ no. Del. no. Mᵈ no. Vᵃ ay. N. C. no. S. C. no. Geo. ay.[1]

Art II. Sect. 2. (paragraph 2) To the end of this, Mʳ Govᵉʳⁿ Morris moved to annex "but the Congress may by law vest the appointment of such inferior officers as they think proper, in the President alone, in the Courts of law, or in the heads of Departments." Mʳ Sherman 2ᵈᵉᵈ the motion

Mʳ Madison. It does not go far enough if it be necessary at all. Superior officers below Heads of Departments ought in some cases to have the appointment of the lesser offices.

Mʳ Govᵗ Morris There is no necessity. Blank commissions can be sent—

On the motion

N. H. ay. Mas. no. Cᵗ ay. N. J. ay. Pᵃ ay. Del. no. Mᵈ divᵈ Vᵃ no. N. C. ay. S C no. Geo. no.[2]

The motion being lost by the[3] equal division of votes, It was urged that it be put a second time, some such provision being too necessary to be omitted, and on a second question it was agreed to nem. con.

Art II. Sect. 1. The words, "and not per capita"—were struck out as superfluous—and the words "by the Representatives" also—as improper, the choice of a[4] President being in another mode as well as eventually by the House of Repᵗ

Art. II. Sect. 2. After[5] "officers of the U. S. whose appointments are not otherwise provided for." were added the words "and which shall be established by law."

Art III. Sect. 2. parag: 3. Mʳ Pinkney & Mʳ Gerry moved to annex to the end, "And a trial by jury shall be preserved as usual in civil cases."

Mʳ Gorham. The constitution of Juries is different in different States and the trial itself is *usual* in different cases in different States.

Mʳ King urged the same objections

---

[1] In the transcript the vote reads: "Virginia, Georgia, aye—2; New Hampshire, Massachusetts, New Jersey, Pennsylvania, Delaware, Maryland, North Carolina, South Carolina, no—8; Connecticut, divided."

[2] In the transcript the vote reads: "New Hampshire, Connecticut, New Jersey, Pennsylvania, North Carolina, aye—5; Massachusetts, Delaware, Virginia, South Carolina, Georgia, no—5; Maryland, divided."

[3] The word "an" is substituted in the transcript for "the."

[4] The word "a" is omitted in the transcript.

[5] The expression "the words" is here inserted in the transcript.

Gen! PINKNEY also. He thought such a clause in the Constitution would be pregnant with embarrassments.

The motion was disagreed to nem: con:

Art. IV. Sect 2. parag: 3. the term " legally " was struck out, and[1] " under the laws thereof " inserted after the word " State," in compliance with the wish of some who thought the term legal [2] equivocal, and favoring the idea that slavery was legal in a moral view.

Art. IV. Sect 3. " New States may be admitted by the Congress into this Union: but no new State shall be formed or erected within the jurisdiction of any other State; nor any State be formed by the junction of two or more States, or parts of States, without the consent of the Legislatures of the States concerned as well as of the Cong⁵ "

M⁵ GERRY moved to insert after " or parts of States " the words " or a State and part of a State " which was disagreed to by a large majority; it appearing to be supposed that the case was comprehended in the words of the clause as reported by the Committee.

Art. IV. Sect. 4. After the word " Executive " were inserted the words " when the Legislature can not be convened."

Art. V. " The Congress, whenever two thirds of both Houses shall deem necessary, or on the application of two thirds of the Legislatures of the several States shall propose amendments to this Constitution, which shall be valid to all intents and purposes as part thereof, when the same shall have been ratified by three fourths at least of the Legislatures of the several States, or by Conventions in three fourths thereof, as the one or the other mode of ratification may be proposed by the Congress: Provided that no amendment which may be made prior to the year 1808 shall in any manner affect the 1 & 4 clauses in the 9. section of article 1 "

M⁵ SHERMAN expressed his fears that three fourths of the States might be brought to do things fatal to particular States, as abolishing them altogether or depriving them of their equality in the Senate. He thought it reasonable that the proviso in favor of the States importing slaves should be extended so as to provide that no State should be affected in its internal police, or deprived of its equality in the Senate.

Col: MASON thought the plan of amending the Constitution exceptionable & dangerous. As the proposing of amendments is in

---

[1] The expression " the words " is here inserted in the transcript.
[2] The transcript italicizes the word " legal."

both the modes to depend, in the first immediately, in the second, ultimately, on Congress, no amendments of the proper kind would ever be obtained by the people, if the Government should become oppressive, as he verily believed would be the case.

M: Gov: Morris & M: Gerry moved to amend the article so as to require a Convention on application of ⅔ of the Sts.

M: Madison did not see why Congress would not be as much bound to propose amendments applied for by two thirds of the States as to call a call a Convention on the like application. He saw no objection however against providing for a Convention for the purpose of amendments, except only that difficulties might arise as to the form, the quorum &c. which in Constitutional regulations ought to be as much as possible avoided.

The motion of M: Gov: Morris & M: Gerry was agreed to nem: con: [see the first part of the article as finally past] [1]

M: Sherman moved to strike out of art. V. after " legislatures " the words " of three fourths " and so after the word " Conventions " leaving future Conventions to act in this matter, like the present Conventions [2] according to circumstances.

On this motion

N. H. div⁴ Mas. ay. C: ay. N. J. ay. P: no. Del. no. M⁴ no. V: no. N. C. no. S. C. no. Geo. no. [3]

M: Gerry moved to strike out the words " or by Conventions in three fourths thereof "

On this [4] motion

N. H. no. Mas. no. C: ay. N. J. no. P: no. Del. no. M⁴ no. V: no. N. C. no. S. C. no. Geo. no. [5]

M: Sherman moved according to his idea above expressed to annex to the end of the article a further proviso " that no State shall without its consent be affected in its internal police, or deprived of its equal suffrage in the Senate."

M: Madison. Begin with these special provisos, and every State will insist on them, for their boundaries, exports &c.

On the motion of M: Sherman

---

[1] Madison's direction is omitted in the transcript.

[2] The transcript uses the word " Conventions " in the singular.

[3] In the transcript the vote reads: " Massachusetts, Connecticut, New Jersey, aye—3; Pennsylvania, Delaware, Maryland, Virginia, North Carolina, South Carolina, Georgia, no—7; New Hampshire, divided."

[4] The word " which " is substituted in the transcript for " this."

[5] In the transcript the vote reads: " Connecticut, aye—1; New Hampshire, Massachusetts, New Jersey, Pennsylvania, Delaware, Maryland, Virginia, North Carolina, South Carolina, Georgia, no—10."

N. H. no. Mas. no. C! ay. N. J. ay. P! no. Del. ay. M⁴ no.
V! no. N. C. no. S. C. no. Geo. no.¹

M! SHERMAN then moved to strike out art V altogether

M! BREARLEY 2ᵈᵉᵈ the motion, on which

N. H. no. Mas. no. C! ay. N. J. ay. P! no. Del div⁴ M⁴ no.
V! no. N. C. no. S. C. no. Geo. no.²

M! GOV! MORRIS moved to annex a further proviso—"that no State, without its consent shall be deprived of its equal suffrage in the Senate"

This motion being dictated by the circulating murmurs of the small States was agreed to without debate, no one opposing it, or on the question, saying no.

Col: MASON expressing his discontent at the power given to Congress by a bare majority to pass navigation acts, which he said would not only enhance the freight, a consequence he did not so much regard—but would enable a few rich merchants in Philadᵃ N. York & Boston, to monopolize the Staples of the Southern States & reduce their value perhaps 50 Per C!—moved a further proviso "that no law in ³ nature of a navigation act be passed before the year 1808, without the consent of ⅔ of each branch of the Legislature" On this ⁴ motion

N. H. no. Mas. no. C! no. N. J. no. P! no. Del. no. M⁴ ay.
V! ay. N. C. abs! S. C. no. Geo. ay.⁵

M! RANDOLPH animadverting on the indefinite and dangerous power given by the Constitution to Congress, expressing the pain he felt at differing from the body of the Convention, on the close of the great & awful subject of their labours, and anxiously wishing for some accomodating expedient which would relieve him from his embarrassments, made a motion importing "that amendments to the plan might be offered by the State Conventions, which should be submitted to and finally decided on by another general Convention" Should this proposition be disregarded, it would he said be impossible for him to put his name to the instrument. Whether he should oppose it afterwards he would not then decide

---

¹ In the transcript the vote reads: "Connecticut, New Jersey, Delaware, aye—3; New Hampshire, Massachusetts, Pennsylvania, Maryland, Virginia, North Carolina, South Carolina, Georgia, no—8."
² In the transcript the vote reads: "Connecticut, New Jersey, aye—2; New Hampshire, Massachusetts, Pennsylvania, Maryland, Virginia, North Carolina, South Carolina, Georgia, no—8; Delaware, divided."
³ The word "the" is here inserted in the transcript.
⁴ The word "which" is substituted in the transcript for "this."
⁵ In the transcript the vote reads: "Maryland, Virginia, Georgia, aye—3; New Hampshire, Massachusetts, Connecticut, New Jersey, Pennsylvania, Delaware, South Carolina, no—7; North Carolina, absent."

but he would not deprive himself of the freedom to do so in his own State, if that course should be prescribed by his final judgment.

Col: MASON 2^{ded} & followed Mr Randolph in animadversions on the dangerous power and structure of the Government, concluding that it would end either in monarchy, or a tyrannical aristocracy; which, he was in doubt, but one or other, he was sure. This Constitution had been formed without the knowledge or idea of the people. A second Convention will know more of the sense of the people, and be able to provide a system more consonant to it. It was improper to say to the people, take this or nothing. As the Constitution now stands, he could neither give it his support or[1] vote in Virginia; and he could not sign here what he could not support there. With the expedient of another Convention as proposed, he could sign.

Mr PINKNEY. These declarations from members so respectable at the close of this important scene, give a peculiar solemnity to the present moment. He descanted on the consequences of calling forth the deliberations & amendments of the different States on the subject of Government at large. Nothing but confusion & contrariety could[2] spring from the experiment. The States will never agree in their plans, and the Deputies to a second Convention coming together under the discordant impressions of their Constituents, will never agree. Conventions are serious things, and ought not to be repeated. He was not without objections as well as others to the plan. He objected to the contemptible weakness & dependence of the Executive. He objected to the power of a majority only of Cong^s over Commerce. But apprehending the danger of a general confusion, and an ultimate decision by the sword, he should give the plan his support.

Mr GERRY, stated the objections which determined him to withhold his name from the Constitution. 1. the duration and re-eligibility of the Senate. 2. the power of the House of Representatives to conceal their journals. 3. the power of Congress over the places of election. 4 the unlimited power of Congress over their own compensations. 5.[3] Massachusetts has not a due share of Representatives allotted to her. 6.[3] ⅗ of the Blacks are to be represented as if they were freemen. 7.[3] Under the power over commerce, monopolies may be established. 8. The vice president being made

---

[1] The word " or " is changed in the transcript to " nor."
[2] The word " will " is substituted in the transcript for " could."
[3] The word " that " is here inserted in the transcript.

head of the Senate. He could however he said get over all these, if the rights of the Citizens were not rendered insecure 1.[1] by the general power of the Legislature to make what laws they may please to call necessary and proper. 2.[2] raise armies and money without limit. 3.[3] to establish a tribunal without juries, which will be a Star-chamber as to Civil cases. Under such a view of the Constitution, the best that could be done he conceived was to provide for a second general Convention.

On the question on the proposition of M.ʳ Randolph. All the States answered—no

On the question to agree to the Constitution, as amended. All the States ay.

The Constitution was then ordered to be engrossed.

And the House adjourned.

MONDAY SEP.ᴿ 17. 1787:[4] IN CONVENTION

The engrossed Constitution being read,

Doc.ᵗ FRANKLIN rose with a speech in his hand, which he had reduced to writing for his own conveniency,[5] and which M.ʳ Wilson read in the words following.

M.ʳ President

I confess that there are several parts of this constitution which I do not at present approve, but I am not sure I shall never approve them: For having lived long, I have experienced many instances of being obliged by better information, or fuller consideration, to change opinions even on important subjects, which I once thought right, but found to be otherwise. It is therefore that the older I grow, the more apt I am to doubt my own judgment, and to pay more respect to the judgment of others. Most men indeed as well as most sects in Religion, think themselves in possession of all truth, and that wherever others differ from them it is so far error. Steele a Protestant in a Dedication tells the Pope, that the only difference between our Churches in their opinions of the certainty of their doctrines is, the Church of Rome is infallible and the Church of England is never in the wrong. But though many private persons

---

[1] The figure " 1 " is changed in the transcript to " first."
[2] The figure " 2 " is changed in the transcript to " secondly, to."
[3] The figure " 3 " is changed in the transcript to " thirdly."
[4] The year " 1787 " is omitted in the transcript.
[5] The word " conveniency " is changed in the transcript to " convenience."

think almost as highly of their own infallibility as of that of their sect, few express it so naturally as a certain french lady, who in a dispute with her sister, said '' I don't know how it happens, Sister but I meet with no body but myself, that's always in the right— *Il n'y a que moi qui a toujours raison.*''

In these sentiments, Sir, I agree to this Constitution with all its faults, if they are such; because I think a general Government necessary for us, and there is no form of Government but what may be a blessing to the people if well administered, and believe farther that this is likely to be well administered for a course of years, and can only end in Despotism, as other forms have done before it, when the people shall become so corrupted as to need despotic Government, being incapable of any other. I doubt too whether any other Convention we can obtain, may be able to make a better Constitution. For when you assemble a number of men to have the advantage of their joint wisdom, you inevitably assemble with those men, all their prejudices, their passions, their errors of opinion, their local interests, and their selfish views. From such an assembly can a perfect production be expected? It therefore astonishes me, Sir, to find this system approaching so near to perfection as it does; and I think it will astonish our enemies, who are waiting with confidence to hear that our councils are confounded like those of the Builders of Babel; and that our States are on the point of separation, only to meet hereafter for the purpose of cutting one another's throats. Thus I consent, Sir, to this Constitution because I expect no better, and because I am not sure, that it is not the best. The opinions I have had of its errors, I sacrifice to the public good. I have never whispered a syllable of them abroad. Within these walls they were born, and here they shall die. If every one of us in returning to our Constituents were to report the objections he has had to it, and endeavor to gain partizans in support of them, we might prevent its being generally received, and thereby lose all the salutary effects & great advantages resulting naturally in our favor among foreign Nations as well as among ourselves, from our real or apparent unanimity. Much of the strength & efficiency of any Government in procuring and securing happiness to the people, depends, on opinion, on the general opinion of the goodness of the Government, as well as well as of the wisdom and integrity of its Governors. I hope therefore that for our own sakes as a part of the people, and for the sake of posterity, we shall act heartily and unanimously in recommending this Constitution (if approved by Congress & confirmed by the Conventions) wherever our influence may extend, and turn our future thoughts & endeavors to the means of having it well administred.

On the whole, Sir, I can not help expressing a wish that every member of the Convention who may still have objections to it, would with me, on this occasion doubt a little of his own infallibility, and to make manifest our unanimity, put his name to this instrument.—

He then moved that the Constitution be signed by the members and offered the following as a convenient form viz. " Done in Convention by the unanimous consent of *the States* present the 17ᵗʰ of Sepᵗ &c—In Witness whereof we have hereunto subscribed our names."

This ambiguous form had been drawn up by Mᵣ G. M. in order to gain the dissenting members, and put into the hands of Docᵗ Franklin that it might have the better chance of success.

Mᵣ GORHAM said if it was not too late he could wish, for the purpose of lessening objections to the Constitution, that the clause declaring " the number of Representatives shall not exceed one for every forty thousand " which had produced so much discussion, might be yet reconsidered, in order to strike out 40,000 & insert " thirty thousand." This would not he remarked establish that as an absolute rule, but only give Congress a greater latitude which could not be thought unreasonable.

Mᵣ KING & Mᵣ CARROL seconded & supported the ideas of Mᵣ Gorham.

When the PRESIDENT rose, for the purpose of putting the question, he said that although his situation had hitherto restrained him from offering his sentiments on questions depending in the House, and it might be thought, ought now to impose silence on him, yet he could not forbear expressing his wish that the alteration proposed might take place. It was much to be desired that the objections to the plan recommended might be made as few as possible. The smallness of the proportion of Representatives had been considered by many members of the Convention an insufficient security for the rights & interests of the people. He acknowledged that it had always appeared to himself among the exceptionable parts of the plan, and late as the present moment was for admitting amendments, he thought this of so much consequence that it would give [1] much satisfaction to see it adopted *

* Transfer the remarks in brackets, to the bottom margin.²
* [This was the only occasion on which the President entered at all into the discussions of the Convention].

---

[1] The word " him " is here inserted in the transcript.
² Madison's direction is omitted in the transcript.

No opposition was made to the proposition of M: Gorham and it was agreed to unanimously.

On the question to agree to the Constitution enrolled in order to be signed. It was agreed to all the States [1] answering ay.

M: RANDOLPH then rose and with an allusion to the observations of Doc: Franklin apologized for his refusing to sign the Constitution notwithstanding the vast majority & venerable names that would give sanction to its wisdom and its worth. He said however that he did not mean by this refusal to decide that he should oppose the Constitution without doors. He meant only to keep himself free to be governed by his duty as it should be prescribed by his future judgment. He refused to sign, because he thought the object of the Convention would be frustrated by the alternative which it presented to the people. Nine States will fail to ratify the plan and confusion must ensue. With such a view of the subject he ought not, he could not, by pledging himself to support the plan, restrain himself from taking such steps as might appear to him most consistent with the public good.

M: Gov: MORRIS said that he too had objections, but considering the present plan as the best that was to be attained, he should take it with all its faults. The majority had determined in its favor and by that determination he should abide. The moment this plan goes forth all other considerations will be laid aside, and the great question will be, shall there be a national Government or not? and this must take place or a general anarchy will be the alternative. He remarked that the signing in the form proposed related only to the fact that the [2] States present were unanimous.

M: WILLIAMSON suggested that the signing should be confined to the letter accompanying the Constitution to Congress, which might perhaps do nearly as well, and would he found be [3] satisfactory to some members * who disliked the Constitution. For himself he did not think a better plan was to be expected and had no scruples against putting his name to it.

M: HAMILTON expressed his anxiety that every member should sign. A few characters of consequence, by opposing or even refusing to sign the Constitution, might do infinite mischief by kindling the latent sparks which [4] lurk under an enthusiasm in favor of the

* He alluded to M: Blount for one.

---

[1] The word " States " is italicized in the transcript.
[2] The transcript italicizes the word " the."
[3] The words " be found " are substituted in the transcript for " he found be."
[4] The word " which " is changed in the transcript to " that."

Convention which may soon subside. No man's ideas were more remote from the plan than his[1] were known to be; but is it possible to deliberate between anarchy and Convulsion on one side, and the chance of good to be expected from the plan on the other.

M: BLOUNT said he had declared that he would not sign, so as to pledge himself in support of the plan, but he was relieved by the form proposed and would without committing himself attest the fact that the plan was the unanimous act of the States in Convention.

Doc: FRANKLIN expressed his fears from what M: Randolph had said, that he thought himself alluded to in the remarks offered this morning to the House. He declared that when drawing up that paper he did not know that any particular member would refuse to sign his name to the instrument, and hoped to be so understood. He professed a high sense of obligation to M: Randolph for having brought forward the plan in the first instance, and for the assistance he had given in its progress, and hoped that he would yet lay aside his objections, and by concurring with his brethren, prevent the great mischief which the refusal of his name might produce.

M: RANDOLPH could not but regard the signing in the proposed form, as the same with signing the Constitution. The change of form therefore could make no difference with him. He repeated that in refusing to sign the Constitution, he took a step which might be the most awful of his life, but it was dictated by his conscience, and it was not possible for him to hesitate, much less, to change. He repeated also his persuasion, that the holding out this plan with a final alternative to the people, of accepting or rejecting it in toto, would really produce the anarchy & civil convulsions which were apprehended from the refusal of individuals to sign it.

M: GERRY described the painful feelings of his situation, and the embarrassment[2] under which he rose to offer any further observations on the subject w:ch had been finally decided. Whilst the plan was depending, he had treated it with all the freedom he thought it deserved. He now felt himself bound as he was disposed to treat it with the respect due to the Act of the Convention. He hoped he should not violate that respect in declaring on this occasion his fears that a Civil war may result from the present crisis of the U. S. In Massachussetts, particularly he saw the dan-

---

[1] The word " own " is here inserted in the transcript.
[2] The transcript uses the word " embarrassment " in the plural.

ger of this calamitous event—In that State there are two parties, one devoted to Democracy, the worst he thought of all political evils, the other as violent in the opposite extreme. From the collision of these in opposing and resisting the Constitution, confusion was greatly to be feared. He had thought it necessary, for this & other reasons that the plan should have been proposed in a more mediating shape, in order to abate the heat and opposition of parties. As it has been passed by the Convention, he was persuaded it would have a contrary effect. He could not therefore by signing the Constitution pledge himself to abide by it at all events. The proposed form made no difference with him. But if it were not otherwise apparent, the refusals to sign should never be known from him. Alluding to the remarks of Doc[r] Franklin, he could not he said but view them as levelled at himself and the other gentlemen who meant not to sign;

Gen![l] PINKNEY. We are not likely to gain many converts by the ambiguity of the proposed form of signing. He thought it best to be candid and let the form speak the substance. If the meaning of the signers be left in doubt, his purpose would not be answered. He should sign the Constitution with a view to support it with all his influence, and wished to pledge himself accordingly.

Doc[r] FRANKLIN. It is too soon to pledge ourselves before Congress and our Constituents shall have approved the plan.

M[r] INGERSOL did not consider the signing, either as a mere attestation of the fact, or as pledging the signers to support the Constitution at all events; but as a recommendation, of what, all things considered, was the most eligible.

On the motion of Doc[t] Franklin

N. H. ay. Mas. ay. C[t] ay. N. J. ay. P[a] ay. Del. ay. M[d] ay. V[a] ay. N. C. ay. S. C. div[d].[*] Geo. ay.[2]

M[r] KING suggested that the Journals of the Convention should be either destroyed, or deposited in the custody of the President. He thought if suffered to be made public, a bad use would be made of them by those who would wish to prevent the adoption of the Constitution.

---

* Gen![l] Pinkney & M[r] Butler disliked the equivocal form of the [1] signing, and on that account voted in the negative.
* To be transferred hither.[3]

---

[1] The word "the" is omitted in the transcript.
[2] In the transcript the vote reads: "New Hampshire, Massachusetts, Connecticut, New Jersey, Pennsylvania, Delaware, Maryland, Virginia, North Carolina, Georgia, aye—10; South Carolina,* divided."
[3] Madison's direction concerning his note is omitted in the transcript.

M.ʳ Wɪʟsoɴ prefered the second expedient, he had at one time liked the first best; but as false suggestions may be propagated it should not be made impossible to contradict them.

A question was then put on depositing the Journals and other papers of the Convention in the hands of the President, on which,

N. H. ay. M.ᵗᵗˢ ay. C.ᵗ ay. N. J. ay. Pen.ᵃ ay. Del. ay. M.ᵈ * no. V.ᵃ ay. N. C. ay. S. C. ay. Geo. ay.²

The President having asked what the Convention meant should be done with the Journals &c, whether copies were to be allowed to the members if applied for. It was Resolved nem: con: "that he retain the Journal and other papers, subject to the order of the ³ Congress, if ever formed under the Constitution.

The members then proceeded to sign the instrument.⁴

⁵ Whilst the last members were signing it ⁶ Doct.ʳ Fʀᴀɴᴋʟɪɴ looking towards the Presidents Chair, at the back of which a rising sun happened to be painted, observed to a few members near him, that Painters had found it difficult to distinguish in their art a rising from a setting sun. I have said he, often and often in the course of the Session, and the vicisitudes of my hopes and fears as to its issue, looked at that behind the President without being able to tell whether it was rising or setting: But now at length I have the happiness to know that it is a rising and not a setting Sun.

⁵ The Constitution being signed by all the members except M.ʳ Randolph, M.ʳ Mason, and M.ʳ Gerry who declined giving it the sanction of their names, the Convention dissolved itself by an Adjournment sine die—

⁷ The few alterations and corrections made in these debates which are not in my hand writing, were dictated by me and made in my presence by John C. Payne.   Jᴀᴍᴇs Mᴀᴅɪsoɴ.

* This negative of Maryland was occasioned by the language of the instructions to the Deputies of that State, which required them to report to the State, the *proceedings* of the Convention.
* Transfer.¹

---

¹ Madison's direction concerning his note is omitted in the transcript.
² In the transcript the vote reads: "New Hampshire, Massachusetts, Connecticut, New Jersey, Pennsylvania, Delaware, Virginia, North Carolina, South Carolina, Georgia, aye—10; Maryland,* no—1."
³ The word "the" is omitted in the transcript.
⁴ In place of the word "instrument," the transcript inserts the following words: "Constitution, as finally amended, as follows." The Constitution is then inserted.
⁵ These two final paragraphs of Madison's notes are transposed in the transcript to follow the signatures to the Constitution.
⁶ The word "it" is omitted in the transcript.
⁷ This statement and Madison's signature are omitted in the transcript.

APPENDIX I

No. 1. EXTRACT OF LETTER FROM GENERAL KNOX TO GENERAL
WASHINGTON, OCTOBER 23, 1786 [1]

. . . . Our political machine constituted of thirteen independent
sovereignties, have been constantly operating against each other,
and against the federal head, ever since the peace. The powers of
Congress are utterly inadequate to preserve the balance between the
respective States, and oblige them to do those things which are
essential to their own welfare, and for the general good. The human
mind in the local legislatures seems to be exerted, to prevent the
federal constitution from having any beneficial effects. The machine
works inversely to the public good in all its parts. Not only is State
against State, and all against the federal head, but the States within
themselves possess the name only, without having the essential con-
comitant of government, the power of preserving the peace; the
protection of the liberty and property of the citizens.

On the first impression of Faction and licentiousness the fine
theoretic government of Massachusetts has given way, and its laws
arrested and trampled under foot. Men at a distance, who have
admired our systems of government, unfounded in nature, are apt to
accuse the rulers, and say that taxes have been assessed too high and
collected too rigidly. This is a deception equal to any that has
hitherto been entertained. It is indeed a fact, that high taxes are the
ostensible cause of the commotions, but that they are the real cause
is as far remote from truth as light from darkness. The people who
are the insurgents have never paid any, or but every little taxes. But
they see the weakness of government; They feel at once their own
poverty, compared with the opulent, and their own force, and they are
determined to make use of the latter, in order to remedy the former.
Their creed is " That the property of the United States, has been
protected from the confiscation of Britain by the joint exertions of
all, and therefore ought to be the common property of all. And he
that attempts opposition to this creed is an enemy to equity and
justice, and ought to be swept from off the face of the earth." In a
word they are determined to annihilate all debts public and private
and have agrarian Laws, which are easily effected by the means of
unfunded paper money which shall be a tender in all cases whatever.

The numbers of these people may amount in Massachusetts to
about one fifth part of several populous counties, and to them may be
collected, people of similar sentiments, from the States of Rhode
Island, Connecticut and New Hampshire, so as to constitute a body
of 12 or 15000 desperate & unprincipled men. They are chiefly of
the young and active part of the community, more easily collected

---

[1] The text of the above letter is printed from the original among the
Washington manuscripts in the Library of Congress.

than perhaps kept together afterwards— But they will probably commit overt acts of treason which will compell them to embody for their own safety—once embodied they will be constrained to submit to discipline for the same reason. Having proceeded to this length for which they are now ripe, we shall have a formidable rebellion against reason, the principle of all government, and the very name of liberty. This dreadful situation has alarmed every man of principle and property in New England. They start as from a dream, and ask what has been the cause of our delusion? what is to afford us security against the violence of lawless men? Our government must be braced, changed, or altered to secure our lives and property. We imagined that the mildness of our government and *the virtue* of the people were so correspondent, that we were not as other nations requiring brutal force to support the laws— But we find that we are men, actual men, possessing all the turbulent passions belonging to that animal and that we must have a government proper and adequate for him. The people of Massachusetts for instance, are far advanced in this doctrine, and the men of reflection, & principle, are determined to endeavor to establish a government which shall have the power to protect them in their lawful pursuits, and which will be efficient in all cases of internal commotions or foreign invasions. They mean that liberty shall be the basis, a liberty resulting from the equal and firm administration of the laws. They wish for a general government of unity as they see the local legislatures, must naturally and necessarily tend to retard and frustrate all general government.

We have arrived at that point of time in which we are forced to see our national humiliation, and that a progression in this line, cannot be productive of happiness either public or private. Something is wanting and something must be done or we shall be involved in all the horror of faction and civil war without a prospect of its termination. Every tried friend to the liberties of his country is bound to reflect, and to step forward to prevent the dreadful consequences which will result from a government of events. Unless this is done we shall be liable to be ruled by an arbitrary and capricious armed tyranny, whose word and will must be law. . . .

No. 2. EXTRACT OF LETTER FROM JOHN JAY TO GENERAL WASHINGTON, JUNE 27, 1786 [1]

. . . . Our affairs seem to lead to some crisis—some Revolution— something that I cannot foresee, or conjecture. I am uneasy and apprehensive—more so, than during the War. *Then* we had a fixed object, and tho the means and time of attaining it were often problematical, yet I did firmly believe that we should ultimately succeed, because I was convinced that Justice was with us. The case is now

---

[1] The text of the above letter is printed from the original among the Washington manuscripts in the Library of Congress. See also *Correspondence of the American Revolution,* Sparks, Editor, Vol. IV (1853), pp. 135, 136; *The Correspondence and Public Papers of John Jay,* Johnston, Editor, Vol. III (1891), pp. 203-205.

altered—we are going and doing wrong, and therefore I look forward to Evils and calamities, but without being able to grasp at the Instrument Nature or measure of them. That we shall again recover, and things again go well, I have no Doubt—such a variety of circumstances would not almost miraculously have combined to liberate and make us a nation for transient & unimportant Purposes. I therefore believe we are yet to become a great and respectable People—but when or how, the Spirit of Prophecy only can discern.

There doubtless is much Reason to think and to say that we are woefully and in many Instances wickedly misled. private Rage for Property suppresses public considerations, & personal rather than national Interests have become the great objects of attention. Representative Bodies will ever be faithful copies of their originals, and generally exhibit a chequered assemblage of virtue and vice, of abilities and weakness. The Mass of Men are neither wise nor good—and the virtue like the other Resources of a country can only be drawn to a point by strong circumstances ably managed, or strong government ably administred. New Governments have not the aid of Habit and hereditary Respect; & being generally the Result of preceding Tumult and confusion, do not immediately acquire Stability or Strength. Besides, in times of commotion some men will gain confidence & Importance who merit neither; and who like political mountebanks are less sollicitous about the Health of the credulous Crowd, than about making the most of their Nostrums & Prescriptions.

New York was rendered less fœderal, by the opinions of the late President of Congress. This is a singular tho' not unaccountable Fact—indeed human actions are seldom inexplicable. What I most fear is, that the better kind of People (by which I mean the People who are orderly and industrious, who are content with their situations, and not uneasy in their Circumstances,) will be led by the Insecurity of Property, the Loss of Confidence in their Rulers, & the Want of public Faith & Rectitude, to consider the charms of Liberty as imaginary and delusive. A State of uncertainty and Fluctuation must disgust and alarm such men, and prepare their minds for almost any change that may promise them Quiet & Security. . . .

No. 3. Extract of Letter from General Washington to John Jay, August 1, 1786 [1]

. . . . Your sentiments, that our affairs are drawing rapidly to a crisis, accord with my own. What the event will be is also beyond the reach of my foresight. We have errors to correct; we have probably had too good an opinion of human nature in forming our confederation. Experience has taught us, that men will not adopt & carry into execution, measures the best calculated for their own good, without the intervention of a coercive power. I do not conceive

---

[1] The text of the above letter is printed from Washington's letter book, Washington manuscripts in the Library of Congress. See also *The Writings of George Washington*, Ford, Editor, Vol. XI (1891), pp. 53-56; the *Correspondence and Public Papers of John Jay*, Johnston, Editor, Vol. III (1891), pp. 207-209.

we can exist long as a nation without having lodged somewhere a power which will pervade the whole union in as energetic a manner, as the authority of the State Governments extends over the several States. To be fearful of investing Congress, constituted as that body is, with ample authorities for national purposes, appears to me the very climax of popular absurdity & madness. Could Congress exert them for the detriment of the public, without injuring themselves in an equal or greater proportion? Are not their interests inseparably connected with those of their constituents? By the rotation of appointment must they not mingle frequently with the mass of Citizens? Is it not rather to be apprehended, if they were possessed of the powers before described, that the individual members would be induced to use them, on many occasions, very timidly & inefficaciously for fear of losing their popularity and future election? We must take human nature as we find it: perfection falls not to the share of mortals. Many are of opinion that Congress have too frequently made use of the suppliant humble tone of requisition, in applications to the States, when they had a right to assert their imperial dignity and command obedience. Be that as it may, requisitions are a perfect nihility, where thirteen sovereign, independent, disunited States are in the habit of discussing & refusing compliance with them at their option. Requisitions are actually little better than a jest & a bye word throughout the land. If you tell the Legislatures they have violated the Treaty of Peace, & invaded the prerogatives of the confederacy they will laugh in your face. What then is to be done? Things cannot go on in the same train forever. It is much to be feared, as you observe, that the better kind of people being disgusted with the circumstances, will have their minds prepared for any revolution whatever. We are apt to run from one extreme into another. To anticipate & prevent disastrous contingencies, would be the part of wisdom & patriotism.

What astonishing changes a few years are capable of producing. I am told that even respectable characters speak of a monarchical form of Government without horror. From thinking proceeds speaking, thence to acting is often but a single step. But how irrevocable & tremendous! what a triumph for our enemies to verify their predictions—what a triumph for the advocates of despotism to find that we are incapable of governing ourselves, & that systems founded on the basis of equal liberty are merely ideal & fallacious! Would to God that wise measures may be taken in time to avert the consequences we have but too much reason to apprehend.

Retired as I am from the world I frankly acknowledge I cannot feel myself an unconcerned spectator. Yet having happily assisted in bringing the Ship into Port & having been fairly discharged; it is not my business to embark again on a sea of troubles. Nor could it be expected that my sentiments and opinions would have much weight on the minds of my Countrymen;—they have been neglected, tho' given as a last legacy in the most solemn manner:—I had then perhaps some claims to public attention—I consider myself as having none at present . . . .

APPENDIX II

No. 1. Extract of Letter from James Madison to Thomas Jefferson [1]

NEW YORK, March 19ᵗʰ, 1787.

DEAR SIR

My last was of the 11ᵗʰ of Febʸ, and went by the packet. This will go to England in the care of a French gentleman, who will consign it to the care of Mʳ Adams.

The appointments for the Convention go on auspiciously. Since my last, Georgia, S. Carolina, N. York, Massᵗˢ and N. Hampshire, have come into the measure. The first and the last of these States have commissioned their delegates to Congress as their representatives in Convention. The deputation of Massᵗˢ consists of Messʳˢ Gorham, Dana, King, Gerry, and Strong. That of N. York, Messʳˢ Hamilton Yates & Lansing. That of S. Carolina, Messʳˢ J. Rutlidge, Laurens, Pinkney, (General) Butler, and Chaˢ Pinkney, lately member of Congress. The States which have not yet appointed are R. Island, Connecticut, and Maryland. The last has taken measures which prove her intention to appoint, and the two former it is not doubted will follow the example of their neighbours. I just learn from the Governor of Virginia that Mʳ Henry has resigned his place in the deputation from that state, and that Genˡ Nelson is put into it by the Executive, who were authorised to fill vacancies. The Governor, Mʳ Wythe, & Mʳ Blair will attend, and some hopes are entertained of Col. Mason's attendance. Genˡ Washington has prudently authorised no expectations of his attendance, but has not either precluded himself absolutely from stepping into the field if the crisis should demand it.

What may be the result of this political experiment cannot be foreseen. The difficulties which present themselves are on one side almost sufficient to dismay the most sanguine, whilst on the other side the most timid are compelled to encounter them by the mortal diseases of the existing Constitution. These diseases need not be pointed out to you, who so well understand them. Suffice it to say, that they are at present marked by symptoms which are truly alarming, which have tainted the faith of the most orthodox republicans, and which challenge from the votaries of liberty every concession in favor of stable Government not infringing fundamental principles, as the only security against an opposite extreme of our present situation.

I think myself that it will be expedient in the first place to lay the foundation of the new system in such a ratification by the people themselves of the several States as will render it clearly paramount to their Legislative authorities. 2ᵈˡʸ Over & above the positive power

---

[1] The text of the above letter is printed from the original among the Madison manuscripts in the Library of Congress. See also, *The Writings of James Madison*, Hunt, Editor, Vol. II (1901), pp. 324-328.

of regulating trade and sundry other matters in which uniformity is proper, to arm the federal head with a negative *in all cases whatsoever* on the local Legislatures. Without this defensive power experience and reflection have satisfied me that however ample the federal powers may be made, or however clearly their boundaries may be delineated, on paper, they will be easily and continually baffled by the Legislative Sovereignties of the States. The effects of this provision would be not only to guard the national rights and interests against invasion, but also to restrain the States from thwarting and molesting each other, and even from oppressing the minority within themselves by paper money and other unrighteous measures which favor the interest of the majority. In order to render the exercise of such a negative prerogative convenient, an emanation of it must be vested in some set of men within the several States, so far as to enable them to give a temporary sanction to laws of immediate necessity. 3dly To change the principle of Representation in the federal system. Whilst the execution of the acts of Cong? depends on the several Legislatures, the equality of votes does not destroy the inequality of importance and influence in the States. But in case of such an augmentation of the federal power as will render it efficient without the intervention of the Legislatures, a vote in the general Councils from Delaware would be of equal value with one from Mass^{ts} or Virginia. This change, therefore, is just. I think, also, it will be practicable. A majority of the States conceive that they will be gainers by it. It is recommended to the Eastern States by the actual superiority of their populousness, and to the Southern by their expected superiority. And if a majority of the larger States concur, the fewer and smaller States must finally bend to them. This point being gained, many of the objections now urged in the leading States agst renunciations of power will vanish. 4^{thly} To organize the federal powers in such a manner as not to blend together those which ought to be exercised by separate departments. The limited powers now vested in Cong? are frequently mismanaged from the want of such a distribution of them. What would be the case, under an enlargement not only of the powers, but the number, of the federal Representatives?—These are some of the leading ideas which have occurred to me, but which may appear to others as improper as they appear to me necessary. . . .

No. 2. EXTRACT OF LETTER FROM JAMES MADISON TO
EDMUND RANDOLPH [1]

April 8, 1787.

. . . . I am glad to find that you are turning your thoughts towards the business of May next. My despair of your finding the necessary leisure as signified in one of your letters, with the probability that some leading propositions at least would be expected from Virg? had engaged me in a closer attention to the subject than I

---

[1] The text of the above letter is printed from the original among the Madison manuscripts in the Library of Congress. See also, *The Writings of James Madison*, Hunt, Editor, Vol II (1901), pp. 336-340.

should otherwise have given. I will just hint the ideas which have occurred, leaving explanations for our interview.

I think with you that it will be well to retain as much as possible of the old Confederation, tho' I doubt whether it may not be best to work the valuable articles into the new System, instead of engrafting the latter on the former. I am also perfectly of your opinion that in framing a system, no material sacrifices ought to be made to local or temporary prejudices. An explanatory address must of necessity accompany the result of the Convention on the main object. I am not sure that it will be practicable tô present the several parts of the reform in so detached a manner to the States as that a partial adoption will be binding. Particular States may view the different articles as conditions of each other, and would only ratify them as such, others might ratify them as independent propositions. The consequence would be that the ratifications of both would go for nothing. I have not however examined this point thoroughly. In truth my ideas of a reform strike so deeply at the old Confederation and lead to such a systematic change, that they scarcely admit of the expedient.

I hold it for a fundamental point that an individual independence of the States is utterly irreconcilable with the idea of an aggregate sovereignty. I think at the same time that a consolidation of the States into one simple republic is not less unattainable than it would be inexpedient. Let it be tried then whether any middle ground can be taken which will at once support a due supremacy of the national authority, and leave in force the local authorities so far as they can be subordinately useful.

The first step to be taken is I think a change in the principle of representation. According to the present form of the Union, an equality of suffrage if not just towards the larger members of it, is at least safe to them, as the liberty they exercise of rejecting or executing the Acts of Congress, is uncontroulable by the nominal sovereignty of Congress. Under a system which would operate without the intervention of the States, the case would be materially altered. A vote from Delaware would have the same effect as one from Mass^{ts} or Virg?

Let the national Government be armed with a positive & compleat authority in all cases where uniform measures are necessary. As in trade &c. &c.—Let it also retain the powers which it now possesses.

Let it have a negative in all cases whatsoever on the Legislative Acts of the States as the K. of G. B. heretofore had. This I conceive to be essential and the least possible abridgement of the State Sovereignties. Without such a defensive power, every positive power that can be given on paper will be unavailing. It will also give internal stability to the States. There has been no moment since the peace at which the federal assent wd have been given to paper money &c. &c.

Let this national supremacy be extended also to the Judiciary departm? If the judges in the last resort depend on the States & are bound by their oaths to them and not to the Union, the intention of the law and the interests of the nation may be defeated by the obsequiousness of the Tribunals to the policy or prejudices of the States. It seems at least essential that an appeal should lie to some national tribunals in all cases „which concern foreigners, or inhabitants of other States. The admiralty jurisdiction may be fully submitted to the national Government.

A Government formed of such extensive powers ought to be well organized. The Legislative department may be divided into two branches; one of them to be chosen every   years by the Legislatures or the people at large, the other to consist of a more select number, holding their appointments for a longer term and going out in rotation. Perhaps the negative on the State laws may be most conveniently lodged in this branch. A Council of Revision may be superadded, including the great ministerial officers.

A National Executive will also be necessary. I have scarcely ventured to form my own opinion yet either of the manner in which it ought to be constituted or of the authorities with which it ought [to be] cloathed.

An article ought to be inserted expressly guarantying the tranquility of the States agst internal as well as external dangers:

To give the new system its proper energy it will be desirable to have it ratified by the authority of the people, and not merely by that of the Legislatures.

I am afraid you will think this project, if not extravagant, absolutely unattainable and unworthy of being attempted. Conceiving it my self to go no farther than is essential, The objections drawn from this source are to be laid aside. I flatter my self however that they may be less formidable on trial than in contemplation. The change in the principle of representation will be relished by a majority of the States, and those too of most influence. The Northern States will be reconciled to it by the *actual* superiority of their populousness: the Southern by their *expected* superiority in this point. This principle established, the repugnance of the large States to part with power will in a great degree subside, and the smaller States must ultimately yield to the predominant will. It is also already seen by many & must by degrees be seen by all that unless the Union be organised efficiently on Republican principles, innovations of a much more objectionable form may be obtruded, or in the most favorable event, the partition of the Empire into rival & hostile confederacies will ensue. . . .

No. 3. LETTER FROM JAMES MADISON TO GEORGE WASHINGTON [1]

DEAR SIR   NEW YORK April 16 1787.
    I have been honoured with your letter of the 31 of March, and find with much pleasure that your views of the reform which ought to be pursued by the Convention, give a sanction to those which I have entertained. Temporising applications will dishonor the Councils which propose them, and may foment the internal malignity of the

---

    [1] The text of the above letter is printed from the original among the Washington manuscripts in the Library of Congress. See also, *The Writings of James Madison*, Hunt, Editor, Vol. II (1901), pp. 344–349.

disease, at the same time that they produce an ostensible palliation of it. Radical attempts, although unsuccessful, will at least justify the authors of them.

Having been lately led to revolve the subject which is to undergo the discussion of the Convention, and formed in my mind *some* outlines of a new system, I take the liberty of submitting them without apology, to your eye.

Conceiving that an individual independence of the States is utterly irreconcileable with their aggregate sovereignty; and that a consolidation of the whole into one simple republic would be as inexpedient as it is unattainable, I have sought for some middle ground, which may at once support a due supremacy of the national authority, and not exclude the local authorities wherever they can be subordinately useful.

I would propose as the ground-work that a change be made in the principle of representation. According to the present form of the Union in which the intervention of the States is in all great cases necessary to effectuate the measures of Congress, an equality of suffrage, does not destroy the inequality of importance, in the several members. No one will deny that Virginia and Mass^{ts} have more weight and influence both within & without Congress than Delaware or Rho. Island. Under a system which would operate in many essential points without the intervention of the State Legislatures, the case would be materially altered. A vote in the national Councils from Delaware, would then have the same effect and value as one from the largest State in the Union. I am ready to believe that such a change will not be attended with much difficulty. A majority of the States, and those of greatest influence, will regard it as favorable to them. To the Northern States it will be recommended by their present populousness; to the Southern by their expected advantage in this respect. The lesser States must in every event yield to the predominant will. But the consideration which particularly urges a change in the representation is that it will obviate the principal objections of the larger States to the necessary concessions of power.

I would propose next that in addition to the present federal powers, the national Government should be armed with positive and compleat authority in all cases which require uniformity; such as the regulation of trade, including the right of taxing both exports & imports, the fixing the terms and forms of naturalization, &c &c.

Over and above this positive power, a negative *in all cases whatsoever* on the legislative acts of the States, as heretofore exercised by the Kingly prerogative, appears to me to be absolutely necessary, and to be the least possible encroachment on the State jurisdictions. Without this defensive power, every positive power that can be given on paper will be evaded & defeated. The States will continue to invade the National jurisdiction, to violate treaties and the law of nations & to harass each other with rival and spiteful measures dictated by mistaken views of interest. Another happy effect of this prerogative would be its controul on the internal vicisitudes of State policy, and the aggressions of interested majorities on the rights of minorities and of individuals. The great desideratum which has not yet been found for Republican Governments seems to be some disinterested & dispassionate umpire in disputes between different passions & interests in the State. The majority who alone have the right of decision, have frequently an interest real or supposed in abusing it. In Monarchies the sovereign is more neutral to the interests and views of different parties; but, unfortunately he too often forms interests of his own repugnant to those of the whole. Might not the national prerogative here suggested be found sufficiently disinterested for the decision of local questions of policy, whilst it would itself be sufficiently restrained from the pursuit of interests adverse to those of the whole Society? There has not been any moment since the peace at which the representatives of the Union would have given an assent to paper money or any other measure of a kindred nature.

The national supremacy ought also to be extended as I conceive to the Judiciary departments. If those who are to expound & apply the laws, are connected by their interests & their oaths with the particular States wholly, and not with the Union, the participation of the Union in the making of the laws may be possibly rendered unavailing. It seems at least necessary that the oaths of the Judges should include a fidelity to the general as well as local constitution, and that an appeal should lie to some National tribunals in all cases to which foreigners or inhabitants of other States may be parties. The admiralty jurisdiction seems to fall entirely within the purview of the national Government.

The national supremacy in the Executive departments is liable to some difficulty, unless the officers administering them could be made appointable by the supreme Government. The Militia ought certainly to be placed in some form or other under the authority which is entrusted with the general protection and defence.

A Government composed of such extensive power should be well organised and balanced. The legislative department might be divided into two branches; one of them chosen every   years by the people at large, or by the Legislatures; the other to consist of fewer members, to hold their places for a longer term, and to go out in such a rotation as always to leave in office a large majority of old members. Perhaps the negative on the laws might be most conveniently exercised by this branch. As a further check, a council of revision including the great ministerial officers might be superadded.

A National Executive must also be provided. I have scarcely ventured as yet to form my own opinion either of the manner in which it ought to be constituted or of the authorities with which it ought to be cloathed.

An article should be inserted expressly guarantying the tranquility of the States against internal as well as external dangers.

In like manner the right of coercion should be expressly declared. With the resources of Commerce in hand, the National administration might always find means of exerting it either by sea or land. But the difficulty & awkwardness of operating by force on the collective will of a State, render it particularly desireable that the necessity of it might be precluded. Perhaps the negative on the laws might create such a mutuality of dependence between the General and particular authorities, as to answer this purpose or perhaps some defined objects of taxation might be submitted along with commerce, to the general authority.

To give a new System its proper validity and energy, a ratification must be obtained from the people, and not merely from the ordinary authority of the Legislatures. This will be the more essential as inroads on the *existing Constitutions* of the States will be unavoidable. . . .

APPENDIX III

LETTER FROM MERCHANTS, TRADESMEN, ETC., OF PROVIDENCE, RHODE ISLAND, TO THE CHAIRMAN OF THE GENERAL CONVENTION [1]

GENTLEMEN   PROVIDENCE, May 11th 1787.

Since the Legislature of this State have finally declined sending Delegates to Meet you in Convention for the purposes mentioned in the Resolve of Congress of the 21st February 1787, the Merchants, Tradesmen and others of this place, deeply affected with the evils of the present unhappy times, have thought proper to communicate in writing thier approbation of your Meeting, And their regret that it will fall short of a Compleat Representation of the Federal Union.—

The failure of this State was owing to the Nonconcurrence of the Upper House of Assembly with a Vote passed in the Lower House, for appointing Delegates to attend the said Convention, at thier Session holden at Newport on the first Wednesday of the present Month.—

It is the general Opinion here and we believe of the well informed throughout this State, that full power for the Regulation of the Commerce of the United States, both Foreign & Domestick ought to be vested in the National Council.

And that Effectual Arrangements should also be made for giving Operation to the present powers of Congress in thier Requisitions upon the States for National purposes.—

As the Object of this Letter is chiefly to prevent any impressions unfavorable to the Commercial Interest of this State, from taking place in our Sister States from the Circumstance of our being unrepresented in the present National Convention, we shall not presume to enter into any detail of the objects we hope your deliberations will embrace and provide for being convinced they will be such as have a tendency to strengthen the Union, promote Commerce, increase the power & Establish the Credit of the United States.

---

[1] The text of the above letter is printed from the original among the manuscripts of the Constitution in the Department of State. See also *Documentary History of the Constitution*, Vol. I (1894), pp. 275-276.

The result of your deliberations tending to these desireable purposes we still hope may finally be Approved and Adopted by this State, for which we pledge our Influence and best exertions.—

In behalf of the Merchants, Tradesmen &c

We have the Honour to be with perfect Consideration & Respect
Your most Obedient &
Most Humble Servant's

JOHN BROWN	JABEZ BOWEN	
THO! LLOYD HALSEY	NICHO! BROWN	
JOS. NIGHTINGALE	JOHN JENCKES	Comtee.
LEVI HALL	WELCOME ARNOLD	
PHILIP ALLEN	WILLIAM RUSSELL	
PAUL ALLEN	JEREMIAH OLMY,	
	WILLIAM BARTON	

The Honble the Chairman of the General Convention
PHILADELPHIA

APPENDIX IV

THE PINCKNEY PLAN PRESENTED TO THE CONVENTION AT ITS SESSION OF MAY 29, 1787

No. 1. OUTLINE OF THE PLAN [1]

1. A Confederation between the free and independent States of N. H. etc. is hereby solemnly made uniting them together under one general superintending Government for their common Benefit and for their Defense and Security against all Designs and Leagues that may be injurious to their Interests and against all forc[e] [or foes?] and Attacks offered to or made upon them or any of them.

2. The Stile.

---

[1] Reprinted from Professor McLaughlin's *Sketch of Pinckney's Plan for a Constitution, 1787, The American Historical Review*, IX, 1904, 735, 741-747.

Professor J. Franklin Jameson had previously identified among the manuscript papers of James Wilson, deposited in the Pennsylvania Historical Society, certain extracts in Wilson's hand as taken from Pinckney's original draft. See J. Franklin Jameson, *Studies in the History of the Federal Convention of 1787*, Annual Report of the American Historical Association, 1902, I, pp. 128, 132; and for an analysis of Pinckney's views, pp. 111, 128, other than those derived from the extracts.

Professor Jameson thus states his views in the light of his studies and his remarkable discovery:

" Concluding that to a considerable extent, and with more or less confidence, we can reconstruct the actual plan which Pinckney laid before the Convention on May 29, we may now turn, finally, to the question, If the document which Pinckney sent to John Quincy Adams was not his original draft, what was it? The question is really not a very difficult one. The similarity of the supposed draft to the final Constitution has constantly been noticed. Its resemblance to the report of the Committee of Detail is still closer. . . . Practically, in other words, the so-called Pinckney plan consists of the report of the Committee of Detail, as brought in on August 6, minus some of its lesser features, and plus some of those of his real plan. It is not possible to say that Pinckney answered Adams' request by sitting down and copying the printed report of the Com-

3. Mutual intercourse—Community of Privileges—Surrender of Criminals—Faith to Proceedings etc.

4. Two Branches of the Legislature—Senate—House of Delegates —together the U. S. in Congress assembled.

H. D. to consist of one Member for every thousand Inhabitants ¾ of Blacks included.

Senate to be elected from four Districts—to serve by Rotation of four Years—to be elected by the H. D. either from among themselves or the People at large.

5. The Senate and H. D. shall by joint Ballot annually [septennially] chuse the Presid⁺ U. S. from among themselves or the People at large.—In the Presd⁺ the executive authority of the U. S. shall be vested.—His Powers and Duties—He shall have a Right to advise with the Heads of the different Departments as his Council.

6. Council of Revision, consisting of the Presid⁺. S.[ecretary] for for.[eign] Affairs, S. of War, Heads of the Departments of Treasury and Admiralty or any two of them tog⁻ w⁺ the Presid⁺.

7. The members of S. and H. D. shall each have one Vote, and shall be paid out of the common Treasury.

8. The Time of the Election of the Members of the H. D. and of the Meeting of U. S. in C. assembled.

9. No State to make Treaties—lay interfering Duties—keep a naval or land Force Militia excepted to be disciplined etc. according to the Regulations of the U. S.

10. Each State retains its Rights not expressly delegated—but no Bill of the Legislature of any State shall become a law till it shall have been laid before S. and H. D. in C. assembled and received their Approbation.

11. The exclusive Power of S. and H. D. in C. Assembled.

12. The S. and H. D. in C. ass. shall have exclusive Power of regulating trade and levying Imposts—Each State may lay Embargoes in Times of Scarcity.

---

mittee of Detail, paraphrasing to a small extent here and there, and interweaving as he went along some of the best-remembered features of his own plan. But it is possible to declare that if he had done this the result would have been precisely like that which in fact he sent on to Washington. . . . It is perhaps sufficient to remark, in conclusion, that as a maker of the Constitution Charles Pinckney evidently deserves to stand higher than he has stood of late years, and that he would have a better chance of doing so if in his old age he had not claimed so much."

Professor A. C. McLaughlin found among the same papers one likewise in Wilson's hand which he identified as Wilson's summary of the original Pinckney Plan made on its reading in the Session of May 29, 1787, or made by him as a member of the Committee of Detail when the original plan was before that committee.

Professor McLaughlin's conclusions are, "By help of the condensation of the plan which Professor Jameson discovered and from the light thrown on the problem by the document printed below, we can say that Pinckney suggested some thirty-one or thirty-two provisions which were finally embodied in the Constitution; of these, about twelve were originally in the Articles of Confederation, . . ."

For an elaborate defense of Pinckney and the enclosure in his letter of 1818, see *The Mystery of the Pinckney Draught* (1908), by Charles C. Nott, formerly Chief Justice of the United States Court of Claims.

13. —— of establishing Post-Offices.

14. S. and H. D. in C. ass. shall be the last Resort on Appeal in Disputes between two or more States; which Authority shall be exercised in the following Manner etc.

15. S. and H. D. in C. ass. shall institute offices and appoint officers for the Departments of for. Affairs, War, Treasury and Admiralty.

They shall have the exclusive Power of declaring what shall be Treason and Misp. of Treason ag^t U. S.—and of instituting a federal judicial Court, to which an Appeal shall be allowed from the judicial Courts of the several States in all Causes wherein Questions shall arise on the Construction of Treaties made by U. S.—or on the Laws of Nations—or on the Regulations of U. S. concerning Trade and Revenue—or wherein U. S. shall be a Party—The Court shall consist of Judges to be appointed during good Behaviour—S. and H. D. in C. ass. shall have the exclusive Right of instituting in each State a Court of Admiralty, and appointing the Judges etc of the same for all maritime Causes which may arise therein respectively.

16. S. and H. D. in C. Ass shall have the exclusive Right of coining Money—regulating its Alloy and Value—fixing the Standard of Weights and Measures throughout U. S.

17. Points in which the Assent of more than a bare Majority shall be necessary.

18. Impeachments shall be by the H. D. before the Senate and the Judges of the federeal judicial Court

19. S. and H. D. in C. ass. shall regulate the Militia thro' the U. S.

20. Means of enforcing and compelling the Payment of the Quota of each State.

21. Manner and Conditions of admitting new States.

22. Power of dividing annexing and consolidating States, on the Consent and Petition of such States.

23. The assent of the Legislature of   States shall be sufficient to invest future additional Powers in U. S. in C. ass. and shall bind the whole Confederacy.

24. The Articles of Confederation shall be inviolably observed, and the Union shall be perpetual: unless altered as before directed.

25. The said States of N. H. etc guarrantee mutually each other and their Rights against all other Powers and against all Rebellion etc.

No. 2. LETTERS FROM CHARLES PINCKNEY TO JOHN QUINCY ADAMS, SECRETARY OF STATE, RELATING TO THE ALLEGED PINCKNEY PLAN

WINGAW NEAR GEORGETOWN December 12 1818

Sir

I have just had the honour to receive your favour—Being at present absent from Charleston on a visit to my planting interest in this neighbourhood I shall in consequence of your letter shorten my stay here considerably & return to Town for the purpose of complying with your request as soon as possible—From an inspection of my old papers not long ago I know it was then easily in my power to have complied with your request—I still hope it is & as soon as I return to my residence in Charleston will again, or as quickly as I can write you on it to prevent delay.

The Draught of the Constitution proposed by me was divided into a number of articles & was in complete detail—the resolutions offered by Mʳ Randolph were merely general ones & as far as I recollect they were both referred to the same Committee.

With great respect & esteem &c.[1]

Sir [2]

On my return to this City as I promised I examined carefully all the numerous notes & papers which I had retained relating to the federal Convention—among them I found several rough draughts of the Constitution I proposed to the Convention—although they differed in some measure from each other in the wording & arrangement of the articles—yet they were all substantially the same—they all proceeded upon the idea of throwing out of view the attempt to amend the existing Confederation (then a very favorite idea of a number) & proceeding de novo—of a Division of the Powers of Government into legislative executive & judicial & of making the Government to operate directly upon the People & not upon the States– – My Plan was substantially adopted in the sequel except as to the Senate & giving more power to the Executive than I intended—the force of vote which the small & middling states had in the Convention prevented our obtaining a proportional representation in more than one branch & the great powers given to the President were never intended to have been given to him while the Convention continued in that patient & coolly deliberative situation in which they had been for nearly the whole of the preceding five months of their session nor was it until within the last week or ten days that almost the whole of the Executive Department was altered—I can assure you as a fact that for more than Four months & a half out of five the power of exclusively making treaties, appointing for the Ministers & judges of the Supreme Court was given to the Senate after numerous debates & consideration of the subject both in Committee of the whole & in the house—this I not only aver but can prove by printed Documents in my possession to have been the case—& should I ever have the pleasure to see you & converse on the subject will state to you some things relative to this business that may be new & perhaps surprising to you—the veil of secrecy from the Proceedings of the Convention being removed by Congress & but very few of the members alive would make disclosures now of the secrets there acted less improper than before—With the aid of the journal & the numerous notes & memorandums I have preserved should now be in my power to give a View of the almost insuperable

---

[1] The text is reprinted from *The Writings of James Madison*, Hunt, Editor, Vol. III (1902), p. 22.

[2] The text is printed from the original among the manuscripts of the Constitution in the Department of State. See also *Documentary History of the Constitution*, Vol. I (1894), pp. 309-311.

difficulties the Convention had to encounter & of the conflicting opinions of the members & I believe should have attempted it had I not always understood Mr Madison intended it—he alone I believe possessed & retained more numerous & particular notes of their proceedings than myself. I will thank you sir to do me the honour to send me or to get the President to direct a copy of the Journal of the Convention to be sent me as also of the Secret Journals of Congress should it be considered not improper in me to make the request.

I have already informed you I have several rough draughts of the Constitution I proposed & that they are all substantially the same differing only in words & the arrangement of the Articles—at the distance of nearly thirty two years it is impossible for me now to say which of the 4 or 5 draughts I have was the one but enclosed I send you the one I believe was it—I repeat however that they are substantially the same differing only in form & unessentials—It may be necessary to remark that very soon after the Convention met I changed & avowed candidly the change of my opinion on giving the power to Congress to revise the State Laws in certain cases & in giving the exclusive Power to the Senate to declare War thinking it safer to refuse the first altogether & to vest the latter in Congress—I will thank you to acknowledge by a line the receipt of the Draught & this.

With very great respect & esteem

I have the honour to be your most

Obedient servant

CHARLES PINCKNEY.

December 30 1818

In Charleston.

No. 3. TEXT OF THE ALLEGED PLAN SUBMITTED BY PINCKNEY TO JOHN QUINCY ADAMS [1]

We the People of the States of New Hampshire Massachusetts Rhode Island & Providence Plantations—Connecticut New York New Jersey Pennsylvania Delaware Maryland Virginia North Carolina South Carolina & Georgia do ordain, declare & establish the following Constitution for the government of ourselves & Posterity.

ARTICLE 1:

The Stile of this Government shall be The United States of America & the Government shall consist of supreme legislative Executive & judicial Powers.

---

[1] Printed from the original among the manuscripts of the Constitution in the Department of State. See also *Documentary History of the Constitution*, Vol. I (1894), pp. 312-321.

The plan is written upon the same paper as the letter transmitting it and with the same ink and the paper in each case bears the watermark of 1797. Therefore the draft transmitted to Secretary Adams cannot have been written on this paper before 1797—some ten years after the Convention. The letter and the draft appear to have been written in 1818 the year of Adams' request to Pinckney to furnish a copy of the Pinckney Plan.

2

The Legislative Power shall be vested in a Congress to consist of two separate Houses—one to be called the House of Delegates & the other the Senate who shall meet on the   Day of   in every year.

3

The members of the House of Delegates shall be chosen every year by the people of the several States & the qualification of the electors shall be the same as those of the Electors in the several States for their legislatures—each member shall have been a citizen of the United States for   years—shall be of   years of age & a resident in the State he is chosen for   Until a census of the people shall be taken in the manner herein after mentioned the House of Delegates shall consist of   to be chosen from the different States in the following proportions— for New Hampshire,   ; for Massachusetts   for Rhode Island,   for Connecticut,   for New York   for New Jersey,   for Pennsylvania,   for Delaware,   for Maryl.ᵈ   for Virginia,   for North Carolina,   for South Carolina,   for Georgia,   & the Legislature shall hereafter regulate the number of delegates by the number of inhabitiants according to the Provisions herein after made, at the rate of one for every   thousand.— All money bills of every kind shall originate in the house of Delegates & shall not be altered by the Senate. The House of Delegates shall exclusively possess the power of impeachment & shall choose it's officers & vacancies therein shall be supplied by the executive authority of the State in the representation from which they shall happen.

4

The Senate shall be elected & chosen by the House of Delegates which house immediately after their meeting shall choose by ballot   Senators from among the Citizens & residents of New Hampshire   from among those of Massachusetts   from among those of Rhode Island   from among those of Connecticut   from among those of New York   from among those of New Jersey   from among those of Pennsylvania   from among those of Delaware   from among those of Maryland   from among those of Virginia   from among those of North Carolina   from among those of South Carolina &   from among those of Georgia— The Senators chosen from New Hampshire Massachusetts Rhode Island & Connecticut shall form one class—those from New York New Jersey Pennsylvania & Delaware one class—& those from Maryland Virginia North Carolina South Carolina & Georgia one class.

The House of Delegates shall number these Classes one two & three & fix the times of their service by Lot—the first class shall serve for   years—the second for   years & the third for   years—as their times of service expire the House of Delegates shall fill them up by elections for   years & they shall fill all vacancies that arise from death or resignation for the time of service remaining of the members so dying or resigning.

Each Senator shall be   years of age at least—shall have been a Citizen of the United States 4 years before his election & shall be a resident of the State he is chosen from. The Senate shall choose it's own Officers.

5

Each State shall prescribe the time & manner of holding elections by the People for the house of Delegates & the House of Delegates shall be the judges of the elections returns & Qualifications of their members.

In each house a Majority shall constitute a Quorum to do business —Freedom of Speech & Debate in the legislature shall not be impeached or Questioned in any place out of it & the Members of both Houses shall in all cases except for Treason Felony or Breach of the Peace be free from arrest during their attendance at Congress & in going to & returning from it—Both Houses shall keep journals of their Proceedings & publish them except on secret occasions & the yeas & nays may be entered thereon at the desire of one   of the members present. Neither house without the consent of the other shall adjourn for more than   days nor to any Place but where they are sitting

The members of each house shall not be eligible to or capable of holding any office under the Union during the time for which they have been respectively elected nor the members of the Senate for one year after—

The members of each house shall be paid for their services by the States which they represent—

Every bill which shall have passed the Legislature shall be presented to the President of the United States for his revision—if he approves it he shall sign it—but if he does not approve it he shall return it with his objections to the house it originated in, which house if two thirds of the members present, notwithstanding the President's objections agree to pass it, shall send it to the other house with the President's objections, where if two thirds of the members present also agree to pass it, the same shall become a law—& all bills sent to the President & not returned by him within   days shall be laws unless the Legislature by their adjournment prevent their return in which case they shall not be laws.

6th

The Legislature of the United States shall have the power to lay & collect Taxes Duties Imposts & excises

To regulate Commerce with all nations & among the several States—

To borrow money & emit bills of Credit

To establish Post offices.

To raise armies

To build & equip Fleets

To pass laws for arming organizing & disciplining the Militia of the United States

To subdue a rebellion in any State on application of its legislature

To coin money & regulate the Value of all coins & fix the Standard of Weights & measures

To provide such Dock Yards & arsenals & erect such fortifications as may be necessary for the United States & to exercise exclusive Jurisdiction therein

To appoint a Treasurer by ballot

To constitute Tribunals inferior to the Supreme Court

To establish Post & military Roads

To establish & provide for a national University at the Seat of the Government of the United States

To establish uniform rules of Naturalization

To provide for the establishment of a Seat of Government for the United States not exceeding   miles square in which they shall have exclusive jurisdiction

To make rules concerning Captures from an Enemy

To declare the law & Punishment of piracies & felonies at sea & of counterfieting Coin & of all offences against the Laws of Nations

To call forth the aid of the Militia to execute the laws of the Union enforce treaties suppress insurrections & repel invasions.

And to make all laws for carrying the foregoing powers into execution—

The Legislature of the United States shall have the Power to declare the Punishment of Treason which shall consist only in levying War against the United States or any of them or in adhering to their Enemies.—No person shall be convicted of Treason but by the testimony of two witnesses.—

The proportion of direct taxation shall be regulated by the whole number of inhabitants of every description which number shall within   years after the first meeting of the Legislature & within the term of every   year after be taken in the manner to be prescribed by the Legislature

No Tax shall be laid on articles exported from the States—nor capitation tax but in proportion to the Census before directed.

All Laws regulating Commerce shall require the assent of two thirds of the members present in each house—The United States shall not grant any title of Nobility—

The Legislature of the United States shall pass no Law on the subject of Religion, nor touching or abridging the Liberty of the Press nor shall the privilege of the writ of Habeas Corpus ever be suspended except in case of Rebellion or Invasion.

All acts made by the Legislature of the United States pursuant to this Constitution & all Treaties made under the authority of the United States shall be the Supreme Law of the Land & all Judges shall be bound to consider them as such in their decisions.

7

The Senate shall have the sole & exclusive power to declare War & to make treaties & to appoint Ambassadors & other Ministers to foreign nations & Judges of the Supreme Court.

They shall have the exclusive power to regulate the manner of deciding all disputes & controversies now subsisting or which may arise between the States respecting Jurisdiction or Territory.

8

The Executive Power of the United States shall be vested in a President of the United States of America which shall be his stile & his title shall be His Excellency. He shall be elected for years & shall be reeligible.

He shall from time to time give information to the Legislature of the state of the Union & recommend to their consideration the measures he may think necessary—he shall take care that the laws of the United States be duly executed: he shall commission all the officers of the United States & except as to Ambassadors other ministers & Judges of the Supreme Court he shall nominate & with the consent of the Senate appoint all other officers of the United States—He shall receive public Ministers from foreign nations & may correspond with the Executives of the different States. He shall have power to grant pardons & reprieves except in impeachments—He shall be Commander in chief of the army & navy of the United States & of the Militia of the several States & shall receive a compensation which shall not be increased or diminished during his continuance in office. At entering on the Duties of his office he shall take an oath to faithfully execute the duties of a President of the United States.—He shall be removed from his office on impeachment by the house of Delegates & Conviction in the Supreme Court of Treason bribery or Corruption —In case of his removal death resignation or disability the President of the Senate shall exercise the duties of his office until another President be chosen—& in case of the death of the President of the Senate the Speaker of the House of Delegates shall do so.

9

The Legislature of the United States shall have the Power & it shall be their duty to establish such Courts of Law Equity & Admiralty as shall be necessary—The Judges of the Courts shall hold their offices during good behaviour & receive a compensation, which shall not be increased or diminished during their continuance in office—One of these Courts shall be termed the Supreme Court whose jurisdiction shall extend to all cases arising under the laws of the United States or affecting ambassadors other public Ministers & Consuls—to the trial of impeachments of officers of the United States—to all cases of Admiralty & maritime jurisdiction—In cases of impeachment affecting ambassadors & other public Ministers this Jurisdiction shall be original & in all the other cases appellate—

All criminal offences (except in cases of impeachment) shall be tried in the State where they shall be committed—the trials shall be open & public & be by Jury.

10

Immediately after the first census of the people of the United States the House of Delegates shall apportion the Senate by electing for each State out of the citizens resident therein one Senator for every   members such State shall have in the House of Delegates—Each State however shall be entitled to have at least one member in the Senate.

11

No State shall grant letters of marque & reprisal or enter into treaty or alliance of confederation nor grant any title of nobility nor without the Consent of the Legislature of the United States lay any impost on imports—nor keep troops or Ships of War in time of peace —nor enter into compacts with other States or foreign powers or emit bills of Credit or make any thing but Gold Silver or Copper a tender in payment of debts nor engage in War except for self defence when actually invaded or the danger of invasion is so great as not to admit of a delay until the Government of the United States can be informed thereof—& to render these prohibitions effectual the Legislature of the United States shall have the power to revise the laws of the several States that may be supposed to infringe the Powers exclusively delegated by this Constitution to Congress & to negative & annul such as do.

12

The Citizens of each State shall be entitled to all privileges & immunities of Citizens in the several States—Any person charged with Crimes in any State fleeing from justice to another shall on demand of the Executive of the State from which he fled be delivered up & removed to the State having jurisdiction of the offence.

13

Full faith shall be given in each State to the acts of the Legislature & to the records & judicial Proceedings of the Courts & magistrates of every State.

14

The Legislature shall have power to admit new States into the Union on the same terms with the original States provided two thirds of the members present in both Houses agree.

15

On the application of the legislature of a State the United States shall protect it against domestic insurrection.

16

If two thirds of the Legislatures of the States apply for the same the Legislature of the United States shall call a Convention for the Purpose of amending the Constitution—or should Congress, with the Consent of two thirds of each house, propose to the States amendments to the same—the agreement of two thirds of the Legislatures of the States shall be sufficient to make the said amendments parts of the Constitution.

The Ratification of the conventions of   States shall be sufficient for organizing this Constitution.

No. 4. MADISON'S NOTE ON THE PINCKNEY PLAN APPARENTLY WRITTEN TO ACCOMPANY HIS DEBATES [1]

The length of the Document laid before the Convention, and other circumstances having prevented the taking of a copy at the time, that which is inserted in the debates was taken from the paper furnished to the Secretary of State, and contained in the Journal of the Convention published in 1819 which it being taken for granted was a true copy was not then examined. The coincidence in several instances between that and the Constitution as adopted, having attracted the notice of others was at length suggested to mine. On comparing the paper with the Constitution in its final form, or in some of its Stages; and with the propositions, and speeches of M.r Pinckney in the Convention, it was apparent that considerable errour

---

[1] The above document was evidently intended by Madison as a note to his debates of the Session of May 29, 1787. It is here printed from the original manuscript. See also *Documentary History of the Constitution*, Vol. V (1905), pp. 417-419.

For an Editorial Note prepared for the above paper, and so entitled by Madison, see *Documentary History of the Constitution of the United States*, Vol. V (1905), pp. 419-432; see also the analysis of the Pinckney plan made by Madison in 1835, in *The Writings of James Madison*, Hunt, Editor, Vol. IX, pp. 558-567 n.

For further expressions of views concerning the authenticity of the Pinckney draft, see letter of James Madison to Jared Sparks, June 27, 1831, in *Life and Writings of Jared Sparks*, Herbert B. Adams, Editor, Vol. II, 1893, pp. 227-229, *The Records of the Federal Convention*, Max Farrand, Editor, Vol. III (1911), pp. 502-503; to Jared Sparks, November 25, 1831, in *The Writings of James Madison*, Hunt, Editor, Vol. IX, 1910, pp. 464-468, *The Records of the Federal Convention*, Vol. III, pp. 514-515; to Thomas S. Grimke, January 6, 1834, in *Writings of James Madison*, Vol. IX, pp. 528-532, *The Records of the Federal Convention*, Vol. III, pp. 531-532; to W. A. Duer, June 5, 1835, in *The Writings of James Madison*, Vol. IX, pp. 553-558, *The Records of the Federal Convention*, Vol. III, pp. 534-537.

had crept into the paper; occasioned possibly by the loss of the Document laid before the convention (neither that nor the Resolutions offered by M! Patterson being among the preserved papers) and by a consequent resort for a copy to the rough draught, in which erasures and interlineations following what passed in the Convention, might be confounded in part at least with the original text, and after a lapse of more than thirty years, confounded also in the memory of the author.

There is in the paper a similarity in some cases, and an identity in others, with details, expressions, and definitions, the results of critical discussions and modifications in the Convention that could not have been anticipated.

Examples may be noticed in Article VIII of the paper; which is remarkable also for the circumstance, that whilst it specifies the functions of the President, no provision is contained in the paper for the election of such an officer, nor indeed for the appointment of any Executive Magistracy; notwithstanding the evident purpose of the author to provide an *entire* plan of a Federal Government.

Again, in several instances where the paper corresponds with the Constitution, it is at variance with the ideas of M! Pinckney, as decidedly expressed in his propositions, and in his arguments, the former in the Journal of the Convention, the latter in the report of its debates: Thus in Art: VIII of the paper, provision is made for removing the President by impeachment; when it appears that in the convention, July 20, he was opposed to any impeachability of the Executive Magistrate: In Art: III, it is required that all money-bills shall originate in the first Branch of the Legislature; which he strenuously opposed Aug: 8 and again Aug: 11: In Art: V members of each House are made ineligible to, as well as incapable of holding, any office under the Union &c. as was the case at one Stage of the Constitution; a disqualification highly disapproved and opposed by him Aug: 14.

A still more conclusive evidence of errour in the paper is seen in Art: III, which provides, as the Constitution does, that the first Branch of the Legislature shall be chosen by the people of the several States; whilst it appears that on the 6!ᵗʰ of June, according to previous notice, too, a few days only, after the Draft was laid before the Convention, its author opposed that mode of choice, urging & proposing in place of it, an election by the Legislatures of the several States.

The remarks here made tho' not material in themselves, were due to the authenticity and accuracy aimed at, in this Record of the proceedings of a Publick Body, so much an object, sometimes, of curious research, as at all times, of profound interest.

APPENDIX V

Hamilton's Draft of a Constitution for the United States

Copy of a paper communicated to J. M. by Col. Hamilton, about the close of the convention in Philad^a, 1787, which he said delineated the constitution which he would have wished to be proposed by the Convention. He had stated the principles of it in the course of the deliberations: See [1]

The people of the United States of America do ordain & establish this Constitution for the government of themselves and their posterity.

Article I

§ 1. The Legislative power shall be vested in two distinct bodies of men, one to be called the Assembly, the other the Senate, subject to the negative hereinafter mentioned.

§ 2. The Executive power, with the qualifications hereinafter specified, shall be vested in a President of the United States.

§ 3. The Supreme Judicial authority, except in the cases otherwise provided for in this Constitution, shall be vested in a Court to be called the Supreme Court, to consist of not less than six nor more than twelve Judges.

Article II

§ 1. The Assembly shall consist of persons to be called representatives, who shall be chosen, except in the first instance, by the free male citizens & inhabitants of the several States comprehended in the Union, all of whom of the age of twenty one years & upwards shall be entitled to an equal vote.

§ 2. But the first Assembly shall be chosen in the manner prescribed in the last article and shall consist of one hundred members of whom N. Hamshire shall have five, Massachussets thirteen, Rhode Island two, Connecticut seven, N. York nine, N. Jersey six, Pennsylvania twelve, Delaware two, Maryland eight, Virginia sixteen, N. Carolina eight, S. Carolina eight, Georgia four.

§ 3. The Legislature shall provide for the future elections of Representatives, apportioning them in each State, from time to time, as nearly as may be to the number of persons described in the 4§ of the VII article, so as that the whole number of Representatives shall never be less than one hundred, nor more than   hundred. There shall be a Census taken for this purpose within three years after the first meeting of the Legislature, and within every successive period of ten years. The term for which Representatives shall be elected shall be determined by the Legislature but shall not exceed three years. There shall be a general election at least once in three

---

[1] The text of the draft is printed from Madison's copy accompanying his notes of the debates. See also *Documentary History of the Constitution*, Vol. III (1900), pp. 771-788.

years; and the time of service of all the members in each Assembly shall begin, (except in filling vacancies) on the same day, and shall always end on the same day.

§ 4. Forty members shall make a House sufficient to proceed to business; but their number may be increased by the Legislature, yet so as never to exceed a majority of the whole number of Representatives.

§ 5. The Assembly shall choose its President and other officers, shall judge of the qualifications & elections of its own members, punish them for improper conduct in their capacity of Representatives not extending to life or limb; and shall exclusively possess the power of impeachment except in the case of the President of the United States; but no impeachment of a member of the Senate shall be by less than two thirds of the Representatives present.

§ 6. Representatives may vote by proxy; but no Representative present shall be proxy for more than one who is absent.*

§ 7. Bills for raising revenue, and bills for appropriating monies for the support of fleets and armies, and for paying the salaries of the officers of Government, shall originate in the Assembly; but may be altered and amended by the Senate.

§ 8. The acceptance of an office under the United States by a Representative shall vacate his seat in the Assembly.

ARTICLE III

§ 1. The Senate shall consist of persons to be chosen, except in the first instance, by Electors elected for that purpose by the Citizens and inhabitants of the several States comprehended in the Union who shall have in their own right, or in the right of their wifes, an Estate in land for not less than life, or a term of years, whereof at the time of giving their votes there shall be at least fourteen years unexpired.

§ 2. But the first Senate shall be chosen in the manner prescribed in the last Article and shall consist of forty members to be called Senators, of whom N. Hampshire shall have   Mass.ts
R. Island   Connecticut   N. York   N. Jersey
     Pen.a   Delaware   Maryl.d   Virg.a
N. Carol.a   S. Carol.   Geo.

§ 3. The Legislature shall provide for the future elections of Senators, for which purpose the States respectively, which have more than one Senator, shall be divided into convenient districts to which the Senators shall be apportioned. A State having but one Senator shall be itself a district. On the death, resignation or removal from office of a Senator his place shall be supplied by a new election in the district from which he came. Upon each election there shall be not less than six nor more than twelve electors chosen in a district.

§ 4. The number of Senators shall never be less than forty, nor shall any State, if the same shall not hereafter be divided, ever have less than the number allotted to it in the second section of this

---

* Quere, ? (to provide for distant States).

article; but the Legislature may increase the whole number of Senators, in the same proportion to the whole number of Representatives as forty is to one hundred; and such increase beyond the present number, shall be apportioned to the respective States in a ratio to the respective numbers of their representatives.

§ 5.   If States shall be divided, or if a new arrangement of the boundaries of two or more States shall take place, the Legislature shall apportion the number of Senators (in elections succeeding such division or new arrangement) to which the constituent parts were entitled according to the change of situation, having regard to the number of persons described in the 4. §. of the VII article.

§ 6.   The Senators shall hold their places during good behaviour, removeable only by conviction on impeachment for some crime or misdemeanor.   They shall continue to exercise their offices when impeached untill a conviction shall take place.   Sixteen Senators attending in person shall be sufficient to make a House to transact business; but the Legislature may increase this number, yet so as never to exceed a majority of the whole number of Senators.   The Senators may vote by proxy, but no Senator who is present shall be proxy for more than two who are absent.

§ 7.   The Senate shall choose its President and other officers; shall judge of the qualifications and elections of its members, and shall punish them for improper conduct in their capacity of Senators; but such punishment shall not extend to life or limb, nor to expulsion. In the absence of their President they may choose a temporary President.   The President shall only have a casting vote when the House is equally divided.

§ 8.   The Senate shall exclusively possess the power of declaring war.   No Treaty shall be made without their advice and consent; which shall also be necessary to the appointment of all officers, except such for which a different provision is made in this Constitution.

ARTICLE IV

§ 1.   The President of the United States of America, (except in the first instance) shall be elected in manner following—The Judges of the Supreme Court shall within sixty days after a vacancy shall happen, cause public notice to be given in each State, of such vacancy, appointing therein three several days for the several purposes following, to wit, a day for commencing the election of electors for the purposes hereinafter specified, to be called the first electors, which day shall not be less than forty, nor more than sixty days, after the day of the publication of the notice in each State—another day for the meeting of the electors not less forty nor more than ninety days from the day for commencing their election—another day for the meeting of electors to be chosen by the first electors, for the purpose hereinafter specified, and to be called the second Electors, which day shall be not less than forty nor more than sixty days after the day for the meeting of the first electors.

§ 2.   After notice of a vacancy shall have been given there shall be chosen in each State a number of persons, as the first electors in the preceding section mentioned, equal to the whole number of the Representatives and Senators of such States in the Legislature of the United States; which electors shall be chosen by the Citizens of such State having an estate of inheritance or for three lives in land, or a clear personal estate of the value of one thousand Spanish milled dollars of the present Standard.

§ 3. These first electors shall meet in their respective States at the time appointed, at one place; and shall proceed to vote by ballot for a President, who shall not be one of their own number, unless the Legislature upon experiment should hereafter direct otherwise. They shall cause two lists to be made of the name or names of the person or persons voted for, which they or the major part of them shall sign & certify. They shall then proceed each to nominate openly in the presence of the others, two persons as for second electors, and out of the persons who shall have the four highest numbers of nominations, they shall afterwards by ballot by plurality of votes choose two who shall be the second electors, to each of whom shall be delivered one of the lists before mentioned. These second electors shall not be any of the persons voted for as President. A copy of the same list signed and certified in like manner shall be transmitted by the first electors to the Seat of the Government of the United States, under a sealed cover directed to the President of the Assembly, which after the meeting of the Second electors shall be opened for the inspection of the two House of the Legislature.

§ 4. The second electors shall meet precisely on the day appointed and not on another day, at one place. The Chief Justice of the Supreme Court, or if there be no Chief Justice, the Judge senior in office in such Court, or if there be no one Judge senior in office, some other Judge of that Court, by the choice of the rest of the Judges or of a majority of them, shall attend at the same place and shall preside at the meeting, but shall have no vote. Two thirds of the whole number of the Electors shall constitute a sufficient meeting for the execution of their trust. At this meeting the lists delivered to the respective electors shall be produced and inspected, and if there be any person who has a majority of the whole number of votes given by the first electors, he shall be the President of the United States; but if there be no such person, the second electors so met shall proceed to vote, by ballot, for one of the persons named in the lists who shall have the three highest numbers of the votes of the first electors; and if upon the first or any succeeding ballot on the day of their meeting, either of those persons shall have a number of votes equal to a majority of the whole number of second electors chosen, he shall be the President. But if no such choice be made on the day appointed for the meeting either by reason of the non-attendance of the second electors, or their not agreeing, or any other matter, the person having the greatest number of votes of the first electors shall be the President.

§ 5. If it should happen that the Chief Justice or some other Judge of the Supreme Court should not attend in due time, the second electors shall proceed to the execution of their trust without him.

§ 6. If the Judges should neglect to cause the notice required by the first section of this article to be given within the time therein limited, they may nevertheless cause it to be afterwards given; but their neglect if wilful, is hereby declared to be an offence for which they may be impeached, and if convicted they shall be punished as in other cases of conviction on impeachment.

§ 7. The Legislature shall by permanent laws provide such further regulations as may be necessary for the more orderly election of the President; not contravening the provisions herein contained.

§ 8. The President before he shall enter upon the execution of his office shall take an oath or affirmation, faithfully to execute the same, and to the utmost of his Judgment & power to protect the rights of the people, and preserve the Constitution inviolate. This oath or affirmation shall be administered by the President of the Senate for the time being in the presence of both Houses of the Legislature.

§ 9. The Senate and the Assembly shall always convene in Session on the day appointed for the meeting of the second electors and shall continue sitting till the President take the oath or affirmation of office. He shall hold his place during good behavior, removeable only by conviction upon an impeachment for some crime or misdemeanor.

§ 10. The President at the beginning of every meeting of the Legislature as soon as they shall be ready to proceed to business, shall convene them together at the place where the Senate shall sit, and shall communicate to them all such matters as may be necessary for their information, or as may require their consideration. He may by message during the Session communicate all other matters which may appear to him proper. He may, whenever in his opinion the public business shall require it, convene the Senate and Assembly, or either of them, and may prorogue them for a time not exceeding forty days at one prorogation; and if they should disagree about their adjournment, he may adjourn them to such time as he shall think proper. He shall have a right to negative all bills, Resolutions or acts of the two Houses of the Legislature about to be passed into laws. He shall take care that the laws be faithfully executed. He shall be the commander in chief of the army and Navy of the United States and of the Militia within the several States, and shall have the direction of war when commenced, but he shall not take the actual command in the field of an army without the consent of the Senate and Assembly. All treaties, conventions and agreements with foreign nations shall be made by him, by and with the advice and consent of the Senate. He shall have the appointment of the principal or Chief officer of each of the departments of war, naval Affairs, Finance and Foreign Affairs; and shall have the nomination; and by and with the consent of the Senate, the appointment of all other officers to be appointed under the authority of the United States, except such for whom different provision is made by this Constitution; and provided that this shall not be construed to prevent the

Legislature, from appointing by name, in their laws, persons to special & particular trusts created in such laws; nor shall be construed to prevent principals in offices merely ministerial, from constituting deputies.—In the recess of the Senate he may fill vacancies in offices by appointments to continue in force until the end of the next Session of the Senate, and he shall commission all officers. He shall have power to pardon all offences except treason, for which he may grant reprieves, untill the opinion of the Senate & Assembly can be had; and with their concurrence may pardon the same.

§ 11. He shall receive a fixed compensation for his services to be paid to him at stated times, and not to be increased nor diminished during his continuance in office.

§ 12. If he depart out of the United States without the Consent of the Senate and Assembly, he shall thereby abdicate his office.

§ 13. He may be impeached for any crime or misdemesnor by the two Houses of the Legislature, two thirds of each House concurring, and if convicted shall be removed from office. He may be afterwards tried & punished in the ordinary course of law. His impeachment shall operate as a suspension from office until the determination thereof.

§ 14. The President of the Senate shall be vice President of the United States. On the death, resignation, impeachment, removal from office, or absence from the United States, of the President thereof, the Vice President shall exercise all the powers by this Constitution vested in the President, until another shall be appointed, or untill he shall return within the United States, if his absence was with the consent of the Senate and Assembly.

ARTICLE V

§ 1. There shall be a chief Justice of the Supreme Court, who together with the other Judges thereof, shall hold their offices during good behaviour, removeable only by conviction on impeachment for some crime or misdemeanor. Each Judge shall have a competent salary to be paid to him at stated times, and not to be diminished during his continuance in office.

The Supreme Court shall have original jurisdiction in all causes in which the United States shall be a party, in all controversies between the United States, and a particular State, or between two or more States; except such as relate to a claim of territory between the United States, and one or more States, which shall be determined in the mode prescribed in the VI article; in all cases affecting foreign Ministers, Consuls and Agents; and an appellate jurisdiction both as to law and fact in all cases which shall concern the Citizens of foreign nations, in all questions between the Citizens of different States, and in all others in which the fundamental rights of this Constitution are involved, subject to such exceptions as are herein contained and to such regulations as the Legislature shall provide.

The Judges of all Courts which may be constituted by the Legislature shall also hold their places during good behaviour, removeable only by conviction on impeachment for some crime or misdemeanor, and shall have competent salaries to be paid at stated times and not to be diminished during their continuance in office; but nothing herein contained shall be construed to prevent the Legislature from abolishing such Courts themselves.

All crimes, except upon impeachment, shall be tried by a Jury of twelve men; and if they shall have been committed within any State, shall be tried within such State; and all civil causes arising under this constitution of the like kind with those which have been heretofore triable by Jury in the respective States, shall in like manner be tried by jury; unless in special cases the Legislature shall think proper to make different provision, to which provision the concurrence of two thirds of both Houses shall be necessary.

§ Impeachments of the President and and Vice President of the U. States, members of the Senate, the Governours and Presidents of the several States, the Principal or Chief Officers of the Departments enumerated in the 10 §. of the 4th Article, Ambassadors and other like Public Ministers, the Judges of the Supreme Court, Generals, and Admirals of the Navy shall be tried by a Court to consist of the Judges of the Supreme Court, and the Chief Justice or first or senior Judge of the superior Court of law in each State, of whom twelve shall constitute a Court. A majority of the Judges present may convict. All other persons shall be tried on impeachment by a court to consist of the Judges of the Supreme Court and six Senators drawn by lot, a majority of whom may convict.

Impeachments shall clearly specify the particular offence for which the party accused is to be tried, and judgment on conviction upon the trial thereof shall be either removal from office singly, or removal from office and disqualification for holding any future office or place of trust; but no Judgment on impeachment shall prevent prosecution and punishment in the ordinary course of law; provided that no Judge concerned in such conviction shall sit as Judge on the second trial. The Legislature may remove the disabilities incurred by conviction on impeachment.

ARTICLE VI

Controversies about the right of territory between the United States and particular States shall be determined by a Court to be constituted in manner following. The State or States claiming in opposition to the United States as parties shall nominate a number of persons, equal to double the number of the Judges of the Supreme Court for the time being, of whom none shall be citizens by birth of the States which are parties, nor inhabitants thereof when nominated, and of whom not more than two shall have their actual residence in one State. Out of the persons so nominated the Senate shall elect one half, who together with the Judges of the Supreme Court, shall form the Court. Two thirds of the whole number may hear and determine the controversy, by plurality of voices. The States concerned may at their option claim a decision by the Supreme

Court only. All of the members of the Court hereby instituted, shall, prior to the hearing of the Cause take an oath impartially and according to the best of their judgments and consciences, to hear and determine the controversy.

ARTICLE VII

§ 1. The Legislature of the United States shall have power to pass all laws which they shall judge necessary to the common defence and general welfare of the Union: But no Bill, Resolution, or act of the Senate and Assembly shall have the force of a law until it shall have received the assent of the President, or of the vice-President when exercising the powers of the President; and if such assent shall not have been given within ten days, after such bill, resolution or other act shall have been presented to him for that purpose, the same shall not be a law. No bill, resolution or other act not assented to shall be revived in the same Session of the Legislature. The mode of signifying such assent shall be by signing the bill act of resolution, and returning it so signed to either House of the Legislature.

§ 2. The enacting stile of all laws shall be "Be it enacted by the people of the United States of America."

§ 3. No bill of attainder shall be passed, nor any ex post facto law; nor shall any title of nobility be granted by the United States, or by either of them; nor shall any person holding an office or place of trust under the United States without the permission of the Legislature accept any present, emolument office or title from a foreign prince or State. Nor shall any Religious Sect, or denomination, or religious test for any office or place, be ever established by law.

§ 4. Taxes on lands, houses and other real estate, and capitation taxes shall be proportioned in each State by the whole number of free persons, except Indians not taxed, and by three fifths of all other persons.

§ 5 The two Houses of the Legislature may by joint ballot appoint a Treasurer of the United States. Neither House in the Session of both Houses, without the consent of the other shall adjourn for more than three days at a time. The Senators and Representatives in attending, going to and coming from the Session of the respective houses shall be privileged from arrest. except for crimes and breaches of the peace. The place of meeting shall always be at the seat of Government which shall be fixed by law.

§ 6. The laws of the United States, and the treaties which have been made under the articles of the confederation, and which shall be made under this Constitution shall be the supreme law of the Land, and shall be so construed by the Courts of the several States.

§ 7. The Legislature shall convene at least once in each year, which unless otherwise provided for by law, shall be the first monday in December.

§ 8. The members of the two Houses of the Legislature shall receive a reasonable compensation for their services, to be paid out of the Treasury of the United States and ascertained by law. The law for making such provision shall be passed with the concurrence of the first Assembly and shall extend to succeeding Assemblies; and no succeeding assembly shall concur in an alteration of such provision, so as to increase its own compensation; but there shall be always a law in existence for making such provision.

ARTICLE VIII

§ 1.   The Governour or President of each State shall be appointed under the authority of the United States, and shall have a right to negative all laws about to be passed in the State of which he shall be Governour or President, subject to such qualifications and regulations, as the Legislature of the United States shall prescribe.   He shall in other respects have the same powers only which the Constitution of the State does or shall allow to its Governour or President, except as to the appointment of Officers of the Militia.

§ 2.   Each Governour or President of a State shall hold his office until a successor be actually appointed, unless he die, or resign or be removed from office by conviction on impeachment.   There shall be no appointment of such Governor or President in the Recess of the Senate.

The Governours and Presidents of the several States at the time of the ratification of this Constitution shall continue in office in the same manner and with the same powers as if they had been appointed pursuant to the first section of this article.

The officers of the Militia in the several States may be appointed under the authority of the U. States; the Legislature whereof may authorize the Governors or Presidents of States to make such appointments with such restrictions as they shall think proper.

ARTICLE IX

§ 1.   No person shall be eligible to the office of President of the United States unless he be now a Citizen of one of the States, or hereafter be born a Citizen of the United States.

§ 2.   No person shall be eligible as a Senator or Representative unless at the time of his election he be a Citizen and inhabitant of the State in which he is chosen; provided that he shall not be deemed to be disqualified by a temporary absence from the State.

§ 3.   No person entitled by this Constitution to elect or to be elected President of the United States, or a Senator or Representative in the Legislature thereof, shall be disqualified but by the conviction of some offence for which the law shall have previously ordained the punishment of disqualification.   But the Legislature may by law provide that persons holding offices under the United States or either of them shall not be eligible to a place in the Assembly or Senate, and shall be during their continuance in office suspended from sitting in the Senate.

§ 4. No person having an office or place of trust under the United States shall without permission of the Legislature accept any present emolument office or title from any foreign Prince or State.

§ 5. The Citizens of each State shall be entitled to the rights privileges and immunities of Citizens in every other State; and full faith and credit shall be given in each State to the public acts, records and judicial proceedings of another.

§ 6. Fugitives from justice from one State who shall be found in another shall be delivered up on the application of the State from which they fled.

§ 7. No new State shall be erected within the limits of another, or by the junction of two or more States, without the concurrent consent of the Legislatures of the United States and of the States concerned. The Legislature of the United States may admit new States into the Union.

§ 8. The United States are hereby declared to be bound to guarantee to each State a Republican form of Government, and to protect each State as well against domestic violence as foreign invasion.

§ 9. All Treaties, Contracts and engagements of the United States of America under the articles of Confederation and perpetual Union, shall have equal validity under this Constitution.

§ 10. No State shall enter into a Treaty, Alliance, or contract with another, or with a foreign power without the consent of the United States.

§ 11. The members of the Legislature of the United States and of each State, and all officers Executive & Judicial of the one and of the other shall take an oath or affirmation to support the Constitution of the United States.

§ 12. This Constitution may receive such alterations and amendments as may be proposed by the Legislature of the United States, with the concurrence of two thirds of the members of both Houses, and ratified by the Legislatures of, or by Conventions of deputies chosen by the people in, two thirds of the States composing the Union.

ARTICLE X

This Constitution shall be submitted to the consideration of Conventions in the several States, the members whereof shall be chosen by the people of such States respectively under the direction of their respective Legislatures. Each Convention which shall ratify the same, shall appoint the first representatives and Senators from such State according to the rule prescribed in the   § of the   Article. The representatives so appointed shall continue in office for one year only. Each Convention so ratifying shall give notice thereof to the Congress of the United States, transmitting at the same time a list of the Representatives and Senators chosen. When the Constitution shall have been duly ratified, Congress shall give notice of a day and place for the meeting of the Senators and Representatives from the several States; and when these or a majority of them shall have assembled according to such notice, they shall by joint ballot, by plurality of votes, elect a President of the United States; and the Constitution thus organized shall be carried into effect.

APPENDIX VI

RANDOLPH'S PROPOSED COMPROMISE TO THE SMALL STATES [1]
JULY 10, 1787

1.   Resolv^d that in the second branch each State have one vote in the following cases,
>   1. in granting exclusive rights to Ports.
>   2. in subjecting vessels or seamen of the U. States to tonnage, duties or other impositions.
>   3. in regulating the navigation of Rivers.
>   4. in regulating the rights to be enjoyed by citizens of one State in the other States.
>   5. in questions arising on the guarantee of territory.
>   6. in declaring war or taking measures for subduing a Rebellion.
>   7. in regulating Coin.
>   8. in establishing & regulating the post office.
>   9. in the admission of new States into the Union.
>   10. in establishing rules for the government of the Militia.
>   11. in raising a regular army.
>   12. in the appointment of the Executive.
>   13. in fixing the Seat of Government.

That in all other cases the right of suffrage be proportioned according to an equitable rule of representation.

2.   that for the determination of certain important questions in the 2^d branch a greater number of votes than a mere majority be requisite.

3.   that the people of each State ought to retain the perfect right of adopting from time to time such forms of republican Government as to them may seem best, and of making all laws not contrary to the articles of Union; subject to the supremacy of the General Government in those instances only in which that supremacy shall be expressly declared by the articles of the Union.

4.   That altho' every negative given to the law of a particular State shall prevent its operation, any State may appeal to the national Judiciary against a negative; and that such negative if adjudged to be contrary to the powers granted by the articles of the Union, shall be void.

5.   that any individual conceiving himself injured or oppressed by the partiality or injustice of a law of any particular State may resort to the National Judiciary, who may adjudge such law to be void, if found contrary to the principles of equity and justice.

---

[1] The text of the proposal is printed from Mr. Madison's copy "communicated by Mr. Randolph July 10, as an accomodating proposition to small States." See also *Documentary History of the Constitution*, Vol. V (1905), pp. 437-438.

APPENDIX VII

SUBSEQUENT NOTES AND REMARKS BY MADISON TO HIS SPEECH OF AUGUST 7, 1787 ON THE QUESTION OF SUFFRAGE

No. 1. (NOTE TO SPEECH OF J[AMES]. M[ADISON]. IN CONVENTION OF 1787, AUGUS 7TH [1]

As appointments for the General Government here contemplated will, in part, be made by the State Gov^{ts} all the Citizens in States where the right of suffrage is not limited to the holders of property, will have an indirect share of representation in the General Government. But this does not satisfy the fundamental principle that men can not be justly bound by laws in making which they have no part. Persons & property being both essential objects of Government, the most that either can claim, is such a structure of it, as will leave a reasonable security for the other. And the most obvious provision, of this double character, seems to be that of confining to the holders of property the object deemed least secure in popular Gov^{ts}, the right of suffrage for one of the two Legislative branches. This is not without example among us, as well as other constitutional modifica-. tions, favoring the influence of property in the Government. But the U. S. have not reached the Stage of Society in which conflicting feelings of the class with, and the class without property, have the operation natural to them in Countries fully peopled. The most difficult of all political arrangements is that of so adjusting the claims of the two classes as to give security to each, and to promote the welfare of all. The federal principle—which enlarges the sphere of power without departing from the elective bases of and controuls in various ways the propensity in small republics to rash measures & the facility of forming & executing them, will be found the best expedient yet tried for solving the problem.

No. 2. NOTE TO THE SPEECH OF J[AMES]. M[ADISON]. ON THE [7TH] DAY OF [AUGUST] [2]

These observations [in the Speech of J. M. See debates in the Convention of 1787. on the   day of   ] do not convey the speaker's more full & matured view of the subject, which is subjoined. He felt too much at the time the example of Virginia.

The right of suffrage is a fundamental Article in Republican Constitutions. The regulation of it is, at the same time, a task of peculiar delicacy. allow the right exclusively to property, and the rights of persons may be oppressed. The feudal polity alone sufficiently proves

---

[1] The text is printed from the original accompanying Madison's notes to the debates. See also *Documentary History of the Constitution*, Vol. V (1905), pp. 439-440.

[2] The text is printed from the original accompanying Madison's notes to the debates. See also *Documentary History of the Constitution*, Vol. V (1905), pp. 440-449.

it. Extend it equally to all, and the rights of property or the claims of justice may be overruled by a majority without property, or interested in measures of injustice. Of this abundant proof is afforded by other popular Gov^ts and is not without examples in our own, particularly in the laws impairing the obligation of contracts.

In civilized communities, property as well as personal rights is an essential object of the laws, which encourage industry by securing the enjoyment of its fruits: that industry from which property results, & that enjoyment which consists not merely in its immediate use, but in its posthumous destination to objects of choice and of kindred affection.

In a just & a free, Government, therefore, the rights both of property & of persons ought to be effectually guarded. Will the former be so in case of a universal & equal suffrage? Will the latter be so in case of a suffrage confined to the holders of property?

As the holders of property have at stake all the other rights common to those without property, they may be the more restrained from infringing, as well as the less tempted to infringe the rights of the latter. It is nevertheless certain, that there are various ways in which the rich may oppress the poor; in which property may oppress liberty; and that the world is filled with examples. It is necessary that the poor should have a defence against the danger.

On the other hand, the danger to the holders of property can not be disguised, if they be undefended against a majority without property. Bodies of men are not less swayed by interest than individuals, and are less controlled by the dread of reproach and the other motives felt by individuals. Hence the liability of the rights of property, and of the impartiality of laws affecting it, to be violated by Legislative majorities having an interest real or supposed in the injustice: Hence agrarian laws, and other leveling schemes: Hence the cancelling or evading of debts, and other violations of contracts. We must not shut our eyes to the nature of man, nor to the light of experience. Who would rely on a fair decision from three individuals if two had an interest in the case opposed to the rights of the third? Make the number as great as you please, the impartiality will not be increased, nor any further security against injustice be obtained, than what may result from the greater difficulty of uniting the wills of a greater number.

In all Gov^ts there is a power which is capable of oppressive exercise. In Monarchies and Aristocracies oppression proceeds from a want of sympathy & responsibility in the Gov^t towards the people. In popular Governments the danger lies in an undue sympathy among individuals composing a majority, and a want of responsibility in the majority to the minority. The characteristic excellence of the political System of the U. S. arises from a distribution and organization of its powers, which at the same time that they secure the dependence of the Gov^t on the will of the nation, provides better guards than are found in any other popular Gov^t against interested combinations of a Majority against the rights of a Minority.

The U. States have a precious advantage also in the actual distribution of property particularly the landed property; and in the universal hope of acquiring property. This latter peculiarity is among the happiest contrasts in their situation to that of the old world, where no anticipated change in this respect, can generally inspire a like sympathy with the rights of property. There may be at present, a Majority of the Nation, who are even freeholders, or the heirs, or aspirants to Freeholds. And the day may not be very near when such will cease to make up a Majority of the community. But they can not always so continue. With every admissible subdivision of the Arable lands, a populousness not greater than that of England or France, will reduce the holders to a Minority. And whenever the Majority shall be without landed or other equivalent property and without the means or hope of acquiring it, what is to secure the rights of property agst the danger from an equality & universality of suffrage, vesting compleat power over property in hands without a share in it: not to speak of a danger in the mean time from a dependence of an increasing number on the wealth of a few? In other Countries this dependence results in some from the relations between Landlords & Tenants in others both from that source, & from the relations between wealthy capitalists & indigent labourers. In the U. S. the occurrence must happen from the last source; from the connection between the great Capitalists in Manufactures & Commerce and the numbers employed by them. Nor will accumulations of Capital for a certain time be precluded by our laws of descent & of distribution; such being the enterprize inspired by free Institutions, that great wealth in the hands of individuals and associations, may not be unfrequent. But it may be observed, that the opportunities, may be diminished, and the permanency defeated by the equalizing tendency of the laws.

No free Country has ever been without parties, which are a natural offspring of Freedom. An obvious and permanent division of every people is into the owners of the Soil, and the other inhabitants. In a certain sense the Country may be said to belong to the former. If each landholder has an exclusive property in his share, the Body of Landholders have an exclusive property in the whole. As the Soil becomes subdivided, and actually cultivated by the owners, this view of the subject derives force from the principle of natural law, which vests in individuals an exclusive right to the portions of ground with which they have incorporated their labour & improvements. Whatever may be the rights of others derived from their birth in the Country, from their interest in the high ways & other parcels left open for common use, as well as in the national Edifices and monuments; from their share in the public defence, and from their concurrent support of the Gov^t, it would seem unreasonable to extend the right so far as to give them when become the majority, a power of Legislation over the landed property without the consent of the proprietors. Some shield agst the invasion of their rights would not be out of place in a just & provident System of Gov^t The principle of such an arrangement has prevailed in all Gov^{ts} where peculiar privileges or interests held by a part were to be secured agst violation, and in the various associations where pecuniary or other property forms the stake. In the former case a defensive right has been allowed; and if the arrangement be wrong, it is not in the defense, but in the kind of privilege to be defended. In the latter case, the shares of suffrage, allotted to individuals have been with acknowledged justice apportioned more or less to their respective interests in the Common Stock.

These reflections suggest the expediency of such a modification of Gov: as would give security to the part of the Society having most at stake and being most exposed to danger. Three modifications present themselves.

1. *Confining* the right of suffrage to freeholders, & to such as hold an equivalent property, convertible of course into freeholds. The objection to this regulation is obvious. It violates the vital principle of free Gov: that those who are to be bound by laws, ought to have a voice in making them. And the violation w^d be more strikingly unjust as the lawmakers become the minority: The regulation would be as unpropitious also as it would be unjust. It would engage the numerical & physical force in a constant struggle agst the public authority; unless kept down by a standing army fatal to all parties.

2. Confining the right of suffrage for one Branch to the holders of property, and for the other Branch to those without property. This arrangement which w^d give a mutual defence, where there might be mutual danger of encroachment, has an aspect of equality & fairness. But it w^d not be in fact either equal or fair, because the rights to be defended would be unequal, being on one side those of property as well as of persons, and on the other those of persons only. The temptation also to encroach tho' in a certain degree mutual, w^d be felt more strongly on one side than on the other; It w^d be more likely to beget an abuse of the Legislative Negative in extorting concessions at the expence of property, than the reverse. The division of the State into the two Classes, with distinct & independ: Organs of power, and without any intermingled Agency whatever, might lead to contests & antipathies not dissimilar to those between the Patricians & Plebeians at Rome.

3. Confining the right of electing one Branch of the Legislature to freeholders, and admitting all others to a common right with holders of property, in electing the other Branch. This w^d give a defensive power to holders of property, and to the class also without property when becoming a majority of electors, without depriving them in the mean time of a participation in the public Councils. If the holders of property would thus have a twofold share of representation, they w^d have at the same time a twofold stake in it, the rights of property as well as of persons the twofold object of political institutions. And if no exact and safe equilibrium can be introduced, it is more reasonable that a preponderating weight sh^d be allowed to the greater interest than to the lesser. Experience alone can decide how far the practice in this case would accord with the Theory. Such a distribution of the right of suffrage was tried in N. York and has been abandoned whether from experienced evils or party calculations, may possibly be a question. It is still on trial in N. Carolina, with

what practical indications is not known.   It is certain that the trial, to be satisfactory ought to be continued for no inconsiderable period; untill in fact the non freeholders should be the majority.

4. Should Experience or public opinion require an equal & universal suffrage for each branch of the Gov^t, such as prevails generally in the U. S., a resource favorable to the rights of landed & other property, when its possessors become the Minority, may be found in an enlargement of the Election Districts for one branch of the Legislature and a prolongation of its period of service.   Large districts are manifestly favorable to the election of persons of general respectability, and of probable attachment to the rights of property, over competitors depending on the personal solicitations practicable on a contracted theatre.   And altho' an ambitious candidate, of personal distinction, might occasionally recommend himself to popular choice by espousing a popular though unjust object, it might rarely happen to many districts at the same time.   The tendency of a longer period of service would be, to render the Body more stable in its policy, and more capable of stemming popular currents taking a wrong direction, till reason & justice could regain their ascendancy.

5. Should even such a modification as the last be deemed inadmissible, and universal suffrage and very short periods of elections within contracted spheres be required for each branch of the Gov^t, the security for the holders of property when the minority, can only be derived from the ordinary influence possessed by property, & the superior information incident to its holders; from the popular sense of justice enlightened & enlarged by a diffusive education; and from the difficulty of combining & effectuating unjust purposes throughout an extensive country; a difficulty essentially distinguishing the U. S. and even most of the individual States, from the small communities where a mistaken interest or contagious passion, could readily unite a majority of the whole under a factious leader, in trampling on the rights of the Minor party.

Under every view of the subject, it seems indispensable that the Mass of Citizens should not be without a voice, in making the laws which they are to obey, & in chusing the Magistrates, who are to administer them, and if the only alternative be between an equal & universal right of suffrage for each branch of the Gov^t and a confinement of the *entire* right to a part of the Citizens, it is better that those having the greater interest at stake namely that of property & persons both, should be deprived of half their share in the Gov^t; than, that those having the lesser interest, that of personal rights only, should be deprived of the whole.

No. 3. Gen! Remarks on the Convention [1]

For case of suffrage see Deb: Aug. 7.

    1. Its Members of the most select kind & possessing particularly the confidence of y^r Constituents

---

[1] The text is printed from the original accompanying Madison's notes to the debates. See also *Documentary History of the Constitution*, Vol. V (1905), pp. 465-466.

2. do   generally of mature age & much political experience.
3. Disinterestedness & candor demonstrated by mutual concessions, & frequent changes of opinion
4. Few who did not change in the progress of discussions the
   opinions on important points which they carried into the
   Convention
5. Few who, at the close of the Convention, were not ready to
   admit this change as the enlightening effect of the discussions—
6. And how few, whose opinions at the close of the Convention,
   have not undergone changes on some points, under the more
   enlightening influence of experience.
7. Yet how much fewer still who, if now living, with the recollection of the difficulties in the Convention, of overcoming
   or reconciling honest differences of opinion, political biasses,
   and local interests; and with due attention to the varieties
   & discords of opinion, the vicisitudes of parties, and the collisions real or imagined of local interests, witnessed on the
   face of the Nation, would not felicitate their Country on
   the happy result of the original Convention, and deprecate
   the experiment of another with general power to revise its
   work.
8. The restraining influence of the Constiⁿ on the aberrations of
   the States of great importance tho' invisible. It stifles
   wishes & inclinations which wᵈ otherwise ripen into overt &
   pernicious acts. The States themselves are unconscious of
   the effect. Were these Constituᴸ and insuperable obstacles
   out of the way—how many political abuses might not have
   sprung up where not suspected. The Propensities in some
   cases, as Mas: Kentʸ &c have not been altogether contrould,
   and but for foreseen difficulties might have been followᵈ
   by greater.

PART III
THE CONSTITUTION, ITS RATIFICATION AND AMENDMENTS

THE CONSTITUTION OF THE UNITED STATES [1]

We the People of the United States, in Order to form a more perfect Union, establish Justice, insure domestic Tranquility, provide for the common defence, promote the general Welfare, and secure the Blessings of Liberty to ourselves and our Posterity, do ordain and establish this Constitution for the United States of America.

Article. I.

Section. 1. All legislative Powers herein granted shall be vested in a Congress of the United States, which shall consist of a Senate and House of Representatives.

Section. 2. The House of Representatives shall be composed of Members chosen every second Year by the People of the several States, and the Electors in each State shall have ∧ the Qualifications requisite for Electors of the most numerous Branch of the State Legislature.

No Person shall be a Representative who shall not have attained to the Age of twenty five Years, and been seven Years a Citizen of the United States, and who shall not, when elected, be an Inhabitant of that State in which he shall be chosen.

Representatives and direct Taxes shall be apportioned among the several States which may be included within this Union, according to their respective Numbers, which shall be determined by adding to the whole Number of free Persons, including those bound to Service for a Term of Years, and excluding Indians not taxed, three fifths of all other Persons. The actual Enumeration shall be made within three Years after the first Meeting of the Congress of the United States, and within every subsequent Term of ten Years, in such Manner as they shall by Law direct. The Number of Representatives shall not exceed one for every thirty Thousand, but each State shall have at Least one Representative; and until such enumeration shall be made, the State of New Hampshire shall be entitled to chuse three, Massachusetts eight, Rhode-

---

[1] This is a literal copy of the engrossed Constitution as signed. It is in four sheets, with an additional sheet containing the resolutions of transmittal. The note indented at the end is in the original precisely as reproduced here.

Island and Providence Plantations one, Connecticut five, New-York six, New Jersey four, Pennsylvania eight, Delaware one, Maryland six, Virginia ten, North Carolina five, South Carolina five, and Georgia three.

When vacancies happen in the Representation from any State, the Executive Authority thereof shall issue Writs of Election to fill such Vacancies.

The House of Representatives shall chuse their Speaker and other Officers; and shall have the sole Power of Impeachment.

Section. 3. The Senate of the United States shall be composed of two Senators from each State, chosen by the Legislature thereof, for six Years; and each Senator shall have one Vote.

Immediately after they shall be assembled in Consequence of the first Election, they shall be divided as equally as may be into three Classes. The Seats of the Senators of the first Class shall be vacated at the Expiration of the second Year, of the second Class at the Expiration of the fourth Year, and of the third Class at the Expiration of the sixth Year, so that one third may be chosen every second Year; and if Vacancies happen by Resignation, or otherwise, during the Recess of the Legislature of any State, the Executive thereof may make temporary Appointments until the next Meeting of the Legislature, which shall then fill such Vacancies.

No Person shall be a Senator who shall not have attained to the Age of thirty Years, and been nine Years a Citizen of the United States, and who shall not, when elected, be an Inhabitant of that State for which he shall be chosen.

The Vice President of the United States shall be President of the Senate, but shall have no Vote, unless they be equally divided.

The Senate shall chuse their other Officers, and also a President pro tempore, in the Absence of the Vice President, or when he shall exercise the Office of President of the United States.

The Senate shall have the sole Power to try all Impeachments. When sitting for that Purpose, they shall be on Oath or Affirmation. When the President of the United States ∧ ^{is tried,} the Chief Justice shall preside: And no Person shall be convicted without the Concurrence of two thirds of the Members present.

Judgment in Cases of Impeachment shall not extend further than to removal from Office, and disqualification to hold and enjoy any Office of honor, Trust or Profit under the United States: but the Party convicted shall nevertheless be liable and subject to Indictment, Trial, Judgment and Punishment, according to Law.

Section. 4. The Times, Places and Manner of holding Elections for Senators and Representatives, shall be prescribed in each State by the Legislature thereof; but the Congress may at any time by Law make or alter such Regulations, except as to the Places of chusing Senators.

The Congress shall assemble at least once in every Year, and such Meeting shall be on the first Monday in December, unless they shall by Law appoint a different Day.

Section. 5. Each House shall be the Judge of the Elections, Returns and Qualifications of its own Members, and a Majority of each shall constitute a Quorum to do Business; but a smaller Number may adjourn from day to day, and may be authorized to compel the Attendance of absent Members, in such Manner, and under such Penalties as each House may provide.

Each House may determine the Rules of its Proceedings, punish its Members for disorderly Behaviour, and, with the Concurrence of two thirds, expel a Member.

Each House shall keep a Journal of its Proceedings, and from time to time publish the same, excepting such Parts as may in their Judgment require Secrecy; and the Yeas and Nays of the Members of either House on any question shall, at the Desire of one fifth of those Present, be entered on the Journal.

Neither House, during the Session of Congress, shall, without the Consent of the other, adjourn for more than three days, nor to any other Place than that in which the two Houses shall be sitting.

Section. 6. The Senators and Representatives shall receive a Compensation for their Services, to be ascertained by Law, and paid out of the Treasury of the United States. They shall in all Cases, except Treason, Felony and Breach of the Peace, be privileged from Arrest during their Attendance at the Session of their respective Houses, and in going to and returning from the same; and for any Speech or Debate in either House, they shall not be questioned in any other Place.

No Senator or Representative shall, during the Time for which he was elected, be appointed to any civil Office under the Authority of the United States, which shall have been created, or the Emoluments whereof shall have been encreased during such time; and no Person holding any Office under the United States, shall be a Member of either House during his Continuance in Office.

Section. 7. All Bills for raising Revenue shall originate in the House of Representatives; but the Senate may propose or concur with Amendments as on other Bills.

Every Bill which shall have passed the House of Representatives and the Senate, shall, before it become a Law, be presented to the President of the United States; If he approve he shall sign it, but if not he shall return it, with his Objections to that House in which it shall have originated, who shall enter the Objections at large on their Journal, and proceed to reconsider it. If after such Reconsideration two thirds of that House shall agree to pass the Bill, it shall be sent, together with the Objections, to the other House, by which it shall likewise be reconsidered, and if approved by two thirds of that House, it shall become a Law. But in all such Cases the Votes of both Houses shall be determined by yeas and Nays, and the Names of the Persons voting for and against the Bill shall be entered on the Journal of each House respectively. If any Bill shall not be returned by the President within ten Days (Sundays excepted) after it shall have been presented to him, the Same shall be a Law, in like Manner as if he had signed it, unless the Congress by their Adjournment prevent its Return in which Case it shall not be a Law.

Every Order, Resolution, or Vote to which the Concurrence of the Senate and House of Representatives may be necessary (except on a question of Adjournment) shall be presented to the President of the United States; and before the Same shall take Effect, shall be approved by him, or being disapproved by him, shall be re-passed by two thirds of the Senate and House of Representatives, according to the Rules and Limitations prescribed in the Case of a Bill.

Section. 8. The Congress shall have Power To lay and collect Taxes, Duties, Imposts and Excises, to pay the Debts and provide for the common Defence and general Welfare of the United States; but all Duties, Imposts and Excises shall be uniform throughout the United States;

To borrow Money on the credit of the United States;

To regulate Commerce with foreign Nations, and among the several States, and with the Indian Tribes;

To establish an uniform Rule of Naturalization, and uniform Laws on the subject of Bankruptcies throughout the United States;

To coin Money, regulate the Value thereof, and of foreign Coin, and fix the Standard of Weights and Measures;

To provide for the Punishment of counterfeiting the Securities and current Coin of the United States;

To establish Post Offices and post Roads;

To promote the Progress of Science and useful Arts, by securing for limited Times to Authors and Inventors the exclusive Right to their respective Writings and Discoveries;

To constitute Tribunals inferior to the supreme Court;

To define and punish Piracies and Felonies committed on the high Seas, and Offences against the Law of Nations;

To declare War, grant Letters of Marque and Reprisal, and make Rules concerning Captures on Land and Water;

To raise and support Armies, but no Appropriation of Money to that Use shall be for a longer Term than two Years;

To provide and maintain a Navy;

To make Rules for the Government and Regulation of the land and naval Forces;

To provide for calling forth the Militia to execute the Laws of the Union, suppress Insurrections and repel Invasions;

To provide for organizing, arming, and disciplining, the Militia, and for governing such Part of them as may be employed in the Service of the United States, reserving to the States respectively, the Appointment of the Officers, and the Authority of training the Militia according to the discipline prescribed by Congress;

To exercise exclusive Legislation in all Cases whatsoever, over such District (not exceeding ten Miles square) as may, by Cession of particular States, and the Acceptance of Congress, become the Seat of the Government of the United States, and to exercise like Authority over all Places purchased by the Consent of the Legislature of the State in which the Same shall be, for the Erection of Forts, Magazines, Arsenals, dock-Yards, and other needful Buildings;—And

To make all Laws which shall be necessary and proper for carrying into Execution the foregoing Powers, and all other Powers vested by this Constitution in the Government of the United States, or in any Department or Officer thereof.

Section. 9. The Migration or Importation of such Persons as any of the States now existing shall think proper to admit, shall not be prohibited by the Congress prior to the Year one thousand eight hundred and eight, but a Tax or duty may be imposed on such Importation, not exceeding ten dollars for each Person.

The Privilege of the Writ of Habeas Corpus shall not be suspended, unless when in Cases of Rebellion or Invasion the public Safety may require it.

No Bill of Attainder or ex post facto Law shall be passed.

No Capitation, or other direct, Tax shall be laid, unless in Proportion to the Census or Enumeration herein before directed to be taken.

No Tax or Duty shall be laid on Articles exported from any State.

No Preference shall be given by any Regulation of Commerce or Revenue to the Ports of one State over those of another: nor shall Vessels bound to, or from, one State, be obliged to enter, clear, or pay Duties in another.

No Money shall be drawn from the Treasury, but in Consequence of Appropriations made by Law; and a regular Statement and Account of the Receipts and Expenditures of all public Money shall be published from time to time.

No Title of Nobility shall be granted by the United States: And no Person holding any Office of Profit or Trust under them, shall, without the Consent of the Congress, accept of any present, Emolument, Office, or Title, of any kind whatever, from any King, Prince, or foreign State.

Section. 10. No State shall enter into any Treaty, Alliance, or Confederation; grant Letters of Marque and Reprisal; coin Money; emit Bills of Credit; make any Thing but gold and silver Coin a Tender in Payment of Debts; pass any Bill of Attainder, ex post facto Law, or Law impairing the Obligation of Contracts, or grant any Title of Nobility.

No State shall, without the Consent of ⋏ the Congress, lay any Imposts or Duties on Imports or Exports, except what may be absolutely necessary for executing it's inspection Laws: and the net Produce of all Duties and Imposts, laid by any State on Imports or Exports, shall be for the Use of the Treasury of the United States; and all such Laws shall be subject to the Revision and Controul of ⋏ the Congress.

No State shall, without the Consent of Congress, lay any Duty of Tonnage, keep Troops, or Ships of War in time of Peace, enter into any Agreement or Compact with another State, or with a foreign Power, or engage in War, unless actually invaded, or in such imminent Danger as will not admit of delay.

Article. II.

Section. 1. The executive Power shall be vested in a President of the United States of America. He shall hold his Office during the Term of four Years, and, together with the Vice President, chosen for the same Term, be elected as follows

Each State shall appoint, in such Manner as the Legislature thereof may direct, a Number of Electors, equal to the whole Number of Senators and Representatives to which the State may be entitled in the Congress: but no Senator or Representative, or Person holding an Office of Trust or Profit under the United States, shall be appointed an Elector.

The Electors shall meet in their respective States, and vote by Ballot for two Persons, of whom one at least shall not be an Inhabitant of the same State with themselves. And they shall make a List of all the Persons voted for, and of the Number of Votes for each; which List they shall sign and certify, and transmit sealed to the Seat of the Government of the United States, directed to the President of the Senate. The President of the Senate shall, in the Presence of the Senate and House of Representatives, open all the Certificates, and the Votes shall then be counted. The Person having the greatest Number of Votes shall be the President, if such Number be a Majority of the whole Number of Electors appointed; and if there be more than one who have such Majority, and have an equal Number of Votes, then the House of Representatives shall immediately chuse by Ballot one of them for President; and if no Person have a Majority, then from the five highest on the List the said House shall in like Manner chuse the President. But in chusing the President, the Votes shall be taken by States, the Representation from each State having one Vote; A quorum for this Purpose shall consist of a Member or Members from two thirds of the States, and a Majority of all the States shall be necessary to a Choice. In every Case, after the Choice of the President, the Person having the greatest Number of Votes of the Electors shall be the Vice President. But if there should remain two or more who have equal Votes, the Senate shall chuse from them by Ballot the Vice President.

The Congress may determine the Time of chusing the Electors, and the Day on which they shall give their Votes; which Day shall be the same throughout the United States.

No Person except a natural born Citizen, or a Citizen of the United States, at the time of the Adoption of this Constitution, shall be eligible to the Office of President; neither shall any Person be eligible to that Office who shall not have attained to the Age of thirty five Years, and been fourteen Years a Resident within the United States.

In Case of the Removal of the President from Office, or of his Death, Resignation, or Inability to discharge the Powers and Duties of the said Office, the Same shall devolve on the Vice President, and the Congress may by Law provide for the Case of Removal, Death, Resignation or Inability, both of the President and Vice President, declaring what Officer shall then act as President, and such Officer shall act accordingly, until the Disability be removed, or a President shall be elected.

The President shall, at stated Times, receive for his Services, a Compensation, which shall neither be encreased nor diminished during the Period for which he shall have been elected, and he shall not receive within that Period any other Emolument from the United States, or any of them.

Before he enter on the Execution of his Office, he shall take the following Oath or Affirmation:—"I do solemnly swear (or affirm) that I will faithfully execute the Office of President of the United States, and will to the best of my Ability, preserve, protect and defend the Constitution of the United States."

Section. 2. The President shall be Commander in Chief of the Army and Navy of the United States, and of the Militia of the several States, when called into the actual Service of the United States; he may require the Opinion, in writing, of the principal Officer in each of the executive Departments, upon any Subject relating to the Duties of their respective Offices, and he shall have Power to grant Reprieves and Pardons for Offences against the United States, except in Cases of Impeachment.

He shall have Power, by and with the Advice and Consent of the Senate, to make Treaties, provided two thirds of the Senators present concur; and he shall nominate, and by and with the Advice and Consent of the Senate, shall appoint Ambassadors, other public Ministers and Consuls, Judges of the supreme Court, and all other Officers of the United States, whose Appointments are not herein otherwise provided for, and which shall be established by Law: but the Congress may by Law vest the Appointment of such inferior Officers, as they think proper, in the President alone, in the Courts of Law, or in the Heads of Departments.

The President shall have Power to fill up all Vacancies that may happen during the Recess of the Senate, by granting Commissions which shall expire at the End of their next Session.

Section. 3. He shall from time to time give to the Congress Information of the State of the Union, and recommend to their Consideration such Measures as he shall judge necessary and expedient; he may, on extraordinary Occasions, convene both Houses, or either of them, and in Case of Disagreement between them, with Respect to the Time of Adjournment, he may adjourn them to such Time as he shall think proper; he shall receive Ambassadors and other public Ministers; he shall take Care that the Laws be faithfully executed, and shall Commission all the Officers of the United States.

Section. 4. The President, Vice President and all civil Officers of the United States, shall be removed from Office on Impeachment for, and Conviction of, Treason, Bribery, or other high Crimes and Misdemeanors.

Article III.

Section. 1. The judicial Power of the United States, shall be vested in one supreme Court, and in such inferior Courts as the Congress may from time to time ordain and establish. The Judges, both of the supreme and inferior Courts, shall hold their Offices during good Behaviour, and shall, at stated Times, receive for their Services, a Compensation, which shall not be diminished during their Continuance in Office.

Section. 2. The judicial Power shall extend to all Cases, in Law and Equity, arising under this Constitution, the Laws of the United States, and Treaties made, or which shall be made, under their Authority;—to all Cases affecting Ambassadors, other public Ministers and Consuls;—to all Cases of admiralty and maritime Jurisdiction;—to Controversies to which the United States shall be a Party;—to Controversies between two or more States;—between a State and Citizens of another State;—between Citizens of different States,—between Citizens of the same State claiming Lands under Grants of different States, and between a State, or the Citizens thereof, and foreign States, Citizens or Subjects.

In all Cases affecting Ambassadors, other public Ministers and Consuls, and those in which a State shall be Party, the supreme Court shall have original Jurisdiction. In all the other Cases before mentioned, the supreme Court shall have appellate Jurisdiction, both as to Law and Fact, with such Exceptions, and under such Regulations as the Congress shall make.

The Trial of all Crimes, except in Cases of Impeachment, shall be by Jury; and such Trial shall be held in the State where the said Crimes shall have been committed; but when not committed within any State, the Trial shall be at such Place or Places as the Congress may by Law have directed.

Section. 3. Treason against the United States, shall consist only in levying War against them, or in adhering to their Enemies, giving them Aid and Comfort. No Person shall be convicted of Treason unless on the Testimony of two Witnesses to the same overt Act, or on Confession in open Court.

The Congress shall have Power to declare the Punishment of Treason, but no Attainder of Treason shall work Corruption of Blood, or Forfeiture except during the Life of the Person attainted.

Article. IV.

Section. 1. Full Faith and Credit shall be given in each State to the public Acts, Records, and judicial Proceedings of every other State. And the Congress may by general Laws prescribe the Manner in which such Acts, Records and Proceedings shall be proved, and the Effect thereof.

Section. 2. The Citizens of each State shall be entitled to all Privileges and Immunities of Citizens in the several States.

A Person charged in any State with Treason, Felony, or other Crime, who shall flee from Justice, and be found in another State, shall on Demand of the executive Authority of the State from which he fled, be delivered up, to be removed to the State having Jurisdiction of the Crime.

No Person held to Service or Labour in one State, under the Laws thereof, escaping into another, shall, in Consequence of any Law or Regulation therein, be discharged from such Service or Labour, but shall be delivered up on Claim of the Party to whom such Service or Labour may be due.

Section. 3. New States may be admitted by the Congress into this Union; but no new State shall be formed or erected within the Jurisdiction of any other State; nor any State be formed by the Junction of two or more States, or Parts of States, without the Consent of the Legislatures of the States concerned as well as of the Congress.

The Congress shall have Power to dispose of and make all needful Rules and Regulations respecting the Territory or other Property belonging to the United States; and nothing in this Constitution shall be so construed as to Prejudice any Claims of the United States, or of any particular State.

Section. 4. The United States shall guarantee to every State in this Union a Republican Form of Government, and shall protect each of them against Invasion; and on Application of the Legislature, or of the Executive (when the Legislature cannot be convened) against domestic Violence.

Article. V.

The Congress, whenever two thirds of both Houses shall deem it necessary, shall propose Amendments to this Constitution, or, on the Application of the Legislatures of two thirds of the several States, shall call a Convention for proposing Amendments, which, in either Case, shall be valid to all Intents and Purposes, as Part of this

Constitution, when ratified by the Legislatures of three fourths of the several States, or by Conventions in three fourths thereof, as the one or the other Mode of Ratification may be proposed by the Congress; Provided that no Amendment which may be made prior to the Year One thousand eight hundred and eight shall in any Manner affect the first and fourth Clauses in the Ninth Section of the first Article; and that no State, without its Consent, shall be deprived of it's equal Suffrage in the Senate.

Article. VI.

All Debts contracted and Engagements entered into, before the Adoption of this Constitution, shall be as valid against the United States under this Constitution, as under the Confederation.

This Constitution, and the Laws of the United States which shall be made in Pursuance thereof; and all Treaties made, or which shall be made, under the Authority of the United States, shall be the supreme Law of the Land; and the Judges in every State shall be bound thereby, any Thing in the Constitution or Laws of any State to the Contrary notwithstanding.

The Senators and Representatives before mentioned, and the Members of the several State Legislatures, and all executive and judicial Officers, both of the United States and of the several States, shall be bound by Oath or Affirmation, to support this Constitution; but no religious Test shall ever be required as a Qualification to any Office or public Trust under the United States.

Article. VII.

The Ratification of the Conventions of nine States, shall be sufficient for the Establishment of this Constitution between the States so ratifying the Same.

The Word, "the," being interlined between the seventh and eighth Lines of the first Page, The Word "Thirty" being partly written on an Erazure in the fifteenth Line of the first Page, The Words "is tried" being interlined between the thirty second and thirty third Lines of the first Page and the Word "the" being interlined between the forty third and forty fourth Lines of the second Page.

done in Convention by the Unanimous Consent of the States present the Seventeenth Day of September in the Year of our Lord one thousand seven hundred and Eighty seven and of the Independance of the United States of America the Twelfth   In witness whereof We have hereunto subscribed our Names,

G? WASHINGTON—Presid.
and deputy from Virginia

Attest WILLIAM JACKSON Secretary

New Hampshire	JOHN LANGDON NICHOLAS GILMAN
Massachusetts	NATHANIEL GORHAM RUFUS KING
Connecticut	W^M SAM^L JOHNSON ROGER SHERMAN
New York . .	ALEXANDER HAMILTON
New Jersey	WIL: LIVINGSTON DAVID BREARLEY. W^M PATERSON. JONA: DAYTON
Pensylvania	B FRANKLIN THOMAS MIFFLIN ROB^T MORRIS GEO. CLYMER THO^S FITZSIMONS JARED INGERSOLL JAMES WILSON GOUV MORRIS
Delaware	GEO: READ GUNNING BEDFORD jun JOHN DICKINSON RICHARD BASSETT JACO: BROOM
Maryland	JAMES M^CHENRY DAN OF S^T THO^S JENIFER DAN^L CARROLL
Virginia	JOHN BLAIR— JAMES MADISON Jr.
North Carolina	W^M BLOUNT RICH^D DOBBS SPAIGHT. HU WILLIAMSON
South Carolina	J. RUTLEDGE CHARLES COTESWORTH PINCKNEY CHARLES PINCKNEY PIERCE BUTLER.
Georgia	WILLIAM FEW ABR BALDWIN

LETTER OF THE PRESIDENT OF THE FEDERAL CONVENTION, DATED SEPTEMBER 17, 1787, TO THE PRESIDENT OF CONGRESS, TRANSMITTING THE CONSTITUTION.[1]

IN CONVENTION, SEPTEMBER 17, 1787.[2]

Sir,

We have now the honor to submit to the consideration of the United States in Congress assembled, that Constitution which has appeared to us the most adviseable.

The friends of our country have long seen and desired, that the power of making war, peace, and treaties, that of levying money and regulating commerce, and the correspondent executive and judicial authorities should be fully and effectually vested in the general government of the Union: But the impropriety of delegating such extensive trust to one body of men is evident—Hence results the necessity of a different organization.

It is obviously impracticable in the federal government of these states, to secure all rights of independent sovereignty to each, and yet provide for the interest and safety of all: Individuals entering into society, must give up a share of liberty to preserve the rest. The magnitude of the sacrifice must depend as well on situation and circumstance, as on the object to be obtained. It is at all times difficult to draw with precision the line between those rights which must be surrendered, and those which may be reserved; and on the present occasion this difficulty was encreased by a difference among the several states as to their situation, extent, habits, and particular interests.

In all our deliberations on this subject we kept steadily in our view, that which appears to us the greatest interest of every true American, the consolidation of our Union, in which is involved our prosperity, felicity, safety, perhaps our national existence. This important consideration, seriously and deeply impressed on our minds, led each state in the Convention to be less rigid on points of inferior magnitude, than might have been otherwise expected; and thus the Constitution, which we now present, is the result of a spirit of amity, and of that mutual deference and concession which the peculiarity of our political situation rendered indispensible.

---

[1] Reprinted from *Documentary History of the Constitution*, Vol. II (1894), pp. 1, 2.
[2] From Washington's copy of the Journal of Congress (Vol. XII, p. 164), the original not having been found among the papers of the Continental Congress up to the time of going to press.

That it will meet the full and entire approbation of every state is not perhaps to be expected; but each will doubtless consider, that had her interest been alone consulted, the consequences might have been particularly disagreeable or injurious to others; that it is liable to as few exceptions as could reasonably have been expected, we hope and believe; that it may promote the lasting welfare of that country so dear to us all, and secure her freedom and happiness, is our most ardent wish.

With great respect, We have the honor to be, Sir,
Your Excellency's
most obedient and humble servants,

GEORGE WASHINGTON, *President.*
By unanimous Order of the Convention.
His Excellency the PRESIDENT of CONGRESS.

RESOLUTION OF THE FEDERAL CONVENTION SUB-MITTING THE CONSTITUTION TO CONGRESS, SEPTEMBER 17, 1787.[1]

IN CONVENTION MONDAY SEPTEMBER 17th 1787.

Present

The States of

New Hampshire, Massachusetts, Connecticut, Mr Hamilton from New York, New Jersey, Pennsylvania, Delaware, Maryland, Virginia, North Carolina, South Carolina and Georgia. Resolved,

That the preceeding Constitution be laid before the United States in Congress assembled, and that it is the Opinion of this Convention, that it should afterwards be submitted to a Convention of Delegates, chosen in each State by the People thereof, under the Recommendation of its Legislature, for their Assent and Ratification; and that each Convention assenting to, and ratifying the Same, should give Notice thereof to the United States in Congress assembled.

Resolved, That it is the Opinion of this Convention, that as soon as the Conventions of nine States shall have ratified this Constitution, the United States in Congress assembled should fix a Day on which Electors should be appointed by the States which shall have ratified the same, and a Day on which the Electors should assemble to vote for the President, and the Time and Place for commencing Proceedings under

---

[1] Reprinted from *Documentary History of the Constitution*, Vol. II (1894), pp. 20, 21.

this Constitution. That after such Publication the Electors should be appointed, and the Senators and Representatives elected: That the Electors should meet on the Day fixed for the Election of the President, and should transmit their Votes certified, signed, sealed and directed, as the Constitution requires, to the Secretary of the United States in Congress assembled, that the Senators and Representatives should convene at the Time and Place assigned; that the Senators should appoint a President of the Senate, for the sole Purpose of receiving, opening and counting the Votes for President; and, that after he shall be chosen, the Congress, together with the President, should, without Delay, proceed to execute this Constitution.

By the Unanimous Order of the Convention

G° WASHINGTON Presid[t]

W. JACKSON Secretary.

RESOLUTION OF CONGRESS OF SEPTEMBER 28, 1787, SUBMITTING THE CONSTITUTION TO THE SEVERAL STATES.[1]

FRIDAY SEPT 28. 1787 [2]

Congress assembled present Newhampshire Massachusetts Connecticut New York New Jersey Pensylvania, Delaware Virginia North Carolina South Carolina and Georgia and from Maryland M[r] Ross

Congress having received the report of the Convention lately assembled in Philadelphia

Resolved Unanimously that the said Report with the resolutions and letter accompanying the same be transmitted to the several legislatures in Order to be submitted to a convention of Delegates chosen in each state by the people thereof in conformity to the resolves of the Convention made and provided in that case.

---

[1] Reprinted from *Documentary History of the Constitution*, Vol. II (1894), p. 22.
[2] From the "Rough" Journal of Congress (No. 1, Vol. 38).

THE FIRST TEN AMENDMENTS TO THE CONSTITUTION.

ARTICLE I.

Congress shall make no law respecting an establishment of religion, or prohibiting the free exercise thereof; or abridging the freedom of speech, or of the press; or the right of the people peaceably to assemble, and to petition the Government for a redress of grievances.

ARTICLE II.

A well regulated Militia, being necessary to the security of a free State, the right of the people to keep and bear Arms, shall not be infringed.

ARTICLE III.

No Soldier shall, in time of peace be quartered in any house, without the consent of the Owner, nor in time of war, but in a manner to be prescribed by law.

ARTICLE IV.

The right of the people to be secure in their persons, houses, papers, and effects, against unreasonable searches and seizures, shall not be violated, and no Warrants shall issue, but upon probable cause, supported by Oath or affirmation, and particularly describing the place to be searched, and the persons or things to be seized.

ARTICLE V.

No person shall be held to answer for a capital, or otherwise infamous crime, unless on a presentment or indictment of a Grand Jury, except in cases arising in the land or naval forces, or in the Militia, when in actual service in time of War or public danger; nor

---

By the State of Rhode Island and Providence Plantations.—Agreed to the whole of the said twelve articles.

By the State of New Jersey.—Agreed to the whole of the said amendments, except the second article.

By the State of Virginia.—Agreed to the whole of the said twelve articles. (Elliot's *Debates*, Vol. I, pp. 339-340.)

No returns were made by the states of Massachusetts, Connecticut, Georgia and Kentucky.

The amendments thus proposed became a part of the constitution—the first and second of them excepted; which were not ratified by a sufficient number of the state legislatures. (*Journal of the Federal Convention*, 1819, Supplement, p. 481.)

shall any person be subject for the same offence to be twice put in jeopardy of life or limb; nor shall be compelled in any criminal case to be a witness against himself, nor be deprived of life, liberty, or property, without due process of law; nor shall private property be taken for public use, without just compensation.

ARTICLE VI.

In all criminal prosecutions, the accused shall enjoy the right to a speedy and public trial, by an impartial jury of the State and district wherein the crime shall have been committed, which district shall have been previously ascertained by law, and to be informed of the nature and cause of the accusation; to be confronted with the witnesses against him; to have compulsory process for obtaining witnesses in his favor, and to have the Assistance of Counsel for his defence.

ARTICLE VII.

In Suits at common law, where the value in controversy shall exceed twenty dollars, the right of trial by jury shall be preserved, and no fact tried by a jury, shall be otherwise re-examined in any Court of the United States, than according to the rules of the common law.

ARTICLE VIII.

Excessive bail shall not be required, nor excessive fines imposed, nor cruel and unusual punishments inflicted.

ARTICLE IX.

The enumeration in the Constitution, of certain rights, shall not be construed to deny or disparage others retained by the people.

ARTICLE X.

The powers not delegated to the United States by the Constitution, nor prohibited by it to the States, are reserved to the States respectively, or to the people.

INDEX

INDEX

Account of expenditures, proposed to be published, 566; from time to time agreed to, 567.

Acts of States, mutual recognition of, by States, committed, 482.

Adams, John Quincy, letters to, from Charles Pinckney, relating to the Pinckney plan, 598; text of plan submitted to, by Charles Pinckney, 600.

Address to people, referred to Committee on style, 544; proposed, 567; rejected, 568.

Adjournment of legislature, provision for, 381.

Admission of new States, 58, 573; debated, 487; agreed to, 488; not to be made out of old States, 488; clause agreed to, 492.

Admission of States, basis for, 213.

Amendments to constitution, provision for, postponed, 58; agreed to, 304; method of making, agreed to, 495; convention for, reconsidered, 539; clause agreed to, 540, 573.

Appointments, power to make, 529; motion that none be made to any offices not created by law, lost, 535; to be referred to State executives, rejected, 470; to office, by Senate, 455; may be vested in lower officers, 572.

Armies, power to raise, debated, 423; limit in time of peace, rejected, 424; appropriation for, to be limited, 512; precaution against, rejected, 565.

Baldwin, Abraham, Ga., attends convention, 84; thinks Senate should represent property, 190; on committee on representation in Senate, 205; favors ineligibility of members of legislature to offices, 505; thinks members of first Congress may create offices for themselves, 562; would discriminate against foreigners, 388; on grand committee on assumption of State debts, 423; defends slavery, 445; on committee on navigation acts, 448; moves amendment relative to imposts, 468; clause to Western country, 493; on committee on postponed measures, 502; approves mode of election of President, 510.

Bankruptcies, uniform laws, 482, 503, clause agreed to, 504.

Bassett, Richard, Del., attends, 17.

Bedford, Gunning, Del., attends, 18; favors short term for executive, 40; favors removal of executive on petition of State legislatures, 46; opposes restrictions on legislature, 53; opposes power of legislature to negative State laws, 78; insists on rights of small States, 198; on committee on representation in Senate, 205; moves definition of power of legislature, 265; would increase representation, 568; denies desire for foreign help, 210; opposes appointment of judges by executive, 276; opposes provision against army, 565.

Bill of Rights, proposed, 556; rejected, 557.

Bills of attainder, 449; forbidden to States, 567.

Bills of credit, 478; forbidden to States, 567.

Bills for revenue, to originate in House, 512.

Bills, originating, 404; question postponed, 438.

Bills, return of, ten days allowed, amendment lost, 559.

Blair, John, Va., attends, 17.

Blount, William, N. C., attends, 131; announces he will sign constitution, 581.

Brearley, David, N. J., attends, 17; seconds resumption of clause relating to rule of suffrage in legislature, 80; moves New Hampshire be urged to send delegates, 190; on committee on representation, 226; opposes election of President by joint ballot, 461; on committee on postponed measures, 502; reports from committee on postponed measures, 502; reports from committee of eleven, 506, 512; would strike out clause for amendments, 575.

647

Broome, Jacob, Del., attends, 17; favors term during good behavior for executive, 271; seconds election of executive by electors, 287; moves ratio electors be committed, 289; seconds motion to postpone question of ineligibility of executive for second term, 315; moves to refer term and duties of President to committee, 463; thinks executive may correspond with States, 470; seconds motion for nine years for Senate, 167; favors equal vote in Senate, 230; thinks legislature may pay themselves, 402; seconds motion to make wages same for both branches of legislature, 403; seconds motion for sole power over treason and legislature, 433; seconds power in legislature to negative State laws, 456; opposes adjournment, 262.

Butler, Pierce, S. C., attends, 17; favors single executive, 49; opposes absolute negative of executive on laws, 53; moves power of executive to suspend laws, 55; opposes short term for executive, 288; favors election of executive by electors, 321; moves to commit clause relating to executive, 324; approves mode of election of President, 509; thinks election by people to legislature impracticable, 33; asks ratio of representation in Senate, 70; opposes power of legislature to negative State laws, 79; favors wealth as basis of representation, 84, 214, 226; moves addition of quotas of contribution to motion relating to representation, 88; postponed, 88; moves that Senate members serve without salary, 96; rejected, 96; moves national compensation of legislature, 149; thinks ineligibility of members of first branch of legislature to offices necessary, 152; moves to consider representation in Senate, 164; opposes ineligibility of Senators to State offices, 173; proposes three years' inhabitancy for members of legislature, 357; would exclude foreigners from Senate, 368; moves postponement of question of eligibility of members of legislature, 401; favors payment of legislature by States, 401; agrees treaties of peace ought to be made with majority of Senate, 530; thinks Congress should consent to inspection duties, 558; insists blacks should count equally with whites, 233; insists slaves equal in labor to freemen, 234; insists blacks be counted in representation, 241; seconds proposition of three-fifths blacks in representation, 243; insists on security for slaves, 250; opposes inferior tribunals in national judiciary, 61; sees no necessity for inferior judicial tribunals, 278; approves money bills originating in Senate, 97; opposes originating money bills in first branch of legislature, 208; favors money bills in first branch, 362; opposes power to emit bills of credit, 413; opposes paper money, 414; moves rule for attendance of members and secrecy, 21; is willing to give power to national government, 28; moves to consider national government, 28; asks extent of limitation of States, 34; fears powers of States may be destroyed, 36; thinks fit persons for offices will be found, 154; moves increase in representation from South Carolina, 228; asks definition of power to legislate where States are incompetent, 260; thinks capital should be fixed in constitution, 332; opposes restriction of franchise, 351; would bar foreigners; 385; opposes war power in Senate, 419; favors power over militia, 425; favors taxation by representation, 437; opposes power over exports, 439; opposed to taxation of exports, 446; fears payment of debts to holders of certificates, 457; would preserve value of debts, 466; on committee on imposts, 470; moves fugitive slaves be delivered up, 481; would allow navigation acts by majority, 484; opposes creation of new States within old, 488; favors nine States for ratification, 496; on committee on postponed measures, 502.

Canals, power to cut, proposed, 563; rejected. 564.

Capital. See Seat of government.

Capitation tax, referred to committee, 448; proposed to prohibit, 566.

Captures on land and water, rules agreed to, 415.

Carroll, Daniel, Md., attends, 223; seconds motion for election of electors for executive by lot, 317; moves election of President by the people, 461; seconds motion that President be elected by electors chosen by the people, 463; on committee on representa-

tends, 17; moves question of election of executive, 310.

Houstoun, William, Ga., attends, 37; moves postponement of term for executive, 270; moves eligibility of executive to second term, 270; seconds motion for increase ratio of electors, 289; moves election of electors for executive by State legislatures, 311; on committee on representation, 226; moves increase in representation of Georgia, 228; does not wish to perpetuate existing constitutions, 281.

Impeachments, provision struck out, 279; mode of, 429; of judges, 449; of President, question postponed, 472; power of, 535; to high crimes and misdemeanors, agreed to, 535; motion not to try in Senate, lost, 537; clause agreed to, 537; to include other civil officers, 537; proposed to suspend persons impeached, lost, 561.

Imports, tax on, 479.

Imposts, power to lay, 409; to be uniform, 470, 563.

Incorporation, power of, 420; charters for, proposed, 564.

Indian affairs, 420.

Ingersoll, Jared, Penn., attends, 18; does not regard signing constitution as pledge to support it, 582.

Invasion, guarantee against article, agreed to, 493.

Inventions, power to encourage, 420.

Jackson, William, elected secretary of convention, 18.

Jefferson, Thomas, extract of letter from James Madison, 589.

Jenifer, Daniel of St. Thomas, Md., attends, 41; moves members of first branch be elected every three years, 91; favors ineligibility of members of legislature to offices, 154; moves postponement of question of money bills, 216; insists vessel must clear from its own State, 501.

Jersey plan. See Patterson's plan.

Johnson, William Samuel, Conn., attends, 41; favors preserving States, 139; thinks State governments must be preserved, 164; thinks States must be preserved, 182; favors wealth and numbers as basis for representation, 242; on definition of treason, 431; insists offense against nation, 432; on committee on navigation acts, 448; thinks provision against *ex post*

facto laws unnecessary, 450; opposes ratification of treaties, 458; thinks provision for State controversies unnecessary, 460; insists on validity of debts, 466; suggests judicial power extend to equity, 473; moves jurisdiction of supreme court extend to cases under constitution, 475; on committee on mutual recognition by States of public acts, 483; thinks Vermont must come into the Union, 489; moves admission of States already formed, 491; on committee on style, 538; submits report of committee on style, 545; favors power to pass sumptuary laws, 558; on committee on sumptuary laws, 558; reports provision for ratification, 560.

Journals of convention, disposition of, 582.

Journals of legislature, publication of, 380, 381; secrecy only in Senate, proposed and rejected, 562.

Judiciary, national, agreed to, 56; single court proposed, 57; changes in clause relating to, made, 96; to be bound by national law, 266; qualifications for, committed, 328.

Appointment by legislature considered, 56; mode considered, 57, 58; by Senate, 97, 274, 303; by executive, 277; by executive with consent of Senate, 277, 300, 303.

Compensation, 58, 277, 474; not to be changed during office, 277; may be increased, 278; may be changed, 474.

Impeachment of, 449, 475; removal of, rejected, 474.

Inferior tribunals, considered, 60, 279; provision for, struck out, 61; legislature to have power to institute, 61, 62; agreed to, 279, 415.

Jurisdiction discussed, 97, 279, 449; power to declare laws unconstitutional, discussed, 51; power to declare law void, denied, 406, 407; supreme court, 428; to extend to equity, 473; appellate jurisdiction, 475; to extend to cases under constitution, 475.

Juries, crimes to be tried by, 477; in civil cases, 556; trial by, to be preserved, rejected, 573.

Revisionary power, as council of revision, 51; revisionary power, 300, 405; with executive, 51, 56, 67, 69, 294; negatived, 406.

Supreme tribunal, agreed to, 274; tenure of office of, 58, 277, 474.

Juries in civil cases, 556.

large branch of legislature by people essential, 33; on elections to Senate, 35; on definition of powers of national legislature, 36; considers election of one branch of legislature by the people necessary, 64; favors small Senate, 70; opposes election of Senate by State legislatures, 73; seconds motion to elect members of first branch every three years, 91; moves legislature fix compensation for members, 92; passed, 93; approves seven years as Senate term, 95; opposes annual elections for first branch of legislature, 145; favors national compensation of legislature, 147; wants compensation of legislature fixed in constitution, 148; moves ineligibility of members of first branch of legislature during term and for one year, 152; opposes absolute ineligibility of members of legislature to offices, 153; proposes rule of voting in Senate, 164; seconds motion to consider representation in Senate, 164; explains object of Senate, 167; opposes compensation of Senators by States, 172; objects to equal vote of States in legislature, 177; contends for proportional representation in Senate, 193; insists on proportional representation in Senate, 198; opposes commitment of question of representation in Senate, 205; insists that representation of States be considered, 221; proposes numbers as basis of representation in first branch of legislature and wealth for Senate, 225; on committee on representation, 226; moves increase in representation, 229; favors fixing standard of representation, 236; favors Pinckney's proposition for Senate, 254; insists on proportional representation, 256; favors continuance of Congress, 280; would exclude debtors from legislature, 327; suggests annual meeting of legislature, 348; wishes legislature to meet in May, 350; favors inhabitants for members of legislature, 356; opposes seven years' residence in State for members of legislature, 356; objects to rule of representation, 359; moves to limit representation, 359; moves vacancies in Senate be filled by legislatures or executives, 364; thinks legislature can fix question of citizenship for Senate, 367;

moves first branch of legislature name time of meeting, 371; thinks legislature should regulate elections, 371; thinks qualifications for legislature should be fixed, 374, 375; moves legislature compel attendance, 378; moves expulsion of members of legislature, 378; on journals of legislature, 380; insists on compensation of members of legislature by nation, 401; moves power of legislature to declare war, 418; representation only temporary, 437; proposes two-thirds of Senate for quorum, 534; seconds motion for reconsideration of number of representatives, 538; doubts if legislature should judge privileges of members, 511; thinks Congress can propose amendments, 574; moves revision of acts by executive and judiciary, 56, 405; favors appointment of judiciary by Senate, 57; favors inferior tribunals in national judiciary, 60; moves legislature have power to institute inferior tribunals, 61; favors association of judiciary with executive in revision of laws, 67, 295, 298; moves that judges of national judiciary be appointed by Senate, 97; agreed to, 97; moves that jurisdiction of national judiciary should extend to cases involving revenue and impeachment, 97; agreed to, 97; suggests appointment of judges by executive and Senate, 276; moves appointment of judges by executive with two-thirds of Senate, 277; favors appointment of judges by executive with consent of Senate, 301, 302; thinks salaries of judges should not be increased, 277, 474; doubts if jurisdiction of judiciary should extend to cases under constitution, 475; moves for term "judicial power," 475; favors qualified negative of executive on laws, 53; favors negative on State laws by legislature, 75, 78, 266, 478, 558; favors qualification mutual negative of both branches of legislature, 347; moves negative extend to resolutions, 408; favors negative on State laws, 456; favors three-fourths vote to set aside President's negative, 556; defends taxation by representation, 247; favors tax on exports, 410, 440; proposes taxation of exports by two-thirds vote, 441; insists on power of legislature to tax

tive being appointed by executives of States, 80; opposes eligibility of executive for second term, 284; seconds motion restricting President's power of appointment, 464; objects to mode of election of President, 509; thinks eventual election of President should be in legislature, 511; thinks President should not have pardoning power over treason, 571; favors small Senate, 34; will not give indefinite powers to national legislature, 36; approves seven years' for Senate term, 95; favors two years for service in first branch of legislature, 144; opposes State compensation for legislature, 147; suggests rotation in Senate, 165; favors commitment of question of representation, 204, 225; on committee on representation, 215; wishes legislature to arrange basis of representation, 243; moves reconsideration of question of representation, 248; opposes police power of legislature, 265; opposes fixing time for meeting of legislature, 349; thinks vacancies in Senate may be filled by executive, 363; moves to postpone question of vote in Senate, 364, 365; thinks vote in Senate should be postponed, 365; opposes fourteen years' citizenship for Senate, 368; agrees to nine years' citizenship for Senate, 370; moves legislature compel attendance, 378; approves expulsion of members of legislature, 378; thinks one member may call for yeas and nays, 379; proposes four years' citizenship for first branch of legislature, 384; agrees to allow eligibility of members of legislature to army or navy, 401; favors ineligibility of members of legislature to offices, 505; doubts if legislature should judge privileges of members, 511; opposes Vice President for president of Senate, 527; would exclude Senate from pardoning power, 571; moves that jurisdiction of national judiciary should extend to cases involving revenue and impeachment, 97; agreed to, 97; favors appointment of judges by Senate, 276; favors inferior judicial tribunals, 279; favors appointment of judges by executive with Senate, 301; favors fixed compensation for judges, 474; moves to reconsider question of money bills, 363; favors money bills in first

branch of legislature, 383; opposes amendment of money bills by Senate, 388; insists on restricting money bills to first branch of legislature, 393; moves to extend negative to resolutions, 409; moves to consider clause for national government, 27, 28; opposes consent of legislature to be necessary to amend constitution, 90; consideration postponed, 90; opposes requiring oaths from members of State governments to observe constitution, 90; upholds national plan, 109: accepts supreme government instead of national, 132; proposes sermon on 4th of July, 182; thinks new States should not be discriminated against, 213; urges compromise, 216; opposes reduction of representation of New Hampshire, 228; moves census as basis for representation, 230; favors census, 233; explains adjournment proposal, 262; favors guarantee of republican constitution, 280; moves that States must have republican government, 281; opposes ratification by legislatures, 305; defines treason, 413; moves power to define piracies, etc., 416; favors power to punish piracies, 416; favors British definition of treason, 432; favors commitment of question of slave trade, 447; thinks provision to fulfill engagements of old government necessary, 450; favors national control of militia, 453; moves provision for State debts, 460; moves validity of debts, 466; moves mutual acceptance of States of public acts, 482; on committee on mutual recognition of public acts by States, 483; finds odious features in constitution, 486; proposes nine States may ratify constitution, 495; thinks State conventions should amend constitution, 500; thinks powers too lossely defined, 503; wants second convention, 541, 544, 575; states objections to constitution, 543; moves to strike out servitude, 559; favors power to grant charters of incorporation, 564; regards armies as dangerous in time of peace, 565; states why he will not sign constitution, 580, 581; does not sign, 583; extract of letter from James Madison, 590.

Ratifying constitution by conventions, discussed, 59, 460; by plurality of States, proposed, 60; by nine

thinks property qualifications for legislature should be fixed, 373; moves qualifications for legislature to be the same as for State legislatures, 375; on journals of legislature, 380; thinks Senate should participate in money bills, 394; seconds motion to postpone question of money bills, 404; wishes one supreme court, 57; opposes inferior tribunals in national judiciary, 60; opposes revisionary power for judges, 300; objects to power of removal of judges, 473; opposes sending for delegates from New Hampshire, 190; opposes adjournment, 262; thinks provision against domestic violence unnecessary, 281; on committee of detail, 318; delivers report of committee of detail, 337; opposes franchise limited to freeholders, 354; thinks foreigners should not hold office, 386; favors measure to guard funds, 421; moves committee to consider State debts, 421; moves assumption of State debts, 421; moves longer sessions of convention, 423; opposes tax on importation of slaves, 442; insists on slave trade, 446; introduces additions to report, 448; moves constitution be supreme law, 455; opposes negative on State laws, 457; thinks provision for controversies between States unnecessary, 460; would prohibit retrospective laws, 479; would preserve *habeas corpus*, 477; on committee to consider mutual recognition of public acts by States, 483; favors navigation acts, 486; says States can not be divided without their consent, 490; proposes bankruptcy laws, 502; moves treaties shall require two-thirds of whole Senate, 533; opposes power to amend clause relating to slavery, 540; thinks Congress need not approve constitution, 543; proposes suspension from office of persons impeached, 561; moves Treasurer be appointed by executive, 562; opposes address to the people, 567.

Seat of government, provision for, discussed, 332; jurisdiction over, 420, 512; clause agreed to, 513.
Senate. *See* Legislature, Senate.
Sherman, Roger, Conn., attends, 27; thinks executive must carry out will of legislature, 38; favors election of executive by legislature,

40, 267; favors three years' term for executive, 40; thinks national legislature should remove executive at pleasure, 46; proposes executive council, 50; seconds motion for eligibility of executive for second term, 270; opposes tenure during good behavior for executive, 271; objects to election of President by ballot, 461; objects to President's power of appointment, 464; favors eventual election of President from seven candidates, 517; thinks greater powers for Congress necessary, 28; opposes election to first branch of legislature by people, 31; favors election of one member of Senate by each State legislature, 35; seconds motion to elect Senate by State legislatures, 69; thinks proportion of suffrage in first branch should be based on free inhabitants, 84; moves each State should have one vote in second branch, 88; rejected, 89; opposes requiring oaths from members of State governments to observe constitution, 90; moves members of first branch be elected annually, 91; approves five years for Senate term, 95; favors single legislative assembly, 136; prefers election to legislature by State legislatures, 143; accepts biennial elections to first branch of legislature, 145; favors State compensation for legislature, 147; opposes ineligibility of members of first branch of legislature to offices, 151, 153; seconds motion for six years for Senators, 165; opposes seven years for Senators, 166; favors frequent elections, 168; thinks States have equal rights, 180; thinks Congress needs more power, 195; favors commitment of question of representation in Senate, 202; favors equal vote in Senate, 220; opposes ratio of representation, 223; on committee on representation, 226; opposes increase in representation, 229; would not shackle legislature, 231; favors numbers as basis of representation, 235; favors representation proposed, 239; thinks legislature should fix representation, 247; insists on equal vote in Senate, 254; thinks legislature will require quotas from States, 259; wishes powers of legislature defined, 264; thinks time for meeting of legislature ought to be fixed, 349; wishes members of legislature to be inhabitants, 356; moves to limit representation, 359; thinks legislature may regulate elections, 372; thinks yeas and nays unnecessary, 379; on journals of legislature, 380, 381; favors ineligibility of members of legislature to offices, 398; thinks nation and State may pay members of legislature, 402; thinks members of legislature ineligible to offices with increased salaries, 505; thinks when legislature votes for President it should vote by States, 519; favors including Senate in treaty making power, 528; moves treaties require majority of whole Senate, 534; opposes reconsideration of representation, 538; moves amendments by legislature proposed to States, 539; thinks Congress has no power over press, 565; opposes inferior tribunals in national judiciary, 61; wishes power to remain with State governments. 63; moves that judges of national judiciary be appointed by legislature, 97; withdrawn, 97; insists on appointment of judges by Senate, 275; favors appointment of judges by Senate, 276; wishes State tribunals to be used when possible, 279; favors power of removal of judges, 473; moves to extend judicial powers to land cases, 476; appellate jurisdiction of supreme court, 476; trial by jury, 477; thinks supreme court should not try President, 536; moves postponement of question of money bills, 222; wishes to consider money bills and vote in Senate together, 252; favors originating money bills in House, 513; defends slave representation, 359, 361; would permit slave trade, 443, 446; objects to use of word "slaves," 468; opposes delivering up of fugitive slaves, 481; opposes negative of executive on laws, 52; power of legislature to negative State laws, 76; opposes negative on State laws by legislature, 265, 266; favors mutual negative by both branches of legislature, 347; opposes negative on laws for judges, 407; thinks negative on State laws unnecessary, 456; favors two-thirds vote to overrule President's negative, 554; opposes power of direct taxation, 264; thinks exports should not be taxed, 412; opposed to tax on exports, 439; objects to taxing men as property,

468; says tax on slaves not a discouragement to importation, 469; moves power to tax exports with consent of States, 479; would leave power to tax imports with legislature, 479; opposes ratification by conventions, 59; thinks constitution can be ratified by State legislatures, 59; favors prayers in convention, 182; would not discriminate against West, 252; thinks United States under no obligations to foreigners, 386; objects to appointment of Treasurer by joint ballot, 415; favors appointment of Treasurer by legislature, 562; to authorize legislature to assume State debts, 422; on grand committee on assumption of State debts, 423; opposes assumption State debts, 436; moves payment of old debts, 467; thinks States should control militia, 425, 426, 451; moves uniformity for militia, 452; opposes State appointment of lower militia officers, 454; favors State power over treason, 433; moves general contributions of States according to representation, 436; thinks provision for State controversies unnecessary, 460; on committee on imposts, 470; proposes regulation of commerce, 476; moves prohibition of paper money, 478; thinks States may lay embargoes, 479; favors navigation acts, 484; favors equality of new States, 487; thinks a State can not be dismembered, 488; moves admission and formation of new States, 490; on claims to Western country, 492; thinks religious test unnecessary, 495; thinks ten States may ratify constitution, 495; thinks all States must agree to constitution, 497; moves ratification by ten States, 498; brings in report on commercial regulations, 501; moves committee to consider postponed propositions, 502; on committee on postponed measures, 502; opposes federal bankruptcy laws, 504; favors mode of electing Vice President, 508; wants army limited, 512; favors Vice President for president of Senate, 527; would submit constitution to Congress, 542; thinks State bills of rights still in force, 557; objects to power to cut canals, 567; favors occasional publication of expenditures, 567; opposes address to people, 568; thinks power of nation supreme in regulating

members of legislature, 357; moves to reconsider seven years' residence for members of legislature, 363; thinks qualifications for legislature should not be fixed, 375; thinks quorum should not be fixed, 376; on right of dissent in legislature, 379; on journals of legislature, 381; proposes four years' citizenship for first branch of legislature, 384, 385; proposes nine years' citizenship for Senate, 388; opposes equal votes in Senate, 390; favors eligibility of members of legislature to offices, 399, 400; favors revisionary power over acts, 408; opposes appointments by Senate, 455; opposes Senate power to make treaties, 458; opposes ineligibility of members of legislature to offices, 505; thinks legislature is judge of privileges of members, 511; wishes council to share in making appointments, 528; would include House in treaty power, 528; thinks majority of Senate may agree to treaties, 530; wants treaties agreed to by majority of Senate, 532; opposes power to convene either house of Congress, 537; proposes amendments agreed to by two-thirds of States, 539; proposes judiciary with executive to have revisionary power, 56, 294, 406; opposes appointment of judiciary by national legislature, 56; moves legislature have power to institute inferior tribunals, 61; favors appointment of judges by executive, 275; insists on revisionary power for judges, 300; opposes power of removal of judges, 473; favors absolute negative of executive on laws, 51, 53; approves power of legislature to negative State laws, 76; agrees to three-fourths of legislature to overrule President's negative, 408; favors negative on State laws, 456; thinks money bills may originate in either branch of legislature, 216, 217; favors publicity in money bills, 218; wishes Senate to originate money bills, 362; opposes provision for money bills, 365, 366; favors ratification of constitution by a plurality of States, 60; proposes seven States may ratify constitution, 495; thinks majority necessary for ratification, 498; proposes eight States may ratify constitution, 496; thinks only ratifying States will be bound, 496; thinks assent of

Congress to constitution unnecessary, 542; favors taxation by representation, 244; favors tax on exports, 411, 440, 441; moves amendment relative to direct taxation, 559; nominates Temple Franklin for secretary of convention, 18; wishes to preserve the States, 66; contrasts Virginia and Jersey plans, 107; discusses national government, 129, 130; thinks States will encroach on national government, 140; opposes sending for delegates from New Hampshire, 190; supports rights of West, 250; favors guarantee of republican constitution to States, 280; moves guarantee of republican government and against rebellion in States, 281; government to act separately, 299; does not favor oath to support government, 304; on committee of detail, 318; would disqualify debtors for office, 330; favors liberal policy to foreigners, 368; favors immigration, 385; on naturalized citizens in Pennsylvania, 387; defines duties and imposts, 410; opposes paper money, 414, 477; thinks definition of felonies unnecessary, 416; favors striking out punishment for piracies, 416; on definition of treason, 431; thinks proof of treason difficult, 433; favors sole power in legislature, 433; opposes slave trade, 445; favors navigation acts by majority, 447, 485; opposes mention of ex post facto laws, 449; moves pardon before conviction, 471; would not allow new States to violate contracts, 478; opposes delivery up of fugitive slaves, 481; on committee on mutual recognition by States of public acts, 482; opposes power to divide a State, 489; thinks States can not be divided, 490; opposes motion on Western country, 492; would not define law of nations, 563; favors power to cut canals, 564; favors university, 564; favors occasional publication of accounts of expenditures, 567; proposes to hand journals to President, 583.

Wythe, George, Va., attends, 17; on committee on rules, 18; reports rules, 18, 21.

Yeas and nays in legislature considered, 379; by one member, rejected, 379.

Yates, Robert, N. Y., attends, 17; on committee on representation, 205, 226.